EFFECTIVE TREATMENTS FOR PTSD

EFFECTIVE TREATMENTS FOR PTSD

Practice Guidelines from the International Society for Traumatic Stress Studies

Edited by

Edna B. Foa
Terence M. Keane
Matthew J. Friedman

THE GUILFORD PRESS
New York   London

© 2000 The Guilford Press
A Division of Guilford Publications, Inc.
72 Spring Street, New York, NY 10012
www.guilford.com

Part II, Treatment Guidelines, ©2000 International Society for Traumatic Stress Studies.

Paperback edition 2004

Printed in the United States of America

Last digit is print number: 10 9 8 7 6 5 4

Library of Congress Cataloging-in-Publication Data

Effective treatments for PTSD : practice guidelines from the International Society for
    Traumatic Stress Studies / edited by Edna B. Foa, Terence M. Keane, Matthew J. Friedman.
        p. ; cm.
    Includes bibliographical references and index.
    ISBN 1-57230-584-3 (cloth)   ISBN 1-59385-014-X (paper)
    1. Post-traumatic stress disorder—Treatment.   2. Psychic trauma—Treatment.
3. Psychotherapy.   I. Foa, Edna B.   II. Keane, Terence Martin.   III. Friedman, Matthew J.
IV. International Society for Traumatic Stress Studies.
    [DNLM: 1. Stress Disorders, Post-Traumatic—therapy.   2. Psychotherapy—methods.
WM 170 E269 2000]
RC552.P67 E35 2000
616.85'21—dc 21   00-026468

About the Editors

Edna B. Foa, PhD, Professor of Clinical Psychology in Psychiatry at the University of Pennsylvania and Director of the Center for the Treatment and Study of Anxiety, is an internationally renowned authority on the psychopathology and treatment of anxiety. Her research aiming at delineating etiological frameworks and targeted treatment has been highly influential, and she is currently one of the leading experts on posttraumatic stress disorders. She has published several books and over 200 articles and book chapters, has lectured extensively around the world, and was the chair of the PTSD work group of DSM-IV. Dr. Foa is the recipient of numerous awards and honors, including the Distinguished Scientist Award from the Scientific section of the American Psychological Association, the First Annual Outstanding Research Contribution Award from the Association for Advancement of Behavior Therapy, the Distinguished Scientific Contributions to Clinical Psychology Award from the American Psychological Association, and the Lifetime Achievement Award from the International Society for Traumatic Stress Studies.

Terence M. Keane, PhD, is Professor and Vice Chairman of Psychiatry at the Boston University School of Medicine. He is also the Chief of Psychology and the Director of the National Center for PTSD at the VA Boston Healthcare System. The past president of the International Society for Traumatic Stress Studies (ISTSS), Dr. Keane has published extensively on the assessment and treatment of PTSD. His contributions to the field have been recognized by many honors, including the Robert Laufer Award for Outstanding Scientific Achievement from ISTSS, a Fulbright Scholarship, Outstanding Research Contributions from the Division of Public Sector Psychol-

ogy of the American Psychological Association, and the Weisband Distinguished Alumnus Award from Binghamton University. Dr. Keane is a Fellow
of the American Psychological Association and the American Psychological
Society. A regular contributor to the literature, he has edited several books
and more than 130 scientific publications.

Matthew J. Friedman, MD, PhD, is Executive Director of the U.S. Department of Veterans Affairs National Center for Posttraumatic Stress Disorder and Professor of Psychiatry and of Pharmacology at Dartmouth Medical
School. He has worked with patients with PTSD as a clinician and researcher
for 25 years and has published extensively on stress and PTSD. Throughout
his professional career, he has tried to combine strong concerns about psychiatric care with a scientific commitment to understanding the etiology, diagnosis, and treatment of clinical phenomena. As a result, his publications span
a variety of topics in addition to PTSD, such as biological psychiatry, psychopharmacology, and clinical outcome studies on depression, anxiety, schizophrenia, and chemical dependency. He has coedited or written books and
monographs on the neurobiological basis of stress, on ethnocultural aspects
of PTSD, on the controversy concerning recovered memories, and on disaster mental health services. Listed in *The Best Doctors in America*, he is past president of the ISTSS, and has served on many VA and NIMH research, education, and policy committees. Among Dr. Friedman's many honors is the 1999
ISTSS Lifetime Achievement Award.

Contributors

Lucy Berliner, MSW, Harborview Medical Center, Center for Sexual Assault and Traumatic Stress, Seattle, Washington

Jonathan I. Bisson, DM, Department of Liaison Psychiatry, Gabalfa Clinic, Cardiff, United Kingdom

Arthur S. Blank, Jr., MD, Department of Psychiatry, George Washington University, Washington, DC, and Department of Psychiatry, Uniformed Services University of Health Sciences, Bethesda, Maryland

Sandra L. Bloom, MD, The Sanctuary®, Hersham Clinic, Philadelphia, Pennsylvania

Etzel Cardeña, PhD, Departments of Psychology and Anthropology, University of Texas-Pan American, Edinburg, Texas

Claude M. Chemtob, PhD, Stress Disorders Research Laboratory, Department of Veterans Affairs, National Center for PTSD, Honolulu, Hawaii

Judith A. Cohen, MD, Department of Psychiatry, Allegheny General Hospital, Pittsburgh, Pennsylvania

Christine A. Courtois, PhD, THE CENTER: Posttraumatic Disorders Program, The Psychiatric Institute of Washington, Washington, DC

Jonathan R. T. Davidson, MD, Psychiatric Outpatient Clinic, Duke University, Durham, North Carolina

Raymond B. Flannery, Jr., PhD, Massachusetts Department of Mental Health, and Department of Psychiatry, Harvard Medical School, Boston, Massachusetts

Edna B. Foa, PhD, Center for the Study and Treatment of Anxiety, Department of Psychiatry, University of Pennsylvania, Philadelphia, Pennsylvania

David W. Foy, PhD, Graduate School of Education and Psychology, Pepperdine University, Culver City, California, and the Headington Program in International Trauma, Fuller Graduate School of Psychology, Pasadena, California

Matthew J. Friedman, MD, PhD, National Center for PTSD, Veterans Affairs Medical Center, White River Junction, Vermont, and Departments of Psychiatry and Pharmacology, Dartmouth Medical School, Hanover, New Hampshire

Shirley M. Glynn, PhD, Research Service, Greater Los Angeles Veterans Affairs Healthcare System at West Los Angeles, Los Angeles, California

Fred D. Gusman, MSW, National Center for PTSD, Department of Veterans Affairs Medical Center, Palo Alto, California

Mary K. Jankowski, PhD, National Center for PTSD, Veterans Affairs Medical Center, White River Junction, Vermont, and Department of Psychiatry, Dartmouth Medical School, Hanover, New Hampshire

David Read Johnson, PhD, Post-Traumatic Stress Center, New Haven, Connecticut

Terence M. Keane, PhD, Department of Psychiatry, Boston University, Boston, Massachusetts, and National Center for PTSD, Boston VA Medical Center, Boston, Massachusetts

Janice L. Krupnick, PhD, Department of Psychiatry, Georgetown University, Washington, DC

Harold S. Kudler, MD, Department of Psychiatry and Behavioral Sciences, Duke University, Durham, North Carolina, and VA Medical Center, Durham, North Carolina

Jose Maldonado, MD, Department of Psychiatry, Stanford University, Stanford, California

John S. March, MD, MPH, Department of Psychiatry, Duke University Medical Center, Durham, North Carolina

Charles R. Marmar, MD, Department of Psychiatry, University of California, San Francisco, California, and Department of Veterans Affairs Medical Center, San Francisco, California

Alexander C. McFarlane, MD, Department of Psychiatry, University of Adelaide, Woodville, South Australia

Elizabeth A. Meadows, PhD, Department of Psychology, Central Michigan University, Mt. Pleasant, Michigan

Thomas A. Mellman, MD, Department of Psychiatry, Dartmouth Medical School, Hanover, New Hampshire

Walter Penk, PhD, Department of Psychiatry, Edith Nourse Rogers Memorial

Veterans Hospital, Bedford, Massachusetts, and Department of Psychiatry, Boston University, Boston, Massachusetts

Roger K. Pitman, MD, Department of Psychiatry, Veterans Affairs Medical Center, Manchester, New Hampshire, and Department of Psychiatry, Harvard Medical School, Boston, Massachusetts

Patricia Resick, PhD, Psychology Department, University of Missouri, St. Louis, Missouri

David S. Riggs, PhD, National Center for PTSD, Boston Veterans Affairs Medical Center, Boston, Massachusetts, and Department of Psychiatry, Boston University, Boston, Massachusetts

Suzanna Rose, PhD, MA, RN, Department of Psychology, West Berkshire Traumatic Stress Service, Reading, United Kingdom

Barbara Olasov Rothbaum, PhD, Department of Psychiatry, Emory University School of Medicine, Atlanta, Georgia

Paula P. Schnurr, PhD, National Center for PTSD, Veterans Affairs Medical Center, White River Junction, Vermont, and Department of Psychiatry, Dartmouth Medical School, Hanover, New Hampshire

Arieh Y. Shalev, MD, Department of Psychiatry, Hadassah University Hospital, Jerusalem, Israel

Stephen M. Southwick, MD, National Center for PTSD, Veterans Affairs Medical Center, West Haven, Connecticut, and Department of Psychiatry, Yale University School of Medicine, New Haven, Connecticut

David Spiegel, MD, Department of Psychiatry and Behavioral Sciences, Stanford University, Stanford, California

David F. Tolin, Center for Treatment and Study of Anxiety, University of Pennsylvania, Philadelphia, Pennsylvania

Onno van der Hart, PhD, Department of Psychiatry, University of Utrecht, Utrecht, The Netherlands

Bessel A. van der Kolk, MD, Trauma Clinic, Boston University, Boston, Massachusetts

Melissa S. Wattenberg, PhD, Psychology Service, Department of Veterans Affairs Healthcare System–Outpatient Clinic, Boston, Massachusetts, and Department of Psychiatry, Tufts University, Boston, Massachusetts

Frank W. Weathers, PhD, Department of Psychology, Auburn University, Auburn, Alabama

Daniel S. Weiss, PhD, Department of Psychiatry, University of California, San Francisco, California, and Veterans Affairs Medical Center, San Francisco, California

Contents

1. Introduction   1
   Edna B. Foa, Terence M. Keane,
   and Matthew J. Friedman

2. Diagnosis and Assessment   18
   Terence M. Keane, Frank W. Weathers,
   and Edna B. Foa

I. TREATMENT APPROACHES
FOR PTSD: LITERATURE REVIEWS

3. Psychological Debriefing   39
   Jonathan I. Bisson, Alexander C. McFarlane,
   and Suzanna Rose

4. Cognitive-Behavioral Therapy   60
   Barbara Olasov Rothbaum, Elizabeth A. Meadows,
   Patricia Resick, and David W. Foy

5. Pharmacotherapy   84
   Matthew J. Friedman, Jonathan R. T. Davidson,
   Thomas A. Mellman, and Stephen M. Southwick

6. Treatment of Children and Adolescents   106
   Judith A. Cohen, Lucy Berliner, and John S. March

Contents   xi

7. Eye Movement Desensitization and Reprocessing   139
Claude M. Chemtob, David F. Tolin,
Bessel A. van der Kolk, and Roger K. Pitman

8. Group Therapy   155
David W. Foy, Shirley M. Glynn, Paula P. Schnurr,
Mary K. Jankowski, Melissa S. Wattenberg,
Daniel S. Weiss, Charles R. Marmar,
and Fred D. Gusman

9. Psychodynamic Therapy   176
Harold S. Kudler, Arthur S. Blank Jr.,
and Janice L. Krupnick

10. Inpatient Treatment   199
Christine A. Courtois and Sandra L. Bloom

11. Psychosocial Rehabilitation   224
Walter Penk and Raymond B. Flannery Jr.

12. Hypnosis   247
Etzel Cardeña, Jose Maldonado,
Onno van der Hart, and David Spiegel

13. Marital and Family Therapy   280
David S. Riggs

14. Creative Therapies   302
David Read Johnson

II. TREATMENT GUIDELINES

15. Psychological Debriefing   317
Jonathan I. Bisson, Alexander C. McFarlane,
and Suzanna Rose

16. Cognitive-Behavioral Therapy   320
Barbara Olasov Rothbaum, Elizabeth A. Meadows,
Patricia Resick, and David W. Foy

17. Pharmacotherapy   326
Matthew J. Friedman, Jonathan R. T. Davidson,
Thomas A. Mellman, and Stephen M. Southwick

18. Treatment of Children and Adolescents   330
      Judith A. Cohen, Lucy Berliner, and John S. March

19. Eye Movement Desensitization and Reprocessing   333
      Claude M. Chemtob, David F. Tolin,
      Bessel A. van der Kolk, and Roger K. Pitman

20. Group Therapy   336
      David W. Foy, Shirley M. Glynn, Paula P. Schnurr,
      Mary K. Jankowski, Melissa S. Wattenberg,
      Daniel S. Weiss, Charles R. Marmar,
      and Fred D. Gusman

21. Psychodynamic Therapy   339
      Harold S. Kudler, Arthur S. Blank Jr.,
      and Janice L. Krupnick

22. Inpatient Treatment   342
      Christine A. Courtois and Sandra L. Bloom

23. Psychosocial Rehabilitation   347
      Walter Penk and Raymond B. Flannery Jr.

24. Hypnosis   350
      Etzel Cardeña, Jose Maldonado,
      Onno van der Hart, and David Spiegel

25. Marital and Family Therapy   354
      David S. Riggs

26. Creative Therapies   356
      David Read Johnson

27. Integration and Summary   359
      Arieh Y. Shalev, Matthew J. Friedman,
      Edna B. Foa, and Terence M. Keane

Index   380

1

Introduction

Edna B. Foa, Terence M. Keane,
and Matthew J. Friedman

The treatment guidelines presented in this book were developed under the auspices of the PTSD Treatment Guidelines Task Force established by the Board of Directors of the International Society for Traumatic Stress Studies (ISTSS) in November 1997. Our goal was to develop a set of treatment guidelines based on an extensive review of the clinical and research literature prepared by experts in one field. The book consists of two parts. The first comprises the position papers that describe the salient literature; the second, the much briefer treatment guidelines. These guidelines are intended to inform the clinician on what we determined were the best practices in the treatment of individuals with a diagnosis of posttraumatic stress disorder (PTSD). PTSD is a serious psychological condition that occurs as a result of experiencing a traumatic event. The symptoms that characterize PTSD are reliving the traumatic event or frightening elements of it; avoidance of thoughts, memories, people, and places associated with the event; emotional numbing; and symptoms of elevated arousal. Often accompanied by other psychological disorders, PTSD is a complex condition that can be associated with significant morbidity, disability, and impairment of life functions.

In the development of these practice guidelines, the Task Force *acknowledged* that traumatic experiences can lead to the development of several different disorders, including major depression, specific phobias, disorders of extreme stress not otherwise specified (DESNOS), personality disorders such as borderline anxiety disorder, and panic disorder. Yet the focus of these guidelines is specifically on the treatment of PTSD and its symptoms as defined in the fourth edition of the *Diagnostic and Statistical Manual of Mental Disorders* (DSM-IV) of the American Psychiatric Association (1994).

It is also recognized that the PTSD diagnostic framework is inherently limiting and these limitations may be particularly salient for survivors of early childhood sexual and physical abuse. Sometimes referred to as DESNOS, people with these histories display a wide range of relational and interpersonal problems that contribute to distressed lives and disability. Yet relatively little is known about the successful treatment of patients with these trauma histories. There is a growing clinical consensus, with a degree of empirical support, that some patients with these histories require multimodal interventions applied consistently over a longer time period.

The Task Force also recognized that PTSD is often accompanied by other psychological conditions and that such comorbidity requires clinical sensitivity, attention, and evaluation at the point of diagnosis and throughout the process of treatment. Disorders of particular concern are substance abuse and major depression, the most frequently co-occurring conditions. Practitioners are referred to the guidelines for these disorders in the development of treatment plans for individuals who manifest multiple disorders and to the integration and summary comments in Chapter 27.

These guidelines are intended for adults, adolescents, and children who have developed PTSD. Their objective is to assist the clinician in providing treatment to these individuals. Because clinicians with diverse professional backgrounds provide mental health treatment for PTSD, the guidelines were developed with interdisciplinary input. Psychologists, psychiatrists, social workers, creative arts therapists, marital therapists, and others actively contributed to, and participated in, the developmental process. Accordingly, the guidelines are suitable for the diversity of clinicians who treat PTSD.

The Task Force explicitly excluded from consideration individuals who are currently involved in violent or abusive relationships. These individuals, ranging from children who are living with an abusive caregiver, to women or men who are currently targets of domestic abuse or violence, to those still living in a war zone, may well meet diagnostic criteria for PTSD. Yet their treatment, and the related forensic and ethical issues that arise, differs fundamentally from those individuals whose traumatic events are over. Individuals who are in the midst of a traumatic situation require special considerations from the clinician. Other practice guidelines will need to be developed for these circumstances.

Little is known about the treatment of PTSD in nonindustrialized countries. Research and scholarly treatises on the topic come largely from the Western industrialized nations. The Task Force acknowledges this cultural limitation explicitly. There is growing recognition that PTSD is a universal response to exposure to traumatic events that is observed in many different cultures and societies. Yet there is a need for systematic research to determine the extent to which the treatments, both psychological and psychopharmacological, that have proven efficacy in Western societies are effective in non-Western cultures.

Finally, clinicians following these guidelines should not limit themselves to only these approaches and techniques. Creative integration of new approaches that have been found to be helpful in other conditions and that have a theoretically sound foundation are encouraged in an effort to optimize treatment outcome.

THE PROCESS OF DEVELOPING THE GUIDELINES

The process of developing these guidelines was as follows. The Task Force cochairs assembled the Task Force by identifying experts in the major schools of therapy and treatment modalities that are currently used with patients who suffer from PTSD. The Task Force was expanded as additional relevant treatment approaches were identified. Thus, the Task Force represented experts across approaches, theoretical orientations, schools of therapy, and professional training. The focus of the guidelines and their format was determined by the Task Force in a series of meetings.

The Task Force cochairs commissioned position papers on the major treatment areas or modalities from Task Force members. Each paper was to be written by a designated member with assistance from other members or clinicians of their choosing as deemed necessary by that member. The position papers included literature reviews of research and clinical practice.

The literature reviews on each of the topics involved the use of online literature searches such as Published International Literature on Traumatic Stress (PILOTS), MEDLINE, and PsycLIT. The resulting papers adhered to a standard format and were restricted in length. Authors reviewed the literature in their assigned area, presented the clinical findings, reviewed critically the scientific support for the approach, and presented the papers to the Chairs. Completed papers were then distributed to all Task Force members for comments and active discussion. These reviews resulted in further revisions to the papers and these eventually became the chapters in this book.

On the basis of the position papers and careful attention to the literature review, a draft of the brief practice guidelines for each treatment approach was developed. These appear in Part II. In these guidelines, each treatment approach or modality was assigned ratings with respect to strength of evidence regarding its efficacy. These ratings were standardized using a coding system adapted from the Agency for Health Care Policy and Research (AHCPR; U.S. Department of Health and Human Services, Public Health Service). This rating system, presented below, represents an effort to formulate recommendations for practitioners based on the available scientific evidence.

The guidelines were reviewed by all members of the Task Force for concurrence and then presented to the Board of Directors of the ISTSS, sent for review to a broad range of professional associations, presented at a public forum at the annual meeting of the ISTSS, and placed on the ISTSS website for comments from the membership. Feedback obtained from this iterative process was incorporated into the guidelines.

There are limitations that exist in the scientific literature on PTSD as well as for other mental disorders. Specifically, most studies use inclusion and exclusion criteria in order to define participants appropriately; accordingly, each study may not fully represent the complete spectrum of patients seeking treatment. It is customary, for example, in studies of PTSD treatment to exclude patients with active substance dependence, acute suicidal ideation, neuropsychological deficits, retardation, or cardiovascular disease. Generalization of the findings, and the resulting guidelines, to these populations would not be appropriate.

CLINICAL ISSUES

Type of Trauma

Most randomized clinical trials (RCTs) with combat (mostly Vietnam) veterans showed less treatment efficacy than RCTs with nonveterans whose PTSD was related to other traumatic experiences (e.g., sexual assaults, accidents, natural disasters). Therefore, some experts believe that combat veterans with PTSD are less responsive to treatment than survivors of other traumas. Such a conclusion is premature. The difference between veterans and other PTSD patients may be related to the greater severity and chronicity of their PTSD rather than to differences inherent to combat traumas. Furthermore, the poor treatment response in veterans may be a sampling artifact, since veterans currently receiving treatment at VA hospitals may constitute a self-selected group of chronic patients with multiple impairments. In short, there is no conclusive evidence at this time that PTSD following certain traumas is especially resistant to treatment.

Single versus Multiple Traumas

No clinical studies have been designed to address the question of whether the number of previous traumas predicts treatment response among PTSD patients. Since most treatment studies have been conducted with either military veterans or female adult survivors of sexual assault, many of whom have a history of multiple assaults, it appears that much of the current knowledge about treatment efficacy applies to people who have been traumatized more than once. It would be of great interest to conduct studies comparing individuals with single versus multiple traumas in order to find out whether, as expected, the former would be more responsive to treatment. Recruitment for such studies could be very difficult, however, since the research design would have to control for PTSD severity and chronicity, as well as for comorbid diagnoses—each of which may be more predictive of treatment response than number of traumas experienced.

Chronicity of PTSD

There is growing interest in clinical approaches that emphasize prevention, identification of risk factors, early detection of PTSD, and acute intervention. This is because of the idea that, as with many medical and mental disorders, PTSD has a better prognosis if clinical intervention is implemented as early as possible. However, the few studies available to date do not support this view. On the other hand, there is abundant evidence that many people who develop PTSD continue to suffer from the disorder indefinitely. Although it is unclear whether chronic PTSD is inherently (e.g., psychobiologically) different than more acute clinical presentations, it is generally believed that chronic PTSD is more difficult to treat.

Some patients with chronic PTSD develop a persistent incapacitating mental illness marked by severe and intolerable symptoms; marital, social, and vocational disability; as well as extensive use of psychiatric and community services. Such patients may benefit more from case management and psychosocial rehabilitation than from psycho- or pharmacotherapy (see Chapter 11).

Gender

Although lifetime prevalence rates of PTSD are twice as high for women as for men (10.4% vs. 5%) and women are four times more likely to develop PTSD when exposed to the same trauma, gender differences in response to treatment have not been studied systematically. Therefore, we do not know whether gender is predictive of treatment outcome. It is important to emphasize this point, since, as noted earlier, a superficial review of the treatment literature suggests that women are more responsive to treatment than men. On further inspection, however, several differences between treatment studies with men and women can be noted, making direct comparisons difficult. First, the PTSD of women studied has usually been caused by (childhood or adult) sexual trauma, whereas studies with men have usually involved war veterans. Second, since there are few data on men who are not Vietnam veterans, one cannot generalize the published data regarding veterans to men with other trauma histories. Finally, other factors such as treatment modality, PTSD severity/chronicity, or the presence of comorbid disorders will need to be systematically controlled in future studies before differences in treatment outcome can be attributed to gender. In short, it is impossible to conclude that gender is predictive of treatment response at this time.

Age

Two questions are relevant concerning the effects of age on treatment outcome: (1) Does the age at which the trauma occurred influence response to treatment? and (2) Does the age when treatment began affect treatment outcome? Neither question has been studied systematically; hence, there are no conclusive data on either question. Adults and children have responded to some treatments and not others. Age of traumatization has not predicted treatment outcome in studies published to date.

Children

Children present so many distinct challenges for assessment and treatment that an entire chapter in this volume has been devoted to treatment of children with PTSD . Developmental level is particularly important, since it may influence both the clinical phenomenology of PTSD in children as well as the choice of treatment. In addition, parental factors must be carefully considered when treating children. Developmental biological factors may also influence choice of drug, if pharmacotherapy is indicated, while developmental cognitive factors may influence both assessment strategies and choice of psychotherapy.

Elder Adults

PTSD may have its onset or reoccurrence at any point in the life cycle. It may persist for decades and even intensify in old age. Developmental factors unique to older adults may influence susceptibility to PTSD among the aged. These include a sense of helplessness produced by illness, diminished functional capacity, or social marginalization. Death of loved ones can trigger intrusive recollections of traumatic losses, thereby precipitating a relapse of PTSD symptoms that may have been in remission for decades. Retirement and the life review process of old age can also increase vulnerability to PTSD exacerbation or relapse. Developmental biological factors may influence both the choice and recommended dosage of any drug selected for pharmacotherapy, while cognitive status may influence the approach to both assessment and psychotherapy for older PTSD patients.

FACTORS AFFECTING TREATMENT DECISIONS

At present, few empirical data exist to guide us in the question of how to decide the course of treatment for PTSD. However, some clinical considerations are discussed below, as well as in Chapter 27.

Treatment Goals

All treatments presented in these guidelines have proponents who claim that they are clinically useful for patients with PTSD. The therapeutic goals for each treatment, however, are not necessarily the same. Some treatments (e.g., cognitive-behavioral therapy, pharmacotherapy and eye movement desensitization and reprocessing) target PTSD symptom reduction as the major clinical outcome by which efficacy should be judged. Other treatments (e.g., hypnosis, art therapy, and, possibly, psychoanalysis) emphasize the capacity to enrich the assessment or therapeutic process rather than the ability to improve PTSD symptoms. Still other treatments (e.g., psychosocial rehabilitation) emphasize functional improvement with or without reduction of PTSD symptoms. Finally, some interventions (e.g., hospitalization, substance abuse treatment) focus primarily on severe disruptive behaviors or comorbid disorders that must be addressed before PTSD treatment per se can be initiated.

Treatment of PTSD

Treatment of PTSD is the major criterion by which all clinical practice is evaluated in these guidelines. Some treatments appear to reduce all clusters of PTSD symptoms, while others seem to be effective in attenuating one symptom cluster (e.g., intrusion [B], avoidant/numbing [C], or arousal [D] symptoms) but not others. Chapter 2 discusses state-of-the-art methods for assessing and monitoring PTSD symptom severity during a treatment trial. Some experts have challenged the focus on specific symptoms when evaluating various therapeutic approaches, arguing that the best gauge of clinical efficacy is the capacity of a given treatment to produce global improvement in PTSD rather than specific symptom reduction. In these guidelines, however, the major criterion for treatment efficacy is reduction of PTSD symptoms, although clinical global improvement is indicated when available.

Comorbidity

As with other mental disorders, patients with PTSD usually have at least one other psychiatric disorder. Indeed, U.S. epidemiological findings indicate that 80% of patients with lifetime PTSD suffer from lifetime depression, another anxiety disorder, or chemical abuse/dependency. Good clinical practice dictates that the best treatment is one that might be expected to ameliorate both PTSD and comorbid symptoms. Therefore, the presence of a specific comorbid disorder may prompt a clinician to choose one particular treatment rather than another. This matter is addressed in more detail in Chapter 27. Again, it must be emphasized, however, that treatment of PTSD is the major criterion by which all the clinical practices have been evaluated.

Suicidality

Self-destructive and impulsive behaviors, while not part of the core PTSD symptom complex, are recognized as associated features of this disorder that may profoundly affect clinical management. Therefore, the routine assessment of all patients presenting with PTSD should include a careful evaluation of current suicidal ideation and past history of suicidal attempts. Risk factors for suicide should also be assessed, such as current depression and substance abuse. If significant suicidality is present, it must be addressed before any other treatment is initiated. If the patient cannot be safely managed as an outpatient, hospitalization should be the immediate clinical focus. If suicidality is secondary to depression and/or substance abuse, clinical attention must focus on either or both conditions before initiating treatment for PTSD.

Chemical Abuse/Dependence

Lifetime prevalence rates of alcohol abuse/dependence among men and women with PTSD are approximately 52% and 28%, respectively, while lifetime prevalence rates for drug abuse/dependence are 35% and 27%, respectively. Such comorbid disorders not only complicate treatment but in some cases might also exacerbate PTSD itself. In addition, a number of legal substances such as nicotine, caffeine, and sympathomimetics (e.g., nasal decongestants) may interfere with treatment and, therefore, should be carefully assessed with all PTSD patients. In many cases, if significant chemical abuse/dependency is present, it should be addressed before PTSD treatment is initiated.

Concurrent General Medical Conditions

There is mounting evidence that traumatized individuals appear to be at greater risk of developing medical illnesses. Compared to nontraumatized individuals, trauma survivors report more medical symptoms, use more medical services, have more medical illnesses detected during a physical examination, and display higher mortality. A few studies suggest that such adverse medical consequences may be mediated by PTSD. This has generated recent interest in screening primary and specialty medical patients for both a trauma history and for PTSD symptoms. This work is in its infancy, however, and there are no data on treatment of PTSD among patients seeking medical or surgical care.

Disability and Functional Impairment

PTSD sufferers differ greatly from one another with respect to symptom severity, chronicity, complexity, comorbidity, associated symptoms, and functional impairment. These differences may affect both the choice of treatment and the clinical goals. For some patients with chronic PTSD, functional improvement may be much more important than reduction of PTSD symptoms. In others (especially those who have been subjected to protracted child sexual abuse or torture), clinical interventions often need to focus primarily on symptoms of dissociation, impulsivity, affect liability, somatization, interpersonal difficulties, or pathological changes in identity. Therefore, although the major emphasis in these guidelines is on reduction of core PTSD symptoms, clinicians may find that functional improvement is the most important or appropriate clinical priority for some patients.

Indications for Hospitalization

Inpatient treatment should be considered when the individual is in imminent danger of harming self or others, has destabilized or relapsed significantly in the ability to function, is in the throes of major psychosocial stressors, and/or is in need of specialized observation/evaluation in a secure environment. Elective hospitalization on a specialized inpatient treatment program is reviewed at length in a chapter devoted entirely to this topic (see Chapter 10). The general recommendation is that such a hospitalization must occur in collaboration with outpatient providers and be integrated into the overall long-term treatment plan that has been developed. Our basic philosophy is that a focus on the past trauma is only in the interest of the future. The goal of treatment is to facilitate efforts to create a life that can move beyond the current immobilization and preoccupation produced by the trauma.

WHAT TREATMENTS ARE INCLUDED IN THE GUIDELINES?

The treatment for trauma-related disturbances has been discussed extensively in the literature for over 100 years. This rich literature has provided us with much clinical wisdom. In the last two decades, several treatments for PTSD have been studied using experimental and statistical methods. Thus, at the present time, we have both clinical and scientific knowledge about what treatment modalities help patients with posttrauma problems. Accordingly, the guidelines contain a variety of psychotherapies and pharmacotherapies that have been practiced with trauma victims who suffer trauma-related symptoms.

The scientific and clinical evidence for the efficacy of these therapies in reducing PTSD and related symptoms vary greatly from one another. However, the study of treatment efficacy for PTSD is still in its initial stage relative to other mental disorders; consequently, the Task Force decided to include in the guidelines both therapies that have been found effective by well-controlled studies and therapies that have long history of practice with traumatized individuals but have not yet been subjected to empirical testing.

CLINICAL RESEARCH ISSUES

What Are Well-Controlled Studies?

Many studies have been conducted to ascertain the efficacy of various treatments in reducing PTSD, only relatively few studies to date have employed rigorous methods. Well-controlled studies should have the following features:

1. *Clearly defined target symptoms.* Merely experiencing a trauma is not an indication for treatment in and of itself. Significant trauma-related symptoms, such as the presence of PTSD or depression, should be present to justify treatment. Whatever the target symptom or syndrome, it should be defined clearly so that appropriate measures can be employed to assess improvement. In addition to ascertaining diagnostic status, it is also important to specify a threshold of symptom severity as an inclusion criterion for entering treatment.

A related issue to target symptoms is the importance of delineating inclusion and exclusion criteria. Delineation of inclusion–exclusion criteria can be of assistance both in examining predictors of outcome and in evaluating the efficacy of the treatment and its generalizability beyond the studied sample. If a treatment is effective regardless of sample differences, it proves more robust and therefore a more useful treatment.

2. *Reliable and valid measures.* Once target symptoms have been identified and the population defined, measures with good psychometric properties should be employed (see earlier discussion on measures). For studies targeting a particular diagnosis, assessment should include instruments designed to yield diagnoses as well as instruments that assess symptom severity.

3. *Use of blind evaluators.* Early studies of treatment of traumatized individuals relied primarily on therapist and patient reports to evaluate treatment efficacy and introduced expectancy and demand biases into the evaluation. The use of blind evaluators is a current requirement for a credible treatment outcome study. Two procedures are involved in keeping an evaluator blind. First, the evaluator should not be the same person conducting the treatment. Second, patients should be trained not to reveal their treatment condition during the evaluation so as not to bias the blind evaluator's ratings.

4. *Assessor training.* The reliability and validity of an assessment depends largely on the skill of the evaluator; thus, training of assessors is critical and a minimum criterion should be specified. This includes demonstrating inter-

rater reliability and calibrating assessment procedures over the course of the study to prevent evaluator drift.

5. *Manualized, replicable, specific treatment programs.* It is also important that the treatment chosen is designed to address the target problem defined by inclusion criteria. Thus, if PTSD is the disorder targeted for treatment, employing a treatment specifically developed for PTSD would be most appropriate. Detailed treatment manuals are of utmost importance in evaluating treatment efficacy because they help to ensure consistent treatment delivery across patients and across therapists, and afford replicability of the treatment to determine generalizability.

6. *Unbiased assignment to treatment.* To eliminate one potential source of bias, neither patients nor therapists should be allowed to choose the patient's treatment condition. Instead, patients should be assigned randomly to treatment condition, or assigned via a stratified sampling approach. This helps to ensure that observed differences or similarities among treatments are due to the techniques employed rather than to extraneous factors. To separate the effects of treatment from therapists, each treatment should be delivered by at least two therapists, and patients should be randomly assigned to therapists within each condition.

7. *Treatment adherence.* The final component of a well-controlled study is the use of treatment adherence ratings. These ratings inform as to whether the treatments were carried out as planned, and whether components of one treatment condition drifted into another.

Limitations of Well-Controlled Studies

While controlled studies are essential for evaluating the efficacy of a given treatment approach, the data emerging from such studies are by no means without problems. The stringent requirements of such studies can render unrepresentative samples; therefore, the generalizablity of the results may be limited. For example, the requirement of random assignments to studies that include placebo may be acceptable to some patients but not to others and the factors that lead someone to enroll in such studies may be germane to how well he or she responds to treatment. Differential rates of dropout also need to be considered when evaluating the studies that have been completed. Some treatments by their very nature are powerful and/or may not be consistent with the patient's expectations of treatment, leading to dropouts. This can and should influence conclusions.

Another source of bias in knowledge derived from controlled studies is that certain treatment approaches are more amenable for some studies than others. For example, short-term and structured treatments such as cognitive-behavioral therapy and medication are more suitable for controlled trials than longer, less structured treatments. As a result, knowledge about the efficacy of the former is more available than that of the latter.

What Is Effect Size?

There are many ways to calculate the effectiveness of a given treatment in ameliorating the target disorder. One way is to examine how many treated people lose their diagnosis. Another way is to calculate reduction in symptom severity from pre- to posttreatment or to follow-up. Effect size is a statistical method that was developed to evaluate in a standardized manner how much, on the average, a given treatment program reduced the severity of the target symptoms severity. Using an effect size method enables us to compare efficacy of different types of treatments across studies. This method was applied to all empirical studies discussed in this volume.

To enhance comparability among the position papers, procedures for calculating and presenting effect sizes were standardized in two ways. First, a single effect size statistic was adopted: a member of Cohen's d family of effect size estimators known as Hedges's unbiased g. Like Cohen's d, Hedges's unbiased g is easy to conceptualize. It is based on the standardized difference between two means, typically the mean of a treatment sample minus the mean of a comparison sample divided by pooled standard deviations of the two samples. Therefore, each whole number represents one standard deviation away from the comparison sample mean. For example, if $g = 0.5$, the mean of the treatment sample would be estimated to be one-half standard deviation above the comparison sample. Unlike Cohen's d, which systematically overestimates when used with small samples, Hedges's unbiased g includes a mathematical adjustment for small sample bias. To further ease comparability, the signs of all effect sizes were then adjusted such that positive effect sizes always represent better outcome than the comparison group.

Second, a hierarchical procedure was adopted for selecting the studies to be included in each position paper. This was done because studies that utilize different kinds of comparison groups produce effect sizes that are not directly comparable, even when utilizing the same effect size statistic. If enough studies that utilized comparison groups such as a waiting list or a nonspecific control treatment were available for inclusion in a position paper, studies utilizing other comparison group types were not included. If the number of "no treatment" comparison studies was inadequate for drawing conclusions, studies utilizing "placebo" comparison groups were included with the caution that the effect sizes calculated from these studies would tend to be smaller in comparison, even if the treatments were equally effective. Only if enough studies of either type were not available would purely within-subjects design in which there was no comparison group be included. In these designs, the only way to calculate a standardized difference effect size is to estimate a comparison group's scores by using the pretreatment scores of the treatment group. Because these estimated scores are not independent, effect sizes resulting from these calculations are inflated compared to effect sizes from the other two comparison group types and should not be compared directly with them.

The State of Current Knowledge
About Treatment of PTSD

Research on treatment efficacy for PTSD began in the early 1980s, with the introduction of the disorder into DSM-III. Since then, many case reports and studies have been published. These studies vary with respect to their methodological rigor; therefore, the strength of conclusions that can be drawn from them is different for different treatments. In general, psychotherapy, specifically, cognitive-behavioral therapy, and medication, specifically, selective serotonin reuptake inhibitors, have both been shown to be effective treatments for PTSD. However, the absence of evidence for a technique or approach does not imply that it does not work, only that it has not yet been subjected to rigorous scientific scrutiny.

There is some research evidence that psychodynamic psychotherapy, hypnotherapy, and eye movement desensitization and reprocessing are also effective, but the studies are either less numerous or less well controlled. Controlled research on other approaches to treating PTSD is needed and many ongoing projects exist internationally at the time of publication of these guidelines. Most conclusions on the treatment of PTSD are based upon efficacy trials and should be viewed cautiously as a result. The field awaits the completion of effectiveness trials to determine the extent to which findings in controlled treatment trials generalize to other clinical environments. As with all disorders, periodic updates of these guidelines are needed to track progress in the field.

Combined Treatments

There are no studies that systematically examined the value of combining psychotherapy with medication, or combinations of medications. Research on other disorders (e.g., depression) has shown benefits from combination approaches. Only a couple of studies examine whether programs that include a wide variety of cognitive-behavioral therapy techniques yield better outcome over programs that include fewer techniques. On the whole, these studies do not support the administration of more complex programs. Despite the scarcity of knowledge, clinical wisdom dictates the use of combined treatments for some patients. Many patients with PTSD also suffer from depression. If the depression is moderate to severe, a combination of psychotherapy and medication is often desired.

THE CODING SYSTEM

To help the clinician in evaluating the treatment approaches presented in the guidelines, the following coding system was devised to denote the strength of the evidence for each approach.

Each recommendation is identified as falling into one of six categories of endorsements, each indicated by a letter. The six categories represent varying levels of evidence for the use of a specific treatment procedure, or for a specific recommendation. This system was adopted from the Agency of Health Care Policy and Research (AHCPR) classification of Level of Evidence.

> *Level A:* Evidence is based upon randomized, well-controlled clinical trials for individuals with PTSD.
>
> *Level B:* Evidence is based upon well-designed clinical studies, without randomization or placebo comparison for individuals with PTSD.
>
> *Level C:* Evidence is based on service and naturalistic clinical studies, combined with clinical observations that are sufficiently compelling to warrant use of the treatment technique or follow the specific recommendation.
>
> *Level D:* Evidence is based on long-standing and widespread clinical practice that has not been subjected to empirical tests in PTSD.
>
> *Level E:* Evidence is based on long-standing practice by circumscribed groups of clinicians that has not been subjected to empirical tests in PTSD.
>
> *Level F:* Evidence is based on recently developed treatment that has not been subjected to clinical or empirical tests in PTSD.

TREATMENT CONSIDERATIONS

Therapist Training

To utilize most appropriately the information contained in these guidelines, individuals should be professionally trained and licensed in their state or country. Typical training would include a graduate-level degree, a clinical internship or its equivalent, and past supervision in the specific technique or approach employed.

Choice of Treatment Setting

Most treatments for PTSD take place in an outpatient setting, such as psychiatric or psychological clinics and counseling centers. However, an inpatient setting may be required when the patient manifests a significant tendency for suicidality or severe comorbid disorders (e.g., psychotic episode, severe borderline personality). The treatment setting should be determined during the initial diagnostic evaluation. Careful monitoring of the patient's mental status throughout treatment may indicate the appropriateness of changes in the treatment setting.

Treatment Management

A comprehensive diagnostic evaluation should precede treatment to determine the presence of PTSD and whether PTSD symptoms constitute the predominant problem of the patient. Once the diagnosis is ascertained, irrespective of the treatment chosen, the clinician should establish a professional milieu. First, the clinician must form and maintain a therapeutic alliance. Special attention should be given to trust and safety issues. Many individuals with PTSD have difficulties trusting others, especially if the trauma had interpersonal aspects (e.g., assault, rape). Other patients have related problems in recognizing and respecting personal boundaries when they enter a therapeutic relationship. Therefore, during the first stage of therapy, attention should be directed to these sensitive issues, providing reassurance that the patient's welfare is the priority in the therapeutic relationship. Second, the therapist should demonstrate concern with the patient's physical safety when planning the treatment, such as appraising the safety of places selected for exposure exercises, or monitoring the safety of the woman who has just left an abusive relationship. Third, the clinician should provide education and reassurance with regard to the PTSD symptoms and related problems. Fourth, the patient's PTSD symptoms and general functioning should be monitored over time. Fifth, comorbid conditions should be identified and addressed. When necessary, it is important to work with other health professionals and with the patient's family members and significant others. Many patients with PTSD require dependable and steady therapeutic relationships because their symptoms do not remit completely and can exacerbate with anniversary reactions and trauma reminders. For these reasons, it is important to assure the patient of the continued availability of his or her therapist. Finally, many patients with PTSD have ongoing crises in their lives and may need to rely intermittently upon a supportive therapist. Crises that arise during the course of therapy have clear implications for the sequencing of treatments for that patient. For some patients, starts and pauses in treatment may characterize the only way that they can engage the process of change. Acknowledging this and accounting for this in designing a treatment plan may avert problems during the intensive therapeutic phase. Additional treatment considerations are presented in Chapter 27.

Treatment Resistance

Despite the progress that has been achieved in the treatment of PTSD, many patients do not benefit from the first line of treatment. The phenomenon of treatment resistance has been particularly noted among Vietnam War veterans receiving VA treatment in the United States, but other trauma populations have their share of treatment failures. It seems that patients with pervasive dysfunction and/or high comorbidity are especially resistant to first-line therapy. These patients may be especially good candidates for programs that include multiple treatment modalities such as meditation, psychotherapy, family therapy, and rehabilitation therapy.

Readiness for Treatment

Several factors deter many traumatized individuals with acute PTSD from seeking treatment for the disorder: They assume that the symptoms will dissipate with time; they feel that nothing can help them, or that there is an element of shame surrounding their traumatic experiences. Accordingly, attempts to offer treatment in this initial stage often fail. Even when PTSD becomes chronic, many sufferers do not seek treatment or present to treatment with related symptoms such as depression. Therefore, after diagnosing the disorder, a crucial first step in preparing the patient for treatment of PTSD is educating him or her about the disorder and its high rates among trauma survivors. Many sufferers are reluctant to enter treatment because they view their PTSD symptoms as a personal failure. For many patients, normalization of their symptoms results in immediate relief and reduces their reluctance to enter treatment.

Some patients are reluctant to enter treatment because it often entails discussing the traumatic event either during the assessment or in therapy. The clinician should encourage patients to express their misgivings and be sensitive to the distress they experience when discussing or recounting their traumatic experiences, so that their concerns can be addressed in the first stage of therapy.

VALIDITY OF MEMORIES OF TRAUMATIC EVENTS

To receive the diagnosis of PTSD, one must first be exposed to a traumatic event. Treatment of PTSD typically involves the processing of this event, its meaning, and its consequences. All the methods in the guidelines presuppose the existence of a verifiable and valid traumatic event. The guidelines do not address the use of any of these approaches in an effort to recover unconscious memories of past traumatic events.

The Task Force does acknowledge that memories for traumatic events are sometimes not reported, or are forgotten by individuals who seek mental health treatment. Yet because of lack of scientific evidence, the Task Force does *not* support the position that the presence of some of the symptoms of PTSD (e.g., emotional numbing, concentration problems, etc.) is clear evidence that the patient experienced a traumatic event. Therefore, the Task Force does not support the use of these guidelines to assist in the recovery of forgotten traumatic memories.

HOW TO USE THE GUIDELINES

These guidelines summarize the state of the art in the treatment of PTSD to inform mental health professionals of the care of patients with PTSD. They begin at the point where the patient has been diagnosed as having PTSD, according to the criteria in DSM-IV. The guidelines also assume that the patient has been evaluated for comorbid disorders. The guidelines include treatments with various degrees of evidence for their efficacy, indicated by the coding system described earlier and the conclusions section for each treatment approach.

The clinician is encouraged to adopt treatments that have been proven effective. However, it is important to remember that several treatments with proven efficacy (e.g., medication, cognitive-behavioral therapy) are available. Also, many treatments that have not been evaluated in well-controlled studies have been practiced extensively and, thus, have accumulated clinical evidence for their efficacy. The distinction between clinical wisdom and scientific knowledge is emphasized here. Not all of the art of psychotherapy has been examined in randomized, controlled clinical trials. Experienced and sensitive clinicians are often in the best position to determine the nature and the timing of specific psychological and psychopharmacological interventions.

We recognize that not all treatments are universally effective. Even the best treatments we have to offer fail in certain circumstances. Clinicians are encouraged to assess systematically patients who are not responding to interventions to determine the presence of undisclosed or undetected conditions that might be responsible for a nonresponse. Detection of factors related to a lack of full participation in a treatment plan may also assist the clinician in understanding a poor outcome. Given that several treatments for PTSD have empirical support, the clinician can sequentially apply these to optimize treatment success.

Finally, the choice of treatment approach should be decided by the clinical circumstances presented by the specific patient (e.g., the presence of comorbid disorders and the patient's preferences) as well as by the efficacy of the treatment modality. Much has been learned about the treatment of PTSD in the past 20 years, and much more still needs to be learned. Clinicians are encouraged to incorporate into their clinical practice the approaches that have proven efficacy. In this way, the public health of society will be enhanced. This is the goal of the ISTSS and its production of these treatment guidelines.

2

Diagnosis and Assessment

Terence M. Keane, Frank W. Weathers,
and Edna B. Foa

Posttraumatic stress disorder (PTSD) is a psychological condition that reflects the development of characteristic symptoms following exposure to high-magnitude life stressors (*Diagnostic and Statistical Manual of Mental Disorders*, fourth edition [DSM-IV]; American Psychiatric Association, 1994). These symptoms include distressing thoughts, feelings, and images that recapitulate the traumatic event; a persistent avoidance of cues associated with the traumatic event; emotional numbing of responsiveness; and a collection of symptoms that represent a persistent increase in stress and arousal. Typically, the disturbance is experienced for longer than 1 month and it causes clinically significant distress or impairment in occupational and social functioning.

To qualify for this diagnosis an individual must be exposed to a traumatic event that involved life-endangering components and the individual's response had to include intense fear, helplessness, or horror. If symptom duration is less than 3 months, then a diagnosis of acute PTSD is conferred, while if duration extends beyond 3 months, the condition is deemed chronic. Occasionally, symptoms emerge months or even years following the exposure to the traumatic event. In these cases, a diagnosis of PTSD with delayed onset is warranted.

DIAGNOSTIC CRITERIA

Fortunately, most people who are exposed to a traumatic event do seem to recover over time. Yet for a sizeable minority, symptoms of PTSD seem to occur and in the absence of treatment can cascade into the development of a serious and persistent psychiatric condition. PTSD is characterized by reex-periencing symptoms that include (1) recurrent and intrusive recollections of the event, (2) recurrent dreams of the event, (3) acting as if the event were re-curring, (4) intense distress at exposure to cues that symbolize the event, and (5) physiological reactivity to cues or reminders of the event.

The disorder also encompasses symptoms of avoidance and emotional numbing. These can include (1) efforts to avoid thoughts, feelings, or even conversations of the event; (2) efforts to avoid activities, places, or people as-sociated with the event; (3) an inability to recall important details surround-ing the event; (4) a diminished interest in formerly enjoyable activities of life; (5) a feeling of detachment, estrangement, or alienation from other people; (6) a restricted range of emotional experiences; and (7) a sense of a shortened future accompanied by a notable lack of preparation for the future.

Additionally, symptoms of arousal that were not present prior to the traumatic event conclude the symptom picture. These arousal symptoms can be (1) sleep difficulties, (2) irritability or anger outbursts, (3) difficulty concen-trating, (4) hypervigilance for danger or a reoccurrence of a life-threatening situation, and (5) an exaggerated and distressing startle response.

PREVALENCE OF EXPOSURE
TO TRAUMATIC EVENTS

Once thought to be relatively rare, recent epidemiological research on the prevalence of exposure to traumatic events has challenged this notion. Norris (1992) surveyed four urban areas in southeastern United States and found that 69% of the adults reported experiencing one or more traumatic events in their lives. Similarly, Resnick, Kilpatrick, Dansky, Saunders, and Best (1993) conducted a nationwide survey of criminal victimization among women and found that 69% of them reported being victimized at least once in their lives. Breslau, Davis, Andreski, and Peterson (1991) found a preva-lence of 39% of people experiencing a traumatic event in a relatively young, well-educated, and insured population. Even college-student populations re-ported high rates of exposure to traumatic events. Vrana and Lauterbach (1994) found that 84% of the undergraduate population at a major Midwest-ern university reported exposure, with 33% stating that they had experienced four or more traumatic events. Clearly, exposure to traumatic events is far more commonplace than experts originally anticipated.

PREVALENCE OF PTSD

Fortunately, people who are exposed to traumatic life events do not always develop PTSD. In the Breslau, Davis, Andreski, and Peterson (1991) study, approximately 25% of those exposed to a traumatic event ultimately developed PTSD, yielding a nearly 9% lifetime prevalence of the disorder. Norris (1992) found a current rate of PTSD of 5%, while Resnick and collegues (1993) reported a 9% current rate of PTSD among women, accompanied by a 12% lifetime rate. General population estimates have also yielded high rates of PTSD. In the Kessler, Sonnega, Bromet, Hughes, and Nelson (1995) National Comorbidity Survey, lifetime PTSD was found in 8% of the adult population. Prevalence rates of PTSD in children have received little empirical attention to date; this is an area in clear need of additional research.

PTSD also seems to occur at higher rates in populations that we characterize as high risk for the disorder. The National Vietnam Veterans Readjustment Study, a landmark epidemiological effort and the first attempt by any country to quantify the psychological toll of a war on its soldiers, found that 30% of the 3.1 million Vietnam veterans developed PTSD at some time following the war. Fifteen percent of them still had PTSD 15 years after the war concluded.

Similarly, individuals who have experienced rape are also at greater risk for developing PTSD. The Kilpatrick, Edmonds, and Seymour (1992) National Women's Study found that 13% of American women had experienced a completed rape at some time in their life. Nearly one-third of them eventually developed PTSD as a result. This study yielded an astoundingly high national rate of 4% rape-related PTSD among American women.

Disasters also seem to induce PTSD at high rates. Green, Lindy, Grace, and Leonard (1992) studied the effects of the dam collapse in Buffalo Creek, West Virginia. They found a 59% lifetime rate of PTSD among survivors and a 25% current rate 14 years after the flooding.

Clearly, exposure to traumatic events is common in the United States and it seems that the prevalence of PTSD in the general population is high, ranking behind only substance abuse disorders, major depression, and social phobia in frequency. As a result, trauma exposure and PTSD represent a major challenge to the public health delivery system in Western developed countries.

Most of the major, well-controlled studies of the prevalence of traumatic events and PTSD have occurred in the United States. Many scholars feel that the prevalence of trauma exposure and PTSD is higher in the developing world in part due to the lack of resources present there to avert disasters and to mitigate their aftermath (De Girolamo & McFarlane, 1996). Future research will determine the extent to which this is an accurate assessment of the situation in developing countries.

Gender differences in exposure and in the development of PTSD are suggested by the results of several epidemiological studies. As found in the National Comorbidity Survey, it seems that males (60%) are more likely to be exposed to traumatic events than females (50%). Yet females (12%) were more likely to develop PTSD than were males (6%). This distinction may be a real gender difference in the susceptibility to PTSD, possibly linked to biological, psychological, or social differences. Alternatively, it may be a direct function of the types of events to which men and women are differentially exposed. For example, women are more than 10 times as likely to be raped, and men are twice as likely to have experienced a dangerous accident. The capacity of different events to induce PTSD at different rates is only now being explored systematically. These studies may very well inform us about the mechanisms associated with the preliminary gender differences in exposure and PTSD observed to date.

In a recent study on this topic, Breslau and colleagues (1998) indeed found that assaultive violence (including rape) induced the highest rate of PTSD of all the traumatic events measured. Yet the sudden and unexpected death of a loved one contributed the highest proportion of PTSD cases (31%) due to its high frequency in the population (60%). This study also found that PTSD persisted longer in women than men, often longer than 6 months (74%), and longer when the traumatic event was directly rather than indirectly experienced. This study also found racial differences in the development of PTSD in that nonwhites were almost twice as likely to develop PTSD following exposure than were whites, findings that again require continued study to understand more fully the mechanisms involved.

ASSESSMENT OF PTSD

PTSD is thus a disorder with high frequency in the general population. Increasingly, clinicians are recognizing that a sizable portion of members of their clinical practice has experienced traumatic events for which they are requesting services. An additional portion of patients' care is complicated by the presence of PTSD. Accordingly, there has been great interest among clinicians in the proper assessment and evaluation of patients with PTSD. Clearly, PTSD is assessed for many different purposes, and the goals of a particular assessment can determine the approach selected by the professional. Clinicians often have as their objective a diagnostic workup that includes a differential diagnosis and treatment planning. They may also be involved in forensic evaluations in which diagnostic accuracy is of utmost importance. Researchers may be interested in the frequency of occurrence, the risk factors, and the complications associated with PTSD (as in epidemiological studies). Moreover, researchers may seek high levels of diagnostic accuracy when studying biological and psychological parameters of the disorder, as in case–control types of studies. Each clinical and research situation requires a different solution depending upon the assessment goals of the professional. For this reason, we present a general overview of the methods by which clinicians can evaluate the quality of available instruments.

Psychometric Theory and Principles

The quality of psychological assessment is examined through two psychometric characteristics: reliability and validity. Reliability is the consistency or replicability of test scores. Validity is the meaningfulness or accuracy inferences, interpretations, or decisions made upon the basis of scores on tests or instruments. Test developers often report the consistency of tests over time (test–retest reliability), over different interviewers or raters (interrater reliability), or over the many items comprising a particular test (internal consistency). Reliability is reported for continuous measures as a simple correlation coefficient that can vary between 0 and 1. Reliability for dichotomous measures such as diagnostic interviews (indicating the presence or absence of a disorder) often is reported as a kappa coefficient (Cohen, 1960) which is also reported as 0–1 and interpreted as the percent agreement above chance.

Measures of validity include content validity, which represents the extent to which a test provides coverage of the domain of symptoms of a condition. The better the coverage of key symptoms, the better the content validity. If the measure of a disorder predicts something of interest or importance, such as response to an intervention, it is said to have good criterion-related validity. Finally, if a measure is correlated with other measures of the same disorder, it is said to have good construct validity.

Diagnostic instruments in the field of mental health are usually evaluated on the basis of their diagnostic utility, a type of criterion-related validity pertaining to a test's capacity to predict diagnostic status (Kraemer, 1992). There are three steps in determining the diagnostic utility of a given instrument. First, a "gold standard" is selected. In psychological research, this is ordinarily a diagnosis based on a clinical interview, but it may also be a determination based on several sources of information. Second, both the gold standard and the newly developed test are administered to the experimental group of participants. Finally, a variety of cutoff scores are examined to determine their diagnostic utility or, in other words, their ability to predict the diagnosis provided by the gold standard. Optimal cutoff scores for the test are those that predict the greatest number of cases and noncases from the original sample.

All measures of a psychological disorder are imperfect (Gerardi, Keane, & Penk, 1989). Two measures of the error contained within a test are false positives and false negatives. A false positive occurs when a patient scores above the cutoff, but is not a true case. A false negative occurs when a patient scores below the given cutoff yet is in fact a true case. Diagnostic utility is often described in terms of a test's sensitivity and specificity. These are measures of a test's performance that take into account errors made in prediction. Sensitivity is the measure of a test's true positive rate, or the probability that those with the disorder will score above a given cutoff score. Specificity is the true negative rate of a test, or the probability that those without the disorder will score below the cutoff for the test. Sensitivity is low if the test yields too many false negatives, whereas specificity is low if the test yields too many false positives.

Selection of tests and diagnostic instruments should include an examination by the clinician of relevant data on their psychometric properties. Inspection of rates of false positives, false negatives, sensitivity, and specificity will also inform the clinician as to how the instrument performs. Conclusions drawn in the clinical assessment are most accurate if they take into account these limitations.

Structured Diagnostic Interviews

It is standard practice in clinical research to employ a structured diagnostic interview to ensure that all PTSD symptomatology is reviewed in detail. Diagnostic interviews combine the virtues of defining precisely how a diagnosis was made with the use of interviews that have known psychometric properties (i.e., reliability and validity). The use of structured diagnostic interviews in the clinical setting is less common, with perhaps the single exception of clinical forensic practice, in which it is strongly encouraged (Keane, 1995). Nonetheless, the use of diagnostic interviews in clinical settings may well improve diagnostic accuracy and improve treatment planning (Litz & Weathers, 1994). The use of broad-based diagnostic interviews that cover the range of high-frequency diagnoses assists the clinician in that it will provide not only an evaluation of the target disorder but also of the extent of clinical comorbidity that is present (Keane & Wolfe, 1990; Weiss & Marmar, 1997). Some of the available diagnostic interviews and their psychometric properties are presented here.

Structured Clinical Interview for DSM (SCID)

The SCID is the most widely used interview to assess Axis I and Axis II psychiatric disorders. It consists of separate modules for the most common diagnostic categories. While the administration of the full SCID can be time-consuming, it does provide information across a broad range of clinical conditions. In many clinical settings, the SCID is used to assess systematically only those conditions that are most frequently encountered. This is economical in terms of time and still provides an examination across key conditions. In working within the context of a trauma clinic, it is recommended that the anxiety disorder, affective disorder, substance abuse disorder modules, and the psychotic screen be employed. This provides a fairly comprehensive examination of those conditions that are frequently comorbid and a systematic way to ensure that a patient does not endorse signs of schizophrenia, a condition that would require a different initial set of clinical interventions.

The PTSD module of the SCID appears to be both clinically sensitive and reliable. Keane and colleagues (1998) examined the interrater reliability of the SCID by asking a second interviewer to listen to audiotapes of an initial interview. They found a kappa of .68 and agreement across lifetime, current, and never PTSD of 78%. Similarly, in a sample of patients who were reinterviewed within a week by a different clinician, they found a kappa of .66 and diagnostic agreement of 78%.

The SCID's primary limitation is that it permits only a dichotomous rating of a symptom (present or absent), placing clinicians in a forced choice situation. Most clinicians agree that the psychological symptoms occur in a dimensional rather than dichotomous fashion, so the SCID seems limited by the use of the present–absent scoring algorithm. Several options have evolved in the field as a result of this limitation.

Anxiety Disorders Interview Schedule—Revised (ADIS-R)

Developed by DiNardo and Barlow (1988), the ADIS-R is a structured diagnostic interview that focuses primarily on the anxiety and affective disorders. The ADIS-R uses a Likert-type scaling procedure for symptoms and is thus capable of being analyzed in multiple ways to determine the extent to which a symptom is present or absent. Assessment of the psychometric properties of the ADIS-PTSD module in two separate studies produced mixed results. In the first study, a small group of combat veterans was assessed by two independent interviewers. Blanchard, Gerardi, Kolb, and Barlow (1986) found excellent sensitivity (1.0) and specificity (.91). In a community-based study with less impressive results, the hit rates were less stable (DiNardo, Moras, Barlow, Rapee, & Brown, 1993).

PTSD Interview

Watson and colleagues' (1991) PTSD Interview yields both dichotomous and continuous scores. The authors report strong test–retest reliability (.95) and internal consistency (alpha = .92), as well as strong sensitivity (.89), specificity (.94), and kappa (.82) when compared with the Diagnostic Interview Schedule (Robins, Helzer, Croughan, & Ratcliff, 1981).

The PTSD Interview appears to have excellent psychometric properties but differs in administrative format from most other structured diagnostic clinical interviews. With it, patients are provided a copy of the scale to read along with the interviewer. From this copy of the scale, they are asked to give to the clinician their rating on the Likert-type scale for each of the symptoms. This format shares much in common with self-report questionnaires, yet deviates from the other diagnostic scales in that it does not allow clinicians to make ratings of their own and utilize their expertise and experience.

Structured Interview for PTSD (SI-PTSD)

The SI-PTSD was developed by Davidson, Smith, and Kudler (1989). As with the PTSD Interview, the SI-PTSD also yields both dichotomous and continuous measures of PTSD symptoms. As a result, it appears to be a useful instrument for diagnosing PTSD and measuring symptom severity. Symptoms are rated by the clinician on 5-point Likert-type scales, and the focus for the clinician is on symptom severity. It possesses initial probe questions and provides helpful follow-up questions to promote a more thorough understanding of the patient's symptom experiences. In a study of male combat veterans, the authors found sensitivity of .96 and specificity of .80, suggesting sound performance.

Clinician-Administered PTSD Scale (CAPS)

Developed by the National Center for PTSD in Boston, the CAPS was designed for use by trained, experienced clinicians (Blake et al., 1990). Consisting of 30 items, the CAPS assesses all 17 symptoms of PTSD as well as a range of associated, frequently observed features. Also contained in the CAPS are ratings for social and occupational functioning and an assessment of the validity of patient responses. Like the PTSD Interview and the SI-PTSD, the CAPS provides both dichotomous and continuous scores. Unique features of the CAPS are that it contains separate ratings for frequency and intensity of each symptom and possesses behaviorally anchored probe questions and scale values. Interviewers are trained to ask their own follow-up questions and use their clinical judgment in arriving at the best ratings.

If administered completely (i.e., all questions regarding associated features, functional impairments, validity ratings), the CAPS takes approximately 1 hour to complete. If only the diagnostic symptoms are assessed, the time for administration is cut in half.

Psychometric data on the performance of the CAPS demonstrate unusual strength in identifying cases and noncases of PTSD. Across three clinicians and 60 separate male veteran subjects, Weathers and colleagues (1992) found test–retest correlations between .90 and .98. Internal consistency was equally impressive, with alpha at .94 across all three primary symptom clusters. Correlations with other established measures of PTSD yielded strong evidence for the construct validity of the CAPS. The correlation of the CAPS was .91 with the Mississippi Scale, .77 with the Keane PTSD Scale of the MMPI-2, and .89 with the SCID-PTSD symptom score. Correlations with a measure of antisocial personality disorder were low, as predicted by the multitrait–multimethod study design.

Using the CAPS as a continuous measure, it was found to have 84% sensitivity, 95% specificity, 89% efficiency, and a kappa of .78 against the SCID. Using the CAPS as a diagnostic measure, a kappa of .72 was found, as compared with the SCID diagnosis. Whether used as a diagnostic or a continuous measure, these findings establish the CAPS as a sound measure of PTSD with excellent psychometric properties. Replications of these findings with male and female motor vehicle accident survivors (Blanchard et al., 1995) and patients with serious mental illnesses of both genders (Mueser et al., 1999) indicated the generalizability of these results across populations, races, and genders. A recent publication carefully explicated nine different scoring algorithms for the CAPS and their implications for diagnostic accuracy, reliability, and validity coefficients (Weathers, Ruscio, & Keane, 1999).

PTSD Symptom Scale Interview (PSS-I)

Developed by Foa, Riggs, Dancu, and Rothbaum (1993), the PSS-I possesses many strong clinical features that warrant its consideration for clinical and research use. Consisting of the 17 criteria of the PTSD diagnosis, the PSS-I uses Likert-type rating scales for each of the criterion symptoms. It can be scored as a continuous and dichotomous measure of PTSD and takes approximately 20 minutes to complete. Administering this measure to 118 women with sexual assault histories, Foa and colleagues (1993) found excellent interrater reliability, diagnostic sensitivity of .88, and specificity of .96. Test–retest reliability over 1 month was also reported to be strong.

The advantages of the PSS-I are its relative brevity, its promising psychometric properties, and its use of Likert-type rating scales that provide both a dichotomous and a continuous scoring routine. Another strength of this interview is its development and validation with sexual assault survivors, a population of great interest and importance clinically.

Self-Report Questionnaires

Several self-report measures have been developed as a time- and cost-efficient method for obtaining information on PTSD symptomatology. These measures enjoy widespread acceptance and use due to ease of administration and scoring, and they are also useful adjuncts to the structured diagnostic instruments. They can also be invaluable when used as screens for PTSD and are most frequently used as continuous measures of PTSD, but specific cutoff scores can be used in order to arrive at a diagnosis of PTSD.

Impact of Event Scale—Revised (IES-R)

Initially developed by Horowitz, Wilner, and Alvarez (1979), the IES was revised by Weiss and Marmar (1997) to incorporate the symptoms of hyperarousal for PTSD (Criterion D). The original scale, which contained only reexperiencing symptoms and avoidance/numbing symptoms, needed to be revised in order to parallel more closely the diagnostic picture. While the authors have provided some preliminary data, more information is needed about the revised version's reliability and validity. The most frequently used measure of PTSD, the original IES possessed good psychometric properties. Similar studies with the revised instrument will ensure its continued use in clinics and research settings.

Mississippi Scale for Combat-Related PTSD

The Mississippi Scale (Keane, Caddell, & Taylor, 1988) is a 35-item scale designed to measure combat-related PTSD. The items were selected from an initial pool of 200 items generated by experts to closely match the DSM-III criteria for the disorder. The Mississippi Scale has excellent psychometric properties, with an alpha of .94 and test–retest reliability of .97 over a 1-week interval. Using a cutoff score of 107, the Mississippi Scale had strong sensitivity (.93) and specificity (.89).

These results were replicated in an independent laboratory by McFall and colleagues (1990a), who found that the Mississippi Scale was highly correlated with the SCID-PTSD module. These findings suggest that the Mississippi Scale, widely used in clinical and research settings serving veterans, is a valuable self-report tool.

Keane PTSD Scale of the MMPI-2

Originally derived from the Minnesota Multiphasic Personality Inventory (MMPI) Form R, the Keane PTSD Scale (PK) now consists of 46 items empirically drawn from the MMPI-2 (Keane, Malloy, & Fairbank, 1984; Lyons & Keane, 1990). The original report on the scale indicated that the PK correctly classified some 82% of the 200 subjects in the study. Subsequent studies have confirmed these findings in combat veteran populations (Watson, Kucala, & Manifold, 1986).

In terms of reliability, Graham (1990) found the PK to have strong internal consistency (.85–.87) and test–retest reliability (.86–.89). Although only a few studies to date have been conducted on the PK in nonveteran populations, the data appear to be promising (Koretzky & Peck, 1990). More research is needed in this area, especially in the area of forensic psychology, where the MMPI-2 is frequently employed because of its validity indexes.

Penn Inventory for Posttraumatic Stress

The Penn Inventory is a 26-item questionnaire developed by Hammerberg (1992). Its psychometric properties have been examined in multiple trauma populations, and its specificity is comparable to that of the Mississippi Scale, while its sensitivity is only slightly lower. Used with accident victims, veterans, and general psychiatric patients, it has primarily been employed with samples of male patients.

Posttraumatic Diagnostic Scale (PTDS)

Developed by Foa, Cashman, Jaycox, and Perry (1997), the PTDS is derived directly from DSM criteria. The items of the PTDS map directly onto the DSM-IV criteria for PTSD; thus, the questionnaire consists of 17 questions. The PTDS begins with a 12-question checklist to elucidate the traumatic events to which an individual might have been exposed. Next, patients are asked to indicate which of the events experienced has bothered them most in the past month. Patients then rate their reactions to the event at the time of its occurrence in order to determine if the event fits both Criterion A1 and A2.

The patient then rates on a 4-point scale the *frequency* of each of the 17 symptoms of PTSD they have experienced in the past 30 days. The final section of the scale asks for self-ratings of impairment across nine areas of life functioning. This scale was validated using several populations, including combat veterans, accident victims, sexual- and non-sexual-assault survivors, and survivors of a range of other traumatic events.

The psychometric analyses proved to be exceptional. For internal consistency, the coefficient alpha was .92 overall; test–retest reliability for the diagnosis of PTSD over a 2- to 3-week interval was also high (kappa = .74). For symptom severity, the test–retest correlation was .83. When compared to a SCID diagnosis of PTSD, a kappa coefficient of .65 was obtained with 82% agreement; the sensitivity of the test was .89, whereas its specificity was .75. Clearly, this self-report scale functioned well in comparison to the clinician ratings obtained in the SCID. It is a useful self-report and screening device for measuring PTSD and its symptom components.

PTSD Checklist (PCL)

Also developed by researchers at the National Center for PTSD in Boston, the PCL comes in two versions: one for civilians, and the other for military personnel. The scale contains the 17 items contained in the DSM diagnostic criteria scored on a 5-point Likert-type scale. Weathers, Litz, Herman, Huska, and Keane (1993) examined its psychometric properties and found excellent internal consistency (alpha = .97), excellent test–retest reliability over a 2- to 3-day period (.96), and strong correlations with other measures of PTSD: .93 with the Mississippi Scale, .77 with the PK scale, and .90 with the IES. Blanchard, Jones-Alexander, Buckley, and Forneris (1996) used the PCL in their studies of motor vehicle accident victims and found that its correlation with the CAPS was .93, and its overall diagnostic efficiency was .90 compared to the CAPS. The properties of the PCL compared with other populations have yet to be reported in the literature.

Los Angeles Symptom Checklist (LASC)

Consisting of 43 items scored on Likert-type scales, the LASC has been extensively studied across different populations (males and females, adults and adolescents, various trauma types). King, King, Leskin, and Foy (1995) examined the psychometric properties of the LASC and found it to possess high internal consistency (alphas ranging from .88 to .95) and test–retest reliability over a 2-week interval (.90 and .94). Its strengths include the various ways in which it can be scored (continuously or dichotomously) and its inclusion of a range of associated features, signs of distress, and functional problems. Using only the 17-item PTSD index, King and colleagues (1995) found sensitivity of .74, specificity of .77, and an overall hit rate of 76% compared to a SCID diagnosis.

The use of these self-report questionnaires in a wide range of clinical and research contexts seems well supported by extant data. It is clear that they can be successfully employed to measure PTSD symptoms when administering a structured diagnostic interview is not feasible or practical. Many of the measures can be used interchangeably, as the findings appear to be robust for the minor variations in methods and approaches involved. In selecting a particular instrument, the clinician is encouraged to examine the data for that instrument on the population for which it is to be employed. In so doing, the clinician is apt to maximize the accuracy and efficiency of the test employed.

Psychophysiological Measures

Research on biologically based measures of PTSD has grown tremendously in the past 10 years. Findings suggest that PTSD alters a wide range of physiological functions (Yehuda, 1997) and may also affect structural components of the brain (Bremner et al., 1995). To date, these findings have not been subjected to rigorous psychometric testing to determine the extent to which the deviations are predictive of PTSD and non-PTSD cases. The primary exception to this conclusion is in the area of psychophysiological reactivity, which from the start examined diagnostic accuracy (see, e.g., Blanchard, Kolb, Pallmeyer, & Gerardi, 1982; Malloy, Fairbank, & Keane, 1983; Pitman, Orr, Forgue, deJong, & Claiborn, 1987).

The findings in this area clearly point to the capacity of psychophysiological indices to identify and classify cases of PTSD on the basis of reactivity to audio-, audiovisual-, and imagery-based cues. Measures have included heart rate, blood pressure, skin conductance, and electromyography (EMG). Studies covered the range of trauma survivors and include victims of motor vehicle accidents, combat veterans from available eras, and survivors of female sexual assault and terrorism. In perhaps the largest study of its kind, Keane and colleagues (1998) examined the responses of over 1,000 combat veterans to audiovisual- and imagery-based cues of combat experiences. The results supported the presence of elevated psychophysiological arousal and reactivity in the participants, more than two-thirds of whom were correctly classified as PTSD or non-PTSD.

Clearly, psychophysiological assessment is costly in terms of time, patient burden, and cost. Yet in cases where much is at stake, it might be helpful to employ this assessment strategy clinically (cf. Prins, Kaloupek, & Keane, 1995). Widespread adoption of this method of assessment is not anticipated due to the costs, the expertise required, and the success of other, economical methods of assessment such as the diagnostic interviews and the psychological tests that are available.

RECOMMENDATIONS FROM THE NIMH–NATIONAL CENTER FOR PTSD CONFERENCE ON ASSESSMENT STANDARDIZATION

In November 1995, 45 clinicians and researchers from across the world met in Boston, Massachusetts, in conjunction with the annual meeting of the International Society for Traumatic Stress Studies to discuss and debate various approaches to the assessment of PTSD (Keane, Solomon, & Maser, 1996). While their task was to provide guidance for conducting clinical research in the field, their recommendations bear on the development of standards for assessing PTSD in many different settings and for a variety of purposes. The conference participants reached consensus on several parameters of the assessment process, described as follows:

1. Clinician-administered structured diagnostic interviews provide valuable clinical information. Clinicians should evaluate their quality using as a guideline the psychometric properties of reliability, validity, and clinical utility.

2. Structured diagnostic interviews that provide both a dichotomous and continuous rating of PTSD symptoms are preferred.

3. Symptom frequency, intensity, and duration of a particular episode are dimensions that should be assessed. It is important to determine levels of distress as articulated by patients regarding their symptom presentation.

4. Ratings of impairment and disability secondary to the symptom complex provide important information regarding the severity of the condition.

5. Measures that evaluate both components of the traumatic event (i.e., A1 and A2) are preferred and even essential.

6. Instruments whose reliability and validity studies contain information regarding their performance across gender, racial, and ethnic groups are

to be given preference, especially when the instrument is to be used with males and females of different cultures and races.

7. Self-report instruments for PTSD should meet the standards for psychometric instruments established by the American Psychological Association's *Standards for Educational and Psychological Tests* (1986).

8. When examining for the presence of traumatic events in the history of a person, the committee "recommended a set of carefully worded items that cover a range of types of events as a minimum." Furthermore, the committee recommended that "in-depth questions need to be asked about event occurrences, perceived life threat, harm, injuries, frequency, duration, and age." The events identified as key to review include war-zone stressors, sexual assault in adulthood and childhood, robbery, accidents, technological disasters, natural disasters or hazardous exposures, sudden death of a loved one, life-threatening illnesses, and witnessing or experiencing violence.

9. The committee also recommended that comorbidity be closely examined because response to treatment can vary depending upon the presence of additional psychological conditions. The committee recommended a full assessment of Axis I disorders using a structured clinical interview such as the SCID or something comparable in scope and efficiency.

10. Finally, the committee recommended that "in evaluating stressors, careful behaviorally-anchored terminology should be used, avoiding jargon such as abuse, rape, etc., terms which are inherently imprecise and not universally understood in the same way within and across cultures."

SUMMARY

Assessment of traumatic events and PTSD is a topic of growing interest and concern in the mental health field (Wilson & Keane, 1997). Since the inclusion of PTSD in the diagnostic nomenclature of the American Psychiatric Association, there has been considerable progress in understanding and evaluating the psychological consequences of exposure to traumatic events. Conceptual models of PTSD assessment have evolved (Keane, Wolfe, & Taylor, 1987; Sutker, Uddo, & Allain, 1991), psychological tests have been developed (Foa, Cashman, Jaycox, & Perry, 1997; Norris & Riad, 1997), diagnostic interviews have been validated (Davidson, Smith, & Kudler, 1989; Foa, Riggs, Dancu, & Rothbaum, 1993; Weathers et al., 1992), and subscales of existing tests have been created to assess PTSD (i.e., MMPI-2: Keane, Malloy, & Fairbank, 1984; Symptom Checklist 90—Revised: Saunders, Arata, & Kilpatrick, 1990). We can rightly conclude that the assessment devices available to assess PTSD are comparable to or better than those available for any disorder in the DSM. Multiple instruments have been developed to cover the range of needs of the clinician. The data on these instruments are nothing short of outstanding.

Clearly, the assessment of PTSD in clinical settings focuses on more than the presence, absence, or severity of PTSD. A comprehensive assessment strategy would purport to gather information about an individual's family history, life context, symptoms, beliefs, strengths, weaknesses, support system, and coping abilities. This would assist in the development of an effective treatment plan for the patient. The primary purpose of this review has been to examine the quality of a range of different instruments used to diagnose PTSD. It should also be clear to the reader that the comprehensive assessment of a patient certainly needs to include indices of social and occupational functioning. Finally, a satisfactory assessment ultimately relies upon the clinical and interpersonal skills of the clinician, since many topics related to trauma are inherently difficult for the patient to disclose and to share with others.

The present review is not intended to be comprehensive in its review of all instruments available for the assessment of PTSD. Many more exist. The intent of the review has been to provide a heuristic structure that clinicians might employ when selecting a particular instrument for their clinical or research purposes. By carefully examining the psychometric properties of an instrument, the clinician can make an informed decision about the appropriateness of a particular instrument for the task at hand. Instruments that provide a full utility analysis (i.e., sensitivity, specificity, hit rate, etc.) for the examination do much to assist clinicians in making their final judgments. Furthermore, instruments that are developed and evaluated on multiple trauma populations, across different genders, and with different racial, cultural, and age groups are highly desirable. This inclusiveness should be the ultimate goal for all instruments.

REFERENCES

American Psychiatric Association. (1994). *Diagnostic and statistical manual of mental disorders* (4th ed.). Washington, DC: Author.

American Psychological Association. (1986). *Standards for educational and psychological testing.* Washington, DC: Author.

Blake, D. D., Weathers, F. W., Nagy, L. M., Kaloupek, D. G., Klauminzer, G., Charney, D. S., & Keane, T. M. (1990). A clinical rating scale for assessing current and lifetime PTSD: The CAPS–1. *Behavior Therapist, 18,* 187–188.

Blanchard, E. B., Gerardi, R. J., Kolb, L. C., & Barlow, D. H. (1986). The utility of the Anxiety Disorders Interview Schedule (ADIS) in the diagnosis of the post-traumatic stress disorder in Vietnam veterans. *Behaviour Research and Therapy, 24,* 577–580.

Blanchard, E. B., Hickling, E. J., Taylor, A. E., Forneris, C. A., Loos, W., & Jaccard, J. (1995). Effects of varying scoring rules of the Clinician-Administered PTSD Scale (CAPS) for the diagnosis of post-traumatic stress disorder in motor vehicle accident victims. *Behaviour Research and Therapy, 33,* 471–475.

Blanchard, E. B., Jones-Alexander, J., Buckley, T. C., & Forneris, C. A. (1996). Psychometric properties of the PTSD checklist (PCL). *Behaviour Research and Therapy, 34,* 669–673.

Blanchard, E. B., Kolb, L. C., Pallmeyer, T. P., & Gerardi, R. J. (1982). A psychophysiological study of post traumatic stress disorder in Vietnam veterans. *Psychiatric Quarterly, 54,* 220–229.

Bremner, J. D., Randall, P. K., Scott, T. M., Bronen, R. A., Seibyl, J. P., Southwick, S. M., Delaney, R. C., McCarthy, G., Charney, D. S., & Innis, R. B. (1995). MRI-based measurement of hippocampal volume in patients with combat-related posttraumatic stress disorder. *American Journal of Psychiatry, 152,* 973–981.

Breslau, N., Davis, G. C., Andreski, P., & Peterson, E. (1991). Traumatic events and posttraumatic stress disorder in an urban population of young adults. *Archives of General Psychiatry, 48,* 216–222.

Breslau, N., Kessler, R. C., Chilcoat, H. D., Schultz, L. R., Davis, G. C., & Andreski, P. (1998). Trauma and posttraumatic stress disorder in the community: The 1996 Detroit area survey of trauma. *Archives of General Psychiatry, 55,* 626–632.

Cohen, J. (1960). A coefficient of agreement for nominal scales. *Educational and Psychological Measurement, 20,* 37–46.

Davidson, J., Smith, R., & Kudler, H. (1989). Validity and reliability of the DSM-III criteria for posttraumatic stress disorder: Experience with a structured interview. *Journal of Nervous and Mental Disease, 177,* 336–341.

De Girolamo, G., & McFarlane, A. C. (1996). The epidemiology of PTSD: A comprehensive review of the international literature. In A. Marsella, M. Friedman, E. Gerrity, & R. Scurfield (Eds.), *Ethnocultural aspects of posttraumatic stress disorder* (pp. 33–85). Washington, DC: American Psychological Association.

DiNardo, P. A., & Barlow, D. H. (1988). *Anxiety Disorders Interview Scale-Revised.* Albany, NY: Center for Phobia and Anxiety Disorders.

DiNardo, P. A., Moras, K., Barlow, D. H., Rapee, R. M., & Brown, T. (1993). Reliability of DSM-III-R anxiety disorder categories: Using the Anxiety Disorders Interview Scale-Revised (ADIS-R). *Archives of General Psychiatry, 50,* 251–256.

Foa, E. B., Cashman, L., Jaycox, L., & Perry, K. (1997). The validation of a self-report measure of posttraumatic stress disorder: The Posttraumatic Diagnostic Scale. *Psychological Assessment, 9,* 445–451.

Foa, E. B., Riggs, D. S., Dancu, C. V., & Rothbaum, B. O. (1993). Reliability and validity of a brief instrument for assessing post-traumatic stress disorder. *Journal of Traumatic Stress, 6,* 459–473.

Gerardi, R., Keane, T. M., & Penk, W. E. (1989). Sensitivity and specificity in developing diagnostic tests of combat-related post-traumatic stress disorder (PTSD). *Journal of Clinical Psychology, 45,* 6–18.

Graham, J. R. (1990). *MMPI-2: Assessing personality and psychopathology.* New York: Oxford University Press.

Green, B. L., Lindy, J. D., Grace, M. C., & Leonard, A. C. (1992). Chronic posttraumatic stress disorder and diagnostic comorbidity in a disaster sample. *Journal of Nervous and Mental Disease, 180,* 760–766.

Hammerberg, M. (1992). Penn Inventory for Posttraumatic Stress Disorder: Psychometric properties. *Psychological Assessment, 4,* 67–76.

Horowitz, M. J., Wilner, N., & Alvarez, W. (1979). Impact of Event Scale: A measure of subjective distress. *Psychosomatic Medicine, 41,* 209–218.

Keane, T. M. (1995). Guidelines for the forensic psychological assessment of PTSD claimants. In R. I. Simon (Ed.), *Post-traumatic stress disorder in litigation* (pp. 99–116). Washington, DC: American Psychiatric Press.

Keane, T. M., Caddell, J. M., & Taylor, K. L. (1988). Mississippi Scale for Combat-Related PTSD: Three studies in reliability and validity. *Journal of Consulting and Clinical Psychology, 56,* 85–90.

Keane, T. M., Kolb, L. C., Kaloupek, D. G., Orr, S. P., Blanchard, E. B., Thomas, R. G., Hsieh, F. W., & Lavori, P. W. (1998). Utility of psychophysiological measurement in the diagnosis of post-traumatic stress disorder: Results from a Department of Veterans Affairs Cooperative Study. *Journal of Consulting and Clinical Psychology, 66,* 914–923.

Keane, T. M., Malloy, P. F., & Fairbank, J. A. (1984). Empirical development of an MMPI subscale for the assessment of combat-related posttraumatic stress disorder. *Journal of Consulting and Clinical Psychology, 52,* 888–891.

Keane, T. M., Solomon, S., & Maser, J. (1996, November). *NIMH–National Center for PTSD assessment standardization conference.* Paper presented at the 12th annual meeting of the International Society for Traumatic Stress Studies, San Francisco, CA.

Keane, T. M., & Wolfe, J. (1990). Comorbidity in post-traumatic stress disorder: An analysis of community and clinical studies. *Journal of Applied Social Psychology, 20,* 1776–1788.

Keane, T. M., Wolfe, J., & Taylor, K. L. (1987). Posttraumatic stress disorder: Evidence for diagnostic validity and methods of psychological assessment. *Journal of Clinical Psychology, 43,* 32–43.

Kessler, R. C., Sonnega, A., Bromet, E., Hughes, M., & Nelson, C. B. (1995). Posttraumatic stress disorder in the National Comorbidity Survey. *Archives of General Psychiatry, 52,* 1048–1060.

Kilpatrick, D., Edmonds, C. N., & Seymour, A. K. (1992). *Rape in America: A report to the nation.* Arlington, VA: National Victims Center.

King, L. A., King, D. W., Leskin, G., & Foy, D. W. (1995). The Los Angeles Symptom Checklist: A self-report measure of posttraumatic stress disorder. *Assessment, 2,* 1–17.

Koretzky, M. B., & Peck, A. H. (1990). Validation and cross-validation of the PTSD subscale of the MMPI with civilian trauma victims. *Journal of Clinical Psychology, 46,* 296–300.

Kraemer, H. C. (1992). *Evaluating medical tests: Objective and quantitative guidelines.* Newbury Park, CA: Sage.

Litz, B. T., & Weathers, F. (1992). The diagnosis and assessment of post-traumatic stress disorder in adults. In M. B. Williams & J. F. Sommer (Eds.), *The handbook of post-traumatic therapy* (pp. 20–37). Westport, CT: Greenwood Press.

Lyons, J. A., & Keane, T. M. (1992). Keane PTSD Scale: MMPI and MMPI–2 update. *Journal of Traumatic Stress, 5,* 111–117.

Malloy, P. F., Fairbank, J. A., & Keane, T. M. (1983). Validation of a multimethod assessment of posttraumatic stress disorders in Vietnam veterans. *Journal of Consulting and Clinical Psychology, 51*(4), 488–494.

McFall, M. E., Smith, D. E., Mackay, P. W., & Tarver, D. J. (1990a). Reliability and validity of Mississippi Scale for Combat-Related Posttraumatic Stress Disorder. *Psychological Assessment, 2,* 114–121.

McFall, M. E., Smith, D. E., Roszell, D. K., Tarver, D. J., & Malas, K. L. (1990b). Convergent validity of measures of PTSD in Vietnam combat veterans. *American Journal of Psychiatry, 147,* 645–648.

Mueser, K. T., Salyers, M., Rosenberg, S. D., Ford, J., Fox, L., & Auciello, P. (1999). *Reliability of trauma and PTSD assessments in persons with severe mental illness.* Manuscript submitted for publication.

Norris, F. (1992). Epidemiology of trauma: Frequency and impact of different potentially traumatic events on different demographic groups. *Journal of Consulting and Clinical Psychology, 60,* 409–418.

Norris, F. H., & Riad, J. K. (1997). Standardized self-report measures of civilian trauma and posttraumatic stress disorder. In J. P. Wilson & T. M. Keane (Eds.), *Assessing psychological trauma and PTSD* (pp. 7–42). New York: Guilford Press.

Pitman, R. K., Orr, S. P., Forgue, D. F., deJong, J., & Claiborn, J. (1987). Psychophysiological assessment of posttraumatic stress disorder imagery in Vietnam combat veterans. *Archives of General Psychiatry, 44,* 970–975.

Prins, A., Kaloupek, D. G., & Keane, T. M. (1995). Psychophysiological evidence for autonomic arousal and startle in traumatized adult populations. In M. J. Friedman, D. S. Charney, & A. Y. Deutch (Eds.), *Neurobiological and clinical consequences of stress: From normal adaptation to post-traumatic stress disorder.* Philadelphia: Lippincott-Raven.

Resnick, H. S., Kilpatrick, D. G., Dansky, B. S., Saunders, B. E., & Best, C. L. (1993). Prevalence of civilian trauma and posttraumatic stress disorder in a representative national sample of women. *Journal of Consulting and Clinical Psychology, 61,* 984–991.

Robins, L. N., Helzer, J. E., Croughan, J. L., & Ratcliff, K. S. (1981). National Institute of Mental Health Diagnostic Interview Schedule: Its history, characteristics, and validity. *Archives of General Psychiatry, 38,* 381–389.

Saunders, B. E., Arata, C. M., & Kilpatrick, D. G. (1990). Development of a crime-related post-traumatic stress disorder scale for women within the Symptom Checklist–90—Revised. *Journal of Traumatic Stress, 3,* 439–448.

Sutker, P. B., Uddo, M., & Allain, A. N. (1991). Clinical and research assessment of posttraumatic stress disorder: A conceptual overview. *Psychological Assessment, 3,* 520–530.

Vrana, S., & Lauterbach, D. (1994). Prevalence of traumatic events and post-traumatic psychological symptoms in a nonclinical sample of college students. *Journal of Traumatic Stress, 7,* 289–302.

Watson, C., Juba, M. P., Manifold, V., Kucala, T., & Anderson, P. E. (1991). The PTSD Interview: Rationale, description, reliability, and concurrent validity of a DSM-III-based technique. *Journal of Clinical Psychology, 47,* 179–188.

Watson, C. G., Kucala, T., & Manifold, V. (1986). A cross-validation of the Keane and Penk MMPI scales as measures of post-traumatic stress disorder. *Journal of Clinical Psychology, 42,* 727–732.

Weathers, F. W., Blake, D. D., Krinsley, K. E., Haddad, W., Huska, J. A., & Keane, T. M. (1992, November). *The Clinician-Administered PTSD Scale: Reliability and construct validity.* Paper presented at 26th annual convention of the Association for Advancement Behavior Therapy, Boston, MA.

Weathers, F. W., Litz, B. T., Herman, D. S., Huska, J. A., & Keane, T. M. (1993, October). *The PTSD Checklist (PCL): Reliability, validity, and diagnostic utility.* Paper presented at the 9th Annual Meeting of the International Society for Traumatic Stress Studies, San Antonio, TX.

Weathers, F. W., Ruscio, A., & Keane, T. M. (1999). Psychometrics properties of nine scoring rules for the Clinician-Administered PTSD Scale (CAPS). *Psychological Assessment, 11,* 124–133.

Weiss, D. S., & Marmar, C. R. (1997). The Impact of Event Scale—Revised. In J. P. Wilson & T. M. Keane (Eds.), *Assessing psychological trauma and PTSD* (pp. 399–428). New York: Guilford Press.

Wilson, J. P., & Keane, T. M. (Eds.). (1997). *Assessing psychological trauma and PTSD*. New York: Guilford Press.

Yehuda, R. (1997). Sensitization of the hypothalamic–pituitary–adrenal axis in PTSD. In R. Yehuda & A. McFarlane (Eds.), *Psychobiology of posttraumatic stress disorder* (pp. 57–75). New York: Annals of the New York Academy of Sciences.

I

TREATMENT APPROACHES FOR PTSD: LITERATURE REVIEWS

3

Psychological Debriefing

Jonathan I. Bisson, Alexander C. McFarlane, and Suzanna Rose

The desire to rescue and protect those in danger is one of the most powerful human motivations. Many health professionals are motivated by this drive to help. In contrast to many areas of mental health, the field of trauma offers an unusual opportunity to prevent the onset and relapse associated with many psychological disorders. In the field of trauma, there is an imperative to prevent and minimize chronic posttraumatic reactions.

This chapter focuses on psychological debriefing (PD) as an example of an intervention provided shortly after a traumatic event to prevent later psychological sequelae. Over the last decade, critical incident stress debriefing (CISD), first described by Mitchell (1983), and other forms of debriefing have become the most written about, widely practiced, and well-recognized forms of early psychological intervention following trauma. Advocation of the routine use of early debriefing following traumatic events has been fueled by anecdotal reports of its effectiveness. Others have presented reviews of the literature cautioning against the reliance on these reports as reliable evidence of efficacy (see, e.g., Bisson & Deahl, 1994; Raphael, Meldrum, & McFarlane, 1995). In this chapter, we therefore decided to focus on debriefing rather than other forms of early intervention. The review considers the theoretical/conceptual framework for debriefing before discussing the different models that have been used and the currently available research in this area. Particular attention is given to research that has employed reliable methodology such as randomized controlled trials.

THEORETICAL/CONCEPTUAL FRAMEWORK

Acute preventive interventions can only be implemented if there is a broad acceptance of a notion of collective responsibility and the value of group survival and care for individuals. Hence, the effectiveness and theoretical underpinning of debriefing are critically dependent upon the general systems of leadership and the management of morale. It entails an essential series of beliefs about the dignity of the individual and his or her importance to the broader social group. The clinical practice of debriefing has often been driven by the immediacy of the imperative to help rather than the development of a sophisticated theory that is being carefully tested for its widespread implementation. In many ways, acute preventive interventions could be seen to be as much social movements as interventions emerging from refinement in clinical practice. However, theoretical origins of debriefing appear to come from a variety of sources.

The Proximity, Immediacy, and Expectancy (PIE) Model

The management of acute combat stress disorders was a school of treatment that emerged in World War I and was then rediscovered in World War II. The PIE model is based on the three principles of proximity, immediacy and expectancy, as described by Kardiner and Spiegel (1947) and also used in more recent conflicts (e.g., Israeli soldiers during the Lebanon War; see Solomon & Benbenishty, 1988) where individuals were treated close to the battle zone (proximity), as soon as possible (immediacy), and with the expectation of returning to duty (expectancy).

The Narrative Tradition

During World War II, General Marshall, the chief historian of the U.S. Army at that time, used and subsequently wrote about debriefing (Marshall, 1944). He advocated holding debriefing sessions on the battlefield as soon as possible after the action and estimated that 7 hours were needed to debrief one fighting day. Although one of the main functions of these meetings was information gathering, Marshall noted that the emotional effects of the debriefing were a "spiritually purging," "morale-building" experience, and one that the men usually relished. Marshall's debriefing method provided a structured intervention that recognized and respected individuals' experiences, grief, and expression of emotional responses. He believed that the debriefing technique was relatively simple and could be performed by commanders without the need for specialist training. In a sense, his exploration of the events of battle gave the troops an opportunity to develop a narrative, or internal verbal representation, of the experience.

Group Psychotherapy

Another paradigm employed in the critical incident debriefing model is that of group psychotherapy. Lindy, Green, Grace, and Titchener (1983) have spoken of the trauma membrane that forms around the community involved in disaster. This notion refers to the mutual and tacit understanding that envelops people who have similarly suffered. These principles are central to the efficacy of group intervention. Groups use the therapeutic forces within the group and the constructive support and interaction to heal people and modify their reactions. The adaptive outcome of the group is the primary aim rather than the focus on individuals.

Crisis Intervention

Social psychiatry has a particular focus on the role of life events as a cause of psychiatric illness. The accompanying arm of intervention was crisis intervention championed by Caplan and Lindemann. The essence of crisis intervention is that a clear precipitant exists and that the individual's distress is clear. It attempts to remove such distress from the domain of illness and presumes that the patient has experienced an offense that has caused this disequilibrium because of its suddeness, which has not allowed the individual time to master his or her emotional response. The essence of the intervention is that the temporary support of the mental health professional will bring about mastery. It is a model of intervention based on the premise that the event is over and the symptoms exibited by the patient are no longer appropriate. The therapist provides a reorganizing influence that assists the individual who is feeling overwhelmed. The critical dimension is to assist the person in reestablishing rational problem solving.

Grief Counseling

The concepts of crisis intervention rapidly extended into the management of the bereaved. Lindemann's work (1944) after the Coconut Grove nightclub fire led to both an investigation of the stages of grief and the interventions that might be successful. Progressively, grief counseling grew away from crisis intervention as a separate discipline. First, Raphael's work (1977) with widows at high risk of negative outcomes following bereavement highlighted the value of interventions in this context. These therapies included an educational component aimed at normalizing the feelings and behaviors associated with grief. Second, the importance of expression of the range of complex emotions associated with loss was often assisted by visiting memorials and handling possessions of the dead person. Focusing on the relationship with the deceased allowed the development of the individual's new sense of identity and integrated self concept. Raphael's use of this approach to assist the bereaved following the Granville train disaster led her to advocate the importance of acute interventions and support following disasters.

Cognitive-Behavioral Therapies

Although behavioral therapy only became a clinical practice of the last half of the 20th century, the principles were well understood in the first half of the century. Two aspects have contributed particularly to debriefing. First, the idea of desensitization is an explicit rationale for minimizing avoidance, particularly in the immediate aftermath of traumatic experiences. A further contribution in this field has been the exploration of the cognitive schemas associated with the traumatic memories. The role of cognitive-behavioral therapy in PTSD has emerged with roughly the same time frame as preventive interventions. Therefore, this area of clinical practice has not had a major theoretical impact. However, the idea of manualized treatments was brought to psychotherapy research by behavioral therapy. Manualized debriefings have become an important component of this field.

Psychoeducation

In many regards, debriefing is a form of psychoeducation. This is an important component of many cognitive-behavioral treatments. It questions the extent to which treatments of psychological trauma owe their treatment effects to nonspecific factors. There appears to be little doubt that giving traumatized individuals a psychological map to understand their reactions does much to contain their distress and to allow them to institute a series of self-regulatory processes.

Catharsis

The expression of affect associated with the memory of an event is also a central component of debriefing. The notion of catharsis goes back to Breuer and Freud's (1893) first lecture, "On the Psychical Mechanism of Hysterical Phenomena: Preliminary Communications."

An Eclectic Model

This brief review shows that debriefing has its origins in a variety of sources. It has a clear intellectual and practical lineage with the original theories about traumatic neurosis from the 1890s, but it has been significantly modified by crisis theory and models of group intervention. These owe their influence to the models of intervention provided in the services in World War II. Much of the interest in disaster research and, subsequently, post traumatic stress disorder (PTSD) came out of the social psychiatry movement. One of the intellectual struggles that emerged during this period of time was whether symptoms arising in relation to an event were simply a distress response or were indicative of a more substantial psychiatric disorder. The psychoanalytic school has strongly argued for the role of social and intrapsychic factors as being the critical determinants of psychological symptoms. Implicit in this idea, the modulation and direction of the individual's processing of the event would minimize or prevent any pathological or prolonged distress.

The theoretical difficulty with this argument emerges with the evidence that in people with PTSD, it appears that there is an abnormal acute stress response of a biological nature (Yehuda, McFarlane, & Shalev, 1998). If individuals with a normal biological stress response do not develop PTSD, the question is whether early and immediate interventions may modify the nature of their acute stress response in such a way as to increase the risk of PTSD. Given the dictum "First, do no harm," the challenge is to demonstrate that in individuals who have a predicted normal outcome, some form of acute intervention does not modify the adaptive restorative response.

In their separate domains, the theories that contribute to debriefing appear sound. Hence, the issue arises as to whether the practice of debriefing has been molded appropriately.

DESCRIPTION OF THE DEBRIEFING METHOD

CISD was first described by Mitchell (1983) as a group intervention for ambulance personnel following exposure to traumatic situations in their work. It was described as a form of crisis intervention as opposed to a form of psychological treatment, and therefore does not have the same philosophy (i.e., debriefing does not explicitly treat a pathological response). CISD and other models of PD have become recognized as semistructured interventions designed to reduce initial distress and to prevent the development of later psychological sequelae such as PTSD following traumatic events by promoting emotional processing through the ventilation and normalization of reactions, and preparation for possible future experiences. Further aims are to identify individuals who may benefit from more formalized treatment and to offer such treatment to them and provide early support. It has generally been considered that any individual exposed to the traumatic event is eligible for PD irrespective of the presence of psychological symptoms. It is, however, apparent that many participants of debriefings would have fulfilled the criteria for acute stress disorder or have sympoms of PTSD, anxiety, and depression. Debriefings have been used with survivors, victims, emergency care workers, and providers of psychological care. The focus of a PD is on the present reactions of those involved in a trauma rather than earlier experiences that may shape their individual reactions. Psychiatric "labeling" is avoided and the emphasis is placed on normalization. The participants are assured that they are normal people who have experienced an abnormal event. Mitchell and Everly (1995) have argued that debriefing should be considered one part of a comprehensive, systematic, multicomponent approach to the management of traumatic stress (critical incident stress management; CISM) and that it should not be used as a one-time stand-alone intervention. Despite this assertion, many practitioners have used debriefing as a stand-alone intervention.

Mitchell's (1983) CISD is a 7-phase technique. The introduction phase of CISD concerns explanation of the purpose of the debriefing, guidelines, and some introductions. During the fact phase, a factual description of exactly what happened is produced, with acknowledgment of accompanying emotions if they are expressed, but these are not considered in detail at this time. The thought phase considers participants' thoughts at the time of the incident. The reaction phase focuses on participants' emotions associated with the event. The symptoms phase aims to help move participants from the emotional reaction to a more cognitively orientated stage in which various trauma-related symptoms are discussed. The teaching phase flows from the symptoms phase and is led by the facilitators who discuss typical symptoms and coping strategies for stress. The reentry phase clarifies issues, gives the opportunity for questions, provides a summary of the debriefing, and ends with closure.

Since Mitchell's initial description of CISD, several other authors have described other, different forms of psychological debriefing (Rose, 1997). Dyregrov (1989) described PD, which represents his interpretation of Mitchell's technique and is indeed very similar, although it specifically discusses sensory information experienced at the time. Dyregrov also appears to devote more attention to individual reactions and to the normalization of reactions. The seven stages of PD as described by Dyregrov are detailed as follows:

1. *The introduction.* The debriefer(s) states that the purpose of the meeting is to review the participant(s) reactions to the trauma, to discuss them, and to identify methods of dealing with them to prevent future problems. The debriefer assumes control and specifies his or her own competence in order to lend confidence to those attending. Three rules are made explicit: (a) Partipants are under no obligation to say anything except why they are there and what their role was vis-à-vis the traumatic event; (b) confidentiality is emphasized in groups and the members understand not to divulge outside the group what others have said; and (c) the focus of the discussions is on the impressions and reactions of the participants.

2. *Expectations and facts.* The details of what actually happened are discussed in considerable detail without focusing on thoughts, impressions, and emotional reactions. Participants are encouraged to describe their expectations; that is, did they expect what happened? (This is believed to focus the

individuals on their experiences at the time and may help them to understand why they reacted in the way they did. This is felt to be extremely important in certain situations, for example, unexpectedly encountering injured children can magnify the intensity of a traumatic situation.)

3. *Thoughts and impressions.* When the facts are being described, thoughts and impressions are elicited by asking questions such as "What were your thoughts when you first realized you were injured?" and "What did you do?" This information aims to (a) construct a picture of what happened, (b) put individual reactions into perspective, and (c) help with the integration of traumatic experiences. Sensory impressions in all five modalities are elicited, for example, "What did you see, hear, touch, smell, taste?" The aim is to produce a more realistic reconstruction of the trauma.

4. *Emotional reactions.* This is usually the longest stage in the PD. The earlier questions concerning thoughts and impressions lead to answers concerning emotions. The debriefer attempts to aid the release of emotions with questions about some of the common reactions during the trauma, such as fear, helplessness, frustration, self-reproach, anger, guilt, anxiety, and depression. Emotional reactions experienced since the event are also discussed.

5. *Normalization.* After the emotional reactions have been expressed, the debriefer aims to facilitate their acceptance. This is done by stressing that the reactions are entirely normal. When more than one person is present in the PD, it is likely that emotions will be shared. This universality aims to help with normalization. The debriefer stresses that individuals do not have to experience all of the emotions that normally occur after a trauma, but it is normal to react after a critical incident. The debriefer also describes common symptoms that individuals may experience in the future: intrusive thoughts and images, distress when reminded of what happened; attempts to avoid thoughts, feelings, and reminders; detachment from others; loss of interest in things that once gave pleasure; anxiety and depressed mood; sleep disturbance, including nightmares; irritability, shame, guilt, and anger; hypervigilance and increased startle reactions.

6. *Future planning/coping.* This stage allows the debriefer to focus on ways of managing symptoms should they arise and to attempt to mobilize internal support mechanisms (e.g., discussing coping mechanisms) and external support (e.g., family and friends). Emphasis is on the importance of open discussion of feelings with family and friends and highlights the possibility of needing additional support from them for a while.

7. *Disengagement.* In this stage, other topics are discussed. Leaflets describing normal reactions and how to cope with them, such as the British Red Cross's *Coping with Personal Crisis*, can be distributed. Guidance is also given regarding the need for further help and where it may be obtained if necessary. Participants are advised to seek further help if, for example, (a) psychological symptoms do not decrease after 4–6 weeks; (b) psychological symptoms

increase over time; (c) there is ongoing loss of function and occupation/family difficulties; (d) others comment on marked personality changes.

Raphael (1986) described a psychological debriefing that was less structured than the Mitchell and Dyregrov models, yet still had much in common with them, including the fact that it was designed as a group intervention for secondary rather than primary victims. She suggested particular topics for discussion that may be useful during the debriefing, including personally experienced disaster stressors such as death encounter, survivor conflict and loss dislocation; positive and negative feelings, victims and their problems, and the special nature of disaster work and personal experiences. Another model, the Multiple Stressor Debriefing Model, designed for use with American Red Cross personnel (Armstrong, O'Callahan, & Marmar, 1991), contains elements from the other debriefings but for the first time focuses on pretrauma strategies adopted by individuals to deal with stressful situations. Four stages are completed. The first stage, disclosure of events, is followed by consideration of feelings and reactions. Coping strategies are then discussed, including the previous ways individuals have dealt with stressful events. Finally, the termination phase considers what it will be like leaving the disaster, the positive work done, and the need to talk to significant others about experiences and feelings.

In more recent years, these group PD models have been modified for use with groups of primary victims and also for developing interventions for individuals who have recently been exposed to a trauma (see, e.g., Hobbs, Mayou, Harrison, & Warlock, 1996; Lee, Slade, & Lygo, 1996). The individual debriefings described in the literature to date have adopted a 7-stage model very similar to that of Mitchell. With the group factors obviously missing, the debriefings focus directly on one individual's experiences and reactions. Some authors have commented that because group factors are of essential importance to the process of PD, the technique should not be transferred for use with individuals (see, e.g., Dyregrov, 1998). In individual PD, the facilitator normalizes the individual's reactions by sharing information gained from previous trauma victims and the literature, rather than by highlighting common reactions within a group. Most reported individual debriefings have been for primary victims with physical injuries. When dealing with individuals who have sustained significant physical injury, attention has also centered on discussion of physical concerns, and possible emotions and reactions associated with disability/disfigurement (Bisson, Jenkins, Alexander, & Bannister, 1997).

In addition to describing an early, brief crisis intervention, the term "psychological debriefing" has also been used to describe a variety of other interventions. For example, Hayman and Scaturo (1992) described an 8-session "psychological debriefing" for military personnel following the Gulf War. Busuttil and colleagues (1995) described debriefing as an integral part of a group treatment package for chronic PTSD. Such diverse use of the term has resulted in a somewhat confused literature and these applications are beyond the scope of this chapter. Here, we use the term to denote a brief preventive technique that occurs shortly after a traumatic event.

METHOD OF COLLECTING DATA

This review draws on the results of a recent systematic review of randomized, controlled trials of brief, early psychological interventions following trauma (Rose & Bisson, 1998; Wessely, Rose, & Bisson, 1998) as well as other studies examining the efficacy of PD and other early interventions. Nine electronic databases were searched (MEDLINE, EMBASE, PsycLIT, PILOTS, Biosis, Pascal, Occ. Safety and Health, CDSR, and the Trials Register of the Cochrane Collaboration Depression, Anxiety and Neurosis Group). The *Journal of Traumatic Stress* was looked at by one author (S. R.) to identify any randomized controlled trials of psychological debriefing, and researchers were also asked if any trials should be included. All appropriate studies were identified and critically read.

SUMMARY OF LITERATURE

Psychological Debriefing

Evidence from Randomized Controlled Clinical Trials

Hobbs, Mayou, Harrison, and Warlock (1996) reported a randomized controlled trial of individual PD for victims of motor vehicle accidents (MVAs). Their study included 106 individuals randomly allocated to a 1-hour individual debriefing undertaken within 24–48 hours of the accident in most cases. The debriefing combined a review of the traumatic experience, encouragement of emotional expression, and promotion of cognitive processing of the experience. They provided advice about common emotional reactions, the value of talking about the experience, and an early, graded return to normal road travel. A leaflet reiterating these messages was also distributed. There was no evidence that any measures apart from supervision were taken to encourage consistency of intervention. Assessment 4 months after the MVA revealed no significant differences between the intervention and control groups in terms of the main outcome measures—Impact of Event Scale (IES; Horowitz, Wilner, & Alvarez, 1979) (effect size = −0.21); General Severity Index of the Brief Symptom Inventory (BSI; Derogatis & Melisaratos, 1983) (effect size = −0.37); interview ratings on intrusive thoughts and travel anxiety (effect size = −0.12); clinical diagnosis of PTSD or phobic anxiety disorder. The intervention group had a worse outcome ($p < .05$) on two subscales of the BSI and showed a nonsignificant trend for poorer outcome in terms of global distress and depression. The authors argued that there was no evidence that PD had helped and, indeed, highlighted indications that it may have been disadvantageous. This study has several good methodological factors, including the use of validated measures and a larger sample size than many studies, but it still has limitations. Unfortunately, reassessment was performed by the same individuals who performed the intervention, which might have led to bias, as might the fact that the debriefed group had a higher mean injury score than the control group and may have been expected to have done worse as a result.

Lee, Slade, and Lygo (1996) studied women over the age of 18 who had miscarried between the 6th and 19th week of pregnancy. Twenty-one women received a 1-hour, individual debriefing, based on the Mitchell and Dyregrov methods, approximately 2 weeks after the miscarriage, and 19 women received no intervention. Follow-up at 4 months revealed no significant difference in symptomatology as judged by the IES (effect size = 0.43 for Intrusion subscale and 0.18 for Avoidance subscale) and the Hospital Anxiety and Depression Scale (HADS; Zigmond & Snaith, 1983) (effect size = 0.11 for Anxiety subscale and 0.28 for Depression subscale) between intervention and control groups. At the 4-month follow-up, two factor analyses of variance (ANOVAs) showed significant main effects of time on all outcome measures, but there were no main effects of the intervention. Multiple regression analyses revealed that emotional distress scores at 1 week predicted scores at 4 months. Significantly more of the PD group (71%) felt that they had been given the opportunity to talk about how they felt compared with 29% of the non-PD group. Women who received the PD were asked to rate its helpfulness on a 100-mm scale, from *Extremely unhelpful* (0) to *Extremely helpful* (100). The mean score was 74. The women on the whole showed a tendency toward being satisfied with their hospital care. Significantly more people in the control group (78%) had tried to obtain additional information about their miscarriage, as opposed to 29% in the PD group, when asked at follow-up. This is another reasonably good study, although the number of participants was small and there were no interview measures at follow-up.

Bisson, Jenkins, Alexander, and Bannister (1997) studied 130 acute burn trauma victims admitted to a regional burn unit. Individuals were randomly allocated to no intervention or to an individual PD, modified from Dyregrov's description, 2–19 days post-burn trauma. A trend toward worse outcome in the PD group at 3-month follow-up was reported (IES effect size = −0.22). At 13-month follow-up, PD was associated with a significantly worse outcome ($p < .05$) as judged by scores on both the anxiety (effect size = −0.42) and depression (effect size = −0.43) subscales of the HADS, the IES (effect size = −0.55), and rate of PTSD determined by the Clinician-Administered PTSD Scale (Blake, Weathers, & Nagy, 1990). The severity of the burn trauma was slightly more extreme in the PD group, and almost twice as many of the PD group, 14 individuals (25%), described significant previous trauma (although previous trauma did not affect outcome). Initial levels of distress influenced outcome far more than presence or absence of PD. However, using ANOVA with the initial IES score as covariate, IES scores remained significantly higher ($p < 05$) in the PD group at 13-month follow-up. Additionally, the length of PD was associated with worse outcome (Pearson's correlation coefficient $= .44$, $p = .001$), as was the closer the PD was to the burn trauma (Pearson's correlation coefficient $= .29$, $p = .03$). Fifty-two percent of the debriefed group said they had found the PD "definitely useful." This study also has its flaws, including a debriefed group that was more traumatized than the control group, as judged by greater percentage burns and subjective life threat, and a power of 53% at a significance level of .05—again low.

Chemtob, Tomas, Law, and Cremniter (1997) examined a single-session group PD and education session for secondary victims 6 and 9 months after a hurricane. The debriefing/educational session, which lasted a total of 5 hours, was shown to result in a significant reduction in IES scores that could not be accounted for by the passage of time. This randomized controlled trial again has its flaws. The combination of PD and an educational package makes it difficult to determine the efficacy of PD alone, and the timing of the intervention makes it difficult to compare PD directly with debriefings that occurred within 1 month of the traumatic event.

Other Evidence: Open Trials and Case Reports

Comparison studies consider a group of individuals involved in a traumatic event(s) and then compare group members according to whether or not they received PD. Findings are weakened by the absence of random allocation to intervention or nonintervention groups: the reasons that determine whether or not individuals attend PD may be extremely important and result in considerable sample bias, markedly affecting the outcome. Prospective studies have shown that the majority of individuals involved in traumatic events do not go on to develop PTSD and, indeed, usually recover from initial symptoms naturally in the following months (see, e.g., Blanchard et al., 1996; Riggs, Rothbaum, & Foa, 1995). It therefore follows that most people given PD following a traumatic event will not develop PTSD. These facts are likely to generate a spurious sense of efficacy regarding the preventive value of PD unless adequately controlled trials are performed.

McFarlane (1988) examined a subgroup of 50 subjects randomly selected from 315 firefighters exposed to a natural disaster 8 months previously and at high risk of developing PTSD as measured by three variables: (1) high exposure (exposure score > 6), (2) significant psychological symptoms as determined by the General Health Questionnaire (GHQ; Goldberg & Hillier, 1979) (> 4), and (3) intrusive thoughts and imagery (IES > 26). This sample was in fact matched with another 96 firefighters who were not interviewed but compared on the basis of exposure, and IES and GHQ scores at 4 months. Therefore, this subgroup was only randomly selected as defined by various combinations of exposure, imagery, and symptoms. This study could not be described as a true randomized clinical trial (RCT).

Although not the main focus of the paper, McFarlane (1988) found that those who received PD shortly after the incident were less likely to develop an acute posttraumatic stress reaction than those who were not debriefed. However, the effectiveness of the debriefing process was thrown into doubt by his finding that individuals who developed a delayed-onset posttraumatic stress reaction were more likely to have attended a debriefing than those who had suffered no psychological disorder at any time during the follow-up period. This led McFarlane to comment that PD may have immediate protective value but little effect in the longer term.

Deahl, Gillham, Thomas, Searle, and Srinivasan (1994) considered the effectiveness of group PD in soldiers who acted as gravediggers during the Gulf War. Seventy-four soldiers took part in the study. For operational reasons, only 55 members of the sample received PD following the Dyregrov method, so the rest formed the control group. In addition, no baseline measures were taken. Twenty (50%) of the PD sample reported finding the intervention helpful, but IES and GHQ-28 scores showed no significant difference between the PD and control group at 9-month follow-up. Hyton and Hasle (1989) similarly questioned the effectiveness of PD as a result of their study of 58 nonprofessional firefighters exposed to dead bodies following a major hotel fire in Norway. They found no difference in psychological symptoms 2 weeks later between formally debriefed firefighters and those who had talked with colleagues.

Stallard and Law (1993) considered group PD that took place 6 months after the trauma. The subjects were 7 adolescent and 1 adult survivor of a minibus collision. In comparison with adolescent survivors from another study, on post-follow-up at 3 months, the PD group showed a significant overall reduction in the Intrusive subscale of the IES, anxiety and depression scores as measured on the Birleson Depression Inventory (Birleson, 1981) and the Revised Children's Manifest Anxiety Scale (Reynolds & Richmond, 1978). In contrast, however, the avoidance scale of this group's IES had increased slightly. This study was neither a RCT nor did the intervention take place in the first month. Jenkins (1996) reported less depression and anxiety at 1 month among 15 emergency services workers debriefed after a mass shooting compared to 15 who declined the debriefing. Kenardy and colleagues (1996) performed a naturalistic study of 195 helpers following an earthquake in Australia. Sixty-two individuals were debriefed; the remaining 133 were not. Individuals completed the GHQ-12 and the IES on four occasions over the next 2 years. There was no evidence of improved rate of recovery in either group.

The final studies containing data lack any control or comparison groups and are therefore even less satisfactory in their methodology. Sloan (1988) described 30 survivors of a nonfatal plane crash who received PD. All of them initially experienced high levels of symptomatology, the intensity of which decreased rapidly over the first 8 weeks, and then more slowly. Robinson and Mitchell (1993) assessed the efficacy of PD among 172 emergency workers in Australia. Two weeks after the PD, 60% completed questionnaires. Overall, the respondents found the PD to be of "considerable value" and the majority believed it had helped to reduce their stress-related symptoms. Very few subjects voiced criticisms, although some participants complained that it was "too political" and gave them a sense of "lack of control."

Flannery, Fulton, Tausch, and DeLoffi (1991) described the debriefing of psychiatric staff members who had been assaulted by patients. This occured immediately after the incident and was followed up by further contact at 3 and 10 days. Over the 90-day study period, there were 67 assaults, and debriefing was offered to 62 victims. Five victims refused to participate. Sixty-nine percent were reported as "regaining a sense of control" within 10 days and only 7 participants required further support, which was offered in the form of a group. The same researchers reported that violence and attacks from patients within a psychiatric setting was reduced by 63% over a 2-year period, along with reductions in medical and legal expenses, following the introduction of a CISM program (cited in Everly & Mitchell, 1999).

Everly and Mitchell (1999) performed a nonsystematic review of studies. They concluded positively about the effectiveness of debriefing, although it is apparent that the studies quoted have significant shortcomings. Among the positive studies cited is Western Management Consultants in Canada, who reported positively about a comprehensive CISM program for nurses. Twenty-four percent of those involved in a PD reported a decline in personnel turnover, and 99% reported a decline in sick-leave days. Dyregrov (1998) anecdotally reported similar experiences with PD as part of a CISM program in Norway and commented that the effectiveness seemed related to the experience of the facilitator.

Alexander (1993) described 35 Grampian police officers involved in the Piper Alpha disaster and the retrieval and identification of human remains. Most were free from evidence of psychological morbidity at follow-up, and Alexander argued that organizational and managerial practices appeared to be powerful antidotes to adverse posttraumatic stress reactions. The officers received daily "debriefing" during their active service and this was cited as important. Searle and Bisson (1992) described 8 soldiers who were severely traumatized during the Gulf War and received PD within 5 days of the trauma. Six subjects satisfied the DSM-III-R criteria for PTSD at 5 weeks. Five subjects required prolonged treatment before their symptoms improved.

Other One-Time Psychological Interventions

These interventions are not labeled as PD but have many common features. In particular, they involve subjects' focusing on what happened during a traumatic event and discussing emotional reactions shortly afterward. Therefore, randomized controlled trials of these interventions are included in this review.

Bordow and Porritt (1979) described a study of 70 males who had been inpatients on a trauma ward in Australia for at least 1 week as a result of involvement in a road traffic accident. The first 30 consecutive subjects, considered "delayed controls," received no intervention and were contacted for interview 3- to 4-months posttrauma. The other 40 subjects were assessed immediately and either contacted 3 months later, with no further intervention, or randomly allocated to a social worker intervention lasting between 2 and 10 hours. The immediate assessment was described as "a structured interview to review the experience of injury and hospitalisation and the subject's emotional reactions to these" (Bordow & Porritt, 1979, p. 252). At 3- to 4-month follow-up, the researchers found that the more prolonged input group fared better than the immediate assessment group, who fared better than the no-assessment group. They argued that their results supported the notion that brief early interventions could help reduce psychological sequelae following trauma and that some individuals needed more than just a single intervention. The immediate assessment did not equate exactly to a PD, as described earlier, but they did have much in common. However, there are several problems within the study. It is not clear why only 10 individuals received a one-time intervention, why the measures used were administered by the same individuals who administered the interventions, why there were no females in the study group, and why the statistical analysis compared differences among all three groups as opposed to between-individual groups. Not enough information was available to calculate effect sizes.

Bunn and Clarke (1979) studied 30 relatives of seriously ill or injured individuals who had been brought for admission to the emergency ward of a hospital in Australia. Subjects were randomly allocated to an intervention or control group. The intervention was a 30-minute semistructured counseling session in which subjects were encouraged to express their feelings and concerns about the crisis. Bunn and Clarke described their intervention as "supportive, empathetic. . . . Subjects were encouraged to express their feelings and concerns about the crisis. Information about the injury or illness and its prognosis was provided" (p. 192). Individuals were interviewed immediately after the intervention, and members of the control group were interviewed 20 minutes after their original recruitment. The results revealed a reduced level of anxiety in the counseled group when compared with the noncounseled group using anxiety-content analysis scales. Unfortunately, this study is seriously flawed. The 5-minute follow-up was inadequate, and the measures used were not ideal. It is impossible to determine whether there were any long-lasting effects of the intervention, as there was no longitudinal follow-up and data provided in the paper did not allow for calculation of effect size.

Stevens and Adshead (cited in Hobbs & Adshead, 1996) described a study of individuals who had presented to an Accident and Emergency department following acute physical trauma. Forty-four males and 19 females were recruited; 21 subjects were lost to follow-up. Within 24 hours of attendance, those in the intervention group received a standardized interview that reviewed the experience and their emotions. Although not adhering to a specific PD technique, the interview contained several of the components described earlier. Individuals were reassessed 1-week, 1-month, and 3-months postattendance. There was no significant difference between patients who were counseled and those who were not in terms of IES score, Beck Depression Inventory (BDI; Beck, Ward, Mendelson, Mack, & Erbaugh, 1961) score, Spielberger Self-Evaluation Questionnaire (SEQ; Spielberger, 1983) score, or development of PTSD, except for those showing high initial SEQ and BDI scores who did better if in the counseled group. Two-thirds said that they found the intervention good, whereas one-third stated that they did not. The latter group's members felt that the counseling had been offered too early, or felt that, personally, they had not needed it. A major flaw in this study is that those individuals who displayed significant emotional responses during the counseling session were excluded from follow-up. This may have caused significant bias, probably resulting in the intervention seeming more effective than was actually the case. Unfortunately, lack of data has again prevented calculation of effect size.

SUMMARY

Early PD has been widely advocated for routine use following major traumatic events. The studies identified in this review vary greatly in quality, but, overall, the quality of the studies, including the randomized controlled trials, is poor. Common methodological shortcomings include small sample size, absence of control group, absence of randomization, varying degrees of trauma, ignoring other confounding variables, low response rates, sampling bias, and lack of uniformity of intervention and timing variance. Overall, the studies provide little evidence that early PD prevents psychopathology following trauma but confirm that, on the whole, PD is well received by participants. It may be that PD is a useful intervention to facilitate the screening of individuals who are at risk, to disseminate education and referral information, and to assist organizational morale. Some negative outcomes following individual PD were found, but, overall, PD did not affect later psychological outcome, when the studies were considered collectively.

The two single-intervention RCTs with a positive outcome (Bunn & Clarke, 1979; Bordow & Porritt, 1979) used a non-PD intervention and were the weakest methodologically. It may be that the intense reexposure involved in a PD can retraumatize some individuals without allowing adequate time for habituation, resulting in a more negative outcome. This result would concur with the findings of Vaughan and Tarrier (1992) and Pitman (1991), who reported similar adverse reactions in some people following exposure therapy and suggested that care should be taken in the selection of individuals for PD if it is to be offered.

Other variables are likely to be far more important than the presence or absence of PD in determining outcome following trauma. This was certainly the case with Bisson, Jenkins, Alexander, and Bannister (1997) and Lee, Slade, and Lygo (1996), where initial levels of distress were much better predictors of outcome than the presence or absence of PD. A recently completed RCT evaluating individual PD of victims of violent crime (Rose, Brewin, Andrews, & Kirk, 1999) again highlighted the lack of preventive effect of the PD intervention, despite reported subjective satisfaction. In this study (Brewin, Andrews, Rose, & Kirk, 1998) it was again noted that persisting high levels of symptoms (measured on average 3-weeks postcrime) were the most potent predictors of continuing disorder. Findings also suggested that later PTSD (recorded 6-months posttrauma) could be relatively well predicted by either of two methods. One method was to diagnose acute stress disorder (ASD) and, in fact, this part of the study was designed to confirm the predictive utility of ASD in a longitudinal study. The other method was to establish the presence (again, on average, 3 weeks following the trauma of violent crime) at moderate levels of intensity, of either three or more reexperiencing or three or more arousal symptoms. The individual's subjective sense of shame as well as anger with others following the traumatic event also had predictive value. From this prospective data set, a short trauma screening questionnaire has been designed. Harvey and Bryant (1998) developed a similar instrument for the diagnosis of ASD and also performed a randomized controlled study of cognitive-behavioral therapy versus intensive nondirective counseling for ASD sufferers. Cognitive-behavioral therapy was shown to prevent the development of PTSD; nondirective counseling did not. These findings suggest that more complex interventions for those individuals at highest risk may be the best way to prevent the development of PTSD following trauma.

RECOMMENDATIONS

Indications

Given the current state of knowledge, neither one-time group nor individual PD can be advocated as being able to prevent the subsequent development of PTSD following a traumatic event (AHCPR Level B). However, there may be benefits to aspects of PD, particularly when employed as part of a comprehensive management program (AHCPR Level C). There appears to be good evidence that it is a well-received intervention for most people (AHCPR

Level A) and even though it may not prevent later psychological sequelae, it may still be useful for screening, education, and support. It may be that appeals for "flexibility" in the therapeutic approach to immediate trauma survivors, as published following the Kings Cross fire (Turner, Thompson, & Rosser, 1989), are important. The possibility that group PD in combination with an educational session several months after a traumatic event may be effective has been raised by one positive study but clearly needs replicating.

Contraindications

Some studies of individual PD have raised the possibility that the intense reexposure involved in PD can retraumatize some individuals without allowing adequate time for habituation, resulting in a negative outcome (individual—AHCPR Level B). It therefore seems essential that if PD or any similar intervention is to be employed, it should be provided by experienced, well-trained practitioners, should not be mandatory, and potential participants should be properly clinically assessed. If employed, the intervention should be accompanied by clear and objective evaluation procedures to ensure meeting the objectives set for it.

CONCLUSIONS

The absence of rigorous research in this area is disappointing, and it is essential that efforts be made to determine what, if anything, should be offered to individuals following traumatic events. Given the results of this review, it appears important only to use methods that have been shown to work. This can only be done through rigorous research, making the need for such research in this area a priority. Studies are few to date and data are scant. There has been a bias toward the more systematic study of individual PD as a standalone intervention, as opposed to group PD as part of a more comprehensive traumatic stress management program, which has been argued as being most effective by several authors (see, e.g., Dyregrov, 1998). There are also many potentially important factors that have not been adequately, systematically evaluated in the studies to date, including time between the trauma and the PD, nature of the trauma, and facilitator experience/quality and nature of the PD. To focus solely on the later reduction of PTSD and other psychological symptoms is probably too simplistic an approach to take to determine whether PD is beneficial as an early intervention. It would therefore be premature at present to conclude that PD should be discontinued as a possible intervention following trauma.

While there is no evidence to support the preventive value of debriefing delivered in a single session, there is a strong argument for providing acute psychological first aid and forming a treatment alliance as early as is practical following a traumatic event. Early contact may provide a method of addressing the major problem of the general reluctance of people with PTSD to accept treatment. It may be that debriefing is not appropriate as a stand-alone intervention or for all types of survivors, and that the target populations for the currently available, randomized controlled trials have been incorrect (e.g., CISD was recommended for groups of rescue teams or help providers, not for primary victims or as part of a comprehensive management program). There is an urgent need for randomized controlled trials to be performed, especially with group interventions (e.g., the efficacy of group PD as part of an overall traumatic stress management program, particularly in relation to emergency workers), studies involving children, multiple-session interventions, and methods of crisis intervention that do not involve intense reexposure to the traumatic event. It also seems important to focus interventions on individuals who appear to be at highest risk of developing psychological disorders, for example, individuals who suffer from ASD, as they appear to be at highest risk of developing PTSD. There is a clinical consensus that the earlier treatment is provided, the better the long-term prognosis, and that the treatment principles for emerging PTSD are similar to those for established PTSD. Whatever the outcome of future research, McFarlane's (1989) warning—that overenthusiasm for primary preventative methods might delay the institution of diagnosis and effective treatment for those who do suffer psychological sequelae—must not be allowed to become a reality.

REFERENCES

Alexander, A. (1993). Stress among police body handlers: A long-term follow-up. *British Journal of Psychiatry, 163,* 806–808.

Armstrong, K., O'Callahan, W., & Marmar, C. R. (1991). Debriefing Red Cross disaster personnel: The multiple stressor debriefing model. *Journal of Traumatic Stress, 4,* 581–593.

Beck, A., Ward, C., Mendelson, M., Mock, J., & Erbaugh, J. (1961). An inventory for measuring depression. *Archives of General Psychiatry, 4,* 561–571.

Birleson, P. (1981). The validity of depressive disorder in childhood and the development of a self-rated scale: A research report. *Journal of Child Psychology and Psychiatry, 22,* 73–78.

Bisson, J., & Deahl, M. (1994). Psychological debriefing and prevention of post-traumatic stress: More research is needed. *British Journal of Psychiatry, 165,* 717–720.

Bisson, J., Jenkins, P., Alexander, J., & Bannister, C. (1997). A randomised controlled trial of psychological debriefing for victims of acute burn trauma. *British Journal of Psychiatry, 171,* 78–81.

Blake, D. D., Weathers, F. W., & Nagy, A. G. Y. (1990). A clinician rating scale for assessing current and life-time PTSD: The CAPS-1. *Behavior Therapist, 18,* 187–188.

Blanchard, E. B., Hickling, E. J., Barton, K. A., Taylor, A. E., Loos, W. R., & Jones-Alexander, J. (1996). One-year prospective outcome of motor vehicle accident victims. *Behaviour Research and Therapy, 34,* 775–786.

Bordow, S., & Porritt, D. (1979). An experimental evaluation of crisis intervention. *Social Science and Medicine, 13a,* 251–256.

Breuer, J., & Freud, S. (1893). On the psychical mechanism of hysterical phenomena: Preliminary communication. In S. Freud & J. Breuer, *Studies on hysteria* (pp. 53–69). London: Penguin.

Brewin, C. R., Andrews, B., Rose, S., & Kirk, M. (1998). Acute stress disorder and posttraumatic stress disorder in victims of violent crime. *American Journal of Psychiatry, 156,* 360–366.

Bunn, T., & Clarke, A. (1979). Crisis intervention: An experimental study of the effects of a brief period of counselling on the anxiety of relatives of seriously injured or ill hospital patients. *British Journal of Medical Psychology, 52,* 191–195.

Busuttil, W., Turnbull, G., Neal, L., Rollins, J., West, A., Bland, N., & Herepath, R. (1995). Incorporating psychological debriefing techniques within a brief group psychotherapy programme for the treatment of posttraumatic stress disorder. *British Journal of Psychiatry, 167,* 495–502.

Chemtob, C., Tomas, S., Law, W., & Cremniter, D. (1997). Postdisaster psychosocial interventions: A field study of the impact of debriefing on psychological distress. *American Journal of Psychiatry, 154,* 415–417.

Deahl, M., Gillham, A., Thomas, J., Searle, M., & Srinivasan, M. (1994). Psychological sequelae following the Gulf War: Factors associated with subsequent morbidity and the effectiveness of psychological debriefing. *British Journal of Psychiatry, 165,* 60–65.

Derogatis, I., & Melisaratos, N. (1983). The Brief Symptom Inventory: An introductory report. *Psychological Medicine, 3,* 595–605.

Dyregrov, A. (1989). Caring for helpers in disaster situations: Psychological debriefing. *Disaster Management, 2,* 25–30.

Dyregrov, A. (1998). Psychological debriefing—an effective method? *Traumatology, 4*(2).

Everly, G. S., Jr., & Mitchell, J. T. (1999). *Critical incident stress management (CISM): A new era and standard of care in crisis intervention.* Ellicot City, MD: Chevron.

Flannery, R. B., Fulton, P., Tausch, J., & DeLoffi, A. Y. (1991). A program to help staff cope with psychological sequelae of assaults by patients. *Hospital and Community Psychiatry, 42,* 935–938.

Goldberg, D., & Hillier, V. (1979). A scaled version of the General Health Questionnaire. *Psychological Medicine, 9,* 139–145.

Harvey, A. G., & Bryant, R. A. (1998). The relationship between acute stress disorder and posttraumatic stress disorder: A prospective evaluation of motor vehicle accident survivors. *Journal of Consulting and Clinical Psychology, 66,* 507–512.

Hayman, P. M., & Scaturo, D. J. (1992). *Psychological debriefing of returning military personnel: A protocol for post combat intervention.* Paper presented at the 25th International Congress of Psychology, Brussels.

Hobbs, M., & Adshead, G. (1996). Preventive psychological intervention for road crash survivors. In M. Mitchell (Ed.), *The aftermath of road accidents: Psychological, social and legal perspectives* (pp. 159–171). London: Routledge.

Hobbs, M., Mayou, R., Harrison, B., & Warlock, P. (1996). A randomised trial of psychological debriefing for victims of road traffic accidents. *British Medical Journal, 313,*1438–1439.

Horowitz, M., Wilner, N., & Alvarez, W. (1979). Impact of Event Scale: A measure of subjective stress. *Psychosomatic Medicine, 41,* 209–218.

Hyton, K., & Hasle, A. (1989). Fire fighters: A study of stress and coping. *Acta Psychiatrica Scandinavica, 80* (Suppl. 355), 50–55.

Jenkins, S. R. (1996). Social support and debriefing efficacy among emergency medical workers after a mass shooting incident. *Journal of Social Behavior and Personality, 11,* 477–492.

Kardiner, A., & Spiegel, H. (1947). *War stress and neurotic illness.* New York: Paul B. Hoeber.

Kenardy, J., Webster, R., Lewin, T., Carr, V., Hazell, P., & Carter, G. (1996). Stress debriefing and patterns of recovery following a natural disaster. *Journal of Traumatic Stress, 9,* 37–49.

Lee, C., Slade, P., & Lygo, V. (1996). The influence of psychological debriefing on emotional adaption in women following early miscarriage: A preliminary study. *British Journal of Medical Psychology, 69,* 47–58.

Lindemann, E. (1944). Symptomatology and management of acute grief. *American Journal of Psychiatry, 101,* 141–148.

Lindy, J. D., Green, B. L., Grace, M., & Titchener, J. (1983). Psychotherapy with survivors of the Beverly Hills fire. *American Journal of Psychotherapy, 37,* 593–610.

McFarlane, A. C. (1988). The longitudinal course of post-traumatic morbidity: The range of outcomes and their predictors. *Journal of Nervous and Mental Disease, 176,* 30–39.

McFarlane, A. (1989). The prevention and management of the psychiatric morbidity of natural disasters: An Australian experience. *Stress Medicine, 5,* 29–30.

Marshall, S. L. (1944). *Island victory.* New York: Penguin Books.

Mitchell, J. T. (1983). When disaster strikes. . . . *Journal of Emergency Medical Services, 8,* 36–39.

Mitchell, J. T., & Everly, G. S. (1995). *Critical incident stress debriefing: An operations manual for the prevention of traumatic stress among emergency services and disaster workers.* Ellicot City, MD: Chevron.

Raphael, B. (1977). Preventive intervention with the recently bereaved. *Archives of General Psychiatry, 34,* 1450–1454.

Raphael, B. (1986). *When disaster strikes: A handbook for caring professions.* London: Hutchinson.

Raphael, B., Meldrum, L., & McFarlane, A. C. (1995). Does debriefing after psychological trauma work? *British Medical Journal, 310,* 1479–1480.

Reynolds, C., & Richmond, B. (1978). What I think and feel: A revised measure of children's manifest anxiety. *Journal of Abnormal Child Psychology, 6,* 271–280.

Riggs, D. S., Rothbaum, B. O., & Foa, E. B. (1995). A prospective examination of symptoms of posttraumatic stress disorder in victims of non-sexual assault. *Journal of Interpersonal Violence, 10,* 201–213.

Robinson, R., & Mitchell, J. T. (1993). Evaluation of psychological debriefings. *Journal of Traumatic Stress, 6*(3), 367–382.

Rose, S. (1997). Psychological debriefing: History and methods counselling. *Journal of the British Association of Counselling, 8*(1), 48–51.

Rose, S., & Bisson, J. I. (1998). Brief early psychological interventions following trauma: A systematic review of the literature. *Journal of Traumatic Stress, 11,* 697–710.

Rose, S., Brewin, C. R., Andrews, A., & Kirk, M. (1999). A randomized controlled trial of psychological debriefing for victims of violent crime. *Psychological Medicine, 29,* 793–799.

Searle, M. M., & Bisson, J. I. (1992). Psychological sequelae of friendly fire. *Proceedings Of Military Psychiatry Conference on Stress, Psychiatry and War*, 78–83.

Sloan, P. (1988). Post traumatic stress in survivors of an airplane crash landing. *Journal of Traumatic Stress, 1*, 211–229.

Solomon, Z., & Benbenishty, R. (1988). The role of proximity, immediacy and expectancy in frontline treatment of combat stress reaction among Israelis in the Lebanon War. *American Journal of Psychiatry, 143*, 613–617.

Spielberger, C. (1983). The State–Trait Anxiety Questionnaire: A comprehensive bibliography. Palo Alto, CA: Consultant Psychologist Press.

Stallard, P., & Law, F. (1993). Screening and psychological debriefing of adolescent survivors of life-threatening events. *British Journal of Psychiatry, 163*, 660–665.

Turner, S. W., Thompson, J. A., & Rosser, R. M. (1989). The King's Cross Fire: Planning a "phase two" psychosocial response. *Disaster Management, 2*, 31–37.

Wessely, S., Rose S., & Bisson J. (1998). A systematic review of brief psychological interventions ("debriefing") for the treatment of immediate trauma related symptoms and the prevention of posttraumatic stress disorder [CD-ROM]. Oxford, UK: Update Software.

Yehuda, R., McFarlane, A. C., & Shalev, A. Y. (1998). Predicting the development of posttraumatic stress disorder from the acute response to a traumatic event. *Biological Psychiatry, 44*, 1305–1313.

Zigmond, A. S., & Snaith, R. P. (1983). The Hospital Anxiety and Depression Scale. *Acta Psychiatrica Scandinavia, 67*, 361–370.

4

Cognitive-Behavioral Therapy

Barbara Olasov Rothbaum, Elizabeth A. Meadows,
Patricia Resick, and David W. Foy

This chapter focuses on a review of the extant literature on cognitive-behavioral therapy (CBT) for posttraumatic stress disorder (PTSD). Due to the strength of the literature base in this area, only empirical studies are included. Based on this review, suggestions are offered regarding decision making for the use of CBT for PTSD. As in all of the chapters, the reader should consult the source documents or treatment manuals for more details.

THEORY

CBT for PTSD encompasses numerous diverse techniques. Earlier therapies (systematic desensitization, relaxation training, biofeedback) focused primarily on Mowrer's two-factor theory of conditioned fear and operant avoidance. With the later insurgence of other therapy procedures specifically focused on PTSD symptoms (prolonged exposure, cognitive therapy, cognitive processing therapy) emotional/information-processing theories of PTSD predominated over learning theory. Social-cognitive theories focus on the content of cognitions within a social context. Recently, there have been efforts to integrate the two theories in Brewin's dual representation theory. There is supporting research evidence for all three theoretical approaches.

Contemporary learning theory attempts to account for much of the development and maintenance of the PTSD symptoms (Hayes, Follette, & Follette, 1996; Hayes, Wilson, Gifford, Follette, & Strosahl, 1996; Naugle & Follette, 1998). Reexperiencing and arousal symptoms are viewed as conditioned emotional responses that result from classical conditioning and are elicited by environmental stimuli. According to behavioral theory, although initial symptoms may be caused by the trauma, many current symptoms may represent attempts to manage trauma-induced distress. These attempts, then, respond to current situational contingencies and become functionally autonomous. Avoidance behaviors, behavioral excesses, and behavioral deficits are under operant control. Appropriate reinforcers in the environment may be lacking, or reinforcers may be ineffective or aversive. Clinical problems can also result from inappropriate stimulus control, whereby the response is appropriate but occurs under the wrong conditions. Problematic behavior is under the control of antecedent and reinforcing stimuli that affect the probability of the occurrence of the behavior. Thoughts, feelings, and physiological responses are classified as private events that can serve as antecedent stimuli or consequences. Therefore, as a result of applied behavioral analysis, the focus for treatment may not necessarily be on the trauma itself, but on the maladaptive behavior that developed in the aftermath of the trauma. However, exposure to conditioned stimuli in the absence of the negative consequences is hypothesized to extinguish conditioned emotional reactions. Therefore, in behavioral theory as well as information-processing theories, exposure is presumed to be the appropriate treatment for reexperiencing and arousal symptoms, while contingency management would be implemented for avoidance and other behavioral problems.

Emotional processing theory (Foa & Kozak, 1986) holds that PTSD emerges due to development of a pathological fear structure concerning the traumatic event (Foa, Steketee, & Rothbaum, 1989). Like other fear structures, this structure includes representations about stimuli, responses, and their meaning. Any information associated with the trauma activates the fear structure. The fear structure in people with PTSD is thought to include a particularly large number of stimuli elements and therefore is easily accessed. Attempts to avoid this activation result in the avoidance symptoms of PTSD. Emotional processing theory proposes that successful therapy involves correcting the pathological elements of the fear structure, and that this corrective process is the essence of emotional processing. Two conditions have been proposed to be required for fear reduction. First, the fear structure must be activated. Second, new information must be provided that includes elements incompatible with the existing pathological elements so they can be corrected. Exposure procedures consist of assisting the patient in confronting trauma-related material, thus activating the trauma memory. This activation constitutes an opportunity to integrate corrective information, and thus modify the pathological elements of the trauma memory. Of particular relevance to PTSD is a study demonstrating that fear activation during treatment promotes successful outcome (Foa, Riggs, Massie, & Yarczower, 1995).

Foa and Rothbaum (1998) posited several mechanisms that are involved in the specific changes relevant to improvement of PTSD. First, repeated imaginal reliving of the trauma is thought to promote habituation and thus reduce anxiety previously associated with the trauma memory and correct the erroneous idea that anxiety stays forever unless avoidance or escape is realized. Second, the process of deliberately confronting the feared memory blocks negative reinforcement connected with the fear reduction following cognitive avoidance of trauma-related thoughts and feelings. Third, reliving the trauma in a therapeutic, supportive setting incorporates safety information into the trauma memory, thereby helping the patient to realize that remembering the trauma is not dangerous. Fourth, focusing on the trauma memory for a prolonged period helps the patient to differentiate the trauma event from other, nontraumatic events, thereby rendering the trauma as a specific occurrence rather than as a representation of a dangerous world and of an incompetent self. Fifth, the process of imaginal reliving helps change the meaning of PTSD symptoms from a sign of personal incompetence to a sign of mastery and courage. Sixth, prolonged, repeated reliving of the traumatic event affords the opportunity to focus on details central to negative evaluations of themselves and modify them. Many of the mechanisms discussed here also operate in *in vivo* exposure. However, the mechanisms most salient during *in vivo* exposure are the correction of erroneous probability estimates of danger and habituation of fearful responses to trauma-relevant stimuli.

Social-cognitive theories are also concerned with information processing, but they focus on the impact of trauma on a person's belief system and the adjustment that is necessary to reconcile the traumatic event with prior beliefs and expectations. These theories focus on a range of emotional reactions, both primary (fear, sadness, anger) and secondary (guilt, shame), and not just fear. They are the basis for cognitive therapies for PTSD. New information that is congruent with prior beliefs about self or world is assimilated quickly and without effort because the information matches schemas, and little attention is needed to incorporate it. However, when schema discrepant events occur, individuals must reconcile the event with their beliefs about themselves and the world. Their schemas must be altered, accommodated, to incorporate this new information. However, this process is often avoided because of strong affect associated with the trauma and, frequently, because altering beliefs may leave people feeling more vulnerable to future traumatic events. Thus, rather than accommodating their beliefs to incorporate the trauma, victims may distort (assimilate) the trauma to keep their beliefs intact.

An alternative to assimilation or accommodation is overaccommodation (Resick & Schnicke, 1992). In this case, trauma victims alter their belief structure to the extreme in an attempt to prevent future traumas. Overaccommodated beliefs may take the form of extreme distrust and poor regard for self and others. Prior traumatic events or negative preexisting beliefs contribute to "the evidence" that these extreme statements are true. Overaccommodated beliefs interfere with natural emotions that emanate from the event (e.g., fear, sadness) and therefore prevent appropriate processing of the emotions and beliefs. Furthermore, overgeneralized negative statements can produce secondary emotions that originally might not have been associated with the event (e.g., shame, guilt). Given this social-cognitive model, affective expression is needed, not for habituation, but in order for the trauma memory to be processed fully. It is assumed that natural affect, once accessed, will dissipate rather quickly, and that the work of accommodating the memory with schemas can begin. Once faulty beliefs regarding the event and overaccommodated beliefs about oneself and the world are challenged, secondary emotions also diminish along with the intrusive reminders.

In an attempt to reconcile the theories of PTSD, Brewin, Dalgleish, and Joseph (1996) have proposed a dual representation theory that incorporates both the information-processing and social-cognitive theories. They proposed that sensory input is subject to both conscious and nonconscious processing. Dual representation theory describes two types of emotional reactions. One type of emotional reaction, conditioned during the event (e.g., fear, anger), is activated along with reexperienced sensory and physiological information. Other emotions (e.g., fear, anger, guilt, shame, sadness) are secondary, resulting from the consequences and implications of the trauma. Brewin and colleagues propose that emotional processing of the trauma has two elements: the activation of nonconscious memories (as suggested by the information processing theories) and the conscious attempt to search for meaning, to ascribe cause or blame, and to resolve conflicts between the event and prior expectations and beliefs. The goal of this process is to reduce the negative emotions and to restore a sense of relative safety and control in one's environment. This theory suggests that both exposure and cognitive therapy may be needed in some cases.

DESCRIPTION OF TECHNIQUES

Eight different cognitive-behavioral treatments for PTSD were reviewed, along with several additional studies of treatment programs that combine one or more of these eight treatments. Brief descriptions of each of these treatments are provided here. The techniques included exposure therapy (EX); systematic desensitization (SD); stress inoculation training (SIT); cognitive processing therapy (CPT); cognitive therapy (CT); assertiveness training (AT); biofeedback (BIO); relaxation training (Relax); combined SIT/EX; combined EX/Relax/CT; and combined CT/EX.

Exposure Therapy

A variety of terms have been used to describe prolonged exposure to anxiety-provoking stimuli without relaxation or other anxiety-reducing methods, including flooding/imaginal/*in vivo*/prolonged/directed; in this chapter, these are referred to collectively as exposure (EX). As in systematic desensitization, EX typically begins with the development of an anxiety hierarchy. In some forms of EX (i.e., flooding), treatment sessions are begun with exposure to the highest item on the hierarchy; others begin with items rated as moderately anxiety provoking. EX methods share the common feature of confrontation with frightening stimuli that continues until the anxiety is reduced. By continuing to expose oneself to a frightening stimulus, anxiety diminishes, leading to a decrease in escape and avoidance behavior that was maintained via negative reinforcement (Mowrer, 1960). As noted earlier, a different conceptualization of EX's mechanism of action with the introduction of emotional processing theory for anxiety disorders in general was offered by Foa and Kozak (1986) and by Foa and Rothbaum (1998) for PTSD in particular.

As noted earlier, there are several variants of EX. In imaginal EX, clients confront their memories of the traumatic event. Some imaginal methods (see, e.g., Foa, Rothbaum, Riggs, & Murdock 1991; Foa et al., 1999) involve clients' providing their own narrative by discussing the trauma in detail in the present tense for prolonged periods of time (e.g., 45–60 minutes), with prompting by the therapist for omitted details. Other forms of imaginal exposure (see, e.g., Cooper & Clum, 1989; Keane, Fairbank, Caddell, & Zimering, 1989) have involved the therapist presenting a scene to the client based on information gathered prior to the EX exercise. The duration and number of EX sessions has also varied, sometimes within the same study. These details are provided in Table 4.1, which summarizes CBT treatment outcome studies for PTSD. Finally, most EX treatments do not consist solely of exposure but include other components such as psychoeducation or relaxation training. The treatments that combine such components typically include vastly more time on Exposure than on these other components, which are often presented as preliminary ways of building up to the exposure. Details on the implementation of EX for PTSD have been provided in Foa and Rothbaum (1998).

Systematic Desensitization

SD is a form of EX that is paired with relaxation. It was first developed by Wolpe (1958) and is based on the principle of reciprocal inhibition. Specifically, the relaxation response was thought to be incompatible with the anxiety response elicited by exposure; thus, short exposures were interrupted by relaxation as anxiety increased. Over time, this allowed clients to confront anxiety-provoking stimuli without an anxiety response. SD has most often been conducted using imaginal exposure. However, it has also been conducted using *in vivo* (i.e., in real life) stimuli, with some indication that this produces greater improvement than imaginal stimuli (Barlow, Leitenberg, Agras, & Wincze, 1969). Typically, the first step in SD is to develop an anxiety hierarchy in which anxiety-provoking stimuli are rank-ordered to allow for gradual increases in difficulty. Relaxation training is taught until clients become proficient in this technique prior to beginning the exposures. Upon gaining this proficiency, the exposure sessions begin, each pausing for initiation of relaxation when anxiety begins to mount. Following the relaxation, the exposure begins again until the client is able to tolerate all stimuli on the hierarchy without anxiety.

Stress Inoculation Training

SIT was developed by Meichenbaum (1974) as an anxiety management treatment. Later Kilpatrick, Veronen, and Resick (1982) modified the program to treat rape victims, although this was prior to the widespread use of the PTSD diagnosis to describe postrape symptomatology. The modified SIT program included education, muscle relaxation training, breathing retraining, role playing, covert modeling, guided self-dialog, and thought stopping. Some applications did not include some of the original SIT strategies, such as assertiveness training, since these were included in treatments compared with SIT in the initial studies. Similarly, in some studies that have compared SIT with EX, clients are not given instructions to confront frightening situations, although this might otherwise be included within several SIT strategies, such as role playing. The rationale underlying SIT focuses on anxiety that becomes conditioned at the time of the trauma and generalizes to many situations. Clients learn to manage this anxiety by using these new skills, thus decreasing avoidance and anxiety.

Cognitive Processing Therapy

CPT was developed by Resick and Schnicke (1992, 1993) to target specifically rape-related PTSD. It incorporates elements of CT therapy and EX. The cognitive component includes training clients in challenging problematic cognitions, particularly self-blame, and attempts to mentally undo the event. Using the skills obtained in challenging thoughts and beliefs, clients are asked to work on overgeneralized beliefs emanating from the rape. Among them are beliefs about safety, trust, power/control, esteem, and intimacy (McCann & Pearlman, 1990). The EX component consists of writing a detailed account of the trauma and reading it to the therapist as well as at home. Aside from the expression of affect, the account is used to generate the client's "stuck points," moments during the assault that cause conflict with previously held beliefs or are particularly hard to accept. These points receive particular attention during cognitive therapy.

Cognitive Therapy

CT, initially developed by Beck (1976) to treat depression, was then developed further as a treatment for anxiety (Clark, 1986). CT is based on Beck's (1976) theory that the interpretation of an event, rather than the event itself, is what determines mood states. Thus, interpretations that are negatively biased lead to negative mood states. These erroneous or unhelpful interpretations, generally referred to as automatic (dysfunctional) thoughts, are typically seen as either inaccurate or too extreme for the situation that prompted them. CT aims to modify automatic thoughts. This occurs in steps wherein clients are taught to identify these dysfunctional thoughts, challenge those evaluated as inaccurate or unhelpful, and, finally, to replace them with more logical or beneficial thoughts. With respect to trauma survivors, much attention is paid to their appraisals of safety–danger, trust, and views of themselves.

Assertiveness Training

It has been suggested that assertive responses, as well as relaxation, may inhibit fear (Wolpe, 1969). AT, as administered in the study by Resick, Jordan, Girelli, Hutter, and Marhoefer-Dvorak (1988), was conducted as a 6-week-long (2-hour sessions) group therapy. Lange and Jakubowski's 1976 book *Responsible Assertive Behavior* was used as the basis for skills-building exercises and assertiveness techniques. Some CT was also used to teach the connection between thoughts, emotions, and behaviors, and to identify faulty thinking patterns. Interpersonal problems that emanate in the wake of trauma were emphasized and clients were helped through CT and role playing to be assertive rather than passive or aggressive in talking to people about their assaults, in asking for social support, or in correcting misinformation.

Biofeedback and Relaxation Training

Both of the anxiety management techniques, BIO and Relax, have been used to treat PTSD. As with the other anxiety management methods such as SIT, these methods provide a way for clients to reduce anxiety that may be elicited by trauma-related stimuli. Both also provide tools with which clients can reduce physiological responses.

METHOD OF COLLECTING DATA

Information was gathered in several ways. First, each of the four authors contributed a summary of recent literature reviews of CBT for PTSD. These reviews were developed via PsycLIT, PsycINFO, and PILOTS searches, analyzing relevant reference lists from articles, chapters, and books, and personal communication with PTSD researchers. The four reviews were then combined into one comprehensive summary and recent studies were added. The individual studies were examined in detail when more information was necessary to judge their methodology or results accurately and this information was then added to the comprehensive summary.

SUMMARY OF LITERATURE

Treatment outcome studies have been conducted on the efficacy of each of these treatments for PTSD. These studies are summarized in Table 4.1. Additionally, a number of case reports and uncontrolled studies have supported the use of several of these treatments. However, because substantial evidence of those techniques exists from controlled studies, case reports and uncontrolled investigations have generally not been included. Only published or in-press reports are included.

In the consideration of space, the studies are not reviewed here in great detail. Table 4.1 contains many of the important details to determine the methodological rigor and thus the strength of the conclusions to be drawn from each study, including the gold standards ratings and Agency for Health Care Policy and Research (AHCPR) ratings. The reader is referred to Foa and Meadows (1997) for a critical review of treatments of PTSD, evaluating studies in terms of the gold standards for clinical studies. These gold standards include (1) clearly defined target symptoms; (2) reliable and valid measures; (3) blind evaluators; (4) assessor training; (5) manualized, replicable, specific treatment programs; (6) unbiased (random) assignment to treatment; and (7) treatment adherence. Many of these CBT studies fare particularly well on this classification according to methodological rigor. The studies are discussed by treatment technique. Studies described as "very well-controlled" or "methodologically rigorous" received a Level A rating on the AHCPR scale and meet all or most of the gold standards. These studies provide strong evidence for their findings. Studies described as "less well-controlled" received a Level B or lower rating on the AHCPR scale and meet fewer of the gold standards. Conclusions drawn from these studies are less strong than those drawn from well-controlled studies. The conclusions drawn from uncontrolled studies are weakest.

Exposure Therapy

Exposure therapy has been tested in 12 studies reviewed in Table 4.1, all of which found positive results for this treatment with PTSD. Of these generally

TABLE 4.1. CBT Studies of PTSD

Study	Treatments[a]	Population/n	No./duration of sessions	Results	Standards met[b]	Rating[c]	Effect sizes[d]
Boudewyns & Hyer (1990)	1. Standard tx + EX 2. Standard tx + traditional counseling	Vietnam veterans, 51	12–14 sessions; 50 min	At follow-up patients who displayed decreased physiological responding also showed improvement on community adjustment measure of anxiety/depression, alienation, vigor, and confidence in skills. 75% of successes were in EX, as were 25% of failures.	1, 4, 5, 6	A	
Bowen & Lambert (1986)	1. SD 2. No tx	Combat veterans, 10	Large no. of sessions, over long time	SD showed significant decrease at posttreatment relative to no treatment.		C	
Brom, Kleber, & Defares (1989)	1. SD 2. Hypnotherapy 3. Psychodynamic tx 4. WL	Various traumas (majority was losing loved ones), 112	15 sessions for SD, 14.4 for hypnosis, 18.8 for psychodynamic	All treatments equally significant and better than WL.	1 (somewhat), 2, 4 (somewhat), 6	A	SD: 1.02 (modified IES)
Cooper & Clum (1989)	1. Standard tx 2. Standard tx + EX	Vietnam veterans, 26 (16 completers, results are from 14)	Imaginal flooding, 6–14 sessions; 90 min ea.	ST + EX showed significant improvement over ST only on self-report symptoms directly related to the trauma, state anxiety, subjective anxiety in response to trauma stimuli, and sleep.	1, 5, 6	A	**EX: 2.15 (reported SUDS during BAT)**
Deblinger, McLeer, & Henry (1990)	1. "CBT program"	Sexually abused girls, 19		Significant improvements pre to post.	1, 2, 4, 5	B	

68

Study	Treatments	Sample	Sessions	Results	Criteria	Rating	Effect size
Devilly & Spence (1999)	1. EMDR 2. CBT	Various traumas, 23	1. 8 sessions, unknown duration 2. 9 sessions, unknown duration	CBT improved more at posttreatment and follow-up than did EMDR.	1, 2, 4, 5, 7	B	CBT: 0.65 at post, 1.03 at follow-up (on PTSD Symptom Scale, relative to EMDR)
Echeburua, de Corral, Sarasua, & Zubizarreta (1996)	1. Relax 2. Coping skills training (EX, Relax, some SIT components)	Women with recent (1–3 mo post) sexual assault, 20	5 sessions; 1 hr ea.	Both groups improved, about equally at posttreatment. At 12-mo follow-up, coping skills training outperformed Relax.	1, 2 (mostly), 4, 5, 6	A	**CST: 0.79 (on PTSD Symptoms Scale, relative to Relax)**
Echeburua, de Corral, Zubizarreta, & Sarasua (1997)	1. Relax 2. EX/CT	Women with CSA or nonrecent adulthood sexual assault, 20	6 sessions; 7 hr total for EX/CT and 4.15 hr total for Relax	Both groups improved, but EX/CT improved more than did Relax, and continued to improve during follow-up period.	1, 2 (mostly), 4, 5, 6	A	**EX/CT: 1.44 (on PTSD Symptoms Scale, relative to Relax)**
Foa, Dancu, Hembree, Jaycox, Meadows, & Street (1999)	1. EX 2. SIT 3. SIT/EX 4. WL	Sexual and physical assault	9 sessions; 90 minutes	All three treatments superior to WL, with no difference between them on most measures. On end-state functioning, PE was best. PE was also best when comparing groups with and without PE.	1, 2, 3, 4, 5, 6, 7	A	PE: 1.91 SIT: 1.57 SIT/PE: 1.45 (PSS-I)
Foa, Hearst-Ikeda, & Perry (1995)	1. "Brief prevention" (BP: EX/Relax/CT) 2. Assessment control (AC)	Sexual assault, 20	4 sessions; 2 hr ea.	At posttreatment, BP better than AC. Of BP, 10% met PTSD diagnosis and 70% of AC met PTSD diagnosis. At follow-up, BP significantly better than AC on depression and severe reexperiencing symptoms.	1, 2, 3, 4, 5	A	**BP: 1.22 (PSS-I; relative to AC)**

(continued)

TABLE 4.1. (continued)

Study	Treatments[a]	Population/n	No./duration of sessions	Results	Standards met[b]	Rating[c]	Effect sizes[d]
Foa, Rothbaum, Riggs, & Murdock (1991)	1. EX 2. SIT 3. Supportive counseling 4. WL	Sexual assault, 45	9 sessions, 90 min	At posttreatment, SIT was better than supportive counseling and WL, and slightly better than EX. At 3-mo follow-up, EX slightly better than SIT.	1 (but no threshold), 2, 3, 4, 5, 6, 7	A	EX: 0.42 SIT: 1.48 (PSS-I)
Frank, Anderson, Stewart, Dancu, Hughes, & West (1988)	1. CT 2. SD 3. WL	Rape trauma, 84	4 wk	SD and CT showed significant improvement at posttreatment relative to WL, with no differences between them.	1, 2, 3, 5, 7	B	(ES not calculated because WL was via separate study at other sites)
Fruch, Turner, Beidel, Mirabella, & Jones (1996)	1. EX	Vietnam combat veterans, 15 males	29 sessions over 17 wk; 90 min ea.	Treatment reduced anxiety.	1, 2, 3, 5, 7	B	
Hickling & Blanchard (1997)	1. SIT/EX (+ a few other small components)	MVA, 10	10–12 sessions	Treatment reduced CAPS severity by 68%.	1, 2, 5, 7	B	
Hyer, Woods, Bruno, & Boudewyns (1989)	1. SD	Vietnam veterans with chronic PTSD, 50	5 wk	Stable personality measure improvement not seen.	1, 2, 4	B	
Keane, Fairbank, Caddell, & Zimering (1989)	1. EX 2. WL	Vietnam veterans, 24	14–16 sessions; 45 per 90 min	EX showed significant improvement at posttreatment and 6-mo follow-up over WL on PTSD reexperiencing symptoms, depression, anxiety; also, therapist ratings of startle memory concentration, impulsivity, irritability, and legal problems all lower than WL.	1, 2, 4, 5, 6	A	EX: 0.22 (MMPI-PTSD scale)

Study	Treatment conditions	Sample	Sessions	Results	Outcome measures	Rating	Effect sizes
Kilpatrick, Veronen, & Resick (1982)	1. SIT 2. Peer counseling 3. (SD—was offered but no one chose this tx)	Sexual assault, 15		SIT effective in reducing rape-related fear/anxiety/avoidance at post and 3-mo follow-up.	1 (somewhat), 2, 5	B	
Marks, Lovell, Noshirvani, Livanou, & Thrasher (1998)	1. EX 2. EX/CT 3. Relax	Variety of traumas, 87 (77 completers)		CT, EX, EX/CT all better than Relax and otherwise equal at posttreatment and at 6-mo follow-up on most, but not all, measures. On CAPS, EX/CT was inferior to either individual treatment (see effect sizes). Relax produced moderate significant improvement.	1, 2, 3, 4, 5, 6, 7	A	**EX: 0.14 CT: 0.08 EX/CT: -0.24 (on CAPS; relative to Relax)**
Peniston & Kulkosky (1991)	1. SD/BIO (brain-wave neurofeedback tx) 2. Traditional medical tx group	Vietnam veterans with PTSD, 29	30 sessions	SD/BIO resulted in a decrease in MMPI clinical scales. The traditional medical tx group showed decreases only in the schizophrenia scale. At 3-mo follow-up all traditional tx subjects relapsed, and 3 of 15 brain-wave neurofeedback subjects relapsed.	1, 2, 5, 6	A	**SD/BIO: 2.50 (on MMPI-PTSD Scale, relative to traditional medical therapy)**
Peniston (1986)	1. SD/BIO 2. No tx	Veterans, 16	Large no. over long period of time	SD/BIO showed significant decrease at posttreatment relative to no treatment on nightmares, flashbacks, muscle tension, and hospital readmissions.	1, 5, 6	B	

(continued)

TABLE 4.1. (continued)

Study	Treatments[a]	Population/n	No./duration of sessions	Results	Standards met[b]	Rating[c]	Effect sizes[d]
Pitman, Orr, Altman, Longpre, Poire, Macklin, Michaels, & Steketee (1996)	1. EX	Vietnam veterans with PTSD, 20	Average of 10.2 (6 sessions for 6 subjects, 12 sessions for 14 subjects)	Evidence of emotional processing, but only 13% overall decrease on outcome measures; 26% reduction in intrusive combat memories on self-monitoring.		C	
Resick & Schnicke (1992)	1. CPT 2. WL (naturally occurring)	Sexual assault, 19	12 sessions	CPT showed significant improvement on PTSD, depression, and social adjustment at posttreatment and 6-mo follow-up. All CPT clients lost diagnosis by 6-mo follow-up.	2, 3, 4, 5	B	CPT: 0.62 (SCL-90-R PTSD scale)
Resick, Jordan, Girelli, Hutter, & Marhoefer-Dvorak (1988)	1. AT 2. SIT 3. Supportive tx	Sexual assault, 37	6 wk of 2-hr sessions	All treatments equally effective.	2 (somewhat), 5, 6 (somewhat)	B	AT: 0.33 (intrusive) AT: 0.57 (avoidant) SIT: 0.07 (intrusive) SIT: 0.60 (avoidant) (IES)
Richards, Lovell, & Marks (1994)	1. EX (each subject had IMF and IVF, with order counterbalanced)	Variety of traumas, 14	8 sessions (4 ea. of IMF and IVF) weekly; 60 min	Both groups did well: 65–80% symptom reduction. At posttreatment and 12-mo follow-up, none retained diagnosis. Only difference between groups is on phobic avoidance: *in vivo* EX was more effective than imaginal EX, regardless of order.	1, 2, 5, 6	B	

Study	Treatment conditions	Population, N	Sessions	Results	Gold standards[b]	Type[c]	ES[d]
Silver, Brooks, & Obenchain (1995)	1. Milieu + BIO 2. Milieu + EMDR 3. Milieu + Relax 4. Milieu (control)	Veterans, 100		Neither BIO nor Relax showed any significant differences relative to the control group.	1, 5, 6	A	**BIO: −0.14 Relax: 0.20 (intrusive thoughts question on Problem Report Form)**
Tarrier, Pilgrim, Sommerfield, Faragher, Reynolds, Graham, & Barrowclough (1999)	1. CT 2. EX	Variety of traumas, 62	16 sessions; 1 hr ea.	Both CT and EX showed significant improvements at posttreatment and follow-up relative to pretreatment, with no differences between them.	1, 2, 3, 5, 6, 7	A	
Thompson, Charlton, Kerry, Lee, & Turner (1995)	1. EX	Traumatized individuals, 23	8 sessions	EX showed significant improvement at posttreatment: 42% on IES, 61% on GHQ, 38% on SCL–90, 35% on CAPS.	1, 2, 5, 7	B	
Watson, Tuorila, Vickers, Gearhart, & Mendez (1997)	1. Relax 2. Relax + breathing 3. Relax + breathing + BIO	Vietnam veterans, 90	10 sessions; 30 min ea.	All groups showed only mild improvement on only a few measures—no differences between groups.	1, 2, 5, 6	A	**Relax/BRT: −0.18 Relax/BIO: 0.35 (on PTSD-I, relative to Relax only)**

[a]AT, assertiveness training; BIO, biofeedback; CPT, cognitive processing therapy; CT, cognitive therapy; EX, exposure; IMF, imaginal flooding; IVF, *in vivo* flooding; PE, prolonged exposure; Relax, relaxation; SD, systematic desensitization; SIT, stress inoculation training; WL, wait-list; tx, treatment; ST, standard treatment.

[b]Gold standards listed are based on what was in paper; only explicitly stated items are included here. 1, clear target symptoms; 2, reliable, valid measures; 3, blind evaluations; 4, assessor training; 5, manualized specific tx; 6, unbiased assignment to tx; 7, adherence.

[c]Study type codes: A, randomized controlled studies; B, well-designed studies without randomization or placebo comparison; C, service/naturalistic studies combined with clinical observations.

[d]**ES in bold** indicates that control was comparison, not WL, group. Items in parentheses refer to the main PTSD measure used, with which effect sizes were calculated.

methodologically controlled studies, eight received the AHCPR Level A rating, and several met many of the gold standards for clinical outcome studies (Foa & Meadows, 1997); thus, the strength of evidence for EX is very conclusive.

Four studies that investigated EX with Vietnam veterans were generally well controlled, while two were uncontrolled. Keane, Fairbank, Caddell, and Zimmering (1989) compared exposure to a wait-list control for 24 veterans and found beneficial effects for reexperiencing symptoms in a well-controlled study. Cooper and Clum (1989) compared EX to standard treatment for 14 completers and found that EX improved self-report of symptoms directly related to the trauma. Boudewyns and Hyer (1990) compared EX to traditional counseling in 51 veterans and found that 75% of those designated as treatment successes had received EX. Glynn and colleagues (1999) compared EX alone with EX plus behavioral family therapy to a wait-list control and found that both groups who had received EX were more improved than the wait-list control group. In an uncontrolled study with no comparison group, Frueh, Turner, Beidel, Mirabella, and Jones (1996) found that treatment with EX reduced anxiety in 15 male veterans. Pitman and colleagues (1996) found equivocal results with EX in an uncontrolled report, but EX was conducted relative to guilt-producing rather than anxiety-producing incidents, which may account for the lack of positive results. Thus, five of six EX studies with Vietnam veterans found positive effects for EX, and four of these were well-controlled.

Two very well-controlled studies examined EX with female sexual assault survivors (Foa et al., 1991, 1999). Both studies received AHCPR Level A ratings and met all seven of the gold standards for clinical outcome studies; thus, firm conclusions can be drawn from the results that EX was efficacious. In the first study, EX was compared to SIT, supportive counseling, and a wait-list control group for 45 female sexual assault survivors with PTSD. In the second study, EX was compared to SIT and the combination of EX plus SIT compared to a wait-list control group for 78 female sexual assault survivors with PTSD.

Four studies examined the efficacy of EX for a mixed variety of traumas. Two were very well controlled (Marks, Lovell, Nochirvani, Livanou, & Thrasher, 1998; Tarrier et al., 1999) and two were moderately well controlled (Richards, Lovell, & Marks, 1994; Thompson, Charlton, Kerry, Lee, & Turner, 1995). In the Marks and colleagues (1998) study, EX alone was compared to CT alone, the combination of EX and CT, and to Relax for 77 completers. All three active treatments led to more improvement than relaxation. The Tarrier and colleagues (1999) study compared imaginal EX to CT for 72 patients and found that both treatments were equally effective in reducing symptoms from pretreatment, although the overall effects were smaller than in other studies. A within-subjects design counterbalanced the order and examined the specific contributions of imaginal EX and *in vivo* EX for 14 survivors of various traumas (Richards et al., 1994), and found that both treatments led to improvements. The only difference was that *in vivo* EX was more effective on phobic avoidance than imaginal EX, regardless of the order of presentation. In the Thompson and colleagues (1995) report, EX was effective for 23 survivors of a variety of traumas, but there was no comparison group.

In summary, compelling evidence from many well-controlled trials with a mixed variety of trauma survivors indicates that EX is quite effective. In fact, no other treatment modality has evidence this strong indicating its efficacy.

Systematic Desensitization

Six studies have examined SD for posttrauma reactions, although most of these studies suffer from methodological problems. The only well-controlled study of SD is by Brom, Kleber, and Defares (1989). They compared SD, hypnotherapy, and psychodynamic treatments to a wait-list control for 112 survivors of various traumas and found no difference between SD and the other treatments. Unfortunately, in this study, not all of the traumas necessarily met DSM criteria for a trauma, as many were due to loss of a loved one.

Four of the remaining five studies examined SD with Vietnam veterans, although none were well controlled. Bowen and Lambert (1986) found that SD produced changes at posttreatment as compared to pretreatment in 10 veterans but used a large number of sessions over a long period of time. Peniston (1986) found SD effective for 16 veterans, also employing a large number of sessions over a long period of time. Peniston and Kulkowsky (1991) used 30 sessions of brain-wave neurofeedback in their SD compared to traditional medical group therapy for 29 veterans and reported decreases in the MMPI scores. The Peniston studies have recently received scathing criticism (Graap & Freid, 1998), calling into question the validity of the data. Hyer, Woods, Bruno, and Boudewyns (1989) did not find improvement on personality measures following 5 weeks of SD with 50 Vietnam veterans. The only study of SD with female assault survivors found a significant improvement after 4 weeks of SD that was not significantly different from CT (Frank et al., 1988). However, this study is confounded by the fact that many subjects were recent survivors (thus, their symptoms would be expected to decrease naturally with time), no PTSD measures were used, and it is not clear that all subjects participated in the same study at the same site.

In summary, although several studies have found that SD was effective in reducing posttrauma symptoms, the studies are not well controlled, and in some cases, we have reason to doubt the validity of the findings. Thus, SD has not received strong support from well-controlled studies. It has been largely abandoned in favor of EX without Relax.

Stress Inoculation Training

Four studies have examined the efficacy of SIT, all with female sexual assault survivors. Of these, two are well controlled and receive AHCPR Level A ratings (Foa et al., 1991, 1999), and two are less well controlled. The Foa studies were discussed earlier, comparing SIT to EX to counseling, to a wait-list control in the first study, and comparing SIT alone to EX alone, and the two combined to wait-list control in the second study. Both studies found that nine 90-minute sessions of SIT were effective in reducing PTSD and related symptoms. In less well-controlled designs, SIT was found as effective as peer counseling (Kilpatrick, Veronen, & Resick, 1982), AT, and supportive therapy (Resick, Jordan, Girelli, Hutter, & Marhoefer-Dvorak, 1988).

In summary, all four studies found SIT effective, but only two were well-controlled and all were with female sexual assault survivors, leaving open the question of SIT's efficacy with other trauma populations.

Cognitive Processing Therapy

Only one study has been published investigating CPT (Resick & Schnicke, 1992). CPT was effective in reducing PTSD and related symptoms in 19 female sexual assault survivors as compared to a naturally occurring wait list control group. This study meets four of the seven gold standards and receives the AHCPR Level B rating due to lack of randomization. CPT is designed specifically for female sexual assault survivors, and thus would have to be modified if applied to other trauma populations.

Cognitive Therapy

Three studies have examined CT for trauma survivors, two of which were reviewed earlier (Frank et al., 1988; Marks, Lovell, Noshirvani, Livanou, & Thrasher, 1998). The Marks and colleagues study is well controlled, receiving an AHCPR Level A rating, and did not find differences between CT, EX, or the combination, but all three were more effective than Relax for 77 treatment completers from a variety of trauma populations. Frank and colleagues (1988) did not find differences between CT and SD, but found that both were better than wait-list controls. However, this study suffers from some severe methodological problems. It should be noted that CPT (discussed earlier) includes a strong cognitive component. Tarrier and colleagues (1999) compared CT to EX for 62 survivors of a variety of traumas and found them equally effective in producing improvement relative to pretreatment.

In summary, CT has been effective in reducing posttrauma symptoms in two controlled studies.

Assertiveness Training

Only one study (Resick et al., 1988) has tested AT for PTSD, and found that it was not significantly different from comparison treatments for female sexual assault survivors. This study received an AHCPR Level B rating. Thus, AT has not received strong support in the treatment of PTSD.

Biofeedback and Relaxation Training

Only one study has examined BIO in a controlled design (Silver, Brooks, & Obenchain, 1995) comparing it to eye movement desensitization and reprocessing (EMDR) plus milieu and Relax plus milieu in 100 Vietnam veterans. BIO was not supported, as EMDR plus milieu was more effective.

Relax is generally included as a control treatment and has been found less effective than comparison treatments (Echeburua, de Corral, Sarasua, & Zubizarreta, 1996; Echeburua, de Corral, Zubizarreta, & Sarasua, 1997; Mark, Lovell, Noshirvani, Livanou, & Thrasher, 1998; Silver et al., 1995).

In summary, BIO and Relax have not received support as effective treatments for PTSD.

Combination Approaches

Combination treatments (e.g., EX combined with SIT) have not resulted in significantly more improvements on PTSD and related symptoms when compared to the single treatments (Foa et al., 1999; Marks et al., 1998). They have been shown to be effective when compared to an assessment control for female sexual assault survivors soon after the assault, when they did not yet meet PTSD criteria (Foa, Hearst-Ikeda, & Perry, 1995), and when compared to Relax (Echeburua et al., 1997). In uncontrolled investigations, combination approaches were effective for 19 sexually abused girls (Deblinger, McLeer, & Henry, 1990) and for 10 survivors of motor vehicle accidents (Blanchard & Hickling, 1997). In summary, combination approaches have received support as effective treatments for PTSD but do not appear to be more effective than their single components.

Cognitive-Behavioral Therapy versus EMDR

Devilly and Spence (1999) compared a CBT program that included prolonged imaginal EX, SIT, and CT to EMDR (for details about this treatment, see Chapter 7) in a sample of males and females who had PTSD following various traumas. All patients received nine treatment sessions of either treatment. The results showed that CBT was statistically and clinically more efficacious than EMDR at both posttreatment and follow-up. Although the two treatments were rated as equally distressing, CBT was rated as more credible and generated higher expectancies for change. Patients rated both treatments as "moderately" distressing, and there were no significant differences in dropout rates.

RECOMMENDATIONS

Comparing the numbers and types of studies supporting each type of treatment, EX has the most studies and the greatest number of well-controlled studies to support its use. EX has been tested in 12 studies reviewed in Table 4.1, all finding positive results for this treatment with PTSD. These are also generally methodologically controlled studies, with eight of these studies receiving the AHCPR Level A rating and several meeting many of the gold standards for clinical outcome studies (Foa & Meadows, 1997); thus, the strength of evidence for EX is very conclusive. In one study, EX was superior to SIT and SIT/PE. Additionally, EX has been tested in a wider range of trauma populations and more studies than have any of the other treatments. Thus, we strongly recommend the use of some form of EX in the treatment of PTSD unless otherwise indicated. In conclusion, the evidence is very compelling from many well-controlled trials, with a mixed variety of trauma survivors, that EX is effective. In fact, no other treatment modality has such strong evidence for its efficacy.

Of the four studies that have examined the efficacy of SIT, all found SIT effective, but only two were well-controlled, and all were with female sexual assault survivors, leaving open the question of SIT's efficacy with other trauma populations. The use of SIT for non-assault-related PTSD has not yet been studied, although there is no reason it should not be effective with these individuals as well. CPT was found effective in one published study, but due to its focus on rape-related issues, it would be inappropriate with other trauma-related populations unless modified for them. CT has been effective in reducing posttrauma symptoms and receives support from two controlled studies. AT has not received strong support in the treatment of PTSD. SD has generally been replaced by EX and would not be recommended. BIO has not yielded improvement in PTSD; thus, we do not recommend its use at this time. One study found Relax to be somewhat effective, but significantly less so than EX, CT, or a combination of the two. Another study found Relax to be effective only on the arousal symptoms with recent trauma survivors. BIO and Relax may be useful as anxiety management components within a more comprehensive program, but they have not received support as effective treatments for PTSD and are therefore not recommended.

LIMITATIONS

Each of the reviewed treatments has its limitations. These include the following:

1. *Exposure.* Some trauma survivors are reluctant to confront trauma reminders and to tolerate the high anxiety and temporarily increased symp-

toms that sometimes accompany exposure. Thus, not everyone may be a candidate for EX. There is some preliminary evidence that EX is not effective for perpetrators of harm, especially patients in which guilt is the primary emotion (Pitman et al., 1991). There is also evidence that individuals whose primary emotional response is anger (Foa, Riggs, Massie, & Yarczower, 1995) may not profit as much from EX as individuals whose primary emotional response is anxiety. However, EX has received the strongest evidence for PTSD and thus should be considered as the first line of treatment unless reasons exist for ruling it out. Litz, Blake, Gerardi, and Keane (1990) and Foa and Rothbaum (1998) have discussed which patients are good candidates for EX.

2. *Systematic desensitization.* Due to findings that longer exposures tend to outperform shorter exposures, and that the use of Relax during exposure does not enhance treatment effectiveness, SD has largely fallen out of favor relative to EX.

3. *Stress inoculation training.* To date, SIT has only been examined in female assault survivors; thus, its efficacy with regard to PTSD caused by other traumas is not known. Some SIT elements may be inappropriate for some clients (i.e., Relax may lead to relaxation-induced anxiety in some). With its many components, therapists require a great deal of training.

4. *Cognitive processing therapy.* CPT was specifically designed as a treatment for rape victims; thus, it may be inappropriate for other trauma victims. To date, all CPT studies have been conducted by the group that developed the treatment, so more studies by other groups are needed.

5. *Cognitive therapy.* Three CT studies were reviewed, and all found CT as effective as comparison treatments, with two of those studies well-controlled. This evidence supports the use of CT for PTSD. However, many PTSD clinicians and researchers feel strongly that an EX component is recommended.

6. *Assertiveness training.* The only study incorporating AT reviewed here was not well-controlled and included only female assault victims; thus, more information is needed before strong conclusions can be drawn. At most, AT should be considered a component of treatment rather than a comprehensive treatment for PTSD.

7. *Biofeedback.* Only one BIO study was reviewed; thus, more studies are needed before conclusions can be drawn. BIO has not been demonstrated to be as effective as other treatments, and is not recommended as a treatment for PTSD.

8. *Relaxation.* Relax may lead to relaxation-induced anxiety in some clients. It has been found to be less effective than the other therapies but may have some limited utility for arousal symptoms. Relax is not recommended as a treatment for PTSD.

9. *Combined programs.* These programs generally have not been shown to be better or worse than the individual treatments comprising the combination program. This may be due to the decrease in time spent on each compo-

nent, but this has yet to be tested. Combined programs are generally more complicated to deliver.

AREAS REQUIRING FURTHER EXPLORATIONS

Issues of comorbidity were not addressed specifically in many of the studies reviewed, although a number of studies demonstrated decreases in depression and anxiety symptoms, in addition to symptoms of PTSD. This was true of EX, SD, SIT, CPT, and combination treatments. A common comorbid condition of PTSD, substance dependence, was often an exclusion criteria for entry into these studies. Many of these studies only focused on one trauma population, such as rape survivors, and only treated clients on an outpatient basis. These factors that limit the generalizability of the findings should thus be addressed in future studies. Preliminary evidence from a case study indicates that virtual reality EX may hold promise (Rothbaum et al., 1999), but this technique awaits controlled testing for PTSD. To date, no controlled study comparing cognitive-behavioral techniques to psychopharmacological approaches has been conducted, but such a study would yield very useful information. More studies of efficient and effective treatments for PTSD are needed.

ACKNOWLEDGMENTS

This chapter was supported in part by Grant Nos. NIMH 1R21MH55555-01, NIMH 1R01MH56351-01 NIMH, and 1R41MH58493-01 awarded to Barbara Olasov Rothbaum and NIH-1-R01-MH51509 awarded to Patricia Resick. We gratefully acknowledge the assistance of Kelly Phipps, Laura Dreer, Josh Scribner, and Doug Fogel.

REFERENCES

Barlow, D. H., Leitenberg, H., Agras, W. S., & Wincze, J. P. (1969). The transfer gap in systematic desensitization: An analogue study. *Behaviour Research and Therapy, 7,* 191–196.

Beck, A. T. (1976). *Cognitive therapy and the emotional disorders.* New York: International Universities Press.

Boudewyns, P. A., & Hyer, L. (1990). Physiological response to combat memories and preliminary treatment outcome in Vietnam veterans: PTSD patients treated with direct therapeutic exposure. *Behavior Therapy, 21,* 63–87.

Bowen, G. R., & Lambert, J. A. (1986). Systematic desensitization therapy with posttraumatic stress disorder cases. In C. R. Figley (Ed.), *Trauma and its wake* (Vol. 2, pp. 280–291). New York: Brunner/Mazel.

Brewin, C. R., Dalgleish, T., & Joseph, S. (1996). A dual representational theory of posttraumatic stress disorder. *Psychological Review, 103,* 670–686.

Brom, D., Kleber, R. J., & Defares, P. B. (1989). Brief psychotherapy for posttraumatic stress disorders. *Journal of Consulting and Clinical Psychology, 57*, 607–612.

Clark, D. M. (1986). A cognitive approach to panic. *Behaviour Research and Therapy, 24*, 461–470.

Cooper, N. A., & Clum, G. A. (1989). Imaginal flooding as a supplementary treatment for PTSD in combat veterans: A controlled study. *Behavior Therapy, 3*, 381–391.

Deblinger, E., McLeer, S. V., & Henry, D. (1990). Cognitive behavioral treatment for sexually abused children suffering from post-traumatic stress: Preliminary findings. *Journal of the American Academy of Child and Adolescent Psychiatry, 29*, 747–752.

Devilly, G. J., & Spence, S. H. (1999). The relative efficacy and treatment distress of EMDR and a cognitive behavioral trauma treatment protocol in the amelioration of post traumatic stress disorder. *Journal of Anxiety Disorders, 13*, 131–158.

Echeburua, E., de Corral, P., Sarasua, B., & Zubizarreta, I. (1996). Treatment of acute posttraumatic stress disorder in rape victims: An experimental study. *Journal of Anxiety Disorders, 10*, 185–199.

Echeburua, E., de Corral, P., Zubizarreta, I., & Sarasua, B. (1997). Psychological treatment of chronic posttraumatic stress disorder in victims of sexual aggression. *Behavior Modification, 21*, 433–456.

Foa, E. B., Dancu, C. V., Hembree, E. A., Jaycox, L. H., Meadows, E. A., & Street, G. P. (1999). The efficacy of exposure therapy, stress inoculation training and their combination in ameliorating PTSD for female victims of assault. *Journal of Consulting and Clinical Psychology, 67*, 194–200.

Foa, E. B., Hearst-Ikeda, D., & Perry, K. J. (1995). Evaluation of a brief cognitive-behavioral program for the prevention of chronic PTSD in recent assault victims. *Journal of Consulting and Clinical Psychology, 63*, 948–955.

Foa, E. B., & Kozak, M. J. (1986). Emotional processing of fear: Exposure to corrective information. *Psychological Bulletin, 99*, 20–35.

Foa, E. B., & Meadows, E. A. (1997). Psychosocial treatments for post-traumatic stress disorder: A critical review. In J. Spence, J. M. Darley, & D. J. Foss (Eds.), *Annual review of psychology* (Vol. 48, pp. 449–480). Palo Alto, CA: Annual Reviews.

Foa, E. B., Riggs, D. S., Massie, E. D., & Yarczower, M. (1995). The impact of fear activation and anger on the efficacy of exposure treatment for PTSD. *Behavior Therapy, 26*, 487–499.

Foa, E. B., & Rothbaum, B. O. (1998). *Treating the trauma of rape: Cognitive-behavioral therapy for PTSD*. New York: Guilford Press.

Foa E. B., Rothbaum B. O., Riggs D., & Murdock T. (1991). Treatment of post-traumatic stress disorder in rape victims: A comparison between cognitive-behavioral procedures and counseling. *Journal of Consulting and Clinical Psychology, 59*, 715–723.

Foa, E. B., Steketee, G., & Rothbaum, B. O. (1989). Behavioral/cognitive conceptualizations of post-traumatic stress disorder. *Behavior Therapy, 20*, 155–176.

Frank, E., Anderson, B., Stewart, B. D., Dancu, C., Hughes, C., & West, D. (1988). Efficacy of cognitive behavior therapy and systematic desensitization in the treatment of rape trauma. *Behavior Therapy, 19*, 403–420.

Frueh, B. C., Turner, S. M., Beidel, D. C. C., Mirabella, R. F., & Jones, W. J. (1996). Trauma management therapy: A preliminary evaluation of a multicomponent behavioral treatment for chronic combat-related PTSD. *Behaviour Research and Therapy, 34*, 533–543.

Glynn, S. M., Eth, S., Randolph, E. T., Foy, D. W., Urbatis, M., Boxer, L., Paz, G. B.,

Leong, G. B., Firman, G., Salk, J. D., Katzman, J. W., & Crothers, J. (1999). A test of behavioral family therapy to augment exposure for combat-related PTSD. *Journal of Consulting and Clinical Psychology, 67,* 243–251.

Hayes, S. C., Follette, W. C., & Follette, V. M. (1996). Behavior therapy: A contextual approach. In A. S. Gurman & S. B. Messer (Eds.), *Essential psychotherapies: Theory and practice* (pp. 128–181). New York: Guilford Press.

Hayes, S. C., Wilson, K. G., Gifford, E., Follette, V. M., & Strosahl, K. D. (1996) Emotional avoidance and behavioral disorders: A functional dimensional approach to diagnosis and treatment. *Journal of Consulting and Clinical Psychology, 64,* 1152–1168.

Hickling, E. J., & Blanchard, E. B. (1997). The private practice psychologist and manual-based treatments: Post-traumatic stress disorder secondary to motor vehicle accidents. *Behaviour Research and Therapy, 35,* 191–203.

Hyer, L., Woods, M. G., Bruno, R., & Boudewyns, P. (1989). Treatment outcomes of Vietnam veterans with PTSD and the consistency of the MCMI. *Journal of Clinical Psychology, 45,* 547–552.

Graap, K., & Friedes, D. (1998). Regarding the data basis for the Peniston Alpha-Theta protocol. *Applied Psychophysiology and Biofeedback, 23,* 265–275.

Keane, T. M., Fairbank, J. A., Caddell, J. M., & Zimering, R. T. (1989). Implosive (flooding) therapy reduces symptoms of PTSD in Vietnam combat veterans. *Behavior Therapy, 20,* 245–260.

Kilpatrick, D. G., Veronen, L. J., & Resick, P. A. (1982). Psychological sequelae to rape: Assessment and treatment strategies. In D. M. Dolays & R. L. Meredith (Eds.), *Behavioral medicine: Assessment and treatment strategies* (pp. 473–497). New York: Plenum Press.

Lang, A. J., & Jakubowski, P. (1976). *Responsible assertive behavior.* Champaign, IL: Research Press.

Litz, B. T., Blake, D. D., Gerardi, R. G., & Keane, T. M. (1990). Decision making guidelines for the use of direct therapeutic exposure in the treatment of post-traumatic stress disorder. *Behavior Therapy, 13,* 91–93.

Marks, I., Lovell, K., Noshirvani, H., Livanou, M., & Thrasher, S. (1998). Treatment of post-traumatic stress disorder by exposure and/or cognitive restructuring: A controlled study. *Archives of General Psychiatry, 55,* 317–325.

McCann, I. L., & Pearlman, L. A. (1990). *Psychological trauma and the adult survivor: Theory, therapy, and transformation.* New York: Brunner/Mazel.

Meichenbaum, D. (1974). Self-instructional methods. In F. H. Kanfer & A. P. Goldstein (Eds.), *Helping people change* (pp. 357–391). New York: Pergamon Press.

Mowrer, O. A. (1960). *Learning theory and behavior.* New York: Wiley.

Naugle, A. E., & Follette, W. C. (1998). A functional analysis of trauma symptoms. In V. M. Follette, J. I. Ruzek, & F. R. Abueg (Eds.), *Cognitive-behavioral therapies for trauma* (pp. 48–73). New York: Guilford Press.

Peniston, E. G. (1986). EMG biofeedback-assisted desensitization treatment for Vietnam combat veterans' post-traumatic stress disorder. *Clinical Biofeedback Health, 9,* 35–41.

Peniston, E. G., & Kulkosky, P. J. (1991). Alpha–theta brainwave neuro-feedback therapy for Vietnam veterans with combat-related post-traumatic stress disorder. *Medical Psychotherapy: An International Journal, 4,* 47–60.

Pitman, R. K., Altman, B., Greenwald, E., Longpre, R. E., Macklin, M. L., Poire, R. E., & Steketee, G. S. (1991). Psychiatric complications during flooding therapy for post-traumatic stress disorder. *Journal of Clinical Psychiatry, 52,* 17–20.

Pitman, R. K., Orr, S. P., Altman, B., & Longpre, R. E., Poire, R. E., Macklin, M. L., Michaels, M. J., & Steketee, G. S. (1996). Emotional processing and outcome of imaginal flooding therapy in Vietnam veterans with chronic posttraumatic stress disorder. *Comprehensive Psychiatry, 37,* 409–418.

Resick, P. A., Jordan, C. G., Girelli, S. A., Hutter, C. K., & Marhoefer-Dvorak, S. (1988). A comparative victim study of behavioral group therapy for sexual assault victims. *Behavior Therapy, 19,* 385–401.

Resick, P. A., & Schnicke, M. K. (1993). *Cognitive processing therapy for rape victims: A treatment manual.* Newbury Park, CA: Sage.

Resick, P. A., & Schnicke, M. K. (1992). Cognitive processing therapy for sexual assault victims. *Journal of Consulting and Clinical Psychology, 60,* 748–756.

Richards, D. A., Lovell, K., & Marks, I. M. (1994). Post-traumatic stress disorder: Evaluation of a behavioral treatment program. *Journal of Traumatic Stress, 7,* 669–680.

Rothbaum, B. O., Hodges, L., Alarcon, R., Ready, D., Shahar, F., Graap, K., Pair, J., Hebert, P., Gotz, D., Wills, B., & Baltzell, D. (1999). Virtual reality exposure therapy for PTSD Vietnam veterans: A case study. *Journal of Traumatic Stress, 12,* 263–271.

Silver, S. M., Brooks, A., & Obenchain, J. (1995). Treatment of Vietnam war veterans with PTSD: A comparison of eye movement desensitization and reprocessing, biofeedback, and relaxation training. *Journal of Traumatic Stress, 8,* 337–342.

Tarrier, N., Pilgrim, H., Sommerfield, C., Faragher, B., Reynolds, M., Graham, E., & Barrowclough, C. (1999). A randomised trial of cognitive therapy and imaginal exposure in the treatment of chronic post traumatic stress disorder. *Journal of Consulting and Clinical Psychology, 67,* 13–18.

Thompson, J. A., Charlton, P. F. C., Kerry, R., Lee, D., & Turner, S. W. (1995). An open trial of exposure therapy based on deconditioning for post-traumatic stress disorder. *British Journal of Clinical Psychology, 34,* 407–416.

Watson, C. G., Tuorila, J. R., Vickers, K. S., Gearhart, L. P., & Mendez, C. M. (1997). The efficacies of three relaxation regiments in the treatment of PTSD in Vietnam War veterans. *Journal of Clinical Psychology, 53,* 917–923.

Wolpe, J. (1958). *Psychotherapy by reciprocal inhibition.* Stanford, CA: Stanford University Press.

Wolpe, J. (1969). *The practice of behavior therapy.* Oxford, UK: Pergamon Press.

5

Pharmacotherapy

Matthew J. Friedman, Jonathan R. T. Davidson,
Thomas A. Mellman, and Steven M. Southwick

THEORY/CONCEPTUAL FRAMEWORK

Posttraumatic stress disorder (PTSD) appears to be a very complex disorder that is associated with stable and profound alterations in many psychobiological systems that have evolved for coping, adaptation, and survival of the human species (Friedman, 1999; Friedman, Charney, & Deutch, 1995; Rasmusson & Charney, 1997; Yehuda & McFarlane, 1997). Given the number of fundamental psychobiological systems that appear to be altered, it may be that PTSD is not a unitary psychobiological abnormality but that (as with fever and edema) there are a number of possible mechanisms through which this disorder might evolve. Another possibility is that there are different psychobiological subtypes of a common PTSD disorder. Indeed, some investigators have concluded that because of this complexity, there is no single animal model that is applicable to PTSD (Rasmusson & Charney, 1997).

Table 5.1 summarizes psychobiological abnormalities in PTSD that involve specific neurotransmitter, neurohormonal, or neuroendocrine systems. Such information is relevant to understanding why certain drugs might be effective therapeutic agents. It might also guide the development of future drugs designed specifically for use in PTSD. Ideally, such an approach would lead to rational pharmacotherapy in which specific classes of drugs are selected because of their actions on specific psychobiological systems. As we consider PTSD from this conceptual perspective, it should be kept in mind

TABLE 5.1. Psychobiological Abnormalities Possibly Associated with PTSD

Proposed psychobiological abnormality	Possible clinical effect
Adrenergic hyperreactivity	Hyperarousal, reexperiencing, dissociation, rage/aggression abnormal information/memory processes, panic/anxiety
Hypothalamic–pituitary–adrenocortical enhanced negative feedback	Stress intolerance
Opioid dysregulation	Numbing
Elevated corticotropin-releasing factor levels	Hyperarousal, reexperiencing, panic/anxiety
Sensitization/kindling	Hyperarousal, reexperiencing
Glutamatergic dysregulation	Dissociation, impaired information and memory processing
Serotonergic dysregulation	Numbing, reexperiencing, hyperarousal, poorly modulated stress responses, associated symptoms[a]
Increased thyroid activity	Hyperarousal

[a]Associated symptoms: Rage, aggression, impulsivity, depression, panic/anxiety, obsessional thoughts, chemical abuse/dependency.

that most of our current information about pharmacotherapy for PTSD is based on empirical trials with established antidepressant and anxiolytic drugs rather than agents specifically targeting putative neurobiological mechanisms underlying the pathophysiology of PTSD.

Some proposed psychobiological abnormalities listed in Table 5.1 are well established (e.g., adrenergic hyperreactivity and hypothalamic–pituitary–adrenocortical [HPA] enhanced negative feedback). Other proposed mechanisms have little empirical support or are primarily theoretical and can only be considered speculative at this time. This is a large and rapidly expanding area of research. More details can be found elsewhere (Friedman, 1999; Friedman, Charney & Deutch, 1995; Yehuda & McFarlane, 1997). We present the following very brief summary of current research findings that may be relevant to pharmacotherapy for PTSD:

1. Adrenergic hyperreactivity appears to be associated with hyperarousal, reexperiencing, panic/anxiety symptoms, and probably associated with dissociation and rage/aggression. Adrenergic mechanisms also play a key role in processing traumatic memories. An alpha-2 adrenergic agonist such as clonidine or a beta-adrenergic antagonist such as propranolol might be expected to attenuate this abnormality. Tricyclic antidepressants (TCAs)

and monoamine oxidase inhibitors (MAOIs) also reduce adrenergic activity through more indirect mechanisms. As shown in studies on treatment of panic disorder, the antiadrenergic effects of both TCAs and MAOIs can be clinically significant.

2. HPA-enhanced negative feedback is a well-established alteration that has not been linked to a specific clinical abnormality. One speculation is that this may be associated with the low tolerance for stress seen in PTSD patients but no data support this hypothesis. Drugs that act on either the adrenergic or serotonergic systems might normalize HPA function.

3. It has been hypothesized that opioid dysregulation might be associated with psychic numbing. In one study, narcotic antagonists appeared to reduce numbing in some patients but produced increased reexperiencing and hyperarousal symptoms for others (Glover, 1993).

4. Elevated corticotropin-releasing factor (CRF) may, etiologically, be the most important abnormality in PTSD because of its central role in the human stress response. Since CRF is uniquely positioned to simultaneously ignite a cascade of adrenergic, HPA, immunological, and other biological responses to stress, appropriate treatment, theoretically, might be to blockade CRF's actions with CRF antagonists or other drugs that inhibit these actions. This is an important area for further research.

5. Sensitization and kindling result when repeated exposure to the same stimulus produces a progressive intensification of neurophysiological, behavioral, or psychobiological response. Sensitization/kindling has been proposed (Post, Weiss, & Smith, 1995) as an animal model for PTSD. Anticonvulsant agents such as carbamazepine and valproate have been suggested as PTSD treatments specifically because of their antikindling properties. There is also interest in the possibility that the new anticonvulsant, lamotrigene, will also have a clinically significant antikindling effect.

6. Glutamatergic dysregulation has been postulated as etiologically responsible for dissociation and for the information- and memory-processing abnormalities associated with PTSD. Normalization could theoretically be achieved with newer anticonvulsants (such as lamotrigene) that modulate glutamatergic transmission (Krystal, Bennett, Bremner, Southwick, & Charney, 1995).

7. As noted in Table 5.1, serotonin (5-HT) appears to have a direct or indirect role in mediating a number of core (DSM-IV B, C, and D) PTSD as well as associated, clinically relevant symptoms. This may be why selective serotonin reuptake inhibitors (SSRIs) have shown such early promise as effective drugs for PTSD. SSRIs might also normalize the poor modulation of the stress response that is associated with a serotonin deficiency (Weissman & Harbert, 1972).

8. Although elevated in PTSD, increased thyroid activity is usually in the high normal rather than thyrotoxic range. Therefore, it would probably be inadvisable to consider an antithyroid agent but, rather, to consider using

a beta-adrenergic antagonist such as propranolol to reverse hyperarousal symptoms due possibly to this abnormality.

THE TECHNIQUE OF PHARMACOTHERAPY

The major techniques in pharmacotherapy involve (1) selecting a drug whose pharmacological actions might be expected to normalize the psychobiological abnormalities associated with a specific disorder; (2) choosing the most appropriate therapeutic agent based on proven efficacy against a specific symptom, cluster of symptoms, and/or comorbid disorder; (3) monitoring and readjusting the dosage in order to optimize therapeutic efficacy and onset of action while minimizing the likelihood of side effects; and (4) knowing when there has been an adequate therapeutic trial of a given drug in order to supplement treatment with an additional drug or to switch to a different pharmacological agent.

There is a strong rationale for pharmacotherapy as an important treatment in PTSD. As noted previously, a number of animal models and neurobiological mechanisms seem pertinent to this disorder. In addition, PTSD patients exhibit abnormalities in several key neurobiological systems (see Table 5.1). Furthermore, there is considerable overlap of symptoms between PTSD, depression, and other anxiety disorders. Finally, PTSD is frequently comorbid with psychiatric disorders that are responsive to drug treatment (e.g., major depression and panic disorder). Drug treatment is one of the most feasible treatments for PTSD. It is generally accepted by most patients although the occurrence of side effects, lack of patient compliance with prescribed drug regimens, and the high commercial cost of new therapeutic agents (e.g., SSRIs, nefazodone, valproate, etc.) may diminish feasibility.

The cost of drug treatment is difficult to compare with the cost of psychotherapy, since it depends on the duration of treatment, the cost of the drug itself, and many other factors. Compliance is generally good during the initial weeks of treatment; it may remain high if there is clinical improvement, but it also may not, even if there is a favorable response to medication. Finally, although it is very easy to disseminate the necessary information about drug treatment to prescribing physicians, it is quite difficult to detect and correct improper prescribing practices.

PTSD is often associated with at least one comorbid psychiatric disorder (e.g., depression, other anxiety disorders and/or chemical abuse/dependency). It is often also associated with clinically significant disruptive symptoms (e.g., impulsivity, mood lability, irritability, aggressiveness and/or suicidal behavior). Some of the drugs to be reviewed in this practice guideline have proven or probable efficacy in ameliorating some of these comorbid disorders or associated symptoms when they, not PTSD, have been the primary targets for treatment. (It should be emphasized, however, that there are scarcely any published findings regarding PTSD drug trials in which comorbid disorders or associated symptoms were systematically controlled and evaluated). Ideally, a practicing pharmacotherapist would select a drug that might be expected to ameliorate such comorbid disorders and associated symptoms at the same time that it reduces PTSD symptom severity. This is pharmacotherapeutic technique at its best.

Because of the many biological abnormalities presumed to be associated with PTSD (Table 5.1), and because of the overlap between symptoms of PTSD and other comorbid disorders, almost every class of psychotropic agent has been administered to PTSD patients. Based on the published data, the following classes of drugs are reviewed in this chapter: SSRIs, other serotonergic agents, antiadrenergic agents, MAOIs, TCAs, benzodiazepines, anticonvulsants, and antipsychotics. Their clinical and pharmacological actions are discussed in a later section.

METHODS OF COLLECTING DATA

These practice guidelines were developed after a comprehensive literature review of all randomized clinical trials (RCTs), open trials, and case reports on pharmacotherapy for PTSD included in PILOTS. The search was conducted using the following keywords: PTSD, pharmacotherapy, antidepressants, anxiolytics, antiadrenergic agents, anticonvulsants, and antipsychotics, as well as the specific names of each drug mentioned in this report. Data from RCTs were given the greatest weight; such findings are summarized in Table 5.2 and include effect sizes for each RCT. Table 5.3 is much more inclusive and summarizes results from all drug trials because of the theoretical as well as clinical interest generated by such data. Table 5.4 presents our recommendations on drug treatment, the strength of the published evidence, indications, and contraindications.

SUMMARY OF THE LITERATURE

Evidence from Randomized Clinical Trials

A summary of randomized clinical drug trials is shown in Table 5.2. Results have clearly been mixed. Given the fact that study populations differed with respect to trauma type, severity, and chronicity, as well as gender, veteran status, outcome measures, and (probably) comorbidity, it is difficult to make any generalizations with confidence. Three studies with clinically meaningful effect sizes (e.g., approximately 1.0) involve an MAOI (phenelzine), and two trials with an SSRI (fluoxetine). Modest improvements were seen with a TCA

TABLE 5.2. Randomized Clinical Trials of PTSD: Drug versus Placebo Treatment

Drug[a]	Class	n	Duration (wk)	Subjects	Sex	Outcome	Drug–placebo response rates[b]	Drug–placebo differences[b]	PTSD-specific drug effects[c]	Effect size[c]
Amitriptyline[1]	TCA	46	8	Mil	M	IES total	47%/19%	28%	+	0.64
Desipramine[2]	TCA	18	4	Mil	M	IES avoidance	2%/0%	2%	−	0.16
Desipramine[2]	TCA	18	4	Mil	M	IES intrusion	4%/1%	3%	−	0.05
Imipramine[3]	TCA	60	8	Mil	M	IES total	65%/28%	37%	−	0.25
Phenelzine[3]	MAOI	60	8	Mil	M	IES total	68%/28%	40%	++	1.08
Phenelzine[4]	MAOI	13	4	Mil/civ	?	IES total	35%/36%	0%	−	0.10
Brofaromin[5d]	MAOI/SSRI	113	10	Mil/civ	M/F	CAPS total	60%/40%	18%	−	0.01
Brofaromine[6d]	MAOI/SSRI	45	14	Civ/mil	M/F	CAPS total	52%/29%	23%	+	0.52
Fluoxetine[7e]	SSRI	24	5	Mil	M	CAPS	15%/10%	5%	−	0.37
Fluoxetine[7e]	SSRI	23	5	Civ	F/M	CAPS	41%/21%	20%	++	1.12
Fluoxetine[8]	SSRI	53	12	Civ	F	CGI	85%/62%	23%	++	0.92
Sertraline[9]	SSRI	208	12	Civ	F/M	DTS	60%/39%	21%	++	0.40
Sertraline[10]	SSRI	187	12	Civ	F/M	CAPS	55%/35%	20%	++	0.30
Alprazolam[11]	BZD	10	5	Mil/civ	?	IES total	14%/4%	10%	−	0.28
Inositol[12]	2nd Mess	13	4	Mil/civ	M/F	IES total	11%/0%	11%	−	0.25

Note. TCA, tricyclic antidepressant; MAOI, monoamine oxidase inhibitor; SSRI, selective serotonin reuptake inhibitor; BZD, Benzodiazepine; 2nd Mess, second messenger; IES, Impact of Event Scale; CAPS, Clinician-Administered PTSD Scale; CGI, Clinical Global Improvement Scale; DTS, Davidson Trauma Scale.
[a]References to studies: 1. Davidson et al. (1990); 2. Reist et al. (1989); 3. Kosten et al. (1991); 4. Shestatzky, Greenberg, & Lerer (1988); 5. Baker et al. (1995); 6. Katz et al. (1994/1995); 7. van der Kolk et al. (1994); 8. Davidson et al. (1997); 9. Davidson, Malik, & Sutherland (1996); 10. Brady et al. (2000); 11. Braun et al. (1990); 12. Kaplan et al. (1995).
[b]From Davidson et al. (1997).
[c]From Friedman (1997).
[d]Not available commercially.
[e]Drug–placebo response rates approximated from a graph.

(amitriptyline; effect size = 0.64) and an MAOI/SSRI (brofaromine; effect size = 0.52).

The two largest studies are multisite RCTs with the SSRI sertraline, which tested approximately 200 subjects in each trial. Although effect sizes were modest, drug–placebo differences in both studies were highly significant ($p < .001$), showing that sertraline reduced PTSD DSM-IV B, C, and D symptoms (Brady et al., 2000; Davidson et al., 1997). The positive findings from these large studies impressed the United States Food and Drug Administration (FDA) sufficiently so that sertraline was approved in December 1999 as an indicated treatment for PTSD. It is the first and only medication to receive such FDA approval. Therefore, the strength of evidence favoring the efficacy for sertraline is given a full Agency for Health Care Policy and Research (AHCPR) Level A rating at this time (see Table 5.4). On the other hand, the mixed results from the small, randomized clinical trials with fluoxetine (van der Kolk et al., 1994) indicate an AHCPR Level A/B rating is appropriate for that drug at this time.

In summary, dramatic responses to medication have been the exception rather than the rule. MAOIs and SSRIs have been more successful than other drugs. It is important to recognize that there have been negative as well as positive clinical trials with SSRIs, MAOIs, and TCAs. Most notably, there have been negative RCTs with phenelzine, desipramine, fluoxetine, and alprazolam, as shown in Table 5.2. Many of the marginal or negative results may have been due to methodological factors (e.g., research design, subjects tested, treatment duration, outcome instruments, etc.) rather than because the drugs, themselves, are ineffective. We have many more questions than answers at this time. Much more research is definitely needed to clarify these questions.

Other Evidence: Open Trials and Case Reports

A fair number of open trials and case reports have been published in addition to randomized clinical trials. As shown in Table 5.3, evidence for the efficacy of many drugs can only be found in these open trials and case reports.

Selective Serotonin Reuptake Inhibitors

In addition to RCTs with sertraline and fluoxetine, which effectively reduce all clusters (DSM-IV B, C, and D) of PTSD symptoms and produce clinical global improvement (Davidson, Malik, & Sutherland, 1997) a number of successful open trials and case reports have been published concerning SSRIs such as fluoxetine, sertraline, paroxetine, and fluvoxamine (see Friedman, 1996, for references). In general, investigators have been impressed by the capacity of SSRIs to reduce the numbing symptoms of PTSD, since other drugs tested thus far do not seem to have this property. In recent, open-label studies with sertraline in rape trauma survivors (Rothbaum, Ninan, &

TABLE 5.3. Summary of Published Results on Pharmacotherapy for PTSD

Drug class	Specific drugs	Daily dose	Probable mechanism of action	No. of RCT	Remarks
SSRIs	Sertraline	50–200 mg	SSRI	2	Whereas earlier studies suggested that SSRIs were primarily effective on DSM-IV PTSD numbing (C) symptoms, more recent RCT and open trials suggest that they produce global improvement and reduce all PTSD (B, C, D) symptom clusters. They are also effective in comorbid disorders such as depression, panic disorder; obsessive–compulsive disorder and chemical dependency/abuse. Finally SSRIs may reduce symptoms associated with PTSD such as rage, impulsivity, suicidal thoughts, depressed mood, obsessional thinking, and alcohol/drug behavior.
	Fluoxetine	20–80 mg	SSRI	3	
	Fluvoxamine	250–300 mg	SSRI	0	
	Paroxetine	10–40 mg	SSRI	0	
Other	Trazodone	25–500 mg	SSRI/5-HT$_2$ blockade	0	Often combined with SSRIs to reverse SSRI-induced insomnia. In one small, open trial, trazodone reduced B, C, and D symptoms. A large multisite randomized clinical trial is underway. Results from two published open-label studies suggest that nefazodone produces global improvement, better sleep, and anxiety reduction in PTSD patients.
	Nefazodone	100–600 mg		0	
Serotonergic	Cyproheptadine	4–28 mg	5-HT antagonist	0	Anecdotal reports indicate that it suppresses nightmares and flashbacks.
	Buspirone	30–60 mg	5-HT$_1$A partial agonist	0	A few case reports suggest reduced B and D symptoms.
Antiadrenergic	Clonidine	0.2–0.6 mg	Alpha-2 agonist	0	Reduces B and D symptoms. Patients may become tolerant.
	Guanfacine	1–3 mg	Alpha-2 agonist	0	Promising case reports in patients who had become tolerant to clonidine.
	Propranolol	40–160 mg	Beta blocker	A-B-A	Successful A-B-A study in which B and D symptoms were reduced in children with sexual-/physical-abuse-related PTSD. Two other studies with mixed results.

(*continued*)

TABLE 5.3. (continued)

Drug class	Specific drugs	Daily dose	Probable mechanism of action	No. of RCT	Remarks
MAOIs	Phenelzine	45–75 mg	Irreversible	2	Good global improvement and reduction of intrusive recollection (B) symptoms and some efficacy against C symptoms. Patients must adhere to MAOI dietary restrictions.
	Tranylcypromine	20–40 mg	MAOI	0	Positive case report—little data.
	Isocarboxazide[a]	10–30 mg	MAOI	0	Positive case report—little data.
	Moclobemide	300–600 mg	Reversible MAO-A inhibitor	0	One open trial—reduced B and C symptoms.
TCAs	Imipramine	150–300 mg	NE/5-HT reuptake inhibitors	1	Not as potent as MAOIs but similar action profile.
	Amitriptyline			1	Good global improvement and reduction of B symptoms. Amitriptyline most effective against C symptoms.
	Desipramine			1	Desipramine was ineffective in a randomized clinical trial.
Benzodiazepines (BZD)	Alprazolam	0.5–6 mg	BZD agonist	1	Few studies. No effect on B or C symptoms. Reduce insomnia, anxiety, and irritability. Clinically significant withdrawal syndrome.
	Clonazepam	1–6 mg	BZD agonist	0	
Anticonvulsants	Carbamazepine	600–1,000 mg	Antikindling action	0	Carbamazepine effective on B and D symptoms. Valproate effective on C and D symptoms.
	Valproate	750–1,750 mg		0	
Antipsychotics	Thioridazine	200–800 mg	D$_2$ antagonist 5HT2/D2 antagonist	0	Case reports—effective on B and D symptoms.
	Clozapine			0	
	Risperidone				

[a]No longer commercially available.

92

Thomas, 1996), fluvoxamine in Vietnam combat veterans (Marmar et al., 1996), and paroxetine in nonveterans with a mixture of traumatic experiences (e.g., rape, criminal assault, and accidents; Marshall et al., 1998), all three clusters (reexperiencing, avoidant/numbing and hyperarousal) of PTSD symptoms were dramatically reduced by SSRI treatment. The paroxetine and fluvoxamine studies are particularly noteworthy because the veterans complained very little about insomnia or arousal side effects, as has been the case with other SSRIs tested. Although SSRIs are generally regarded as having fewer side effects than other drugs, some patients cannot tolerate them because of gastrointestinal symptoms and sexual dysfunction in addition to insomnia and agitation.

SSRIs are also an attractive choice because they may improve comorbid disorders such as depression, panic, and obsessive–compulsive disorder, and reduce alcohol consumption (Brady, Sonne, & Roberts, 1995).

SSRIs may also be clinically useful because a number of symptoms associated with PTSD may be mediated by serotonergic mechanisms such as rage, impulsivity, suicidal intent, depressed mood, panic symptoms, obsessional thinking, and behaviors associated with alcohol or drug abuse/dependency (Fava et al., 1996; Friedman, 1990).

Other Serotonergic Agents

As shown in Table 5.3, there have been two open-label trials with nefazodone but very few data on trazodone, cyproheptadine, and buspirone. Nefazodone, an SSRI plus 5-HT$_2$ antagonist, has shown promise in open-label trials of combat veterans and may be of particular help in improving sleep and decreasing anger (Davidson, Weisler, Malik, & Conner, 1998; Hertzberg, Feldman, Beckham, Moore, & Davidson, 1998). Trazodone (which is also an SSRI plus 5-HT$_2$ antagonist) has shown only modest effectiveness against PTSD symptoms in a small open trial (Hertzberg, Feldman, Beckham, & Davidson, 1996) but has been prescribed mostly because of its capacity to reverse the insomnia caused by SSRI agents such as fluoxetine and sertraline. As a result, many PTSD patients receiving SSRI treatment also receive trazodone (25–500 mg) at bedtime. Trazodone's advantage over conventional hypnotics is that its major serotonergic mode of action is synergistic with overall SSRI treatment and its sedative properties promote sleep (Cook & Conner, 1995).

Antiadrenergic Agents: Propranolol, Clonidine, and Guanfacine

Although it is well established that adrenergic dysregulation is associated with chronic PTSD (for details and references, see Friedman, Charney, & Deutch, 1995; Yehuda & McFarlane, 1997), there has been little research with the alpha-2 agonist, clonidine, or with the beta adrenergic antagonist, propranolol, despite the fact that positive findings with both drugs were reported as early as 1984 (Kolb, Burris, & Griffiths, 1984). Indeed, there are no randomized clinical trials with either drug.

In four open trials with clonidine (see Friedman & Southwick, 1995, for references), successful reduction of many PTSD and associated symptoms was observed, including traumatic nightmares, intrusive recollections, hypervigilance, insomnia, startle reactions, and angry outbursts; in addition, patients in these trials reported improved mood and concentration.

Sometimes, patients who have a favorable initial response to clonidine appear to develop tolerance to this drug, resulting in a return of PTSD symptoms. There are two recent case reports in which clonidine was replaced by the adrenergic alpha-2 agonist, guanfacine (which has a longer half-life, 18–22 hours), after tolerance had developed. In both cases, complete suppression of PTSD symptoms was again achieved and maintained over the subsequent course of treatment (Harmon & Riggs, 1996; Horrigan, 1996).

In an A-B-A design (6 weeks off–6 weeks on–6 weeks off medication), propranolol was administered to eleven physically and/or sexually abused children with PTSD. Significant reductions in reexperiencing and arousal symptoms were observed during drug treatment but symptoms relapsed to pretreatment severity following discontinuation of medication (Famularo, Kinscherff, & Fenton, 1988). Results were mixed in two other trials with propranolol.

Monoamine Oxidase Inhibitors

In addition to two randomized clinical trials with phenelzine (one of which had serious methodological flaws) reported previously, there have been two successful open trials of phenelzine, a number of positive case reports (see De Martino, Mollica, & Wilk, 1995, for references), and one negative open trial with phenelzine (Weizman et al., 1996).

A comprehensive review of all published findings on MAOI treatment (Southwick, Yehuda, Giller, & Charney, 1994) found that MAOIs produced moderate to good global improvement in 82% of all patients, primarily due to reduction in reexperiencing symptoms such as intrusive recollections, traumatic nightmares, and PTSD flashbacks. Insomnia also improved. No improvement was found, however, in PTSD avoidant/numbing, PTSD hyperarousal, and depressive or anxiety/panic symptoms.

The use of MAOIs has traditionally been limited when there are legitimate concerns that patients may ingest alcohol or pharmacologically contraindicated illicit drugs, or that they may not adhere to necessary dietary restrictions. The most serious consequence of lack of compliance is a hypertensive crisis, which is a medical emergency. Such concerns do not apply to reversible MAO-A inhibitors such as moclobemide (which are not currently available in the United States). Indeed, moclobemide produced significant reductions in PTSD reexperiencing and avoidant symptoms in a recent open trial with 20 patients (Neal, Shapland, & Fox, 1997).

Tricyclic Antidepressants

In addition to the randomized clinical trials (showing positive results with imipramine and amitriptyline, and negative results with desipramine) reported previously, there are numerous case reports and open trials with TCAs (see Ver Ellen & van Kammen, 1990, for references). Results have been mixed and generally modest in magnitude. In their analysis of 15 randomized trials, open trials, and case reports involving TCA treatment for PTSD, Southwick and associates (1994) found that 45% of patients showed moderate to good global improvement following treatment, whereas MAOIs produced global improvement in 82% of patients who received them. As with MAOIs, most improvement was due to reductions in reexperiencing rather than avoidant/numbing or arousal symptoms.

To summarize, TCAs appear to reduce PTSD reexperiencing and/or avoidant symptoms but have not demonstrated the same degree of efficacy as SSRIs or MAOIs. Furthermore, their side effects are not tolerated well by many PTSD patients. It is because of their relative lack of potency, their side effects, and their failure to reduce avoidant/numbing symptoms that TCAs have been replaced by SSRIs as first-line drugs in PTSD treatment. This may be a rush to judgment, however, since TCAs have been tested primarily on veterans with severe and chronic PTSD, while SSRIs have been tested mostly on nonveteran cohorts. Indeed, TCAs have actually outperformed SSRIs in reducing PTSD severity among combat veterans (Davidson et al., 1997).

Benzodiazepines

There are only three publications on benzodiazepine treatment for PTSD in addition to the randomized clinical trial with alprazolam reported previously (Braun et al., 1990). These include open trials with alprazolam and clonazepam, respectively. In each study, however, patients reported reduced insomnia, anxiety, and irritability but no improvement in PTSD reexperiencing, avoidant, or numbing symptoms. In addition, there is a risk of prescribing these agents for many patients with comorbid alcohol or drug abuse/dependence, and a serious withdrawal syndrome has been reported following abrupt discontinuation of alprazolam among PTSD patients (see Friedman & Southwick, 1995).

In summary, the evidence does not support benzodiazepines as first-line treatment for PTSD. A preliminary open-label report in which the benzodiazepine hypnotic, temazepam, was administered at bedtime to trauma survivors with acute stress disorder (e.g., 1 to 3 months after the traumatic event) found that pharmacotherapy specifically targeting disrupted sleep was associated with marked reduction in PTSD symptoms (Mellman, Byers, & Angenstein, 1998). On the other hand, a prospective study with alprazolam and clonazepam in recently traumatized emergency room patients found that early treatment with benzodiazepines did not appear to prevent the later development of PTSD (Gelpin, Bonne, Peri, Brandes, & Shalev, 1996).

Anticonvulsants

There have been a number of open trials of anticonvulsant drugs with PTSD patients initially tested because of their antikindling action. In five studies, carbamazepine produced reductions in reexperiencing and arousal symptoms, while in three studies, valproate produced reductions in avoidant/numbing and arousal (but not reexperiencing) symptoms (see Friedman & Southwick, 1995, for references).

Antipsychotics

The current thinking is that antipsychotic medications should only be prescribed for the rare PTSD patients who fail to respond to other drugs and who exhibit psychotic symptoms. Some preliminary anecdotal observations have shown that PTSD patients who exhibit extreme hypervigilance/paranoia, physical aggression, social isolation, and trauma-related hallucinations, and are refractory to SSRIs, antiadrenergics, and other drugs described previously (see Friedman & Southwick, 1995), may respond to antipsychotic agents such as thioridazine (Dillard, Bendfeldt, & Jernigan, 1993) and clozapine (Hamner, 1996). Further reports can be expected in the future, especially with atypical antipsychotic drugs such as olanzapine, risperidone, and quetiapine, because clinicians have begun to prescribe them for refractory PTSD patients.

AREAS REQUIRING FURTHER EXPLORATION

Although there are promising results with a number of drugs, much more research is needed. Among the important questions that demand additional attention are the following:

1. Has generalizing too much from results with the most chronic, severe, and treatment refractory patients led us to underestimate the potential usefulness of pharmacotherapy in PTSD?

2. Have we been utilizing the best outcome measures (e.g., should we pay more attention to clinical global improvement, functional improvement, and clinical utilization rather than PTSD symptom reduction)?

3. Should we consider new kinds of pharmacological agents rather than established antidepressant/anxiolytic agents that were not developed initially for the treatment of PTSD)? Consideration of the unique pathophysiology of PTSD would suggest that drugs acting on key mechanisms of the human stress response, itself, might have potential usefulness in PTSD treatment. This might include currently experimental drugs that reduce the actions of CRF, such as CRF antagonists, neuropeptide Y agonists, or drugs that enhance the actions of neuropeptide Y.

4. Are there different subtypes of PTSD that might require different drugs for treatment? Clinical evidence suggests that there may be depressive and anxious subtypes of PTSD. Laboratory findings suggest that there may be subtypes of PTSD that specifically involve adrenergic versus serotonergic mechanisms. Evidence from sensitization and kindling models of PTSD (Post, Weiss, & Smith, 1995) have demonstrated that the psychobiology of stress-induced abnormalities changes over time, suggesting that some drugs might be effective in early stages of the disorder while different drugs might be more effective in chronic PTSD. Finally, the clinical phenomenology of complex PTSD (Herman, 1992, with the prominence of impulsive, dissociative, and somatic symptomatology, suggests that different pharmacotherapeutic approaches might be more effective than those that are useful in standard PTSD treatment.

5. Ethnopharmacological concerns have rarely been addressed. Lin, Poland, Anderson, and Lesser (1996) have shown that Caucasian versus Asian patients exhibit different pharmacokinetic responses to the same dose of the same drug. Furthermore, dietary habits, beliefs about drug efficacy, and social/familial factors affecting compliance all suggest that ethnocultural concerns must be considered when prescribing a drug for PTSD.

6. We continue to search for a "magic bullet" for PTSD—a single drug that will alleviate all symptom clusters with equal efficacy. Although that is a reasonable goal, it may not turn out to be a practical one. Much published literature suggests that certain drugs may be more effective against some PTSD clusters than others. For example, it has been suggested (Friedman & Southwick, 1995) that MAOIs/TCAs are best for reexperiencing symptoms, SSRIs for avoidant/numbing symptoms, and clonidine/propranolol for hyperarousal symptoms. Should this turn out to be the case, the best approach might consist of individualized selection from an array of drugs with complementary actions rather than a single "magic bullet." There is plenty of precedent for such an approach in standard medical treatment. For example, some patients with arteriosclerotic cardiovascular disease may require a diuretic, a calcium channel blocker, and digoxin. As we learn more about the complex pathophysiology of PTSD, we may also conclude that such an approach may provide the most cost-effective treatment for some of our patients.

SUMMARY

Currently, we know four things with certainty about pharmacotherapy for PTSD:

1. Many people are receiving medication.
2. Clinical trials usually show that some patients benefit greatly from pharmacotherapy.
3. SSRIs are currently the best established drug treatment for PTSD and can be recommended as a first-line treatment.
4. Much more research is needed.

At a more speculative level, drugs seem to have at least three potential benefits for PTSD patients: amelioration of PTSD symptoms; treatment of comorbid disorders; and reduction of associated symptoms that interfere with psychotherapy and/or daily function.

Treatment of PTSD

Table 5.4 summarizes our recommended use of drugs for PTSD treatment. It shows the strength of evidence (AHCPR Level A–F) to support these recommendations as well as specific indications, contraindications, and other pertinent information about each drug. A brief summary of Table 5.4 can be found in "Practice Guidelines for Pharmacotherapy" (Part II of this volume). The most substantial available evidence supports the use of the broad category of antidepressant medications, especially SSRIs, that appear to promote global improvement in most, but not all, randomized clinical trials. It is not as clear whether antidepressants are effective treatment for specific (intrusive, avoidant/numbing, or arousal) PTSD symptom clusters or whether they have a broad spectrum of action against all PTSD symptoms and associated symptoms of depression and anxiety disorders.

SSRIs clearly appear most promising for benefiting all three symptom clusters in civilian PTSD populations. Results with chronic veteran populations are much more difficult to interpret because of the severity and chronicity of their PTSD. TCAs and MAOIs have produced modest, substantial, therapeutic benefits, respectively, in drug trials with veterans, although relatively few patients have participated in such trials. These studies have not been replicated because there has been little active research interest in TCAs or MAOIs in recent years, since SSRIs appear to have advantages with respect to efficacy and tolerability.

Antiadrenergic agents such as clonidine, guanfacine, and propranolol may prove to ameliorate arousal and reexperiencing symptoms by reducing the excessive adrenergic activity associated with PTSD. Unfortunately, at present very little clinical data substantiate this speculation. Anticonvulsants

TABLE 5.4. Evidence for Efficacy of Drugs in the Treatment of PTSD Based on the Published Literature

Drug class	Specific drugs	Strength of evidence[a]	Indications	Contraindications	Remarks
SSRIs	Sertraline[b] Fluoxetine Paroxetine Fluvoxamine	A A/B B B	• Reduce B, C, and D symptoms. • Produce clinical global improvement. • Effective treatment for depression, panic disorder, and obsessive–compulsive disorder. • Reduce associated symptoms.	• May exacerbate insomnia and agitation. • May produce sexual dysfunction	• Current evidence is stronger for SSRI efficacy among civilian rather than Vietnam veteran cohorts.
Other serotonergic	Trazodone Nefazodone	C B	• Trazodone/nefazodone may reduce B, C, and D symptoms. • Trazodone is synergistic with SSRIs and reverses SSRI-induced insomnia. • Effective antidepressants, few side effects.	• May be too sedating.	• Very few published reports on either of these agents.
	Cyproheptadine	F	• Reduces flashbacks and nightmares.	• Sedation	• Supporting data are anecdotal.
	Buspirone	F	• Reduces B and D symptoms.		• Supporting data are anecdotal.

(continued)

TABLE 5.4. (continued)

Drug class	Specific drugs	Strength of evidence[a]	Indications	Contraindications	Remarks
Antiadrenergic	Clonidine	C	• Reduces B and D symptoms.	• May lower blood pressure or slow pulse rate too much.	• Few studies. • Tolerance may develop to clonidine.
	Guanfacine	C	• Reduces B and D symptoms.	• Must use cautiously with patients on hypotensive medications.	• Anecdotal evidence.
	Propranolol	C	• Reduces B and D symptoms.	• May produce depressive symptoms or psychomotor slowing.	• Few studies. • Some negative results.
MAOIs	Phenelzine	A/B	• Reduces B symptoms. • Produces global improvement. • Effective antidepressant and antipanic agent.	• Patients must follow a strict dietary regimen. • Contraindicated in patients with alcohol/substance abuse/dependency. • May produce insomnia, hypotension, and anticholinergic and hepatotoxic side effects.	
	Moclobemide	B	• Reduces B and C symptoms.	• May produce insomnia, headache, dizziness, fatigue, nausea, and diarrhea.	• Only one open trial to date. • Not available in United States. • No dietary restrictions.

Class	Drug	Level	Effectiveness	Cautions	Comments
TCAs	Imipramine Amitriptyline Desipramine	A A A	• Reduce B symptoms. • Produce global improvement. • Effective antidepressant and antipanic agents.	• Anticholinergic side effects. • May produce EKG abnormality. • May produce hypotension, arousal, or sedation.	• Not as effective as SSRIs or MAOIs with civilian cohorts. • May be more effective with Vietnam veteran cohorts. • Desipramine was ineffective in a randomized clinical trial.
Benzodiazepines	Alprazolam Clonazepam	B C	• Reduce D symptoms only. • Effective anxiolytics and antipanic agents.	• Should not be prescribed to patients with past or present alcohol/drug abuse/dependency. • May exacerbate depressive symptoms.	• Few studies. • Specific usefulness in PTSD not well established.
Anticonvulsants	Carbamazepine	B	• Effective on B and D symptoms. • Effective in bipolar affective disorder.	• May produce neurological symptoms, luekopenia, hyponatremia, and thrombocytopenia.	• Open but no randomized trials for either drug. • May have a unique role in PTSD with comorbid bipolar (and possibly unipolar) affective disorder.
	Valproate	B	• Effective on C and D symptoms. • Effective in bipolar affective disorders.	• May produce gastrointestinal problems and tremor.	
Antipsychotics	Thioridazine Clozapine Risperidone	F F F	• Possible effectiveness on B and D symptoms. • Effective antipsychotic agents.	• Sedation, hypotension, and anticholinergic effects. • Extropyramidal effects (thioridazine primarily).	• Anecdotal reports only. • Not first-line drugs in PTSD but may have unique role for hypervigilant/paranoid, extremely agitated or psychotic patients refractory to other drugs.

[a] Level A, randomized clinical trials; Level B, well-designed clinical studies without randomization or placebo comparison; Level C, service and naturalistic clinical studies, combined with clinical observations that are sufficiently compelling to warrant use of this drug; Level F, a few observations that have not been subjected to clinical or empirical tests.

[b] Approved by FDA as an indicated treatment for PTSD (December 1999).

101

have also shown promise in open clinical trials. Empirical evidence suggests that benzodiazepines are not useful for treating DSM-IV B or C PTSD symptoms. Finally, there is no evidence to recommend antipsychotic agents for monotherapy of PTSD.

Treatment of Comorbid Disorders

A great deal of evidence suggests that pharmacotherapy will successfully reduce most disorders that are comorbid with PTSD. SSRIs, TCAs, and MAOIs have proven efficacy against depression and panic disorder. SSRIs are also effective treatment for obsessive–compulsive disorder and alcohol abuse/dependence. Anticonvulsants are useful in bipolar affective disorder, and propranolol has been shown to be effective in panic disorder.

Treatment of Associated Disruptive Symptoms: Drugs as an Adjunct to Psychotherapy

Since compelling and consistent evidence exists demonstrating the efficacy of cognitive-behavioral treatment for PTSD, medication need not always be considered a first-line intervention. When disruptive symptoms interfere with a patient's ability to participate in psychotherapy, pharmacotherapy has an important potential role as an adjunct to psychotherapy. SSRIs are effective in this regard, since they have been shown to reduce impulsivity, mood lability, irritability, aggressiveness, and suicidal behavior. Antiadrenergic drugs reduce arousal and, possibly, dissociative symptoms. Anticonvulsive mood stabilizers such as carbamazepine or valproate might also be expected to reduce aggressive and impulsive behaviors. And atypical antipsychotics might significantly reduce hypervigilant/paranoid behavior, but there is very little current evidence demonstrating such efficacy with PTSD patients.

The recent development of SSRIs and other novel drugs that might be expected to reduce psychobiological abnormalities associated with PTSD has ushered in a new interest in pharmacotherapy for this disorder. There is good reason to anticipate exciting breakthroughs in the foreseeable future that should equip clinicians with a greater variety of effective drugs that will benefit patients with PTSD.

REFERENCES

Baker, D. G., Diamond, B. I., Gillette, G., Hamner, M., Katzelnick, D., Keller, T., Mellman, T. A., Pontius, E., Rosenthal, M., Tucker, P., van der Kolk, B. A., & Katz, R. (1995). A double-blind, randomized placebo-controlled multi-center study of brofaromine in the treatment of post-traumatic stress disorder. *Psychopharmacology, 122,* 386–389.

Brady, K., Pearlstein, T., Asnis, G. M., Baker, D., Rothbaum, B., Sikes, C. R., & Farfel, G. M. (2000). Double-blind placebo-controlled study of the efficacy and safety of sertraline treatment of posttraumatic stress disorder. *Journal of the American Medical Association, 283,* 1837–1844.

Brady, K. T., Sonne, S. C., & Roberts, J. M. (1995). Sertraline treatment of comorbid posttraumatic stress disorder and alcohol dependence. *Journal of Clinical Psychiatry, 56,* 502–505.

Braun, P., Greenberg, D., Dasberg, H., & Lerer, B. (1990). Core symptoms of posttraumatic stress disorder unimproved by alprazolam treatment. *Journal of Clinical Psychiatry, 51,* 236–238.

Cook, M. D., & Conner, J. (1995). Retrospective review of hypnotic use in combination with fluoxetine or sertraline. *Clinical Drug Investigation, 9,* 212–216.

Davidson, J., Kudler, H., Smith, R., Mahorney, S. L., Lipper, S., Hammett, E. B., Saunders, W. B., & Cavenar, J. Jr. (1990). Treatment of post-traumatic stress disorder with amitriptyline and placebo. *Archives of General Psychiatry, 47,* 259–266.

Davidson, J., Landburg, P. D., Pearlstein, T., Weisler, R., Sikes, C., & Farfel, G. M. (1997, December). Double-blind comparison of sertraline and placebo in patients with posttraumatic stress disorder (PTSD). *Abstracts of the American College of Neuropsychopharmacology 36th Annual Meeting.* San Juan, Puerto Rico.

Davidson, J. R. T., Malik, M. L., & Sutherland, S. M. (1996). Response characteristics to antidepressants and placebo in post-traumatic stress disorder. *International Clinical Psychopharmacology, 12,* 291–296.

Davidson, J. R. T., Weisler, R. H., Malik, M. L., & Connor, M. K. (1998). Treatment of posttraumatic stress disorder with nefazodone. *International Clinical Psychopharmacology, 13,* 111–113.

DeMartino, R., Mollica, R. F., & Wilk, V. (1995). Monoamine oxidase inhibitors in posttraumatic stress disorder. *Journal of Nervous and Mental Disease, 183,* 510–515.

Dillard, M. L., Bendfeldt, F., & Jernigan, P. (1993). Use of thioridazine in post-traumatic stress disorder. *Southern Medical Journal, 86,* 1276–1278.

Famularo, R., Kinscherff, R., & Fenton, T. (1988). Propranolol treatment for childhood post-traumatic stress disorder, acute type: A pilot study. *American Journal of Diseases of Children, 142,* 1244–1247.

Fava, M., Alpert, J., Nierenberg, A., Ghaemi, N., O'Sullivan, R., Tedlow, J., Worthington, J., & Rosenbaum, J. (1996). Fluoxetine treatment of anger attacks: a replication study. *Annals of Clinical Psychiatry, 8,* 7–10.

Friedman, M. J. (1996). Biological alterations in PTSD: Implications for pharmacotherapy. In E. Giller & L. Weisaeth (Eds.), *Bailliere's clinical psychiatry: International practice and research: Post-traumatic stress disorder* (pp. 245–262). London: Bailliere Tindall.

Friedman, M. J. (1997). Drug treatment for PTSD: Answers and questions. *Annals of the New York Academy of Sciences, 821,* 359–371.

Friedman, M. J. (1990). Interrelationships between biological mechanisms and pharmacotherapy of post-traumatic stress disorder. In M. E. Wolfe & A. D. Mosnaim (Eds.), *Post-traumatic stress disorder: Etiology, phenomenology, and treatment* (pp. 204–225). Washington, DC: American Psychiatric Press.

Friedman, M. J. (Guest Ed.). (1999). Progress in psychobiological research on PTSD. *Seminars in clinical neuropsychiatry, 4,* 229–316.

Friedman, M. J., Charney, D. S., & Deutch, A. Y. (1995). *Neurobiological and clinical consequences of stress: From normal adaptation to PTSD.* Philadelphia: Lippincott–Raven.

Friedman, M. J., & Southwick, S. M. (1995). Towards pharmacotherapy for PTSD. In M. J. Friedman, D. S. Charney, & A. Y. Deutch (Eds.), *Neurobiological and clinical consequences of stress: From normal adaptation to PTSD* (pp. 465–481). Philadelphia: Lippincott–Raven.

Gelpin, E., Bonne, O., Peri, T., Brandes, D., & Shalev, A. (1996). Treatment of recent trauma survivors with benzodiazepines: A prospective study. *Journal of Clinical Psychiatry, 57,* 390–394.

Glover, H. (1993). A preliminary trial of nalmefane for the treatment of emotional numbing in combat veterans with post-traumatic stress disorder. *Israel Journal of Psychiatry and Related Sciences, 30,* 255–263.

Hamner, M. B. (1996). Clozapine treatment for a veteran with comorbid psychosis and PTSD [Letter]. *American Journal of Psychiatry, 153,* 841.

Harmon, R. J., & Riggs, P. D. (1996). Clonidine for posttraumatic stress disorder in preschool children. *Journal of American Academy of Child and Adolescent Psychiatry, 35,* 1247–1249.

Herman, J. L. (1992). *Trauma and recovery.* New York: Basic Books.

Hertzberg, M. A., Feldman, M. E., Beckham, J. C., & Davidson, J. R. T. (1996). Trial of trazodone for posttraumatic stress disorder using a multiple baseline group design. *Journal of Clinical Psychopharmacology, 16,* 294–298.

Hertzberg, M. A., Feldman, M. E., Beckham, J. C., Moore, S. D., & Davidson, J. R. T. (1998). Open trial of nefazodone for combat-related posttraumatic stress disorder. *Journal of Clinical Psychiatry, 59,* 460–464.

Horrigan, J. P. (1996). Guanfacine for PTSD nightmares [Letter]. *Journal of American Academy of Child and Adolescent Psychiatry, 35,* 975–976.

Kaplan, Z., Amir, M., Swartz, M., & Levine, J. (1995). Inositol treatment of PTSD. *Anxiety, 2,* 51–52.

Katz, R. J., Lott, M. H., Arbus, P., Croq, L., Lingjaerde, O., Lopez, G., Loughrey, G. C., MacFarlane, D. J., Nugent, D., Turner, S. W., Weisaeth, L., & Yule, W. (1994/1995). Pharmacotherapy of post-traumatic stress disorder with a novel psychotropic. *Anxiety, 1,* 169–174.

Kolb, L. C., Burris, B. C., & Griffiths, S. (1984). Propranolol and clonidine in the treatment of the chronic post-traumatic stress disorders of war. In B. A. van der Kolk (Ed.), *Post-traumatic stress disorder: Psychological and biological sequelae* (pp. 97–107). Washington, DC: American Psychiatric Press.

Kosten, T. R., Frank, J. B, Dan, E., McDougle, C. J., & Giller, E. L. (1991). Pharmacotherapy for post-traumatic stress disorder using phenelzine or imipramine. *Journal of Nervous and Mental Disease, 179,* 366–370.

Krystal, J. H., Bennett, A., Bremner, J. D., Southwick, S. M., & Charney, D. S. (1995). Toward a cognitive neuroscience of dissociation and altered memory functions in posttraumatic stress disorder. In M. J. Friedman, D. S. Charney, & A. Y. Deutch (Eds.), *Neurobiological and clinical consequences of stress: From normal adaptation to PTSD* (pp. 239–270). Philadelphia: Lippincott–Raven.

Lin, K.-M., Poland, R. E., Anderson, D., & Lesser, I. M. (1996). Ethnopharmacology and the treatment of PTSD. In A. J. Marsella, M. J. Friedman, E. T. Gerrity, & R. M. Scurfield (Eds.), *Ethnocultural aspects of posttraumatic stress disorder* (pp. 505–528). Washington, DC: American Psychological Association.

Marmar, C. R., Schoenfeld, F., Weiss, D. S., Meltzler, T., Zatzick, D., Wu, R., Smiga, S., Tecott, L., & Neylan, T. (1996). Open trial of fluvoxamine treatment for combat related posttraumatic stress disorder. *Journal of Clinical Psychiatry, 57*(Suppl. 8), 66–72.

Marshall, R. D., Schneier, F. R., Fallon, B. A., Knight, C. G., Abbate, L. A., Goetz, D., Campeas, R., & Liebowitz, M. R. (1998). An open trial of paroxetine in patients with noncombat-related, chronic posttraumatic stress disorder. *Journal of Clinical Psychopharmacology, 18,* 10–18.

Mellman, T. A., Byers, P. M., & Augenstein, J. S. (1998). Pilot evaluation of hypnotic medication during acute traumatic stress response. *Journal of Traumatic Stress, 11,* 563–569.

Neal, L. A., Shapland, W., & Fox, C. (1997). An open trial of moclobemide in the treatment of post-traumatic stress disorder. *International Clinical Psychopharmacology, 12,* 231–237.

Post., R. M., Weiss, S. R B., & Smith, M. A. (1995). Sensitization and kindling: Implications for the evolving neural substrate of PTSD. In M. J. Friedman, D. S. Charney, & A. Y. Deutch (Eds.), *Neurobiological and clinical consequences of stress: From normal adaptation to PTSD* (pp. 203–224). Philadelphia: Lippincott–Raven.

Rasmusson, A. M., & Charney, D. S. (1997). Animal models of relevance to PTSD. *Annals of the New York Academy of Sciences, 821,* 332–351.

Reist, C., Kauffman, C. D., Haier, R. J., Sangdahl, C., DeMet, E. M., Chicz-DeMet, A., & Nelson, J. N. (1989). A controlled trial of desipramine in 18 men with post-traumatic stress disorder. *American Journal of Psychiatry, 146,* 513–516.

Rothbaum, B. O., Ninan, P. T., & Thomas, L. (1996). Sertraline in the treatment of rape victims with posttraumatic stress disorder. *Journal of Traumatic Stress, 9,* 865–871.

Shestatzky, M., Greenberg, D., & Lerer, B. (1988). A controlled trial of phenelzine in post-traumatic stress disorder. *Psychiatry Research, 24,* 149–155.

Southwick, S. M., Yehuda, R., Giller, E. L., & Charney, D. S. (1994). Use of tricyclics and monoamine oxidase inhibitors in the treatment of PTSD: A quantitative review. In M. M. Murburg (Ed.), *Catecholamine function in post-traumatic stress disorder: Emerging concepts* (pp. 293–305). Washington, DC: American Psychiatric Press.

van der Kolk, B. A., Dryfuss, D., Michaels, M., Shera, D., Berkowitz, R., Fisler, R., & Saxe, G. (1994). Fluoxetine in post-traumatic stress disorder. *Journal of Clinical Psychiatry, 55,* 517–522.

Ver Ellen, P., & van Kammen, D. P. (1990). The biological findings in post-traumatic stress disorder: A review. *Journal of Applied Social Psychology, 20*(21), 1789–1821.

Weissman, A., & Harbert, C. A. (1972). Recent developments relating serotonin and behavior. *Annual Reports in Medicinal Chemistry, 7,* 47–52.

Weizman, R., Laor, N., Schujovitsky, A., Wolmer, L., Abramovitz-Schnaider, P., Freudstein-Dan, A., & Rehavi, M. (1996). Platelet imipramine binding in patients. *Psychiatry Research, 63,* 143–150.

Yehuda, R., & McFarlane, A. C. (1997). Psychobiology of posttraumatic stress disorder. *Annals of the New York Academy of Sciences, 821,* New York: New York Academy of Sciences.

6

Treatment of Children
and Adolescents

Judith A. Cohen, Lucy Berliner, and John S. March

THEORETICAL POSITION

Overview

Since posttraumatic stress disorder (PTSD) entered the psychiatric lexicon
with DSM-III (American Psychiatric Association, 1980), followed shortly by
Terr's (1983) pioneering studies of the children of Chowchilla, many studies
have shown that exposure to a variety of stressors can lead to serious and often debilitating PTSD in children and adolescents. As child mental health
workers have increasingly come to appreciate the extent to which children
are exposed to traumatic situations, the severity of their acute distress, and
the potential for serious, long-term psychiatric sequelae, researchers have begun to conduct empirical studies of childhood PTSD within a sound developmental framework (Pynoos, Steinberg, & Wraith, 1995). Partly as a result,
the DSM-IV PTSD diagnostic criteria, unlike those for DSM-III, now explicitly reflect accommodations for the presentation of symptoms in children
(although it should be noted that field trials for DSM-IV PTSD criteria did
not include children; see American Psychiatric Association, 1994). In this
chapter, we briefly survey the context in which PTSD treatment occurs and
describe the types of treatment that are typically implemented with traumatized children and adolescents. We then review in detail the limited empirical

106

data regarding evidence-based treatments for pediatric PTSD and, in some cases, non-PTSD sequelae of childhood trauma.

PTSD in Children

Careful attention to the nature of the stressor is mandatory when considering treatment interventions, especially since many sexually abused children do not meet diagnostic criteria for PTSD (Kendall-Tackett, Williams, & Finkelhor, 1993) while still showing profound psychological impairments warranting treatment (Cahill, Llewelyn, & Pearson, 1991). Hence, many treatment approaches and outcome studies that have been designed for sexually abused children include subjects not meeting full PTSD diagnostic criteria (Cohen & Mannarino, 1996a), whereas a diagnosis of PTSD is more commonly an entry criterion in studies of PTSD after sudden trauma (March, Amaya-Jackson, Murray, & Schulte, 1998). It should also be noted that the severity of different traumatic experiences varies greatly and is not always proportional to chronicity. For example, war often exposes children to trauma of immensely greater magnitude (e.g., repeatedly witnessing violent death, sudden loss of parents and friends, loss of home, refugee conditions) than other chronic stressors. Thus, Terr's (1991) differentiation between single and chronic traumas may not adequately distinguish between very different levels of traumatic experience.

A recent review of 25 studies indicates that three factors have been found consistently to predict the development of PTSD symptom levels in children: the severity of the trauma exposure, parental trauma-related distress, and temporal proximity to the traumatic event (American Academy of Child and Adolescent Psychiatry [AACAP], 1998; Foy, Madvig, Pynoos, & Camilleri, 1996). However, very few studies have been sufficiently well designed or adequately powered to identify variables that might predict the development of PTSD symptoms in children. In particular, little attention has been paid to variables that might moderate or mediate the outcome of treatment (March & Curry, 1998). A *moderator variable* affects the direction or strength of the relationship between an independent and a dependent variable (Barron & Kenny, 1986; Holmbeck, 1997). A *mediator variable* explains the relationship between an independent and a dependent variable. It defines the mechanism through which the former affects the latter. The theoretical influence of such variables has been described in detail by Yule (1992b). With a few notable exceptions (Cohen & Mannarino, 1996b), few of the cited treatment outcome studies have examined predictors of treatment outcome or distinguished between baseline moderator (e.g., race or gender) or mediator (e.g., compliance with or dose of treatment) effects.

Not surprisingly, PTSD symptoms themselves vary considerably with developmental stage (American Academy of Child and Adolescent Psychiatry, 1998). Developmental themes also influence children's appraisals of

threat, attribution of meaning, emotional and cognitive means of coping, tol-
eration of their reactions, expectations about recovery, and effectiveness in
addressing secondary life changes (Amaya-Jackson, 1995; Pynoos, Steinberg,
& Wraith, 1995). Thus, it is imperative that clinicians and researchers frame
current knowledge about child and adolescent exposure to traumatic stress
within a developmental framework that recognizes the intricate matrix of a
changing child and environment, evolving familial and societal expectations,
and an essential linkage between disrupted and normal development.

In general, as children mature, they are more likely to exhibit adult-like
PTSD symptoms. Thus, adolescents with PTSD may meet standard DSM-
IV criteria with reexperiencing symptoms, avoidance and numbing, and hyperarousal. Adolescents with chronic PTSD who have experienced prolonged or repeated stressors may also present with predominantly dissociative
features, including derealization, depersonalization, self-injurious behavior,
substance abuse, and intermittent angry or aggressive outbursts (Goodwin,
1988; Hornstein, 1996). Children may be more likely than adolescents to
show posttraumatic reenactment behaviors in play, drawings, or verbaliza-
tions. Sleep disturbances may be especially common in prepubertal children
(Benedek, 1985). While Terr (1983) also has described "omen formation" in
these children (i.e., they come to believe that certain "signs" were warnings of
the traumatic event approaching and that if they are alert enough, they will
be able to see "omens" predicting future disasters), there is little empirical literature to support this assertion, nor has a sense of a foreshortened future received empirical support (McNally, 1993). Very young children may present
with relatively few DSM-IV PTSD symptoms. In part, this is because, as
Scheeringa, Zeanah, Drell, and Larrieu (1995) point out, eight out of 18
DSM-IV criteria "require verbal descriptions from patients of their experiences and internal states. . . . Limited cognitive and expressive language skills
[in young children] make inferring their thoughts and feelings difficult" (p.
191). Therefore, infants, toddlers, and preschoolers may present with generalized anxiety symptoms (separation fears, stranger anxiety, fears of monsters
or animals), avoidance of situations that may or may not have an obvious link
to the original trauma, sleep disturbances, and preoccupation with certain
words or symbols that may or may not have an apparent connection to the
traumatic event (Drell, Siegel, & Gaensbauer, 1993). Almquist and Brandell-
Forsberg's (1997) demonstration that formal and objective assessment of play
content aids in the diagnosis of PTSD in preschoolers illustrates the general
principle that assessment methods in children younger than age 8 represent
an area that is ripe for methodological innovation.

Clinically Relevant Subtypes

DSM-IV specifies three subtypes of PTSD: acute, chronic, and delayed-
onset. Due to the difficulty in eliciting some PTSD symptoms from children

and the tendency of some parents to minimize PTSD symptomatology in their children (which may contribute to a delay in having the child evaluated), a careful history should be taken before using the delayed-onset specifier in children or adolescents. It also should be noted that if PTSD symptoms have appeared within 1 month of exposure to an extreme traumatic stressor but have not lasted beyond 1 month, and there are dissociative features, a diagnosis of acute stress disorder (ASD) should be made. If symptoms then extend beyond 1 month, the diagnosis should be changed to PTSD.

Comorbidity

Traumatized children frequently exhibit symptoms of disorders other than PTSD, and children with other disorders may have PTSD as a comorbid diagnosis. Careful questioning, not only of parents and teachers but also of the child regarding his or her internal experiences, is often necessary to clarify the diagnostic picture. This is especially important because parents may not be aware of the existence or severity of their child's PTSD symptoms. Children may minimize these symptoms in order to protect parents or to avoid discussions of the traumatic event. Thus, it is essential to question the child carefully in a developmentally appropriate manner about PTSD symptoms he or she may be experiencing. Because of the high prevalence of comorbid symptomatology in children with PTSD, it is crucial to include non-PTSD outcomes as targets for treatment and predictors of treatment response in treatment outcome studies. On the other hand, while multiple diagnoses should be made (where appropriate) in order to facilitate treatment planning, it is important to keep the focus on the traumatic event when considering the overall symptom picture.

In children with PTSD, depression may be an especially common comorbid problem. Brent and colleagues (1995) noted that there is a large overlap in symptom criteria between PTSD and major depressive disorder (MDD), and went on to suggest that the "core features" of PTSD may be much narrower than the DSM-IV criteria suggest. The study by Brent and colleagues as well as others (Goenjian et al., 1995; Green, 1985; Hubbard, Realmuto, Northwood, & Masten, 1995; Kinzie, Sack, Angell, Manson, & Rath, 1986; Kiser, Heston, Milsap, & Pruitt, 1991; Looff, Grimley, Kuiler, Martin, & Shunfield, 1995; Singer, Anglin, Song, & Lunghofer, 1995; Stoddard, Norman, & Murphy, 1989; Weine et al., 1995; Yule & Udwin, 1991) have noted comorbidity between PTSD and depressive disorders (MDD and dysthymic disorder). Several authors have hypothesized that PTSD precedes and predisposes individuals to the onset of MDD rather than the reverse (Goenjian et al., 1995). Investigators have documented comorbidity between PTSD and substance abuse in older children (Arroyo & Eth, 1985; Brent et al., 1995; Clark et al., 1995; Looff et al., 1995; Sullivan & Evans, 1994), and PTSD and other anxiety disorders (DSM-III-R overanxious disorder, agoraphobia, separation anxiety disorder, and generalized anxiety disorder; see Brent et al., 1995; Clark et al., 1995; Goenjian et al., 1995; Kiser et al., 1991; Lonigan, Shannon, Taylor, Finch, & Sallec, 1994; Singer et al., 1995; Yule & Udwin, 1991).

Both externalizing and internalizing symptoms are also common. For example, authors such as Malmquist (1986) have noted that numbing or avoidance may take many forms in children, including restlessness, hyper alertness, poor concentration, and behavioral problems. Anxiety symptoms in young children may take the form of hyperactivity, distractibility, and increased impulsivity, which are hallmarks of attention-deficit/hyperactivity disorder (ADHD). This may in part explain why comorbidity has also been found between PTSD and ADHD (Cuffe, McCullough, & Pumariega, 1994; Famularo, Fenton, Kinscherff, & Augustyn, 1996; Glod & Teicher, 1996; McCullough & Pumariega, 1994). In addition, ADHD may in itself be a risk factor for traumatic exposure (Famularo et al., 1996). A high prevalence of other externalizing disorders, such as conduct disorder and oppositional defiant disorder, also has been noted in clinical and population samples of children with PTSD (Arroyo, & Eth, 1985; Green, 1985; Steiner, Garcia, & Matthews, 1997; Stoddard, Norman, & Murphy, 1989). Steiner and colleagues (1997) suggest that PTSD may result in loss of impulse control and diminished control of aggression and anger, which may explain this comorbidity. Pelcovitz and colleagues (1994) hypothesize that externalizing symptoms may be an initial response to ongoing stressors such as physical abuse, and that there may be a "sleeper" effect in the emergence of PTSD symptoms.

Comorbidity between PTSD and borderline personality disorder (BPD) is not uncommon in sexually abused adolescents or those children who have multiyear, multistressor traumas and PTSD histories. Studies have indicated that 60–80% of females diagnosed as having BPD report a history of childhood sexual abuse (Herman, Perry, & van der Kolk, 1989; Stone, 1990). Goodwin (1985) and Herman and van der Kolk (1987) have suggested that BPD may represent a very severe and chronic manifestation of PTSD. Other authors have indicated the predominance of dissociative and interpersonal problems associated with chronic PTSD (Famularo, Fenton, Kinscherff, & Augustyn, 1996; Spiegel, 1984; Terr, 1991). For these reasons, Goodwin (1985) recommends that diagnosis of personality disorders should be deferred until PTSD symptoms have resolved.

DESCRIPTION OF TECHNIQUES

Play Therapy

The term "play therapy" traditionally refers to the use of play as a projective technique. However, most descriptions of trauma-focused treatment advocate the use of play and other nonverbal techniques (use of drawings, puppets, dolls, etc.) as a means of enhancing the child's comfort and ability to communicate in therapy, in order to accomplish specific therapeutic goals rather than as a projective technique (Deblinger & Heflin, 1996; Gil, 1991). This use of play in therapy is incorporated into many of the therapeutic interventions described below.

Psychological Debriefing

Pynoos and Nader (1988) describe a "psychological first aid" approach for children exposed to community violence, which may be offered in schools as well as in traditional treatment settings shortly following the traumatic event. This model emphasizes clarifying the facts about the traumatic event, normalizing children's PTSD reactions, encouraging expression of feelings, teaching problem-solving techniques, and referring the most symptomatic children for ongoing treatment. Such interventions can serve a screening function to identify children at high risk for the development of PTSD (see, e.g., Yule & Udwin, 1991). Unfortunately, therapists themselves sometimes avoid directly discussing certain traumatic events (e.g., child abuse) for a variety of reasons, including the fear of tainting the child's potential testimony in subsequent legal proceedings or concern that repeated questioning may influence children's memory regarding the factual aspects of an event (see, e.g., Ceci, Leichtman, & White, 1996).

Psychoeducation

Most treatment approaches include some degree of psychoeducation for parents, children, and sometimes teachers (Blom, 1986; Butler, Rizzi, & Handwerger, 1996; Galante & Foa, 1986; LaGreca, Vemberg, Silverman, & Prinstein, 1996; Molta, 1995; Nir, 1985; Rigamer, 1986). In particular, education about the traumatic experience (common emotional reactions to this kind of event, how to respond/protect oneself if this event were to recur, etc.) is considered beneficial to children, as well as their parents, and is a common component of many treatment approaches (see, e.g., Deblinger & Heflin, 1996).

Psychoanalytic/Psychodynamic Approaches

Despite a large and sometimes clinically compelling literature, there is little evidence apart from descriptive case studies that psychodynamic psychotherapy is effective for pediatric PTSD or other sequelae of severe trauma (Bleiberg, 1994). Nonetheless, a variety of authors advocate psychoanalytic interventions for traumatized children (see, e.g., Gaensbauer, 1994; McElroy & McElroy, 1989) as a primary intervention. Case studies have reported on the impact of trauma and the treatment response with reference to object relations (Seinfeld, 1989), the use of defense mechanisms (McElroy & McElroy, 1989), and resistance (Van Leeuwen, 1988). In these approaches, longer term, individual therapy is used as the vehicle for processing the impact and meaning of the traumatic event, but, again, empirical support is weak at best.

Cognitive-Behavioral Techniques

Like other cognitive-behavioral approaches to treating mentally ill children and adolescents, cognitive-behavioral therapy (CBT) for traumatized children generally blends both cognitive and behavioral interventions, including exposure techniques (direct discussions of the traumatic event), stress management/relaxation techniques, and exploration and correction of inaccurate attributions regarding the trauma (see, e.g., Berliner, 1997; Cohen & Mannarino, 1993; Friedrich, 1996a). However, some strictly behavioral intervention such as *in vitro* flooding have also been used to decrease PTSD symptoms in children (Saigh, 1989), and these interventions should be distinguished from the more commonly used, combined CBT methods.

1. *Controlled exposure to traumatic cues* likely is therapeutic for children, as it is with adults (Saigh, 1992). Unfortunately, clinicians may be hesitant to take such an approach with children because of reservations about increasing child symptomatology or because of desire to avoid the negative affect associated with such discussion (Benedek, 1985). Many children are very avoidant of talking about the trauma and may in fact become transiently more symptomatic during exposure interventions. Hence, authors vary in the degree to which they advocate explicit exposure techniques. While Deblinger and Heflin (1996) and March, Amaya-Jackson, Murray, and Schulte (1998) recommend systematic gradual exposure to increasingly upsetting aspects of the trauma, other protocols (see, e.g., Cohen & Mannarino, 1993) do not include hierarchical exposure. Regardless of the specific manner in which exposure-based interventions are accomplished, most authors consider behavioral and narrative exposure to be a critical component of treatment for PTSD in children (Azarian, Miller, & Skriptchenko-Gregorian, 1996; Benedek, 1985; Berliner, 1997; Friedrich, 1996a; Galante & Foa, 1986; Parson, 1995; Pynoos & Eth, 1985, 1986; Pynoos & Nader, 1988; Rigamer, 1986; Saigh, 1989; Saigh, Yule, & Inamdar, 1996; Silvern, Karyl, & Landis, 1995; Snodgrass, Yamamoto, & Frederick, 1993; Terr, 1990). However, no controlled empirical study to date has demonstrated exposure techniques per se to be efficacious in decreasing PTSD symptoms in children.

2. *Stress management* strategies are frequently paired with direct discussion of the traumatic event. Siegel (1995) has provided a neurocognitive explanation of why stress management may alleviate PTSD symptoms. It is often recommended that progressive muscle relaxation, thought stopping, positive imagery, and controlled breathing be taught to children prior to detailed discussions of the trauma (Berliner, 1997; Cohen & Mannarino, 1993; Deblinger & Heflin, 1996; Parson, 1995; Saigh, 1992; Saigh et al., 1996;

Snodgrass et al., 1993). Mastering these skills may give children a sense of control over thoughts and feelings rather than being overwhelmed by them and allows them to approach the direct discussion of the traumatic event with confidence and not lead to uncontrollable reexperiencing symptoms and fear. Stress management techniques also are useful outside the therapeutic context if and when reexperiencing phenomena occur.

3. *Cognitive therapy (CT) techniques* have also proven useful in the treatment of pediatric PTSD. Besides straightforward cognitive restructuring regarding aberrant risk appraisal and overresponsibility, CT often targets evaluation and reconsideration of negative cognitive assumptions that children may have made with regard to the traumatic event (Berliner, 1997; Cohen & Mannarino, 1993; Deblinger & Heflin, 1996; Joseph, Brewin, Yule, & Williams, 1993; Pynoos & Eth, 1986; Spaccarelli, 1995). Beyond mere reassurances, faulty attributions regarding the trauma (e.g., "It was my fault," "Nothing is safe anymore") are explored and challenged. Most often this is accomplished through step-by-step logical analysis of the cognitive distortions, replacing them with more accurate and functional attributions. Other trauma-related beliefs, such as survivor's guilt and omen formation, may also respond to cognitive methods. Based on findings that children's trauma-related attributions and perceptions strongly predict psychological symptomatology (Mannarino, Cohen, & Berman, 1994), some authors believe the cognitive component to be at least as important as exposure in reducing postttraumatic symptoms.

Eye Movement Desensitization and Reprocessing (EMDR)

EMDR, which many consider a variant of CBT, is an intervention that combines components of exposure and cognitive therapy with directed eye movements (Shapiro, 1996). Patients are instructed to recall aspects of the traumatic event while visually following back-and-forth hand movements by the therapist. Studies with adults have shown some evidence for effectiveness in the treatment of PTSD, although the value of the eye movement procedure has not been specifically demonstrated (see, e.g., Lohr, Tolin, & Lilienfeld, 1998; Pitman et al., 1996), nor is it likely to be essential (Hyer & Brandsma, 1997). Considerable case lore (Tinker & Wilson, 1988) and, more recently, an unpublished study by Chemtob and colleagues suggest that brief treatment with EMDR may benefit traumatized youth (Chemtob, Nakashima, Hamada, & Carlson, n.d.-b).

Medication

Although PTSD has an exogenous origin and likely requires psychological treatment, the disorder is nevertheless a true psychophysiological disorder (Perry, 1994) and psychotropic medication may, in selected cases, prove helpful in relieving PTSD and collateral symptoms (Davidson & March, 1997). Ideally, medications should decrease intrusions, avoidance, and anxious arousal; minimize impulsivity and improve sleep; treat secondary disorders; and facilitate cognitive and behavioral interventions. Unfortunately, other than clinical lore, little data exist to guide medicating children and adolescents (March, Amaya-Jackson, & Pynoos, 1996; Pfferbaum, 1997). A variety of psychopharmacological agents have been used to treat childhood posttraumatic stress symptoms and the associated symptoms of depression or panic, including propranolol (Famularo, Kinscherff, & Augustyn, 1988), carbamazepine (Looff, Grimley, Kuiler, Martin, & Shunfield, 1995), clonidine (DeBellis et al., 1994; Harmon & Riggs, 1996), and antidepressants (Brent et al., 1995). In adults, case reports and uncontrolled trials suggests that the benefits of conventional drug treatments in PTSD are quite modest (Davidson & March, 1997); clinical experience is similar for children and adolescents.

Inclusion of Parents

Parental emotional reaction to the traumatic event and parental support of the child are potentially powerful influences on the child's PTSD symptomatology (Cohen & Mannarino, 1996b; Burton, Foy, Bwanausi, Johnson, & Moore, 1994; Meyer, Blakeney, & Moore, 1994). Hence, most experts assert that inclusion of parents and/or supportive others in treatment is important for resolution of PTSD symptoms for children (American Academy of Child and Adolescent Psychiatry, 1998). At a minimum, including parents in treatment helps them monitor the child's symptomatology and learn appropriate behavioral management techniques, both in the intervals between treatment sessions and after therapy is terminated. In addition, helping parents resolve their emotional distress related to the trauma, to which they usually have had either direct or vicarious exposure, can help them be more perceptive and responsive to the child's emotional needs (Burman & Allen-Meares, 1994; Rizzone, Stoddard, Murphy, & Kruger, 1994). Many parents benefit from specific psychoeducation regarding their child's PTSD symptoms and how to manage them (Cohen & Mannarino, 1993; Deblinger & Heflin, 1996; Rigamer, 1986). Not surprisingly, parent interventions are considered imperative in the child abuse literature, where most authors recommend one or more parent-directed components (Berliner, 1997; Blom, 1986; Brent et al., 1995; Burman & Allen-Meares, 1994; Butler, Rizzi, & Handwerger, 1996; Cohen & Mannarino, 1993; Deblinger & Heflin, 1996; Friedrich, 1996b; Galante & Foa, 1986; Macksoud & Aber, 1996; Rigamer, 1986; Simons & Silveira, 1994; Terr, 1989).

Integrated Treatments

It is widely recognized that, of necessity, assessment and treatment of PTSD must address a variety of symptoms or dysfunctions beyond those related to

PTSD per se. For example, Friedrich (1996a) advocates an approach for sexually abused children that targets attachment issues, affect regulation, and self-perception. Sullivan and Evans (1994) argue for integrating trauma-focused interventions with 12-step interventions for use in adolescents with PTSD and chemical dependence. On the other hand, little or no empirical evidence supports combining treatments within or across treatment modalities. In particular, no empirical evidence supports the common clinical belief that the combination of medication management and psychotherapy is superior to psychotherapy alone.

Length of Treatment

Clinically, most children and adolescents with uncomplicated PTSD make substantial improvement with 12–20 sessions of PTSD-specific psychotherapy. Some authors have reported success with as few as three to six sessions of highly specific treatments (Chemtob, Nakashima, Hamada, & Carlson, n.d.-b; Saigh, 1986). A smaller number of children require long-term treatment. Children exposed to massive violence, intrafamilial homicide or suicide, prolonged abuse, or exposure to repetitively distressing events may require longer treatment than children who have experienced less traumatic exposure. The presence of preexisting psychopathology in the child or a parent, prior history of abuse, or ongoing exposure to a disruptive living situation may also suggest a need for intensive, longer term intervention. Long-term treatment can occur weekly or as "pulsed intervention" based on the child's response to treatment and clinical symptoms. Pulsed intervention assumes that brief therapy is suspended (rather than terminated) until further treatment becomes necessary—such as during developmental transitions, changes in living situation, or additional traumatic exposure. "Pulsing" the treatment helps encourage the development of child and parental competence by expressing confidence in the parent's ability to help the child through difficult episodes without reliance on therapy. Unfortunately, severe PTSD often requires arduous and critical dedication to treatment on the part of the child, parent, and therapist. Longer term therapy also may be necessary when issues related to capacity to trust and to form meaningful relationships are present. The length of treatment should be determined on an individual basis, with consideration given to the child's symptomatic improvement and achievement of age-appropriate development tasks.

METHOD OF COLLECTING DATA

This ensuing literature review has been adapted from the PTSD practice parameters developed by the American Academy of Child and Adolescent Psychiatry (1998), supplemented by new research identified through the following searches and expert review. Sources included searching MEDLINE and Psychological Abstracts, reviewing the bibliographies of book chapters and review articles, soliciting source materials from colleagues with expertise in PTSD in children, and a search of the National Center on PTSD PILOTS database. The searches of MEDLINE and Psychological Abstracts were conducted in May 1998, using the text terms "posttraumatic stress disorder," "children," and "adolescents." References from these articles and chapters were then reviewed, as were 12 full-length books.

SUMMARY OF LITERATURE

Clinical Evidence

While it is beyond the scope of this chapter to review the extensive clinical literature on the treatment of pediatric PTSD, numerous techniques have proven valuable in clinical work (Yule & Canterbury, 1994). In general, a "prevention–intervention" model incorporating triage for children exposed to stressor events, supporting and strengthening coping skills for anticipated grief/trauma responses, treating other disorders that may develop or exacerbate in the context of PTSD as well as acute PTSD symptoms, is recommended (Pynoos & Nader, 1993). While the horror of the trauma can never be undone—hence, "cure" may not be the appropriate treatment goal—victims can become well-functioning survivors if appropriate treatment is given and facilitation of healing takes place.

A number of authors have focused on the value of providing an acute crisis response to parents, teachers, and/or children in groups at school, in the hospital, or in other community settings (Blom, 1986; Galante & Foa, 1986; Goenjian et al., 1997; LeGreca, Vemberg, Silverman, & Prinstein, 1996; Pynoos & Nader, 1988; Rigamer, 1986; Stallard & Law, 1993; Stoddard, 1996; Sullivan & Evans, 1994; Yule & Udwin, 1991). Many of these interventions used convenience samples in schools or towns exposed to a common traumatic event. Group interventions in such situations provide a timely intervention to the largest possible number of exposed children. The rationale for crisis intervention following this type of trauma is that immediate discussion of the event and its impact may prevent the development of avoidance and other PTSD symptoms in large numbers of exposed children. The opportunity for screening and referral may be particularly helpful. Yule (1992a) and Yule and Udwin (1991) found that screened children in high-risk groups were far more likely to follow up when offered treatment.

Trauma-focused psychosocial interventions from a variety of theoretical perspectives are widely described in the clinical literature (see, e.g., Cohen & Mannarino, 1993; Deblinger & Heflin, 1996; James, 1989; Saigh, 1992; Terr, 1990; Yule & Canterbury, 1994). These approaches do not always focus only on PTSD or posttraumatic stress symptoms, but often include a range of trauma impacts. The treatments may be delivered in a variety of modalities (individual, group, family), use directive or more nondirective approaches, rely on verbal or nonverbal methods, and be short- or long-term. They all focus specifically on emotional and cognitive processing of the traumatic event.

Preliminary studies have indicated that some children with PTSD exhibit physiological abnormalities similar to those seen in adults with PTSD (see, e.g., Perry, 1994). These reports have led clinicians to prescribe a variety of medications for children with PTSD. Marmar, Foy, Kagan, and Pynoos (1993) and DeBellis and colleagues (1994a; DeBellis, Lefter, Trickett, & Putnam, 1994b) suggested, but did not empirically evaluate, the possibility that an alpha-2 adrenergic agonist such as clonidine might be more effective than psychostimulants for ADHD symptoms in sexually abused and other children with comorbid PTSD. Brent and colleagues (1995) argued that antidepressants might be helpful for some children with PTSD, particularly those with a predominance of depressive or panic disorder symptoms. To date, there have been no randomized controlled trials of antidepressants or other drug treatments for PTSD in children.

Identification, much less treatment, of dissociative symptoms described in some children with chronic PTSD is controversial. Clinicians should be aware that some children with PTSD have prominent dissociative symptoms that may take the form of hallucinations or disorganized thinking and behavior. These symptoms may be difficult to distinguish from psychotic states and should be ruled out as manifestations of PTSD. There have been no controlled studies evaluating treatment approaches for dissociation. Because of the complexity of treating PTSD complicated by dissociative symptoms, clinicians should consult additional references such as Putnam (1997) and Silberg (1996).

Not all behavioral and emotional problems in children with PTSD are caused by traumatic events. In treating children with PTSD or PTSD symptoms, it is essential that the clinician recognize the presence of preexisting and comorbid psychiatric disorders and their interaction with PTSD symptoms. When trauma-focused therapy does not result in improvement or directly target these other difficulties, therapists should administer proven interventions for these conditions as well.

Empirical Evidence

Very few empirical studies of trauma-focused interventions in children and adolescents have been conducted to date. These studies have not always required that subjects meet diagnostic criteria for PTSD but have instead assessed PTSD symptoms, as well as other related conditions, including depressive symptoms, and general emotional and behavioral problems. Thus, the degree of methodological rigor varies considerably in the following studies, with some of the single-case studies showing greater methodological sophistication than randomized designs, but all use defined targeted symptoms and at least attempt to assess change using valid and reliable measures. Tables 6.1, 6.2, and 6.3 present estimates of effect sizes for studies involving true untreated, treated, and within-group comparisons, respectively. We summarize the literature based on strength of evidence for treatment efficacy.

Clinical Trials (Pre–Post; No Comparison Group)

PSYCHOSOCIAL TREATMENTS

Single-Case Subject-Level Designs. Saigh (1986, 1989) used a multiple baseline across traumatic scenes design to show reductions in posttraumatic stress as a result of a multifaceted behavioral treatment package (parent–child education, *in vitro* and relaxation training, and debriefing) with children traumatized in a war zone. Similarly, Farrell, Hains, and Davies (1998) evaluated effectiveness of cognitive-behavioral interventions with 4 sexually abused children using a multiple baseline design, with pretreatment, posttreatment, and 3-month follow-up assessments. PTSD symptomatology decreased in all of the children. There are numerous pre–post treatment studies with groups of sexually abused children, almost all of which of which demonstrate improvement for at least some symptoms (Finkelhor & Berliner, 1995).

Single-Case Group Designs. Using a single case across time, setting, and age design, March, Amaya-Jackson, Murray, and Schulte (1998) examined the efficacy of an 18-week, group-administered, school-based, manualized cognitive-behavioral intervention with 17 youth who had experienced a single-incident stressor. The authors used a schoolwide selection to treatment procedure conducted in two elementary and two junior high schools, and entered children who were positive for PTSD into the therapeutic regimen. Fourteen of 17 subjects completed treatment. Of these, 8 (57%) no longer met DSM-IV criteria for PTSD immediately posttreatment; 12 of 14 subjects (86%) were free of PTSD at 6-month follow-up. On intent-to-treat analyses, treatment produced a robust beneficial effect at posttreatment on the Clinician-Administered PTSD Scale—Child Version (CAPS-C), with additional improvement accruing at follow-up. Improvements of a similar magnitude were seen for depression, anxiety, and anger. Locus of control remained external from pre- to posttreatment but became strongly internal at follow-up.

Extended Pretreatment Baseline Designs. Two studies with sexually abused children and one study of children suffering a single-incident stressor specifically targeted posttraumatic stress symptoms and attempted to address the problem of having no comparison group. Lanktree and Briere (1995)

TABLE 6.1. Comparisons with Control Groups

Study quality	Authors	Target population	Sessions	Dependent measure	Type of treatment	Sample size	Effect size	Comment
A[c]	Deblinger, Lippman, & Steer (1996)	Sexually abused children	12	Diagnostic interview	Individual Parent COMB Community	22 22 24 21	C vs. P 0.42 C vs. COMB 0.04 P vs. COMB 0.33 Pending data	Significantly greater decrease in PTSD sx in children receiving experimental tx.
A[c]	Cohen & Mannarino (1996a)	Sexually abused preschool children	12	CSBI	CBT Community	CBT 39 NST 28	0.59	PTSD sx, sexualized and nonsexualized behavior problems decreased significantly only in the experimental tx group with group × time differences in PTSD and behavior sx.
A	Berliner & Saunders (1996)	Sexually abused children	10	CITES-R	Enhanced sexual-abuse-specific CBT; group. Children randomized to standard sexual-abuse-specific CBT	80	N/A	No group × time differences in PTSD or anxiety sx.
A[i]	Celano, Hazzard, Webb, & McCall (1996)	32; sexually abused children	8	CITES-R	CBT Usual tx	15 17	0.21	No group × time differences in self-report or parent-reported PTSD sx.
A[c]	Cohen & Mannarino (1998)	49; sexually abused children	12	CSBI	Sexual-abuse-specific CBT; individual child and parent	CBT 30 NST 19	0.2	No group × time differences in PTSD or anxiety sx. Group × time differences in depression and social competence.
B[c]	Field, Seligman, Scafedi, & Schanberg (1996)	Children exposed to a hurricane	8	No PTSD-dependent measure	Massage therapy, attention control	60	N/A	No PTSD-dependent measure.

Note. Superscript *i* indicates intent-to-treat analyses; superscript *c* indicates completer analyses. tx, treatment; sx, symptoms; C, community; P, parent; COMB, combination; CBT, cognitive-behavioral therapy; CSBI, Child Sexual Behavior Inventory; NST, nondirective supportive therapy; CITES-R, Children's Impact of Events Scale—Revised.

TABLE 6.2. Comparisons with No-Treatment Controls

Study quality	Authors	Target population	Sessions	Dependent measure	Type of treatment	Sample size	Effect size	Comment
A[c]	Chemtob, Hamada, & Nakashima (n.d.)	Children exposed to a hurricane	4 weekly group or individual sessions in school	PTSD Reaction Inventory	CBT WLC	—	—	PTSD sx decreased acutely and at follow-up in CBT condition relative to WLC
A[c]	Chemtob, Nakashima, Hamada, & Carlson (in press)	Children exposed to a hurricane	4 weekly individual sessions	PTSD Reaction Inventory	EMDR WLC	17 15	1.34	PTSD sx and anxiety decreased compared to wait list; 56% no longer met PTSD criteria
B[i]	Goenjian et al. (1997)	Adolescents exposed to massive earthquake	4½-hr group sessions; 2 individual sessions over 3 wk	PTSD Reaction Inventory	Trauma tx Comparison schools	35 29	0.41	PTSD sx decreased in tx group, worsened in comparison group; control group became more depressed

Note. Superscript *i* indicates intent-to-treat analyses; superscript *c* indicates completer analyses. tx, treatment; sx, symptoms; CBT, cognitive-behavioral therapy; EMDR, eye movement desensitization and reprocessing; WLC, wait-list control.

TABLE 6.3. Pre- to Posttreatment Comparisons

Study quality	Authors	Target population	Sessions	Dependent measure	Type of treatment	Sample size	Effect size	Comment
B[c]	Deblinger, McLeer, & Henry (1990)	Sexually abused children	12 weekly	Diagnostic interview	Individual CBT	19	2.8	Depression and behavior problems decreased.
B[i]	March, Amaya-Jackson, Murray, & Schulte (1998)	Adolescents with PTSD after single-incident stressor	18 weekly	CAPS	Group CBT	17	1.15	Depression, behavior problems, anger decreased; locus of control external to internal.
C	Stallard & Law (1993)	Survivors of a minibus crash	3	Psychological debriefing	None; compared pre-tx scores with other treated traumatized children.	7	N/A	PTSD sx, anxiety, and depression decreased.

Note. Superscript *i* indicates intent-to-treat analyses; superscript *c* indicates completer analyses. BT, cognitive-behavioral therapy; CAPS, Clinician-Administered PTSD Scale.

121

followed 105 children receiving a "trauma-specific" treatment. The treatment was not manualized, nor were there procedures for treatment adherence. Only 19 children were still in treatment at the 1-year assessment point. The authors found that children improved on a trauma-specific symptom checklist. Controlling for time since the abuse, the authors concluded that the period of treatment accounted for improvement. Deblinger, McLeer, and Henry (1990) tested a 12-session cognitive-behavioral, sexual-abuse-specific treatment that was manualized with 19 sexually abused girls. The authors used a repeated pretreatment assessment method to demonstrate that symptom abatement only occurred following active therapeutic intervention.

Historical Control Designs. Two studies of acute school-based interventions with disaster survivors used comparative data to demonstrate preliminary effectiveness results. Yule (1992a) compared children in a school that welcomed intervention and held a debriefing meeting for all survivors and two small, open-ended, cognitive-behaviorally based groups, with children in a school where there had been no outside help. The children in the treatment school had significantly lower posttraumatic stress scores and fear scores. Stallard and Law (1993) assessed adolescents receiving a group-administered psychological debriefing for minibus crash survivors and reported significant reductions at posttest in trauma, anxiety, and depression symptoms, using the scores of children in the Yule (1992a) study for comparison purposes.

PSYCHOPHARMACOLOGICAL TREATMENTS

Case Reports. Horrigan (1996) reported an open study in which a long-acting alpha-2 agonist, guanfacine, was successful in reducing nightmares in a 7-year-old child with PTSD. Famularo, Kinscherff, and Fenton (1988) described modest decreases in PTSD symptomatology in 11 sexually and/or physically abused children following a 5-week course of propranolol, although symptoms reappeared following cessation of the medication. Looff, Grimley, Kuiler, Martin, and Shunfield (1995) reported that carbamazepine at serum levels of 10.0 to 11.5 μg/ml resulted in complete remission of symptoms in 22 out of 28 children with PTSD. These findings were complicated by the fact that several of the children were concurrently taking Ritalin, clonidine, selective serotonin reuptake inhibitors (SSRIs), or tricyclic antidepressants. Harmon and Riggs (1996) reported a decrease in at least some PTSD symptoms in all 7 children included in an uncontrolled clinical trial using clonidine patches.

Single-Case or Between-Group Controlled Studies. There are no between-group or single-case controlled studies of medications for pediatric PTSD.

Controlled Clinical Trials (Pre–Post; Comparison Group)

PSYCHOSOCIAL TREATMENTS

Nonrandomized Comparison Group. Goenjian and colleagues (1997) tested a school-based grief/trauma-focused cognitive-behavioral intervention to decrease chronic PTSD and depressive symptoms in 64 adolescents following a catastrophically destructive earthquake. Children in four schools near the epicenter of the earthquake were evaluated 1½ years after the earthquake; children in two of the schools were then provided with treatment, while children in the remaining two schools were untreated. Pretreatment levels of PTSD symptoms and depression were high in both groups. The treatment included direct exploration of the trauma, relaxation and desensitization procedures, resolution of grief through focusing on nontraumatic memories, and group support through recognition of the commonality of PTSD symptoms among peers. The treated group experienced significant improvement in PTSD and depressive symptoms, whereas these symptoms significantly worsened in the untreated group.

Randomized Clinical Trial with No-Treatment Control Conditions. Three studies have randomized children to an experimental and a no-treatment condition. In all three cases, the experimental treatment produced positive results. Because no alternative treatment was tested, it is not possible to ascribe the results to the specific nature of the intervention versus nonspecific effects of an active treatment.

Field, Seligman, Scafedi, and Schanberg (1996) investigated the impact of massage therapy with children exposed to a hurricane. The authors randomly assigned 50 children to massage therapy or to a video attention-control condition. Prior to treatment, both groups scored in the severe range for posttraumatic stress symptoms. The massage therapy group experienced significantly more improvement than the control group on posttreatment scores, one of which was the Revised Children's Manifest Anxiety Scale (RCMAS). For a variety of reasons, including no PTSD-specific dependent measure and the lack of blind evaluations, this study is less convincing with respect to potential efficacy than some of the single-case designs.

Two years after a catastrophic natural disaster (hurricane), Chemtob and colleagues used a repeated-measures, randomized, lagged-groups design to evaluate a brief, manual-guided group psychosocial intervention that, by description, was largely cognitive-behavioral, administered by specially trained school counselors to highly symptomatic children identified via schoolwise screening (Chemtob, Hamada, & Nakashima, n.d.). Children awaiting treatment served as wait-list controls and provided treatment replications when treated. Treatment effectiveness was assessed using (1) a children's self-report inventory of trauma symptoms, (2) a semistructured clinical interview, and (3) teachers' ratings of classroom behaviors. In the follow-up 1 year later, consistent with self-reports, interviewer evaluation indicated that the treated children had significantly fewer trauma symptoms than untreated (wait-list) children. Similarly, teacher ratings indicated that among treated children, a number of key classroom behaviors significantly improved compared to wait-list children. Reduction in symptoms was maintained at 1-year follow-up.

Using a similar randomized, lagged-groups design, Chemtob and colleagues later provided three individual sessions of EMDR treatment to 32 children who were (1) treatment nonresponders to the earlier treatment intervention and (2) met clinical criteria for PTSD (Chemtob, Nakashima, Hamada, & Carlson, in press). The Children's Reaction Inventory (CRI) was the primary measure of the treatment's effect on PTSD symptoms. Associated symptoms were measured using the RCMAS and the Children's Depression Inventory (CDI). There were substantial reductions in both groups' CRI scores following treatment. Also significant, though more modest, reductions occurred in RCMAS and CDI total scores. Treatment gains were maintained at 6-month follow-up.

Randomized Clinical Trials against Comparison Treatments. Recently, studies contrasting the treatment of PTSD in sexually abused children with CBT and control treatments have entered the literature. While the published investigations are not free of methodological problems (e.g., lack of blind evaluators and use of completer rather than intent-to-treat [ITT] analyses), they are significantly strengthened by rigorous assessment methods, randomized treatment assignment, and manualized treatment and adherence/fidelity procedures.

Deblinger, Lippman, and Steer (1996) examined the target of an experimental study using a 12-week trauma-focused, cognitive-behavioral treatment with 100 sexually abused children. The experimental treatment was manualized, and rigorous treatment adherence procedures were used. Subjects were randomly assigned to one of four treatment conditions: child only, parent only, child and parent, or routine community service. Results indicated that although all groups improved on PTSD symptoms, children in the two conditions that received direct, trauma-specific treatment demonstrated significantly greater improvement in PTSD symptoms than children in the other two conditions. This study also found that when the parent received treatment, there was significantly more improvement in parent-reported externalizing symptoms and child-reported depressive symptoms.

Several studies have examined alternative treatments. Three studies have compared a sexual abuse–specific, trauma-focused treatment with a nonspecific supportive therapy, while one study compared a standard and an enhanced trauma-specific treatment.

Cohen and Mannarino (1996a) evaluated trauma-focused cognitive-behavioral treatment for 68 sexually abused preschoolers and their parents. Children were randomly assigned to either the CBT intervention or a nondirective support therapy condition. The treatments were manualized and rigorous adherence procedures were used. Child PTSD symptoms and sexually inappropriate behaviors, as reported by parents, significantly decreased by posttreatment in the CBT group only (Cohen & Mannarino, 1996a).

Two other controlled studies with school-age children comparing manualized CBT trauma-specific and nonspecific treatments failed to find significant group × time effects in impact on anxiety or PTSD symptoms (Celano, Hazzard, Webb, & McCall, 1996; Cohen & Mannarino, 1998). Cohen and Mannarino (1998) randomly assigned 49 sexually abused children and their caretakers to a 12-session, individually administered intervention, and Celano and colleagues (1996) randomly assigned 32 sexually abused girls and their parents to an 8-session intervention in which therapy time was either split between children and parents or conjoint. Both studies used manuals, rigorous treatment-adherence procedures, and blind evaluators. One explanation for the null findings is that older children in therapy for sexual abuse spontaneously engage in exposure-type activities, thus reducing the likelihood of finding a treatment-specific effect. Another explanation may be that the number of subjects completing treatment in these studies did not provide adequate power to detect group × time effects. The studies did find that trauma-specific treatment was more effective in reducing depression and improving social competence (Cohen & Mannarino, 1998), in reducing parental self-blame and expectations of negative impact of abuse, and in increasing abuse-related parental support to the child (Celano et al., 1996).

Berliner and Saunders (1996) examined whether the addition of the specific techniques of gradual exposure and stress inoculation training improved outcomes compared to a standard, abuse-focused treatment for 80 school-age sexually abused children. The treatments were manualized and rigorous treatment adherence procedures were used. Contrary to the hypothesis, there were no group × time differences in PTSD or anxiety symptoms. These authors concluded that since most children did not exhibit high pretreatment levels of these symptoms, there may have been either a floor effect or the standard treatment contained sufficient exposure and coping skills components to obviate the need for more specific strategies with children who have moderate symptom levels. Another explanation for the lack of significant differences is that the standard, abuse-focused control-group treatment contained inadvertent exposure elements, which made the two treatments insufficiently distinct to detect differences.

Cross-Modality Comparative Treatment Trials

Data on the comparative efficacy of psychotherapy versus medication, or the combination of the two approaches, are not yet practical given the limited state of knowledge regarding the efficacy of psychotherapy even more so medication treatment for pediatric PTSD. Two probably underpowered and otherwise poorly designed studies of different psychotherapy approaches have, however, been published. A randomized trial comparing group and individual play therapy for sexually abused children, without specific reference to PTSD symptoms, found differences in improvement for group therapy on only one outcome measure (Perez, 1998). In a study comparing sexually abused children randomly assigned to family network therapy and family network therapy plus group therapy, Monck and colleagues (1994) reported no differences in child treatment outcomes. PTSD symptoms were not specifically assessed and no firm conclusions regarding treatment approach (individual, group, or family) can yet be drawn.

SUMMARY

Like adults, children and adolescents develop PTSD or PTSD symptoms following a variety of severe stressors. Because DSM-IV PTSD criteria may not be sufficiently sensitive to developmental issues, especially in younger children, questions have been appropriately raised about whether current diagnostic criteria adequately capture posttrauma impacts in children. A variety of moderator and mediator variables also have been proposed vis-à-vis the development of PTSD after exposure to a high-magnitude stressor; none have been adequately explored with respect to tracking treatment outcome. No evidence exists that a particular treatment approach (e.g., individual, group, or family) for delivery of the psychotherapeutic treatment is superior. The best available evidence supports outpatient, trauma-focused psychotherapy containing cognitive-behavioral components, including exposure strategies, stress management/relaxation, cognitive/narrative restructuring, and a parental treatment component as the preferred treatment approach. While psychotropic medications, particularly clonidine and the SSRIs are widely used for pediatric PTSD, current empirical support is inadequate to justify the use of any particular medication to treat PTSD symptoms in children or adolescents. Involvement of parents in treatment has not been shown specifically to ameliorate child PTSD symptoms except in preschoolers, but is likely to be necessary for improvements in PTSD, general emotional/behavioral functioning, and reduction of depressive symptoms in many, if not most, traumatized youth.

PROPOSED GUIDELINES FOR TREATMENT

Overview

The following recommendations regarding clinical interventions for children with PTSD symptoms are based on the available empirical evidence and supported by clinical experience. Because of the diagnostic uncertainties associated with PTSD in children, many experts believe that treatment for significant posttraumatic symptomatology is likely to prove helpful even when full DSM-IV diagnostic criteria for PTSD are not met. In particular, children and adolescents who have PTSD symptoms and concomitant functional impairment secondary to the symptoms (e.g., in family or school role performance, social relationships, moods/behaviors) can benefit from the recommended interventions. With the caveat that preschool children require adaptation of diagnostic methods, if not criteria, future treatment–outcome research in this area might profitably focus on children and adolescents with a DSM-IV diagnosis of PTSD using randomized designs and rigorous assessment methods.

Assessment

A careful assessment beginning with the presenting complaint and moving through a DSM-IV five-axis diagnostic assessment to a tailored treatment plan based on a systematic assessment of problem areas is the cornerstone of treatment planning. It is essential to interview the child, in addition to the parents, with regard to the presence of PTSD and related symptoms (Earls, Smith, Reich, & Jung, 1988).

Assessment and treatment with traumatized children, regardless of the condition, disorder, or functional impairment, should be conducted in a developmentally sensitive manner (McNally, 1996). This means that the modalities and mechanisms for communication should be adjusted to the child's developmental level. For example, young children often rely on non-verbal methods of communication and participate more fully when play, drawing, or acting out are used as the vehicle for clinical strategies. On the other hand, older children and adolescents can be offended when therapists assume that they prefer to play rather than talk, or infantilize the treatment process. Therapists must also be aware of the tasks and issues of particular developmental stages, and the potential for developmental derailment that is associated with the impact of traumatic events. Restoring normal developmental functioning is always a goal of child treatment (Pynoos & Nader, 1993).

Parental involvement in treatment is highly relevant to developmental trajectory. Parents should routinely be included in the assessment process, but the level and nature of involvement in treatment should be based on developmental stage, level of family functioning independent of PTSD, the extent to which PTSD disrupts family processes, and the type of emotional or behavioral problem targeted for treatment. Parents or other primary caretakers necessarily must be included in the therapeutic process when externalizing behaviors (due to PTSD or other sources) require behavioral contingency management to carry out effective interventions.

Treatment Setting

Children with PTSD symptomatology should be the direct recipients of interventions to ensure maximum treatment gains. While empirical evidence does not support a preference for individual, family, or group therapy, in most cases, treatment likely will be administered as individual therapy. For abused children, interventions may initially be delivered as individual therapy and subsequently be reinforced by rehearsal and practice with parents. This approach may also be helpful for other groups of traumatized children, as it enhances communication with and reliance on parents if traumatic exposure or symptoms recur in the future. Group therapy in the school setting may be optimal for children who have experienced a common trauma, for example, a hurricane or school shooting. Community- and school-based brief interventions also can serve as a screening mechanism to identify high-risk children who should be referred for formal therapy. While psychological debriefing following a disaster is ordinarily group administered in school or community settings, it is important to note that psychological debriefing after sudden trauma lacks adequate empirical support in the pediatric population and has the potential to exacerbate traumatic reactions rather than to facilitate rapid recovery.

Psychoeducation

All recommended treatment approaches incorporate psychoeducation as a component, usually at the beginning of treatment. Posttraumatic reactions are explained and normalized, and children and adults are provided an opportunity to express feelings, ask questions, and receive support.

Level A–B Treatment

As of this writing, cognitive-behavioral treatment approaches (CBT) have the strongest empirical evidence for efficacy in resolving PTSD symptoms in children. CBT may, therefore, be considered the first-line approach, either alone or in combination with other forms of treatment. It is unclear from the existing research, however, which components of CBT are the "active ingredients." Although most evaluated forms of CBT have used exposure techniques, it is not yet established how much and how explicit the exposure component needs to be, or how many repetitions are necessary to obtain therapeutic effect. There is some evidence from the research that the opportunity to talk about the traumatic event in a supportive environment, even without structured, hierarchical, or prolonged exposure, may be helpful. In other instances, the avoidance or reluctance may not be due to anxiety; therefore, insistence on repeated recounting of the details may be unnecessary and even cause iatrogenic side effects (e.g., reluctance due to embarrassment, irritation about having to describe the event to so many professionals).

Similarly, the role of cognitive restructuring or anxiety management training (e.g., relaxation training, constructive self-talk) relative to exposure-based interventions has not been adequately evaluated empirically in children.

Other Treatments

Other psychosocial treatments, such as psychodynamic psychotherapy, art therapy, or group psychotherapy, are supported by anecdotal evidence but cannot on this basis be recommended as first-line treatments for pediatric PTSD.

Similarly, due to the lack of adequate empirical data, clinicians must rely on judgment to determine the appropriateness of psychopharmacological interventions, usually basing intervention strategies on the pattern of comorbidity in children with PTSD who have prominent depressive, anxiety, panic, and/or ADHD symptoms (Donnelly, Amaya-Jackson, & March, 1999). As a general practice, medication should be selected on the basis of established practice in treating the comorbid condition (e.g., antidepressants for children with prominent depressive symptoms). Because of their favorable side-effects profile and evidence supporting effectiveness in treating both depressive and anxiety disorders, SSRIs often are the first psychotropic medication chosen for treating pediatric PTSD. Clonidine may be helpful for some children and adolescents with prominent hyperarousal symptoms, especially elevated startle responses.

Level of Care

There is currently no clear evidence regarding the proper length of treatment. Some acute interventions, including psychological debriefing, consist of one to several sessions. As with most cognitive-behavioral interventions for pediatric mental disorders (Hibbs & Jensen, 1996), the majority of empirically evaluated interventions have been between 8 and 16 sessions. This does not mean that some children, especially those who have experienced prolonged victimization, have poor premorbid adjustment, comorbid conditions, or exhibit chronic PTSD with predominantly dissociative features, will not require much longer interventions. Clinical judgment based on intervention target and progress should be used in determining treatment length.

Indications and Contraindications

Indications for the interventions described earlier, except for psychological debriefing, are the presence of significant PTSD symptoms with some degree of functional impairment. It is not yet clear whether all children with such symptoms require treatment, since some children appear to recover over time without formal intervention. However, because there are currently no reliable means of predicting, in individual cases, which children will have persistent symptomatology or develop symptoms at a later point, it is recommended by most, but not all, experts that symptomatic youth with Criterion A experiences be offered treatment.

Contraindications are generally specific to the treatment modality in question. For example, cognitive therapy is unlikely to be helpful in the severely retarded child; clonidine would be contraindicated in the child at risk for hypotension secondary to medical (heart disease) or nonmedical (dehydration with athletics) causes. With respect to PTSD per se, comorbidity may be the primary problem—defined as causing the greatest degree of present-state functional impairment—and must, as a result, be addressed before specific PTSD treatment(s) can be applied. For example, children with comorbid depression and suicidality should probably not receive a trauma-focused, exposure-based intervention until the depressive symptomatology has abated with either psychotherapy, medication with an SSRI, or both. Similarly, children with substance abuse disorders should be treated for those problems prior to the initiation of trauma-focused interventions. Though not without controversy, most experts believe that children who do not report or recall a traumatic event, even if they may exhibit some posttraumatic symptoms, probably should not have a treatment focused on a presumed traumatic event.

FUTURE DIRECTIONS

There are several important areas for future inquiry with regard to the optimal treatment of PTSD and PTSD symptoms in children. One area concerns the nature and assessment of PTSD in children (American Academy of Child and Adolescent Psychiatry, 1998; March, 1999). Currently, there is not an ideal instrument for determining the presence or absence of PTSD in children. The existing measures have been used primarily in research contexts and may not be easily incorporated into clinical settings. In addition, there are questions about the diagnosis of PTSD and whether further modification of DSM-IV criteria is necessary to reflect the developmental differences in posttraumatic impact, especially for young children. Consensus has not yet been achieved regarding the level and severity of PTSD symptoms that are clinically significant or require formal intervention.

Most treatment outcome research so far has focused on cognitive-behavioral interventions. The findings are consistent with the therapy-outcome literature in general that finds cognitive-behavioral interventions to be effective. However, it has yet to be established whether it is specific components of this approach that are the active ingredients in reducing PTSD symptoms and whether different components are more effective with certain symptom patterns or for children of specific developmental stages. Studies that analyze and compare the different treatment elements with a range of ages and symptom presentations would be especially helpful in designing optimal treatment regimens.

Trials of different medicines, alone or in combination with other forms of treatment, would be especially desirable to elucidate the comparative risks and benefits of psychotropic medications with this population.

Having demonstrated that treatment outcome studies are possible in this population, treatment research within and across modalities must move toward greater methodological rigor, as exemplified in other studies of pediatric anxiety disorders (Chorpita, Barlow, Albano, & Daleiden, 1998). Furthermore, larger multisite trials will be needed to examine potential moderators and mediators of treatment outcome (March & Curry, 1998).

Identifying effective interventions in controlled studies is only one step toward improving treatment outcomes among children who suffer from PTSD or PTSD symptoms. It is necessary that proven treatments be transported from the laboratory to the clinic (Kendall & Southam-Gerow, 1995). Field studies that evaluate how treatments are delivered under more usual conditions, or with children and families who may have more complicated circumstances, will be necessary, as will attention to the cost-effectiveness of different treatment approaches.

REFERENCES

Almquist, K., & Brandell-Forsberg, M. (1997). Refugee children in Sweden: Posttraumatic stress disorder in Iranian preschool children exposed to organized violence. *Child Abuse and Neglect, 21,* 351–366

Amaya-Jackson, L. (1995). Post-traumatic stress disorder in adolescents. *Adolescent Medicine, 6*(2), 251–270.

American Academy of Child and Adolescent Psychiatry. (1998). Summary of the practice parameters for the assessment and treatment of children and adolescents with post-traumatic stress disorder. *Journal of the American Academy of Child and Adolescent Psychiatry, 37*(9), 997–1001.

American Psychiatric Association. (1980). *Diagnostic and statistical manual of mental disorders* (3rd ed.). Washington, DC: Author.

American Psychiatric Association. (1994). *Diagnostic and statistical manual of mental disorders* (4th ed.). Washington, DC: Author.

Arroyo, W., & Eth, S. (1985). Children traumatized by Central American warfare. In S. Eth & R. S. Pynoos (Eds.), *Posttraumatic stress disorder in children* (pp. 101–120). Washington, DC: American Psychiatric Press.

Azarian, A., Miller, T. W., & Skriptchenko-Gregorian, V. (1996). Baseline assessment of children traumatized by the Armenian earthquake. *Child Psychiatry and Human Development, 27,* 29–41

Barron, R., & Kenny, D. (1986). The moderator–mediator variable distinction in social psychological research: Conceptual, strategic and statistical considerations. *Journal of Personality and Social Psychology, 51*(6), 1173–1182.

Benedek, E. (1985). Children and psychic trauma: A brief review of contemporary thinking. In S. Eth & R. S. Pynoos (Eds.), *Posttraumatic stress disorder in children* (pp. 1–16). Washington, DC: American Psychiatric Press.

Berliner, L. (1997). Intervention with children who experience trauma. In D. Cicchetti & S. Toth (Eds.), *The effects of trauma and the developmental process* (pp. 491–514). New York: Wiley.

Berliner, L., & Saunders, B. E. (1996). Treating fear and anxiety in sexually abused children: Results of a controlled 2 year follow-up study. *Child Maltreatment, 1,* 294–309

Bleiberg, E. (1994). Borderline disorders in children and adolescents: The concept, the diagnosis, and the controversies. *Bulletin of the Menninger Clinic, 58*(2), 169–196.

Blom, G. A. (1986). A school disaster—intervention and research aspects. *Journal of the American Academy of Child and Adolescent Psychiatry, 25,* 336–345.

Brent, D. A., Perper, J. A., Moritz, G., Liotus, L., Richardson, D., Cannobio, R., Schweers, J., & Roth, C. (1995). Posttraumatic stress disorder in peers of adolescent suicide victims. *Journal of the American Academy of Child and Adolescent Psychiatry, 34,* 209–215.

Burman, S., & Allen-Meares, P. (1994). Neglected victims of murder: Children's witness to parental homicide. *Social Work, 39,* 28–34.

Burton, D., Foy D., Bwanausi, C., Johnson, J., & Moore, L. (1994). The relationship between traumatic exposure, family dysfunction, and posttraumatic stress symptoms in male juvenile offenders. *Journal of Traumatic Stress, 7,* 83–93.

Butler, R. W., Rizzi, L. P., & Handwerger, B. A. (1996). The assessment of posttraumatic stress disorder in pediatric cancer patients and survivors. *Journal of Pediatric Psychology, 21,* 499–504.

Cahill, C., Llewelyn, S. P., & Pearson, C. (1991). Long-term effects of sexual abuse which occurred in childhood: A review. *British Journal of Clinical Psychology, 30,* 117–130.

Ceci, S. J., Leichtman, M., & White, T. (1996). Interviewing preschoolers: Remembrance of things planted. In D. P. Peters (Ed.), *The child witness in context: Cognitive, social, and legal perspectives.* Dordrecht, Netherlands: Kluwer Academic.

Celano, M., Hazzard, A., Webb, C., & McCall, C. (1996). Treatment of traumagenic beliefs among sexually abused girls and their mothers: An evaluation study. *Journal of Abnormal Child Psychology, 24,* 1–16.

Chemtob, C., Hamada, R., & Nakashima, J. (n.d.). *Psychosocial intervention for post-disaster trauma symptoms in elementary school children: A controlled field study.* Unpublished manuscript.

Chemtob, C., Nakashima, J., Hamada, R., & Carlson, J. (in press). Brief treatment for elementary school schildren with disaster-related posttraumatic stress disorder: A field study. *Journal of Clinic Psychology.*

Chorpita, B., Barlow, D., Albano, A., & Daleiden, E. (1998). Methodological strategies in child clinical trials: Advancing the efficacy and effectiveness of psychosocial treatments. *Journal of Abnormal Child Psychology, 26*(1), 7–16.

Clark, D. B., Bukstein, O. G., Smith, M. G., Kaczynski, N. A., Mezzich, A. C., & Donovan, J. E. (1995). Identifying anxiety disorders in adolescents hospitalized for alcohol abuse or dependence. *Psychiatric Services, 46,* 618–620.

Cohen, J. A., & Mannarino, A. P. (1993). A treatment model for sexually abused preschoolers. *Journal of Interpersonal Violence, 8,* 115–131.

Cohen, J. A., & Mannarino, A. P. (1996a). A treatment outcome study for sexually abused preschool children: Initial findings. *Journal of the American Academy of Child and Adolescent Psychiatry, 35,* 42–50.

Cohen, J. A., & Mannarino, A. P. (1996b). Factors that mediate treatment outcome of sexually abused preschool children. *Journal of the American Academy of Child and Adolescent Psychiatry, 35*(10), 1402–1410.

Cohen, J. A., & Mannarino, A. P. (1998). Interventions for sexually abused children: Initial treatment outcome findings. *Child Maltreatment, 3,* 17–26.

Cuffe, S. P., McCullough, E. L., & Pumariega, A. J. (1994). Comorbidity of attention deficit hyperactivity disorder and posttraumatic stress disorder. *Journal of Child and Family Studies, 3,* 327–336.

Davidson, J. R. T., & March, J. S. (1997). Traumatic stress disorders. In A. Tasman, J. Kay, & J. A. Lieberman (Eds.), *Psychiatry* (Vol 2, pp. 1085–1098). Philadelphia: Saunders.

DeBellis, M. D., Chrousos, G. P., Dorn, L. D., Burke, L., Helmers, K., Kling, M. A., Trickett, P. K., & Putnam, F. W. (1994). H-P-A axis dysregulation in sexually abused girls. *Journal of Clinical Endocrinology and Metabolism, 78,* 249–255.

DeBellis, M. D., Lefter, L., Trickett, P. K., & Putnam, F. W. (1994). Urinary catecholamine excretion in sexually abused girls. *Journal of the American Academy of Child and Adolescent Psychiatry, 33,* 320–327.

Deblinger, E., & Heflin, A. H. (1996). *Cognitive behavioral interventions for treating sexually abused children.* Thousand Oaks, CA: Sage.

Deblinger, E., Lippman, J., & Steer, R. (1996). Sexually abused children suffering posttraumatic stress symptoms: Initial treatment outcome findings. *Child Maltreatment, 1,* 310–321.

Deblinger, E., McLeer, S. V., & Henry, D. (1990). Cognitive behavioral treatment for sexually abused children suffering posttraumatic stress: Preliminary findings. *Journal of the American Academy of Child and Adolescent Psychiatry, 29,* 747–752.

Donnelly, C. L., Amaya-Jackson, L., & March, J. S. (1999). Psychopharmacology of pediatric posttraumatic stress disorder. *Journal of Child and Adolescent Psychopharmacology, 9*(3), 203–220.

Drell, M. J., Siegel, C. H., & Gaensbauer, T. J. (1993). Posttraumatic stress disorder. In C. H. Zeanah (Ed.), *Handbook of infant mental health* (pp. 291–304). New York: Guilford Press.

Earls, F., Smith, E., Reich, W., & Jung, K. G. (1988). Investigating psychopathological consequences of a disaster in children: A pilot study incorporating a structured diagnostic interview. *Journal of the American Academy of Child and Adolescent Psychiatry, 27,* 90–95.

Famularo, R., Kinscheiff, R., & Fenton, T. (1988). Propanolol treatment for childhood posttraumatic stress disorder, acute type: A pilot study. *American Journal of Disabled Children, 142,* 1244–1247.

Famularo, R., Fenton, T., Kinscherff, R., & Augustyn, M. (1996). Psychiatric comorbidity in childhood posttraumatic stress disorder. *Child Abuse and Neglect, 20*(10), 953–961.

Farrell, S. P., Hains, A. A., & Davies, W. H. (1998). Cognitive behavioral interventions for sexually abused children exhibiting PTSD symptomatology. *Behavior Therapy, 29,* 241–255.

Field, T., Seligman, S., Scafedi, F., & Schanberg, S. (1996). Alleviating posttraumatic stress in children following Hurricane Andrew. *Journal of Applied Developmental Psychology, 17,* 37–50.

Finkelhor, D., & Berliner, L. (1995). Research on the treatment of sexually abused children: A review and recommendations. *Journal of the American Academy of Child and Adolescent Psychiatry, 34*(11), 1408–1423.

Foy, D. W., Madvig, B. T., Pynoos, R. S., & Camilleri, A. J. (1996). Etiologic factors in the development of posttraumatic stress disorder in children and adolescents. *Journal of School Psychology, 34,* 133–145.

Friedrich, W. N. (1996a). An integrated model of psychotherapy for abused children. In J. Briere, L. Berliner, J. Bulkely, C. Jenny, & T. Reid (Eds.), *The APSAC handbook on child maltreatment* (pp. 104–118). Thousand Oaks, CA: Sage.

Friedrich, W. N. (1996b). Clinical considerations of empirical treatment studies of abused children. *Child Maltreatment, 1,* 343–347.

Gaensbauer, T. J. (1994). Therapeutic work with a traumatized toddler. *Psychoanalytic Study of the Child, 49,* 412–433.

Galante, R., & Foa, D. (1986). An epidemiological study of psychic trauma and treatment effectiveness for children after a natural disaster. *Journal of the American Academy of Child and Adolescent Psychiatry, 25,* 357–363.

Gil, E. (1991). *The healing power of play.* New York: Guilford Press.

Glod, C. A., & Teicher, M. H. (1996). Relationship between early abuse, PTSD, an activity levels in prepubertal children. *Journal of the American Academy of Child and Adolescent Psychiatry, 35,* 1384–1393.

Goenjian, A. K., Karayan, I., Pynoos, R. S., Minassian, D., Najarian, L. M., Steinberg, A. M., & Fairbanks, L. A. (1997). Outcome of psychotherapy among early adolescents after trauma. *American Journal of Psychiatry, 154,* 536–542.

Goenjian, A. K., Pynoos, R. S., Steinberg, A. M., Najarian, L. M., et al. (1995). Psychiatric comorbidity in children after the 1988 earthquake in Armenia. *Journal of the American Academy of Child and Adolescent Psychiatry, 34,* 1174–1184.

Goodwin, J. (1985). Post-traumatic symptoms in incest victims. In S. Eth & R. S. Pynoos (Eds.), *Posttraumatic stress disorder in children* (pp. 155–168). Washington, DC: American Psychiatric Press.

Goodwin, J. (1988). Post-traumatic stress symptoms in abused children. *Journal of Traumatic Stress, 1,* 475–488.

Green, A. H. (1985). Children traumatized by physical abuse. In S. Eth & R. S. Pynoos (Eds.), *Posttraumatic stress disorder in children* (pp. 133–154). Washington, DC: American Psychiatric Press.

Harmon, R. J., & Riggs, P. D. (1996). Clinical perspectives: clonidine for posttraumatic stress disorder in preschool children. *Journal of the American Academy of Child and Adolescent Psychiatry, 35,* 1247–1249.

Herman, J. L., Perry, J. C., & van der Kolk, B. A. (1989). Childhood trauma in borderline personality disorder. *American Journal of Psychiatry, 146,* 490–495.

Herman, J. L., & van der Kolk, B. A. (1987). Traumatic antecedents of borderline personality disorder. In B. A. van der Kolk (Ed.), *Psychological trauma* (pp. 303–327). Washington, DC: American Psychiatric Press.

Hibbs, E., & Jensen, P. (1996). *Psychosocial treatments for child and adolescent disorders.* Washington, DC: American Psychological Press.

Holmbeck, G. N. (1997). Toward terminological, conceptual, and statistical clarity in the study of mediators and moderators: Examples from the child-clinical and pediatric psychology literatures. *Journal of Consulting and Clinical Psychology, 65*(4), 599–610.

Hornstein, N. L. (1996). Complexities of psychiatric differential diagnosis in children with dissociative symptoms and disorders. In J. Silberg (Ed.), *The dissociative child* (pp. 27–46). Lutherville, MD: Sidran Press.

Horrigan, J. P. (1996). Guanfacine for posttraumatic stress disorder nightmares [Letter to the editor]. *Journal of the American Academy of Child and Adolescent Psychiatry, 35,* 975–976.

Hubbard, J., Realmuto, G. M., Northwood, A. K., & Masten, A. S. (1995). Comorbidity of psychiatric diagnoses with posttraumatic stress disorder in survivors of childhood trauma. *Journal of the American Academy of Child and Adolescent Psychiatry, 34,* 1167–1173.

Hyer, L., & Brandsma, J. M. (1997). EMDR minus eye movements equals good psychotherapy. *Journal of Traumatic Stress, 10*(3), 515–22.

James, B. (1989). *Treating traumatized children.* Lexington, MA: Lexington Books.

Joseph, S., Brewin, C., Yule, W., & Williams, R. (1993). Causal attributions and posttraumatic stress disorder in adolescents. *Journal of Child Psychology and Psychiatry, 34,* 274–253.

Kendall, P. C., & Southam-Gerow, M. A. (1995). Issues in the transportability of treatment: The case of anxiety disorders in youths. *Journal of Consulting and Clinical Psychology, 63*(5), 702–8.

Kendall-Tackett, K. A., Williams, L. M., & Finkelhor, D. (1993). Impact of sexual abuse on children: A review and synthesis of recent empirical studies. *Psychological Bulletin, 113*(1), 164–180.

Kinzie, J. D., Sack, W. H., Angell, R. H., Manson, S., & Rath, B. (1986). The psychiatric effects of massive trauma on Cambodian children: I. The children. *Journal of the American Academy of Child and Adolescent Psychiatry, 25,* 370–376.

Kiser, L. J., Heston, J., Milsap, P. A., & Pruitt, D. B. (1991). Physical and sexual abuse in childhood: Relationships with posttraumatic stress disorder. *Journal of the American Academy of Child and Adolescent Psychiatry, 30,* 776–783.

LaGreca, A. M., Vemberg, E. M., Silverman, W. K., & Prinstein, M. J. (1996). Symptoms of posttraumatic stress in children after Hurricane Andrew: A prospective study. *Journal of Consulting and Clinical Psychology, 64,* 712–723.

Lanktree, C. B., & Briere, J. (1995). Outcome of therapy for sexually abused children: A repeated measures study. *Child Abuse and Neglect, 19,* 1145–1155.

Lohr, J. M., Tolin, D. F., & Lilienfeld, S. O. (1998). Efficacy of eye movement desensitization and reprocessing: Implications for behavior therapy, *Behavior Therapy, 29,* 123–156.

Lonigan, C. J., Shannon, M. P., Taylor, C. M., Finch, A. J., & Sallec, F. R. (1994). Children exposed to disaster: II. Risk factors for the development of post-traumatic symptomatology. *Journal of the American Academy of Child and Adolescent Psychiatry, 33,* 94–105.

Looff, D., Grimley, P., Kuiler, F., Martin, A., & Shunfield, L. (1995). Carbamazepine for posttraumatic stress disorder [Letter]. *Journal of the American Academy of Child and Adolescent Psychiatry, 34,* 703–704.

Macksoud, M. S., & Aber, J. L. (1996). The war experiences and psychosocial development of children in Lebanon. *Child Development, 67,* 70–88.

Malmquist, C. P. (1986). Children who witness parental murder: Posttraumatic aspects. *Journal of the American Academy of Child and Adolescent Psychiatry, 25,* 320–325.

Mannarino, A. P., Cohen, J. A., & Berman, S. R. (1994). The Children's Attribution and Perception Scale: A new measurement of sexual abuse-related factors. *Journal of Clinical Child Psychology, 23,* 204–211.

March, J. (1999). Assessment of pediatric posttraumatic stress disorder. In P. A. Saigh & J. D. Bremner (Eds.), *Posttraumatic stress disorder: A comprehensive text* (pp. 199–218). Boston: Allyn & Bacon.

March, J., Amaya-Jackson, J., & Pynoos, R. (1996). Pediatric post-traumatic stress disorder. In J. Weiner (Ed.), *Textbook of child and adolescent psychiatry* (2nd ed.). Washington, DC: American Psychiatric Press.

March, J., Amaya-Jackson, L., Murray, M., & Schulte, A. (1998). Cognitive-behavioral psychotherapy for children and adolescents with post-traumatic stress disorder following a single incident stressor. *Journal of the American Academy of Child and Adolescent Psychiatry, 37*(6), 585–593.

March, J., & Curry, J. (1998). The prediction of treatment outcome. *Journal of Abnormal Child Psychology, 26*(1), 39–52.

Marmar, C. K., Foy, D., Kagan, B., & Pynoos, R. S. (1993). An integrated approach for treating posttraumatic stress. In R. S. Pynoos (Ed.), *Posttraumatic stress disorder: A clinical review* (pp. 239–272). Lutherville, MD: Sidran Press.

McCullough, E. L., & Pumariega, A. J. (1994). Comorbidity of attention deficit hyperactivity disorder and posttraumatic stress disorder. *Journal of Child and Family Studies 3,* 327–336.

McElroy, L. P., & McElroy, R. A. (1989). Psychoanalytically oriented psychotherapy with sexually abused children. *Journal of Mental Health Counseling, 11,* 244–257.

McNally, R. (1993). Stressors that produce posttraumatic stress disorder in children. In J. R. T. Davidson & E. B. Foa (Eds.), *Posttraumatic stress disorder: DSM IV and beyond* (pp. 57–74). Washington DC: American Psychiatric Association.

McNally, R. J. (1996). Assessment of posttraumatic stress disorder in children and adolescents. *Journal of School Psychology, 34*(2), 147–161.

Meyer, W. J., Blakeney, P., & Moore, P. (1994). Parental well-being and behavioral adjustment of pediatric survivors of burns. *Journal of Burn Care and Rehabilitation, 15,* 62–68.

Molta, R. W. (1995). Childhood posttraumatic stress disorder and the schools. *Canadian Journal of School Psychology, 11,* 65–78.

Monck, E., Bentovim, A., Goodall, G., Hyde, C., Lewin, B., & Sharland, E. (1994). *Child sexual abuse: A descriptive and treatment outcome study.* London: Her Majesty's Stationery Office.

Nir, Y. (1985). Posttraumatic stress disorder in children with cancer. In S. Eth & R. S. Pynoos (Eds.), *Posttraumatic stress disorder in children* (pp. 121–132). Washington, DC: American Psychiatric Press.

Parson, E. R. (1995). Post-traumatic stress and coping in an inner-city child. *Psychoanalytic Study of the Child, 50,* 272–307.

Pelcovitz, D., Kaplan, S., Goldenberg, B., Mandel, F., Lehane, J., & Guarrero, J. (1994). Posttraumatic stress disorder in physically abused adolescents. *Journal of the American Academy of Child and Adolescent Psychiatry, 33,* 305–312.

Perez, C. L. (1998). A comparison of group play therapy and individual therapy for sexually abused children (Doctoral dissertation, University of Northern Colorado, 1988). *Dissertation Abstracts International, 48,* 3079.

Perry, B. (1994). Neurobiological sequelae of childhood trauma: PTSD in children. In M. Marburg (Ed.), *Catecholamines in PTSD* (pp. 233–255). Washington, DC: American Psychiatric Press.

Pfferbaum, B. (1997). Posttraumatic stress disorder in children: A review of the last ten years. *Journal of the American Academy of Child and Adolescent Psychiatry, 36*(11), 1503–1511.

Pitman, R. K., Orr, S. P., Altman, B., Longrpree, R. E., Poire, R. E., & Macklin, M. L. (1996). Emotional processing during eye-movement desensitization and reprocessing therapy of Vietnam veterans with chronic post-traumatic stress disorder. *Comprehensive Psychiatry, 37,* 419–429.

Putnam, F. W. (1997). *Dissociation in children and adolescents: A developmental perspective.* New York: Guilford Press.

Pynoos, R., & Eth, S. (1986). Witness to violence: The child interview. *Journal of the American Academy of Child and Adolescent Psychiatry, 25,* 306–319.

Pynoos, R. S., & Eth, S. (1985). Children traumatized by witnessing acts of personal violence: Homicide, rape or suicidal behavior. In S. Eth & R. S. Pynoos (Eds.), *Posttraumatic stress disorder in children* (pp. 17–44). Washington, DC: American Psychiatric Press.

Pynoos, R. S., & Nader, K. (1988). Psychological first aid and treatment approach to children exposed to community violence: Research implications. *Journal of Traumatic Stress, 1,* 445–473.

Pynoos, R. S., & Nader, K. (1993). Issues in the treatment of posttraumatic stress in children and adolescents. In J. P. Wilson & B. Raphael (Eds.), *International handbook of traumatic stress syndromes* (pp. 535–549). New York: Plenum Press.

Pynoos, R., Steinberg, A., & Wraith, R. (1995). A developmental model of childhood traumatic stress. In D. Cicchetti & D. Cohen (Eds.), *Manual of developmental psychopathology: risk disorder, adaptation* (pp. 72–95). New York: Wiley.

Rigamer, E. F. (1986). Psychological management of children in a national crisis. *Journal of the American Academy of Child and Adolescent Psychiatry, 25,* 364–369.

Rizzone, L. P., Stoddard, F. J., Murphy, J. M., & Kruger, L. T. (1994). Posttraumatic stress disorder in mothers of children and adolescents with burns. *Journal of Burn Care Rehabilitation, 15,* 158–163.

Saigh, P. A. (1986). *In vitro* flooding in the treatment of a 6-yr-old boy's posttraumatic stress disorder. *Behaviour Research and Therapy, 24*(6), 685–688.

Saigh, P. A. (1989). The use of an *in vitro* flooding package in the treatment of traumatized adolescents. *Journal of Developmental and Behavioral Pediatrics, 10*(1), 17–21.

Saigh, P. A. (1992). The behavioral treatment of child and adolescent posttraumatic stress disorder. *Advances in Behaviour Research and Therapy, 14*(4), 247–275.

Saigh, P. A., Yule, W., Inamdar, S. C. (1996). Imaginal flooding of traumatized children and adolescents. *Journal of School Psychology, 34,* 163–183.

Scheeringa, M. S., Zeanah, C. H., Drell, M. J., & Larrieu, J. A. (1995). Two approaches to diagnosing posttraumatic stress disorder in infancy and early childhood. *Journal of the American Academy of Child and Adolescent Psychiatry, 34,* 191–200.

Seinfeld, J. (1989). Therapy with a severely abused child: An object relations perspective *Clinical Social Work Journal, 17,* 40–49.

Shapiro, F. (1996). Eye movement desensitization and reprocessing (EMDR): Evaluation of controlled PTSD research. *Journal of Behavior Therapy and Experimental Psychiatry, 27*(3), 209–18.

Silberg, J. L. (1996). *The dissociative child.* Lutherville, MD: Sidran Press.

Siegel, D. J. (1995). Memory, trauma and psychotherapy: A cognitive science view. *Journal of Psychotherapy Practice and Research, 4,* 93–122.

Silvern, L., Karyl, J., & Landis, T. Y. (1995). Individual psychotherapy for the traumatized children of abused women. In E. Peled, P. G. Jaffe, P. L. Edleson (Eds.), *Ending the cycle of violence: Community responses to children of battered women* (pp. 43–76). Thousand Oaks, CA: Sage.

Simons, D., & Silveira, W. R. (1994). Posttraumatic stress disorder in children after television programmes. *British Medical Journal, 305,* 389–390.

Singer, M. I., Anglin, T., Song, L., & Lunghofer, L. (1995). Adolescents' exposure to violence and associated symptoms of psychological trauma. *Journal of the American Medical Association, 273,* 477–482.

Snodgrass, L., Yamamoto, J., & Frederick, C. (1993). Vietnamese refugees with posttraumatic stress disorder symptomatology: Intervention via a coping skills model. *Journal of Traumatic Stress, 6,* 569–574.

Spaccarelli, S. (1995). Measuring abuse stress and negative cognitive appraisals in child sexual abuse: Validity data on two new scales. *Journal of Abnormal Child Psychology, 23,* 703–727.

Spiegel, D. (1984). Multiple personality as a post-traumatic stress disorder. *Psychiatric Clinics of North America, 7,* 101–110.

Stallard, P., & Law, F. (1993). Screening and psychological debriefing of adolescent survivors of life threatening events. *British Journal of Psychiatry, 163,* 660–665.

Steiner, H., Garcia, I. G., & Matthews, Z. (1997). Posttraumatic stress disorder in incarcerated juvenile delinquents. *Journal of the American Academy of Child and Adolescent Psychiatry, 36,* 357–365.

Stoddard, F. J. (1996). Psychiatric care of burned infants, children and adolescents. In M. Lewis (Ed.), *Child and adolescent psychiatry* (pp. 1016–1033). Washington, DC: American Psychiatric Press.

Stoddard, F. J., Norman, D. K., & Murphy, M. (1989). A diagnostic outcome study of children and adolescents with severe burns. *Journal of Trauma, 29,* 471–477.

Stone, M. H. (1990). Abuse and abusiveness in borderline personality disorder. In P. S. Links (Ed.), *Family environment and borderline personality disorder.* Washington, DC: American Psychiatric Press.

Sullivan, J. M., & Evans, K. (1994). Integrated treatment for the survivor of childhood trauma who is chemically dependent. *Journal of Psychoactive Drugs, 26,* 369–378.

Terr, L. C. (1983). Chowchilla revisited: The effect of psychic trauma four years after a school bus kidnapping. *American Journal of Psychiatry, 140,* 1543–1550.

Terr, L. C. (1989). Treating psychic trauma in children: A preliminary discussion. *Journal of Traumatic Stress, 2*(1), 3–20.

Terr, L. C. (1990). *Too scared to cry.* New York: Harper & Row.

Terr, L. C. (1991). Childhood traumas: An outline and overview. *American Journal of Psychiatry, 148*(1), 10–20.

Tinker, R., & Wilson, S. (1988). *Through the eyes of a child: EMDR with children.* New York: Norton.

Van Leeuwen, K. (1988). Resistances in the treatment of a sexually molested 6-year-old girl. *International Review of Psycho-Analysis, 15,* 149–156.

Weine, S., Becker, D. F., McGlashan, T. H., Vojvoda, D., Hartman, S., & Robbins, J. P. (1995). Adolescent survivors of "ethnic cleansing": Observations on the first year in America. *Journal of the American Academy of Child and Adolescent Psychiatry, 34,* 1153–1159.

Yule, W. (1992a). Post-traumatic stress disorder in child survivors of shipping disasters: The sinking of the "Jupiter." *Psychotherapy and Psychosomatics, 57,* 200–205.

Yule, W. (1992b). Resilience and vulnerability in child survivors of disasters. In B. Tizard & V. Varma (Eds.), *Vulnerability and resilience: A Festschrift for Ann and Alan Clark* (pp. 182–198). London: Taylor & Francis.

Yule, W., & Udwin, O. (1991). Screening child survivors for posttraumatic stress disorder: Experiences from the "Jupiter" sighting. *British Journal of Clinical Psychology, 30,* 131–138.

Yule, W., & Canterbury, R. (1994). The treatment of post traumatic stress disorder in children and adolescents. *International Review of Psychiatry, 6*(2–3), 141–151.

7

Eye Movement Desensitization and Reprocessing

Claude M. Chemtob, David F. Tolin, Bessel A. van der Kolk, and Roger K. Pitman

Eye movement desensitization and reprocessing (EMDR), an emerging therapy for psychological trauma, has been in use for nearly a decade. Although it has stimulated strong interest and enthusiasm, EMDR has also received intense critical scrutiny. This chapter provides an overview of the history and theory of EMDR. Next, the EMDR procedure is summarized, followed by a review of the outcome literature. Dismantling studies of the contribution of eye movements to the efficacy of the EMDR procedure are then reviewed, followed by an overall rating reflecting the current knowledge of EMDR's efficacy, along with recommendations for its use. The chapter concludes with suggestions for further research.

HISTORY AND DEVELOPMENT OF EMDR

Rather than having been generated from a specific theoretical position, EMDR originated in a serendipitous observation by Dr. Francine Shapiro in 1987. In her book, Shapiro (1995) described how she noticed during a walk that back-and-forth movements of her eyes were associated with reductions in the aversiveness of troublesome thoughts. In a first attempt to test the therapeutic effect of eye movements on "traumatic memory symptomatology," Shapiro formulated a desensitization procedure that included asking trauma survivors to think of a troublesome thought or memory while tracking her fingers as she moved them back and forth across the individual's visual field. Participants reported that during the procedure, their thoughts became less distressing. The report of this first experience with "eye movement desensitization" (EMD) created considerable interest (Shapiro, 1989). Shapiro subsequently changed the procedure's name to "eye movement desensitization and reprocessing" (EMDR) to reflect an increased emphasis on fostering cognitive and emotional changes in the participant through a more highly developed procedure.

EMDR THEORY

EMDR theorists characterize EMDR as an integrative treatment informed by such diverse concepts as network theories of emotion (Lang, 1979) and of PTSD (Chemtob, Roitblat, Hamada, Carlson, & Twentyman, 1988; Foa, Steketee, & Rothbaum, 1989), dissociation (Janet, 1973), mood-dependent learning (Bower, 1981), assimilation and accommodation (Piaget, 1950), nonverbal representation of traumatic memories (van der Kolk, 1994), incorporation of corrective information (Foa & Kozak, 1986), and the "tendency to completion" from Horowitz's (1976) seminal analysis of information processing in trauma. EMDR theorists regard their treatment as incorporating a dynamic view of information processing that is consistent with newer models of learning and cognition, including connectionist theories.

Shapiro (1995) has proposed an "accelerated information-processing" model to account for the resolution of traumatic memories. The model includes the following key propositions:

1. Traumatization entails interference with psychological and biological processes that normally promote adaptation to memories of events. Traumatic memories are at least partially dissociated from the broader semantic–affective network and represented in a "state-dependent" form. This leads to distortions in perception, feeling, and response.

2. An intrinsic self-healing mechanism exists within people that when activated reintegrates traumatic memories into a normalized form. Conjugate eye movements (or other stimulation such as tone or taps) performed within the context of the EMDR procedure activate this self-healing mechanism. A number of hypotheses have been proposed to account for the possible contribution of such stimulation (for a review, see Shapiro, 1999).

3. Information about self–other attributions is encoded along with cognitive, affective, and physiological response elements. Self-representations play a key role in preserving the distortions inherent in traumatic memories.

4. In cases of multiple traumatization, EMDR treatment dosage is determined by the number of traumatic memories to be accessed and resolved. Sometimes, but not always, these memories can be grouped thematically.

THE EMDR PROCEDURE

EMDR treatment requires the patient to identify multiple aspects of the traumatic memory, including the images associated with the event, the affective and physiological response elements, the negative self-representation induced by the traumatic experience, and an alternate, desired, positive self-representation. Shapiro (1995) describes EMDR as a structured, multicomponent treatment package that incorporates the following eight stages:

1. *Patient history and treatment planning.* In this phase, the clinician thoroughly evaluates patient readiness, barriers to treatment (which may include secondary gains from the maintenance of the trauma-related pathology), dysfunctional behaviors, symptoms, and illness characteristics. The clinician then identifies suitable trauma memories ("targets") as foci for treatment. The EMDR treatment plan addresses not only the trauma-specific memories implicated in the psychopathology, but also present reminders of the traumatic event. It also seeks to identify remedial skills and behaviors for the patient's future use.

2. *Preparation.* This stage is used to establish an appropriate treatment relationship, provide education about trauma, inform the patient of the rationale behind EMDR, teach specific coping skills for processing trauma-related material as it emerges, and assist the patient in learning to maintain perspective in the face of trauma reactivation.

3. *Assessment.* In this stage, the patient is asked to bring together the components of the traumatic memory in a structured manner. This process includes (a) identifying a distressing image in memory, (b) identifying an associated negative cognition, (c) identifying an alternate positive cognition, (d) rating the validity of the positive cognition (VoC) using a 7-point scale, (e) identifying the emotions associated with the traumatic memory, (f) rating the subjective level (or units) of disturbance (SUD) using an 11-point scale, and (g) identifying trauma-related physical sensations and their bodily location (e.g., a flutter in the stomach).

For example, a rape victim with PTSD might generate an unpleasant mental image of the rape and the thought, "It's my fault." Next, the patient might identify an alternate positive cognition such as, "I did the best I could under the circumstances." The patient would then rate the felt "truth" of this positive cognition on the VoC scale. Next, the patient might identify emotions of fear and anger. The intensity of these and other emotions elicited by the target memory would be assessed via the SUD scale. Then, the client might note that palpitations and a choking feeling are the primary sensations associated with the traumatic memory. In preparation for skills building, the patient might note that becoming more able to say "no" might help her avoid future, dangerous situations.

4. *Desensitization and reprocessing.* During this critical stage of treatment, the patient is initially asked to hold in mind the disturbing image, the negative cognition, and the bodily sensations associated with the traumatic memory. The clinician moves his or her fingers back and forth, approximately 12 inches in front of the patient's face, while the patient tracks the moving fingers with his or her eyes. Procedural alternatives to using the eye movements include other stimulation, such as auditory tones or hand taps. After approximately 20 back-and-forth eye movements, the clinician stops and asks the patient to let go of the memory, take a deep breath, and provide feedback about any changes in the image, bodily sensations, emotions, or thoughts about the self. Often, patients will report the emergence of new memories, emotions, sensations, or cognitions. After each set of eye movements (or other stimulation), depending on the patient's response, the therapist instructs the patient on what to attend to next. Usually, minimum direction by the therapist is recommended; however, in some instances, where processing of the traumatic memory appears blocked, the therapist may be required to intervene with procedural variations intended to support cognitive and/or emotional change.

5. *Installation of positive cognition.* Once the SUD rating has been reduced as far as possible toward zero (no discomfort), the positive cognition described in Stage 4 is again assessed using the VoC scale. The patient is instructed to think of the target image while covertly rehearsing the positive cognition. Another set of eye movements is performed, followed by another assessment of the validity of the positive cognition. This cycle is repeated until the VoC rating rises as far as possible toward 7 (completely valid). Specific coping skills designed to deal with past memories and present emotions, as well as optimal behavioral responses to future situations (e.g., saying "no" to undesired advances from men in the case of the hypothetical rape victim) may also be rehearsed within the EMDR framework (Shapiro, 1995).

6. *Body scan.* In this stage, the patient is asked to check for any signs of residual physical tension or discomfort. If such are reported, they are taken to be indicators of incomplete trauma processing. The patient is then instructed to attend to the physical sensations while additional sets of eye movements are performed.

7. *Closure.* This stage is designed to prepare the patient for leaving each session. Because the activation of traumatic memories can provoke strong emotions, techniques such as relaxation or visualization are occasionally used to help the patient reach closure. The patient is encouraged to keep a journal of feelings, thoughts, and dreams related to the trauma in between sessions and to utilize self-control techniques.

8. *Reevaluation.* Each subsequent session incorporates an assessment of whether treatment goals have been reached and maintained. Trauma-related material that has emerged since the last session may be addressed. Additional sessions are scheduled as needed to address trauma memories, current reminders, and skills development.

EMDR TREATMENT EFFICACY

This section reviews the empirical literature bearing on the efficacy of EMDR as a treatment for PTSD. Other recent reviews include Feske (1998), Lohr, Tolin, and Lilienfeld (1998), Shapiro (1996), and Spector and Read (1999). The articles reviewed here were identified via literature searches on PsycLIT, PsycINFO, PILOTS, and MEDLINE. We also searched the reference lists in relevant publications. The relatively large number of studies conducted to date on the efficacy of EMDR enabled us to select those that met many of Foa and Meadows's (1997) "gold standard" criteria for treatment studies. Accordingly, we used the following criteria for inclusion in this review:

1. The study was published (or in press) in a peer-reviewed journal. This criterion excluded, for example, the study of Boudewyns, Stwertka, Hyer, Albrecht, and Sperr (1993).
2. The study employed a control condition that allowed differentiation of specific effects of the treatment from nonspecific effects due to the passage of time or the performance of repeated assessments (Mahoney, 1978). This criterion excluded, for example, open trials by Forbes, Creamer, and Rycroft (1994) and Lazrove, Triffleman, Kite, McGlashan, and Rounsaville (1998).
3. The study employed random assignment to the EMDR or control condition. This criterion excluded, for example, the study of Devilly and Spence (1999). Although the authors characterized their procedure as "stratified randomization," treatment was provided in blocks, with the majority of the non-EMDR patients treated in the first block, and the majority of the EMDR patients treated in the second block. This represents a substantial departure from standard randomization strategies. An earlier study by Devilly, Spence, and Rapee (1998) also employed stratified randomization. However, because the potentially confounding recruitment heterogeneities and treatment order effects introduced by the subject blocking in the earlier study were less dramatic than in the later study, the earlier study is included in this review. Also excluded was a multiple-baseline dismantling study by Montgomery and Ayllon (1994) that treated subjects first in a non-eye-movement condition, followed by an eye-movement condition.
4. The dependent variables included at least one standard measure of PTSD symptoms. This resulted in the exclusion, for example, of studies by Shapiro (1989) and Silver, Brooks, and Obenchain (1995), as well as a dismantling study by Wilson, Silver, Covi, and Foster (1996).

Table 7.1 provides additional details regarding the studies reviewed here, including control conditions, samples, session number and duration, outcome measures, effect sizes, and comments. Table 7.1 also provides a key for outcome measure abbreviations used there and in the following text.

TABLE 7.1. EMDR Treatment Studies Reviewed

Study	Treatments	Sample	No./duration of session	Outcome measures	Effect sizes (g)	Comments
		Studies of EMDR versus wait list (or continuing standard care)				
Jensen (1994)	1. EMDR 2. SC	25 male combat veterans with PTSD	1. 2 sessions, 50 min	SI-PTSD[1], MISS[2]	Post-tx: EMDR vs. SC = 0.97[1], −0.36[2]	a, b, d, f, g
Wilson, Becker, & Tinker (1995)	1. EMDR 2. Wait list	40 male and 40 female civilians, 46% PTSD	1. 3 sessions, 90 min	IES-int[1], IES-avd[2]	Post-tx: EMDR vs. WL = 1.32[1], 1.01[2]	
Rothbaum (1997)	1. EMDR 2. Wait list	18 female rape victims with PTSD	1. 3 sessions, 90 min	PSS-I[1], IES-int[2], IES-avd[3]	Post-tx: EMDR vs. WL = 2.68[1], 2.19[2], 2.70[3]	e
Chemtob, Nakashima, Hamada, & Carlson (in press)	1. EMDR 2. Wait list	32 male and female children with PTSD	1. 3 sessions, 40 min	CSI[1]	Post-tx: EMDR vs. WL = 1.29[1]	f
		Studies of EMDR versus other treatment (or newly initiated standard care)				
Vaughan et al. (1994)	1. EMD 2. IHT 3. AMT	13 male and 23 female civilians, 78% PTSD	1. 3–5 sessions, 50 min 2. 3–5 sessions, 50 min, with homework 3. 3–5 sessions, 50 min, with homework	SI-PTSD[1], IES-int[2], IES-avd[3]	Post-tx: EMD vs. IHT = 0.70[1], 0.71[2], −0.33[3] EMD vs. AMT = 0.62[1], 1.03[2], 0.14[3] Follow-up: EMD vs. IHT = 0.43[1], −0.02[2], 0.35[3] EMD vs. AMT = 0.42[1], 0.30[2], 0.47[3]	a

Study	Conditions	Sample	Sessions	Measures	Results	Notes
Carlson, Chemtob, Rusnak, Hedlund, & Muraoka (1998)	1. EMDR 2. BF-REL 3. SC	35 male combat veterans with PTSD	1. 12 sessions, 60–75 min 2. 12 sessions, 40 min, with homework	MISS[1], IES-int[2], IES-avd[3], CAPS-freq[4], CAPS-intsty[5],	<u>Post-tx:</u> EMDR vs. BF-REL = 1.08[1], 0.47[2], 0.36[3] EMDR vs. SC = 0.91[1], 0.41[2], 0.02[3] <u>Follow-up:</u> EMDR vs. BF-REL = 0.97[1], 0.70[2], 0.90[3], 1.90[4], 1.88[5]	
Marcus, Marquis, & Sakai (1997)	1. EMDR 2. SC	14 male and 53 female civilians with PTSD	1. 6 sessions, 50 min	MISS[1], IES[2]	<u>Post-tx:</u> EMDR vs. SC = 0.75[1], 0.92[2]	g
Scheck, Schaeffer, & Gillette (1998)	1. EMDR 2. AL	60 young women, 77% PTSD	1. 2 sessions, 90 min 2. 2 sessions, 90 min	IES[1], PENN[2]	<u>Post-tx:</u> EMDR vs. AL = 0.75[1], 0.71[2]	h

Dismantling studies controlling for eye movements

Study	Conditions	Sample	Sessions	Measures	Results	Notes
Renfrey & Spates (1994)	1. EMDR 2. Automated EMDR 3. EMDR – EM	5 male and 18 female civilians, 91% PTSD	1. 2–6 sessions, unknown duration 2. 2–6 sessions, unknown duration 3. 2–6 sessions, unknown duration	CAPS, IES, Phys	Insufficient information	a, g
Boudewyns & Hyer (1996)	1. EMDR + SC 2. (EMDR – EM) + SC 3. SC	61 male combat veterans with PTSD	1. 5–7 sessions, unknown duration 2. 5–7 sessions, unknown duration	CAPS, IES, Phys	Insufficient information	b, d

(continued)

145

TABLE 7.1. *(continued)*

Study	Treatments	Sample	No./duration of session	Outcome measures	Effect sizes (g)	Comments
			Dismantling studies controlling for eye movements			
Pitman et al. (1996)	1. EMDR 2. (EMDR – EM)	17 male combat veterans with PTSD	1. 6 sessions, 70–110 min 2. 6 sessions, 70–110 min	CAPS[1], MISS[2], IES-int[3], IES-avd[4]	Post-tx: EMDR vs. (EMDR – EM) = –0.03[1], 0.14[2], 0.11[3] –0.02[4] Follow-up: EMDR vs. (EMDR – EM) = 0.19[1], 0.22[2], 0.39[3], 0.14[4]	a, b, d
Devilly, Spence, & Rapee (1998)	1. EMDR + SC 2. (EMDR – EM) + SC 3. SC	51 male combat veterans with PTSD	1. 2 sessions, 90 min 2. 2 sessions, 90 min	MISS[1]	Post-tx: (EMDR + SC) vs. [(EMDR – EM) + SC] = 0.31[1] (EMDR + SC) vs. SC = 0.03[1] Follow-up: (EMDR + SC) vs. [(EMDR – EM) + SC] = 0.25[1]	b, c, d, e, h

Note. Effect sizes are given as Hedges's unbiased *g* and represent the magnitude of the difference between the EMDR and control group at the posttreatment (and in some studies follow-up) assessment, *not* the magnitude of change scores. Positive effect sizes indicate that the EMDR group was less symptomatic than control group at the time of the assessment; negative effect sizes indicate the opposite. *Treatments*: EMDR, eye movement desensitization and reprocessing; WL, wait list; SC, standard care; BF-REL, biofeedback-assisted relaxation; AMT, applied muscle relaxation training; AL, active listening; IHT, imagery habituation training. *Standardized PTSD outcome measures*: SI-PTSD, Structured Interview for PTSD; PSS-I, PTSD Symptom Scale—Interviewer Version; PTSD-I, PTSD Interview; CAPS, Clinician-Administered PTSD Scale; freq, frequency; intsty, intensity; MISS, Mississippi Scale for PTSD; IES, Impact of Event Scale; int, intrusion; avd, avoidance; PENN, Penn Inventory for PTSD; CSI, Childhood Symptom Inventory. (See respective studies in text for references.) *Comments*: a–d, Interpretation of negative results limited by a, small samples; b, treatment-refractory participants; c, questionable randomization; d, questionably adequate treatment dosage duration, and/or fidelity; e, single therapist; f, missing or incomplete baseline assessment; g, nonblind outcome evaluator(s); h, some outcome assessments by telephone or mail.

The reviewed studies are divided into two categories: those that employed a wait-list control, and those that employed control treatments. Included in the wait-list category are studies in which the control group received continuing standard care. A limitation of these studies is that they do not control for the possibility of nonspecific effects due to a newly introduced treatment. Included in the control treatment category are studies in which the control group received newly initiated (as opposed to continuing) standard care.

Studies Employing a Wait-List (or Continuing Standard Care) Control

Jensen (1994) studied 25 male Vietnam combat veterans with PTSD who were receiving psychiatric services at a VA Medical Center. Thirteen were selected to receive two sessions of EMDR in addition to their current treatment. Neither group showed significant symptom reductions following treatment; in fact, both groups worsened somewhat. As noted in the "Comments" column of Table 7.1, this study suffered from several limitations (e.g., a treatment refractory sample and inexperienced therapists).

Wilson, Becker, and Tinker (1995) assigned 40 male and 40 female trauma survivors of diverse, mainly civilian, traumatic events to three sessions of EMDR or wait list. Wait-list participants subsequently received EMDR. Results indicated that patients who received EMDR improved on all measures, particularly those that reflected trauma-related symptoms, whereas wait-list patients did not. Pre–post effect sizes were large and continued to improve at follow-up for five of the nine measures. This study's participants were largely single-event trauma survivors, which limits generalizability of the results to patients with multiple traumas. A 15-month follow-up study of 66 of the original participants treated with EMDR (Wilson, Becker, & Tinker, 1997) indicated that treatment gains were maintained. Eighty-four percent of participants who originally had PTSD no longer met criteria for this disorder after only three EMDR sessions.

Rothbaum (1997) assigned 18 female rape victims with PTSD to either three sessions of EMDR or wait list. Patients treated with EMDR showed a greater decrease in trauma-related symptoms than did wait-list patients, with very large effect sizes. At posttreatment, 90% of EMDR patients, compared to 12% of wait-list patients, no longer met criteria for PTSD.

Using a lagged-groups design, Chemtob, Nakashima, Hamada, and Carlson (in press) evaluated the efficacy of EMDR for 32 elementary-school-age children meeting criteria for PTSD 3 years after a catastrophic hurricane. EMDR resulted in substantial reductions in scores on the Children's Reaction Inventory (CRI), which was employed as a structured interview, as well as significant but lesser reductions in depressive and anxiety symptoms. Gains were maintained at 6-month follow-up. Health visits to the school nurse were also significantly reduced following successful treatment with EMDR.

Studies Employing Control Treatments (or Newly Initiated Standard Care)

Vaughan and colleagues (1994) compared EMDR to two other treatments in 36 trauma victims. Seventeen participants were first chosen for a wait list. All participants were then assigned to one of three treatment conditions: EMDR, imagery habituation training (IHT), or applied muscle relaxation training (AMT). The last two therapies, but not EMDR, included daily homework between sessions. All active treatment groups improved significantly compared to the wait list at both posttreatment and follow-up. There were no group differences with regard to improvement in total PTSD symptoms. However, only EMDR produced significant improvement in flashbacks and nightmares. This finding was reinforced by superior results for EMDR on the Impact of Event Scale (IES) intrusion subscale at posttreatment; at follow-up, EMDR produced further improvement on this subscale, but its significant superiority was lost due to improvement in the two other groups.

Marcus, Marquis, and Sakai (1997) conducted a study of PTSD treatment in 67 patients being seen in a large health maintenance organization (HMO). Help-seeking patients who had not previously received PTSD treatment were referred for evaluation. Following assessment, patients meeting diagnostic criteria for PTSD were assigned to EMDR or standard clinical care, which included individual treatment, medication, and/or group therapy. Patients in both groups received medications, day treatment, and hospitalization as needed. The design did not predetermine the number of sessions in either treatment condition, which permitted the authors to consider the number of sessions received as a health care utilization outcome variable. Results indicated that patients who received EMDR showed significantly faster and greater improvement on measures of PTSD, depression, and anxiety. At posttreatment, 77% of EMDR patients no longer met criteria for PTSD compared to 50% in the standard care condition. EMDR patients used fewer supplementary treatment and medication management sessions than did standard care patients.

Scheck, Schaeffer, and Gillette (1998) assigned 60 young women exhibiting traumatic memories and dysfunctional behavior, such as promiscuity and running away from home, to two sessions of either EMDR or Rogerian active listening (AL), administered by different groups of therapists. There was statistically significant improvement on all measures for both treatment conditions. At posttreatment, the EMDR group showed lower symptom severity than did the AL group on four of the five measures employed. Although AL was efficacious in reducing symptoms, the effect size for EMDR was twice as large.

Carlson, Chemtob, Rusnak, Hedlund, and Muraoka (1998) assigned 35 male combat-veteran outpatients to standard care only, 12 sessions of biofeedback-assisted relaxation, or 12 sessions of EMDR. At posttreatment, the EMDR group showed significantly greater symptom reduction than the other two groups. Physiological arousal decreased following treatment, but there were no group differences. At 3-month follow-up, the standard care group was no longer in the study, but the EMDR group continued to show lower symptoms than the biofeedback-assisted relaxation group. At 9-month follow-up, 90% of the EMDR, but only 46% of the biofeedback, participants were retained. The EMDR group continued to show lower symptoms than did the biofeedback group on most measures. Seventy-five percent of EMDR-treated participants no longer met criteria for PTSD at 9-month follow-up. Evaluators rated the EMDR patients as significantly more satisfied with their treatment experience.

In closing this review of controlled efficacy studies, a perusal of the effect sizes of EMDR versus control treatments in Table 7.1 reveals that nearly all are positive and many are large.

DISMANTLING STUDIES EXPLORING
THE ROLE OF EYE MOVEMENTS

The contribution of eye movements to EMDR's effects has been the subject of speculation, critical review, and several controlled studies since the introduction of the procedure by Shapiro (1989), who initially proposed a central role for eye movements performed while the patient concentrated on the memory to be desensitized. In order to evaluate the specific effect of the eye movements on treatment outcome, several "dismantling" studies have been conducted comparing procedures that adhere to the EMDR protocol to varying degrees with control procedures that replace eye movements with patients' either closing their eyes or focusing their gaze on a nonmoving target.

Renfrey and Spates (1994) assigned 5 male and 18 female civilians with intrusive PTSD symptoms, all but two of which met criteria for PTSD, to one of three treatment conditions: EMD ($n = 8$), a protocol employing eye movements induced by left–right–left flashing lights ($n = 8$), and a protocol employing active visual attention to a fixed, flashing light ($n = 7$). All groups rehearsed traumatic memories per Shapiro's (1989) original EMD protocol. Between two and six sessions were provided, depending on participants' responses. Although specific supporting data were not reported, all groups showed effects in the direction of improvement on the PTSD outcome measures, with no differences among groups.

In a preliminary report of a study described as in progress, Boudewyns and Hyer (1996) randomly assigned 61 male combat veterans to standard care only, standard care plus 5–7 sessions of EMDR, or standard care plus 5–7 sessions of an EMDR analogue that was procedurally similar to EMDR, except that patients were asked to keep their eyes closed rather than move them back and forth. On the Clinician-Administered PTSD Scale (CAPS), all three groups' symptoms dropped significantly at posttreatment, with no significant differences among groups. There were also no significant group differences on the IES, which did not significantly change as a function of treatment. Both the EMDR and analogue groups showed significantly lower heart rate responses and less self-reported anxiety after treatment than the standard care group, which actually showed increases.

Devilly, Spence, and Rapee (1998) treated veterans with chronic combat-related PTSD with two sessions of EMDR ($n = 19$), two sessions of a similar procedure in which a fixed, flashing light was substituted for the eye movements ($n = 16$), or standard psychiatric support ($n = 16$). Although all three groups improved on all outcome measures, the EMDR and EMDR analogue groups combined showed more improvement than the standard care group, but they did not differ from each other. At 6-month follow-up, symptoms had reverted to pretreatment levels.

Pitman and colleagues (1996) randomly assigned 17 male outpatient Vietnam combat veterans with PTSD to either EMDR or an identical control condition with fixed (rather than moving) gaze. During the control treatment, the therapist moved his fingers in front of the patient's face, but the patient was instructed not to follow them with his eyes but, instead, to tap a finger of each hand rhythmically. Six sessions of one treatment focusing on a specific combat event were provided, followed by six sessions of the other treatment focusing on another combat event, in a crossover design. Both groups showed modest improvements. There were no differences between EMDR with and without eye movements, except on IES-avoidance, where the eyes-fixed treatment was superior. At 5-year follow-up (Macklin et al., 2000), the improvements had disappeared, and participants did not differ from a previously unstudied group that had not undergone such treatment. In this study, restricting the focus to two clearly delineated traumatic events may have reduced the impact of the treatment procedure on overall PTSD symptoms.

Overall, the studies reviewed here provide little support for the hypothesis that eye movements are critical to the effects of EMDR. However, a final conclusion regarding this issue is precluded by methodological limitations of the various studies (listed under "Comments" in Table 7.1), including treatment refractory subjects, questionably adequate treatment dosage and fidelity, and limited power due to small samples. Kazdin and Bass (1989) discuss the problem of evaluating competing treatments in designs and samples that confer inadequate power, and they specifically note the implication for dismantling studies of psychotherapy. Additional research in designs that rectify these limitations using carefully defined control conditions, establishing high levels of treatment fidelity, and incorporating large numbers of patients drawn from treatment responsive populations, is indicated.

EFFICACY RATING AND CLINICAL RECOMMENDATIONS

Based upon this review of seven published, randomized, controlled, efficacy studies, we assign EMDR an AHCPR Level A/B rating. The "A" component of this rating means that the reviewed studies found EMDR to be more efficacious for PTSD than wait-list, routine-care, and active-treatment controls. Studies of EMDR treatment have generally yielded large effect sizes. The "B" component of this rating means that additional studies that employ more extensive controls addressing the limitations of studies to date, and that compare EMDR to other focused PTSD treatments, are needed to establish the highest level of confidence in EMDR's efficacy. As might be expected for any treatment, the evidence is stronger for the beneficial effect of EMDR on persons with single-event civilian trauma than on multiply traumatized, treatment refractory, chronically ill war veterans who are often inpatients, substance dependent, compensation seeking, and/or previously unresponsive to treatment.

It is important to distinguish the treatment of a single traumatic memory from the treatment of PTSD. In some early studies, this distinction was not preserved, leading to unrealistic expectations. Accordingly, EMDR dosage (i.e., number of sessions) should be consistent with the complexity of the trauma and the number of traumatic memories.

QUESTIONS IN NEED OF FURTHER RESEARCH

To date, few EMDR studies have benefited from external funding. As a result, the extant studies have been conducted in field settings, resulting in studies with higher external than internal validity. In this sense, EMDR treatment research has not fully matured. For example, EMDR proponents maintain that treatment fidelity strongly influences efficacy. However, most EMDR studies to date have not used sophisticated tools such as multirater evaluations or checklists to assess fidelity. This creates difficulties in interpreting results. Such methodological controls represent the next needed step in evaluating EMDR's efficacy as a treatment for PTSD and are strongly encouraged.

Support for EMDR's therapeutic efficacy does not necessarily imply support either for its underlying theory or for the postulated role of eye movements or other specific EMDR components. On the other hand, the finding that a procedure employing multiple, brief, interrupted exposures to traumatic material can be efficacious, calls for a reexamination of traditional theoretical notions that prolonged, continuous exposure is required (Eysenck, 1979). Further investigation of such issues promises to deepen our understanding of trauma treatment mechanisms. Additional properly designed dismantling studies also need to be conducted in order to identify what components of EMDR are beneficial. Ideally, such studies should be conducted with patients who are likely to be responsive to treatment (e.g., single trauma, more acute), because it is difficult to compare differences in induced changes in minimally responsive patients.

Comparisons of EMDR with other PTSD treatments in larger samples are indicated. These should not be restricted to efficacy but should also examine other important issues such as treatment efficiency (cf. Marcus, Marquis, & Sakai, 1997), and patient tolerance and comfort (Pitman et al., 1996; see also Cahill & Frueh, 1997), which may be advantages of this therapy. It is also important to determine which patient characteristics predict improvement with which treatment modality. EMDR's efficacy in the treatment of childhood PTSD needs to be investigated further. Finally, an extraordinarily large number of therapists have been trained in EMDR, a highly standardized treatment modality. These therapists represent a potentially valuable resource for mounting large, field-based effectiveness trials of PTSD treatment.

REFERENCES

Boudewyns, P. A., & Hyer, L. A. (1996). Eye movement desensitization and reprocessing (EMDR) as treatment for post-traumatic stress disorder (PTSD). *Clinical Psychology and Psychotherapy, 3,* 185–195.

Boudewyns, P. A., Stwertka, S. A., Hyer, L. A., Albrecht, J. W., & Sperr, E. V. (1993). Eye movement desensitization for PTSD of combat: A treatment outcome pilot study. *Behavior Therapist, 16,* 29–33.

Bower, G. H. (1981). Mood and memory. *American Psychologist, 36,* 129–148.

Cahill, S. P., & Frueh, B. C. (1996). Flooding versus eye movement desensitization and reprocessing therapy: Relative efficacy has yet to be investigated (comment on Pitman et al.). *Comprehensive Psychiatry, 38,* 300–303.

Carlson, J. G., Chemtob, C. M., Rusnak, K., Hedlund, N. L., & Muraoka, M. Y. (1998). Eye movement desensitization and reprocessing (EMDR) treatment for combat-related posttraumatic stress disorder. *Journal of Traumatic Stress, 11,* 3–24.

Chemtob, C. M., Nakashima, J., Hamada, R., & Carlson, J. (in press). Brief treatment for elementary school children with disaster-related PTSD: A field study. *Journal of Clinical Psychology.*

Chemtob, C. M., Roitblat, H. L., Hamada, R. S., Carlson, J. G., & Twentyman, C. T. (1988). A cognitive action theory of post-traumatic stress disorder. *Journal of Anxiety Disorders, 2*(3), 253–275.

Devilly, G. J., & Spence, S. H. (1999). The relative efficacy and treatment distress of EMDR and a cognitive-behavior trauma treatment protocol in the amelioration of posttraumatic stress disorder. *Journal of Anxiety Disorders, 13,* 131–157.

Devilly, G. J., Spence, S. H., & Rapee, R. M. (1998). Statistical and reliable change with eye movement desensitization and reprocessing: Treating trauma within a veteran population. *Behavior Therapy, 29,* 435–455.

Eysenck H. J. (1979). The conditioning model of neurosis. *Behavioral and Brain Sciences, 2,* 155–199.

Feske, U. (1998). Eye movement desensitization and reprocessing treatment for posttraumatic stress disorder. *Clinical Psychology: Science and Practice, 5,* 171–181.

Foa, E. B., & Kozak, M. J. (1986). Emotional processing of fear: Exposure to corrective information. *Psychological Bulletin, 99,* 20–35.

Foa, E. B., & Meadows, E. A. (1997). Psychosocial treatments for posttraumatic stress disorder: A critical review. *Annual Review of Psychology, 48,* 449–480.

Foa, E. B., Steketee, G., & Rothbaum, B. O. (1989). Behavioral/cognitive conceptualizations of post-traumatic stress disorder. *Behavior Therapy, 20,* 155–176.

Forbes, D., Creamer, M., & Rycroft, P. (1994). Eye movement desensitization and reprocessing in posttraumatic stress disorder: A pilot study using assessment measures. *Journal of Behavior Therapy and Experimental Psychiatry, 25,* 113–120.

Horowitz, M. J. (1976). *Stress response syndromes.* New York: Aronson.

Janet, P. (1973). *L' automatisme psychologique.* Paris: Société Pierre Janet.

Jensen, J. A. (1994). An investigation of eye movement desensitization and reprocessing (EMD/R) as a treatment for posttraumatic stress disorder (PTSD) symptoms of Vietnam combat veterans. *Behavior Therapy, 25,* 311–325.

Kazdin, A. E., & Bass, D. (1989). Power to detect differences between alternative treatments in comparative psychotherapy outcome research. *Journal of Consulting and Clinical Psychology, 57,* 138–147.

Lang, P. J. (1979). A bio-informational theory of emotional imagery. *Psychophysiology, 16,* 495–512.

Lazrove, S., Triffleman, E., Kite, L., McGlashan, T., & Rounsaville, B. (1998). An open trial of EMDR as treatment for chronic PTSD. *American Journal of Orthopsychiatry, 69,* 601–608.

Lohr, J. M., Tolin, D. F., & Lilienfeld, S. O. (1998). Efficacy of eye movement desensitization and reprocessing: Implications for behavior therapy. *Behavior Therapy, 29,* 123–156.

Macklin, M. L., Metzger, L. J., Lasko, N. B., Berry, N. J., Orr, S. P., & Pitman, R. K. (2000). Five-year follow-up study of eye movement desensitization and reprocessing therapy for combat-related posttraumatic stress disorder. *Comprehensive Psychiatry, 41*(1), 24–27.

Mahoney, M. J. (1978). Experimental methods and outcome evaluation. *Journal of Consulting and Clinical Psychology, 46,* 660–672.

Marcus, S. V., Marquis, P., & Sakai, C. (1997). Controlled study of treatment of PTSD using EMDR in an HMO setting. *Psychotherapy, 34,* 307–315.

Montgomery, R. W., & Ayllon, T. (1994). Eye movement desensitization across subjects: Subjective and physiological measures of treatment efficacy. *Journal of Behavior Therapy and Experimental Psychiatry, 25,* 217–230.

Piaget, J. (1950). *The psychology of intelligence.* New York: Harcourt, Brace & World.

Pitman, R. K., Orr, S. P., Altman, B., Longpre, R. E., Poire, R. E., & Macklin, M. L. (1996). Emotional processing during eye movement desensitization and reprocessing (EMDR) therapy of Vietnam veterans with post-traumatic stress disorder. *Comprehensive Psychiatry, 37,* 419–429.

Renfrey, G., & Spates, C. R. (1994). Eye movement desensitization: A partial dismantling study. *Journal of Behavior Therapy and Experimental Psychiatry, 25,* 231–239.

Rothbaum, B. O. (1997). A controlled study of eye movement desensitization and reprocessing in the treatment of posttraumatic stress disordered sexual assault victims. *Bulletin of the Menninger Clinic, 61,* 317–334.

Scheck, M. M., Schaeffer, J. A., & Gillette, C. (1998). Brief psychological intervention with traumatized young women: The efficacy of eye movement desensitization and reprocessing. *Journal of Traumatic Stress, 11,* 25–44.

Shapiro, F. (1989). Eye movement desensitization: A new treatment for post-traumatic stress disorder. *Journal of Behavior Therapy and Experimental Psychiatry, 20,* 211–217.

Shapiro, F. (1995). *Eye movement desensitization and reprocessing: Basic principles, protocols, and procedures.* New York: Guilford Press.

Shapiro, F. (1996). Eye movement desensitization and reprocessing (EMDR): Evaluation of controlled PTSD research. *Journal of Behavior Therapy and Experimental Psychiatry, 27,* 209–218.

Shapiro, F. (1999). Eye movement desensitization and reprocessing (EMDR) and the anxiety disorders: Clinical and research implications of an integrated psychotherapy treatment. *Journal of Anxiety Disorders, 13,* 35–67.

Silver, S. M., Brooks, A., & Obenchain, J. (1995). Treatment of Vietnam War veterans with PTSD: A comparison of eye movement desensitization and reprocessing, biofeedback, and relaxation training. *Journal of Traumatic Stress, 8,* 337–342.

Spector, J., & Read, J. (1999). The current status of eye movement desensitization and reprocessing (EMDR). *Clinical Psychology and Psychotherapy, 6,* 165–174.

van der Kolk, B. A. (1994). The body keeps the score: Memory and the evolving psychobiology of posttraumatic stress. *Harvard Review of Psychiatry, 1,* 253–265.

Vaughan, K., Armstrong, M. S., Gold, R., O'Connor, N., Jenneke, W., & Tarrier, N. (1994). A trial of eye movement desensitization compared to image habituation training and applied muscle relaxation in post-traumatic stress disorder. *Journal of Behavior Therapy and Experimental Psychiatry, 25,* 283–291.

Wilson, D. L., Silver, S. M., Covi, W. G., & Foster, S. (1996). Eye movement desensitization and reprocessing: Effectiveness and autonomic correlates. *Journal of Behavior Therapy and Experimental Psychiatry, 27,* 219–229.

Wilson, S. A., Becker, L. A., & Tinker, R. H. (1995). Eye movement desensitization and reprocessing (EMDR) treatment for psychologically traumatized individuals. *Journal of Consulting and Clinical Psychology, 63,* 928–937.

Wilson, S. A., Becker, L. A., & Tinker, R. H. (1997). Fifteen-month follow-up of eye movement desensitization and reprocessing (EMDR) treatment for posttraumatic stress and psychological trauma. *Journal of Consulting and Clinical Psychology, 65,* 1047–1056.

8

Group Therapy

David W. Foy, Shirley M. Glynn, Paula P. Schnurr,
Mary K. Jankowski, Melissa S. Wattenberg, Daniel S. Weiss,
Charles R. Marmar, and Fred D. Gusman

The purpose of this chapter is to present a critical review of group therapy approaches currently used in the treatment of chronic posttraumatic stress disorder (PTSD). A brief overview of the historical development of group treatment for PTSD is first presented, followed by a discussion of three commonly utilized group treatment approaches. Data on the empirical support for group treatment for PTSD are next detailed; indications and contraindications for the use of group interventions with specific survivors are described; and areas of necessary further investigation are then identified.

Given the contemporaneous recognition of PTSD as a psychiatric diagnosis and the growth of the self-help movement and group treatment modalities in the 1970s, it is perhaps not a coincidence that group therapy attracted great interest as a front-line treatment for PTSD during this epoch (see, e.g., Horowitz & Solomon, 1975). The appeal of group interventions for PTSD rests, to a large extent, on the clear relevance of joining with others in therapeutic work when coping with a disorder marked by isolation, alienation, and diminished feelings (Allen & Bloom, 1994). A group intervention seems even more suitable for populations such as Vietnam veterans or sexual assault survivors, who often feel ostracized from the larger society or even judged and blamed for their predicament. Furthermore, it is not at all surprising that among these individuals who felt alienated from the greater community, group interventions originally tended to adopt a "survivor helping survivor" or "band of sisters/brothers" model, in which the group facilitator(s) in fact shared the same traumatic exposure history as those seeking counseling

(Lifton, 1973; Shatan, 1973). These interventions emphasized communality and mutual commitment. The genesis of veterans' "rap groups" and the creation of the VA Readjustment Counseling Service, in which Vietnam veterans were hired to assist other veterans outside of the traditional hospital setting, epitomizes this type of approach.

While informal rap groups have a place historically in the evolution of group treatment methods for PTSD, there have been no controlled trials to establish an empirical basis for their efficacy in promoting recovery from traumatic events. However, mental health professionals from several theoretical orientations have refined and tested a number of more systematic group interventions for PTSD over the past 20 years. In contrast to rap groups, these interventions hold to clearly delineated lines between therapist and clients and are intended for group members who share a specific, well-diagnosed, acknowledged psychiatric disorder. Some have argued that they are especially appropriate in more chronic forms of PTSD (Walker & Nash, 1981).

From a broad theoretical perspective, these group approaches might be classified as "supportive," "psychodynamic," or "cognitive-behavioral." While they may differ in their underlying formulations of symptom etiology and maintenance, these approaches share some similar features: (1) homogeneous membership in the group by survivors of the same type of trauma (e.g., combat veterans or sexual assault survivors); (2) acknowledgment and validation of the traumatic exposure; (3) normalization of traumatic responses; (4) utilization of the presence of other individuals with a similar traumatic history to dispel the notion that the therapist cannot be helpful to the survivors because he or she has not shared the experience; and (5) adoption of a nonjudgmental stance toward behavior required for survival at the time of the trauma. Incorporating these principles facilitates the development of a psychologically safe, respectful therapeutic environment.

The theoretical contributions of Yalom's (1975) principles of group process to the conduct of each of the three types of group treatment have often been acknowledged (e.g., the importance of instilling hope). Nevertheless, it is imperative to note that none of these approaches is, strictly defined, "process-oriented"; that is, the critical therapeutic ingredient is not thought to be the corrective recapitulation of the primary family group, nor is it expression of intense affect between members about their relationship. In terms of how group treatments are designed specifically to address the traumatic experiences of their members, distinctions have been made between "covering" and "uncovering" methods. Supportive groups represent a "covering" approach in which the emphasis is placed on addressing current life issues, while psychodynamic and cognitive-behavioral approaches are designed to address members' specific traumatic experiences and memories directly (i.e., "uncover" the trauma). In fact, current group treatments from either psychodynamic or cognitive-behavioral perspectives are often described as "trauma focus" groups, wherein members' recounting of their traumatic experiences is a primary feature. Trauma focus groups of either type are more likely to be conducted as "closed" or cohort groups, while supportive groups are amenable to an "open" format in which members can be added after the group begins. Some clinicians have posited that a combination of approaches, tailored to the individual's specific phase of the disorder and clinical status, may be most appropriate (see, e.g., Herman, 1992).

DESCRIPTION OF TECHNIQUES

Brief descriptions are provided for each of these three different kinds of group treatment types: supportive group therapy, psychodynamic group therapy, and cognitive-behavioral group therapy.

Supportive Group Therapy

While diverse in purpose and theoretical orientation, groups within the supportive modality bear a "family resemblance," tending to share certain characteristic and distinguishing features. Unlike uncovering therapies, supportive groups include little focus on the actual details of traumatic experiences, although they acknowledge and validate the impact of trauma. Interventions aim at exploring middle-range affects (e.g., frustration, sadness, happiness, hurt), diffusing more extreme affects related to hyperarousal (e.g., rage, terror). While supportive groups may incorporate structured material, the purpose of such information is generally to enhance the comfort level of the group in contrast to the use of content in cognitive-behavioral skills training and formal psychoeducational groups. Demand on clients is typically low to moderate, with little or no homework or testing for mastery of material. Supportive groups are designed to maintain a sense of interpersonal comfort and to keep transference at a low to moderate level.

As an alternative to exposure-based, uncovering, and skills-building treatments, supportive group therapy provides a context that orients members toward current coping. For individuals with PTSD, struggles with intrusions, avoidance and numbing, and hyperarousal may disrupt present-day living. Over time, this disruption from the traumatic past can interfere with attention and response to current circumstances, leading to deterioration in functioning. Relying on many of the intrinsic therapeutic factors of group psychotherapy (Yalom, 1975), supportive PTSD groups mobilize the strengths and competence of group members to reduce or control interference from symptoms and trauma-based attitudes as they affect social, emotional, occupational, recreational, and health-related functioning.

"Supportive" is an umbrella term covering a variety of modified-process group approaches that focus on current life issues and problems. Sup-

portive groups can be conducted in a range of clinical and paraclinical settings as a means of engendering in members a sense of community for otherwise isolating chronic conditions and circumstances. In PTSD programs,
supportive groups may serve as the primary therapy modality, as introduction
and preparation for further therapy, or as support for compliance with other
concurrent treatment (e.g., individual or group trauma work, or formal skills
building). In intensive outpatient, partial hospitalization, or inpatient programs for PTSD, this modality is often the "glue" that holds the overall treatment package together, providing the cohesion that increases patients' comfort with more demanding therapies.

Psychodynamic Group Therapy

The goal of psychodynamic group treatment for PTSD is to give each survivor new understanding about what it means to have been exposed to
trauma and to have reacted the way he or she did, and to help the survivor
confront the continuing issues presented by the experience. From a psychodynamic perspective, a clarification of the working model of self and other(s)
involved in reactions to the traumatic event is a key therapeutic ingredient.
These clarifications may be in the form of cognitive appraisal of internal di-
alogue about the meaning of the event, "lessons learned," or personal meaning attributed to an event, or an aspect of an event. This process involves the
exploration of conscious and unconscious self-concepts related to weak and
strong self-representations evoked by the trauma, as these self-concepts are
related to current conflicted views of the self and connected to the self-representations from early development. As well, clarification of frequently implicit assumptions (e.g., someone has to be blameworthy) about the meaning
of the trauma for the individual can be as important as the actual process of
being in a group treatment where discussion of what happened occurs in a
safe context.

Effective treatment involves integration of an accurate recounting of
traumatic events, to the degree possible, including pre- and posttrauma issues that are an important components of the story. The latter may include
responses by family or significant others, or other issues, in the social milieu
in which the event occurred. Appropriate affective involvement, monitored
to control patients' feelings of being overwhelmed and offset the risk for precipitating dissociative reactions, is a fundamental requirement of the approach. This affective involvement usually proceeds from initial anxiety pri-
or to recounting the incident, anxiety and/or tears of pain during the
telling, to a kind of "calm after the storm," during which some consolidation
occurs. In the psychodynamic approach, the painful affects are traced back
to views, frequently irrational, of self and other. These irrational views include the need for omnipotent control, the assumption that betrayal is in-
evitable, the belief that trauma happens only for a good or understandable

reason, and that avoidance of strong feelings is a necessary or positive protective strategy.

Cognitive-Behavioral Group Therapy

The primary objective of cognitive-behavioral group therapy is to reduce PTSD symptoms directly or to enhance members' control of their chronic symptoms. Improving self-control and quality of life in those whose lives have been controlled by their symptoms is seen as equally important to immediate symptom reduction. Emphasizing these objectives takes into account the frequent intractable nature of chronic PTSD insofar as lifelong risk for symptom exacerbation is concerned. However, the approach challenges members to adopt realistic goals of living fuller lives while managing risks of periodic symptom exacerbation.

Cognitive-behavioral focus group therapy emphasizes application of systematic, prolonged exposure and cognitive restructuring to each individual's traumatic experience, and relapse prevention training to enhance members' coping skills and resources for maintaining control over specific PTSD and related symptoms (Foy, Ruzek, Glynn, Riney, & Gusman, 1997). The cognitive-behavioral model of trauma focus group therapy may be set in a developmental perspective, taking into account important relationships and experiences occurring across the entire life span (over pretrauma, trauma, and posttrauma time frames) for group members who may now be in middle adulthood (Gusman et al., 1996). Thus, cognitive-behavioral models may feature an autobiographical emphasis that combines both individual narrative construction and the group concept of others bearing witness nonjudgmentally as members publicly recount their significant life experiences. In addition, by encouraging group members repeatedly to experience their personal tragic events, as well as being exposed vicariously to the experiences of other group members, the model incorporates trauma processing. Relapse prevention planning is a final core component of cognitive-behavioral trauma focus groups. Emphasis on mobilizing coping resources to be used in predictable, high-risk situations is intended to help maintain treatment gains between sessions and after group therapy is completed.

Differences between Psychodynamic and Cognitive-Behavioral Approaches

While the two uncovering approaches share a common emphasis on direct trauma processing, there are notable differences between them regarding treatment goals, methods, and assumed mechanisms. Psychodynamic group treatments are oriented toward increasing understanding (insight) of survivors' traumatic experiences and reactions, and giving meaning to current life. In contrast, cognitive-behavioral treatments are primarily intended to

decrease or improve control over trauma-related symptoms. Carefully recounting the traumatic event with controlled affective arousal is typical of the
psychodynamic treatment method, while cognitive-behavioral methods utilize prolonged, repeated exposure to the traumatic experience. Restructuring
self–other representations is likely to be described as the assumed treatment
mechanism in psychodynamic treatment, in contrast with the principles of
habituation and extinction that are invoked by cognitive-behavioral theorists.

METHOD OF COLLECTING DATA

The primary method used to identify empirical studies of group treatment
for PTSD was a literature search using the PILOTS database at the National
Center for PTSD in White River Junction, Vermont. Additionally, members
of the group treatment subcommittee and others were asked to submit other
studies that, to their knowledge, were not initially identified. Standards to
evaluate study methodologies were derived from Kazdin and Bass (1989) and
Foa and Meadows (1997).

SUMMARY OF LITERATURE

In this section, clinical trials of group psychotherapy for adult trauma survivors are briefly reviewed. The review excludes case studies and reports on
the efficacy of multicomponent inpatient programs in which combinations of
various types of group therapy are delivered. Table 8.1 lists the reviewed
studies, along with information about selected methodological features and
major findings. Treatment typically was delivered in 10–15 weekly sessions
(range = 6 weeks to 1 year), and session length was usually set at 1½ or 2
hours. Tables 8.2 and 8.3 display effect sizes for those studies whose data permitted these calculations. Almost all of the studies were conducted with female survivors of childhood or adulthood sexual abuse; very few studies were
found to be conducted with male participants.

Supportive Group Therapy

Table 8.1 shows three studies (Cryer & Beutler, 1980; Richter, Snider, &
Gorey, 1997; Tutty, Bidgood, & Rothery, 1993) designed to evaluate supportive group therapy, sampling adult female survivors of childhood sexual abuse
(2 studies) or survivors of domestic violence (1 study). With treatment duration ranging from 10 to 15 sessions, these studies examined treatment outcome through measures of self-esteem, depression, and anxiety. None of
these studies measured PTSD symptoms directly. Favorable results were
reported in each study, and Tables 8.2 and 8.3 show that the effect sizes

TABLE 8.1. Studies of Group Psychotherapy for Trauma Survivors: Cognitive-Behavioral, Psychodynamic, and Supportive Types

Study (type)	Treatment group (% of enrolled)	Comparison group (% of enrolled)	No. of sessions/ group sizes	Population	Major findings
Randomized designs					
Alexander, Neimeyer, Follette, Moore, & Harter (1989) (psychodynamic)	16 interpersonal transaction 20 process group (84% across treatment groups)	21 wait-list control (% NA)	10 weekly/ NA	Female CSA survivors	Not controlling for pretest scores, both treatment groups improved more than controls in depression and distress; only the process group improved in social adjustment; gains were generally maintained at 6-month follow-up.
Zlotnik et al. (1997) (cognitive-behavioral)	17 affect management (71%)	16 wait-list control (67%)	15 weekly/ 6–8	Female CSA survivors w/PTSD who had received individual psycho- and/or pharmacotherapy	Controlling for pretest scores, affect management improved more than controls in PTSD and dissociation.
Nonrandomized designs					
Hall, Mullee, & Thompson (1995) (psychodynamic)	53 analytic (open enrollment) (56%)	18 no-treatment control (53%)	6 months weekly (varied)/ ≤ 12	Female CSA survivors	Not controlling for pretest scores, posttest service utilization decreased in the treatment group but not in the comparison group. Within the treatment group, depression decreased over time.

(continued)

TABLE 8.1. (continued)

Study (type)	Treatment group (% of enrolled)	Comparison group (% of enrolled)	No. of sessions/ group sizes	Population	Major findings
Nonrandomized designs (cont.)					
Resick & Schnicke (1992) (cognitive–behavioral)	19 cognitive processing therapy (90%)	20 wait-list control	12 weekly/ 5–8	Female sexual assault survivors	Not controlling for pretest scores, cognitive processing treatment improved more than controls in PTSD and depression scores. Within the treatment group only: relative to pretest scores, posttest scores improved in PTSD, depression, distress, and social adjustment; changes were maintained at 3- and 6-month follow-up, and depression continued to improve from posttreatment to 3 months.
Resick, Jordan, Girelli, Hutter, & Marhoefer-Dvorak (1988) (cognitive–behavioral)	12 stress inoculation 13 assertiveness training 12 supportive psychotherapy (86% across treatment groups)	13 wait-list control, all of whom were included in treatment groups	6 weekly/ 4–8	Female sexual assault survivors	No improvement from pretest to posttest in wait-list group; not controlling for pretest scores, all groups improved similarly from pre- to posttest on anxiety; depression, self-esteem, fear, and PTSD; improvements were generally maintained at 3- and 6-month follow-up.
Richter, Snider, & Gorey (1997) (supportive)	78 problem-solving group, some of whom are counted in comparison group; total n = 115 (87%)	80 wait-list control, some of whom are counted in treatment group	15 weekly/ 4–10	Female CSA survivors	Not controlling for pretest scores (but which were equivalent), active treatment improved more than controls in depression and self-esteem scores.

Study	Treatment group	Control group	Length/sessions	Population	Results
Roth, Dye, & Lebowitz (1988) (psychodynamic)	7 active treatment (78%)	6 no-treatment control (46%)	1 year weekly/ 7	Female sexual assault survivors	Not controlling for pretest scores, active treatment improved less than controls in intrusion scores by Session 8; no differences in five other measures. Within the treatment group only: relative to pretest scores, Session 20 scores improved in rape-related fears, psychosocial functioning, and intrusion; gains generally maintained at end of treatment.
Single-group designs					
Carver, Stalker, Stewart, & Abraham (1989) (psychodynamic)	29 process group (51%)		10 and 15 weekly/ NA	Female CSA survivors	Relative to initial assessment, pretest scores showed no change (n = 20; all 20 did not necessarily complete pre–post assessment). Relative to pretest scores, posttest scores showed improvement in all SCL-90 scores except paranoid ideation but not in (a non-SCL measure of) depression and social behavior.
Cryer & Beutler (1980) (supportive)	9 unspecified treatment (NA)		10 weekly/ 9	Female sexual assault survivors	Relative to pretest scores, posttest scores improved in distress, obsessiveness, anxiety, and expression of control.
Frueh, Turner, Beidel, Mirabella, & Jones (1996) (cognitive-behavioral)	11 social and emotional rehabilitation (group component of trauma management therapy) (73%)		10 weekly and biweekly/ 2–5	Male Vietnam combat veterans	Relative to midtreatment scores (when treatment switched from individual to group), posttest scores improved in clinical global impressions, anxiety, and social activities.

(continued)

TABLE 8.1. (continued)

Study (type)	Treatment group (% of enrolled)	Comparison group (% of enrolled)	No. of sessions/ group sizes	Population	Major findings
Single-group designs (cont.)					
Hazzard, Rogers, & Angert (1993) (psychodynamic)	78 process group (53%)		1 year weekly/ 4–10	Female CSA survivors	Relative to pretest scores, posttest scores improved in locus of control, sexual problems, self-esteem, PTSD symptoms, and distress.
Lubin, Loris, Burt, & Johnson (1998) (cognitive-behavioral)	29 cognitive-behavioral (76%)		16 weekly/ 6–7	Female multiple trauma survivors	Relative to pretest scores, posttest scores improved in intrusion, avoidance, hyperarousal, and depression.
Stauffer & Deblinger (1996) (cognitive-behavioral)	19 cognitive-behavioral (56%)		11 weekly/ NA	Nonoffending females and their sexually abused, 2- to 6-year-old children	Relative to pretest scores, Week 10 scores improved in adult distress, PTSD symptoms, parenting behavior, and child sexual behavior; gains maintained at 3-month follow-up.
Tutty, Bidgood, & Rothery (1993) (supportive)	60 support group (67%) 32 (53%) 6-month follow-up		10–12 weekly/ NA	Female survivors of domestic violence	Relative to pretest scores, posttest scores improved in locus of control, self-esteem, stress and coping, marital relations, and physical and nonphysical violence; improvements maintained at follow-up, although sample was biased toward highest functioning women.

Note. NA, not available; CSA, childhood sexual abuse.

TABLE 8.2. Hedges's Unbiased Effect Size Estimator (g) for Comparisons with Control Groups

Authors (year)	Target population	No. and length of treatment sessions	Dependent measure	Control and treatment groups	Sample and effect sizes for completers	
					n	g
Alexander, Neimeyer, Follette, Moore, & Harter (1989)	Female CSA survivors	10 wk 1½-hr sessions	Modified Fear Survey (MFS)	Wait-list control	21	—
				Interpersonal transaction	16	0.04
				Process format	20	-0.23
Zlotnick et al. (1997)	Female CSA survivors receiving individual therapy concurrently	15 wk 2-hr sessions	Davidson Trauma Scale	Wait-list control	17	—
				Affect management	16	0.83
Resick & Schnicke (1992)	Female sexual assault survivors	12 wk 1½-hr sessions	PTSD subscale of the SCL-90-R	Wait-list control	20	—
				Cognitive processing	19	0.62
Resick, Jordan, Girelli, Hutter, & Marhoefer-Dvorak (1988)	Female sexual assault survivors	6 sessions 2 hr ea.	IES (intrusions)	Wait-list control	13	—
				Assertiveness	13	0.33
				Supportive	12	0.19
				Stress inoculation	12	0.07
			IES (avoidance)	Wait-list control	13	—
				Stress inoculation	12	0.60
				Assertiveness	13	0.57
				Supportive	12	0.50
Richter, Snider, & Gorey (1997)	Female CSA survivors receiving individual therapy concurrently	15 wk 1½-2-hr sessions	BDI	Wait-list control	80	—
				Supportive	78	0.60
Roth, Dye, & Lebowitz (1988)	Female sexual assault survivors receiving individual therapy concurrently	1 yr 2½-hr sessions	IES (intrusions)	Wait-list control	6	—
				Psychodynamic	7	-1.56
Hall, Mullee, & Thompson (1995)[a]	Female CSA survivors	1–45 sessions		Control	34	—
				Psychoanalytic	94	—

Note. SCL-90-R, Symptom Checklist 90—Revised; IES, Impact of Event Scale; BDI, Beck Depression Inventory.
[a]Effect size cannot be calculated with data provided.

TABLE 8.3. Hedges's Unbiased Effect Size Estimator (g) for Pretreatment versus Posttreatment Comparisons

Authors (year)	Target population	No. and length of treatment sessions	Dependent measure	Treatment groups	n	g
Carver, Stalker, Stewart, & Abraham (1989)[a]	Female CSA survivors	10–15 wk	Zung Depression Scale	Psychodynamic	20	—
Cryer & Beutler (1980)	Female sexual assault survivors	10 wk 1½-hr sessions	GSI of the SCL-90	Supportive	9	0.66
Frueh, Turner, Beidel, Mirabella, & Jones (1996)	Male Vietnam combat veterans	12 wk 14 1½-hr sessions	CAPS-1	Trauma management (social and emotional rehabilitation)	11	1.09
Hazzard, Rogers, & Angert (1993)	Female CSA survivors	1 yr 1½-hr weekly sessions	Trauma Symptom Checklist (TSC-33)	Process format	34	0.44
Lubin, Loris, Burt, & Johnson (1998)	Female multiple trauma survivors	16 wk 1½-hr sessions	CAPS	Cognitive-behavioral	29	0.81
Stauffer & Deblinger (1996)	Nonoffending mothers and their sexually abused children ages 2–6 yr	11 wk 2-hr sessions	IES (intrusions) IES (avoidance)	Cognitive-behavioral	19 19	0.24 0.56
Tutty, Bidgood, & Rothery (1993)	Female survivors of domestic violence	10–12 wk 2- to 3-hr sessions	Perceived Stress Scale	Supportive	60	0.54

Note. CAPS, Clinician-Administered PTSD Scale; CAPS-1, Clinician-Administered PTSD Scale; GSI, Global Severity Index of Symptom Checklist.
[a]Effect size cannot be calculated with data provided.

obtained on primary measures in these three studies were highly similar (0.54, 0.60, and 0.66) even though the actual outcome variables were different in each study. An advantage of the studies on supportive therapy is that two of them included relatively large sample sizes ($n = 60$–115).

Psychodynamic Group Therapy

Table 8.1 includes five studies examining psychodynamic group therapy (Alexander, Neimeyer, Follette, Moore, & Harter, 1989; Carver, Stalker, Stewart, & Abraham, 1989; Hall, Mullee, & Thompson, 1995; Hazzard, Rogers, & Angert, 1993; Roth, Dye, & Lebowitz, 1988), four of which included larger group sizes ($n = 29$–78). For all five studies, female adult survivors of childhood sexual abuse were sampled. In this set were three studies using control group designs. As was the case with supportive group therapy, each of the studies of psychodynamic group therapy reported positive treatment outcome associated with that treatment condition. Treatment duration was bimodal in distribution, with two studies in the 10- to 15-session range, while two other studies extended treatment for 1 year. PTSD symptoms were directly assessed in two studies; depression and anxiety were measured in the other three studies.

Tables 8.2 and 8.3 show that effect size calculations were possible for three of the studies (-0.23, -1.56, and 0.44). The negative effect size values for the Alexander and colleagues (1989) and Roth and colleagues (1988) studies do not indicate that the psychodynamic treatment groups worsened with treatment. In both of these studies, there was notable discrepancy between the initial status of treatment and wait-list groups, with the wait-list group being less symptomatic in both cases. In the Alexander and colleagues (1989) study, scores on the fear survey for both wait-list and treatment groups decreased in equivalent amounts. In the Roth and associates (1988) study, both the wait-list and treatment groups remained the same over the interval of 8 weeks, the last time point at which the wait-list group was assessed.

Cognitive-Behavioral Group Therapy

There are six studies examining cognitive-behavioral treatment listed in Table 8.1 (Frueh, Turner, Beidel, Mirabella, & Jones, 1996; Lubin, Loris, Burt, & Johnson, 1998; Resick, Jordan, Girelli, Hutter, & Marhoefer-Dvorak, 1988; Resick & Schnicke, 1992; Stauffer & Deblinger, 1996; Zlotnik et al., 1997). There is some variability in the trauma populations sampled in these studies. Three studies sampled adult female survivors of childhood sexual abuse. Combat veterans, female survivors of multiple trauma, and mothers with their sexually abused children were sampled in the other three studies. While the group sample sizes in these studies are relatively small ($n = 11$–37), the results pattern is the same as for the other two types of treatment; that is, every study showed positive treatment outcome for the cognitive behavioral group(s) relative to wait-list controls (three studies) or comparing pre- to post-treatment scores. In this set of studies, treatment duration was relatively short in every case, ranging from 6 to 16 sessions. In every study, direct measures of PTSD were employed, and four studies used equivalent instruments, making direct comparison of results possible. Tables 8.2 and 8.3 show effect sizes ranging from 0.33 to 1.09, with a mean of 0.68 obtained for the set of six studies. Two studies (Resick et al., 1988; Stauffer & Deblinger, 1996) that reported separate measures for intrusion and avoidance symptoms produced similar findings, showing relatively larger treatment effects for avoidance symptoms.

Comparisons across Treatment Types

To date, only one study (Resick, Jordan, Girelli, Hutter, & Marhoefer-Dvorak, 1988) has made a direct comparison between types of group treatment. Resick and her colleagues compared stress inoculation, assertion training, and supportive group therapy to each other as well as to a wait-list condition (all of whose members subsequently were included in one of the three treatment groups). Similar improvements were obtained across therapy conditions, although there was some variability in treatment effect sizes shown on intrusion measures.

Even though effect sizes were calculated on 12 of the 14 studies on group treatment, differences in study design and, most notably, nonequivalence of primary outcome measures constrain direct comparisons of results and conclusions of relative efficacy. In terms of design and methodology, supportive and cognitive-behavioral group treatments were found to be shorter in duration (6–15 weeks in every study) compared to psychodynamic treatments (up to 1 year in three studies). For supportive and psychodynamic treatments, outcome was more likely to be measured as broader aspects of distress or adjustment, while all six cognitive-behavioral treatment studies used direct measures of PTSD severity. Sample sizes for studies of supportive and psychodynamic therapies were typically larger than those in studies of cognitive behavioral therapy. In general, the data show that group psychotherapy, regardless of the nature of the therapy, is associated with favorable outcomes in a range of symptom domains. PTSD and depression are the most commonly included outcomes, but efficacy has been demonstrated for a range of other symptoms as well, including anxiety, self-esteem, and fear.

Methodological Limitations

Despite this generally favorable body of findings, however, significant methodological issues constrain inferences that can be drawn about the efficacy of group treatment generally, or about superiority of one type of group treatment over the others. The strongest inferences may be drawn from the randomized studies that have been conducted. Both Alexander and colleagues (1989) and Zlotnik and colleagues (1997) found that treatment, relative to a wait-list condition, was associated with favorable changes in female survivors of sexual abuse. Using a study design that includes a wait-list comparison group is highly appropriate for evaluating the efficacy of treatment that has not been studied, because inclusion of this group controls for history, maturation, testing, instrumentation, regression to the mean, selection, attrition, and interactions of participant characteristics with these threats to internal validity. However, it is notable that only some of the threats are controlled if random assignment is not used. Because a wait-list comparison group differs in so many ways from a treated group, such designs limit our ability to know whether, or to what extent, observed effects are due to the particular treatments delivered, as opposed to the fact that any treatment was delivered—a problem of construct validity. Although Alexander and associates (1989) found some evidence of treatment specificity (process group treatment, but not interpersonal transaction group treatment, was associated with gain in social adjustment), the problem of interpreting treatment effects generally remains.

Most studies that have not used random assignment also have found that treatment is associated with improvements in symptoms and functioning (Hall, Mullee, & Thompson, 1995; Resick & Schnicke, 1992; Resick, Jordan, Girelli, Hutter, & Marhoefer-Dvorak, 1988; Richter, Snider, & Gorey, 1997; Roth, Dye, & Lebowitz, 1988). Non-randomized designs yield data that are somewhat ambiguous because of the threats to internal validity inherent in the comparison of nonequivalent groups (e.g., maturation, selection). An important method of addressing (but not eliminating) these threats—statistical control for pretreatment differences—was not used in any of the studies in this category. Adding to the interpretation difficulties is the fact that most of these studies had only wait-list/no-treatment comparison groups.

Among studies that did not employ a comparison group (Carver, Stalker, Stewart, & Abraham, 1989; Cryer & Beutler, 1980; Frueh, Turner, Beidel, Mirabella, & Jones, 1996; Hazzard, Rogers, & Angert, 1993; Stauffer & Deblinger, 1996; Tutty, Bidgood, & Rothery, 1993), all found pre- to posttreatment improvements in outcomes. By themselves, these studies have limited interpretability because almost all threats to internal validity cannot be controlled. The study by Carver and colleagues (1989) provides some stronger evidence that the improvements are specific to therapy and not to other factors, especially maturation or regression to the mean. Carver and colleagues made *two* pretest assessments, 7 weeks apart, and found no change in symptoms, while symptom changes were observed posttreatment. The extended baseline observation does not completely rule out threats to validity, but it does substantially strengthen the conclusion that the changes were due to treatment; this is similar to Resick and colleagues' (1988) wait-list condition.

In a conservative interpretation of these findings, the data suggest that group therapy is associated with positive outcomes. A remaining concern is with construct validity—why, or how, group therapy works. Are the observed outcomes merely due to placebo effects? Further studies are needed to determine the mechanisms by which positive outcomes are achieved.

Conducting research on the effectiveness of group psychotherapy is challenging, and our comments about the existing research are not meant to be harsh criticisms of the authors, who, in fact, have done an excellent job in advancing research to its present state. Only because of their work can we recommend that additional research be done, because their demonstrations of efficacy provide a basis for going forward. Although a detailed methodological critique is beyond the scope of this chapter, we later call attention to key issues that are particularly important for future research in this area.

SUMMARY

In the past 20 years since the inception of PTSD as a diagnostic entity, relatively little research attention has been given to evaluating group therapy techniques designed for treating the disorder. Despite an exhaustive search, less than 20 studies of group psychotherapy outcome were identified. Only two of these studies employed randomization in their design methodology. Additionally, other methodological limitations were identified that limit the scientific conclusions that can be drawn from the results of these studies. Most studies sampled populations displaying chronic PTSD symptoms. Nevertheless, positive treatment outcomes were reported in most studies, lending general support to the use of group therapy with trauma survivors. While three distinct types or combinations of group therapies are represented in the literature, treatment outcome findings do not presently favor a particular type. Since research on group therapy for PTSD is in its infancy stage, much more research activity is warranted before techniques producing superior outcomes are clearly identified.

RECOMMENDATIONS

Individuals recovering from PTSD can experience great emotional volatility. Thus, the development of a comprehensive, effective treatment plan, well-suited to the individual, is of paramount importance. Generally, group treatment for PTSD is recommended as potentially effective, based upon consistent evidence from the studies reviewed in this chapter. The levels of evidence for this recommendation range from two studies using randomized control designs (AHCPR Level A), and five studies using nonrandomized control designs (AHCPR Level B), to seven studies using single-group designs in which pre–post differences were examined (AHCPR Level C).

In evaluating an individual's characteristics for appropriateness for participation in a group intervention, two pivotal issues must be addressed: (1) Is a group approach suitable for this individual? and (2) If a group approach is suitable in this case, which type of group would be most appropriate?

Tables 8.4 and 8.5 present factors identified in the literature as important considerations in matching trauma survivors to group treatment. Since these selection factors are primarily rationally derived, they do not constitute hard-and-fast criteria so much as they represent useful guidelines for informing the matching process. Relative to individual forms of therapy for PTSD, group therapies tend to be more structured and place more rigid requirements upon the individual for participation. There is less flexibility for accommodating individual needs that may arise over the course of therapy in the group format. For some individuals, extreme social interaction anxiety may block beneficial participation in group therapy activities.

Comparing selection factors for trauma focus groups to supportive groups, it is evident that there are more stringent requirements for assignment to the "uncovering" modality. Generally, individuals need to be psychologically stable and willing to undergo reexperiencing their traumas. Supportive group therapy may be a better match for less stable individuals or for those who do not accept the rationale for personal trauma processing. Assignment considerations for the two types of trauma focus group therapy appear to be very similar. Clear factors for differentiating between assignment to psychodynamic or cognitive-behavioral group therapies have not been identified.

TABLE 8.4. Indications and Contraindications for Group Therapy

Indications for group therapy

1. Flexible in personal schedule in order to meet group at appointed times
2. Able to establish interpersonal trust with other group members and leaders
3. Prior group experience, including 12-step groups
4. Completion of a preparatory course of individual therapy
5. Not actively suicidal or homicidal
6. Shares similar traumatic experiences with other group members
7. Compatible for gender, ethnicity, and sexual orientation with other members
8. Willing to abide by rules of group confidentiality
9. Not severely paranoid or sociopathic
10. Has stable living arrangements

Contraindications for group therapy

1. Active psychosis
2. Severe organicity or limited cognitive capacity
3. Pending litigation or compensation seeking

TABLE 8.5. Indications for Trauma Focus versus Supportive Groups

1. Individual can tolerate high anxiety arousal or other strong affects
2. No active suicidality or homicidality
3. Substance abuse or other comorbidities are under control
4. Individual accepts rationale for trauma uncovering work
5. Willingness to self-disclose personal traumatic experiences
6. No current life crises

AREAS REQUIRING FURTHER EXPLORATION

In evaluating the utility of a psychotherapy format such as a group intervention, three questions are critical: (1) Does participation in the format yield symptom improvements? (2) Does participation in specific applications of the format (e.g., the psychodynamic group or the supportive group) yield differential improvements? and (3) How might validated applications be best generalized from the research laboratory to clinic practice? Additional systematic research on group treatment for PTSD would be useful on all three topics.

With regard to the first question—Does group therapy improve outcomes in PTSD?—the answer seems affirmative. As reflected in the studies reported in Table 8.1, group therapy utilizing diverse approaches appears to yield benefits, especially among female sexual abuse survivors. Unfortunately, randomized trials on any type of group therapy for PTSD with males are sorely lacking. Given the current prevalence of group approaches in many VA settings with combat veterans, this paucity of research is especially disturbing and merits attention.

With an acceptance of the hypothesis that group therapy yields improvements in PTSD outcomes, the issue of whether particular client characteristics are predictive of outcome becomes of interest. For example, individuals with multiple traumatic events and/or Axis II diagnoses might be expected to achieve more limited benefits from most therapeutic interventions, including group treatment. The identification of common predictive variables would greatly enhance treatment planning and inform our knowledge base.

The answer to the second question—Does participation in specific applications of group therapy yield differential improvement?—is less clear. Published empirical studies comparing different types of group therapy have been limited to that of Resick and colleagues (1988); this study found no special benefit in any of the group treatment approaches. Comparative outcomes studies are notoriously difficult to conduct (Kazdin, 1986), as they are complicated by significant methodological issues.

In terms of implications of the methodological critique of present work, we wish to call attention to five issues that are particularly important for future comparative outcome research (see Foa & Meadows, 1997; Kazdin & Bass, 1989). The first issue is the use of random assignment, which is essential at this point to expand on existing knowledge. While it is most often applied to assignment of subjects to groups, randomization could also be expanded to include assignment of groups to treatment conditions. The advantage here is that smaller treatment facilities could participate in controlled trials when, otherwise, there would be an insufficient supply of study participants for randomizing individuals to competing treatment groups. Second is the use of comparison groups that permit inferences about why a given treatment works. Third is statistical power, which was inadequate for finding all but very large effect sizes in most published studies presented in Table 8.1. Adequate power is especially important for studies that compare one active treatment with another, where effect sizes are almost certain to be smaller than those for comparisons with a wait-list condition (Kazdin & Bass, 1989). A fourth issue concerns manualization and related therapist competence and adherence monitoring; these are important for standardizing treatment delivery and ensuring that therapist competence is equated across treatment conditions (only the following mentioned the use of manuals: Resick, Jordan, Girelli, Hutter, & Marhoefer-Dvorak, 1988; Resick & Schnicke, 1992; Stauffer & Deblinger, 1996; Zlotnik et al., 1997). The fifth, and final, issue is statistical analysis, which needs to account for the clustering of participants within therapy groups (only Alexander, Neimeyer, Follette, Moore, & Harter, 1989, considered this issue).

The final question—How might validated applications be best generalized from the research laboratory to clinic practice?—incorporates two issues. First, most of the randomized trials presented in Table 8.1 are efficacy trials, with relatively strict control on participant inclusion–exclusion criteria and treatment implementation. Effectiveness trials, in which these interventions are evaluated in nonresearch settings, are clearly needed. Here again, research in settings that emphasize treatment in PTSD, such as the VA, would be especially critical. A second issue involves how specific group treatments might best be integrated in the range of clinical services often offered to individuals with severe (and usually chronic) PTSD. Many trauma survivors experience such severe behavioral dysfunction that they concurrently utilize multiple integrated treatment interventions, such as those described by Frueh, Turner, Beidel, Mirabella, and Jones (1996) and Johnson and colleagues (1996). A variety of group and individual therapies typically play a role in these comprehensive interventions. Data on whether comprehensive programs are beneficial are either preliminary (Frueh et al., 1996) or disappointing (Fontana & Rosenheck, 1997). Dismantling studies to identify effective treatment elements, including specific types of group therapy, will be required if positive reports are forthcoming. Here, the need to integrate individual and group treatment toward mutual treatment objectives (Brende, 1981) requires careful consideration. Similarly, the imperative to match interventions with the participant's ability to tolerate the distress inherent in trauma focus groups (Herman, 1992) is an important issue that requires empirical validation.

REFERENCES

Alexander, P. C., Neimeyer, R. A., Follette, V. M., Moore, M. K., & Harter, S. (1989). A comparison of group treatments of women sexually abused as children. *Journal of Consulting and Clinical Psychology, 57,* 479–483.

Allen, S. N., & Bloom, S. L. (1994). Group and family treatment of posttraumatic stress disorder. *Psychiatric Clinics of North America, 17,* 425–437.

Brende, J. O. (1981). Combined individual and group therapy for Vietnam veterans. *International Journal of Group Psychotherapy, 31,* 367–377.

Carver, C. M., Stalker, C. A., Stewart, E., & Abraham, B. (1989). The impact of group therapy for adult survivors of childhood sexual abuse. *Canadian Journal of Psychiatry, 34,* 753–758.

Cryer, L., & Beutler, L. E. (1980). Group therapy: An alternative treatment approach for rape victims. *Journal of Sex and Marital Therapy, 6,* 40–46.

Foa, E. B., & Meadows, E. A. (1997). Psychosocial treatments for post-traumatic stress disorder: A critical review. In J. Spence, J. M. Darley, & D. J. Foss (Eds.), *Annual review of psychology* (Vol. 48, pp. 449–480). Palo Alto, CA: Annual Reviews.

Fontana, A., & Rosenheck, R. (1997). Effectiveness and cost of the inpatient treatment of post-trauamtic stress disorder: Comparison of three models of treatment. *American Journal of Psychiatry, 154,* 758–765.

Foy, D. W., Ruzek, J. I., Glynn, S. M., Riney, S. A., & Gusman, F. D. (1997). Trauma focus group therapy for combat-related PTSD. *In Session: Psychotherapy in Practice, 3,* 59–73.

Frueh, B. C., Turner, S. M., Beidel, D. C., Mirabella, R. F., & Jones, W. J. (1996). Trauma management therapy: A preliminary evaluation of a multicomponent behavioral treatment for chronic combat-related PTSD. *Behaviour Research and Therapy, 34,* 533–543.

Gusman, F. D., Stewart, J., Young, B. H., Riney, S. J., Abueg, F. R., & Blake, D. D. (1996). *Ethnocultural aspects of posttraumatic stress disorder: issues, research, and clinical applications.* Washington, DC: American Psychological Association.

Hall, Z. M., Mullee, M. A., & Thompson, C. (1995). A clinical and service evaluation of group therapy for women survivors of childhood sexual abuse. In M. Aveline & D. A. Shapiro (Eds.), *Research foundations for psychotherapy practice* (pp. 263–279). New York: Wiley.

Hazzard, A., Rogers, J. H., & Angert, L. (1993). Factors affecting group therapy outcome for adult sexual abuse survivors. *International Journal of Group Psychotherapy, 43,* 453–468.

Herman, J. L. (1992). *Trauma and recovery.* New York: Basic Books.

Horowitz, M. D., & Solomon, G. F. (1975). A prediction of delayed stress response syndrome in Vietnam veterans. *Journal of Social Issues, 4,* 67–79.

Johnson, D. R., Rosenheck, R., Fontana, A., Lubin, H., Southwick, S., & Charney, D. S. (1996). Outcome of intensive inpatient treatment for combat-related posttrauamtic stress disorder. *American Journal of Psychiatry, 153,* 771–777.

Kazdin, A. E. (1986). Comparative outcome studies if psychotherapy: Methodological issues and strategies. *Journal of Consulting and Clinical Psychology, 54,* 95–105.

Kazdin, A. E., & Bass, D. (1989). Power to detect differences between alternative treatments in comparative psychotherapy outcome research. *Journal of Consulting and Clinical Psychology, 57,* 138–147.

Lifton, R. J. (1973). *Home from the war.* New York: Simon & Schuster.

Lubin, H., Loris, M., Burt, J., & Johnson, D. R. (1998). Efficacy of psychoeducational group therapy in reducing symptoms of posttraumatic stress disorder among multiply traumatized women. *American Journal of Psychiatry, 155,* 1172–1177.

Resick, P. A., Jordan, C. G., Girelli, S. A., Hutter, C. K., & Marhoefer-Dvorak, S. (1988). A comparative outcome study of behavioral group therapy for sexual assault victims. *Behavior Therapy, 19,* 385–401.

Resick, P. A., & Schnicke, M. K. (1992). Cognitive processing therapy for sexual assault victims. *Journal of Consulting and Clinical Psychology, 60,* 748–756.

Richter, N. L., Snider, E., & Gorey, K. M. (1997). Group work intervention with female survivors of childhood sexual abuse. *Research on Social Work Practice, 7,* 53–69.

Roth, S. H., Dye, E., & Lebowitz, L. (1988). Group therapy for sexual-assault victims. *Psychotherapy, 25,* 82–93.

Shatan, C. F. (1973). The grief of soldiers: Vietnam combat veterans' self-help movement. *American Journal of Orthopsychiatry, 43,* 640–653.

Stauffer, L. B., & Deblinger, E. (1996). Cognitive behavioral groups for nonoffending mothers and their young sexually abused children: A preliminary treatment outcome study. *Child Maltreatment, 1,* 65–76.

Tutty, L. M., Bidgood, B. A., & Rothery, M. A. (1993). Support groups for battered women: Research on their efficacy. *Journal of Family Violence, 8,* 325–343.

Walker, J. J., & Nash, J. D. (1981). Group therapy in the treatment of Vietnam combat veterans. *International Journal of Group Psychotherapy, 31,* 379–389.

Yalom, I. D. (1975). *The theory and practice of group psychotherapy.* New York: Basic Books.

Zlotnick, C., Shea, M. T., Rosen, K. H., Simpson, E., Mulrenin, K., Begin, A., & Pearlstein, T. (1997). An affect-management group for women with posttraumatic stress disorder and histories of childhood sexual abuse. *Journal of Traumatic Stress, 10,* 425–436.

9

Psychodynamic Therapy

Harold S. Kudler, Arthur S. Blank Jr.,
and Janice L. Krupnick

THEORY STATEMENT

In 1895, Joseph Breuer and Sigmund Freud published their *Studies on Hysteria*, which advanced the proposition that mental disorders are sometimes rooted in psychological trauma. Most of their contemporaries held that psychiatric patients suffered primarily from biological defects. Janet (1886, 1889/1973) was already developing an effective, systematic psychotherapy for trauma survivors, but his premise was that patients were unable to integrate traumatic memories because their brains were degenerate. Breuer and Freud's radical notion was that an idea or experience, in itself, can be pathogenic. They sought the pathogenic thought or memory in order to extract it and thereby provide a cure.

Breuer, who wrote the first case history in the *Studies*, employed hypnosis to probe for, identify, and remove traumatic memories. He found that if he could get his patient to recall the trauma that led to a particular symptom and reexperience that event along with the emotions that accompanied it (*abreaction*), the symptom would disappear. By repeating this process for each of his patient's symptoms, he eventually brought her to health. This cathartic treatment was the first method of analyzing the psyche.

Breuer was Freud's mentor, yet even as the young Freud attempted to follow Breuer's method, he was clearly moving in a very different direction. Freud distrusted hypnosis and, following a patient's advice (Frau Emmy in Breuer & Freud, 1895/1955), began simply to listen to his patients talk about their symptoms (*free association*). Freud hypothesized that hysterical patients repress their awareness of traumatic memories in order to *defend* against them. Repressed memories are not forgotten: they are actively maintained outside of the patient's consciousness. Such memories do, however, remain active at the *unconscious* level of psychic processing. Freud conceived of the interplay between what was conscious and unconscious as a dynamic give-and-take between defense (an *ego* or "myself" function) and what was being defended against (an *id* or "not-myself" function). Psychic balance is maintained by a *compromise* that partially expresses the repressed traumatic memory in the form of a symptom. The symptom also expresses the ego's defense against the memory (and its attendant affect). As an example, a man presented with complaints of a recurrent nightmare in which a local hotel collapsed. He could not understand why he would dream of something that never happened. The nightmare interfered with his sleep and tortured his waking thoughts. In taking a history, his therapist discovered that the patient, who had been a medic during the Gulf War, had been responsible for pulling bodies out of a barracks that had received a direct missile hit. The patient had never associated the dream about his hometown with his horrific war memories. He had generally avoided his war memories in his waking thoughts. (Incidentally, his nightmares ceased after this connection was suggested.)

Psychic balance comes at a price. To the extent that the patient represses, he or she is not dealing with reality. Instead, the patient retreats into a life founded on a wish of how the world should be. Ideally, a survivor will learn to cope with the residua of trauma and achieve a new psychic balance, but if the patient reaches a stalemate, symptoms may grow so severe or so numerous that they become incapacitating. At such times, *psychodynamic psychotherapy* may be indicated.

Like Breuer, Freud originally thought of traumatic memories as foreign objects festering in the psyche. One simply needed to pluck them out and health would ensue. Over time, he realized that it was as important to analyze defenses as it was to analyze repressed material. Thus, Freud replaced the idea of catharsis with the concept of *working through*, which requires thorough, reiterative exploration of the dynamic processes involved in symptom formation. From the psychodynamic perspective, a posttraumatic symptom is not a simple defect: It is an adaptive attempt to manage the trauma. The external world may or may not be a meaningful place (this is a question for philosophy and theology), but mental life is inextricably caught up in meaning and meaning making. Psychodynamic psychotherapy elicits and explicates meanings in order to make unconscious meanings conscious. The patient's increasing understanding of his or her own premises and operating principles provides him or her with an opportunity to cope more effectively. The concept of symptoms as compromises whose meaning must be understood and worked through is a fundamental proposition that distinguishes psychodynamic psychotherapy from the theories and treatments that preceded it.

Another distinguishing proposition of psychodynamic psychotherapy is *transference*. When a patient enters into a working relationship with a therapist, some of the patient's responses reflect a realistic appraisal of the therapist's character and behavior and a practical alliance with the therapist in the service of a successful treatment outcome. Yet, as Freud and subsequent clinicians observed, in each therapeutic relationship, there also develops a very different class of attitudes toward the therapist that primarily repeat the patient's important past relationships in a manner inappropriate to the current situation. Such transference can be positive or negative, dependent or hostile, aggressive or submissive (or a complex mixture of these and other responses). When Freud first encountered transference, he considered it an interference (or *resistance*) and tried to overcome it through appeals to reason or by the weight of his authority. Over time, he realized that, like hysterical symptoms (and dreams), transference is a compromise expression of psychic life. Through mutual effort to understand the transference, patient and therapist gain a clearer view of the underpinnings of the problem that brought them together.

Modern psychoanalytic technique is designed to precipitate transference. Frequent meetings promote an intense relationship. The couch and the therapist's *neutrality* and relative anonymity are meant to provide a *blank screen* onto which transference can be *projected. Psychoanalysis* has become the *analysis of the transference.* All psychodynamic psychotherapies involve transference work but there is a differential in its application across the spectrum of therapies: In supportive psychotherapy, for example, the therapist's interventions are informed by an understanding of the transference, but the therapist rarely seeks to bring the transference to the patient's attention; in formal psychoanalysis, on the other hand, transference interpretations and the patient's working through of transference comprise the core of therapy. This emphasis on interpretation of the transference distinguishes formal psychoanalysis from other psychodynamic psychotherapies.

Forging a therapeutic relationship with a patient is always demanding. It is still more complex when the patient is a trauma survivor (see, e.g., Courtois, 1999; De Wind, 1984). In working closely with survivors, therapists must contend with their personal responses to what the patient has been through and to those demands that the patient makes upon the therapist. This can evoke powerful *countertransference* reactions. Countertransference has been variously defined but, for the purposes of this chapter, it refers to therapist responses (thoughts, feelings, interventions, etc.) that more closely express the therapist's personal issues than they reflect a rational, clinically appropriate response to the patient. At such times, it is the therapist who loses track of reality. Even therapists who do not think of themselves as psychodynamically oriented tend to pay close attention to countertransference. Many important articles and texts have been written on the importance of countertransference in treating trauma survivors (Danieli, 1984; Davies &

Frawley, 1994; Haley, 1974; Pearlman & Saakvitne, 1995; Wilson & Lindy, 1994).

It is generally agreed that therapists should guard against acting on countertransference but, being human, they often discover their counter-transferential responses precisely because they have become enmeshed in these thoughts, feelings and/or enactments. Many therapists seek personal psychodynamic psychotherapy to achieve greater awareness of their personal countertransference tendencies. It is neither possible nor even preferable to eradicate personal reactions to patients. No one can be useful to a patient about whom he or she has no feelings at all, and repression of such feelings only creates blind spots. Learning to acknowledge and work with counter-transference helps the therapist understand what is going on in the therapy.

The relationship between patient and psychotherapist cannot be reduced to transference and countertransference. Patient and therapist also take part in a *real relationship* that is relatively free from distortions and central to their *working alliance* toward the patient's health (Greenson, 1967). Loewald (1960) suggested that the patient–therapist relationship is, itself, the critical therapeutic factor in psychoanalysis. As Bruch points out, "[Psychodynamic] psychotherapy rests on the assumption that problems with an origin in damaging and confusing early experiences are capable of correction through a new and different intimate personal relationship" (1974, p. 19). A distorted sense of self and others can be reworked in the context of that new relationship. The interpersonal aspects of psychotherapy are no less important in psychodynamic work with trauma survivors. The patient–therapist relationship complements the use of other interventions in the therapeutic action of psychodynamic psychotherapy.

The psychoanalytic concept of trauma has evolved steadily over the last century. Early in his clinical work, Freud found that every hysterical patient he treated, male or female, reported a history of sexual abuse (Freud, 1896/1962). Since he presumed that children do not have sexual feelings, he concluded that molestation prematurely and traumatically awakened their sexuality. He later abandoned this "seduction theory" on the grounds that (1) not all hysterical patients had been seduced and (2) children do, indeed, have sexual feelings (Freud, 1905/1953). While Freud, throughout his career, held to the concept that some cases of hysteria do stem from sexual abuse during childhood, he came to believe that hysteria and other kinds of psychological problems could also arise from dynamic conflict between sexual impulses and personal or social inhibitions (Freud, 1925/1959; Gay, 1988). At this point in his career, Freud took a hiatus from trauma theory in order to address more general questions about psychological development.

Freud's attention was drawn back to the problem of psychological trauma by World War I. In *Beyond the Pleasure Principle* (1920/1955), he defined psychological trauma as the result of a breach in a psychic *stimulus barrier*. Like Janet (van der Hart, Brown, & van der Kolk, 1989) Freud understood the survivors' intrusive and avoidant symptoms (later core elements of post-traumatic stress disorder [PTSD]) as a biphasic attempt to cope with trauma. Freud speculated that survivors repeat these memories in the hope of mastering them. He revised his theory of dreams to include a special class of post-traumatic dreams rooted in this *repetition compulsion*. He also hypothesized that while all living things have an inherent instinct for self-preservation, they also strive to nullify any and all noxious stimulation, internal or external, even if it means giving life up entirely (*death instinct*).

One of Freud's colleagues, Abraham Kardiner (1941), treated hundreds of combat veterans in World War I and published his findings on the eve of World War II. Kardiner accepted Freud's premises about psychological trauma but emphasized the interplay between psychological and biological factors that resulted in what he termed the *physioneurosis* of combat survivors. The two world wars forced many clinicians and theorists (Fairbairn, 1943b; Ferenczi, Abraham, Simmel, & Jones, 1921; Greenson, 1949; Grinker & Speigel, 1945; Kardiner & Spiegel, 1947; Lidz, 1946; Lindemann, 1944; Rivers, 1918) to ponder psychodynamic models and forge therapeutic interventions. Abreactive models, employing amytal and hypnosis (well described by Sargant & Slater, 1969, and dramatically chronicled by John Huston, 1948, in his documentary film *Let There Be Light*) were combined with supportive and psychoeducational interventions in highly effective treatments of *combat fatigue*. This successful application of psychoanalytic theory spurred worldwide interest in psychoanalysis in the postwar years.

Another legacy of World War II was the need to consider the effects of massive psychic trauma on noncombatants. Studies on survivors of the Holocaust (Krystal, 1968) and of Hiroshima (Lifton, 1967) demonstrated that overwhelming events could numb basic human capacities and result in a kind of "death in life." Krystal (1988) went on to develop an information-processing model of psychological trauma, which included the idea that overwhelming events can disable the psyche's ability to utilize anxiety as a signal for the mobilization of defense. Once this system is disrupted, anxiety and other affects fail to serve psychic needs. Affects may become muted, overwhelming, or inappropriate. The ego, without its normal signal processing, is virtually defenseless. One possible outcome is *alexithymia* (a profound disconnection between words and feelings).

The work of Melanie Klein (1975) highlighted the psyche's efforts to balance love and hate in the context of the relationship between self and others. While many psychoanalysts fail to find clinical relevance in Freud's death instinct, Kleinian theory demands consideration of how that instinct may underlie imbalances in the posttraumatic modulation of affection and aggression.

Heinz Kohut's *self psychology* theory has also been applied to the problem of psychological trauma (Ulman & Brothers, 1988). A stable sense of self (and the regulatory systems that maintain it) is refined in the course of normal narcissistic development but can be disrupted or even shattered by experiences that threaten the very relevance of the self.

Object relations theory, which seeks to understand how intrapsychic functions and structures develop in the context of interpersonal experiences, offers valuable insights into how shattered personal assumptions, relationships, and social contracts can lead to psychopathology. D. W. Winnicott's (1965) description of the *holding environment*, which enables children to overcome fears of physical and psychological annihilation as they move toward greater autonomy, provides valuable clues as to how adults maintain or fail to maintain psychic balance in the face of trauma. Kudler (1991) has suggested that Winnicott's holding environment essentially *is* Freud's stimulus barrier. Fairbairn (1943a) conceived of trauma as releasing repressed, internalized relationships with so-called *bad objects*. When a hated and feared object (such as a frustrating parent) is also essential for survival, the psyche may become flooded with anxiety. Treatment focuses on regaining balance between acceptable levels of dependence and aggression.

Many commentators have criticized psychoanalysis as being more concerned with intrapsychic reality than with the effects of real external events. The work of Shengold (1989, 1991), Terr (1979), Lindy (1985), and a host of others demonstrates the clinical relevance and conceptual power that modern psychoanalytic perspectives bring to the problem of psychological trauma.

When faced with overwhelming experiences, the mind mobilizes defenses. Among the primary defenses against trauma are an attempt to master traumatic memories through repetition and (paradoxically) an effort to avoid these same memories. These defenses may also be employed in the course of bereavement, adjustment disorders, and acute stress disorder. When such states remit, it may be assumed that the defense was successful and a new balance has been achieved. In PTSD, equilibrium has not been reestablished because the adaptive process, itself, has been overwhelmed. The defenses become entangled with the traumatic impressions against which they were meant to defend. The resulting complexes are symbolically represented as symptoms.

Mind and brain are separate levels of abstraction that can be useful in considering complex human processes. Ultimately, mind and brain are different aspects of a single mental system that integrates experience, manages response, and maintains equilibrium. The smooth operation of this system is as much dependent on the successful navigation of a complex developmental process as it is on the genetic equipment supplied at the moment of conception. It is now apparent that the expression of this genetic endowment is, itself, often dependent on developmental processes and environmental states. Biological psychiatry and psychodynamic principles are often portrayed as locked in competition, but it is more profitable to consider them as complementary (Kandel, 1979; Kudler, 1989; Reiser, 1984). Biological treatments can be profitably combined with psychodynamic treatments. Combining perspectives produces a more complete picture of PTSD. The treatment of this profoundly human problem requires understanding and intervention at the level of human nature. Psychodynamic psychotherapy approaches PTSD by way of the mind. As such, it offers a unique perspective on psychological trauma.

DESCRIPTION OF TECHNIQUES

Psychoanalytic theory has continuously evolved and given rise to a broad array of techniques referred to as psychodynamic psychotherapies. These are grounded in psychoanalytic concepts of defense, conflict, symptoms as meaningful representations, conscious and unconscious levels of mental activity, transference, countertransference, and the therapeutic relationship. Techniques can vary greatly with regard to how these concepts are applied.

In formal psychoanalysis, patient and therapist meet four to five times per week over the course of 2–7 years (or more). Adults and children are treated. Whereas adults are expected to interact with the analyst through free association of ideas on the couch, children generally bring intrapsychic material into analysis through play.

Although analysts vary in their degree of activity, they strive to remain neutral in their responses to the patient. As Anna Freud (1966) pointed out, this means that the analyst avoids siding with any one aspect of the patient's intrapsychic contents, structure, or function (be it wish, defense, or demand to adhere to social standards). The analyst's only investment is in the patient's progress toward autonomy and health.

Progress in psychoanalysis stems from growth in the patient's understanding of his or her own premises, strategies, perceptions, and responses to the external environment. This is accomplished in the context of a strong working alliance with a trustworthy and considerate analyst and a shared commitment to honesty and candor. The patient follows the *fundamental rule* of saying whatever is on his or her mind, no matter how irrelevant, noxious, or banal that thought might appear. The analysis follows these associations and explores dreams, symptomatic acts, transference, and countertransference in order to explicate the complex network of ideas, memories, wishes, fears, and constitutional givens that compose the psyche of this unique person. Another way to think of psychoanalysis is as a constant sifting and sorting of what is true and what is fantasy in the patient's assessment of him- or herself and his or her world. The therapist employs observations, confrontations, and interpretations to test hypotheses with the patient. It is important to emphasize that the therapist is simply a facilitator in this process. Ultimately, it is the patient who analyzes him or her self.

In psychodynamic psychotherapy, meetings may be held once or twice weekly, or even less often. Sessions still tend to run for 45 or 50 minutes. Patient and therapist face one another without benefit of the couch. While therapists tend to be more active (make more comments, be more emotionally available in the hour), they may still strive for neutrality vis-à-vis the patient's conscious and unconscious concerns. The process may or may not center on the interpretation of transference. There may be more emphasis on here-and-now issues as opposed to the developmental and historical issues plumbed in formal psychoanalysis. Fundamental intrapsychic change is not the primary focus. Nonetheless, psychodynamic psychotherapy is primarily an *expressive* therapy that seeks to enlarge the patient's understanding of unconscious issues in the context of a strong therapeutic alliance. Psychodynamic psychotherapy is not "watered down psychoanalysis." It is a different technical application that reflects the patient's specific needs and expectations regarding treatment and the therapist's assessment of how deeply the treatment must go in order to reach the desired effects. Psychodynamic psychotherapy is aimed at improving self-understanding and *ego strength* (intrapsychic integrity and capacity to cope).

In the now considerable body of work describing psychodynamic psychotherapy for survivors of trauma (see, e.g., Briere, 1996; Chu, 1998; Lindy, 1986, 1996; McCann & Pearlman, 1990; Ochberg, 1988; Parson, 1984; Roth & Batson, 1997; van der Kolk, McFarlane, & Weisaeth, 1996), psychoanalytic roots are not always explicit. The boundaries between these treatments and the cognitive-behavioral therapies are sometimes blurred. A variety of interventions may be applied at different phases of treatment. The broad range of psychodynamic techniques acknowledges the variety of survivor populations, the specific needs of individual patients, and the particular treatment goals established by different clinicians. Theories and findings may or may not be generalizable across survivor populations.

Mann (1973) pointed out that patients in long-term therapy often make significant gains as they approach termination. He hypothesized that impending separation from the therapist impelled this final spurt of progress. This led him to develop a *brief psychodynamic therapy* (12 sessions) that exploits the factor of separation by emphasizing how few sessions remain. This technique may be particularly useful when issues of separation and loss are prominent in the patient's presentation (as in work with trauma survivors). A number of manualized, brief dynamic therapies have grown around another idea proposed by Mann: Brief therapies work best when the patient presents a problem that can be understood within a single metaphor or theme (as in Luborsky's [1990] *core conflictual relationship theme*).

Brief psychodynamic psychotherapies have been developed specifically for the treatment of trauma survivors. Horowitz (1974; Horowitz & Kaltreider, 1979) presented a transference-based, 20-session model (later revised to 12 sessions) that takes into account how a survivor's preexisting personality and defensive style interacts with his or her traumatic experience to produce particular conflicts and specific kinds of relationships—including specific therapeutic relationships (see also Horowitz et al., 1984; Horowitz, Marmar, Weiss, De Witt, & Rosenbaum, 1984). Marmar and Freeman (1988) applied Horowitz's ideas in developing a brief treatment method focused on the management of narcissistic regression in the face of trauma. Brom, Kleber, and Defares (1989) also followed Horowitz in developing a manualized, brief psychodynamic psychotherapy for PTSD.

Horowitz (1997b) recently updated his manual for the brief psychodynamic treatment of stress response syndromes. His theory of how interacting systems can either precipitate symptoms or relieve them, advance coping capacity or diminish it, and, ultimately, reconfigure character structure (Horowitz, 1998) is an example of a multimodal brief approach based on reliable, research-validated strategies. In Horowitz's model, a systematic individualized case formulation (based on psychoanalytic concepts of how defense and unconscious information processing affect mood and behavioral patterns) informs the therapist when to use behavioral techniques for guided desensitization (in order to achieve shock mastery), cognitive techniques (to modify dysfunctional conscious beliefs and plan possible futures), and/or supportive and expressive dynamic techniques (to modify defensive resistances to processing of stressful events) (Horowitz, 1997a). The therapist employs this model to guide changes in how the patient's emotions are regulated and to facilitate identity reschematization and affiliation reformation.

Supportive psychotherapy is often characterized as being less expressive than other forms of psychodynamic psychotherapy. Therapists are generally more active in their interventions and less likely to interpret than to "support" the patient's defenses by bolstering self-esteem and allying with those coping strategies that the patient has already found useful. The focus is less on uncovering unconscious conflicts than on restoring intrapsychic equilibrium. Problems are managed in the here and now rather than through extended elaborations of development and intrapsychic structure. While the therapist is less likely to make transference interpretations, interventions are nonetheless informed by a psychodynamic understanding of the patient's problems and relationship patterns (including transference and countertransference issues) and by an appreciation of how supportive interventions affect the intrapsychic balance (Werman, 1984).

Interpersonal psychotherapy (IPT) is a time-limited, manualized treatment that is usually grouped with psychodynamic/expressive therapies but also incorporates supportive elements. The therapist takes an exploratory stance and focuses interventions on the patient's outside relationships rather than on transference. Although IPT was developed for the treatment of individuals with major depression (Klerman, Weissman, Rounsaville, & Chevron, 1984), it has been adapted, in recent years for use with other disorders. At the present time, Krupnick, Green, and Miranda (1998) are developing IPT as a group treatment for women with current PTSD following such interpersonal trauma as sexual and physical assault or abuse, sexual molestation, or relationship violence. IPT is hypothesized to be a useful strategy with this population because of its focus on impairment in relationships. Since interpersonal trauma can lead to PTSD, and PTSD is itself associated with dysfunctional interpersonal function, these researchers propose that an approach that helps survivors find new ways to understand and behave in relationships can reduce PTSD symptoms. This hypothesis is currently being tested in a study comparing subjects who have been randomly assigned to group IPT or a wait-list control group.

Hypnotic and other abreactive techniques are sometimes employed in work with trauma survivors in the hope of uncovering repressed material. These may be useful adjuncts to psychodynamic psychotherapy but despite the historical connections noted earlier, they are not regarded as psychodynamic psychotherapies for PTSD.

This chapter is focused on those techniques described earlier, yet a number of other therapeutic techniques, including several group, family, and cognitive psychotherapies, have also been derived from psychodynamic concepts. Many group and family therapies remain well within the bounds of psychodynamic psychotherapy, while others do not. Cognitive therapy, which emphasizes the role of unconscious schemas in the production of symptoms, has blossomed into a separate form of therapy. Even in strictly behavioral treatment, which owes little to psychodynamic theory, there is a general understanding that without a strong therapeutic alliance (the nature of which has been adduced through psychoanalytic theory), interventions are likely to fail. Many therapists who distance themselves from psychoanalysis and psychodynamic psychotherapy still pay careful attention to unconscious meanings, symbolic acts, and the concepts of transference and countertransference derived from psychoanalysis and practiced in psychodynamic psychotherapy.

METHOD OF COLLECTING DATA

The literature on psychodynamic psychotherapy of PTSD was obtained from searches using MEDLINE, PsycINFO, PILOTS, *Title Key Word and Author Index to Psychoanalytic Journals, 1920–1986* (1987), papers furnished by members of the Working Group, review of most books that include chapters on PTSD treatment published since 1980, review of all issues of the *Journal of Traumatic Stress*, and review of references in published articles and chapters. Items chosen bear directly on theory, technique, and outcome.

The psychodynamic literature is particularly rich in case reports. There is ongoing debate over the relative value of the case report as compared to the double-blind, controlled studies typical of pharmacological research. Our position is that each is a legitimate form of scholarship and neither is suited for application in every field of research. Case reports are valuable because they extract clinical material from a particular case, or a small series of cases, in order to inform theory and practice. Case studies neither provide ultimate tests for psychodynamic hypotheses nor can they define the limits of psychopathology, theory, or technique. They do, however, provide the groundwork for hypotheses that can be tested empirically.

This task force has set standards by which research is to be judged. These favor designs that involve many individuals and tightly controlled variables. This is not the optimal lens for studying psychodynamic research. In order to conform to the other position papers in this series, this section concentrates on the relatively few studies of this nature in the psychodynamic literature. Note that each of these studies involves brief psychodynamic psychotherapy. Their findings may not be generalizable to formal psychoanalysis, to long-term psychodynamic psychotherapy, or to supportive psychotherapy. While most psychodynamic case reports receive low scores in the classification of Level of Evidence chosen by the Agency for Health Care Policy and Research (AHCPR) Guidelines Committee, it must be emphasized that the psychodynamic literature is an essential part of the scientific effort to understand the human impact of psychological trauma.

SUMMARY OF THE LITERATURE

Empirical Studies

Horowitz and colleagues conducted several empirical studies (1993, 1994; Horowitz, 1995) testing the hypothesis that survivors of traumatic events experience heightened intrusive *and* avoidant symptoms related to traumatic memories and themes. These studies employed a manualized, brief psychodynamic psychotherapy. Horowitz holds that this biphasic response generates intense conflict as the survivor attempts to integrate traumatic memories while defending against external and internal dangers. Horowitz and colleagues found that when a conflictual topic (one linked to the traumatic event) emerges in a psychodynamic session, it is accompanied by intrusions and avoidances, emotionality, fragmentation of important ideas, verbal and nonverbal warding off behaviors, and stifling of facial emotional expression (Horowitz et al., 1993 [AHCPR Level D], 1994 [AHCPR Level C]). Recognition of these responses can cue patient and therapist to the emergence of traumatic themes in therapy and better enable them to process this material. Such recognition may also help patients become aware of inadequate or even pathological attempts at coping that have interfered with their working through of a posttraumatic problem. These findings are pertinent to all psychodynamic approaches.

Brom, Kleber, and Defares (1989) constructed a controlled outcome study on the efficacy of three modes of therapy: trauma desensitization, hypnotherapy, and a brief psychodynamic therapy (based on Horowitz's model). The outcome objective was to see which therapy most reduced PTSD symptoms of intrusion and avoidance. The 112 subjects diagnosed with PTSD were randomly assigned to one of the three therapies. Therapists had over 10 years of experience in their respective method. Each therapist was supervised by a recognized expert in the specific treatment. The mean length of treatment in each setting was 15 sessions (desensitization), 14.4 sessions (hypnotherapy), and 18.8 sessions (psychodynamic therapy). The authors concluded that "the treatments do benefit some in comparison with a control group and using stringent methodological techniques but they do not benefit everyone, the effects are not always substantial, and the differences between the therapies are small" (p. 610). While the psychodynamic treatment involved the most sessions and showed the least improvement in terms of intrusion symptoms on initial scores, follow-up data indicated that subjects in the psychodynamic treatment group showed greater improvement during the posttermination phase than did the subjects in the other two therapies. This finding of an accruing posttreatment improvement, similar to that noted by Horowitz, Marmar, Weiss, Kaltreider, and Wilner (1986), suggests that psychodynamic therapy mobilizes coping mechanisms that continue to function following termination. Brom, Kleber, and Defares's (1989) findings are most relevant to brief psychodynamic psychotherapy but may be generalizable to longer-term psychodynamic treatments (AHCPR Level A).

Clinical Studies

Lindy (1988) reported clinical outcomes of his work with 37 combat veterans of the Vietnam War, each of whom met DSM-III criteria for PTSD. The average age of subjects was 35. They were evaluated with regard to combat experience and psychological function, and were compared with a volunteer sample ($n = 200$) of Vietnam veterans culled from clinical and nonclinical sources. There was no placebo comparison group. Patient assignment was not randomized. Treatment involved a psychodynamic psychotherapy engaging traumatic war memories. Completers must have addressed termination issues within the treatment setting. There were 23 completers. The treatment rationale was to help subjects learn to deal with traumatic memories rather than repress them. Treatment objectives looked beyond symptom reduction. The ultimate goal was intrapsychic change. Treatment was manualized and included three phases: opening, working through, and termination. Working alliance, transference, and countertransference factors were monitored. The average number of sessions was 56. Significant changes were noted on the Psychiatric Evaluation Form (based on clinical ratings made by independent clinicians and on global ratings made by both patients and therapists). Significant differences were also noted on other self-report measures including the Symptom Checklist 90, the Impact of Event Scale, and the Cincinnati Stress

Response Schedule. Intrusive phenomena, feelings of alienation and depression, and associated features of hostility and substance abuse were most notably changed. Clinical ratings at the end of treatment indicated that patients were still not at "normal" levels. The author noted that, in their final interview, subjects were generally impressive in their increased capacity to trust and to manage traumatic stress precipitated in an interview. They also seemed to have moved from a state of psychic numbing to an appreciation of being alive. They experienced a greater sense of personal integrity and dignity with regard to their own experiences as combat soldiers. There was less estrangement and more investment in adult roles and socially constructive activities. Subjects also expressed a greater sense of continuity with the person they had been before the war (AHCPR Level B).

Weiss and Marmar (1993) describe a 12-session psychodynamic treatment for adult survivors of single traumatic events. They employed a treatment manual and reported on results in work with over 200 patients. They did not employ systematic outcome measures. The thrust of their article is that this method is "teachable." This finding is most relevant to brief psychodynamic psychotherapy but may be generalizable to longer-term psychodynamic treatments (AHCPR Level C).

Roth and Batson (1997) conducted a systematic evaluation of a yearlong psychodynamic treatment of 6 adult female survivors of childhood incest with PTSD. Markers of improvement in the areas represented by PTSD and other psychiatric diagnoses, trauma themes, and complex PTSD symptoms demonstrated significant clinical change. The therapeutic effect for trauma themes occurred in survivors' processing of the traumatic origins of their fear, shame, alienation, and rage (AHCPR Level B).

Numerous clinical studies were neither controlled nor strict in their choice of outcome measures but are sufficiently compelling to warrant the use of psychodynamic psychotherapy and the application of psychodynamic approaches to survivors of traumatic events (AHCPR Level C). These include Judith Herman's (1992) description of her work with trauma survivors, most of whom were adult women who had survived childhood rape or incest. Treatment involved a combination of expressive and supportive psychodynamic psychotherapy techniques that sequentially emphasized issues of safety, remembrance/mourning, and reconnection in the context of a strong, positive relationship with a trusted therapist. Also, Leonard Shengold describes his experience with the formal psychoanalysis of adult survivors of childhood sexual trauma in his books *Soul Murder* (1989) and *"Father, Don't You See I'm Burning?"* (1991). Shengold makes a strong case for formal psychoanalysis with these patients, many of whom evidenced severe character pathology. He suggests that a child may respond to sexual abuse by isolating and compartmentalizing feelings, thoughts, and identifications. Murderous rage may represent the greatest burden for the patient. This must be carefully confronted and interpreted, so that what has been held apart can be reintegrated. The degree of symptom improvement varied among patients, but Shengold points to progress that patients made in managing feelings, engaging in relationships, and testing reality. De Wind (1971) presented salutary results in 23 cases of Holocaust survivors treated by formal psychoanalysis. Success seemed to depend on the patient's ability to mourn lost love objects and to tolerate his or her own aggression. In addition to better managing posttraumatic symptoms, patients were also reported to have achieved a deeper sense of integration and meaning. Rose (1991) described successful experience with psychodynamic psychotherapy in a series (number unspecified) of adult female patients who had been raped. The treatment emphasized confrontation and management of intense rage. Rose found that patients improved in terms of their posttraumatic symptoms and, in some cases, seemed to make progress in dealing with preexisting conflicts. The findings of these studies are limited to the populations and techniques peculiar to each report, but they are potentially generalizable to other psychodynamic psychotherapies.

Single- or small-series case reports, starting with Breuer and Freud's *Studies on Hysteria*, comprise the bulk of the evidence for the efficacy of more explicitly psychoanalytic approaches for trauma survivors. These are, at best, AHCPR Level D evidence (based on long-standing and widespread clinical practice that has not been subjected to empirical tests in PTSD). Prominent examples include Greenson's (1971) report of his multimodal treatment of a 20-year-old soldier who was tormented by intrusive repetitions of words in his mind that did not make sense to him. A sodium pentothal interview revealed that the words the soldier repeated were the same words that had come into his thoughts when he was on the verge of drowning in a combat incident. The patient subsequently wrote to his mother and found out that these words were from a lullaby she used to sing to him. This very brief treatment utilized abreaction, education, and a psychoanalytic approach on the part of the therapist. The patient reportedly became symptom-free. Goldschmidt (1986) also reported a positive outcome with an adult patient who, as a 4-year-old child, witnessed the suicide of his parents (who also attempted to poison him). The treatment consisted of a 20-session, brief psychodynamic psychotherapy in which the therapist identified and interpreted elements of the traumatic situation that were being relived in the therapy setting. The patient improved in terms of his ability to mourn. He also was able to curtail what had previously been frequent reenactments of the trauma (including urges to hurt himself, extreme avoidance, and marked anxiety). The patient went on to begin formal psychoanalysis. Lindy (1988) also noted the tendency to reenact traumatic events and responses in the transference in his work with Vietnam veterans (as cited earlier). Krupnick (1997) reported a single-case study demonstrating the efficacy of brief (12-session) psychodynamic psychotherapy for PTSD. The treatment was largely of a supportive nature but transference interpretations were also offered. The therapist attempted to help the patient "reestablish a sense of coherence and meaning"

(p. 77). Treatment was meant to alleviate PTSD symptoms but also focused on helping the patient move forward in her life without guilt. By accepting her rageful and aggressive feelings, the patient became able to integrate a more mature sense of self. Taken together, this group of reports suggests that psychoanalysis and psychodynamic psychotherapy have long-standing and widespread efficacy in the treatment of trauma survivors.

SUMMARY

Psychodynamic treatment seeks to reengage normal mechanisms of adaptation by addressing what is unconscious and, in tolerable doses, making it conscious. This is accomplished by exploring the psychological meaning of a traumatic event. It may include sifting and sorting through wishes, fantasies, fears, and defenses stirred up by the event. Psychodynamic treatment requires insight and courage, and is best approached in the context of a therapeutic relationship that emphasizes safety and honesty. Transference and countertransference are universal phenomena that should be recognized by therapists but may or may not be explicitly addressed in the therapy depending on treatment modality and therapist judgment. The therapist–patient relationship is, in itself, a crucial factor in the patient's response.

RECOMMENDATIONS

When a patient is being considered for a psychodynamic psychotherapy, be it formal psychoanalysis, psychodynamic psychotherapy, brief psychodynamic psychotherapy, or supportive psychotherapy, there are certain patient attributes that the therapist needs to evaluate. During the evaluation stage, therapist and patient team up to review the patient's goals. Is the patient hoping simply to reduce symptoms and "get on with life" or is he or she seeking a broader understanding of his or her reactions, life history, goals, and options? What practical considerations (financial factors, available time, career pressures) pertain to the therapy? By the end of the evaluation (which might require anywhere from one to five sessions or more), the therapist should be able to offer the patient a concise statement of the problem and general recommendations for treatment. The final choice of treatment modality is best made collaboratively. Certain guidelines may be helpful in making this decision.

Gabbard (1994) lists the indications for highly expressive psychodynamic psychotherapy (including formal psychoanalysis) as follows:

> 1) a strong motivation to understand oneself, 2) suffering that interferes with life to such an extent that it becomes an incentive for the patient to

endure the rigors of treatment, 3) the ability not only to regress and give up control of feelings and thoughts but also to quickly regain control and reflect on that regression (regression in the service of the ego) (Greenson, 1967), 4) tolerance for frustration, 5) a capacity for insight or psychological mindedness, 6) intact reality testing, 7) meaningful and enduring object relations, 8) reasonably good impulse control, and 9) ability to sustain a job (Bachrach & Leaff, 1978). (p. 111)

Gabbard also emphasizes the patient's ability to form a strong, trusting relationship with the therapist. Luborsky, Crits-Christoph, Mintz, and Auerbach (1988) add that a good outcome is more likely when there is a positive relationship between therapist and patient at the outset of treatment.

PTSD patients may lack one or more of the attributes listed earlier because of the following tendencies: avoidance of traumatic material; fears of being overwhelmed by feelings, thoughts, and images; decreased tolerance for frustration; impaired ability to begin or sustain relationships; weakened impulse control; and difficulty sustaining employment. As Courtois's (1999) review of current trauma-focused models of psychodynamic psychotherapy indicates, vulnerabilities of these kinds can often be addressed by phase-oriented treatments that incorporate multiple techniques and emphasize pacing of the work to the individual's needs and capacities.

Another key indicator for expressive psychodynamic psychotherapy, derived from clinical wisdom, is the patient's ability to stand back from his or her own position and see him- or herself objectively. This capacity, referred to as an *observing ego*, is generally believed to strengthen in the course of treatment and is sometimes used to gauge the patient's readiness to terminate. The combination of a strong observing ego and reasonable self-understanding may equip an individual to maintain or even improve his or her psychic balance without the help of a therapist.

The following characteristics would indicate a more supportive psychodynamic psychotherapy: long-standing ego weakness; acute life crisis; poor tolerance for anxiety and/or frustration; poor capacity for insight; poor reality testing; severely impaired object relations; limited impulse control; low intelligence or organic cognitive dysfunction; difficulty with self-observation; tenuous ability to form a therapeutic alliance (Gabbard, 1994).

The next issue to resolve is whether the therapy should be long term or brief. Expressive therapy and supportive therapy may be either long-term and open-ended or brief and focal. The choice depends to some extent on practical considerations: Managed care concerns and the patient's financial resources may be critical factors. The choice also depends on the agreed-upon goals of treatment and the patient's capacities. Brief therapy demands that the patient be able quickly to form a trusting relationship with the therapist. The patient and therapist must also be able to agree on a clear focus for the work. Luborsky (1990) dubs this a *core conflictual relationship theme* and has demonstrated that brief psychotherapy is more successful when therapists' interpretations are in close congruence with that theme.

Brief psychodynamic therapy is not "less therapy." It is a technically refined, highly focused, psychotherapeutic approach that is indicated when patient and therapist are in close agreement about the nature of the problem and the mode of intervention. It requires a patient with quick intelligence, a high degree of trust, a strong ability to tolerate harsh feelings, and a well-developed ability to think about him- or herself with clarity and perspective. Although the studies by Brom, Kleber, and Defares (1989) and Horowitz, Marmar, Weiss, Kaltreider, and Wilner (1986) suggest that brief therapy can continue to have a salutary effect long after treatment ends, it is also true that brief therapy is most clearly indicated when the problem, itself, is focal.

Many patients who have experienced traumatic events have problems that are much less focal. The concept of *complex PTSD* (Herman, 1992; Pelcovitz et al., 1997) is based on an understanding that trauma experienced during earlier developmental periods has strong implications for later development. For many such survivors, the posttraumatic state combines PTSD symptoms with more general difficulties in regulation of affect, impulsivity, dissociative tendencies, damaging perceptions of self and others, somatization, and alterations in systems of meaning. McCann and Pearlman (1990) and Roth and Batson (1997) have detailed the disruptions in central beliefs and self-image that underlie the psychology of the adult survivor of childhood trauma. McCann and Pearlman note, for example, that transference and countertransference issues are consequently harsh and powerful, and specify difficulties in the areas of safety, trust/dependency, esteem, and independence. Davies and Frawley (1994) have described the defensive use of dissociation in which the adult survivor of childhood incest expresses traumatic material while simultaneously warding off traumatic memories, affects, and fantasies. They also suggest that fear, itself, can become *eroticized* (confused and admixed with sexual excitement) in ways that can profoundly affect the patient's life and the therapeutic relationship. This may be a factor in *revictimization* (a pattern of repeated traumatization throughout the life span). McCann and Pearlman (1990) summarize research suggesting that survivors of childhood trauma may be particularly vulnerable to later victimization and may be at increased risk for PTSD secondary to traumas experienced in later life. Krupnick, Green, and Miranda (1998) have suggested that interpersonal psychotherapy, with its focus on helping patients understand and change relationship patterns, may reduce the potential for revictimization in later relationships.

When the presenting problem is complex, a more open-ended, long-term treatment may be indicated. A number of considerations will dictate whether formal psychoanalysis or another long-term modality is more appropriate. If a patient is to take part in formal psychoanalysis, he or she must be willing to tackle broad issues and possess the prerequisite qualities for participation in psychotherapy based on the precipitation and interpretation of transference. This decision must be based on a careful assessment of the patient's goals and capacities (using the criteria described earlier).

Because traumatic experiences and certain personality disorders predispose to emotional instability, a period of supportive therapy may be required to ready the patient for more intense, expressive modes of therapy. The preparatory phase helps the patient achieve greater mastery of emotional and cognitive responses, and develop a more solid therapeutic alliance as a foundation for expressive work to follow.

Danieli (1989) has suggested that group treatment may be indicated in work with Holocaust survivors and their children. Homogeneous groups of survivors, or of their children, and mixed, intergenerational groups can create a contemporary "family" that helps members reaffirm their identity and rework their relationship to others. Mobilization of internalized and trauma-tainted object relationships within the group may provide sorely needed opportunities for mourning and progression. Danieli's recommendations are echoed by those of Shay (1994), who stressed the importance of the *communalization* of war experience through the sharing of narrative within groups of combat veterans. The reader is referred to Chapter 8 for a more complete discussion of group treatment.

The contraindications to psychodynamic modes of therapy consist largely of the opposites of those indications listed previously. An inability to form a therapeutic alliance, a lack of psychological mindedness, limited observing ego, impaired reality testing, and an inability to tolerate strong emotions are important contraindications to expressive modes of therapy. The patient may simply be unable to contain the issues expected to arise in the course of treatment.

Countertransference for trauma survivors can be profound, and this must always be kept in mind when working with this population. Significant countertransference on the part of the therapist can serve as a relative contraindication to undertaking or continuing a therapy. Appropriate training, continuous self-reflection, collegial support, ongoing supervision, and personal psychotherapy can each play a role in helping a therapist maintain his or her therapeutic stance in the course of work with trauma survivors. Pearlman and Saakvitne (1995) have described the phenomenon of *vicarious traumatization*, which they define as the therapist's response to the stories of childhood abuse told by patient after patient. They consider that vicarious traumatization exists as a special dimension in the therapeutic relationship and needs to be considered in addition to transference and countertransference distortions. The authors offer strategies for avoiding what they call the *countertransference vicarious traumatization cycle* that they warn may otherwise undermine patient, therapist, and therapy.

The literature on the treatment of depression supports the conclusion that the combination of psychodynamic and pharmacological treatments may have synergistic effects (DiMascio et al., 1979; van Praag, 1989). While parallel studies have not been done with PTSD patients, clinical wisdom strongly supports the need to do whatever may work for the patient. Clinical experience suggests that pharmacological interventions that decrease excessive arousal, anxiety, and dysphoria, and improve the ability to sleep are often helpful in readying a patient to deal with stressful memories, thoughts, and feelings in psychodynamic psychotherapy.

AREAS REQUIRING FURTHER EXPLORATION

Psychodynamic researchers have had significant problems employing conventional research paradigms to evaluate their work. Some of the studies cited earlier (especially the work of Brom, Kleber, & Defares; Horowitz; Lindy; and Luborsky) offer ways to make this paradigmatic leap. It is essential that psychodynamic psychotherapists find ways to state their propositions as testable hypotheses. Research would be enriched by more case reports and large-scale studies that describe treatment effects among different populations of survivors. Historical reviews are needed to retrace the evolution of key theoretical concepts, so that they may be reconsidered and, in some cases, redefined. Interdisciplinary efforts are needed to bring psychodynamic perspectives in closer contact with neuroscience and genetics, as well as with developmental, cognitive, and behavioral approaches in psychology. Finally, and perhaps most important, competition among rivals must be reformulated as collaboration among colleagues. This Guidelines Project is a good step in that direction.

ACKNOWLEDGMENTS

We wish to acknowledge the members of the Working Group on Psychodynamic Psychotherapy for PTSD, including Nanette Auerhahn, Ronald Batson, Elizabeth Brett, Richard Gartner, Mardi Horowitz, Nancy Kobrin, Dori Laub, Elana Newman, Laurie Pearlman, Susan Roth, and Bessel van der Kolk. We also thank the reviewers, Matthew Friedman, Patricia Resick, and Susan Roth, for their efforts on behalf of this project.

REFERENCES

Bachrach, H. M. & Leaff, L. A. (1978). "Analyzability": A systematic review of the clinical and quantitative literature. *Journal of the American Psychoanalytic Association, 26,* 881–920.

Breuer, J., & Freud, S. (1955). Studies on hysteria. In J. Strachey (Ed. & Trans.), *The standard edition of the complete psychological works of Sigmund Freud* (Vol. 2, pp. 1–335). London: Hogarth Press. (Original work published 1895)

Briere, J. (1996). *Therapy for adults molested as children: Beyond survival* (2nd ed.). New York: Springer.

Brom, D., Kleber, R. J., & Defares, P. B. (1989). Brief psychotherapy for post-traumatic stress disorders. *Journal of Consulting and Clinical Psychology 57*, 607–612.

Bruch, H. (1974). *Learning psychotherapy: Rationale and ground rules.* Cambridge, MA: Harvard University Press.

Chu, J. A. (1998). *Rebuilding shattered lives: The responsible treatment of complex posttraumatic and dissociative disorders.* New York: Wiley.

Courtois, C. A. (1999). *Recollections of sexual abuse: Treatment principles and guidelines.* New York: Norton.

Danieli, Y. (1984). Psychotherapists' participation in the conspiracy of silence about the Holocaust. *Psychoanalytic Psychology 1*, 23–42.

Danieli, Y. (1989). Mourning in survivors and children of survivors of the Nazi Holocaust: The role of group and community modalities. In D. R. Dietrich & P. C. Shabad (Eds.), *The problem of loss and mourning: Psychoanalytic perspectives* (pp. 427–460). Madison, CT: International Universities Press.

Davies, J. M., & Frawley, M. G. (1994). *Treating the adult survivor of childhood sexual abuse: A psychoanalytic perspective.* New York: Basic Books.

De Wind, E. (1971). Psychotherapy after traumatization caused by persecution. In H. Krystal & W. G. Niederland (Eds.), *Psychic traumatization* (pp. 93–114). Boston: Little, Brown.

De Wind, E. (1984). Some implications of former massive traumatization upon the actual analytic process. *International Journal of Psychoanalysis, 65*, 273–281.

DiMascio, A., Weissman, M. A., Prusoff, B. A., Neu, C., Zwilling, M., & Klerman, G. (1979). Differential symptom reduction by drugs and psychotherapy in acute depression. *Archives of General Psychiatry, 36*, 1450–1456.

Fairbairn, W. R. D. (1943a). The repression and return of bad objects (with special reference to the "war neuroses"). In W. R. D. Fairbairn, *Psychoanalytic studies of the personality* (pp. 59–81). London: Tavistock.

Fairbairn, W. R. D. (1943b). The war neuroses—their nature and significance. In W. R. D. Fairbairn, *Psychoanalytic studies of the personality* (pp. 256–288). London: Tavistock.

Ferenczi, S., Abraham, K., Simmel, E., & Jones, E. (1921). *Psycho-analysis and the war neuroses.* New York: International Psycho-Analytical Press.

Freud, A. (1966). The ego and the mechanisms of defense. In *The writings of Anna Freud* (Vol. 2, pp. 1–191). New York: International Universities Press. (Original work published 1936)

Freud, S. (1953). Three essays on the theory of sexuality. In J. Strachey (Ed. & Trans.), *The standard edition of the complete psychological works of Sigmund Freud* (Vol. 7, pp. 123–245). London: Hogarth Press. (Original work published 1905)

Freud, S. (1955). Beyond the pleasure principle. In J. Strachey (Ed. & Trans.), *The standard edition of the complete psychological works of Sigmund Freud* (Vol. 18, pp. 1–64). London: Hogarth Press. (Original work published 1920)

Freud, S. (1959). An autobiographical study. In J. Strachey (Ed. & Trans.), *The standard edition of the complete psychological works of Sigmund Freud* (Vol. 20, pp. 1–74). London: Hogarth Press. (Original work published 1925)

Freud, S. (1962). The aetiology of hysteria. In J. Strachey (Ed. & Trans.), *The standard edition of the complete psychological works of Sigmund Freud* (Vol. 3, pp. 187–221). London: Hogarth Press. (Original work published 1896)

Gabbard, G. O. (1994). *Psychodynamic psychiatry in clinical practice: The DSM-IV edition.* Washington, DC: American Psychiatric Press.

Gay, P. (1988). *Freud: A life for our time.* New York: Norton.

Goldschmidt, O. (1986). A contribution to the subject of psychic trauma based on the course of a psychoanalytic short therapy. *International Review of Psycho-Analysis, 13,* 181–199.

Greenson, R. R. (1978). The psychology of apathy. In R. R. Greenson, *Explorations in psychoanalysis* (pp. 17–30). New York: International Universities Press. (Original work published 1949)

Greenson, R. R. (1967). *The technique and practice of psychoanalysis.* New York: International Universities Press.

Greenson, R. R. (1978). A dream while drowning. In R. R. Greenson, *Explorations in psychoanalysis* (pp. 415–423). New York: International Universities Press. (Original work published 1971)

Grinker, R., & Spiegel, J. (1945). *Men under stress.* New York: McGraw-Hill.

Haley, S. (1974). When the patient reports atrocities. *Archives of General Psychiatry, 30,* 191–196.

Herman, J. (1992). *Trauma and recovery.* New York: Basic Books.

Horowitz, M. J. (1974). Stress response syndromes: Character style and dynamic psychotherapy. *Archives of General Psychiatry, 31,* 768–781.

Horowitz, M. J. (1995). Defensive control of states and person schemas. In T. Shapiro & R. N. Emde (Eds.), *Research in psychoanalysis: Process, development, outcome* (pp. 67–89). Madison, CT: International Universities Press.

Horowitz, M. J. (1997a). *Formulation as a basis for planning psychotherapy.* Washington, DC: American Psychiatric Press.

Horowitz, M. J. (1997b). *Stress response syndromes* (3rd ed.). Northvale, NJ: Aronson.

Horowitz, M. J. (1998). *Cognitive psychodynamics: From conflict to character.* New York: Wiley.

Horowitz, M. J., & Kaltreider, N. (1979). Brief therapy of the stress response syndrome. *Psychiatric Clinics of North America, 2,* 365–377.

Horowitz, M. J., Marmar, C., Krupnick, J., Wilner, N., Kaltreider, N., & Wallerstein, R. (1984). *Personality styles and brief psychotherapy.* New York: Basic Books.

Horowitz, M. J., Marmar, C., Weiss, D. S., DeWitt, K., & Rosenbaum, R. (1984). Brief therapy of bereavement reactions: The relation of process to outcome. *Archives of General Psychiatry, 41,* 438–448.

Horowitz, M. J., Marmar, C., Weiss, D., Kaltreider, N., & Wilner, N. (1986). Comprehensive analysis of change after brief dynamic psychotherapy. *American Journal of Psychiatry, 143,* 582–589.

Horowitz, M. J., Milbrath, C., Jordan, D., Stinson, C., Ewert, M., Redington, D., Fridhandler, B., Reidbord, S., & Hartley, D. (1994). Expressive and defensive behavior during discourse on unresolved topics: A single case study. *Journal of Personality, 62,* 527–563.

Horowitz, M. J., Stinson, C., Curtis, D., Ewert, M., Redington, D., Singer, J. L., Bucci, W., Merganthaler, E., Milbrath, C., & Hartley, D. (1993). Topics and signs: Defensive control of emotional expression. *Journal of Consulting and Clinical Psychology, 61,* 421–430.

Huston, J. (1948). *Let there be light* (PMF5019). Washington, DC: Film Production of the U. S. Army.

Janet, P. (1886). Les actes inconscients et la mémoire pendant le somnambulisme. *Revue Philosophique, 25*(I), 238–279.

Janet, P. (1973). *L'automatisme psychologique.* Paris: Société Pierre Janet. (Original work published 1889)

Kandel, E. R. (1979). Psychotherapy and the single synapse. *New England Journal of Medicine, 301,* 1029–1037.

Kardiner, A. (1941). *The traumatic neuroses of war.* New York: Paul B. Hoeber.

Kardiner, A., & Spiegel, H. (1947). *War stress and neurotic illness.* New York: Paul B. Hoeber.

Klein, M. (1975). *Envy and gratitude and other works, 1946–1963.* New York: Free Press.

Klerman, G. L., Weissman, M. M., Rounsaville, B. J., & Chevron, E. (1984). *Interpersonal psychotherapy of depression.* New York: Basic Books.

Krupnick, J. (1997). Brief psychodynamic treatment of PTSD. *Session: Psychotherapy in Practice, 3,* 75–89.

Krupnick, J. L., Green, B. L., & Miranda, J. (1998, June). *Group interpersonal psychotherapy for the treatment of PTSD following interpersonal trauma.* Paper presented at the annual meeting of the Society for Psychotherapy Research, Snowbird, UT.

Krystal, H. (Ed.). (1968). *Massive psychic trauma.* New York: International Universities Press.

Krystal, H. (1988). *Integration and self-healing.* Hillsdale, NJ: Analytic Press.

Kudler, H. (1989). The tension between psychoanalysis and neuroscience: A perspective on dream theory in psychiatry. *Psychoanalysis and Contemporary Thought, 12,* 599–617.

Kudler, H. (1991). What is psychological trauma? *National Center for Post-Traumatic Stress Disorder Clinical Newsletter, 2,* 8.

Lidz, T. (1946). Nightmares and the combat neurosis. *Psychiatry, 3,* 37–49.

Lifton, R. J. (1967). *Death in life: Survivors of Hiroshima.* New York: Random House.

Lindemann, E. (1944). Symptomatology and management of acute grief. *American Journal of Psychiatry, 101,* 141–146.

Lindy, J. (1985). The trauma membrane and other clinical concepts derived from psychotherapeutic work with survivors of natural disasters. *Psychiatric Annals, 15,* 153–60.

Lindy, J. (1986). An outline for the psychoanalytic psychotherapy of post-traumatic stress disorder. In C. Figley (Ed.), *Trauma and its wake* (Vol. II, pp. 195–212). New York: Plenum Press.

Lindy, J. (1988). *Vietnam: A casebook.* New York: Brunner/Mazel.

Lindy, J. (1996). Psychoanalytic psychotherapy of post-traumatic stress disorder. In B. van der Kolk, A. C. McFarlane, & L. Weisaeth (Eds.), *Traumatic stress: The effects of overwhelming experiences on mind, body, and society* (pp. 525–536). New York: Guilford Press.

Loewald, H. W. (1960). On the therapeutic action of psychoanalysis. *International Journal of Psychoanalysis, 41,* 16–33.

Luborsky, L. (1990). A guide to the CCRT method. In L. Luborsky & P. Crits-Christoph (Eds.), *Understanding transference: The core conflictual relationship theme method* (pp. 15–36). New York: Basic Books.

Luborsky, L., Crits-Christoph, P., Mintz, J., & Auerbach, A. (1988). *Who will benefit from psychotherapy?: Predicting therapeutic outcomes.* New York: Basic Books.

Mann, J. (1973). *Time-limited psychotherapy.* Cambridge, MA: Harvard University Press.

Marmar, C., & Freeman, M. (1988). Brief dynamic psychotherapy of post-traumatic stress disorders: Management of narcissistic regression. *Journal of Traumatic Stress, 1,* 323–337.

McCann, I. L., & Pearlman, L. A. (1990). *Psychological trauma and the adult survivor: Theory, therapy, and transformation.* New York: Brunner/Mazel.

Mosher, P. W. (Ed.). (1987). *Title key word and author index to psychoanalytic journals, 1920–1986.* New York: American Psychoanalytic Association.

Ochberg, F. M. (Ed.). (1988). *Post-traumatic therapy and victims of violence.* New York: Brunner/Mazel.

Parson, E. R. (1984). The reparation of the self: Clinical and theoretical dimensions in the treatment of Vietnam combat veterans. *Journal of Contemporary Psychotherapy, 14*(1), 4–56.

Pearlman, L. A., & Saakvitne, K. W. (1995). *Trauma and the therapist: Countertransference and vicarious traumatization in psychotherapy with incest survivors.* New York: Norton.

Pelcovitz, D., van der Kolk, B., Roth, S., Mandel, F. S., Kaplan, S., & Resik, P. A. (1997). Development of a criteria set and a structured interview for disorders of extreme stress (SIDES). *Journal of Traumatic Stress, 10,* 3–17.

Reiser, M. F. (1984). *Mind, brain, body.* New York: Basic Books.

Rivers, W. H. R. (1918, February 2). An address on the repression of war experience. *Lancet,* pp. 173–177.

Rose, D. (1991). A model for psychodynamic psychotherapy with the rape victim. *Psychotherapy, 28,* 85–95.

Roth, S., & Batson, R. (1997). *Naming the shadows: A new approach to individual and group psychotherapy for adult survivors of childhood incest.* New York: Free Press.

Sargant, W., & Slater, E. (1969). *An introduction to physical methods of treatment in psychiatry* (4th ed.). Edinburgh and London: Livingstone.

Shay, J. (1994). *Achilles in Vietnam: Combat trauma and the undoing of character.* New York: Atheneum, Macmillan.

Shengold, L. (1989). *Soul murder: The effects of childhood abuse and deprivation.* New Haven, CT: Yale University Press.

Shengold, L. (1991). *"Father, don't you see I'm burning?": Reflections on sex, narcissism, symbolism, and murder.* New Haven, CT: Yale University Press.

Terr, L. (1979). Children of Chowchilla. *Psychoanalytic Study of the Child, 34,* 547–623.

Ulman, R., & Brothers, D. (1988). *The shattered self: Psychoanalytic study of trauma.* Hillsdale, NJ: Analytic Press.

Van der Hart, O., Brown, P., & van der Kolk, B. A. (1989). Pierre Janet's treatment of post traumatic stress. *Journal of Traumatic Stress, 2,* 379–395.

van der Kolk, B. A., McFarlane, A. C., & Weisaeth, L. (Eds.). (1996). *Traumatic stress: The effects of overwhelming experience on mind, body, and society.* New York: Guilford Press.

van Praag, H. (1989). Moving ahead yet falling behind: A critical appraisal of some trends in contemporary depression research. *Neuropsychobiology, 22,* 181–193.

Weiss, D., & Marmar, C. (1993). Teaching time-limited dynamic psychotherapy for post-traumatic stress disorder and pathological grief. *Psychotherapy, 30,* 587–591.

Werman, D. S. (1984). *The practice of supportive psychotherapy.* New York: Brunner/Mazel.

Wilson, J. P., & Lindy J. D. (Eds.). (1994). *Countertransference in the treatment of PTSD.* New York:, Guilford Press.

Winnicott, D. W. (1965). *The maturational processes and the facilitating environment: Studies in the theory of emotional development.* London: Hogarth Press.

10

Inpatient Treatment

Christine A. Courtois and Sandra L. Bloom

THEORY

The contemporary model of inpatient treatment of posttraumatic stress disorder (PTSD) reflects two main influences: (1) developments in the treatment of trauma in both inpatient and outpatient settings (including outcome research on the efficacy of treatment) that have taken place over the course of the past two decades, and (2) the impact of managed care and other cost-containment efforts. Historically, the correlation between traumatic experiences and subsequent psychiatric difficulties has long gone unrecognized. The large epidemiological study of Kessler, Sonnega, Broment, Hughes, and Nelson (1995) has shown that subjects with PTSD are almost eight times as likely to have three or more psychiatric disorders, while 88% of men and 79% of women with PTSD have a history of at least one other disorder. Related findings have been reported by other researchers in studies of combat veterans (Brady, 1997; Orsillo et al., 1996; Southwick, Yehuda, & Giller, 1993), adult abuse survivors (Brown & Anderson, 1991; Ellason, Ross, Sainton, & Mayran, 1996), inpatients (Faustman & White, 1989; Hryvniak & Rosse, 1989), and women (Breslau, Davis, Peterson, & Schultz, 1997; Carlin & Ward, 1992).

Despite the fact that a trauma history and PTSD symptoms are quite prevalent in a significant number of individuals requiring inpatient and outpatient psychiatric care, many mental health practitioners have had little or no training in the treatment of posttraumatic reactions in their professional education, a circumstance that unfortunately persists today. As a result, practitioners often fail to identify the traumatic etiology of the patient's clinical condition. In response to this deficiency, treatment models have developed that are more responsive to the relationship between traumatic experience and later psychiatric difficulties. An assumption underlying specialized approaches is that recognition and direct treatment of the traumatic experience(s) and consequences will assist the individual to work out the trauma. This, in turn, will lead to the lessening and resolution of associated posttraumatic symptoms. In a trauma-based approach, much emphasis is given to the development of a coherent cognitive framework for understanding the general consequences and psychopathological responses that originate with traumatic experience. The patient is viewed not as pathological and as someone to be treated by those in authority, but as a person with normal responses to abnormal stress who is a partner in the treatment process.

Since the late 1970s and early 1980s, specialty units (or treatment tracks within general units) for the inpatient treatment of PTSD have been developed around this treatment philosophy, which serves to distinguish them from more traditional units. These programs are geared to two main traumatized populations: combat veterans and adults abused as children (adult abuse survivors). Both of these populations are likely to have suffered additional experiences of trauma over the life span. Occasionally, victims of other types of acute and/or chronic traumatization (i.e., sexual assault, domestic violence, refugee trauma, torture, etc.) have also been treated in these programs. Early on, many trauma-based programs were of midrange to long-term duration (30-day average length of stay in adult survivor programs in private or community hospitals, and 90 days or longer in veterans programs in the Department of Veterans Affairs) and included intensive group and individual treatment that focused specifically on the past traumatic experiences, in addition to other life issues conducted in rehabilitative, family, and milieu therapies (Bloom, 1994; Johnson, 1997).

More recently, the therapeutic emphasis has shifted from a primary focus on processing and resolving the trauma (although many early programs did attend to a range of issues besides the trauma) to a broader focus on understanding the individual's psychosexual development, object relations, pre- and posttrauma risk and resiliency factors, social support network, symptoms, and functioning—all from a trauma-based perspective. This more comprehensive treatment orientation is due, in part, to the following:

1. The increasing recognition that symptoms associated with chronic PTSD are quite complicated, comorbid with other psychiatric conditions, and thus more difficult to treat and to ameliorate than previously known. A treatment that places primary emphasis on the traumatic experience (especially through the use of techniques that foster regression, abreaction, and re-vivification of the trauma) while neglecting issues of safety, present-day func-

tioning, and reconnection with others, is usually not restorative (this approach has been labeled the "first generation" model of trauma treatment) (Chu, 1992; Johnson, Feldman, Southwick, & Charney, 1994).

2. The development of treatment models that are more comprehensive and oriented toward other issues besides traumatization and PTSD symptoms, including object relations and attachment issues (the "second generation" model) (Johnson et al., 1994).

3. The development of a phase-oriented posttrauma treatment that is sequenced, progressive, and titrated. In this model, crisis management and resolution, personal safety, patient education regarding trauma and the human response to trauma, education and skills building for self-management of symptoms, symptom stabilization, and rational psychopharmacology are given priority (Brown, Scheflin, & Hammond, 1998; Chu, 1998; Courtois, 1999; van der Kolk, McFarlane, & van der Hart, 1996). A focus on reconstructing and reworking traumatic memories is usually only pursued when the patient's posttraumatic symptoms continue unabated and/or lack of resolution contributes to the patient's difficulty establishing and maintaining personal safety. In the phase-oriented model, severe decompensation and/or risk of imminent harm to or from others are the paramount reasons for inpatient treatment.

4. The findings of treatment outcome data that first became available in the late 1980s and early 1990s in the VA.

5. Utilization review, the necessity for cost containment, and the influence of managed care (in both the private sector and the VA).

At the present time, a great diversity can be seen across individual inpatient PTSD programs, as each program offers a unique blend of treatment strategies and modalities. Yet even with this diversity, the overall philosophical orientation of these programs is trauma-responsive, and they utilize many common treatment approaches. All include a primary therapeutic focus on the traumatic experience(s) and its consequences, and then incorporate attention to issues of personal safety, functional improvement, skills-building for self-management and symptom reduction (including relapse planning), rehabilitation, and the reintegration of the individual into everyday family, work, and social life—all core issues for traumatized individuals.

The treatment model is conceptually based on the three central theoretical paradigms identified by Seidel, Gusman, and Abueg (1994): social learning theory, the life-span development model, and the therapeutic community or milieu psychiatry. This is melded with the multimodal and sequenced posttraumatic treatment model described by Brown, Scheflin, and Hammond (1998), Chu (1998), Courtois (1999), Marmar, Foy, Kagan, and Pynoos (1994), and van der Kolk, McFarlane, and van der Hart (1996), and with the model of general psychiatric care, including psychopharmacology that is tai-

lored to the needs of the traumatized population (Friedman, Davidson, Mellman, & Southwick, Chapter 5, this volume). It also incorporates differential
selection of therapeutic targets depending on the type of trauma. Catherall
(1989) identified primary (initial traumatic experience) and secondary types
of trauma (the subsequent breakdown of the survivor's social environment
and connection to others) in many patients with PTSD that call for different
and broadened treatment approaches and strategies. Most recently, the model is incorporating more attention to the individual's object relations, attachment style and capacities, and pre- and posttrauma risk and resiliency factors.

Specific treatment goals include (1) a comprehensive assessment; (2) the
reduction of core PTSD symptoms (intrusion, numbing/dissociation, hyperarousal); (3) the reduction of other PTSD symptoms that might be at subclin-
ical levels but are nevertheless important to the individual's well-being or influence his or her clinical status; (4) the identification and stabilization of
comorbid conditions and symptoms; (5) the stabilization and/or resolution of
suicidal, self-injurious, or homicidal impulses and any other crisis circumstances; (6) the improvement of troublesome personality difficulties; (7) the
reduction of social friction due to interpersonal difficulties and deficits; (8)
the improvement of functional status and the reduction of salient symptoms;
(9) the improvement of specific areas of disability; and (10) extensive discharge planning and relapse prevention.

At present, most programs are of moderate length (in the range of 2–6
weeks) due largely to the pressures of a managed care environment. Additionally, clinical observations and available empirical evidence (reviewed later) suggest that programs of short or midrange duration (4–6 weeks) are possibly more effective than very short-term (days to 2 weeks) or longer-term (6
weeks or more) programs in treating both core PTSD symptoms and other
psychiatric symptoms (although data from a 12-week Australian combat veteran program with inpatient and outpatient components showed treatment
gains in core PTSD and other symptoms [Creamer & Morris, 1997; Creamer, Morris, Biddle, & Elliott, 1999] and reimbursement models currently
available in the VA best support a midlength program of 60 days). Whereas
extended admissions (more than 6 months) used to be the norm in some
programs, this is no longer the case. Decreased length of stays is certainly in
keeping with national trends in the United States regarding the changing
patterns of psychiatric inpatient care (Mechanic, McAlpine, & Olfson,
1998).

Programs of very short duration, of necessity, are usually crisis-oriented
and work to decrease the patient's level of acuity or decompensation through
the use of crisis intervention, intensive therapy, and targeted psychopharmacology, along with focused education, problem solving, and safety planning.
In longer-term programs, admission need not be as crisis-driven and often

occurs on a planned basis. The usual requirement is that the patient have severe enough symptomatology and distress to warrant an intensive treatment
experience and/or around-the-clock monitoring. Longer-term programs
have the luxury of more ambitious goals (e.g., to improve interpersonal skills
and functioning in family, social, and work settings; to lessen and resolve psychiatric symptoms; to address and resolve dysfunctional or irrational cognitions and beliefs associated with traumatization in hopes of lessening core
PTSD symptoms, etc.).

Hospitalization in a specialized program is contraindicated if malingering is suspected, or if the patient suffers from psychosis or significant enough
characterological and/or social impairment to make work in a therapeutic
milieu impossible. Also, patients in the throes of any life-threatening condition without suicidal intent (e.g., substance abuse, eating disorders) are not
good candidates for this type of treatment until their clinical condition has
been stabilized. Patients should be assessed as to their ability and willingness
to participate voluntarily in a treatment setting that addresses their traumatic
history and traumatic stress reactions and where they are expected to actively
create and participate in an emotionally safe and physically nonviolent environment.

In recognition of the ongoing intensive care needs of patients who have
chronic conditions that only occasionally meet criteria for inpatient admission (and yet who might need repeated admissions) or whose admissions are
attenuated due to stringent utilization review and managed care restrictions,
many inpatient programs have developed partial hospital, day-treatment programs, residential rehabilitation programs, and intensive outpatient treatment offerings to provide a continuum of care and a safety net for these patients. This trend seems to be getting stronger in the VA system, where a
movement away from inpatient treatment in favor of intensive outpatient
and residential treatment is under way (F. Gusman, personal communication,
1999).

Preliminary research on the efficacy of partial hospitalization reported
by Perconte (1989), Perconte and Griger (1991), and Perconte, Griger, and
Belluci (1989), similar to the data reported for inpatient treatment, showed
treatment gains at discharge, with partial relapse on 1-year follow-up. These
findings are concordant with those of Long and colleagues (1989), Ronis and
colleagues (1996), and Wang, Wilson, and Mason (1996), whose findings suggest a long-term course of chronic PTSD. Many patients with histories of prolonged traumatization and chronic PTSD require psychiatric and rehabilitative services of long duration; however, according to the findings of Wang and
colleagues, a number of patients need intensive services only on an episodic
basis. Patients in the latter category have been found to have cyclical patterns
of relapse and decompensation (when intensive services are most needed), and
recovery and recompensation (when they are not). Thus, a variety of inpatient,

residential, and intensive outpatient treatment options are necessary to meet the ongoing needs of the most chronic and disabled patients, and the episodic and cyclical needs of those who are better able to cope.

DESCRIPTION OF PROGRAMS AND TECHNIQUES

Over the course of the past decade, a number of program descriptions of individual inpatient PTSD programs have been published (Allen, Kelly, & Glodich, 1997; Bear, 1993; Bloom, 1994, 1997; Courtois, Cohen, & Turkus, 1994; Forman & Havas, 1990; Johnson, 1997; Johnson, Feldman, Lubin, & Southwick, 1995; Johnson & Lubin, 1997; Kluft, 1991, 1996; Putnam, Loewenstein, Silberman, & Post, 1984; Ross, 1987, 1996; Sakheim, Hess, & Chivas, 1988; Seidel, Gusman, & Abueg, 1994; Solt, Chen, & Roy, 1996). Only in the past 5 years have programs been systematically surveyed and assessed as to their treatment components and techniques. Two such studies are available. The most comprehensive survey of inpatient programs for the treatment of adult survivors of sexual abuse ($n = 22$, out of a total of 70 programs identified and contacted) was published by the Safer Society Press (Bear, 1993). This survey, which relied on a convenience sample of program directors who chose to respond to a detailed questionnaire, is therefore not necessarily a representative sample. It is likely that the results are already outdated, because many of the surveyed programs have closed due to market demands and changes; nevertheless, the document provides useful descriptions of program components that defined the treatment model and are likely to apply to existing programs, and are therefore of interest in this review.

In the VA, a comprehensive assessment of program structure, content, and social climate in specialized residential PTSD programs ($n = 19$) was conducted in 1991 to determine whether they differed from general psychiatric units ($n = 18$) (Johnson, Rosenheck, & Fontana, 1997). The content and structure of each type of unit were defined by the program directors, and the social climate was assessed by veteran/patients with a PTSD diagnosis. A review of inpatient treatment for war-related PTSD over the course of 20 years was published by Johnson and colleagues (1996) and Rosenheck, Fontana, and Errara (1997).

The findings of both studies emphasized this type of specialized treatment program's relative newness and rarity, and its distinctiveness from more general psychiatric units. Most programs operate as discrete units, although some are a specialized part (or treatment track) of a more generic unit. The data generated by both studies are used here to describe the program components and techniques most likely to be incorporated in inpatient PTSD programs. By and large, this multimodal treatment model is provided by a multidisciplinary team (psychiatrists, clinical nurse specialists and nursing staff; psychologists, clinical social workers, counselors, expressive arts therapists, occupational and recreational therapists). As noted earlier, this model uses the trauma-based approach as a philosophical foundation to elaborate the concept of the therapeutic milieu as a major part of what differentiates it from the more general psychiatric unit. This orientation stresses the concept of "social healing for social wounds" (Bloom, 1997) and recognizes the critical role of the therapeutic community of peers in offering support to counteract the effects of interpersonal victimization and traumatization. Within the community, patients have the opportunity to be with others who have had similar traumatic experiences and posttraumatic aftereffects in a context that is normalizing, instructive, and supportive. The therapeutic milieu also offers the context for learning new coping and relationship skills, and for reworking some of the problematic interpersonal issues that are so often a consequence of traumatic injury suffered at the hands of other human beings or within institutions.

In specialized programs, attempts are made to provide an intensive therapeutic milieu that, first of all, is physically as well as emotionally safe for its members, all of whom are admitted on a voluntary basis. Clear expectations exist about participation and boundaries, about what is acceptable behavior and what is not. Aggression and violence toward self or others (including staff) are expressly not allowed and the admission is contingent on the agreement to interact safely and without aggression and violence. Violations and boundary testing are quite common, however, and are to be expected in a subset of traumatized individuals. Aggression toward self or others is often part of the posttraumatic aftermath that, paradoxically, may occur in the interest of personal safety and self-soothing. When such safety violations occur in a treatment setting, they must be handled promptly, firmly, and decisively by staff, lest they compromise the safety of all and the integrity of the community and the treatment team (Bills & Bloom, 1998).

Patients are expected to take personal responsibility for their behavior and to attempt to substitute healthier coping skills (that are actively taught to them as part of the treatment, as described later) when they experience compulsive, self-destructive, and/or violent urges. Social safety in the context of the community is also stressed and actively worked on in these programs. Patients are taught about dysfunctional interpersonal behavior that has been found to be associated with traumatization (i.e., common boundary and interaction difficulties; the roles of victim, victimizer, rescuer, and bystander; and reenactment dynamics) and taught new, more assertive, functional, and empowered ways of interacting with others.

To summarize the predominant program structure: The milieu is designed to be predictable, safe, nonrigid and nonauthoritarian, and community-based. It is respectful of the patient, encourages personal empowerment and communal responsibility, collaborative treatment, and clear and open patient-to-patient and patient-to-staff communication. In some programs (VA programs in particular), staff members themselves are trauma survivors who have worked through the effects of their combat experience, a situation that may give them additional credibility with patients while offering them hope for their own recovery. In contrast, the personal trauma history of staff members in adult abuse survivor programs is not as explicitly acknowledged to the patient population.

Some programs have selective admission criteria, most having more to do with the patient's ability to function safely within a therapeutic community than with specific diagnostic criteria. Most programs require voluntary admission (some units are open and unlocked, although most are locked) and a suspected or diagnosed posttraumatic condition (in addition to comorbid conditions and other diagnoses). The most common comorbid Axis I diagnoses are major depression, anxiety disorders, alcohol/substance abuse, eating disorders, somatization disorder, dissociative disorders, atypical psychosis, and intermittent explosive disorder. Consistent with the established connection between trauma and personality disorders (Ellason, Ross, Sainton, & Mayran, 1996; Herman, Perry, & van der Kolk, 1989; Perry, Herman, van der Kolk, & Hoke, 1990; Sabo, 1997), many patients are diagnosed with Axis II disorders, most commonly, borderline, obsessive–compulsive, avoidant, dependent, paranoid, self-defeating, antisocial, and mixed types. Axis III medical conditions are common sequelae for many traumatized patients, since a past history of physical and sexual abuse, and other forms of traumatization have all been correlated with major health consequences (Davidson, Hughes, Blazer, & George, 1991; Friedman & Schnurr, 1995). Patients may also enter treatment due to significant and ongoing psychosocial stressors such as homelessness, unemployment, continued exposure to violence, episodes of revictimization, and so on.

VA programs are obviously open to all veterans who qualify but Johnson, Rosenheck, and Fontana (1997) found that specialized units had stronger external boundaries than more general units and were more likely to screen patients before admission, control admissions, admit in cohort groups for defined lengths of stay, and maintain waiting lists. Bear (1993) reported much less consistency and wide variation in the steps of the admission process among the various adult abuse survivor programs included in her survey. Most of these programs were housed in private, for-profit hospital chains, making it difficult, if not impossible, for destitute adult survivors without some sort of insurance to participate. Some attempts have been made recently, with some gratifying results, to introduce trauma-based programming into general units of state hospital systems serving a mixed treatment population (Bills & Bloom, 1998), but this kind of approach requires ongoing and consistent leadership that can be difficult to maintain in financially stressed hospital systems. (However, at the present time, both New York and Maine are planning and implementing trauma-based programmatic emphases into their respective state mental health systems, including inpatient units.)

The trauma-based understanding that is found in specialized programs is evident from the time of initial evaluation and admission, when the emphasis is on "What happened to you?" as opposed to "What's wrong with you?" (Bloom, 1994). Yet, even with this emphasis, the necessity for a comprehensive multidisciplinary evaluation is recognized. Chronically traumatized patients have complex clinical conditions. Some symptoms and disorders have been found to mimic or obscure others (e.g., PTSD symptoms overlap with symptoms of other psychiatric and medical diagnoses) in ways that make differential diagnosis difficult and misdiagnosis common. Assessment in specialized programs, in contrast to assessment in general units, is more likely to incorporate questions and objective psychometric instruments that assess traumatic experiences and trauma symptoms to assist in differential diagnosis. Conversely, specialized programs may be better able to ascertain if patients have primary diagnoses that are not trauma-related, such as cases of complex comorbitidy, hysteria, or malingering.

The treatment offered in speciality programs is transtheoretical and multimodal. No single theory of therapy is primary, although psychodynamic and cognitive-behavioral perspectives are at the foundation of most, if not all, of the programs. Techniques and strategies are drawn predominantly from the following: insight/self-discovery, posttraumatic stress, cognitive-behavioral (including anxiety management strategies), psychodynamic, and psychosocioeducational treatment models. Cognitive-behavioral approaches include structured psychoeducation about trauma and the normal human response to traumatization. Specialized approaches focus on the identification of feelings, emotional expression and debriefing, anxiety management, cognitive restructuring, imaginal flooding techniques, exposure and desensitization, skills training, behavior modification, and relapse prevention. (In some programs, newly developed techniques such as eye movement desensitization and reprocessing [EMDR] are being utilized.) Hypnosis and guided imagery may be used in some programs for the purposes of ego strengthening and self-soothing but are not used or recommended for either memory retrieval or abreaction. Expressive therapies are critical components of inpatient trauma treatment, since they provide patients with a safe way of expressing the nonverbal and emotionally charged aspects of their experience, while providing them with tools they can continue to use after discharge. A variety of expressive/creative therapies, including art, psychodrama, poetry/writing, video, and movement/dance, are utilized in different programs in recognition of the difficulty that some traumatized individuals have in verbalizing their experiences. In some programs, field trips and other off-unit activities are included, since they provide excellent opportunities for the rehearsal of developing skills. Unfortunately, activities of this sort are not in keeping with managed care limitations, so they are rarely utilized anymore.

Optimally, treatment planning occurs very early in the admission and with the patient's collaboration. Both VA and adult abuse survivor programs stress an intensive treatment milieu that fosters the patient's personal responsibility and active participation. Most programs are highly structured and include some combination of the following in addition to a preliminary multidisciplinary psychosocial assessment: individual therapy (daily or several times per week); several group experiences per day (including community meetings, group therapy, didactic and skills-building groups, expressive therapy, and occupational/recreational therapy groups); psychopharmacology; case management and social work services; attendance at 12-step meetings (as warranted), and, couple and family meetings and therapy sessions. Moreover, in many programs, active efforts are made to closely coordinate treatment goals with the outpatient provider to avoid precipitating splits between providers and to provide the patient with consistency in the transition back to the outpatient setting. Since this population is so complex and demanding, management of acute episodes in the outpatient setting can be quite difficult. Inpatient hospitalization often provides the outpatient therapist with the opportunity for specialized professional input and consultation that is usually unavailable in the outpatient setting. Planning for discharge begins almost immediately upon admission to emphasize to the patient that the length of stay is relatively short and that he or she must settle in and work immediately, because the return to residential or outpatient treatment is imminent.

To summarize, inpatient treatment is a vital, often life saving part of a complete continuum of care, particularly when used as a short-term and limited part of an individual's overall treatment, most of which is expected to occur in an outpatient setting. Many of the programs have evolved to become more comprehensive in their approaches due to the chronicity and corresponding complexity of the needs of this patient population. Additionally, although many programs emphasize reentry into mainstream life, many also recognize that the needs of these patients may be lifelong and episodic, and so they have devised more residential and outpatient treatment modalities, where the bulk of the treatment is expected to occur. Table 10.1 summarizes many of the components of specialized inpatient PTSD programs that differentiate them from general psychiatric units.

A limited number of empirical investigations of inpatient programs have been undertaken to date and others are under way. We next describe the completed studies.

METHOD OF COLLECTING DATA

The data for the following review of the empirical literature were collected in two ways. The first involved a comprehensive literature search of the PILOTS, MEDLINE, and PsycINFO databases of studies published through spring 1999. The second involved a request for data from directors of inpatient trauma programs. Many of the papers identified in the literature

TABLE 10.1. Some Differences between Specialized Inpatient PTSD Treatment Programs and General Psychiatric Units

Admission criteria	Treatments offered	Outcome goals
	General psychiatric unit	
Crisis/severe stressors	Multidisciplinary assessment	Stabilization of precipitating
Harm to self and others	Psychological testing (as ordered)	crisis
Decompensation	Adjunctive assessment (as ordered)	Lessening of stressors
Inability to function	Nursing	Personal and social safety
Psychiatric conditions and	Psychopharmacology	Lessening of symptoms
diagnoses	Social work and case management	Increase in functioning
	Group treatment	Discharge to outpatient
	Individual therapy (some units)	treatment
	General cognitive-behavioral	
	interventions	
	Expressive therapy	
	Occupational/recreational therapy	
	Couple/family education/	
	consultation/treatment	
	Collaboration with outpatient	
	providers?	
	Specialized unit	
Crisis/severe stressors	Multidisciplinary assessment	Personal and social safety
Harm to self and others	Psychological testing (as ordered)	Stabilization of precipitating
Decompensation	Adjunctive assessment (as ordered)	crisis
Inability to function	Specialized philosophy for all	Involvement in treatment
More selective admission	interventions/specialized staff	planning
and ability to select:	training: posttrauma	Active interaction with
PTSD symptoms/	orientation:	treatment team and
diagnosis	"What happened to you?"	treatment program
Willingness to be safe	versus "What's wrong with	Lessening of stressors
on the unit	you?"	Lessening of PTSD symptoms
Willingness to	"Social healing for social	Lessening of other symptoms
participate in the	wounds"	Increase in functioning
milieu and in the	Posttraumatic under-	Education about trauma,
treatment process	standing of symptoms	human response to trauma,
Willingness to discuss	Social and personal safety	self-management of
trauma with others	Personal empowerment	symptoms
Willingness to wait for	Nursing	Skills building in self-
opening on unit	Psychopharmacology	management of symptoms
and/or for cohort	Social work and case management	Personal empowerment and
group to form	Milieu treatment	communal responsibility
Stronger external	Group treatment	Participation in milieu and
boundaries to the rest of	Individual treatment (many	connection with others
the hospital	programs)	Cognitive restructuring
	Specialized and general cognitive-	Graduated exposure to
	behavioral interventions	traumatic
	Focused expressive therapy	material/memory, as
	Occupational/recreational therapy	warranted for resolution
	Couple/family/education/	Comprehensive discharge
	consultation/treatment	planning and relapse
	Collaboration with outpatient	prevention
	providers	
	Specialized techniques, by program	

search were descriptive; however, several available outcome studies (most conducted within the VA) are reviewed in the next section.

SUMMARY OF LITERATURE

The studies reported here, with several exceptions, attempted to investigate the efficacy of the entire treatment program versus program components. A problem is immediately evident in studies of milieu therapy: defining a specific technique and attempting to study the impact of that technique separate from the impact of other techniques and the general influence of the therapeutic community itself. Milieu therapy, rather than being a discrete and separate technique, is actually a setting within which specific and nonspecific techniques are integrated and delivered. Moos's (1974) work on evaluating treatment environments has demonstrated that a consistent treatment philosophy maintains environmental stability over time; therefore, the philosophical underpinning of a program based on trauma may have a large—and difficult to measure—influence on treatment outcome. An additional challenge to the evaluation of a program's overall effectiveness comes from admissions that are crisis-driven versus those that occur on a planned basis. They, too, may result in changes that are difficult to measure (i.e., other crises such as deaths or serious injuries that were are averted or prevented by the hospitalization). Despite various difficulties of this sort that can confound evaluation efforts, a number of studies have researched entire programs and specific program components.

Next, we review the available studies, categorized into the two main program types: those for combat veterans and those for adult abuse survivors.

Empirical Studies

Level A

No randomized control study of the efficacy of inpatient treatment for veterans or adult abuse survivors is currently available.

Levels B and C

Evidence from well-designed clinical studies without randomization or placebo comparison for individuals with PTSD (Level B) and from service and naturalistic clinical studies, combined with clinical observations that are sufficiently compelling to warrant use of the treatment technique or recommendation (Level C), is as follows:

1. *Veterans*. Thirteen studies have been identified (6 at Level B and 7 at Level C) and are listed in Table 10.2. All involve convenience samples of

TABLE 10.2. Results of Available Empirical Studies of Inpatient Programs

Study and rating	N	Subjects	Program type and length	Study purpose	Control and follow-up	Findings and effect size
Creamer, Morris, Biddle, & Elliot (1999) B	419	Australian Vietnam combat vets	Long-term specialty	To study treatment outcome in combat-related PTSD in vets who completed a 12-week hospital-based program.	No control 3 and 9 mo follow-up	Significant improvements in core PTSD symptoms, anxiety, depression, alcohol abuse, social dysfunction, and anger. Treatment gains were variable and, for most veterans, considerable pathology remained post-discharge.
Mellman (1998) C	26	Combat vets	Long-term specialty	To study the value of longer term, inpatient treatment.	No control 4 and 6 mo follow-up	Significant improvements in interpersonal functioning with family members and intimacy; extended treatment involvement may generalize to family functioning post-discharge.
Fontana & Rosenheck (1997) B	785	Vietnam vets	Three types: short-term, long-term specialty, and nonspecialty	To study the effectiveness and cost of three inpatient treatment models.	No control; comparison 1 yr at 4-mo intervals follow-up	Vets in short-term PTSD units and general units showed significant improvement at follow-up. Vets had greatest satisfaction with short-term PTSD programs. Cost, effectiveness and satisfaction suggest short-term PTSD units are inpatient option of choice.
Ford, Fisher, & Larson (1997) C	74	Combat vets	Long-term	To study the role of object relations as a predictor of inpatient treatment outcome.	No control No follow-up	Little evidence of reliable or clinically significant change at discharge on psychological indices, yet treatment associated with reduction of utilization of inpatient and residential services. Role of object relations in treatment outcome suggested.
Johnson et al. (1997) C	51	Vietnam vets	Long-term	To analyze outcome of an intensive inpatient program for combat-related PTSD.	No control 6-, 12-, and 18-mo follow-up	Increase in symptoms and decrease in violent actions, thoughts, and legal problems from admission to follow-up. Improvement in family and interpersonal relationships at discharge but return to pretreatment levels at 18 mo. Study questions whether long-term intensive inpatient treatment is effective and whether other forms of treatment should be considered.

(continued)

TABLE 10.2. *(continued)*

Study and rating	N	Subjects	Program type and length	Study purpose	Control and follow-up	Findings and effect size
Ragsdale, Cox, Finn, & Eisler (1996) B	24	Vietnam vets	Short-term	To study outcome of treatment in a short-term intensive inpatient program versus weekly outpatient group therapy.	Control group of wait-list vets in outpatient group therapy No follow-up	Significant improvements in hopelessness, shame, guilt, loneliness, and emotional expressiveness. No significant change on other indices. No positive changes in wait-list comparison group. Posttreatment effect size, d: 55 (29, −0.81); $r = .26$.
Hammarberg & Silver (1994) B	39	Vets	Long-term	To track patient from admission to discharge (90 days) and to compare with two control groups: (1) PTSD vets out of treatment and (2) non-PTSD nontreatment (over 12 wk).	Two control groups 1-year follow-up of treatment completers	As measured by the Penn Inventory for PTSD, 48% of treatment completers showed some or substantial gains, 39% showed no gain, and 13% showed some increase in symptoms at discharge. At 1-yr follow-up, a return to pretreatment levels on the PTSD symptoms measures was noted. Posttreatment effect size d: 16 (−0.16, −0.49); $r = 0.01$.
Munley, Bains, Frazee, & Schwartz (1994) B	14 and 35	Vietnam vets	Short-term	To study if there are pretreatment differences between patients who complete versus those who do not complete a specialized inpatient PTSD program tract, and between completers and noncompleters rated by their therapists as having the highest versus lowest ratings on overall response to treatment.	Random sample of treatment completers vs. treatment dropouts ($n = 14$) and highest vs. lowest therapist ratings ($n = 35$) No follow-up	No significant differences between samples in either comparison between treatment completers and treatment noncompleters.

Study	N	Population	Term	Purpose	Control/Follow-up	Results
Funari, Piekarski, & Sherwood (1991) C	45	Vietnam vets	Long-term	To study changes on the Millon Clinical Multiaxial Inventory in completers of a specialized inpatient treatment program.	No control / No follow-up	Treatment completers showed decreases on 12 of the 20 scales and increases on 8; PTSD-related symptoms of anxiety and dysthymia decreased significantly and schizoid, avoidant, and passive–aggressive character styles also showed significant decreases.
Boudewyns, Hyer, Woods, Harrison, & McCranie (1990)	58	Vietnam vets	Long-term	To study any pretreatment differences between successful and unsuccessful outcome after inpatient treatment on a specialized unit and to study whether those treated with direct exposure therapy (DET) have better treatment outcomes than those treated with standard treatment (ST).	No control / 3-mo follow-up: DET versus ST (random assignment)	No significant differences between "success" versus "failure" groups on any pretreatment variables. On follow-up, a significant number of subjects treated with DET were identified as "successes" versus those treated with ST. Posttreatment effect size d: .03 (-0.30, -0.36); r: .01. Follow-up effect size d: .54 (-0.21, -1.30); r: .27.
Scurfield, Kenderdine, & Pollard (1990) C	86	War zone veterans	Long-term	To establish a baseline of clinical data on application to the specialized inpatient program versus postdischarge follow-up.	No control / 4- to 16-mo postdischarge follow-up	Significant differences found on one symptom checklist and positive trends toward symptom reduction on another. Positive changes in self-esteem, interpersonal relationships, numbing, and arousal. PTSD-related intrusive symptoms had the least clear-cut improvement.
Starkey & Ashlock (1984, 1886) C	5	Vietnam vets	Short-term	To determine pre- and posttest scores on the MMPI and Post-Vietnam Stress Index (PVSI).	No control / No follow-up	Decrease on PVSI scores; Reversal of MMPI validity scale scores and decrease in hostility and phobic reactions scales in treatment completers.
Bills & Bloom (1998) C	24	Inpatients in a state hospital ward	Long-term	To determine change in minutes of seclusion/restraint per mo and self-harm, aggressive, and accident episodes per mo after implementation of Sanctuary® model general and safety interventions.	No control / No follow-up	Unit restraint/seclusion and violence decreased substantially; relapse at point when leader/change implementer was absent from unit for a period of time.

(continued)

TABLE 10.2. *(continued)*

Study and rating	*N*	Subjects	Program type and length	Study purpose	Control and follow-up	Findings and effect size
Ross (1997) C	134	Adult survivors of childhood trauma with PTSD diagnosis	Long-term	To evaluate whether differences in DSM-IV personality clusters as assessed by MMPI-2 affect outcome for a 6-wk specialized unit for adult survivors of childhood trauma.	No control 3-mo and 1-yr follow-up	Data indicated the program was effective in reducing PTSD and associated symptoms at discharge. Personality type not found to influence treatment gains.
Wright & Woo (1997) C	134	Adult survivors of childhood trauma and PTSD diagnosis	Long-term	To study the outcomes of adult survivors of childhood trauma who enter a 6-wk specialized unit for adult survivors of childhood trauma.	No control 3-mo and 1-yr follow-up	At discharge, frequency and intensity of symptoms did not meet threshold for PTSD diagnosis or for frequency and intensity of symptom clusters B, C, and D. Overall symptom frequency and intensity ratings significantly decreased although declines in gains were also identified at follow-up.
Ellason & Ross (1997) C	54	Adults with DID	Unknown	To study treatment outcome in DID patients following treatment in a specialized PTSD/DID inpatient program.	No control 2 years	Patients showed marked improvement on Schneiderian first-rank symptoms, mood and anxiety disorders, dissociative symptoms, and somatization, with a significant decrease in the number of psychiatric medications prescribed. Patients with DID may respond well to treatment.

inpatients with PTSD treated in a specialty or general psychiatric unit. Only 3 utilized comparison groups. Most studies administered ratings and self-report measures of symptoms (of PTSD and other psychiatric diagnoses) and social functioning at admission and discharge, and occasionally at follow-up some months later (ranging from 3 to 24 months) in an attempt to determine the efficacy of treatment. It is evident that studies are becoming more sophisticated. The earlier studies involved pre- and posttesting of psychiatric symptoms of small samples of inpatients from one single-treatment program using standard psychometric instruments with no follow-up data collection. Although some of the more recent studies still have small sample sizes, some involve larger samples from multiple sites. They also gather a broader range of psychiatric, social, and object relations data, and patient satisfaction data using several different generic and trauma-specific psychometric instruments administered at admission and discharge, and at various intervals postdischarge.

2. *Adult abuse survivors.* Five outcome studies (all Level C) were identified, only two of which are published. Four are included in Table 10.2, since they contain some data and analyses.

Findings can be summarized as follows: In the VA, some data support the assertion that moderate-length specialized programs (ranging from 2 to 12 weeks) and general psychiatric units are more effective than long-term specialized programs, because of changes in objective indices of symptoms (especially on follow-up testing) and patient self-report and level of satisfaction. This finding may be confounded, however, by the fact that the shorter-stay PTSD units and general psychiatric units were both designed for crisis admissions (with correspondingly high initial symptom levels), while the longer-stay programs involved planned admissions (with less high initial symptoms). Mean PTSD severity levels in the former programs were higher and therefore showed considerable change as the crisis was resolved.

Treatment modalities that focused on current life issues (in addition to a general focus on the traumatic circumstance and aftermath) were favored and seen as more effective long term than those that focused predominantly on the trauma. In many of these studies, PTSD symptoms remitted to baseline pretreatment levels upon follow-up assessment. In some studies, life and trauma-related themes and schemas, as well as morale and interpersonal relations, showed improvement that lasted to the time of postevaluation. One study found that object relations constituted a significant predictor of treatment outcome (Ford, Fisher, & Larson, 1997). Based upon the findings of this study, the researchers recommended that patients be carefully screened and matched with a range of treatment or rehabilitative services. They also recommended conceptualizing treatment outcome beyond symptom reduction and noted that "rehabilitation of chronic posttraumatic symptomatology and associated psychosocial impairment may be facilitated by assessment, treatment design, and client–treatment matching on the basis of multidimensional psychological indices" (p. 547). These authors were explicit in their agreement with Johnson and colleagues (1996) that long-term inpatient PTSD treatment should not be seen as the certain and only approach to the rehabilitation of chronic PTSD, and that many patients may be better served by ongoing outpatient, residential, or community-based care that promotes community reintegration (à la "second generation" and secondary trauma conceptual models) and selected interventions (see Rogers [1998] for a critique of this model and additional suggestions for treatment strategies and research). Following this line of reasoning, inpatient admissions would be reserved for serious remissions, crises, and intensive evaluation and/or treatment efforts with interventions tailored to the individual's needs at the time of admission. The findings of the study of a 12-week inpatient–outpatient treatment program for Australian Vietnam veterans (Creamer & Morris, 1997; Creamer, Morris, Biddle, & Elliott, 1999) also supported the use of a short inpatient stay with outpatient follow-up as a better option than traditional long-stay programs. The findings of this study indicated highly variable treatment gains, with considerable pathology remaining at completion of the therapeutic programs.

In contrast to these findings concerning the treatment of traumatized veterans, it is impossible to draw any definitive data-based conclusions about the treatment of adult survivors of childhood abuse due to a dearth of outcome studies and data. Ellason and Ross's (1997) study of the treatment of patients diagnosed with dissociative identity disorder (DID) is of significance because it found positive treatment outcome (marked improvement on Schneiderian first-rank symptoms, mood and anxiety disorders, dissociative symptoms, and somatization, with a significant decrease in the number of psychiatric medications prescribed). In this study, patients treated to the point of personality integration were significantly more improved than those who had not yet reached integration; however, the inpatient treatment model, or its possible impact on the findings, is not discussed in the article. Thus, it is unclear what techniques or mechanisms (including other inpatient and outpatient treatment in the intervening 2 years from discharge to follow-up assessment) accounted for the treatment gain. Bills and Bloom's (1998) findings involved a tabulation of a decline in the number of violent incidents and number of minutes of restraint/seclusion used per month following the implementation of a Sanctuary® model program stressing safety agreements and a secure environment in a state hospital unit. Their findings highlight the importance of a nonretraumatizing environment to personal recovery from traumatic stress disorders. Wright, Woo, and Ross (1996) and Wright and Woo (1997), in the most methodologically sound study of adult survivors to date, reported significant decreases in intensity and frequency of PTSD and associated symptoms, 1-year postdischarge from a 6-week traumatic stress program for self-identified survivors of childhood trauma. The program was organized around a strategy of stabilization and a present-centered focus versus a past-oriented cathartic traumatic recollection strategy. Thus, these findings are similar to those of the veteran samples. The authors highlight the significance of their findings in light of the fact that one-third of the study population met criteria for the diagnosis of borderline personality disorder in addition to the diagnosis of PTSD. Another component of this study examined whether differences in DSM-IV personality clusters as assessed by the Minnesota Multiphasic Personality Inventory—2 (MMPI-2) affected treatment gains for program participants. When findings from instruments measuring PTSD and associated symptoms were compared with MMPI-2 personality clusters, no significant differences were found between personality subtype and treatment gains. Results suggested that personality type did not influence treatment gains (Ross, 1997).

Clinical Studies

Levels C, D, E, and F

Evidence based on naturalistic and clinical studies (Level C), long-standing and widespread clinical practice (Level D), long-standing practice by circumscribed groups of clinicians not subjected to empirical tests (Level E), and recently developed treatment not subjected to clinical or empirical tests in PTSD (Level F) is as follows:

1. *Veterans.* Several studies (included in Table 10.2) and anecdotal articles have been identified that describe and assess the philosophical orientation, structure, content, and perceived social climate of specialized inpatient treatment for PTSD. These provide descriptions of how specialized programs differ from generic psychiatric units, as described previously.

2. *Adult abuse survivors.* A number of individual program descriptions are available that delineate the similarities in philosophical orientation to treatment and milieu management in both specialized inpatient treatment programs for adult survivors of sexual abuse and specialty units for the treatment of patients diagnosed with multiple personality disorder (now dissociative identity disorder). Many write-ups describe special elements and emphases of the program and how they seem to impact the patients and the management of the milieu. As described earlier, the survey of treatment programs for adult abuse survivors conducted by the Safer Society (Bear, 1993) provided the most comprehensive data to date. That report specifically highlighted the dearth of outcome research and data at that time, a situation that, unfortunately, is not very different today.

SUMMARY

Outcome research on specialized inpatient trauma treatment is more developed and more available for programs housed in the VA that treat combat veterans than for programs in freestanding hospitals that treat adult abuse survivors. Although the available findings have value and suggest directions for program design and modification, they are only preliminary and are not strong. Additional outcome studies that use more rigorous methodology involving randomization, control groups, and long-term follow-up are sorely needed.

It is recognized, however, that the very characteristics of inpatient treatment make assessment difficult and call for creative research solutions. Inpatient trauma treatment can best be viewed as a "metatherapy," the provision of a safe and health-promoting context, rather than one specific modality. Inpatient PTSD treatment integrates a posttraumatic perspective with various therapeutic modalities that have been demonstrated to be effective into an overall coordinated treatment plan conducted in a stable, nonviolent environment. When most effective, a coherent system of meaning can emerge from the therapeutic milieu that helps the patient to restore a sense of social connection and purpose. The complex and rich nature of this treatment can provide an opportunity for the rapid acquisition of new knowledge and skills, but it is this complexity that makes careful quantitative research so difficult and so scarce. Prolonged, chronic PTSD is a complicated (and, in some cases, difficult and resistant) disorder to treat; it has a host of associated comorbid disorders and medical conditions that must be given treatment consideration. The risk of suicide and other behaviors that are destructive to self and others is very high in this population and often necessitates hospitalization.

Available research findings to date regarding cost, effectiveness, and satisfaction generally suggest specialized programs of 2- to 12-weeks' duration as the inpatient option of choice for the treatment of chronic PTSD. Within a structured inpatient setting, it is possible to provide the patient with a coherent cognitive framework within which treatment can be planned and carefully orchestrated in stages. The first stage of treatment in any inpatient setting is the establishment of safety, and this step usually dominates specialized PTSD treatment today. In this model, validating and understanding the past are considered to be important, while attempts to treat prolonged PTSD by revisiting the trauma without first establishing safety are recognized to be potentially harmful. The "second generation" approach of carefully sequenced multimodal milieu treatment in a context of personal and social safety with a present and future orientation is recommended as the model of choice. It is recognized that, whatever the program, most inpatient treatment encompasses the tasks of Phase 1 of the posttrauma treatment model. Psychopharmacology is an important component of inpatient care and the management of distressing symptoms, although medication alone has not been demonstrated to be effective in the treatment of trauma-related disorders.

Findings of available studies suggest the need for careful assessment and treatment planning, with differential goals and treatment strategies determined by the individual's object relations, ego strength and self-capacity, pre-

and posttrauma risk and resiliency factors, severity of symptoms, degree of social connection, and level of functioning and disability. Inpatient treatment should be considered when the individual is in imminent danger of harming self or others, has decompensated or relapsed significantly in the ability to function, is suffering from debilitating symptoms of PTSD and/or comorbid diagnoses, is in the throes of major psychosocial stressors, and/or is in need of specialized observation/evaluation in a secure environment. It is contraindicated for individuals who are unwilling or unable to participate in milieu treatment based on a posttrauma treatment model, for those who are actively psychotic and/or characterologically impaired to such a degree that they are unable or unwilling to maintain safety within the therapeutic context, and for those who have life-threatening conditions (e.g., substance abuse, eating disorders) that require preliminary stabilization.

A shorter-term model of inpatient PTSD treatment (ranging anywhere from 2 to 12 weeks' duration) has several significant advantages. It assists in and complies with utilization review and cost-containment efforts, and encourages patients to move to a less restrictive (and less regressive) level of care once their crisis and symptoms are stabilized. It operates in collaboration with the patient's outpatient provider(s) and functions as one component (albeit a very crucial one in times of crisis and decompensation) of the continuum of treatment options for chronic trauma survivors. It responds to the long-term treatment needs of patients with chronic PTSD and associated comorbid and medical conditions by anticipating the need for episodic intensive treatment in a secure environment. Within the environment, it provides to the traumatized patient a philosophy and tailored treatment model that is not usually available on more general units. This orientation assures that the traumatic origin of the patient's difficulties and pathology is not ignored, yet it has a whole-person focus that extends beyond the traumatization. A focus on the past trauma is only in the interest of the future, to a life less encumbered by the trauma or what Shalev (1997) labeled "healing forward."

REFERENCES

Allen, J. G., Kelly, K. A., & Glodich, A. (1997). A psychoeducational program for patients with trauma-related disorders. *Bulletin of the Menninger Clinic, 61*(2), 222–239.

Bear, E. (1993). *Inpatient treatment for adult survivors of sexual abuse: A summary of data from 22 programs.* Brandon, VT: Safer Society Program.

Bills, L. J., & Bloom, S. L. (1998). From chaos to sanctuary: Trauma-based treatment for women in a state hospital system. In B. Labotsky, A. K. Blanch, & A. Jennings (Eds.), *Women's health services: A public health perspective* (pp. 348–367). Thousand Oaks, CA: Sage.

Bloom, S. L. (1994). The sanctuary model: Developing generic inpatient programs for the treatment of psychological trauma. In M. B. Williams & J. F. Sommer (Eds.), *Handbook of post-traumatic therapy* (pp. 474–494). Westport, CT: Greenwood Press.

Bloom, S. L. (1997). *Creating sanctuary: Toward the evolution of sane societies.* New York: Routledge.

Boudewyns, P. A., Hyer, L., Woods, M. G., Harrison, W. R., & McCranie, E. (1990). PTSD among Vietnam veterans: An early look at treatment outcome using direct therapeutic exposure. *Journal of Traumatic Stress, 3,* 359–368.

Brady, K. T. (1997). Posttraumatic stress disorder and comorbidity: Recognizing the many faces of PTSD. *Journal of Clinical Psychiatry, 58*(Suppl. 9), 12–15.

Breslau, N., Davis, G. C., Peterson, E. L., & Schultz, L. (1997). Psychiatric sequelae of posttraumatic stress disorder in women. *Archives of General Psychiatry, 54,* 81–87.

Brown, D., Scheflin, A. W., & Hammond, D. C. (1998). *Memory, trauma treatment, and the law: An essential reference on memory for clinicians, researchers, attorneys, and judges.* New York: Norton.

Brown, G. R., & Anderson, B. (1991). Psychiatric morbidity in adult inpatients with childhood histories of sexual and physical abuse. *American Journal of Psychiatry, 148*(1), 55–61.

Carlin, A. S., & Ward, N. G. (1992). Subtypes of psychiatric inpatient women who have been sexually abused. *Journal of Nervous and Mental Disease, 180,* 392–397.

Catherall, D. R. (1989). Differentiating intervention strategies for primary and secondary trauma in post-traumatic stress disorder: The example of Vietnam veterans. *Journal of Traumatic Stress, 2*(3), 289–304.

Chu, J. A. (1992). The therapeutic roller coaster: Dilemmas in the treatment of childhood abuse survivors. *Journal of Psychotherapy Practice and Research, 1,* 351–370.

Chu, J. A. (1998). *Rebuilding shattered lives: The responsible treatment of complex post-traumatic and dissociative disorders.* New York: Wiley.

Courtois, C. A. (1999). *Recollections of sexual abuse: Treatment principles and guidelines.* New York: Norton.

Courtois, C. A., Cohen, B. M., & Turkus, J. A. (1994). Developing an inpatient dissociative disorders unit. In M. B. Williams & J. F. Sommer (Eds.), *Handbook of post-traumatic therapy* (pp. 463–473). Westport, CT: Greenwood Press.

Creamer, M., & Morris, P. (1997, November). *Treatment outcome in Australian veterans with chronic PTSD: Preliminary findings.* Paper presented at the 8th annual meeting of the International Society for Traumatic Stress Studies, Montreal, Canada.

Creamer, M., Morris, P., Biddle, D., & Elliot, P. (1999). Treatment outcome in Australian veterans with combat-related posttraumatic stress disorder: A cause for cautious optimism? *Journal of Traumatic Stress, 12*(4), 545–558.

Davidson, J., Hughes, D., Blazer, D., & George, L. K. (1991). Post-traumatic stress disorder in the community: An epidemiological study. *Psychological Medicine, 21,* 713–721.

Ellason, J. W., & Ross, C. A. (1997). Two-year follow-up of inpatients with dissociative identity disorder. *American Journal of Psychiatry, 154*(6), 832–839.

Ellason, J. W., Ross, C. A., Sainton, K., & Mayran, L. W. (1996). Axis I and II comorbidity and childhood trauma history in chemical dependency. *Bulletin of the Menninger Clinic, 60*(1), 39–51.

Faustman, W. O., & White, P. A. (1989). Diagnostic and psychopharmacological treatment characteristics of 536 inpatients with posttraumatic stress disorder. *Journal of Nervous and Mental Disease, 177*(3), 154–159.

Fontana, A., & Rosenheck, R. (1997). Effectiveness and cost of the inpatient treatment of posttraumatic stress disorder: Comparison of three models of treatment. *American Journal of Psychiatry, 154*(6), 758–776.

Ford, J. D., Fisher, P., & Larson, L. (1997). Object relations as a predictor of treatment outcome with chronic posttraumatic stress. *Journal of Consulting and Clinical Psychology, 65*(4), 547–559.

Forman, S. I., & Havas, S. (1990). Massachusetts' post-traumatic stress disorder program: A public health treatment model for Vietnam veterans. *Public Health Reports, 105,* 172–179.

Friedman, M. J., & Schnurr, P. (1995). The relationship between trauma, post-traumatic stress disorder, and physical health. In M. J. Friedman, D. S. Charney, & A. Y. Deutch (Eds.), *Neurobiological and clinical consequences of stress: From normal adaptation to PTSD* (pp. 507–524). Philadelphia: Lippincott–Raven.

Funari, D. J., Piekarski, A. M., & Sherwood, R. J. (1991). Treatment outcomes of Vietnam veterans with posttraumatic stress disorder. *Psychological Reports, 68,* 571–578.

Hammarberg, M., & Silver, S. M. (1994). Outcome of treatment for post-traumatic stress disorder in a primary care unit serving Vietnam veterans. *Journal of Traumatic Stress, 7*(2), 195–215.

Herman, J. L., Perry, J. C., & van der Kolk, B. A. (1989). Childhood trauma in borderline personality disorder. *American Journal of Psychiatry, 146,* 490–495.

Hryvniak, M. R., & Rosse, R. B. (1989). Concurrent psychiatric illness in inpatients with post-traumatic stress disorder. *Military Medicine, 154,* 399–401.

Johnson, D. (1997). Inside the specialized inpatient PTSD units of the Department of Veterans Affairs. *Journal of Traumatic Stress, 10*(3), 357–360.

Johnson, D. R., Feldman, S. C., Lubin, H., & Southwick, S. M. (1995). The use of ritual and ceremony in the treatment of post-traumatic stress disorder. *Journal of Traumatic Stress, 8,* 283–289.

Johnson, D. R., Feldman, S. C., Southwick, S. M., & Charney, D. S. (1994). The concept of second generation program in the treatment of posttraumatic stress disorder among Vietnam veterans. *Journal of Traumatic Stress, 7*(2), 217–304.

Johnson, D., & Lubin, H. (1997). Treatment preferences of Vietnam veterans with PTSD. *Journal of Traumatic Stress, 10*(3), 391–406.

Johnson, D., Rosenheck, R., & Fontana, A. (1997). Assessing the structure, content, and perceived social climate of residential PTSD treatment programs. *Journal of Traumatic Stress, 10*(3), 361–367.

Johnson, D., Rosenheck, R., Fontana, A., Lubin, H., Charney, D., & Southwick, S. (1996). Outcome of intensive inpatient treatment for combat-related posttraumatic stress disorder. *American Journal of Psychiatry, 153*(6), 771–777.

Kessler, R., Sonnega, A., Broment, E., Hughes, M., & Nelson, C. B. (1995). Posttraumatic stress disorder in the National Comorbidity Survey. *Archives of General Psychiatry, 52,* 1048–1060.

Kluft, R. P. (1991). Hospital treatment of multiple personality disorder: An overview. *Psychiatric Clinics of North America, 14*(3), 695–719.

Kluft, R. P. (1996). Hospital treatment. In J. L. Spira (Ed.), *Treating dissociative identity disorder* (pp. 275–335). San Francisco: Jossey-Bass.

Long, R., Wine, P., Penk, W., Keane, T., Chew, D., Gerstein, C., O'Neill, J., & Nadelson, T. (1989). Chronicity: Adjustment differences of Vietnam combat veterans differing in rates of psychiatric hospitalization. *Journal of Clinical Psychology, 45*(5), 745–753.

Marmar, C. R., Foy, D., Kagan, B., & Pynoos, R. S. (1994). An integrated approach for treating posttraumatic stress. In R. Pynoos (Ed.), *Posttraumatic stress disorder: A clinical review* (pp. 99–132). Lutherville, MD: Sidran Press.

Mechanic, D., McAlpine, D. D., & Olfson, M. (1998). Changing patterns of psychiatric inpatient care in the United States, 1988–1994. *Archives of General Psychiatry, 55*, 785–791.

Mellman, T. A. (1998). *Outcome following inpatient PTSD treatment at the Miami VA.* Paper presented at the annual meeting of the International Society for Traumatic Stress Studies, Washington DC.

Moos, R. H. (1974). *Evaluating treatment environments: A social ecological approach.* New York: Wiley.

Munley, P. H., Bains, D. S., Frazee, J., & Schwartz, L. T. (1994). Inpatient PTSD treatment: A study of pretreatment measures, treatment dropout, and therapist ratings of response to treatment. *Journal of Traumatic Stress, 7*(2), 319–325.

Orsillo, S. M., Weathers, F. W., Litz, B. T., Steinberg, H. R., Huska, J. A., & Keane, T. (1996). Current and lifetime psychiatric disorders among veterans with war zone-related posttraumatic stress disorder. *Journal of Nervous and Mental Disease, 184*(5), 307–131.

Perconte, S. T. (1989). Stability of positive treatment outcome and symptoms relapse in posttraumatic stress disorder. *Journal of Traumatic Stress, 2,* 127–135.

Perconte, S. T., & Griger, M. L. (1991). Comparison of successful, unsuccessful, and relapsed Vietnam veterans treated for posttraumatic stress disorder. *Journal of Nervous and Mental Disease, 179*(9), 558–562.

Perconte, S. T., Griger, M. L., & Bellucci, G. (1989). Relapse and rehospitalization of veterans two years after treatment for PTSD. *Hospital and Community Psychiatry, 40,* 1072–1073.

Perry, J. C., Herman, J. L., van der Kolk, B. A., & Hoke, L. A. (1990). Psychotherapy and psychological trauma in borderline personality disorder. *Psychiatric Annals, 20,* 33–43.

Putnam, F. W., Loewenstein, R. J., Silberman, E. J., & Post, R. M. (1984). Multiple personality disorder in a hospital setting. *Journal of Clinical Psychiatry, 45,* 172–175.

Ragsdale, K. G., Cox, R. D., Finn, P., & Eisler, R. M. (1996). Effectiveness of short-term specialized inpatient treatment for war-related posttraumatic stress disorder: A role for adventure-based counseling and psychodrama. *Journal of Traumatic Stress, 9*(2), 269–283.

Rogers, S. (1998). An alternative interpretation of "intensive" PTSD treatment failures. *Journal of Traumatic Stress, 11*(4), 769–775.

Ronis, D. L., Bates, E. W., Garfein, A. J., Buit, B. K., Falcon, S. P., & Liberzon, I. (1996). Longitudinal patterns of care for patients with posttraumatic stress disorder. *Journal of Traumatic Stress, 9*(4), 763–781.

Rosenheck, R., Fontana, A., & Errera, P. (1997). Inpatient treatment of war-related posttraumatic stress disorder: A 20-year perspective. *Journal of Traumatic Stress, 10*(3), 407–414.

Ross, C. A. (1987). Inpatient treatment of multiple personality disorder. *Canadian Journal of Psychiatry, 32,* 779–781.

Ross, C. A. (1996). Short-term problem-oriented inpatient treatment. In J. L. Spira (Ed.), *Treating dissociative identity disorder* (pp. 337–365). San Francisco: Jossey-Bass.

Ross, S. (1997). *Differences in MMPI-2 profiles: Treatment outcome for adult survivors of childhood trauma.* Unpublished manuscript.

Sabo, A. N. (1997). Etiological significance of associations between childhood trauma and borderline personality disorder: Conceptual and clinical implications. *Journal of Personality Disorders 11*(1), 50–70.

Sakheim, D. K., Hess, E. P., & Chivas, A. (1988). General principles for short-term inpatient work with multiple personality disorder patients. *Psychotherapy, 25*, 117–124.

Scurfield, R. M., Kenderdine, S. K., & Pollard, R. J. (1990). Inpatient treatment for war-related post-traumatic stress disorder: Initial findings on a longer-term outcome study. *Journal of Traumatic Stress, 3*(2), 185–201.

Seidel, R. W., Gusman, F. D., & Abueg, F. R. (1994). Theoretical and practical foundations of an inpatient post-traumatic stress disorder and alcoholism treatment program. *Psychotherapy, 31*(1), 67–78.

Shalev, A. Y. (1997). Discussion: Treatment of war-related posttraumatic stress disorder: Learning from experience. *Journal of Traumatic Stress, 10*(3), 415–422.

Solt, V., Chen, C., & Roy, A. (1996). Seasonal patterns of posttraumatic stress disorder admissions. *Comprehensive Psychiatry, 37*(1), 40–42.

Southwick, S. M., Yehuda, R., & Giller, E. L. (1993). Personality disorders in treatment-seeking combat veterans with posttraumatic stress disorder. *American Journal of Psychiatry, 150*, 1020–1023.

Starkey, T. W., & Ashlock, L. E. (December, 1984). Inpatient treatment of PTSD: An interim report of the Miami model. *VA Practitioner*, pp. 37–40.

Starkey, T. W., & Ashlock, L. E. (1986). Inpatient treatment of PTSD: Final results of the late, great Miami model. *VA Practitioner, 3*, 41–44.

van der Kolk, B. A., McFarlane, A. C., & van der Hart, O. (1996). A general approach to treatment of posttraumatic stress disorder. In B. A. van der Kolk, A. C. McFarlane, & L. Weisaeth (Eds.), *Traumatic stress: The effects of overwhelming experience on mind, body, and society* (pp. 417–440). New York: Guilford Press.

Wang, S., Wilson, J. P., & Mason, J. W. (1996). Stages of decompensation in combat-related posttraumatic stress disorder: A new conceptual model. *Integrative Physiological and Behavioral Science, 31*, 237–253.

Wright, D. C., & Woo, W. L. (1997, November). *Outcomes of inpatient treatment of chronic PTSD: One year follow-up.* Poster session presented at the 8th annual meeting of the International Society for Traumatic Stress Studies, Montreal, Canada.

Wright, D. C., Woo, W. L., & Ross, S. (1996). Inpatient treatment of chronic post traumatic stress disorder: Outcome of treatment for adult survivors of childhood trauma. *International Journal of Psychology, 31*, 278.

11

Psychosocial Rehabilitation

Walter Penk and Raymond B. Flannery Jr.

This chapter centers on psychosocial rehabilitation services for persons meeting criteria for posttraumatic stress disorder (PTSD). Psychosocial rehabilitation services consist of techniques and interventions for persons with severe mental disorders who display needs in social functioning related to activities in daily living. Services defined as "psychosocial rehabilitation" include, but are not restricted to, interventions that improve daily living skills; social interactions with family and friends, harm-avoidance/health-promoting behaviors, including substance abuse treatment; housing needs; and educational and vocational needs. Detailed descriptions of psychosocial rehabilitation interventions and techniques may be found in program guides and standards published by such professional organizations as the International Association of Psychosocial Rehabilitation Services (IAPRS; 1994), Joint Commission on Accreditation of Healthcare Organizations (JCAHO; 1993), Commission on Accreditation of Rehabilitation Facilities (CARF; 1998), and Veterans Health Administration's (VHA) 1998 Program Guides.

Some clinicians believe psychosocial rehabilitation techniques are appropriate only for schizophrenia and not for other mental disorders, such as PTSD, which also can be quite severe. The approach taken here is problem-focused; that is, if the client identifies that a problem exists, and the clinician concludes that this problem is associated with PTSD, then both the client and the clinician, together, should select an appropriate psychosocial rehabilitation technique and adapt it to address specific problems of the person presenting with PTSD. The course of recovery varies in PTSD: symptoms can range from mild to severe. Selection of type of psychosocial intervention must be tailored and varied to fit the stage in recovery through active, collaborative interactions between the client and clinician (Wang, Wilson, & Mason, 1996). Client self-direction and involvement is essential in psychosocial rehabilitation.

This chapter centers on seven models of psychosocial rehabilitation services that are commonly used in treatment planning for persons with severe mental disorders, including PTSD: (1) patient health and psychoeducation; (2) self-care/independent living skills training; (3) supported housing; (4) family skills training; (5) social skills training; (6) vocational rehabilitation; and (7) case management.

THEORETICAL RATIONALES

As discussed at length in preceding chapters, central to many theories about treating trauma are the notions that techniques should reduce or remove current negative emotions and avoidance behaviors associated with reminders and memories of past traumas. Intrusive reliving of the past trauma in the present time leads to symptomatic behaviors designed to avoid emotionally reexperiencing emotional turmoil, chaos, and helplessness originally experienced when the trauma occurred (McFarlane, 1994; van der Kolk, McFarlane, & van der Hart, 1996).

Theories about treating trauma have been summarized in several key publications (see, e.g., Foa, Rothbaum, Riggs, & Murdock, 1991; Herman, 1992), as well as elsewhere in this volume. Most sources concur that in order to establish positive ways of coping with intrusive reliving of the original trauma, treatment may unfold through a series of stages, for example:

1. Stabilization, including (a) education and (b) identification of feelings through verbalizing somatic states.
2. Deconditioning of traumatic memories and responses.
3. Restructuring of traumatic personal schemes.
4. Reestablishment of secure social connections and interpersonal efficacy.
5. Accumulation of restitutive emotional experiences. (van der Kolk, McFarlane, & van der Hart, 1996, p. 426)

It should be noted that these authors propose a general approach to stage theories of treatment. Such stages are not mutually exclusive and improvement is not necessarily stage-dependent.)

Considering the psychosocial rehabilitation techniques described here, within the context of this stage-by-stage approach to treatment, one can readily conclude that psychosocial rehabilitation services may be more appropriate for later stages in treatment—those stages in which the client is concerned with reestablishing effective social interactions and developing positive emotional experiences to offset trauma and its effects. However, recent studies by Marks, Lovell, Noshirvani, Livanou, and Thrasher (1998) and Tarrier and colleagues (1999) have questioned whether persons in recovery need rigidly to pass through any and/or all of these stages in recovery, particularly the stage of "deconditioning of traumatic memories and responses." By raising questions about the necessity of exposure therapy, findings from both Marks and colleagues (1998) and Tarrier and colleagues (1999) permit us to examine in a new way our dogmas about the necessity of exposure therapy as the only way to decondition habituation to traumatic memories. Such new findings allow us to consider the possibilities of beneficial effects from psychosocial rehabilitation techniques, for example, that may be just as effective without "deconditioning traumatic memories and responses" by the cognitive restructuring that is implicit when, for example, patients return to work after having considered themselves helpless in mastering their environment.

Finally, just as the dream belongs to the dreamer, so does the stage in recovery belong to the client; that is, the process of psychosocial rehabilitation techniques must be centered in the client's identification of which problems to address and in his or her capacities to generate goals to resolve those problems identified during the course of recovery and adjustment.

Treatments described in the preceding chapters are designed to focus upon a person learning specific behavioral techniques to overcome fears of emotions related to trauma, as well as to develop new schemas for integrating memories of trauma into his or her continuing personal experiences and maturation (van der Kolk, McFarlane, & van der Hart, 1996).

However, as persons with PTSD begin to generalize their new ways of coping with trauma-related emotions and memories to new situations, as occurs, for example, when persons with PTSD seek emotional relationships with others as a way of protecting themselves, so psychosocial rehabilitation techniques can serve as one form of intervention to facilitate social interactions and personal integration of troubling emotions and memories of traumatic experiences. Psychosocial rehabilitation techniques that a client learns with the therapist provide the context in which new ways of coping with trauma are tested for their practicality, suitability, and generalizability to the social world—a social world that, theoretically, is needed to buffer and to protect against the memories of trauma. Psychosocial rehabilitation techniques also provide the arena of interaction where new, pleasurable experiences can be learned—those experiences that are needed to offset the profound sense of helplessness and the excruciating pain of psychological and physical injuries from the original trauma (van der Kolk, McFarlane, & van der Hart, 1996).

Psychosocial rehabilitation techniques, then, contain procedures for "reestablishing secure social connections." Hence, psychosocial rehabilitation techniques can become a valuable resource to clients and to therapists, perhaps more so when these techniques are designed to cope with the symptoms of PTSD. However, most psychosocial rehabilitation techniques are general forms of intervention, targeting not the specific symptoms of PTSD but the general by-products of the disorder. In implementing proven psychosocial rehabilitation techniques, clients and clinicians also are encouraged to collaborate in the use of accurate and appropriate skills learned through the rehabilitation process to address the person's memories of past trauma in current situations.

DESCRIPTION OF TECHNIQUES

Before describing the psychosocial rehabilitation techniques that clients and clinicians may find clinically useful in recovering from PTSD, we must state that none of these interventions meet Level A category requirements in the Agency for Health Care Policy and Research (AHCPR) Classification of Level of Evidence; none have been demonstrated as effective using randomized, controlled, clinical trials in the treatment of PTSD. Furthermore, none have been tested at Level B, where effectiveness is based upon a well-designed clinical study without randomization or placebo comparison for persons with PTSD.

However, all psychosocial rehabilitation services described here are supported by AHCPR Level C criteria (i.e., clients' satisfaction with services; clinician's conclusions based upon demonstration projects or services they provide; panel consensus; clinical studies, naturalistic in nature, for program evaluation surveys). Such Level C classifications from surveys and naturalistic clinical studies, combined with clinical observations, are sufficiently compelling to warrant use of psychosocial rehabilitation techniques in treatment planning for PTSD (see, in particular, studies conducted in 1998 at the Northeast Program Evaluation Center by Rosenheck and colleagues).

Psychosocial rehabilitation techniques have been demonstrated as effective when applied to persons with other forms of mental disorders; in some cases, what is demonstrated as beneficial for one kind of mental disorder may generalize with comparable effectiveness to other forms of disorders. Whereas direct testing of psychosocial rehabilitation techniques with PTSD disorders is lacking, positive results in their application to other disorders provide additional support for using these techniques in treatment planning for PTSD.

Furthermore, most clinical studies reviewed and cited here have been conducted with clients that simultaneously meet criteria for several disorders: None have been published for PTSD-only groups. Although psychosocial rehabilitation techniques do not meet either AHCPR Level A or Level B criteria, location of an increasing number of Level C-type reports strongly supports conclusions that psychosocial rehabilitation should be considered in treatment planning—particularly when clients have identified such problems and have selected ways to achieve goals to overcome these problems.

We now describe each of the seven types of psychosocial rehabilitation with promising Level C-type evidence (see Table 11.1) by first asking a question about a possible psychosocial deficit and then briefly describing a psychosocial remedy for which there is evidence of effectiveness.

As noted earlier, the philosophical foundation of rehabilitation (i.e., client self-direction) centers in the process of clients being involved in identifying problems, setting appropriate goals, and selecting relevant psychosocial rehabilitation services. These services are essential in treatment planning for each person meeting PTSD criteria, providing that the client is an active partner with the clinician in selecting services and in evaluating progress in achieving the client's goals. One can readily determine whether any one, or several in combination, of the seven domains of psychosocial rehabilitation are appropriate in PTSD treatment planning by applying the following checklist (based on Veterans Health Administration checklist for determining applicability of psychosocial rehabilitation interventions; Penk & Losonzcy, 1997).

The Psychosocial Rehabilitation Checklist is designed to assess whether the person in recovery from PTSD wants or needs any, some, or all services listed.

TABLE 11.1. Checklist to Determine Whether Psychosocial Rehabilitation Services Are Indicated in Treatment of PTSD

1. *Patient education services.* If client and clinician together conclude that the client is not fully informed about aspects of health needs and does not avoid high-risk behaviors (e.g., PTSD, substance abuse), then activate health education services.

2. *Self-care/independent living skills training.* If client and clinician together conclude that client with PTSD does not have sufficient self-care and independent living skills, refer to self-care/independent living skills training services.

3. *Supported housing services.* If client and clinician together conclude that the client with PTSD does not have safe, decent, affordable, stable housing that is consistent with treatment goals, then use and/or refer to supported housing services.

4. *Supported family skills services.* If client and clinician together conclude that the client's family is not actively supportive and/or knowleddeable about treatment for PTSD, then implement family skills training.

5. *Social skills training.* If client and clinician together conclude that the client with PTSD is not socially active, then implement social skills training.

6. *Supported employment.* If client and clinician together conclude that client with PTSD does not have a job that provides adequate income and/or fully uses his or her training and skills, then implement supportive employment interventions.

7. *Case management.* If client and clinician together conclude that the client with PTSD is unable to locate and coordinate access to services such as those listed above, then use case management services.

Clinicians should note that psychosocial rehabilitation services are initiated increasingly more frequently in outpatient settings, so it is essential that the client and clinician together determine that the client is medically and psychiatrically stabilized before starting a course of psychosocial rehabilitation. Furthermore, the Psychosocial Rehabilitation Checklist should be used in conjunction with other assessments of the person's willingness (i.e., "readiness") and capacities (e.g., status of cognition, memory, judgment, etc.) as they relate to learning such new skills. Finally, some psychosocial rehabilitation depends upon skills acquisition, underscoring the importance of practice as central in this process. Clients and clinicians together may need to redesign and adapt these techniques, emphasizing access to nonverbal emotional experiences, so that the intervention specifically focuses on the client's learning new skills to cope with symptoms of PTSD.

So what does the literature reveal about these psychosocial rehabilitation services? Results presented here refer to key papers that provide more detailed descriptions, along with a brief discussion of the strengths and weaknesses of such techniques. These techniques may be used in an adjunctive manner with other forms of treatment described elsewhere in this volume, or they may be used differentially as the person with PTSD progresses through stages in recovery, based upon considerations of "readiness" and level of intensity for the particular form of psychosocial rehabilitation selected for application. An important tradition in psychosocial rehabilitation techniques is the constant interplay of matching rehabilitation with stage in recovery (Wang, Wilson, & Mason, 1996).

METHODS USED IN REVIEWING LITERATURE

Sources for descriptions about psychosocial rehabilitation services can be found in the above-listed standards (see, e.g., IAPSRS, 1994; JCAHO, 1993; CARF, 1998; VHA Program Guide). Search for outcome studies was facilitated by Fred Lerner, DLS, through the PILOTS program at the National PTSD Center (VA Medical Center, White River Junction, Vermont). PILOTS classifies PTSD research by types of treatment/rehabilitation, case mix, and outcomes.

Furthermore, this chapter is indebted to all VA clinicians and the staff of Birch and Davis in Silver Spring, Maryland, who convened to assess psychosocial rehabilitation techniques and to write algorithms for managing patients. The product of this endeavor—the Psychosocial Rehabilitation module, as chaired by Walter Penk, PhD, and Miklos Losonczy, MD—served as the basis for both the literature reviewed here and the descriptions of techniques and criteria for determining their use (see *The VHA Clinical Guidelines for Management of Persons with Major Depressive Disorder, Post-Traumatic Stress Disor-*

der, and Substance Abuse (Horvath, 1997a) and *The VHA Clinical Guidelines for Management of Persons with Psychoses* (Horvath, 1997b; Thomas Horvath, MD, Chief Consultant, Mental Health Strategic Planning Group, VHA Headquarters, Washington, DC).

SUMMARY OF THE LITERATURE

Psychosocial rehabilitation services, even when used in conjunction with other therapies listed in this volume, may offer the advantage of approaching memories of trauma less directly and with greater structure, being less verbal but still more emotionally centered. The domains discussed begin with techniques that focus on client safety and harm-reduction interventions, and continue progressively through coping skills training for community survival, ending with techniques (i.e., case management) that ensure participation in, and coordination of, psychosocial rehabilitation services along a continuum of care.

Physical Health and Education Psychosocial Rehabilitation Services

When the client and clinician conclude that the client is sufficiently stable and has identified and is both willing and able to learn about PTSD and its treatment, the clinician refers the client to psychosocial rehabilitation services, which provides education for the following: diagnosis and nature of PTSD; treatment expectations and importance of compliance to treatment and rehabilitation regimens; information about medication for PTSD (purposes, benefits, risks, dosage information, medication refills, and appointments); information about other forms of psychosocial and behavioral therapies; socialization programs (social skills training); dual-diagnosis training; and vocational rehabilitation programs (such as transitional or supported employment).

Physical health education techniques may be added to the treatment plan when the client with PTSD and the clinician conclude that the client continues to engage in high-risk behaviors (such as substance abuse) and when he or she is able to participate in educational processes that provide training in harm-avoidance and wellness-promoting behaviors (see, e.g., Allen, Kelly, & Glodich, 1997). Although there is a scarcity of health and education training programs specifically addressing the needs of persons with PTSD, equivalent psychosocial rehabilitation techniques have been developed and tested for patients with chronic conditions such as schizophrenia. Clinical studies among patients with schizophrenia, many of whom have also been traumatized, may provide guidelines for PTSD (see Atkinson, Coia, Gilmour, & Harper, 1996; Eckman et al., 1992; Goldman & Quinn, 1988;

Halford, Harrison, Kalyansundaram, Olive, & Simpson, 1995; Kelly & Scott, 1990; MacPherson, Jerrom, & Hughes, 1996; Runder et al., 1994).

Examples of other forms of patient health and education forms of psychosocial rehabilitation include education about drug use, health, and relapse (Marlatt & Gordon, 1985; Nowinski, Baker, & Carroll, 1994); sexually transmitted diseases (Cates & Graham, 1993; Goisman, Kent, Montgomery, & Cheevers, 1991; Kalichman, Sikkema, Kelly, & Bulto, 1995; Marlow, West, Corrigan, & Pena, 1994); smoking cessation (American Psychiatric Association, 1996); and diet and exercise (Byrne, Brown, Voorberg, & Schofield, 1994; McDougall, 1992).

Several unvalidated self-help manuals for PTSD are available as examples of patient education and to illustrate psychoeducational techniques: Flannery's *Post-Traumatic Stress Disorder: The Victim's Guide to Healing and Recovery* (1992) and, more recently, Flannery's (1998) peer-help program for healthcare staff assaulted by their patients; and Matsakis's *"I Can't Get Over It": A Handbook for Trauma* (1996). Clients and clinicians report that such self-help educational techniques are effective. In addition to a general psychoeducational approach, there are specialty approaches to PTSD. Notable are Bass and Davis's *The Courage to Heal: A Guide for Women Survivors of Child Abuse* (1988), Mitchell and Bray's *Emergency Services Stress: Guidelines for Preserving the Health and Careers of Emergency Services Personnel* (1990), and Harris's *Trauma Recovery and Empowerment: A Clinician's Guide for Working with Women in Groups* (1998).

A prototypical study showing how such self-help books can be validated may be found in recent research comparing aerobic exercise, clomipramine, and placebo in the treatment of panic disorder (Broocks et al., 1998). Subjects were randomized to two conditions—(1) aerobic exercise; (2) either clomipramine or placebo. Whereas the clomipramine condition was associated with greater improvement in a variety of attitudinal and behavioral outcome measures, subjects randomly assigned to the aerobic exercise condition obtained gains in outcomes significantly larger than those for placebo and nearly matched gains found for the clomipramine condition. The investigators concluded, "To our knowledge, this is the first placebo-controlled, randomized study to examine the effects of aerobic exercise in panic disorder with or without agoraphobia as defined by the DSM-III-R or ICD-10 criteria" (Broocks et al., 1998, p. 604). This pioneering study highlights the type of research on patient education and psychoeducational rehabilitation techniques that must be conducted for persons meeting PTSD criteria and, concurrently, demonstrates empirically that the addition of a psychosocial rehabilitation technique such as exercise produces gains in home and community adjustment.

Self-Care and Independent Living Skills Techniques

When the client and clinician conclude that the client with PTSD is deficient in self-care or does not have skills to maintain current living arrangements in the home and community, or if the client is achieving well below anticipated levels of independence in social and personal functioning, then training in independent living skills should be considered. Clients have identified such problems and address goals such as personal care and hygiene, money management, shopping, cooking, using transportation, medication compliance, making and following a schedule, and deficiencies in leisure skills and recreation. Manualized treatments for independent skills training are well developed for persons with schizophrenic disorders and their effectiveness have been empirically validated (e.g., Ayllon & Azrin, 1968; Falloon, 1999; Liberman et al., 1993).

Studies are now needed to test hypotheses that such psychosocial rehabilitation techniques do indeed generalize to and ameliorate problems of avoidance and "learned helplessness" symptoms associated with PTSD. Given the positive impact of independent skills training techniques for mental disorders in general (Halford, Harrison, Kalyansundaram, Olive, & Simpson, 1995), it is highly recommended that PTSD-centered modules be developed and tested empirically for effectiveness. Existing independent skills modules for other mental disorders could be easily adapted to address key symptoms of PTSD, in keeping with the theoretical injunctions that "patients need to expose themselves actively to experiences that provide them with feelings of mastery and pleasure" (van der Kolk, McFarlane, & van der Hart, 1996, p. 433).

Supported Housing Techniques

During the course of treatment, the client and clinician may determine that the client with PTSD has a problem with housing that significantly impacts rehabilitation. Housing problems come in different forms: The client may be homeless or, if not homeless, may have significant problems obtaining a safe, quality, affordable, stable home; or he or she may be completely dissatisfied with current housing conditions. Any such problems with housing might impact other treatment efforts in which the client and clinician are collaborating and, as a consequence, require coordination (see, e.g., Schutt, 1996; Schutt & Garrett, 1992).

Furthermore, difficulties in maintaining a home may be associated with symptoms of PTSD (e.g., homelessness may be implicated as at least an indirect result of avoidance symptoms producing interferences in socialization). Based on estimates that nearly one-third of the nation's homeless are combat veterans, some researchers have speculated that pathways to homelessness are associated with PTSD. Most supported housing interventions involve referring the client to other specialists for purposes of solving homelessness. Such referrals tend to fragment rehabilitation and decrease opportunities to integrate homelessness services with other forms of rehabilitation. Supported housing outcomes may be enhanced if clients and clinicians integrate PTSD treatments into housing services. Furthermore, treating the frequently co-occuring problem of substance use should also be integrated into supported housing interventions when homelessness is associated with PTSD (see, e.g., Goldfinger et al., 1999).

Clinicians treating some clients with PTSD (particularly those who are more impaired or have inadequate resources) will sometimes find themselves asked to collaborate with the client in addressing homelessness or interferences in obtaining housing. Clinicians may be asked whether homelessness is related to PTSD, and, if so, to define the relationship. Furthermore, how should rehabilitation be planned for persons with PTSD who are in need of housing services? Upon such occasions, clinicians must both understand models of supported housing and integrate their treatment of PTSD with such supported housing services.

It is highly likely that controlled studies of supported housing models already include subjects who also meet criteria for PTSD—and many other disorders as well, such as co-occurring substance use. This growing literature, which includes positive outcomes among persons with other forms of mental disorders, empirically demonstrates that certain forms of supported housing, particularly those that provide case management and linkages to specialized clinical services, are more effective than the standard solutions for homelessness—either "single-room occupancy" (e.g., providing a room but not other forms of rehabilitation or case management) or "warehousing" in shelters without other forms of support (see, e.g., Goldfinger et al., 1997).

Forms of housing considered more effective are those in which clinical services are integrated or efforts are made by treating staff to foster community living (see, e.g., Goldfinger et al., 1997; Schutt & Garrett, 1992). Naturalistic studies carried out at the VA's Northeast Program Evaluation Center (NEPEC) of the VA Medical Center, West Haven, Connecticut, continue to provide empirical support for the essential role of clinical services integrated into housing interventions in the treatment of persons with PTSD and other disorders (see, e.g., Rosenheck & Seibyl, 1998).

Psychosocial Rehabilitation Techniques for Family Support

Clinicians treating persons with PTSD will sometimes find that a client reports difficulties in family relationships as a problem. Psychoeducational techniques to improve family support are available if the person with PTSD identifies this problem, agrees to family involvement, and grants the clinician permission to contact family members (i.e., family of origin and/or family of procreation) to obtain their voluntary agreement to participate. When it has been agreed by patient, family, and clinician that family involvement is important in rehabilitation and treatment of PTSD, then a variety of interventions may be selected for application. These techniques range from psychoeducational modules for educating the patient's family about PTSD to techniques for involving families more directly in treatment (see Mueser & Glynn, 1999).

Forms of family intervention are discussed in greater detail elsewhere in this volume, but one of the many objectives in involving the patient's family in treatment is to establish (or reestablish) social supports for a person who has become isolated or has reduced social interactions. Moreover, such techniques may also inform the family about the expected course of rehabilitation and treatment.

Complications arise if one or more family members are perpetrators and the patient has been traumatized by relatives. Such complications require more specialized forms of therapeutic interventions, such as family therapy, which requires the skills of trained therapists and not just family psychoeducation and family support programs. Cynthia Carson Bisbee's *Educating Patients and Families about Mental Illness: A Practical Guide* (1991) is but one of several guides for the clinician in how to design a family education program. Although the model presented by Bisbee is for mental illness in general, it can be readily adapted for families of patients with PTSD.

Common to most such manualized family education approaches are sections about the diagnosis and nature of mental illness; treatment expectations; purposes and management of medication for PTSD; brief descriptions of psychosocial and behavioral therapies for PTSD; practical steps for family involvement as well as recommendations for other forms of socialization and social support programs, with special emphasis upon "networking" to alleviate social isolation and social avoidance in PTSD; establishment of healthy lifestyles; and participation in community-based self-help and advocacy groups (cf. Marsh, 1998).

Naturalistic studies and clinical observations attest to the effectiveness of adding family education to treatment planning. Hypotheses about general versus trauma-specific psychoeducational techniques need to be evaluated. Considering that short-term therapies for PTSD are increasing, the abiding and consistent role of families as participants in the therapeutic alliance is emerging as a rich resource for improving PTSD treatment.

Social Skills Training

If both client and clinician determine that symptoms associated with PTSD causes the client to remain isolated from others and to avoid potentially satisfying social interactions, then some form of social skills training should be implemented. Social skills training has a rich history of application in the treatment of mental disorders (see, e.g., Paul & Lentz, 1977). Interventions are based upon theories of social learning, from which a diversity of manualized interventions have been developed, particularly for persons with serious mental disorders such as schizophrenia.

Effectiveness of social skills training has been well demonstrated over many years in many randomized, controlled studies, but not specifically for PTSD (for an updated evaluation of contemporary approaches to social skills training as well as types of interventions, see Dilk & Bond, 1996). Types of interventions include supportive group discussion to improve socialization; token economies; medication and symptom management, as well as management of leisure time and recreation groups; community survival groups; problem-solving groups; and the community service module (Johnson, Rosenheck, & Fontana, 1997). Given the fact that social skills training has been empirically demonstrated as effective in reducing social isolation of persons with such severe mental disorders as schizophrenia, similar techniques are likely to be promising, particularly if adapted for PTSD to address antecedent conditions involved in trauma and its consequences (Rothbaum & Foa, 1996).

One limitation must be noted. Social skills training techniques require considerable control over consequences and contingencies in the environment, as well as much practice. In the past, before managed care, such techniques were demonstrated as effective for groups undergoing comparatively longer inpatient hospitalization. The question is whether inpatient-based social skills training techniques can be adapted for outpatient, community-based services delivery. One promising avenue is through Telehealth and Telemedicine applications, writing software programs for social skills training based in cognitive-behavioral therapy techniques. Another is the community service module developed by Johnson, Rosenheck, and Fontana (1997), which obtained favorable results. A year after clients were discharged from inpatient services, this "rehabilitative" cluster of interventions was more highly rated than the "psychotherapeutic" services. Social skills training techniques, then, are recommended particularly for persons with severe symptoms of social avoidance associated with PTSD. In keeping with principles of social learning, providing such social skills training techniques can be individually tailored for "avoidance" symptoms.

Vocational Rehabilitation Techniques

Vocational rehabilitation techniques have been demonstrated under controlled experimental conditions as especially effective in treating mental disorders (see, e.g., Bell & Lysaker, 1996; Bell, Lysaker, & Milstein, 1996; Bell, Milstein, & Lysaker, 1993; Bond, Drake, Mueser, & Becker, 1997). Since unemployment, or equally serious "underemployment," frequently accompanies PTSD, problems of work adjustment must be addressed among persons struggling with the aftermaths of trauma. Like many other psychosocial rehabilitation techniques, there are many levels of complexity among voational rehabilitation techniques. Vocational rehabilitation techniques may be conceptualized as graded along a continuum of rehabilitation, proceeding from incentive workshops in highly structured settings (see, e.g., Luo & Yu, 1994;

Sauter & Nevid, 1991) to transitional work (see, e.g., Bell & Lysaker, 1996), designed for the person in rehabilitation to take on increased work responsibilities in a hospital, to the more complex supported employment, in which patients are placed in competitive jobs at competitive wages and provided with specialized support to remain on the job (see, e.g., Bond, 1997; Drake, McHugo, Becker, & Anthony, 1996; Li & Wang, 1994).

This family of vocational rehabilitation interventions can be readily adapted to address not only the social and vocational impairment associated with PTSD but also the primary symptoms of PTSD. As summarized by many therapists treating PTSD, general PTSD indicators include (1) a profound loss of mastery over one's environment; (2) avoidance of social interaction; and (3) loss of one's meaning and purpose in life due to the trauma and its aftermath (see, e.g., Flannery, 1992; van der Kolk, McFarlane, & van der Hart, 1996). Vocational rehabilitation requires that the person with PTSD engage in a productive activity, usually paid, thereby offering him or her opportunities to regain mastery of at least the work environment. Such work programs, which are administered by vocational rehabilitation specialists who work together with patients in groups on a common goal and focus on achieving group objectives, simultaneously reduce social avoidance while emphasizing group sharing and group activities. Finally, vocational rehabilitation confronts issues about meaning and purpose in living by providing experiences that define one as a worker, offer mastery of the environment (or, at least, a significant portion of it) through work, and operationalize meaning in life within a context in which purpose for living may be defined by the products one produces through work. Little wonder that controlled, clinical studies have demonstrated the effectiveness of vocational rehabilitation for the treatment of persons with mental disorders (see, e.g., Anthony, Rogers, Cohen, & Davies, 1995; Drake, 1996; Lehman, 1995; Lysaker, Bell, Milstein, & Bryson, 1993).

Vocational rehabilitation is highly recommended as the psychosocial rehabilitation of choice in the treatment of PTSD for both persons who are unemployed and those who are "underemployed" (Brown & Schulberg, 1995), but it is contraindicated for those not wishing to engage in paid employment because they are retired or disabled (see, e.g., Rosenheck, Frisman, & Sindelar, 1995).

Vocational rehabilitation may be accessed readily in the community by linking persons with PTSD to services provided by state and federal vocational rehabilitation programs. Currently, welfare-to-work programs are increasing. "One-stop shopping" types of supported employment programs, offering a range of needed services, are regarded as more effective than programs providing only brokering and linking services. Results from VHA residential treatment programs (e.g., domiciliary, compensated work therapy, and therapeutic residences) provide empirical justification for integrating services into a "one-stop shopping" model of healthcare delivery—at least for veterans, many with PTSD, who are homeless and unemployed (Siebyl, Rosenheck, Medak, & Corwel, 2000).

Case Management

Case management is recommended when there is evidence that the person with PTSD will not, or cannot locate and schedule the aforementioned services (i.e., supported employment, supported housing, supported education, social skills training, family education services, independent living skills, etc.). Case management is also indicated when the person with PTSD undergoes frequent rehospitalizations because he or she does not follow treatment plans or access recommended community-based services, or is not able to negotiate the complexities of receiving services from many different agencies in a variety of locales.

Case management varies from (1) simple case management limited to linking the client to needed services to (2) intensive case management, in which a well-trained clinician teaches the client needed psychosocial rehabilitation skills in the client's home and community. Among populations with histories of trauma, the assertive community treatment models have been empirically validated under controlled (but not with random assignment) conditions (see, e.g., Mueser, Bond, Drake, & Resnick, 1998).

Most of the research that empirically validates case management has been conducted among persons with severe mental disorders (Mueser, Bond, Drake, & Resnick, 1998), presumably including persons with co-occurring PTSD and other disorders. Evidence to date suggests that outcomes are more favorable for intensive case management than for simple case management that consisting merely of linking clients to several agencies. Case management interventions have been demonstrated to reduce inpatient hospitalizations and severe symptoms, as well as to stabilize housing for formerly homeless persons, but as yet, there is little evidence to suggest that case management improves vocational adjustment or social functioning (cf. Mueser et al., 1998). While it remains unknown why intensive case management services are associated with fewer inpatient hospital stays and symptom reduction, the preponderance of speculation points toward several factors: (1) a more knowledgeable approach to problem solving specifically for the client's needs (as distinguished from mere amorphous linkage to other agencies that may not be so problem-focused as the person providing intensive case management); (2) more integrated, rather than fragmented, services (in keeping with general trends across many studies of psychosocial rehabilitation techniques in which comprehensive approaches yield better outcomes than separated service); (3) clients' periodic need for special interventions due to the comorbidities of substance abuse interfering with success in treatment and rehabilitation (Ashery, 1992); (4) the effects of one, rather than many, coaches developing a relationship with the traumatized person; and, finally but most importantly, (5) case management many times preserves the importance of client choice and proceeds on the basis of consumer self-direction and involvement.

The simpler forms of case management have been devised more as tools of management for purposes of reducing costs by restricting inpatient stays and minimizing outpatient visits; most simple case management is prescriptive (i.e., telling clients what to do). In contrast, intensive case management, usually more interactive, centers on the needs of the client and involves him or her actively in the process of rehabilitation (Mueser, Bond, Drake, & Resnick, 1998). Research studies favor the superiority of intensive case management for the outcomes cited earlier, but only if the target of services is client-based rather than agency-centered. Discerning this trend in clinical studies suggests that intensive case management can be designed to treat PTSD, focusing psychosocial rehabilitation techniques to address problems unique to the disorder.

SUMMARY

Many psychosocial rehabilitation techniques have been developed for the treatment of mental disorders other than PTSD, and these now comprise a rich repository from which clients and clinicians collaboratively may select interventions to address similar problems in devising treatment plans for persons with PTSD. Psychosocial rehabilitation techniques range in bandwidth from those interventions that address a very narrow range of problems (e.g., relapse prevention, medication compliance) to those that are much wider in scope (e.g., generalized symptom reduction).

Surveys, naturalistic studies, and clinical observations indicate that psychosocial rehabilitation techniques are promising for PTSD. However, studies need to be conducted for patients with PTSD to see if the evidence is as favorable as it has been for randomized, controlled studies among patients/subjects meeting non-PTSD criteria for other mental disorders.

Despite the paucity of randomized, controlled studies, psychosocial rehabilitation techniques are enthusiastically endorsed if clinicians incorporate other, empirically validated methods of treating PTSD within the context of psychosocial rehabilitation, and when clinicians ensure client self-direction and client involvement at all stages in the rehabilitation process. Psychosocial rehabilitation techniques, themselves, can readily be criticized as lacking diagnostic specificity in the services rendered to patients. Redesigning psychosocial rehabilitation interventions for persons with PTSD is likely to improve the effectiveness of the intervention. Now, trauma-focused psychosocial rehabilitation techniques must be developed and tested under randomized, controlled, comparison conditions to determine whether trauma-focused adaptations are as effective as these techniques in their original forms.

Current practices for unemployed seriously mentally disordered persons entail adding vocational rehabilitation and employment interventions. Treatment might be improved if the process of seeking and choosing employment were considered in terms how the problems of PTSD were manifested during the course of these job-seeking behaviors. To do this, therapist and client together would develop ways of coping with PTSD as symptoms were experienced while seeking employment and/or while working. Focusing vocational rehabilitation on PTSD requires both client and clinician to know the traumatic cues, or triggers, in the workplace, so that problems resulting from exposure to reminders of trauma can be anticipated and dealt with during the course of employment training and placement.

Examples include designing vocational rehabilitation for female rape victims that involve resocialization programs to address any difficulties in coping with heightened sensitivities in female–male interactions, or designing work readiness programs in schools where combat veterans with PTSD learn skills to teach inner-city children struggling with daily violence.

By integrating and incorporating treatment of PTSD into the process of psychosocial rehabilitation, clinicians are likely to improve both traditional interventions for PTSD and selected psychosocial rehabilitation techniques that are appropriate in each particular case. Such methods, adapted for PTSD, quite naturally promote objectives of improving emotional attachments, increasing social interactions, and providing opportunities to learn new ways of mastering one's environment.

RECOMMENDATIONS

The psychosocial rehabilitation techniques reviewed here are highly recommended once it is determined that clients with PTSD demonstrate a deficit in a particular domain and have identified and set goals to overcome such problems. Structured interviews for classifying PTSD, such as the Clinician-Administered PTSD Scale (CAPS-1), the Structured Clinical Interview for DSM-IV (SCID), or the Diagnostic Interview Schedule (DIS), will yield some information as to whether PTSD has produced other deficits in psychosocial functioning. But additional interviews or administration of other assessment approaches may be necessary that focus on home and community adjustment, such as the Addiction Severity Indices and Quality of Life Scales (Keane, Newman, & Orsillo, 1997). Use of the questions in Table 11.1 usually suffices in determining whether to recommend services. These problems are so basic that the lack of solutions means the void must be filled. Only rarely are any of these problems not identified by both the client and clinician for treatment planning. There are rare exceptions in which clients would not identify such problems: some persons may not wish, need, nor be able to return to work for any of a variety reasons; others may not have the cognitive or emotional capacities to participate in patient education services; others may not have families for which the supported family services would be recommended; still others may feel so helpless that they are completely treatment noncompliant. (However, with regard to treatment/rehabilitation noncompliance, we have found that, at least for unemployed persons with PTSD, vocational rehabilitation services are usually more attractive than referrals to other therapeutic techniques.)

Psychosocial rehabilitation techniques are so basic and fundamental that questions arise as to whether persons with PTSD will actively participate in other forms of treatment interventions if they remain homeless, unemployed, and still engage in high-risk behaviors. When any of these basic problems are identified by the client and the clinician, psychosocial rehabilitation services should be considered.

But in order for these psychosocial rehabilitation techniques to be truly effective, experimental research needs to be designed and studied. Trauma-focused psychosocial rehabilitation techniques must be developed and evaluated for their effectiveness in the treatment of PTSD. The general notions of psychosocial rehabilitation have been designed and tested, much in the same manner as a broad-spectrum antibiotic; but now we must develop PTSD-specific techniques, that is, design an effective psychosocial-deficit-specific intervention. Such new experimental studies of psychosocial rehabilitation techniques for PTSD should compare for relative effectiveness the unrevised, existing, non-PTSD-focused rehabilitation manuals with trauma-focused psychosocial rehabilitation techniques. Trauma-focused techniques have not been empirically validated as more effective than psychosocial rehabilitation techniques in their original forms. So, the next "generation" of research testing the effectiveness of psychosocial rehabilitation for PTSD begins with writing new, and adapting old, trauma-focused manuals and techniques and then designing tests of empirical validation and comparing the "old" with the "new" for different stages in the course of recovery that is unique for PTSD. As empirically validated, manual-guided rehabilitation modules become available from such experimental endeavors, then clinical pathways for the treatment of PTSD can be improved (see, e.g., Wang, Wilson, & Mason, 1996).

AREAS REQUIRING FURTHER EXPLORATION

Areas in psychosocial rehabilitation and PTSD that require further exploration include (but are not restricted to) the following considerations:

1. A "needs assessment" for psychosocial rehabilitation among persons with PTSD should be conducted on a national, representative sample. A prototype justifying this area of exploration can be found in the National Viet-

nam Veterans Readjustment Study (NVVRS), in which many deficits such as housing and employment needs were surveyed in considerable detail. Using the NVVRS's extensive survey for the "Prevalence of Other Postwar Readjustment Problems," a similar needs assessment should be conducted in terms of salient types of PTSD disorders (e.g., victims of violence, natural disasters, etc.) as well as types of co-occurring disorders (e.g., PTSD-only; PTSD and substance abuse, PTSD and schizophrenia). Needs for psychosocial rehabilitation services are expected to vary as a function of differences in socioeconomic status, age, and education, as was found in the NVVRS.

2. As noted throughout the chapter, psychosocial rehabilitation manuals (such as those produced for the National Institute on Alcohol Abuse and Alcoholism's Project MATCH) need to be written and tested through AHCPR Level A experimental designs with randomization and comparison groups. For those forms of psychosocial services that may not be considered "treatment," such as housing placement, then procedural guidelines should be written, incorporating recommendations about working with persons with PTSD.

3. Training in the use of psychosocial rehabilitation techniques must be developed and offered to clinicians treating persons with PTSD. Studies on effectiveness of treating other mental disorders among persons with extensive psychosocial deficits are demonstrating that "one-stop shopping" such as rehabilitation/treatment offerings is associated with more favorable outcomes than fragmenting care into many different locales and agencies. Therapists must learn how to provide services in the communities of patients with PTSD and profound psychosocial deficits. Therapists also need to know how to revise psychosocial rehabilitation services so that these services become a vehicle for learning how to cope with PTSD symptoms. Training for therapists in psychosocial rehabilitation is needed, along with standards to evaluate proficiencies and competencies. Finally, therapists may not be skilled in the philosophical foundations of rehabilitation, with its emphasis upon client choice, consumer self-direction, and client involvement in collaborative rehabilitation planning and implementation.

4. Patient placement criteria, using the concepts of guided level of care determinations in InterQual and American Society of Addiction Medicine (ASAM) criteria, need to be developed for treatment planning purposes. Such criteria should include guidelines for deciding admission, continuation, discharge, and relapse to PTSD psychosocial rehabilitation services, based on objective, standardized indicators of needed level of care.

5. PTSD psychosocial rehabilitation services must be classified in terms of which combination of services should be recommended for which level of care needed by patients with PTSD (and possibly other, co-occurring disorders). Ongoing research in addictions shows that veterans with substance abuse and PTSD actually increase costs of treatment if they are not "matched" with appropriate services during initial admission to treatment.

These data underscore the "needs-to-service" matching that must be explored. The end product of such studies should be computerized algorithms for treatment matching. Comparative cost-for-gain effectiveness of services must be researched using such promising evaluation approaches as the "cumulative block increment" model (Gastfriend & McLelland, 1997).

6. Professional organizations must develop advocacy for empirically validated psychosocial rehabilitation techniques for PTSD. Currently, such techniques are not underwritten in most HMO contracts for care. It would be unfortunate if a promising set of interventions, well-validated for other mental disorders, were not available for therapists treating PTSD.

ACKNOWLEDGMENTS

We express our appreciation to our colleagues at the Edith Nourse Rogers Memorial Veterans Hospital in Bedford, Massachusetts: Arlene Devlin, Gregory Binus, Lawrence Herz, Douglas Bitman, Edward Federman, Dolly Sadow, Christopher Boyd, Charles Drebing, Estee Sharon, Alice van Ormer, Christopher Krebs, and Judith McNamara Bradley.

We are indebted to Terence M. Keane, Morris Bell, Kim Mueser, and William Anthony for their knowledgeable and encouraging readings and recommendations. We also thank Jacquelyn Coggin for her fine editing job.

REFERENCES

Allen, J. G., Kelly, K. A., & Glodich, A. (1997, Spring). A psychoeducational program for patients with trauma-related disorders. *Bulletin of the Menninger Clinic, 61*(2), 222–39.

American Psychiatric Association. (1996). Practice guidelines for the treatment of patients with nicotine dependence. *American Journal of Psychiatry, 153*(10; Suppl.), 1–31.

Anthony, W. A., Rogers, E. S., Cohen, M., Davies, R. R. (1995). Relationships between psychiatric symptomatology, work skills, and future vocational performance. *Psychiatric Services, 46*(4), 353–358.

Ashery, R. S. (Ed.). (1992). *Progress and issues in case management* (NIDA Research Monograph 127, DHHS Publication No. ADM 92–1946). Washington, DC: U.S. Government Printing Office.

Atkinson, J. M., Coia, D. A., Gilmour, W. H., & Harper, J. P. (1996). The impact of education groups for people with schizophrenia on social functioning and quality of life. *British Journal of Psychiatry, 168*, 199–204.

Ayllon, T., & Azrin, N. H. (1968). *The token economy*. New York. Appleton–Century–Crofts.

Bass, E., & Davis, L. (1988). *The courage to heal: A guide for women survivors of child abuse*. New York: Harper & Row.

Bell, M., & Lysaker, P. (1996). Levels of expectation for work activity in schizophrenia: Clinical and rehabilitation outcomes. *Psychiatric Rehabilitation, 19*(3), 71–76.

Bell, M. D., Lysaker, P. H., & Milstein, R. M. (1996). Clinical benefits of paid work activity in schizophrenia. *Schizophrenia Bulletin, 22*(1), 51–67.

Bell, M. D., Milstein, R. M., & Lysaker, P. H. (1993). Pay and participation in work activity: Clinical benefits for clients with schizophrenia. *Psychosocial Rehabilitation, 17*(2), 173–177.

Bisbee, C. C. (1991). *Educating patients and families about mental illness: A practical guide.* Gaithersburg, MD: Aspen.

Bond, G. D. R. (1997). An update on supported employment for people with severe mental illness. *Psychiatric Services, 48*(3), 335–345.

Bond, G. R., Drake, R. E., Becker, D. R., & Mueser, K. T. (1997). *Effectiveness of psychiatric rehabilitation approaches for employment of people with severe mental illness.* Manuscript submitted for publication.

Broocks, A., Bandelow, B., Pekrun, G., George, A., Meyer, T., Bartmann, U., Hillmer-Vogel, U., & Ruther, E. (1998, May). Comparison of aerobic exercise, clomipramine, and placebo in the treatment of panic disorder. *American Journal of Psychiatry, 155*(5), 603–609.

Brown, C., & Schulberg, H. C. (1995). The efficacy of psychosocial treatments in primary care. A review of randomized clinical trials. *General Hospital Psychiatry, 17*(6), 414–424.

Byrne, C., Brown, B., Voorberg, N., & Schofield, R. (1994). Wellness education for individuals with chronic mental illness living in the community. *Issues in Mental Health Nursing, 15*(3), 239–252.

Cates, J. A., & Graham, L. L. (1993). HIV and serious mental illness: Reducing the risk. *Community Mental Health Journal, 29*(1), 35–47.

Committee on Accreditation of Rehabilitation Facilities. (1998). *CARF standards for rehabilitation services.* Tucson, AZ: Author.

Dilk, M. N., & Bond, G. R. (1996). Meta-analysis of skills training research for individuals with severe mental illness. *Journal of Consulting and Clinical Psychology, 64,* 1337–1346.

Drake, R. E. (1996). The New Hampshire study of supported employment for people with severe mental illness. *Journal of Consulting and Clinical Psychology, 64,* 390–398.

Drake, R. E., McHugo, G. J., Becker, D. R., & Anthony, W. A. (1996). The New Hampshire study of supported employment for people with severe mental illness. *Consulting and Clinical Psychology, 64*(2), 391–399.

Eckman, T. A., Wirshing, W. C., Marder, S. R., Liberman, R. P., Johnston-Cronk, K., Zimmermann, K., & Mintz, J. (1992). Technique for training schizophrenic patients in illness self-management: A controlled trial. *American Journal of Psychiatry, 149,* 1549–1555.

Falloon, I. R. H. (1999). Optimal treatment for psychosis in an international demonstration project. *Psychiatric Services, 50,* 615–618.

Flannery, R. B. (1992). *Post-traumatic stress disorder: The victim's guide to healing and recovery.* New York: Crossroads.

Flannery, R. B. (1998). *The Assaulted Staff Action Program (ASAP): Coping with the psychological aftermath of violence.* Ellicot City, MD: Chevron.

Foa, E. B., Rothbaum, B. O., Riggs, D. S., & Murdock, G. B. (1991). Treatment of post-traumatic stress disorder in rape victims: Comparison between cognitive-behavioral procedures and counseling. *Journal of Consulting and Clinical Psychology, 59,* 715–723.

Gastfriend, D. R., & McLellan, A. T. (1997). Treatment matching: Theoretic basis and practical implications. *Medical Clinics of North America: Alcohol and Other Substance Abuse, 81,* 945–966.

Goisman, R. M., Kent, A. B., Montgomery, E. C., & Cheevers, M. M. (1991). AIDS education for patients with chronic mental illness. *Community Mental Health Journal, 27*(3), 189–197.

Goldfinger, S. M., Schutt, R. K., Tolomiczenko, G. S., Turner, W., Ware, N., Penk, W. E., Abelman, M. S., Avruskin, T. L., Breslau, J., Caplan, B., Dickey, B., Gonzalez, O., Good, B., Hellmann, S., Lee, S., O'Bryan, M., & Seidman, L. (1997). Housing persons who are homeless and mentally ill: Independent living or evolving consumer households? In W. R. Breakey & J. W. Thompson (Eds.), *Mentally ill and homeless: Special programs for special needs* (pp. 29–49). Amsterdam: Harwood.

Goldfinger, S. M., Schutt, R. K., Tolomiczenko, G. S., Seidman, L., Penk, W. E., Turner, W., & Caplan, B. (1999). Housing placement and subsequent days homeless among formerly homeless adults with mental illness. *Psychiatric Services, 50,* 674–679.

Goldman, C. R., & Quinn, F. L. (1988). Effects of patient education program in treatment of schizophrenia. *Hospital and Community Psychiatry, 39,* 282–286.

Halford, W. K., Harrison, C., Kalyansundaram M. B., Olive, M., & Simpson, S. (1995). Preliminary results for a psychoeducational program to rehabilitate chronic patients. *Psychiatric Services, 46*(11), 1189–1191.

Harris, M. (1998). *Trauma recovery and empowerment: A clinician's guide for working with women in groups.* New York: Free Press.

Herman, J. L. (1992). *Trauma and recovery.* New York: Basic Books.

Horvath, T. (Chair). (1997a). *The VHA clinical guidelines for major depressive disorder, post-traumatic stress disorder and substance abuse.* Washington, DC: Mental Health Strategic Health Group.

Horvath, T. (Chair). (1997b). *The VHA clinical guidelines for the management of persons with psychoses.* Washington, DC: Mental Health Strategic Health Group.

International Association of Psychosocial Rehabilitation Services. (Eds.). (1994). *An introduction to psychiatric rehabilitation.* Columbia, MD: Author.

Johnson, D. R., Rosenheck, R., & Fontana, A. (1997). Assessing the structure, content, and perceived social climate of residential PTSD treatment programs. *Journal of Traumatic Stress, 10,* 361–376.

Joint Commission on the Accreditation of Healthcare Organizations. (Ed.). (1993). *Principles of biopsychosocial rehabilitation.* Chicago: Author.

Kalichman, S. C., Sikkema, K. J., Kelly, J. A., & Bulto, M. (1995). Use of brief behavioural skills intervention to prevent HIV among chronic mentally ill adults. *Psychiatric Services, 46*(3), 275–280.

Keane, T. M., Newman, E., & Orsillo, S. M. (1997). Assessment of military related post-traumatic stress disorder. In J. P. Wilson & T. M. Keane (Eds.), *Assessing psychological trauma and PTSD* (pp. 267–290). New York: Guilford Press.

Kelly, G. R., & Scott, J. E. (1990). Medication compliance and health education among outpatients with chronic mental disorders. *Medical Care, 28*(12), 1181–1197.

Lehman, A. F. (1995). Vocational rehabilitation in schizophrenia. *Schizophrenia Bulletin, 21*(4), 645–656.

Li, F., & Wang, M. (1994). A behavioral training programme for chronic schizophrenia patients: A three-month randomised controlled trial in Beijing (M. R. Phillips, Trans.). *British Journal of Psychiatry, 165*(Suppl. 24), 58–67.

Liberman, R. P., Wallace, C. J., Blackwell, G. A., Eckman, T. A., Vaccaro, T. V., & Kuehnel, T. G. (1993). *Innovations in skills training: The UCLA Social and Independent Living Skills Modules.* Camarillo, CA: Psychiatric Rehabilitation Consultants.

Luo K., & Yu, D. (1994). Enterprise-based sheltered workshops in Nanjing: A new model for the community rehabilitation of mentally ill workers. *British Journal of Psychiatry, 165*(Suppl. 24), 89–95.

Lysaker, P., Bell, M., Milstein, R., & Bryson, G. (1993). Work capacity in schizophrenia. *Hospital and Community Psychiatry, 44*(3), 278–280.

MacPherson, R., Jerrom, B., & Hughes, A. (1996). A controlled study of education about drug treatment in schizophrenia. *British Journal of Psychiatry, 168*(6), 709–717.

Marks, I., Lovell, K., Noshirvani, H., Livanou, M., & Thrasher, S. (1998). Treatment of posttraumatic stress disorder by exposure and/or cognitive restructuring: A controlled study. *Archives of General Psychiatry, 55*, 317–325.

Marsh, D. T. (1998). *Serious mental illness and the family: The practitioner's guide.* New York: Wiley.

Matsakis, A. (1996). *"I can't get over it": A handbook for trauma survivors* (2nd ed.). Oakland, CA: New Harbinger Press.

Marlatt, G. A., & Gordon, J. R. (Eds.). (1985). *Relapse prevention: Maintenance strategies in the treatment of addictive behaviors.* New York: Guilford Press.

Marlow, R. M., West, J. A., Corrigan, S. A., Pena, J. M., & Cunningham, S. C. (1994). Outcome of psychoeducation for HIV risk reduction. *AIDS Education and Prevention, 6*(2), 113–125.

McDougall, S. (1992). The effect of nutritional education on the shopping and eating habits of a small group of chronic schizophrenic patients living in the community. *British Journal of Occupational Therapy, 55*(2), 62–68.

McFarlane, A. C. (1994). Individual psychotherapy for post-traumatic stress disorder. *Psychiatric Clinics of North America, 17*, 393–408.

Mitchell, J. T., & Bray, G. R. (1990). *Emergency services stress: Guidelines for preserving the health and careers of emergency services personnel.* Englewood Cliffs, NJ: Prentice-Hall.

Mueser, K. T., Bond, G. R., Drake, R. E., & Resnick, S. G. (1998). Models of community care for severe mental illness: A review of research on case management. *Schizophrenia Bulletin, 24*, 37–74.

Mueser, K. T., & Glynn, S. M. (1999). *Behavioral family therapy for psychiatric disorders* (2nd ed.). Oakland, CA: New Harbinger Press.

National Institute on Drug Abuse. (1996). *Therapy manuals for drug addiction: Manual 1. A cognitive-behavioral approach: Treating cocaine addiction.* Washington, DC: U.S. Government Printing Office.

National Institute on Drug Abuse. (1996). *Therapy manuals for drug addiction: Manual 2. A community reinforcement plus vouchers approach: Treating cocaine addiction.* Washington, DC: U.S. Government Printing Office.

Nowinski, J., Baker, S., & Carroll, K. (1994). *Twelve-step facilitation therapy manual* (Vol. 1, NIAA Project MATCH Monograph, NIH Publication No. 94-3722). Washington, DC: U. S. Government Printing Office.

Paul, S. M., & Lentz, R. (1977). *Psychosocial treatment of the chronic mental patient.* Cambridge, MA: Harvard University Press.

Penk, W. E., & Losonzcy, M. (Eds.). (1997). Psychosocial Rehabilitation Checklist in the psychosocial rehabilitation. In T. Horvath (Ed.), *Management of persons with psychoses: Clinical guidelines.* Washington, DC: Department of Veterans Affairs.

Rosenheck, R., Frisman, L., & Sindelar, J. (1995). Disability compensation and work among veterans with psychiatric and nonpsychiatriac impairments. *Psychiatric Services, 46*(4), 359–365.

Rosenheck, R., & Seibyl, C. L. (1998). Participation and outcome in a residential treatment and work therapy program for addictive disorders: The effects of race. *American Journal of Psychiatry, 155*, 1029–1034.

Rothbaum, B. O., & Foa, E. B. (1996). Cognitive-behavioral therapy for posttraumatic stress disorder. In B. A. van der Kolk, A. C. McFarlane, & L. Weisaeth (Eds.), *Traumatic stress: The effects of overwhelming experience on mind, body, and society* (pp. 491–509). New York: Guilford Press.

Runder, B. R., Moe, L., Sollien, T., Fjell, A., Borchgrevink, T., Hallert, M., & Naess, P. O. (1994). The Psychosis Project: Outcome and cost effectiveness of psychoeducational program for schizophrenic adolescents. *Acta Psychiatrica Scandinavica, 89*(3), 211–218.

Sauter, A. W., & Nevid, J. S. (1991). Work skills training with chronic schizophrenic sheltered workers. *Rehabilitation Psychology, 36*(4), 255–264.

Schutt, R. K. (1996). *Investigating the social world.* Los Angeles, CA: Pine Forge Press.

Schutt, R. K., & Garrett, G. R. (1992). *Responding to the homeless: Policy and practice.* New York: Plenum Press.

Siebyl, C. L., Rosencheck, R., Medak, S., & Corwel, L. (2000, May). *Health Care for Homeless Veterans Programs: The eleventh annual report, draft for concurrence.* West Haven, CT: Department of Veterans Affairs, NEPEC, VA Medical Center, West Haven, Connecticut.

Tarrier, N., Pilgrim, H., Sommerfield, C., Faragher, B., Reynolds, M., Graham, E., & Barrowclough, C. (1999). A randomized trial of cognitive therapy and imaginal exposure in the treatment of chronic PTSD. *Journal of Consulting and Clinical Psychology, 67,* 13–18.

van der Kolk, B. A., McFarlane, A. C., & van der Hart, O. V. (1996). A general approach to treatment of posttraumatic stress disorder. In B. A. van der Kolk, A. C. McFarlane, & L. Weisaeth (Eds.), *Traumatic stress: The effects of overwhelming experience on mind, body, and society* (pp. 417–440). New York: Guilford Press.

Wang, S., Wilson, J. P., & Mason, J. W. (1996). Stages in decompensation in combat-related PTSD: A new conceptual model. *Integrative Physiological and Behavioral Science, 31,* 237–253.

12

Hypnosis

Etzel Cardeña, Jose Maldonado,
Onno van der Hart, and David Spiegel

DEFINITIONS

Hypnotic phenomena have been described for centuries, but the systematic development of clinical and research hypnosis had to wait until the 19th century (Ellenberger, 1970). In the specific context of posttraumatic symptomatology, hypnotic techniques have been used for the psychological treatment of shell shock, battle fatigue, traumatic neuroses, their more recent incarnation, posttraumatic stress disorder (PTSD), and dissociative symptomatology (see, e.g., Brende, 1985; Spiegel & Spiegel, 1987). In this section, we review hypnosis and related constructs, relate them to dissociation and posttraumatic symptomatology, and provide the rationale for the use of hypnosis in the treatment of PTSD.

It will clarify matters to distinguish among "hypnosis" as a specific procedure; "hypnotic phenomena," as behavioral and experiential phenomena occurring in the context of the hypnotic procedure; "hypnotic-like phenomena," as phenomena similar to those associated with hypnosis but occurring in other contexts; and "hypnotizability," "hypnotic susceptibility," or "hypnotic responsiveness," as the ability to respond to a series of suggestions within a formal hypnotic procedure.

Hypnosis was defined by Division 30 of the American Psychological Association as "a procedure during which a health professional or researcher suggests that a client, patient, or subject experience changes in sensations, perceptions, thought, or behavior. The hypnotic context is generally established by an induction procedure" (Kirsch, 1994, p. 143). Hypnotic procedures can bring about a state of aroused, attentive focal concentration with a relative suspension of peripheral awareness and heightened sensitivity to suggestions (Spiegel, 1994; Spiegel & Cardeña, 1990). The labeling of the situation as hypnotic and instructions to disregard everyday concerns and focus instead on the hypnotist's suggestions for relaxation, alertness, or a perceptual event such as a metronome ticking, are common ingredients of hypnotic inductions. The induction procedure can be more or less formal. Despite some claims to the contrary, there is no evidence that "indirect" suggestions and lack of a hypnosis context are more effective than direct suggestions and a clear labeling of the context as hypnosis (Matthews, Bennett, Bean, & Gallagher, 1985).

Hypnotic inductions typically involve communications to disregard extraneous concerns and to concentrate on the behaviors and experiences proposed by the hypnotist. The induction for the Harvard Group Scale of Hypnotic Susceptibility (Shor & Orne, 1962) serves as a good illustration of a common approach. Its initial stage includes establishing rapport and briefly explaining the nature of the hypnotic procedure (e.g., that it is based on suggestions and that the hypnotic experience may not be that different from other experiences encountered in everyday life). A more formal procedure then ensues, in which the individual is told that he or she will become more relaxed and hypnotized as he or she attends to suggestions to relax the muscles of the whole body and to close the eyes. Afterward, the hypnotist counts from 1 to 20 to "deepen" the hypnotic experience. The following stage consists of giving specific suggestions to alter sensations, behavior, and cognition. This and other relaxation inductions last many minutes, but there are briefer procedures, such as the induction for the Hypnotic Induction Profile (HIP), which requires about a minute. It involves having the individual roll the eyes upward, slowly closing them while taking a deep breath, letting the breath out and the eyes relax, and experiencing floating sensations (Spiegel & Spiegel, 1987).

Although hypnotic inductions commonly entail suggestions for relaxation, suggestions for activity and alertness are equally effective. In that modality, the hypnotist emphasizes mental alertness and has the participant engage on a physical activity such as riding a stationary bike or moving the hand (Cardeña, Alarcón, Capafons, & Bayot, 1998). Procedures emphasizing mental alertness and physical activity may be a method of choice for individuals who easily fall asleep, are hypotensive, depressed, or just have a preference for activity and alertness over relaxation.

With respect to the clinical use of hypnosis, Division 30's definition states that "hypnosis is not a type of therapy, like psychoanalysis or behavior therapy. Instead, it is a procedure that can be used to facilitate therapy. . . .

Clinical hypnosis should be used only by properly trained and credentialed health care professionals . . . who have also been trained in the clinical use of hypnosis and are working within the areas of their professional expertise" (Kirsch, 1994, p. 143).

Hypnotic phenomena are behavioral, cognitive, and experiential alterations that either emerge or are enhanced by a hypnotic induction. A number of studies have described these common alterations among "hypnotized" individuals: (1) a sense of compulsion or enhanced suggestibility; (2) a diminution in reflective awareness, related to absorption in the suggested experiences; and (3) a number of unusual experiences, including alterations in body image and sense of time, and dissociative experiences such as feeling detached from oneself or the environment (cf. Cardeña & Spiegel, 1991). Because some people are not susceptible to hypnotic procedures, or may actively resist suggestions, there is no guarantee that a hypnotic procedure will evoke hypnotic phenomena in any particular individual.

Hypnotic-like phenomena may occur spontaneously following nonhypnotic events, especially among highly hypnotizable individuals. Hypnotic-like phenomena are behaviors and experiences similar to those found in a hypnotic setting, such as perceptual alterations, enhanced suggestibility, and narrow and continuous attentional focus, but encountered in different contexts. As described later, a number of acute and chronic traumatic reactions share similarities with formally induced hypnotic phenomena. It is important to realize that hypnotic-like phenomena can occur in the absence of a hypnotic context, especially with highly hypnotizable individuals and during traumatic situations.

Finally, *hypnotizability* and *hypnotic susceptibility or responsiveness* refers to the robust evidence of valid and reliable individual differences in response to hypnotic suggestions. Using standardized induction and suggestion procedures, researchers have found that about 25% of individuals show substantial to very high hypnotizability, some 50% have moderate hypnotizability, and 25% have low or no susceptibility (cf. Hilgard, 1965). It has also been observed that some very highly hypnotizable individuals are prone to have hypnotic-like experiences independent of the context (Spiegel & Spiegel, 1987; Tellegen & Atkinson, 1974), and that hypnotizability has a positive correlation with reports of spontaneous and unusual events, including paranormal experiences and a tendency to blur the distinction between different states of consciousness (see, e.g., Cardeña, 1993; Pekala, Kumar, & Marcano, 1995).

Hypnotic responsiveness varies throughout the life cycle. Individuals are more highly hypnotizable during their late childhood years, with a peak in hypnotic capacity around the age of 12. This is followed by a moderate decline, with stabilization later in adulthood (Hilgard, 1965). Hypnotizability does not seem to change much during adult years. A test–retest study found a correlation of .71 for two testings, one conducted during undergraduate years and the other 25 years later (Piccione, Hilgard, & Zimbardo, 1989).

HYPNOSIS, DISSOCIATION, AND POSTTRAUMATIC PHENOMENA

Several pioneers of modern psychopathology (e.g., Pierre Janet, Josef Breuer and Sigmund Freud, Morton Prince) studied the triad of hypnosis–dissociation–trauma and developed theories to account for their relationship (Breuer & Freud, 1895/1982; Janet, 1889/1973; van der Hart & Horst, 1989; van der Kolk & van der Hart, 1989). Spiegel and Cardeña (1991) have remarked that trauma can be seen as the process of being made into an object, the victim of someone else's rage, of organized aggression, or of nature's indifference. The helplessness engendered by traumatic experiences may create sudden challenges to normal ways of processing perception, cognition, affect, and relationships (Maldonado & Spiegel, 1994). Experimental and survey data suggest that, indeed, traumatic and stressful events produce a narrow focus of attention, with a consequent disregard of peripheral information (Cardeña & Spiegel, 1993; Christianson & Loftus, 1987; Classen, Koopman, Hales, & Spiegel, 1998; Koopman, Classen, & Spiegel, 1996), and these attentional processes seem to be similar to those manifested during hypnosis (Cardeña & Spiegel, 1991; Nijenhuis & van der Hart, 1999).

This narrowing of attention, especially if maintained for more than a few moments, is associated with alterations in consciousness, including dissociative phenomena. As a descriptive construct, "dissociation" has been defined as an alteration in consciousness, characterized by an experiential disconnection or disengagement from the self and/or the environment (Cardeña, 1994). More theoretically it was defined as "a structured separation of mental processes . . . that are ordinarily integrated" (Spiegel & Cardeña, 1991, p. 367). Dissociative phenomena include alterations in the sense or perception of self and the environment, the sense of agency or will, memory, emotion, and identity (Butler, Duran, Jasiukaitis, Koopman, & Spiegel, 1996; Cardeña, 1997). Recently, the concept of somatoform dissociation has stressed dissociative somatic symptomatology such as lack of sensations or motor control (Nijenhuis, Spinhoven, Van Dyck, van der Hart, & Vanderlinden, 1996).

Ever since Janet (1889/1973), dissociation has been strongly associated with traumatic events. During, or shortly after a traumatic event, a substantial proportion of individuals experience dissociative alterations, including experiential (or passive) detachment, and alterations in memory and perception (see, e.g., Cardeña & Spiegel, 1993; Foa & Hearst-Ikeda, 1996; Spiegel & Cardeña, 1991). A number of these changes have been often described in the hypnosis literature, including alterations in the sense of time, a narrow focus of attention, experiential detachment, and slowing down of responses (Cardeña, 1995). Relatedly, Nash (1992, p. 150) has remarked that "the description given by patients of some pathological [including, we would add, posttraumatic] states often resembles the report of normal subjects describing their experience during hypnosis."

Furthermore, there is evidence that dissociation around the time of trauma is a significant predictor of later PTSD, an issue addressed by the recent diagnosis of acute stress disorder (see, e.g., Bremner et al., 1992; Classen, Koopman, Hales, & Spiegel, 1998; Koopman, Classen, & Spiegel, 1996; Marmar et al., 1994; Shalev, Peri, Canetti, & Schreiber, 1996; Staab, Grieger, Fullerton, & Ursano, 1996). Although substantial amnesia after single episodes of trauma is not common (see, e.g., Cardeña, Grieger, Staab, Fullerton, & Ursano, 1997), other forms of dissociation may be present. Van der Hart and colleagues have formulated a model distinguishing among three levels of dissociation of the personality (see, e.g., van der Hart, van der Kolk, & Boon, 1998), in which primary dissociation would be the dissociation of the traumatic memory state from the consciously available autobiographical–narrative memory system (i.e., classical amnesia). Secondary dissociation would be a lack of association within the traumatic memory system, that is, compartmentalization and fragmentation of the normally integrated BASK (behavior, affect, sensation, knowledge) components of the memory. Tertiary dissociation would be compartmentalization or fragmentation of the self-representational system, such as in dissociative identity disorder. Most nonchronic dissociative reactions are likely to involve secondary dissociation rather than the other two types.

Not only are trauma victims more prone to experience or even deliberately use dissociation, but it has been observed for a long time that individuals with posttraumatic symptomatology are highly hypnotizable (see, e.g., Ross, 1941), an observation for which Gill and Brenman (1961) found some informal mathematical support. More recent and systematic studies have confirmed these clinical observations. Masked and nonmasked studies with standardized hypnotizability scales have corroborated that, on average, individuals suffering from posttraumatic symptoms or full PTSD tend to be highly hypnotizable and are significantly more hypnotizable than most other clinical and nonclinical groups (Cardeña, 1996; Kluft, 1985; Spiegel, Detrick, & Frischholz, 1982; Spiegel, Hunt, & Dondershine, 1988; Stutman & Bliss, 1985), and have high imagery abilities (Stutman & Bliss, 1985). However, the relationship between hypnotizability and trauma history in nonclinical groups is equivocal (Putnam & Carlson, 1998). Some studies suggest that a positive correlation between history of trauma and hypnotizability is present only in survivors of repeated rather than isolated instances of trauma (Eisen, Anderson, Cooper, Horton, & Stenzel, 1994). There is also some evidence that chronic dissociation is more likely to occur after repeated rather than single instances of trauma (Gold & Cardeña, 1993; Terr, 1991).

RATIONALE FOR USE

Several theoretical and empirical considerations have led experts in hypnosis to suggest that the use of this technique may be a useful addition to the treatment of PTSD:

1. The high hypnotizability of many PTSD patients can be purposefully used in hypnosis. There is evidence that hypnotic techniques usually work best with moderate and highly hypnotizable individuals (Levitt, 1994; Spiegel, Frischholz, Fleiss, & Spiegel, 1993; Spiegel, Frischholz, Maruffi, & Spiegel, 1981), although other factors such as expectancies also seem to mediate response to hypnosis (Schoenberger, Kirsch, Gearan, Montgomery, & Pastyrnak, 1997).

2. Many PTSD patients suffer from dissociative symptoms (Cardeña, 1996; Dracu, Riggs, Hearst-Ikeda, Shoyer, & Foa, 1996; Hyer, Albrecht, Poudewyns, Woods, & Brandsma, 1993). As early as 1920, McDougall had remarked that in the treatment of trauma "the essential therapeutic step is the relief of the dissociation. . . . Emotional discharge is not necessary to this, though it may play some part in contributing to bring it about" (p. 25). Because hypnosis may induce dissociative experience within a structured and controlled setting, patients can learn specific techniques to modulate and bring under control unbidden and distressing phenomena (Benningfield, 1992; Spiegel & Cardeña, 1990; Valdiserri & Byrne, 1982). Furthermore, dissociative phenomena may be reframed and utilized for therapeutic purposes (Edgette & Edgette, 1995; Phillips, 1993).

3. Hypnotic techniques can be easily integrated into diverse approaches, including psychodynamic or cognitive-behavioral therapies, and pharmacotherapy (see, e.g., Kirsch, 1996; Muraoka et al., 1996; Spiegel & Spiegel, 1987). Meta-analyses of the research on the use of hypnosis to treat various clinical conditions have shown that hypnosis can have a synergistic effect on the therapies with which it has been used as an adjunct (Kirsch, Capafons, Cardeña, & Amigó, 1999; Kirsch, Montgomery, & Sapirstein, 1995; Smith, Glass, & Miller, 1980). Although these analyses have been conducted with conditions other than PTSD, hypnotic techniques may also augment the efficacy of other therapies for PTSD, especially considering its dissociative features.

4. Two dominant models in the treatment of PTSD, the psychodynamic and cognitive-behavioral, emphasize the importance of a recollection of the traumatic event, whether within the framework of achieving emotional and cognitive integration or of providing repeated exposure to the traumatic event. This recollection should occur in the context of enhancing alternative, more adaptive responses. Both models require some recollection of the traumatic event and, as described later, hypnosis can facilitate the working

through of traumatic memories by giving the patient techniques to pace and control the intensity and associated distress of the traumatic memory.

5. There is evidence that some traumatized individuals have fragmentary, disorganized or no recall of traumatic events (Brown, Scheflin, & Hammond, 1998). As mentioned earlier, patients with PTSD are likely to have experienced dissociative phenomena at the time of trauma, including alterations of memory. This memory impairment can take various forms: problems encoding new information (Bremner et al., 1993); partial and, more rarely, total amnesia (see, e.g., Cardeña & Spiegel, 1993); a decontextualized recall of the event; or impersonal recollection. Hypnosis and traumatic events can produce similar experiences, and if trauma victims were in a dissociated state at the time of the trauma, using the structured dissociation of hypnosis may facilitate access to trauma-related memories. The theory of state-dependent memory (Overton, 1978) supports the hypothesis that hypnosis may facilitate the retrieval of memories associated with a similar state of mind as that which occurred at the time of the trauma. State-dependent effects may occur especially when no stronger cues are available (Eich, 1995). However, as described later, the use of hypnotic techniques to recall memories needs to be conducted very carefully, because hypnosis may unrealistically enhance the individual's confidence on the reported memory rather than its actual accuracy (Dywan & Bowers, 1983). It is important to develop research models that will test whether hypnotic techniques can indeed enhance accurate recall of traumatic incidents.

DESCRIPTION OF TECHNIQUES

Hypnotic techniques for the treatment of posttraumatic disturbances have been used for more than a century in various ways and include supportive suggestions; uncovering; integrating or abreacting trauma memories (Brende, 1985; Brown & Fromm, 1986); and reconstructing past events (as in Janet's substitution of a more benign memory for a traumatic one; van der Hart, Brown, & van der Kolk, 1989; see also Kardiner & Spiegel, 1947).

Trauma treatment, especially for chronic or otherwise complicated cases, usually follows a phase-oriented model, defined by Brown, Scheflin, and Hammond (1998) as dividing the trauma treatment into phases or stages of treatment, each with its own objectives or goals. Hypnosis can be used during the typical three general stages of trauma treatment (first described by Janet; see van der Hart et al., 1989), which entail (1) establishing the therapeutic relationship and frame, providing short-term relief, and helping stabilize the patient by making symptoms more manageable and enhancing coping skills; (2) working through and integrating the traumatic events; and (3) furthering integration, and self- and relational development. Our clinical observation has been that length of treatment will vary depending on a number of factors, including (1) the nature of trauma (e.g., multiple or single events, natural disaster or caused by humans); (2) how soon treatment starts after the traumatic event; (3) patients' comorbidity, including how affected are self- and relational schemas; and (4) previous history of chronic abuse or neglect. For posttraumatic conditions following a single, uncomplicated recent trauma, our clinical experience is that a few sessions may alleviate the symptoms. For chronic or complicated conditions, treatment is more likely to require a number of months or years. Some clinicians (see, e.g., Fromm & Nash, 1997) have remarked that hypnosis usually shortens the treatment of the therapies to which it is an adjunct, but this assertion has not yet been systematically tested.

Treatment Phase 1: Stabilization and Symptom Reduction

During the initial phase, the focus is on stabilizing and alleviating patients' symptoms, and enhancing self-mastery over symptoms and current concerns and stresses. This initial phase may be revisited even after later phases are being implemented. Hypnotic suggestions can be used to induce relaxation, so that patients can learn to experience a calm and serene state and, through self-hypnosis, learn how to maintain this state outside of the consulting room. Specific suggestions can target symptoms associated with PTSD, including anxiety, physical pain, discomfort, and sleep disturbances (see, e.g., Eichelman, 1985; Jiranek, 1993). Other techniques that may be especially useful at this stage include establishing an imaginal "safe place" (Brown & Fromm, 1986; Watkins & Watkins, 1997) and using "ego strengthening" procedures (Frederick & McNeal, 1993; Hartland, 1965). Brown, Scheflin, and Hammond (1998) provide various signs of stabilization in this phase, including feeling safe, self-soothing, connectedness, alleviation of PTSD symptoms, and so on.

Treatment Phase 2: Treatment of Traumatic Memories

The second phase, after an appropriate therapeutic alliance has been forged and the patient has developed sufficient personal resources to confront difficult issues without being overwhelmed by them, involves working with traumatic memories. Whether to overcome the phobia of traumatic memories (cf. van der Hart, van der Kolk, & Boon, 1998), achieve psychological integration (Brown et al., 1998; Spiegel & Cardeña, 1990), or enhance emotional engagement habituation and cognitive restructuring (cf. Foa & Meadows, 1997; Jaycox, Foa, & Morral, 1998), authors from diverse perspectives agree on the importance of working with trauma memories. It bears mentioning that since the introduction of the term "abreaction" by Breuer and Freud (1895/1982), various authors have used this concept in describing the purpose of trauma treatment. Although a minority still speaks of "abreactive techniques," a more current view is that the main goal is integration of the traumatic memory rather than its abreaction (for a review, see van der Hart & Brown, 1992). In terms of van der Hart's structural model, treating traumatic memories entails integrating the dis-integrated components of the traumatic memory into a structural whole, the self-representational system into a structural whole and, in turn, integrating each with the other.

Occasionally, the focus may be to make conscious apparently forgotten material (see Brown et al., 1998). However, during the integration work of memories, it is likely that more detailed or even new and relevant memories will emerge spontaneously. Greater recollection of accurate, meaningful memories after repeated probes has been demonstrated in the laboratory (see, e.g., Erdelyi, 1994).

Exposing patients to traumatic stimuli or memory requires careful consideration. There is some evidence that exposure therapy for PTSD may exacerbate symptoms among perpetrators (Pitman et al., 1991, cited in Foa & Meadows, 1997), and among chronic PTSD patients in an intensive, residential treatment, the first author observed enhanced distress when they were asked to repeatedly recollect traumatic events. It has also been remarked that revisiting traumatic memories may be counterproductive unless the patient experiences safety and has enough ego strength to deal with such material (Peebles, 1989). Relatedly, van der Kolk, McFarlane, and van der Hart (1996, p. 436) have written that "only when issues of interpersonal security can be safely negotiated can the therapeutic relationship be utilized to hold the patient's psyche together when the threat of physical disintegration is reexperienced. . . . Once the traumatic experiences have been located in time and place, the person can start making distinctions between current life stresses and past trauma, and can decrease the impact of the trauma on present experience."

Spiegel (1992) remarked that this process can be facilitated by appropriate attention to transference and countertransference issues related to the trauma; working through issues of trust and mutual acceptance is a critical part of the psychotherapy of trauma-related symptoms. Hypnotic techniques can also help provide a context in which to accomplish exposure to traumatic memories in a way that does not overwhelm the patient (cf. Scheff, 1980), although exposure therapy has been successfully conducted without hypnosis (Foa & Meadows, 1997).

Therapists using hypnosis during this phase need to remember that, as a group, patients with PTSD have been found to be highly hypnotizable, so therapists should avoid suggestive or misleading questions or comments when eliciting new information. Questions should avoid misinformation or suggestion of a specific answer. Also, patients need help to achieve a controlled processing of memories while maintaining a state of comfort and safety. Adequate hypnotic memory retrieval involves the use of techniques that promote physical levels of relaxation and a sense of cognitive and emotional control.

It has been our observation that working with traumatic memories should proceed at a pace that patients can tolerate. Hypnotic techniques should be tailored to patients' particular needs, with an emphasis on using the occasion to enhance their sense of control over their mental and physical state. Many patients fear that if they recall traumatic memories, they will once again lose control and symbolically reenact the helplessness experienced during the traumatic episode. To some extent, this is not an unreasonable fear. Memories can take over patients' mental lives every time they experience flashbacks, but hypnosis may allow patients to separate themselves from their memories as needed. Part of the therapist's role is to help control and structure the retrieval and expression of painful memories, and the feelings associated with them. Hypnosis can be used to facilitate a therapeutic working through of traumatic memories. Because they often produce feelings of helplessness and powerlessness, the patient can be given appropriate ego-enhancing suggestions and images to generate experiences of personal power, protection, and competence (see, e.g., Ebert, 1988). Other techniques, described for dissociative patients but applicable to PTSD, include "fractionated [or gradual] abreactions," time sense alterations, and trance ratification (Kluft, 1994). We describe here six especially relevant techniques for PTSD: relaxation, projective and restructuring techniques, age regression, affect bridge, and imaginal memory containment (Brown & Fromm, 1986).

Relaxation

After the induction of hypnosis, which may itself contain suggestions for relaxation, a deeper level of physical relaxation may be easily achieved by instructing patients to imagine themselves in a place they associate with relaxation and calmness. This could be a place they have been before, or a place they invent in their minds, such as floating in a hot tub, pool, or space. Once the desired level of relaxation is achieved, and patients are instructed to maintain this state, they are asked to confront emotionally charged traumatic memories. The objective is to process traumatic memories at a pace patients can tolerate, while maintaining the same level of physical and, if possible, emotional relaxation. Hypnotic techniques can be integrated with systematic desensitization if needed (Wilshire, 1996).

Projective Techniques

In these techniques, patients "project" images, sensations, and thoughts away from themselves, onto an imaginary screen. Useful images include a movie or computer screen, the surface of a calm lake, a mirror, or a blue sky. This technique seems to facilitate the process of separating memories from physically painful sensations if necessary, in order to minimize the possibility of overwhelming recollections or retraumatization. The screen may allow for the manipulation of the affect that is mobilized during the retrieval of traumatic memories. Patients are taught to control the intensity of the content by making the images larger or smaller, or by moving the screen closer or farther away from them. They can also transform the images by changing the color (e.g., making images black and white rather than in color), the sound (e.g., lowering the volume or completely eliminating it), the speed (e.g., slowing or fast-forwarding images), or they can choose to turn the screen off if the intensity becomes uncontrollable at any given time. Patients are reminded that, as in a frightening movie, some scenes may be difficult or even repulsive, but they do not have to reexperience the pain associated with the traumatic memories or images. The goal of this technique is to increase patients' sense of control and safety, until they can work through and integrate all of the information, sensations, thoughts, emotions, and so on.

Restructuring

A variation of the previous technique calls for patients to divide the screen in half. While doing this, they are asked to project onto the left side of the screen images of what they need to work on (e.g., memories of the trauma), whereas on the right side of the screen, they may picture something they did in order to protect themselves or someone else (Spiegel, 1981, 1992). On occasion, some patients may have difficulty remembering anything good, and may blame themselves inappropriately for not having done enough. The therapist encourages them to recall anything they might have done to protect themselves and attempts to reinterpret their perception of powerlessness into a useful survival technique. Fighting back, screaming for help, or just "lying still" in order to avoid further abuse are examples of common defensive acts. The goal is to facilitate the restructuring of traumatic memories so as to make them more bearable.

The new cognition involves recognizing both the intensity of the threat and the patient's adaptive response at the time of trauma. At the end, the two images serve to restructure the memory of the trauma. The image on the left symbolizes the summary of the trauma itself. The image on the right may help patients realize that while they were indeed victimized, they were also attempting to master the situation and displayed courage during a time of overwhelming threat. This process may allow patients to realize that the humiliation of the trauma is only one aspect of the experience.

Age Regression

In contrast with projective techniques, hypnotically induced regression to an earlier time may not provide patients with the protective advantage of being able to "project" memories away from themselves; because of this, it may be a more intense experience. In this technique, the therapist suggests that patients, by counting or some other technique, go back in time to a previous self. We have observed that this procedure can help patients understand the origin of long-forgotten bodily symptoms, such as conversion symptoms and somatic flashbacks. Potentially, it may even help them recall dissociated memories. Highly hypnotizable individuals are able to use this technique as a form of "role playing" the events, as if they were happening all over again. This may provide a more complete recall of affects and other elements that may have been dissociated from the memory of the event. A full recollection may even help explain some present behaviors, such as a disproportionate response to seemingly benign stressors. Although it may be very difficult determining to what extent the recalled memory is historically accurate, and, again, misleading questions or remarks should be avoided, it nonetheless is useful in making sense of the individual's interpretation of the traumatic event. It should be pointed out that the "regression" that occurs is an imaginal–experiential event, not a literal regression to a younger age (Nash, 1992). Although, in contrast with Nash, Brown, Scheflin, and Hammond (1998) opine that age regression may bring about significant recovery of accurate memory if misleading questioning is avoided, all of these authors concur that at the very least this technique may be very useful when exploring affect.

Affect Bridge

This technique seems to be particularly useful in cases where patients present with phobic-like symptoms (Watkins, 1987). After achieving a state of physical and emotional relaxation, patients are instructed to go back to the very first time they felt a particular way before (e.g., afraid). Highly hypnotizable individuals often respond by recounting a past experience associated (literally or figuratively) with the current fearful feelings, and the therapist can then help patients figure out associations or explanations for current inappropriate responses such as phobias.

Imaginal Memory Containment

In this technique, imagery is used to contain unresolved (parts of) memories until the patient or client is ready for further memory work. An example is an imagined safe in which the patient places the traumatic memory. The safe is closed and, in the patient's imagination, both the patient and the therapist use separate keys to lock it. A related, more direct hypnotic approach is to suggest posthypnotically that amnesia for traumatic memories be maintained if the patient's current recollection might be too distressing. In general, it is advisable to give permissively formulated suggestions. For example, "Take along from this experience in hypnosis whatever is good to take with you, for which the time is right, and just leave behind whatever is better to be left here for the time being" (van der Hart, Boon, & Van Everdingen, 1990 p. 243).

Treatment Phase 3: Further Personality Reintegration and Rehabilitation

The third phase of treatment emphasizes maintaining the gains of the two previous phases, achieving integration of the traumatic event into an adaptive sense of the self and the world, and enhancing personal and relational development. Brown, Scheflin, and Hammond (1998) have proposed that the work in this phase should include stabilizing the previous integration of various psychological processes, developing the self rather than maintaining it crystallized into the trauma, establishing or reestablishing healthy relationships, modulating impulses and emotions, stabilizing psychophysiological responses, and achieving good cognitive restructuring. It is important to point out that, as much as possible, treatment should not deal exclusively with alleviation of pathology, but should also consider the personal development of the individual. For some patients and therapists, adding a spiritual and community dimension to treatment may be of great benefit.

In this phase, hypnotic techniques are helpful in stabilizing the gains outside of the clinic and in proposing alternative forms of coping that the individual can implement on his or her own, for instance, through self-hypnosis. Other techniques, such as age-progression (to follow), may help break a hopeless sense of the future by providing a goal to achieve a better, albeit realistic, personal future.

An Eight-Process Model to Treat PTSD

We have developed a treatment approach to treat posttraumatic syndromes that details important therapeutic processes and can be easily subsumed under Phases 2 and 3 of the more general phase-oriented treatment described earlier (Spiegel, 1992; Spiegel & Cardeña, 1990). This approach is designed to help patients recognize and understand factors involved in the development of their symptoms, define one or several particularly frightening memories, learn how to control them, and reintegrate the memories into a more adaptive and healthy sense of the self and the world. Of the following eight processes, the first six or seven are particularly indicated for the second, or working-through, stage of trauma therapy, whereas the last step (congruence) is especially useful for the last, or reintegration, stage of treatment. More general hypnotic strategies for relaxing, strengthening the ego, coping, and so on, can be used in the initial stage of treatment (Brown & Fromm, 1986).

1. *Confrontation.* It is important to confront traumatic memories directly instead of trying to avoid them, which, paradoxically, may perpetuate them

and prevent the physical and psychological benefits of verbal elaboration (cf. Foa, Hearst-Ikeda, & Perry, 1995; Wegner & Pennebaker, 1993).

2. *Confession.* It is often advisable to allow patients to confess deeds or emotions that are embarrassing to them and at times repugnant to the therapist. It is important to help these patients distinguish between misplaced guilt and real remorse. Patients often have a retrospective wish to change traumatic circumstances through a fantasy that they could have controlled the past. The price of this fantasy may be irrational guilt, such as patients telling themselves that they were responsible for events that they could not have controlled.

3. *Consolation.* The intensity of traumatic experiences requires an actively consoling approach from the therapist, lest he or she be perceived as judgmental or as minimizing the pain inflicted on the patient. We have observed a kind of traumatic transference in which, for example, rape victims feel that therapists are reinflicting the trauma on patients while working therapeutically with trauma memories. Appropriate expressions of empathic understanding and concern are helpful in acknowledging and diffusing this common reaction.

4. *Conscious experience.* We believe that patients need also to be encouraged to make fully conscious those aspects of the memory that they may experience in a detached way, but that are necessary to understand fully and move past an event. Patients may hold some form of amnesia for aspects of the event, or for their own reactions to it. Permitting this material to come into the open is thought to foster a full account and integration of various emotions, thoughts, and attitudes related to trauma. Hypnotic techniques, such as the split-screen mentioned earlier, may provide patients with some control and organization on how to confront and confess to an experience. A suggestion that lets the patient remember only the material mentioned during hypnosis that he or she can tolerate at that point can facilitate a gradual and tolerable recall of difficult memories.

5. *Condensation.* It is important to find an image that condenses a crucial aspect of the traumatic experience. This representation can make the overwhelming aspects of the trauma more manageable by giving them concrete form. Furthermore, it can be used to facilitate a restructuring of the experience by joining previously disparate images. For example, the person can link the pain associated with the death of a buddy in combat with the happiness experienced during some earlier, shared time. This allows the individual to alter the pain of the loss by understanding it in terms of the positive aspects of the relationship. Using hypnosis techniques, a patient may find an image that provides a good affective and sensory condensation of trauma.

6. *Concentration.* The use of the intense but safe concentration fostered by hypnosis can help contain the effect of the traumatic experience by having the patient learn to voluntarily deploy attention to that or other events, as appropriate. Learning to focus and modulate attention on the loss suggests that

when the hypnotic state has ended, attention can be shifted away from the traumatic experience.

7. *Control.* Since the most painful aspect of severe trauma can be the absolute sense of helplessness and loss of control over one's body and the environment, it is important for therapy to enhance the patient's sense of control over those memories. The experience can be structured so that patients have the opportunity to terminate the working-through process when they feel they have had enough; they can also be given suggestions to remember as much from the hypnosis experience as they care to, and they can be put in charge of their own self-hypnosis experiences, which they should practice outside of the session. These procedures give patients a greater sense of control and mastery.

8. *Congruence.* During this stage, the patient's task is to achieve a good integration of memories, self-images, and sense of the world, allowing for a resumption of congruent and fluid cognitive and memory patterns. Use of such techniques as age progression, in which patients create an image of what type of person they aspire to be in the future, can facilitate a new integration between the old and the emerging self. The goal also includes the elimination of dissociative reactions and the development of a sense of reintegration back into a healthy and normal life. In related terms, Myers (1940) had formulated his overall treatment goal with shell-shocked combat soldiers as the reintegration of the traumatic ("emotional") personality state with the "apparently normal" personality state, a similar goal to that in Phase 3.

Transference Issues

Therapists can provide guidance, support, protection, and comfort as patients go through the difficult task of reprocessing and restructuring traumatic memories (Brown & Fromm, 1986). However, the intense emotions that characterize hypnotic retrieval of traumatic memories may facilitate the expression of inner fantasies and memories. In some patients, hypnosis can facilitate a sense of infantile dependency in which transference expectations are intensified. As in any other therapeutic relationship, the quality and affective content of this reaction may be based on the patient's early object relations.

It is our experience that the presence and intensity of transference reactions during the psychotherapy of trauma victims can be quite strong. The use of hypnosis does not prevent the development of these reactions; on the contrary, it may facilitate its emergence. In many instances, the development of transference reactions may occur earlier than in conventional therapy. Because some therapists may erroneously foster dependency feelings in an overzealous attempt to "take over" and help the patient, we suggest that, instead, they use the transference situation to foster patients' ability to help themselves by creating an environment of self-control and autonomy.

Another form of transference reaction has been termed a "traumatic transference" (Maldonado & Spiegel, 1994; Spiegel, 1989, 1992). It involves the transference of feelings related to the abuser or the circumstances associated with the traumatic experience onto the therapist. Such feelings may be an attempt to experience suppressed anger toward the perpetrator. These feelings should not be minimized or shut off. Doing so might confirm patients' belief that there is something wrong about having these feelings. Unresolved, they can hamper therapy by distancing the patient from the therapist and foster the use of primitive defenses, including acting out.

A Cautionary Note on Memory and Hypnosis

Potential complications of using hypnosis in the treatment of trauma victims include the incorrect assumption that hypnosis will automatically bring forth accurate recollections and the possible creation of pseudomemories or "false memories," especially in highly hypnotizable individuals.

With regard to the assumption of enhanced memory retrieval through hypnosis, a number of controlled studies have shown that hypnosis facilitates improved recall of both true and confabulated material (see, e.g., Dywan & Bowers, 1983). Hypnosis may enhance recall, especially of meaningful material (Brown, Scheflin, & Hammond, 1998), but not all recovered memories are true. Furthermore, enhanced recall might be the product of general heightened concentration or merely repeated testing (Erdelyi, 1994). Hypnotic procedures are more likely to increase the total number of memories, and the confidence placed on their accuracy, than to decrease the ratio of accurate-to-inaccurate statements or produce confabulation (Butler & Spiegel, 1997). Burgess and Kirsch (1997) report that providing participants with a warning about the potentially unwarranted confidence in memories obtained through hypnosis mitigates the usually observed increase in confidence judgments. These types of warnings or clarifications may counteract the often-encountered expectation that hypnosis will uncover the truth "recorded" in the "unconscious mind."

With respect to the possibility of pseudomemory creation, because hypnosis involves a diminution of critical judgment, it may enhance responsivity to social cues and internal stimuli. It can distort memory through confabulation, involving the creation of false memories, which are then reported as real (Laurence & Perry, 1983), or through the unwarranted increased sense of confidence with which hypnotized individuals report their memories ("concreting"), whether these are true or false (Dywan & Bowers, 1983; McConkey & Sheehan, 1995; Orne et al., 1985; Spiegel & Spiegel, 1987).

It is also worth noting that the experimental literature on pseudomemory creation with hypnosis has typically involved creating or distorting minor details, not major life events (Brown, Scheflin, & Hammond, 1998), and that the likelihood of adopting a false memory depends on its normal likelihood of occurrence, and social and contextual factors independent of hypnosis (Lynn, Myers, & Malinoski, 1997). Furthermore, a number of other interrogatory and therapeutic procedures, including misleading questions during a therapeutic or research interaction, can also produce false reports. Some authors have concluded that pseudomemories are not produced by hypnosis per se, but by inappropriate forms of inquiry and inaccurate assumptions about hypnosis (Brown, Scheflin, & Hammond, 1998; McConkey & Sheehan, 1995). Just as hypnosis is only adjunctive to treatment, it is only adjunctive to memory retrieval techniques. After a comprehensive review of their own and others' research, McConkey and Sheehan concluded that "memory distortion is neither unique nor specific to hypnosis. . . . Distortion is probable enough in the normal waking state" (1995, pp. 210, 214). Fromm and Nash (1997, pp. 223–224) concluded:

> Hypnosis has been unfairly singled-out by the media and the courts on this issue. Of the hundreds of expressive therapeutic techniques now extant, hypnosis is the only one for which there are substantial data on memory and its accuracy. . . . The media and the courts focus on the memory-distorting effects of hypnosis precisely because hypnosis researchers are the ones who have most rigorously documented how plastic memory is in treatment. . . . It is not that these factors are absent in other expressive therapies.

Indeed, victims and witnesses repeatedly interrogated by police or other investigators are subject to the same degree of "suggestibility and concreting" as hypnotized individuals. This is especially true when the person being interrogated happens to be a highly suggestible individual (Spiegel & Spiegel, 1987). Because of the possibility for memory inaccuracies, therapists are warned about believing everything a patient recalls. "Therapeutic judgment" should be utilized when analyzing and interpreting hypnotically recovered material (Maldonado & Spiegel, 1998). This approach is similar to that with which (nontraumatic) childhood memories, fantasies, and dreams are handled. Some memories are a more or less accurate representation of reality, while others may be at least partly fantasies that need to be interpreted before a more accurate picture can be obtained. In a related vein, a recent report from the International Society for Traumatic Stress Studies (ISTSS; 1998) concluded that imagery can enhance both false and true memories, that most individuals resist the implantation of false memories, and that situational and personal characteristics may contribute to the creation of pseudomemories.

Therapists must be aware of the legal ramifications of doing trauma work, whether hypnosis is used or not, and remember the limitations inherent in the use of hypnotic enhancement of memories. Some courts have not only banned the product of hypnotic interrogation in court, but also have ruled that the testimony of witnesses who have been previously hypnotized about the facts of a case be excluded per se, instead of evaluating the likely effect of hypnosis in each case.

If there are any legal proceedings pending, we recommend that the therapist do the following: (1) With the consent of the patient, inform the patient's counsel of the therapist's plans before any hypnotic procedures take place; (2) carefully document the participant's knowledge of possible traumatic events before hypnosis is employed; (3) use nonleading questions during hypnotic interrogation; (4) obtain electronic recording of all contacts with patients; and (5) carefully debrief both counsel and patient after completion of the process.

With awareness of the reconstructive nature of memory and the potential effect of misleading questions or cues on recollection, therapists with solid training in hypnosis should feel comfortable using it in the treatment of PTSD whenever warranted. The American Society of Clinical Hypnosis has provided guidelines and informed-consent samples for uses of hypnosis for memory work that might be of use for the clinician or forensic expert (Hammond et al., 1995).

METHOD OF COLLECTING DATA

The major sources for identifying relevant citations were PsycLIT, MEDLINE, and the PILOTS traumatic stress database. These sources were searched using combinations of the following keywords: "hypnosis," "hypnotism," "trauma," "PTSD," "traumatic neurosis," "shell shock," and "combat fatigue." A library search for relevant books and consultation with colleagues in the field were also used. References on the related fields of memory and dissociation were incorporated.

SUMMARY OF THE LITERATURE

Various meta-analyses of studies on the treatment of anxiety, pain, and other conditions imply that hypnosis can substantially enhance the effectiveness of psychodynamic and cognitive-behavioral therapies (Kirsch, 1996; Kirsch, Montgomery, & Sapirstein, 1995, Kirsch, Capafons, Cardeña, & Amigó, 1999; Smith, Glass, & Miller, 1980). However, most of the literature on the use of hypnosis for PTSD entails case studies. The reader should bear in mind the limitations of this method, which include a general lack of systematic assessment and a possible bias toward reporting positive rather than negative results. Nonetheless, case reports consistently suggest that hypnosis can be very helpful when treating PTSD patients. Hypnotic techniques have been reported to be effective for symptoms often associated with PTSD such as pain (Daly & Wulff, 1987; Jiranek, 1993; Richmond et al., 1996), anxiety

(Kirsch et al., 1995), and repetitive nightmares (Eichelman, 1985; Kingsbury, 1993). Also, clinical observations suggest that hypnosis can help modulate and control dissociative processes commonly found among PTSD patients (Benningfield, 1992; Brende & Benedict, 1980; Spiegel, 1981; Spiegel & Cardeña, 1990; Van der Hart, Boon, & Van Everdingen, 1990), although to date, no systematic studies have been conducted to evaluate this claim.

A Brief History of the Use of Hypnosis for Posttraumatic Conditions

Vijselaar and Van der Hart (1992) have described a very early reference (1813) to Dutch physicians using hypnosis to treat traumatic grief. Of the many French therapists using hypnosis around the turn of the century, Pierre Janet was probably the clinician who, more than anybody else, utilized it in the treatment of patients with posttraumatic conditions (see, e.g., Janet, 1898/1990; cf. van der Hart, Brown, & van der Kolk, 1989). Crocq and De Verbizier (1989), examined Janet's major clinical works, and determined that approximately half of his patients had been traumatized. Janet described the successful application of hypnotic techniques in symptom reduction, increase of ego strength, and exploration and treatment of traumatic memories. Breuer and Freud (1895/1982) also employed hypnotic techniques at the turn of the 19th century to treat patients who had reported traumatic events.

Probably the earliest time when hypnosis was widely used for the treatment of posttraumatic conditions was during World War I. Although the French reportedly prohibited the use of hypnosis in military hospitals (Southard & Fenton, 1919), the American, British, and German armies did not (see, e.g., Brown, 1919; McDougall, 1926; Myers, 1916, 1940; Nonne, 1915; Simmel, 1919; Smith & Pear, 1917). In a series of articles in *The Lancet*, Charles Myers (e.g., 1916) described the successful use of hypnosis to alleviate various symptoms of shell shock, including dissociative amnesia, sensory alterations, and speech disturbances. Later on (1940), Myers discussed the benefits and limitations of hypnosis for shell shock: "[Hypnosis] is a perfectly safe and reliable procedure to adopt, provided that it be only employed for psycho-therapeutic purposes, in particular for mental re-integration or re-synthesis of dissociated or repressed memories, and not merely for the removal of bodily 'functional' disorders by suggestion" (p. 57). In an important discussion in the *British Journal of Psychiatry*, shortly after the Great War, Myers (1920–1921), McDougall (1920–1921) and Jung (1921–1922) strongly argued against the use of abreactive techniques. All three agreed, instead, on the importance of psychological "re-integration" or "re-synthesis."

W. H. Rivers (1918) also used hypnosis occasionally and discussed the importance of having patients experience, not repress, the traumatic events, and of cognitively restructuring the patients' interpretation of the trauma ("re-education," in his terms). Southard and Fenton (1919) presented 589 case studies of shell shock, including a "comparatively long" (p. 895) series of 27 cases successfully treated with hypnosis. Although they remarked on the "miraculous" cures after hypnosis, they recommended a longer reeducation process to bring the patient back to normalcy.

Smith and Pear (1917, p. 41) provided keen observations of the objective and subjective components of posttraumatic symptomatology: "In the first place there is the vividness or intensity of the stimulus; in the second, the degree of recency; in the third, the frequency of the stimulus; and in the fourth its relevancy (to the individual's past experience and personality)." They also emphasized the use of hypnosis as an adjunct, concluding that "hypnotic treatment, when used with skill, discretion, and discrimination, has its place in the treatment of shell-shock and similar conditions. . . . Hypnosis *alone* will be of relative slight use" (original emphasis, p. 40).

Around the time of Word War II, Hadfield (1944) conducted probably the only systematic study on the use of hypnosis for shell shock, through a follow-up with 100 of the 500–600 patients he had treated. He found that 90% of patients treated with "hypno-analysis" were working full-time, 18 months after discharge. As used in this study, hypno-analysis emphasized abreaction of a traumatic memory within a psychoanalytic context. A psychiatrist who participated in the Spanish Civil War wrote that "mild hypnosis" was a useful technique for emotional and imaginative (perhaps highly hypnotizable?) patients (Mira, 1943).

World War II brought not only a change in terminology, from shell shock to war neuroses, but also a general shift from the use of hypnosis to such medications as insulin, ether, sodium-amytal, and sodium pentothal to induce sedation and sometimes abreaction. Bleckwenn started using amytal to treat neuropsychiatric disorders in 1930; Lindemann applied it for psychiatric conditions, and Sargant and Slater developed its treatment for "acute war neuroses" (Naples & Hackett, 1978; Sargant, 1942). Some authors expressed a preference for this procedure over hypnosis (see, e.g., Gillespie, 1943; Grinker & Spiegel, 1945), whereas Kardiner and Spiegel (1947) remarked that ordinary therapy, therapy with sedatives, or therapy with hypnosis, had distinct advantages and disadvantages. They concluded that, in any case, the final integration of the clinical material should occur during the ordinary state of consciousness. In their review of the literature, Brenman and Gill (1947), concluded that narcotherapy was more problematic than hypnotherapy in the induction of catharsis because it induces a "less controllable" state.

During World War II, hypnosis was partly replaced by narcotherapy, although hypnosis remained in use, especially for patients with amnesia, fugue, and conversion (see, e.g., Alpern, Carbone, & Brooks, 1946; Fischer, 1943; Kartcher & Korner, 1947; Watkins, 1949). Probably the most thorough description of hypnosis to treat war neuroses during World War II is that of John Watkins (1949, in press) of his experiences at Welch Hospital, where group hypnotic and narcotherapy techniques were used to enhance motivation and develop insight among patients with various posttraumatic symptoms.

(It is worth mentioning that the "ego therapy" hypnotic approach, created by John Watkins [for an overview, see Watkins & Watkins, 1997], has been used with patients with posttraumatic stress [see, e.g., Phillips, 1993]. The main concept, that individuals have organized systems of behavior and experience, with more or less permeable boundaries, seems useful, and many of the hypnotic techniques described by Watkins have been very influential in the treatment of combat veterans and other posttraumatic patients. Nonetheless, some aspects of "ego therapy" could be seen as unnecessarily personalizing psychophysiological states, at least among some dissociative patients [cf. International Society for the Study of Dissociation, 1994]. Systematic inquiry on this particular approach is clearly warranted.)

Kartcher and Korner (1947) reported on the use of hypnosis for approximately one-third of acute patients in a Pacific Island hospital, especially for diminishing or clearing amnesia, confusion, and other symptoms; to enhance insight; and to help with diagnosis and sedation. They remarked that, overall, hypnosis was a better procedure than narcotherapy, but that is should be considered an adjunctive rather than a comprehensive therapy.

In a more recent overview of the literature on narcotherapy, Perry and Jacobs (1982) did not mention the use of amytal interviews for PTSD, but instead recommended it for other conditions (e.g., catatonia, stupor, medically unexplained muteness) when rapid evaluation and treatment are important and patients have been unresponsive to other interventions. In our days, the pendulum seems to have swung again, with a preference for hypnosis over medications in most cases (Putnam, 1992). A number of reasons underlie this shift, including the development of modern tranquilizers, the fact that narcotics are contraindicated for some medical and psychiatric conditions (e.g., for patients with liver, kidney, or heart problems, or paranoia; Naples & Hackett, 1978), and the clinical observation that hypnotic techniques can produce effects similar to narcotherapy without its medical complications (Tinnin, personal communication, Fall 1998).

There have been occasional reports of the use of hypnosis to treat Vietnam War PTSD patients. Balson and Dempster (1980) described the treatment of 15 patients with acute or chronic "war neuroses," consisting of an evaluation and therapy preparation phase, treatment, and follow-up and consolidation. The first phase consisted of 4–10 sessions, and treatment of 8–20 sessions, with booster sessions for all but one of the patients. The framework of treatment was psychodynamic, using hypnosis to foster abreaction. The follow-up, conducted between 4 and 24 months, consisted of a clinical evaluation to determine if symptoms had returned. The authors claim that 12 out of the 15 patients had a successful treatment. More importantly, the authors measured hypnotizability at the beginning of treatment, using the HIP (Spiegel & Spiegel, 1987). Although they did not calculate inferential statistics, a binomial test for $p = 0.5$ we conducted reveals that there was a significant relationship between low hypnotizability and treatment failure ($p < 0.05$, two-tailed). These are the only data known to us that have provided support for the hypothesis that hypnotizability may be positively correlated with good treatment outcome in posttraumatic patients. Nonetheless, the results have to be qualified because the three treatment failures had a "chronic" condition, whereas the successful treatments included both "chronic" and "acute" conditions. Successful case reports with Vietnam veterans have also been provided by Brende and Benedict (1980) and Spiegel (1981). Van der Hart and Spiegel (1993) have described hypnosis-based assessment and treatment of psychotic conditions associated with trauma.

Recent Studies

The only controlled study on hypnosis for PTSD is that of Brom, Kleber, and Defares (1989), who compared hypnosis to systematic desensitization and psychodynamic psychotherapy in the treatment of 112 individuals "who were diagnosed as suffering from posttraumatic stress disorders according to DSM-III" (p. 608). The majority of these patients had experienced the loss of a loved one, whereas the remaining patients had been traumatized directly. Some participants might not have met the current DSM-IV criteria for PTSD.

Before treatment started, patients had elevated scores on many symptoms subscales, including the Impact of Event Scales (IES). The design included random assignment to an expert, and testing at baseline, end of treatment, and 3 months after treatment. There was a wait-list control group whose two testings, parallel to the baseline and end-of-therapy testing of the experimental groups, did not vary significantly. The authors found no significant difference in outcome among the three therapies evaluated (desensitization, hypnosis embedded in a behavioral frame, and psychodynamic therapy). The groups receiving hypnosis and desensitization had fewer sessions on average than the psychodynamic group ($M = 14.4$ and 15 sessions, as compared with 18.8 sessions for psychodynamic therapy). The "hypnotherapy" group had significantly lower IES scores at the end of therapy ($M = 33.7$, $SD = 22.9$) and at follow-up ($M = 31.7$, $SD = 22.0$) as compared with its pretreatment testing ($M = 50.8$, $SD = 11.7$; $p < .05$; unbiased g's of 0.94 and 1.06, respectively). The group treated with hypnosis also had significantly lower IES scores at posttest and follow-up than the control group's baseline ($M = 51.1$, $SD = 14.1$, $p < .05$; unbiased g's of 0.89 and 1.02, respectively). Brom and colleagues concluded that hypnosis and desensitization were especially useful for intrusion symptoms, whereas psychodynamic therapy was particularly useful for avoidance symptoms.

A recent meta-analysis of controlled clinical trials (Sherman, 1998) provides a comparison between the effects of the study by Brom and colleagues (1989) and those of other controlled studies. That comparison suggests that the major advantage of using hypnosis may come at follow-up, rather than at the end of the treatment (pp. 422–423), a consistent result with meta-analyses of hypnosis for conditions other than PTSD (see Kirsch, Capafons, Cardeña, & Amigó, 1999). However, with just one randomized control study on hypnosis for PTSD, any speculation is tentative. Considering that meta-analyses have indicated that hypnosis enhances the effect of other therapies, it would be informative to carry out a design that compares an effective treatment such as exposure and cognitive restructuring techniques (see, e.g., Foa, Hearst-Ikeda, & Perry, 1995), with and without hypnosis. In any case, the advice by Shalev, Bonne, and Eth (1996) to combine various forms of treatment for PTSD is worth heeding.

With respect to specific populations, the majority of recent case studies of hypnosis for PTSD have centered on victims of sexual assault and rape (Benningfield, 1992; Ebert, 1988, Manning, 1996; Phillips, 1993; Roth & Batson, 1993; Smith, 1991; Spiegel, 1989). Hypnotic treatment for victims of car and industrial accidents was reported by Kingsbury (1988) and Leung (1994). Somer (1994) discussed the use of hypnosis with Holocaust survivors, whereas Peebles (1989) described the treatment of a patient whose PTSD was brought on by failure of anesthesia during surgery.

Hypnotic techniques may be effective with individuals from other cultural groups exposed to traumatic events, as exemplified by case reports of Native American Vietnam veterans with PTSD (Krippner & Colodzin, 1989), Asian survivors of mass violence (Lee & Lu, 1989), and Hispanic burn patients (Dobkin de Ríos & Friedmann, 1987).

There are also a few case reports describing the use of hypnotic techniques on children with posttraumatic symptomatology, including those of Kluft (1991) and Rhue and Lynn (1991). The latter describe the joint use of storytelling and hypnosis. Friedrich (1991) describes four case studies, two of which included pre- and posttreatment data on the Child Behavior Checklist, which includes various symptom subscales. We conducted a t test on the subscale scores of the two children whose data were reported, which indicated that they were significantly better after treatment than before (M's = 62.2 and 75.5, respectively; Wilcoxon's $z = 3.62$, $p < .0005$; unbiased $g = 1.18$).

A number of case studies illustrate the integration of hypnotic and other techniques. Ffrench's (1995) described the use of hypnosis within a cognitive-behavioral framework. She treated a moderately hypnotizable victim of armed robbery who, in an informal evaluation, presented with acute stress disorder that was changed to a PTSD diagnosis after 4 weeks. After eight sessions, the patient's scores decreased in the Beck Depression Inventory (from 31 to 4) and the State–Trait Anxiety Inventory (from 99th percentile to 58th percentile in the state scale, and from 99th percentile to 64th percentile in the trait scale). A follow-up 1 month after treatment showed that the therapeutic gains had been maintained.

Using a single-case, multiple-baseline design, Hossack and Bentall (1991) found that two sessions each of relaxation and visual–kinesthetic dissociation (somewhat similar to the split-screen technique described earlier) produced substantial improvement in intrusive and general symptomatology in three patients, partial recovery in one, and no improvement in another. Although the authors did not call their intervention "hypnosis," they used two techniques commonly used in a hypnotic setting.

With regard to the integration of hypnosis with various specific treatments for posttraumatic conditions, there are descriptions of strategic therapy (Kingsbury, 1992), ego state therapy (Phillips, 1993; Watkins & Watkins, 1997), and systematic desensitization (Wilshire, 1996). MacHovec (1984) has written on various techniques of hypnosis for PTSD, and Torem (1992) has described the technique of age progression with two multiply traumatized patients.

Our review of the literature shows that hypnotic techniques have been used for more than 150 years in the treatment of posttraumatic conditions. Although many case reports by clinicians from different eras and countries have consistently endorsed the use of hypnosis for posttraumatic disorders, and there is one randomized control study with PTSD patients according to DSM-III criteria, randomized control studies with current diagnostic criteria are needed before hypnosis can be considered an "empirically supported treatment" for PTSD (Cardeña, 2000). The consistency of positive reports invites further systematic study.

RECOMMENDATIONS

There are compelling theoretical reasons and clinical observations to recommend the use of hypnosis as an adjunct for the treatment of PTSD, but before attempting hypnosis, it may be useful to dispel false beliefs about the nature of hypnosis, for which a set of questions evaluating patients' beliefs and attitudes about hypnosis may be valuable (Keller, 1996). Hypnosis is a procedure that may accelerate the therapeutic relationship, which may be especially useful in the age of managed care. We believe that hypnotic techniques may facilitate the important task of working through traumatic memories and increase coping skills and sense of competency (e.g., through ego-strengthening techniques). They may also be of particular help for patients who exhibit such symptoms as anxiety, dissociation, pain, and sleep problems, for which hypnosis has been effective. And, as mentioned, hypnosis has enhanced their efficacy of various therapeutic approaches

Although systematic outcome research has been limited, there is general evidence that hypnosis can facilitate, intensify, and shorten treatment

(AHCPR Level D). The consistency of clinical reports and observations, going back for almost two centuries, and the control study of Brom and colleagues (1989) suggest that hypnosis may be an effective and safe adjunctive procedure in the treatment of PTSD and other posttraumatic conditions (AHCPR Level C). We hope that a future literature review will contain controlled studies that evaluate the efficacy and effectiveness of hypnosis as an adjunct for the treatment of PTSD.

Following is a list of *contraindications* to the use of traditional hypnotic techniques:

1. In the rare cases of individuals who are refractory or minimally responsive to suggestions, hypnotic techniques may not be the best choice, because there is some evidence that hypnotizability is related to treatment outcome efficacy (Levitt, 1994; Spiegel et al., 1981, 1993). There are brief but effective measures to evaluate hypnotizability in the clinical setting, such as the HIP (Spiegel & Spiegel, 1987) and the Stanford Hypnotic Clinical Scale (Morgan & Hilgard, 1978–1979).

2. Some PTSD patients may be reluctant to undergo hypnosis, either because of religious belief or other reasons. If the resistance is not cleared after dispelling mistaken assumptions, other suggestive techniques can be tried. They include emotional self-regulation therapy (ESRT), which is done with open eyes and uses sensory recall exercises rather than a hypnotic induction (Bayot, Capafons, & Cardeña, 1997; Kirsch, Capafons, Cardeña, & Amigó, 1999).

3. For patients who have low blood pressure or are prone to fall asleep, hypnotic procedures such as "alert hand," which emphasize alertness and activity rather than relaxation, may be substituted (Cardeña, Alarcón, Capafons, & Bayot, 1998).

REFERENCES

Alpern, H. S., Carbone, H. A., & Brooks, J. T. (1946). Hypnosis as a therapeutic technique in the war neuroses. *Bulletin of the U.S. Army Medical Department, 5*, 315–324.

Balson, P. M., & Dempster, C. R. (1980). Treatment of war neuroses from Vietnam. *Comprehensive Psychiatry, 211*, 167–175.

Bayot, A., Capafons, A., & Cardeña, E. (1997). Emotional self-regulation therapy: A new and efficacious treatment for smoking. *American Journal of Clinical Hypnosis, 40*, 146–156.

Benningfield, M. F. (1992). The use of hypnosis in the treatment of dissociative patients. *Journal of Child Sexual Abuse, 1*, 17–31.

Bremner, J. D., Scott, T. M., Delaney, R. C., Southwick, S. M., Mason, J. W., Johnson, D. R., Innis, R. B., McCarthy, G., & Charney, D. S. (1993). Deficits in short-term memory in posttraumatic stress disorder. *American Journal of Psychiatry, 150*, 1015–1019.

Bremner, J. D., Southwick, S., Brett, E., Fontana, A., Rosenheck, R., & Charney, D. S. (1992). Dissociation and posttraumatic stress disorder in Vietnam combat veterans. *American Journal of Psychiatry, 149*, 328–332.

Brende, J. (1985). The use of hypnosis in posttraumatic conditions. In W. E. Kelly (Ed.), *Post-traumatic stress disorder and the war patient* (pp. 193–210). New York: Brunner/Mazel.

Brende, J., & Benedict, B. (1980). The Vietnam combat delayed stress response syndrome: Hypnotherapy of "dissociative symptoms." *American Journal of Clinical Hypnosis, 23*, 38–40.

Brenman, M., & Gill, M. M. (1947). *Hypnotherapy.* New York: International Universities Press.

Breuer, J., & Freud, S. (1982). *Studies on hysteria.* New York: Basic Books. (Original work published 1895)

Brom, D., Kleber, R. J., & Defares, P. B. (1989). Brief psychotherapy for post-traumatic stress disorder. *Journal of Consulting and Clinical Psychology, 57*, 607–612.

Brown, D., Scheflin, A., & Hammond, C. (1998). *Memory, trauma treatment, and the law.* New York: Norton.

Brown, D. P., & Fromm, E. (1986). *Hypnotherapy and hypnoanalysis.* Hillsdale, NJ: Erlbaum.

Brown, W. (1919, June 14). Hypnosis, suggestion, and dissociation. *British Medical Journal*, 734–736.

Burgess, C. A., & Kirsch, I. (1997, November). *Honest warnings mitigate the negative effects of hypnosis on memory.* Paper presented at the 48th Annual Meeting of the Society for Clinical and Experimental Hypnosis, Washington, DC.

Butler, L. D., Duran, R. E. F., Jasiukaitis, P., Koopman, C., & Spiegel, D. (1996). Hypnotizability and traumatic experience: A diathesis–stress model of dissociative symptomatology. *American Journal of Psychiatry, 153*, 41–63.

Butler, L., & Spiegel, D. (1997). Trauma and memory. In L. Dickstein, M. Riba, & J. Oldham (Eds.), *Review of psychiatry* (pp. 11–53). Washington, DC: American Psychiatric Press.

Cardeña, E. (1993). Hypnotizability and mental boundaries: A correlational study. *International Journal of Clinical and Experimental Hypnosis, 41*, 331.

Cardeña, E. (1994). The domain of dissociation. In S. J. Lynn & J. Rhue (Eds.), *Dissociation: Clinical and theoretical perspectives* (pp. 15–31). New York: Guilford Press.

Cardeña, E. (1995, August). *Alterations of consciousness in hypnosis and trauma.* Early Career Award Address at the 103rd Annual Meeting of the American Psychological Association, New York.

Cardeña. E. (1996). Dissociativity in Gulf War PTSD patients. *International Journal of Clinical and Experimental Hypnosis, 44*, 394.

Cardeña, E. (1997). The etiologies of dissociation. In S. Powers & S. Krippner (Eds.), *Broken images, broken selves* (pp. 61–87). New York: Brunner/Mazel.

Cardeña, E. (2000). Hypnosis for the treatment of trauma: A probable but not yet supported efficacious intervention. *International Journal of Clinical and Experimental Hypnosis, 48*, 221–234.

Cardeña, E., Alarcón, A., Capafons, A., & Bayot, A. (1998). Effects on suggestibility of a new method of active-alert hypnosis. *International Journal of Clinical and Experimental Hypnosis, 3*, 280–294.

Cardeña, E., Grieger, T., Staab, J., Fullerton, C., & Ursano, R. (1997). Memory disturbances in the acute aftermath of disasters. In J. D. Read & D. S. Lindsay (Eds.), *Recollection of trauma* (p. 568). New York: Plenum Press.

Cardeña, E., & Spiegel, D. (1991). Suggestibility, absorption and dissociation: An integrative model of hypnosis. In J. F. Schumaker (Ed.), *Human suggestibility: Advances in theory, research and application* (pp. 93–107). New York: Routledge.

Cardeña, E., & Spiegel, D. (1993). Dissociative reactions to the San Francisco Bay Area earthquake of 1989. *American Journal of Psychiatry, 150,* 474–478.

Christianson, S., & Loftus, E. (1987). Memory for traumatic events. *Applied Cognitive Psychology, 1,* 225–239.

Classen, C., Koopman, C., Hales, R., & Spiegel, D. (1998). Acute stress disorder as a predictor of posttraumatic stress symptoms. *American Journal of Psychiatry, 155,* 620–624.

Crocq, L., & De Verbizier, J. (1989). Le traumatisme psychologique dans l'oeuvre de Pierre Janet. *Annales Médico-Psychologiques, 147,* 983–987.

Daly, E., & Wulff, J. (1987). Treatment of a post-traumatic headache. *British Journal of Medical Psychology, 60,* 85–88.

Dobkin de Ríos, M., & Friedmann, J. K. (1987). Hypnotherapy with Hispanic burn patients. *International Journal of Clinical and Experimental Psychology, 35,* 87–94.

Dracu, C. V., Riggs, D. S., Hearst-Ikeda, D., Shoyer, B. G., & Foa, E. B. (1996). Dissociative experiences and posttraumatic stress disorder among female victims of criminal assault and rape. *Journal of Traumatic Stress, 9,* 253–267.

Dywan, J., & Bowers, K. (1983). The use of hypnosis to enhance recall. *Science, 222,* 184–185.

Ebert, B. W. (1988). Hypnosis and rape victims. *American Journal of Clinical Hypnosis, 31,* 50–56.

Edgette, J. H., & Edgette, J. S. (1995). *The handbook of hypnotic phenomena in psychotherapy.* New York: Brunner/Mazel.

Eich, E. (1995). Searching for mood dependent memory. *Psychological Science, 6,* 67–75.

Eichelman, B. (1985). Hypnotic change in combat dreams of two veterans with posttraumatic stress disorder. *American Journal of Psychiatry, 142,* 112–114.

Eisen, M. L., Anderson, A., Cooper, T., Horton, M., & Stenzel, C. (1994, August). *Repeated child abuse, parental addictions, interpersonal trust and hypnotizability.* Paper presented at the 102nd Annual Convention of the American Psychological Association, Los Angeles.

Ellenberger, H. F. (1970). *The discovery of the unconscious.* New York: Basic Books.

Erdelyi, M. H. (1994). Hypnotic hypermnesia: The empty set of hypermnesia. *International Journal of Clinical and Experimental Hypnosis, 42,* 379–390.

Ffrench, C. (1995). The meaning of trauma: Hypnosis and PTSD. *Australian Journal of Clinical and Experimental Hypnosis, 23,* 113–123.

Fischer, C. (1943). Hypnosis in treatment of neuroses due to war and to other causes. *War Medicine, 4,* 565–576.

Foa, E. B., & Hearst-Ikeda, D. (1996). Emotional dissociation in response to trauma. In L. K. Michelson & W. J. Ray (Eds.), *Handbook of dissociation* (pp. 207–226). New York: Plenum Press.

Foa, E. B., Hearst-Ikeda, D., & Perry, K. (1995). Evaluation of a brief cognitive behavioral program for the prevention of chronic PTSD in recent assault victims. *Journal of Consulting and Clinical Psychology, 63,* 948–955.

Foa, E. B., & Meadows, E. A. (1997). Psychosocial treatments for posttraumatic stress disorder: A critical review. *Annual Review of Psychology, 48,* 449–480.

Frederick, C., & McNeal, S. (1993). From strength to strength: "Inner strength" with immature ego states. *American Journal of Clinical Hypnosis, 35,* 250–256.

Friedrich, W. N. (1991). Hypnotherapy with traumatized children. *International Journal of Clinical and Experimental Hypnosis, 39*, 67–81.

Fromm, E., & Nash, M. R. (1997). *Psychoanalysis and hypnosis.* Madison, CT: International Universities Press.

Gill, M. M., & Brenman, M. (1961). *Hypnosis and related states.* New York: International Universities Press.

Gillespie, R. D. (1943). *Psychological effects of war on citizen and soldier.* London: Chapman & Hall.

Gold, J., & Cardeña, E. (1993, August). *Sexual abuse and combat-related trauma: Psychometric and phenomenological resemblance.* Paper presented at the 101st Annual Convention of the American Psychological Association, Toronto, Canada.

Grinker, R. R., & Spiegel, J. P. (1945). *Men under stress.* Philadelphia: Blakiston.

Hadfield, J. A. (1944). Treatment by suggestion and hypno-analysis. In E. Miller (Ed.), *The neuroses in war* (pp. 128–149). New York: Macmillan.

Hammond, D. C., Garver, R. B., Mutter, C. B., Crasilneck, H. B., Frischholz, E., Gravitz, M. A., Hibler, N. S., Olson, J., Scheflin, A., Spiegel, H, & Wester, W. (1995). *Clinical hypnosis and memory: Guidelines for clinicians and for forensic hypnosis.* Des Plaines, IL: American Society of Clinical Hypnosis.

Hartland, J. (1965). The value of ego-strengthening procedures prior to direct symptom removal under hypnosis. *American Journal of Clinical Hypnosis, 8*, 89–93.

Hilgard, E. (1965). *The experience of hypnosis.* New York: Harcourt.

Hossack, A., & Bentall, R. P. (1996). Elimination of posttraumatic symptomatology by relaxation and visual–kinesthetic dissociation. *Journal of Traumatic Stress, 9*, 99–110.

Hyer, L. A., Albrecht, W., Poudewyns, P. A., Woods, M. G., & Brandsma, J. (1993). Dissociative experiences of Vietnam veterans with chronic posttraumatic stress disorder. *Psychological Reports, 73*, 519–530.

International Society for the Study of Dissociation. (1994). *Guidelines for treating dissociative identity disorder.* Chicago: Author.

International Society for Traumatic Stress Studies. (1998). *Childhood trauma remembered.* Northbrook, IL: Author.

Janet, P. (1889). *L'automatisme psychologique.* Paris: F. Alcan. (Reissued: Société Pierre Janet, Paris, 1973)

Janet, P. (1898). *Névroses et idées fixes* (Vol. 1). Paris: F. Alcan. (Reissued: Société Pierre Janet, Paris, 1990)

Jaycox, L. H., Foa, E. B., & Morral, A. R. (1998). Influence of emotional engagement and habituation on exposure therapy for PTSD. *Journal of Consulting and Clinical Psychology, 66*, 185–192.

Jiranek, D. (1993). Use of hypnosis in pain management in post-traumatic stress disorder. *Australian Journal of Clinical and Experimental Hypnosis, 21*, 75–84.

Jung, C. G. (1921–22). The question of the therapeutic value of "abreaction." *British Journal of Psychiatry, 2*, 13–22.

Kardiner, A., & Spiegel, H. (1947). *War stress and neurotic illness.* New York: Hoeber.

Kartchner, F. D., & Korner, I. N. (1947). The use of hypnosis in the treatment of acute combat reactions. *American Journal of Psychiatry, 103*, 630–636.

Keller, R. F. (1996). Assessment of client beliefs and expectations of hypnosis and treatment. *Psychological Hypnosis, 5*, 808–812.

Kingsbury, S. J. (1988). Hypnosis in the treament of posttraumatic stress disorder: An isomorphic intervention. *American Journal of Clinical Hypnosis, 31*, 81–90.

Kingsbury, S. J. (1992). Strategic psychotherapy for trauma: Hypnosis and trauma in context. *Journal of Traumatic Stress, 5,* 85–96.

Kingsbury, S. J. (1993). Brief hypnotic treatment of repetitive nightmares. *American Journal of Clinical Hypnosis, 35,* 161–169.

Kirsch, I. (1994). Defining hypnosis for the public. *Contemporary Hypnosis, 11,* 142–143.

Kirsch, I. (1996). Hypnotic enhancement of cognitive-behavioral weight loss treatments: Another meta-reanalysis. *Journal of Consulting and Clinical Psychology, 64,* 517–519.

Kirsch, I., Capafons, A., Cardeña, E., & Amigó, S. (1999). Clinical hypnosis and self-regulation: An introduction. In I. Kirsch, A. Capafons, E. Cardeña, & S. Amigó (Eds.), *Clinical hypnosis and self-regulation therapy: A cognitive-behavioral perspective* (pp. 3–18). Washington, DC: American Psychological Association.

Kirsch, I., Montgomery, G., & Sapirstein, G. (1995). Hypnosis as an adjunct to cognitive behavioral psychotherapy: A meta-analysis. *Journal of Consulting and Clinical Psychology, 63,* 214–220.

Kluft, R. P. (1985). Dissociation as a response to extreme trauma. In R. P. Kluft (Ed.), *Childhood antecedents of multiple personality* (pp. 66–97). Washington, DC: American Psychiatric Press.

Kluft, R. P. (1991). Hypnosis in childhood trauma. In W. Wester & D. J. O'Grady (Eds.), *Clinical hypnosis with children* (pp. 53–68). New York: Brunner/Mazel.

Kluft, R. P. (1994). Applications of hypnotic phenomena. *Hypnos, 21,* 205–233.

Koopman, C., Classen, C., & Spiegel, D. (1996). Dissociative responses in the immediate aftermath of the Oakland/Berkeley firestorm. *Journal of Traumatic Stress, 9,* 521–540.

Krippner, S., & Colodzin, B. (1989). Multicultural methods of treating Vietnam veterans with post-traumatic stress disorder. *International Journal of Psychosomatics, 36,* 79–85.

Laurence, J. R., & Perry, C. (1983). Hypnotically created memory among highly hypnotizable subjects. *Science, 222,* 523–524.

Lee, E., & Lu, F. (1989). Assessment and treatment of Asian-American survivors of mass violence. *Journal of Traumatic Stress, 2,* 93–120.

Leung, J. (1994). Treatment of post-traumatic stress disorder with hypnosis. *Australian Journal of Clinical and Experimental Hypnosis, 22,* 87–96.

Levitt, E. E. (1994). Hypnosis in the treatment of obesity. In S. J. Lynn, J. W. Rhue, & I. Kirsch (Eds.), *Handbook of clinical hypnosis* (pp. 533–553). Washington, DC: American Psychological Association.

Lynn, S. J., Myers, B., & Malinoski, P. (1997). Hypnosis, pseudomemories, and clinical guidelines. In J. D. Read & D. Lindsay (Eds.), *Recollections of trauma* (pp. 305–336). New York: Plenum Press.

MacHovec, F. (1984). The use of brief hypnosis for posttraumatic stress disorders. *Emotional First Aid, 1,* 14–22.

Maldonado, J. R., & Spiegel D. (1994). Treatment of post traumatic stress disorder. In S. J. Lynn & J. W. Rhue (Eds.), *Dissociation: Clinical and theoretical perspectives* (pp. 215–241). New York: Guilford Press.

Maldonado, J. R., & Spiegel, D. (1998). Trauma, dissociation and hypnotizability. In R. Marmar & D. Bremmer (Eds.), *Trauma, memory and dissociation* (pp. 57–106). Washington, DC: American Psychiatric Press.

Manning, C. (1996). Treatment of trauma associated with childhood sexual assault. *Australian Journal of Clinical and Experimental Hypnosis, 24,* 36–45.

Marmar, C. R., Weiss, D. S., Schlenger, W. E., Fairbank, J. A., Jordan, B. K., Kulka, R. A.,

& Hough, R. L. (1994). Peritraumatic dissociation and posttraumatic stress in male Vietnam theater veterans. *American Journal of Psychiatry, 15,* 902–907.

Matthews, W. J., Bennett, H., Bean, W., & Gallagher, M. (1985). Indirect versus direct hypnotic suggestions—an initial investigation: A brief communication. *International Journal of Clinical and Experimental Hypnosis, 33,* 219–223.

McConkey, K. M., & Sheehan, P. W. (1995). *Hypnosis, memory, and behavior in criminal investigation.* New York: Guilford Press.

McDougall, W. (1920–1921). The revival of emotional memories and its therapeutic value (III). *British Journal of Psychology, 1,* 23–29.

McDougall, W. (1926). *An outline of abnormal psychology.* London: Methuen.

Mira, E. (1943). *Psychiatry in war.* New York: Norton.

Morgan, A. H., & Hilgard, E. R. (1978–1979). The Stanford Hypnotic Clinical Scale for Adults. *American Journal of Clinical Hypnosis, 21,* 134–147.

Muraoka, M., Komiyama, H., Hosoi, M., Mine, K., & Kubo, C. (1996). Psychosomatic treatment of phantom limb pain with posttraumatic stress disorder: A case report. *Pain, 66,* 385–388.

Myers, C. S. (1916, March 18). Contributions to the study of shell-shock (III). *Lancet,* pp. 608–613.

Myers, C. S. (1920–1921). The revival of emotional memories and its therapeutic value (II). *British Journal of Psychiatry, 1,* 20–22.

Myers, C. S. (1940). *Shell shock in France 1914–18.* Cambridge, UK: Cambridge University Press.

Naples, M., & Hackett, T. P. (1978). The Amytal interview: History and current uses. *Psychosomatics, 19,* 98–105.

Nonne, M. (1915). Zur therapeutischen Verwendung der Hypnose bei Fällen von Kriegshysterie. *Medizinische Klinik, 11,* 1391–1396.

Nash, M. R. (1992). Hypnosis, psychopathology, and psychological regression. In E. Fromm & M. R. Nash (Eds.), *Contemporary hypnosis research* (pp. 149–169). New York: Guilford Press.

Nijenhuis, E. R. S., Spinhoven, P., Van Dyck, R., van der Hart, O., & Vanderlinden, J. (1996). The development and psychometric characteristics of the Somatoform Dissociation Questionnaire (SDQ-20). *Journal of Nervous and Mental Disease, 184,* 688–694.

Nijenhuis, E. R. S., & van der Hart, O. (1999). Forgetting and reexperiencing trauma: From anesthesia to pain. In J. M. Goodwin & R. Attias (Eds.), *Splintered reflections: Images of the body in trauma* (pp. 39–65). New York: Basic Books.

Orne, M. T., Axelrad, D., Diamond, B. L., Gravitz, M. A., Heller, A., Mutter, C. B., Spiegel, D., & Spiegel, H. (1985). Scientific status of refreshing recollection by the use of hypnosis. *Journal of the American Medical Association, 253,* 1918–1923.

Overton, D. A. (1978). Major theories of state dependent learning. In B. T. Ho, D. W. Richards, & D. L. Chute (Eds.), *Drug discrimination and state dependent learning* (pp. 283–318). New York: Academic Press.

Peebles, M. J. (1989). Through a glass darkly: The psychoanalytic use of hypnosis with posttraumatic stress disorder. *International Journal of Clinical and Experimental Hypnosis, 37,* 192–206.

Pekala, R. J., Kumar, V. K., & Marcano, G. (1995). Anomalous/paranormal experiences, hypnotic susceptibility, and dissociation. *Journal of the American Society for Psychical Research, 89,* 313–332.

Perry, J. C., & Jacobs, D. (1982). Overview: Clinical applications of the amytal interview in psychiatric emergency settings. *American Journal of Psychiatry, 135*, 552–559.

Phillips, M. (1993). Turning symptoms into allies: Utilization approaches with posttraumatic symptoms. *American Journal of Clinical Hypnosis, 35*, 179–180.

Piccione, C., Hilgard, E. R., & Zimbardo, P. G. (1989). On the degree of stability of measured hypnotizability over a 25 year period. *Journal of Personality and Social Psychology, 56*, 289–295.

Putnam, F. W. (1992). Using hypnosis for therapeutic abreactions. *Psychiatric Medicine, 10*, 51–65.

Putnam, F. W., & Carlson, E. B. (1998). Hypnosis, dissociation, and trauma: Myths, metaphors, and mechanisms. In J. D. Bremner & C. R. Marmar (Eds.), *Trauma, memory, and dissociation* (pp. 27–55). Washington, DC: American Psychiatric Press.

Rhue, J., & Lynn, S. J. (1991). Storytelling, hypnosis and the treatment of sexually abused children. *International Journal of Clinical and Experimental Hypnosis, 39*, 198–214.

Richmond, K., Berman, B. M., Docherty, J. P., Holdstein, L. B., Kaplan, G., Keil, J. E., Krippner, S., Lyne, S., Mosteller, F., O'Connor, B. B., Rudy, E. B., & Schatzberg, A. F. (1996). Integration of behavioral and relaxation approaches into the treatment of chronic pain and insomnia. *Journal of the American Medical Association, 276*, 313–318.

Rivers, W. H. (1918, February 2). The repression of war experience. *Lancet*, pp. 173–177.

Ross, T. A. (1941). *Lectures on war neuroses*. London: Edward Arnold.

Roth, S. H., & Batson, R. (1993). The creative balance: The therapeutic relationship and thematic issues in trauma resolution. *Journal of Traumatic Stress, 6*, 159–177.

Sargant, W. (1942, November 19). Physical treatment of acute war neuroses. *British Medical Journal*, pp. 574–576.

Scheff, T. (1980). *Catharsis in healing, ritual, and drama*. Los Angeles: University of California Press.

Schoenberger, N., Kirsch, I., Gearan, P., Montgomery, G., & Pastyrnak, S. (1997). Hypnotic enhancement of a cognitive behavioral treatment for public speaking anxiety. *Behavior Therapy, 28*, 127–140.

Shalev, A. Y., Bonne, O., & Eth, S. (1996). Treatment of posttraumatic stress disorder: A review. *Psychosomatic Medicine, 58*, 165–182.

Shalev, A. Y., Peri, T., Canetti, L., & Schreiber, S. (1996). Predictors of PTSD in injured trauma survivors: A prospective study. *American Journal of Psychiatry, 153*, 219–225.

Sherman, J. J. (1998). Effects of psychotherapeutic treatment for PTSD: A meta-analysis of controlled clinical trials. *Journal of Traumatic Stress, 11*, 413–436.

Shor, R. E., & Orne, E. C. (1962). *Harvard Group Scale of Hypnotic Susceptibility. Manual*. Palo Alto, CA: Consulting Psychologists Press.

Simmel, E. (1919). *Kriegs-Neurosen und psychisches Trauma*. München & Leipzig: Otto Nemnich.

Smith, G. E., & Pear, T. H. (1917). *Shell shock and its lessons*. London: University Press.

Smith, M. L., Glass, G. V., & Miller, T. I. (1980). *The benefits of psychotherapy*. Baltimore: Johns Hopkins University Press.

Smith, W. H. (1991). Antecedent of posttraumatic stress disorder: Wasn't being raped enough? *International Journal of Clinical and Experimental Hypnosis, 39*, 129–133.

Somer, E. (1994). Hypnotherapy and regulated uncovering in the treatment of older survivors of Nazi persecution. *Clinical Gerontologist, 14*, 47–65.

Southard, E. E., & Fenton, N. (1919). *Shell-shock and other neuropsychiatric problems*. Boston: W. M. Leonard.

Spiegel, D. (1981). Vietnam grief work using hypnosis. *American Journal of Clinical Hypnosis, 24,* 33–40.

Spiegel, D. (1989). Hypnosis in the treatment of victims of sexual abuse. *Psychiatric Clinics of North America, 12,* 295–305.

Spiegel, D. (1992). The use of hypnosis in the treatment of PTSD. *Psychiatric Medicine, 10,* 21–30.

Spiegel, D. (1994). Hypnosis. In R. E. Hales, S. C. Yudofsky, & J. A. Talbott (Eds.), *The American Psychiatric Press textbook of psychiatry* (pp. 1115–1142). Washington, DC: American Psychiatric Press.

Spiegel, D., & Cardeña, E. (1990). New uses of hypnosis in the treatment of posttraumatic stress disorder. *Journal of Clinical Psychiatry, 51,* 39–43.

Spiegel, D., & Cardeña, E. (1991). Disintegrated experience: The dissociative disorders revisited. *Journal of Abnormal Psychology, 100,* 366–78.

Spiegel, D., Detrick, D., & Frischholz, E. (1982). Hypnotizability and psychopathology. *American Journal of Psychiatry, 139,* 431–437.

Spiegel, D., Frischholz, E. J., Fleiss, J. L., & Spiegel, H. (1993). Predictors of smoking abstinence following a single-session restructuring intervention with self-hypnosis. *American Journal of Psychiatry, 150,* 1090–1097.

Spiegel, D., Frischholz, E. J., Maruffi, B., & Spiegel, H. (1981). Hypnotic responsivity and the treatment of flying phobia. *American Journal of Clinical Hypnosis, 23,* 239–247.

Spiegel, D., Hunt, T., & Dondershine, H. E. (1988). Dissociation and hypnotizability in posttraumatic stress disorder. *American Journal of Psychiatry, 145,* 301–305.

Spiegel, H., & Spiegel, D. (1987). *Trance and treatment: Clinical uses of hypnosis.* Washington, DC: American Psychiatric Press.

Staab, J. P., Grieger, T. A., Fullerton, C. S., & Ursano, R. J. (1996). Acute stress disorder, subsequent posttraumatic stress disorder and depression after a series of typhoons. *Anxiety, 2,* 219–225.

Stutman, R. K., & Bliss, E. L. (1985). Posttraumatic stress disorder, hypnotizability, and imagery. *American Journal of Psychiatry, 142,* 741–743.

Tellegen, A., & Atkinson, G. (1974). Openness to absorbing and self-altering experiences ("absorption"), a trait related to hypnotic susceptibility. *Journal of Abnormal Psychology, 83,* 268–277.

Terr, L. (1991). Childhood traumas: An outline and overview. *American Journal of Psychiatry, 148,* 10–20.

Torem, M. S. (1992). "Back from the future": A powerful age progression technique. *American Journal of Clinical Hypnosis, 35,* 81–88.

Valdiserri, E. V., & Byrne, J. P. (1982). Hypnosis as emergency treatment for a teenage rape victim. *Hospital and Community Psychiatry, 33,* 767–769.

van der Hart, O., Boon, S., & Van Everdingen, G. B. (1990). Writing assignments and hypnosis in the treatment of traumatic memories. In M. L. Fass & D. Brown (Eds.), *Creative mastery in hypnosis and hypnoanalysis* (pp. 231–253). Hilsdale, NJ: Erlbaum.

van der Hart, O., & Brown, P. (1992). Abreaction re-evaluated. *Dissociation, 5,* 127–140.

van der Hart, O., Brown, P., & van der Kolk, B. A. (1989). Pierre Janet's treatment of post-traumatic stress. *Journal of Traumatic Stress, 2,* 379–396.

van der Hart, O., & Horst, R. (1989). The dissociation theory of Pierre Janet. *Journal of Traumatic Stress, 2,* 397–412.

van der Hart, O., & Spiegel, D. (1993). Hypnotic assessment and treatment of trauma-induced psychoses. *International Journal of Clinical and Experimental Hypnosis, 41,* 191–209.

van der Hart, O., van der Kolk, B. A., & Boon, S. (1998). Treatment of dissociative disorders. In J. D. Bremner & C. R. Marmar (Eds.), *Trauma, memory, and dissociation* (pp. 253–283). Washington, DC: American Psychiatric Press.

van der Kolk, B. A., McFarlane, A. C., & van der Hart, O. (1996). A general approach to treatment of posttraumatic stress disorder. In B. A. van der Kolk, A. C. McFarlane, & L. Weisaeth (Eds.), *Traumatic stress* (pp. 417–440). New York: Guilford Press.

van der Kolk, B. A., & van der Hart, O. (1989). Pierre Janet and the breakdown of adaptation in psychological trauma. *American Journal of Psychiatry, 146,* 1530–1540.

Vijselaar, J., & van der Hart, O. (1992). The first report of hypnotic treatment of traumatic grief: A brief communication. *International Journal of Clinical and Experimental Hypnosis, 40,* 1–6.

Watkins, J. (1949). *Hypnotherapy of war neuroses.* New York: Ronald Press.

Watkins, J. (1987). *Hypnotherapeutic techniques: Clinical hypnosis* (Vol. 1). New York: Irvington.

Watkins, J. (in press). The psychodynamic treatment of combat neuroses (PTSD) with hypnosis during World War II. *International Journal of Clinical and Experimental Hypnosis.*

Watkins, J. & Watkins, H. (1997). Overt–covert dissociation and hypnotic ego-state therapy. In L. K. Michelson & W. J. Ray (Eds.), *Handbook of dissociation* (pp. 431–448). New York: Plenum Press.

Wegner, D. M., & Pennebaker, J. W. (1993). *Handbook of mental control.* Englewood Cliffs, NJ: Prentice-Hall.

Wilshire, D. (1996). Trauma and treatment with hypnosis. *Australian Journal of Clinical and Experimental Hypnosis, 24,* 125–136.

13

Marital and Family Therapy

David S. Riggs

Clinicians have long recognized that marital and family relationships serve a potentially important role in recovery from traumatic events (Barrett & Mizes, 1988; Beiser, Turner, & Ganesan, 1989; Davidson, Hughes, Blazer, & George, 1991; Solomon, Waysman, & Mikulincer, 1990). Similarly, it has been noted that traumatic events and the aftereffects of such events can significantly affect the partners and families of those directly exposed to the trauma (see, e.g., Figley, 1985; Waysman, Mikulincer, Solomon, & Weisenberg, 1993). This recognition has led numerous authors to suggest that marital and family therapy be included, or at least considered, when developing comprehensive treatment programs for posttraumatic stress disorder (PTSD) and other psychological sequelae of trauma (see, e.g., Figley, 1988, 1989; Glynn et al., 1995). Unfortunately, despite the many suggestions about how to incorporate marital and/or family therapy into comprehensive treatment programs, no controlled studies and very few empirical data exist to address the impact of including such treatments in programs aimed at alleviating the effects of trauma. Therefore, the present review relies heavily on the theoretical and clinical writings extant in the literature on the treatment of PTSD and other trauma-related problems.

Although marital and family therapy are distinct forms of intervention with their own histories and somewhat different emphases, they share certain theoretical assumptions and characteristics (e.g., systemic focus, multiple participants). Authors who have suggested the incorporation of marital or family therapy into programs for treating posttraumatic symptoms have largely relied on the same arguments for the value of such interventions. Therefore, in the present chapter, I use the term "marital/family therapy" to refer to those arguments offered to support the utility of these interventions. In cases where arguments or suggestions appear specific to either marital therapy or family therapy, the individual terms are used.

ORIENTATION OF REVIEW

Because systematic examination of marital/family therapies for PTSD is generally lacking, the bulk of the current review focuses on the rationale and specific goals of therapies that have been suggested in the existing literature.

The body of the present review is separated into two sections, reflecting two philosophies or arguments that appear to guide much of the literature on marital/family therapy for trauma-related symptoms. The first argument for using marital/family therapy as a treatment for posttraumatic symptoms is based on the recognition that trauma and its aftereffects can impact directly and indirectly on the families and relationships of exposed individuals (Carroll, Rueger, Foy, & Dohohoe, 1985; Jordan et al., 1992; Solomon, Mikulincer, Fried, & Wosner, 1987; Waysman, Mikulincer, Solomon, & Weisenberg, 1993). The focus of these approaches is to address the systemic disruption resulting from both the trauma exposure and the manifestation of posttraumatic symptoms by one or more family members. Thus, the intervention focuses more on relieving the distress in the traumatized relationship or family than on reducing a particular individual's symptoms. The approaches suggested by this argument are clearly based on the marital and family therapies that have been developed to address issues in other populations. For the purposes of this review, I refer to these treatment approaches as *systemic* treatments.

The second argument for including marital/family therapy approaches in the treatment of trauma-related symptoms focuses on the role of the spouse and family members in helping the trauma survivor to recover from the symptoms arising from the traumatic experience (Barrett & Mizes, 1988; Beiser, Turner, Ganesan, 1989; Davidson, Hughes, Blazer, & George, 1991; Solomon, Waysman, & Mikulincer, 1990). In this formulation, the spouse or family members represent an important source of social support for the identified patient. Marital/family treatment approaches within this formulation focus on improving the efficacy of the spouse or family in providing support to the patient. This model of marital/family treatment relies heavily on educational and skills-training approaches to treatment and draws little from the marital and family therapy traditions or the theories underlying such therapies. For the purposes of this review, I refer to these treatment approaches as support treatments.

These two approaches to marital/family therapy for trauma-related symptoms incorporate different treatment techniques and different targets of intervention. Systemic treatments tend to focus on the family or relationship distress resulting from the trauma. In contrast, support treatments tend to focus on the symptoms of the individual who was exposed to the traumatic event. These distinctions also lead to differences in the methods used to evaluate the efficacy of treatment. Outcome evaluations for systemic treatments focus on improvements in family or relationship functioning, with a particular focus on communication. Support treatments, on the other hand, tend to evaluate outcome based on changes in the trauma-related symptoms of the identified patient.

Notably, these approaches are not mutually exclusive and there is some overlap in techniques and outcome evaluation. For example, authors who suggest systemic treatments recognize the role of the family in providing social support and (ideally) a safe recovery environment. Similarly, authors who approach the issue from the perspective of educating and training the spouse or family members acknowledge that trauma can significantly impact on members of the family who were not directly exposed to the trauma (or on multiple family members exposed to the same trauma). However, because the different philosophies lead to the use of different treatment approaches, units of analysis (system vs. individual) and measures of outcome success, they are summarized separately here.

THEORETICAL RATIONALE

Rationale for Systemic Treatment Approaches

In some cases (e.g., natural disasters, motor vehicle accidents, homicide of a family member), couples or entire families experience the same trauma. In these cases, the family system is likely to be disrupted, and the logic behind offering treatment to the family is relatively straightforward. However, even in cases where only one member of a family directly experiences the trauma, there is growing empirical evidence that the effect of trauma extends to the families of these individuals. For example, combat veterans with PTSD appear at risk for significant relationship problems (Card, 1987; Carroll, Rueger, Foy, & Donohoe, 1985; Jordan et al., 1992; Waysman, Mikulincer, Solomon, & Weisenberg, 1993). Veterans with PTSD tend to be less satisfied with their intimate relationships (Carroll et al., 1985; Jordan et al., 1992). Furthermore, these relationships are less cohesive and expressive, and more conflictual and violent than are the relationships of veterans without PTSD (Carroll et al., 1985; Jordan et al., 1992; Solomon et al., 1987). Partners of Vietnam veterans with PTSD also report significantly less satisfaction with their lives than do partners of Vietnam veterans without PTSD (Jordan et al., 1992). The impact of PTSD on the partners of veterans, however, may extend beyond the detrimental effect on the relationship. Beckham, Lytle, and Feldman (1996) found that psychological distress among the partners of

Vietnam veterans with PTSD was significantly associated with the severity of symptoms reported by the veteran. Also, Waysman and colleagues (1993) found that wives of Israeli veterans with PTSD reported greater psychiatric symptoms and impaired social relations compared to the wives of veterans without PTSD. The authors attributed this difference to rigid and conflictual family interactions. The presence of significant family and marital disruption provides the impetus for the application of many of the marital/family therapy approaches to posttraumatic symptoms reviewed here.

By definition, systemic treatments are focused on the responses of the marital or family system to the traumatic event rather than on the posttraumatic symptoms of one or more of the family members. Successful outcome is evaluated via improvement in family functioning (primarily on the basis of improved communication and reduced conflict). Within this framework, two intervention strategies have been suggested: (1) family therapy—focused on alleviating conflict and promoting communication with the entire family system, and (2) marital therapy—focused on aiding dyadic communication and reducing conflict between spouses.

Rationale for Supportive Treatment Approaches

The primary rationale offered for providing supportive therapy to the spouses and family members is the recognition that these persons serve as important source of social support for trauma survivors. Indeed, intimate partners typically serve as an individual's primary source of social support (Beach, Martin, Blum, & Roman, 1993; McLeod, Kessler, & Landis, 1992; Syrotuik & D'Arcy, 1984). This is particularly important given the role of social support in the recovery from a traumatic experience (Barrett & Mizes, 1988; Beiser, Turner, & Ganesan, 1989; Davidson, Hughes, Blazer, & George, 1991; Solomon, Waysman, & Mikulincer, 1990). It is argued that educating and supporting family members of trauma survivors may help them to provide more useful support to the victim, fostering recovery. Another argument for attending to the needs of family members is the suggestion that the partners of trauma survivors may knowingly or unintentionally sabotage treatment of the survivor (Foa & Rothbaum, 1998).

METHODS OF COLLECTING DATA

As the literature does not appear to include a comprehensive review of the use of marital/family therapy in the context of trauma, the current review relies exclusively on original sources. As an initial attempt to identify articles and chapters, searches were conducted using the PsycLIT and PILOTS databases. Articles and chapters that included at least one of the terms "marital therapy," "couples therapy," or "family therapy," and at least one of the terms "PTSD," "posttraumatic stress disorder," "trauma," "disaster," "combat," "rape," or "assault" were identified. This search resulted in a list of approximately 150 publications. Titles and abstracts of the identified articles were then reviewed to identify those most likely to include empirical data and/or specific descriptions of therapeutic approaches. Because issues pertaining to the treatment of children are to be addressed in a separate review, articles and chapters that addressed the treatment of childhood trauma specifically were eliminated from this review. The remaining articles and chapters were used for the bulk of the present review. In addition, relevant works cited in these articles and chapters were identified; these works were obtained if they were not already included in the review.

Although many authors have been willing to discuss the potential value of incorporating marital/family therapy into programs to treat trauma survivors, few have outlined specific techniques or approaches that might be of value in this endeavor. Instead, marital/family therapy is often included among a variety of other potential adjunct therapies that could be incorporated into a comprehensive treatment program. In many cases, the suggestion to include marital/family therapy constituted a single paragraph or brief section in a much larger discussion of treatment issues. In such cases, the authors seemed to rely on readers' existing knowledge of marital/family interventions, or they referred readers to sources for general descriptions of such approaches. For the purposes of the present review, I summarize marital/family techniques and approaches that have been suggested specifically for the treatment of trauma survivors.

SUMMARY OF THE LITERATURE

Systemic Treatment Approaches

Family Interventions

By far, the most detailed delineation of systemic family therapy with trauma survivors has been put forth by Figley (1983, 1985, 1986, 1988, 1995). This program has as its goal to "*empower* the family to overcome and learn from their ordeal and, in so doing, be more prepared to handle future adversities" (Figley, 1995, p. 351; original emphasis). Within this framework, the therapist works to foster skills that lead to the effective exchange of information, problem solving, and conflict resolution. Figley (1986, 1995) describes five phases of family therapy with traumatized families: (1) commitment to therapeutic objectives, (2) framing the problem, (3) reframing the problem, (4) developing a healing theory, and (5) closure and preparedness. This therapy, as it is conceptualized, is relatively brief, and the therapist serves primarily as a facilitator, encouraging family members to develop and refine their own skills for dealing with extreme stressors. Success is measured not only by improvement in current family functioning, but also in the family's ability to better cope with future difficulties (Figley, 1995).

Initial sessions are devoted to establishing rapport and trust between the therapist and family members, as well as defining the therapist's role as a consultant to the family. The second phase of therapy focuses on identifying and addressing the family's trauma-related difficulties. This includes examining family members' previous attempts to cope with their problems and reactions, and the obstacles to successful coping. The therapist then works to enhance family supportiveness and communication skills to enhance the exchange of ideas and self-disclosure. The family then spends time reviewing troubling memories associated with the trauma. As family members share their reactions to the trauma, a new consensus view of the trauma and the family's reaction begins to develop. Finally, the individual perspectives are brought together to form a family healing theory—or a single story about the trauma and its aftermath—that allows the family to agree on what has happened and how it will cope with a similar event in the future (Figley, 1985).

To date, there are no published controlled studies that examine the efficacy of Figley's treatment. The intervention appears to use techniques that have been developed within the tradition of family therapy with a focus on the trauma. None of the papers describing this therapy (Figley, 1983, 1985, 1986, 1988, 1995) included data from validated measures to support the efficacy of this treatment in alleviating the symptoms of PTSD or the systemic disruption associated with the disorder. None of the papers presented case studies to provide support for the efficacy of the treatment. Case descriptions were provided to illustrate the treatment techniques.

RECOMMENDATIONS

This family systems approach appears most appropriate for addressing disruptions in the family following trauma. It is recommended that it be used in conjunction with (or following) other techniques that are designed to address PTSD symptoms more specifically. *Strength of evidence: D.*

A similar, though slightly different approach to family therapy is offered by Erickson (1989), who describes an adaptation of Williamson's (1982a, 1982b) consultation process. This model of family therapy was developed to intervene in families where young adults are struggling to become independent from their parents. Thus, this treatment may be most applicable when young adults are traumatized and must then struggle to claim (or reclaim) independence from a family that becomes overprotective. Erickson (1989) applies this treatment program in the case of a family whose oldest daughter (approximately 22 years of age) had recently been raped. However, it is suggested that the approach would be equally viable with couples, extended families, and close friends. Notably, Erickson suggests that this approach to treatment is most appropriate for "those families who were functioning adequately before the [trauma] and whose dynamics and interaction can incorporate the kind of self-disclosure and supportiveness demanded" (p. 273). Erickson includes a brief description of assessment issues pertinent to this decision.

Similar to Figley's (1995) treatment described earlier, the goal of Erickson's (1989) therapy is to aid the family in integrating the trauma into the family system and thereby strengthen family cohesion through more effective communication skills and mutual support. Within this treatment program, tasks are designed to help family members to (1) recognize the trauma as a family crisis that requires a shared response, (2) recognize and respond to the needs of each family member, (3) encourage appropriate self-disclosure and affective responses, and (4) understand that the damage caused by the trauma is not irreparable. With these goals in mind, Erickson describes a treatment that incorporates both individual and family sessions to address the needs of the rape survivor and her family.

Initially, the survivor is seen separately from her family for sessions in which she is encouraged to talk about her rape experience. The family is seen (independent of the rape survivor) and each member is encouraged to share his or her reactions to the rape. In the second stage of treatment, the survivor and the family are seen in separate, small groups, where family members are again encouraged to explore the events of the rape and the impact on the family. Each family member, including the survivor, is then asked to write an unstructured "autobiography" of his or her experience of the rape. The therapist then evaluates the readiness of the family for sharing and supporting the victim as she shares her story. When it is determined that the family is ready (this may first require traditional family therapy), the victim invites the family to join her. The survivor briefly shares her story of the rape. Then, over the course of 3 consecutive days, the survivor and the family discuss in detail the events of the rape and its impact on the family.

To date, there are no published controlled studies that examine the efficacy of Erickson's (1989) treatment. There were no data presented in the paper describing this therapy to support its efficacy in the treatment of posttraumatic symptoms at the systemic or individual level. There were no clinical case studies presented to support the efficacy of this treatment. The techniques were illustrated with a case example, but no outcome data were presented.

RECOMMENDATIONS

As the only illustration of this treatment approach presented it as an adjunct to individual treatment of the rape survivor, it is recommended that the family therapy be used only in conjunction with (or following) other techniques designed to address PTSD symptoms more directly. *Strength of evidence: F.*

Harris (1991) presents a family crisis intervention model for dealing with posttraumatic reactions arising from a recent trauma. Illustrating the treatment with the case of a family whose 18-year-old daughter was raped, Harris describes a 5-step problem-solving intervention for families in crisis as a result of a trauma. These stages bear a strong resemblance to the stages delineated by Figley (1989). The first stage of therapy is devoted to building rapport and trust between the therapist and family. The second stage involves (1) identifying problems that must be addressed immediately, (2) improving communication, and (3) improving family social support. The third stage of treatment consists of examining possible solutions to the problems. With the survivor's permission, this stage includes a discussion of his or her psychological problems. In the fourth stage, the therapist works to encourage the family to take concrete action in order to solve previously identified problems. If it is deemed necessary by the family and/or therapist, the final stage of the intervention, follow-up, allows for further treatment of the family following the crisis.

To date, there are no published controlled studies that examine the efficacy of Harris's (1991) treatment. No data were presented to support the efficacy of this therapy in the treatment of posttraumatic symptoms at the systemic or individual level. One brief, clinical case study is presented to illustrate the techniques used in this treatment. One telephone contact 3 months after treatment indicated that the rape survivor felt that the rape was "no longer a major issue to be overtly confronted" and that the family "reported a general feeling of happiness and comfort with one another" (p. 206). It should be noted that the rape survivor was seen in individual therapy during the time that the family was treated, and that this individual treatment was still going on at the time of the 3-month telephone call.

RECOMMENDATIONS

As the only illustration of this treatment approach presented it as an adjunct to individual treatment of the rape survivor, it is recommended that the family therapy be used only in conjunction with (or following) other techniques designed to address PTSD symptoms more directly. *Strength of evidence: F.*

Several other authors have presented general guidelines, but not specific techniques, for conducting family therapy with trauma survivors and their families. The guidelines/goals suggested for such treatments are similar to those included in the treatment strategies described earlier and include the following:

Removing the survivor from the role of identified patient (Williams & Williams, 1980)

Educating families as to the impact of trauma (Mio & Foster, 1991; Williams & Williams, 1980)

Use of both individual and family sessions (Mio & Foster, 1991; Rosenheck & Thompson, 1986)

Developing mutual support and communication skills (Williams &
Williams, 1980)

Clarifying roles and values (Mio & Foster, 1991; Williams & Williams,
1980)

Resolving specific emotional disruptions such as rage, shame, or guilt
(Brende & Goldsmith, 1991; Williams & Williams, 1980)

Identifying and breaking patterns of trauma repetition (Brende & Goldsmith, 1991)

Marital Interventions

Several authors have proposed the use of systemic interventions that focus on
the marital dyad rather than on the larger family system. However, only two
of these studies have been presented in any detail in published works. One of
these interventions, critical interaction therapy (Johnson, Feldman, & Lubin,
1995), is conceptualized as operating within the larger framework of family
therapy as described by Figley (1989, 1995). The other, emotion-focused
marital therapy (Johnson, 1989; Johnson & Williams-Keeler, 1998), presents
the application of an established treatment for marital distress to cases where
one member of the couple has been traumatized.

Johnson, Feldman, and Lubin (1995) present a treatment approach that
focuses on general patterns of marital interaction that commonly occur
among Vietnam veteran's families. Notably, these authors present this approach as an alternative to holding disjointed sessions (i.e., separate sessions
with the veteran and family members) (Rosenheck & Thompson, 1986). At a
general level, Johnson and colleagues argue that families of trauma survivors
engage in a pattern of behavior that they term the "critical interaction." The
interaction is a "repetitive conflict that is covertly associated with the traumatic memory" (p. 404). Critical interactions are described as following a set
sequence of events. Specifically, a marital conflict arouses distressing emotions, leading the veteran to focus his attention on a parallel event from Vietnam. The veteran then withdraws from the spouse (or has an explosive rage
reaction) that effectively ends all communication between the partners. Partners experience feelings of fear, anger, and hopelessness that prevent attempts to resolve the conflict and develop their own narratives of the conflict.
The lack of resolution leads to a repetition of the conflict. Critical interaction therapy utilizes a specific series of interventions with the goals of (1)
teaching the couple about their interactional process, (2) pointing out the
connections to the veteran's traumatic experiences, (3) allowing the veteran
and spouse to stop blaming one another and, instead, to offer support, and
(4) promoting better problem solving and communication. The sequence of
interventions described by Johnson and colleagues is as follows:

The couple engages in free discussion.

A conflict occurs that results in the veteran withdrawing (this can be a subtle behavior).

The therapist inquires about the traumatic memory that the conflict elicited.

The spouse is asked to physically comfort the veteran (e.g., hold his hand).

The veteran is asked to tell the traumatic story to his spouse.

The therapist points out how this memory is related to the repetitive conflict.

The veteran is asked to check with and comfort the spouse.

The therapist reviews the sequence of events.

The therapist assigns homework to help the couple structure behavior around conflicts at home.

These behaviors are rehearsed in session.

To date, there are no published controlled studies that examine the efficacy of critical interaction therapy (Johnson et al., 1995). The paper describing this therapy did not include data to support its efficacy in the treatment of posttraumatic symptoms at the systemic or individual level. There were no clinical case studies presented to support the efficacy of this treatment. The techniques were illustrated with case examples.

RECOMMENDATIONS

This approach appears most appropriate for addressing disruptions in the relationship that are associated with trauma or posttraumatic symptoms. However, the increase in support offered by the partner may be helpful in reducing PTSD symptoms. In the absence of data to support this contention, though, it is recommended that it be used in conjunction with (or following) other techniques that are designed to address PTSD symptoms more specifically. *Strength of evidence: F.*

The second approach to conducting marital therapy with trauma survivors, emotion-focused marital therapy, represents an attempt to apply a treatment program with established efficacy for treating marital distress to the situation in which one member of the couple has experienced trauma. The techniques of emotionally focused couple therapy (EFT) are described in detail elsewhere (see Johnson, 1996; Johnson & Greenberg, 1994). Briefly stated, the approach is short term (12–20 sessions) and experiential, with a focus on "reprocessing the emotional responses that organize attachment behaviors" (Johnson & Williams-Keeler, 1998, p. 29). EFT has been divided into nine steps that Johnson and Williams-Keeler (1998) suggest parallel the three stages of therapy for trauma survivors described by McCann and Pearlman (1990). Specifically, Johnson and Williams-Keeler describe the first four steps of EFT (assessment, identification of interaction patterns, identification of underlying feelings, and labeling negative interaction patterns as the problem) as representing the stabilization phase of treatment. Steps 5 through 7 of EFT (owning the fears that arise in a relationship, acceptance of these by the partner, and asking for needs to be met appropriately) reflect the stage of building capacities in treatment of trauma survivors. Finally, Steps 8 (developing new ways of coping) and 9 (integrating new interaction patterns into the relationship) parallel the integration stage of McCann and Pearlman's (1990) treatment.

To date, there are no published controlled studies that examine the efficacy of EFT with trauma survivors. However, ample data support the efficacy of EFT with distressed couples more generally (Dunn & Schwebel, 1995; Johnson & Greenberg, 1985) and also in cases where the woman in the couple is depressed (Dessaulles, 1991). Johnson and Williams-Keeler (1998) suggest that EFT has been used effectively with couples in which one or both partners have been traumatized by abuse, violent crime, natural disasters, and combat, but they cite only one published case study (Johnson, 1989). Johnson (1989) describes the successful treatment of a couple in which the woman was an incest survivor; however, no standardized assessments were included to support this claim. The techniques of EFT, as they pertain to work with trauma survivors, are illustrated with case examples by Johnson and Johnson and Williams-Keeler.

RECOMMENDATIONS

Emotion-focused marital therapy has been found effective in reducing marital distress generally, and these papers suggest that it also is effective in the context of trauma. The increase in support offered by the partner may be helpful in reducing PTSD symptoms. However, in the absence of data to support this contention, it is recommended that it be used in conjunction with (or following) other techniques that are designed to address PTSD symptoms more specifically. *Strength of evidence: D.*

Two systematic studies of marital therapy with Vietnam combat veterans were found in the literature search. Both were conducted as dissertation studies.

Cahoon (1984) examined the impact of offering couples counseling to veterans attending rap group treatment at local Vet Centers. The couples treatment was adapted from existing marital therapy techniques and focused on communication and problem-solving skills training. Couples treatment was conducted in a group format in seven weekly sessions, lasting 90–120 minutes each. Participants were not randomly assigned to treatment groups. Participants in the couples groups were veterans recommended for the treatment by therapists at the Vet Centers. A small minority of the veterans who were approached agreed to enter couples treatment, and only nine couples completed the seven-session treatment.

Veterans who completed the seven-session course of couples therapy showed some improvement on self-reports of affective and problem-solving communication. Due to the small sample size, these changes failed to reach statistical significance ($p < .10$). The effect sizes were 0.18 and 0.41 for affective and problem-solving communication, respectively. The partners who completed the couples treatment reported statistically significant improvements ($p < .05$) in global marital distress and problem-solving communication. The effect sizes for the partners were 0.34 and 0.56 for general distress and problem-solving communication, respectively. These gains were accompanied by significant improvements in rap group leaders' ratings of coping ability (effect size = 0.72) and PTSD symptoms (effect size = 0.47).

RECOMMENDATIONS

As the only illustration of this treatment approach presented it as an adjunct to group treatment of the combat veteran, it is recommended that the marital therapy be used only in conjunction with (or following) other techniques designed to address PTSD symptoms more directly. *Strength of evidence: B.*

In the only controlled study of marital therapy with traumatized individuals, Sweany (1988) randomly assigned 14 couples, in which the male partner suffered from combat-related PTSD, to an 8-week marital treatment or a wait-list condition in which treatment was delayed by 8 weeks. The marital intervention consisted of eight weekly, 2-hour sessions based on behavioral marital therapy (Jacobson & Margolin, 1979). This intervention focused on improving communication, increasing positive marital interactions, teaching problem-solving skills, and enhancing intimacy.

The groups were compared immediately posttreatment using standardized self-report measures of marital adjustment, depression, and PTSD symptoms. Results indicated marginally significant group differences, with the treated group showing some improvement in marital satisfaction, depression, and PTSD symptoms. However, the improvements were relatively small (effect sizes were not calculable given the data reported). Changes in veterans' and partners' reports of marital satisfaction showed significant differences. Participants in the treatment group showed greater improvement that did those in the wait-list group. The treated group of veterans reported a significantly larger reduction in PTSD symptoms than did veterans in the control group. None of the other 13 comparisons reached the level of statistical significance.

RECOMMENDATIONS

Behavioral marital therapy has been found effective in reducing marital distress in general, and this result suggest that it is effective in reducing distress in the context of trauma. In addition, the study suggests that marital therapy may be effective in reducing symptoms of PTSD. However, as most of the veterans in this study received prior (or concurrent) individual or group treatment focused on PTSD symptoms, it is recommended that the marital therapy be used only in conjunction with (or following) other techniques designed to address PTSD symptoms more directly. *Strength of evidence: A.*

Supportive Treatment Approaches

Most of the suggestions to incorporate support treatments for spouses and/or family members occur in the context of treatment programs aimed at reducing symptoms of PTSD. In this context, specific suggestions for the treatment of partners and/or family members are rarely spelled out in detail. Rather, they are briefly mentioned as potential adjuncts to the treatment techniques used to address the PTSD symptoms (see, e.g., Blanchard & Hickling, 1997; Foa & Rothbaum, 1998; Keane, Albano, & Blake, 1992). When specific suggestions are made as to what should be included in such treatments, they typically include education of the family members about PTSD and/or the treatment being undertaken with the survivor, support groups, and stress management programs.

The most detailed description of supportive therapy for spouses of trauma survivors involves the Koach program developed in Israel (Solomon, Bleich, Shoham, Nardi, & Kotler, 1992a). The Koach project includes a monthlong, extensive, multifaceted treatment program with a variety of intervention approaches (the reader is referred to Solomon et al., 1992a, for a detailed account of the program). The component of interest to the present review is the inclusion of veterans' wives in the treatment. The strategies used with the wives are detailed by Rabin and Nardi (1991). Briefly, wives were invited to attend two treatment sessions prior to the initiation of the veterans' program. In the first session, the wives were allowed to discuss the difficulties that they were experiencing as a result of their husbands' symptoms. The second session involved a discussion of posttraumatic symptoms and information about basic behavioral and cognitive principals as they relate to chronic PTSD symptoms. During the first week of the veterans' treatment program, wives were invited to a daylong workshop in which cognitive coping skills, effective use of operant strategies to reinforce husbands' positive behavior, and communication skills were taught. During the second week of the veterans' program, wives and family members participated in a "family day," for which the veterans organized entertaining activities for the families. At this time, staff members held informal talks with the wives of the veterans. During the last 2 weeks of the program, veterans and their wives participated in three couples groups aimed at sharing common problems, improving communication and problem solving skills, and encouraging the veterans to view their partners as sources of support. Finally, these couples groups served as the basis for continuing self-help groups after the 1-month treatment was completed. The efficacy of the Koach program is unclear (see Solomon et al., 1992b). The effect of including the wives and the couples aspect of the treatment program has not been examined.

RECOMMENDATIONS

Among those who treat trauma survivors, there is clear, rationally derived support for the inclusion of some supportive marital/family treatment. However, the absence of any empirical support for the inclusion of such programs makes strong recommendations difficult. At this point, it would seem reasonable to include such supportive treatment when it is requested by the survivor and/or the partner and to work carefully with the survivor to coordinate such an intervention with the treatment of the survivor. *Strength of evidence: D.*

SUMMARY

In summary, the literature on the use of marital and family therapies with survivors of trauma is severely lacking. A number of authors suggest the use of such treatments to address disruption in the family or to increase the support available to the trauma survivor. These treatments tend to be skills-focused, with much emphasis placed on improving communication, problem solving, coping, and mutual support. Unfortunately, there have been very few empirical examinations of the efficacy of such interventions. Even in the clinically focused literature, careful case studies with standard assessments are lacking.

The two methodologically sound empirical examinations that were found in the literature included very small samples ($N = 9$ couples and $N = 14$ couples). However, the results of these studies suggest that marital treatment focused on communication and problem-solving skills may help reduce marital distress and (in one case) PTSD symptoms. These studies are also limited in that they included only trauma survivors identified as Vietnam combat veterans. Until the results of these studies are replicated with larger samples and survivors of other types of trauma, it remains premature to recommend marital therapy for the treatment of PTSD or PTSD-related marital distress.

Most of the other marital and family treatments described in the existing literature on the treatment of trauma survivors are limited to clinical descriptions without systematic data collection to support their efficacy. Authors provide substantial rationale for the use of family and marital therapies either alone or in conjunction with other treatments for trauma-related symptoms, and there is general consensus on the techniques that might be used in such an approach. However, the lack of empirical support for such treatments means that it is difficult to know if and when they should be used or how they should be incorporated into other treatment programs.

At the present time, then, it is recommended that marital and family therapy be used as adjuncts to treatments that are focused on the alleviation of PTSD symptoms, and not be seen themselves as treatments for PTSD. However, as marital and family disruption is frequently a problem among trauma survivors, it is also recommended that clinicians evaluate the need for marital and family therapy when treating trauma survivors. When such a need is identified, it is recommended that marital/family therapy occur concurrently or following treatment of the survivor's PTSD symptoms. Furthermore, it is recommended that marital/family therapy focus on improving communication and reducing conflict among family members. This may entail communication around current problems or issues related to the trauma and its aftermath. It is important to note that though these therapies tend to focus on functioning of the dyad or family, improvements made in these areas may contribute to alleviation of PTSD symptoms. Also, several of the techniques outlined here incorporate some form of exposure to the traumatic material (i.e., telling family members of the trauma, discussions of traumatic themes). To the extent that such discussions constitute effective exposure exercises or other reparative experiences, it is possible that marital and family interventions could serve directly to reduce PTSD symptoms.

FURTHER CONSIDERATIONS

Indications and Contraindications

The general absence of any empirical data regarding marital/family therapy for PTSD means that decision criteria for when to incorporate these therapies into other treatment programs, or the consequences of not including such treatment when it is warranted, are largely unknown. However, some guidelines can be derived from the descriptive literature reviewed here. The authors generally suggested that family therapy is most appropriate when the family system is largely intact and functioning well prior to the traumatic event. In these cases, treatment can focus on the impact of the trauma on the system. When the system is dysfunctional prior to the trauma, more traditional family therapy may be necessary prior to addressing the trauma-related problems.

Only rarely, and almost exclusively in the case of traumatized children, have authors suggested that marital/family therapy represent the exclusive, or even primary, mode of treatment for posttraumatic psychological symptoms. Rather, authors tend to suggest that marital/family therapy may be an important adjunct to other forms of treatment that are aimed more directly at alleviating posttraumatic symptoms. Even in cases where family therapy is recommended as the primary form of therapy (see, e.g., Erickson, 1989; Figley, 1995), concurrent or preliminary individual treatment with the trauma survivor is often recommended to help address specific PTSD symptoms or difficulties around initial retelling of the traumatic experience. Nothing is known about the efficacy of marital and family interventions alone as treatments for PTSD or other posttraumatic symptoms. Thus, pending further investigation, it is recommended at this time that, in the case of traumatized adults, marital and family therapy be conducted only in conjunction with (or following) treatment of the traumatized individual (or individuals) with interventions shown effective in reducing symptoms of PTSD.

Systemic approaches to marital and family intervention assume disruption in the system. Although it is clear that a large number of traumatized individuals experience difficulties in their intimate relationships (see, e.g., Jordan et al., 1992; Riggs, Byrne, Weathers, & Litz, 1998), there are clearly some families that find satisfactory ways to cope with trauma. Thus, the decision to include marital or family therapy in a treatment plan for a traumatized individual should be based on the identification of a significant disruption or dissatisfaction in the family.

The inclusion of interventions aimed at increasing spousal or family support during individually focused treatment for PTSD has not been carefully examined. It would seem clear that offering education about the disorder and information about the chosen treatment approach to a spouse or other family member could be helpful for the treatment, but it is not clear that it is necessary in all cases. Interventions with significant others should be attempted when the therapist and traumatized client agree that it might aid the treatment being conducted to address the trauma symptoms. When a therapist suspects that family members might interfere with treatment, intentionally or inadvertently, intervention with the family members also seems warranted. It is important to note that family interference may be motivated by a variety of factors and the intervention strategy chosen to address the problem should reflect the issues in the particular family in question.

Family Violence

Many authors have noted the distress that may arise as a result of living with a family member who has been traumatized (see, e.g., Figley, 1985; Waysman, Mikulincer, Solomon, & Weisenberg, 1993). Indeed, this distress represents one of the primary rationales for engaging in marital or family therapy. However, in some cases, the distress arises from the actions of the traumatized individual. For example, rates of family violence are significantly higher among veterans with PTSD than among those who do not have the disorder (Jordan et al., 1992; Riggs, Byrne, Weathers, & Litz, 1998). There is considerable debate within the field of family violence as to whether it is appropriate to conduct marital or family therapy when violence is occurring within the family or dyad. The identification of what treatment for family violence is most effective and safest remains unclear and is likely dependent on a complex decision process based on factors such as the severity and frequency of the violence as well as its objective and subjective consequences. Generally, we recommend that clinicians proceed cautiously in applying marital and family therapy in trauma-related cases where violence is occurring within the family. Consultation with professionals familiar with the treatment of family violence is highly recommended.

Separation/Lack of Commitment

Though not discussed explicitly, except in the case of emotion-focused marital therapy, the lack of commitment to the current relationship on the part of the survivor and/or the spouse is probably a contraindication for the use of marital therapy for PTSD.

Other Considerations in Using Marital/Family Therapy with Trauma Survivors

No discussion of comorbid disorders as they relate to the use of marital/family therapies was found in the literature reviewed here. However, marital therapy has been found helpful in treating depression (see, e.g., Jacobson, Dobson, Fruzetti, Schmaling, & Salusky, 1991) and alcohol abuse (see, e.g., O'Farrell, 1994) either alone or in conjunction with other interventions. As these disorders represent much of the comorbid psychopathology associated with PTSD, it is possible that such interventions will prove helpful in the case of PTSD with comorbid depression and/or substance use. However, clear recommendations regarding the use of marital or family therapy in cases of PTSD with comorbid psychological disorders are not possible at this time.

As mentioned earlier, there are times when couples or entire families experience a particular trauma simultaneously (or one member is directly traumatized, while the others are traumatized indirectly by the same event). It is also possible for more that one member of a family to have experienced distinct traumas (e.g., the wife of a combat veteran is raped). Little is written about the added complexity of conducting marital/family therapy when multiple members of the family have experienced different traumas (see Balcom, 1996, for an exception). It would seem likely that cases in which multiple family members have experienced traumas would be more amenable to the systemic interventions than to the supportive interventions described earlier. However, it may be important to incorporate some supportive techniques into the intervention. Alternatively, it might be possible to conceptualize treatment of multiply traumatized families as constituting a "group treatment" for traumatized individuals. Regardless of the specific approach taken with these cases, it is likely that the marital or family intervention will prove significantly more complicated than in cases where a single member of the family is the direct victim of trauma. As is the case with regard to comorbidity, specific recommendations about how best to treat multiply traumatized families needs further study.

FUTURE DIRECTIONS

In general, the use of marital and family interventions to address the problems of trauma survivors has been neglected by clinicians and researchers alike. Although a number of authors have suggested that addressing the needs of families and couples in the aftermath of trauma is a good idea, only a few have described specific interventions that might be used. Almost none of these approaches have been investigated empirically, and only one small, randomized, controlled clinical trial was identified in the literature. Clearly, this is an area in need of substantial research and development. Clinical experience and empirical data indicate that trauma and posttraumatic symptoms create substantial disruption in the relationships and families of survivors (see, e.g., Jordan et al., 1992; Riggs, Byrne, Weathers, & Litz, 1998). It is also apparent that social support plays an important role in recovery from trauma. Thus, it seems likely that interventions aimed at reducing family distress and improving support within the family could be very useful in alleviating some of the problems faced by trauma survivors.

The absence of systematic research as to the efficacy of marital and family therapy in treating posttraumatic difficulties means that many questions regarding the application of such treatments are also unanswered. There is little or no guidance offered regarding decisions as to when and with whom marital/family therapy should be incorporated into a treatment program (or represent the primary form of therapy) for PTSD. In the absence of clear guidelines, it would seem important for clinicians to evaluate the presence of marital/family disruption and the functional link between the family problems and the individual's PTSD symptoms. The decision to included marital/family treatment and how to combine such treatment with individual PTSD-focused treatment depends on the presumed impact of each treatment on both family and individual distress; that is, if the marital/family problems appear to result from the PTSD symptoms but would not interfere with the individual's treatment for PTSD, marital and/or family treatment might be postponed until after the individual treatment. It is possible that the alleviation of PTSD symptoms may result in improved family functioning. Alternatively, if it seems that the marital/family problems will interfere with individual treatment, the two may have to occur concurrently. A few contraindications for this approach have been suggested (e.g., family violence, lack of commitment, prior family dysfunction), but these arise from general issues related to marital and family therapy. There are no empirical data to support these contentions in the specific case of PTSD.

As might be expected based on the limited literature examining marital and family therapy for survivors of trauma, numerous questions remain regarding specific aspects of the application of these treatments. Many of these issues reflect the status of trauma-related treatments in general; however, the lack of empirical studies examining marital and family therapies leaves therapists with very little guidance for making decisions in these areas. First, it is not clear whether certain forms of marital/family therapy would be more successful than others for survivors of specific trauma; that is, would it be possible to specify marital/family treatments that are more appropriate for working with survivors of child abuse and others that would be more appropriate for families of combat veterans? Similarly, it is not clear whether some treatments would be better than others when treating a family exposed to a particular trauma compared to a family coping with the aftermath of a trauma directly experienced by a single member. It is also unclear whether the treatment of a family that was intact prior to the trauma (e.g., a family trying to cope with the daughter's rape) is different or similar to the treatment of a family that formed subsequent to a trauma (e.g., a couple that married after a veteran returned from combat). The impact of the chronicity of PTSD symptoms (i.e., whether the treatment is begun in the immediate aftermath of the trauma or years later) has also not been examined with regard to marital/family treatments.

One additional issue that arose in the context of this review has to do with the unit of analysis in terms of treatment outcome. Some approaches to marital/family therapy attend to the disruption in the dyad or family resulting from trauma, and treatment outcome is evaluated in terms of family functioning. Other approaches focus on treatment of the spouse and/or family as a means of augmenting individual treatment for PTSD, and outcome is evaluated in terms of reduced PTSD symptoms. This difference in outlook raises significant issues with regard to the direction of future research in marital/family therapy, but it may also impact on outcome evaluations of other treatment approaches. Given the strong evidence that trauma is disruptive to family functioning, it seems potentially valuable to include marital/family functioning as one measure of outcome in future treatment studies, regardless of the treatment modality under examination.

REFERENCES

Balcom, D. (1996). The interpersonal dynamics and treatment of dual trauma couples. *Journal of Marital and Family Therapy, 22*(4), 431–442.

Barrett, T. W., & Mizes, J. S. (1988). Combat level and social support in the development of posttraumatic stress disorder in Vietnam veterans. *Behavior Modification, 12,* 100–115.

Beach, S. R., Martin, J. K., Blum, T. C., & Roman, P. M. (1993). Effects of marital and co-worker relationships on negative affect: Testing the central role of marriage. *American Journal of Family Therapy, 21,* 313–323.

Beckham, J. C., Lytle, B. L., & Feldman, M. E. (1996). Caregiver burden in partners of Vietnam War veterans with posttraumatic stress disorder. *Journal of Consulting and Clinical Psychology, 64,* 1068–1072.

Beiser, M., Turner, R. J., & Ganesan, S. (1989). Catastrophic stress and factors affecting its consequences among Southeast Asian refugees. *Social Science and Medicine, 28,* 183–195.

Blanchard, E. B., & Hickling, E. J. (1997). *After the crash: Assessment and treatment of motor vehicle accident survivors.* Washington, DC: American Psychological Association.

Brende, J. O., & Goldsmith, R. (1991). Post-traumatic stress disorder in families. *Journal of Contemporary Psychotherapy, 21*(2), 115–124.

Cahoon, E. P. (1984). *An examination of relationships between post-traumatic stress disorder, marital distress, and response to therapy by Vietnam veterans.* Unpublished doctoral dissertation, University of Connecticut, Storrs, CT.

Card, J. J. (1987). Epidemiology of PTSD in a national cohort of Vietnam veterans. *Journal of Clinical Psychology, 43*(1), 6–17.

Carroll, E. M., Rueger, D. B., Foy, D. W., & Donohoe, C. P. (1985). Vietnam combat veterans with PTSD: Analysis of marital and cohabitating adjustment. *Journal of Abnormal Psychology, 94,* 329–337.

Davidson, J. R., Hughes, D., Blazer, D. G., & George, L. K. (1991). Post-traumatic stress disorder in the community: An epidemiological study. *Psychological Medicine, 21,* 713–721.

Dessaulles, A. (1991). *The treatment of clinical depression in the context of marital distress.* Unpublished doctoral dissertation, University of Ottawa, Canada.

Dunn, R. L., & Schwebel, A. I. (1995). Meta-analytic review of marital therapy outcome research. *Journal of Family Psychology, 9* (1), 58–68.

Erickson, C. A. (1989). Rape and the family. In C. R. Figley (Ed.), *Treating stress in families* (pp. 257–289). New York: Brunner/Mazel.

Figley, C. R. (1983). Catastrophes: An overview of family reactions. In C. R. Figley & H. I. McCubbin (Eds.), *Stress and the family: Volume II. Coping with catastrophe* (pp. 3–20). New York: Brunner/Mazel.

Figley, C. R. (1985). From victim to survivor: Social responsibility in the wake of catastrophe. In C. R. Figley (Ed.), *Trauma and its wake: The study and treatment of PTSD* (pp. 398–415). New York: Brunner/Mazel.

Figley, C. R. (1986). Traumatic stress: The role of the family and social support system. In C. R. Figley (Ed.), *Trauma and its wake: Volume II. The study and treatment of post-traumatic disorder* (pp. 39–54). New York: Brunner/Mazel.

Figley, C. R. (1988). A five-phase treatment of post-traumatic stress disorder in families. *Journal of Traumatic Stress, 1*(1), 127–141.

Figley, C. R. (1989). *Helping traumatized families.* San Francisco: Jossey-Bass.

Figley, C. R. (Ed.). (1995). *Compassion fatigue: Coping with secondary traumatic stress disorder in those who treat the traumatized.* New York: Brunner/Mazel.

Foa, E. B., & Rothbaum, B. O. (1998). *Treating the trauma of rape: Cognitive-behavioral therapy for PTSD.* New York: Guilford Press.

Glynn, S. M., Eth, S., Randolph, E. T., Foy, D. W., Leong, G. B., Paz, G. G., Salk, J. D., Firman, G., & Katzman, J. W. (1995). Behavioral family therapy for Vietnam combat veterans with posttraumatic stress disorder. *Journal of Psychotherapy Practice and Research, 4,* 214–223.

Harris, C. J. (1991). A family crisis–intervention model for the treatment of post-traumatic stress reaction. *Journal of Traumatic Stress, 4,* 195–207.

Jacobson, N. S., Dobson, K., Fruzetti, A. E., Schmaling, K. B., & Salusky, S. (1991). Marital therapy as a treatment for depression. *Journal of Consulting and Clinical Psychology, 59,* 547–557.

Johnson, D. R., Feldman, S. C., & Lubin, H. (1995). Critical interaction therapy: Couples therapy in combat-related posttraumatic stress disorder. *Family Process, 34,* 401–412.

Johnson, S. M. (1996). *The practice of emotionally focused marital therapy: Creating connection.* New York: Brunner/Mazel.

Johnson, S. M. (1989). Integrating marital and individual therapy for incest survivors: A case study. *Psychotherapy, 21*(6), 96–103.

Johnson, S. M., & Greenberg, L. S. (1985). Emotionally focused couples therapy: An outcome study. *Journal of Marital and Family Therapy, 11,* 313–317.

Johnson, S. M., & Greenberg, L. S. (Eds.). (1994). *The heart of the matter: Perspectives on emotion in marital therapy.* New York: Brunner/Mazel.

Johnson, S. M., & Williams-Keeler, L. (1998). Creating healing relationships for couples dealing with trauma: The use of emotionally focused marital therapy. *Journal of Marital and Family Therapy, 24,* 25–40.

Jordan, B. K., Marmar, C. R., Fairbank, J. A., Schlenger, W. E., Kulka, R. A., Hough, R. L., & Weiss, D. S. (1992). Problems in families of male Vietnam veterans with posttraumatic stress disorder. *Journal of Consulting and Clinical Psychology, 60*(6), 916–926.

Keane, T. M., Albano, A., & Blake, D. D. (1992). Current trends in the treatment of posttraumatic stress symptoms. In M. Basoglu (Ed.), *Torture and its consequences: Current treatment approaches* (pp. 363–401). Cambridge, UK: Cambridge University Press.

McCann, I. L., & Pearlman, L. A. (1990). *Psychological trauma and the adult survivor: Theory, therapy, and transformation.* New York: Brunner/Mazel.

McLeod, J. D., Kessler, R. C., & Landis, K. R. (1992). Speed of recovery from major depressive episodes in a community sample of married men and women. *Journal of Abnormal Psychology, 101,* 277–286.

Mio, J. S., & Foster, J. D. (1991). The effects of rape upon victims and families: Implications for a comprehensive family therapy. *American Journal of Family Therapy, 19*(2), 147–159.

O'Farrell, T. J. (1994). Marital therapy and spouse-involved treatment with alcoholic patients. *Behavior Therapy, 25,* 391–406.

Rabin, C., & Nardi, C. (1991). Treating post traumatic stress disorder couples: A psychoeducational program. *Community Mental Health Journal, 27*(3), 209–224.

Riggs, D. S., Byrne, C. A., Weathers, F. W., & Litz, B. T. (1998). The quality of intimate relationships of male Vietnam veterans: Problems associated with posttraumatic stress disorder. *Journal of Traumatic Stress, 11,* 87–102.

Rosenheck, R., & Thompson, J. (1986). "Detoxification" of Vietnam War trauma: A combined family–individual approach. *Family Process, 25,* 559–570.

Solomon, Z., Bleich, A., Shoham, S., Nardi, C., & Kotler, M. (1992a). The "Koach" project for treatment of combat-related PTSD: Rationale, aims, and methodology. *Journal of Traumatic Stress, 5*(2), 175–193.

Solomon, Z., Mikulincer, M., Fried, B., & Wosner, Y. (1987). Family characteristics and posttraumatic stress disorder: A follow-up of Israeli combat stress reaction casualties. *Family Process, 26*(3), 383–394.

Solomon, Z., Shalev, A., Spiro, S. E., Dolev, A., Bleich, A., Waysman, M., & Cooper, S. (1992b). Negative psychometric outcomes: Self-report measures and a follow-up telephone survey. *Journal of Traumatic Stress, 5*(2), 225–246.

Solomon, Z., Waysman, M., & Mikulincer, M. (1990). Family functioning, perceived social support, and combat-related psychopathology: The moderating role of loneliness. *Journal of Social and Clinical Psychology, 9,* 456–472.

Sweany, S. L. (1987). *Marital and life adjustment of Vietnam combat veterans: A treatment outcome study.* Unpublished doctoral dissertation, University of Washington, Seattle.

Syrotuik, J., & D'Arcy, C. (1984). Social support and mental health: Direct, protective and compensatory effects. *Social Science and Medicine, 18,* 229–236.

Waysman, M., Mikulincer, M., Solomon, Z., & Weisenberg, M. (1993). Secondary traumatization among wives of posttraumatic combat veterans: A family typology. *Journal of Family Psychology, 7,* 104–118.

Williams, C. M., & Williams, T. (1980). Family therapy for Vietnam veterans. In T. Williams (Ed.), *Post-traumatic stress disorder of the Vietnam veteran* (pp. 221–231). Cincinnati, OH: Disabled American Veterans.

Williamson, D. S. (1982a). Personal authority via termination of the intergenerational hierarchical boundary: Part II. The consultation process and the therapeutic methods. *Journal of Marital and Family Therapy, 8,* 23–37.

Williamson, D. S. (1982b). Personal authority in family experiences via termination of the intergenerational hierarchical boundary: Part III. Personal authority defined, and the power of play in the change process. *Journal of Marital and Family Therapy, 8,* 309–323.

14

Creative Therapies

David Read Johnson

AIM AND SCOPE

The aim of this chapter is to review the existent knowledge base regarding the use of the creative arts therapies in the assessment and treatment of psychological trauma. Wherever possible, summary statements are made with reference to more detailed articles, books, or reports. It is important to note that the creative arts therapies consist of several modalities, each of which is represented by separate professional associations, journals, and traditions. At times, this chapter refers to specific modalities; however, we have attempted to highlight information that is relevant to the creative arts therapies as a whole.

This chapter focuses only on the creative arts therapies, that is, art therapy, dance/movement therapy, drama therapy, music therapy, poetry and bibliotherapy, and psychodrama. The related field of body therapies (e.g., Feldenkrais, Alexander, Pesso–Boyden psychomotor, Rubenfeld synergy work, among others) are not covered but could be the focus in a future study.

METHOD OF COLLECTING DATA

The material gathered for this chapter was derived from an extensive review of existing literature on the creative arts therapies (including PILOTS and PsycLIT databases), as well as reports from two previous International Society for Traumatic Stress Studies (ISTSS) Task Forces on Curriculum. Drafts of this chapter were reviewed by members of the Creative Arts committee who represent the major modalities of the creative arts therapies (see Acknowledgments).

DEFINITION

The creative arts therapies are the intentional use by a trained therapist of art, music, dance/movement, drama, and poetry in psychotherapy, counseling, special education, or rehabilitation.

HISTORICAL BACKGROUND

Creative arts therapies, as professions, began during the 1940s, when a number of psychotherapists and artists began collaborating in the treatment of severely disturbed clients. Since many severely disturbed patients were unable to utilize the highly verbal modality of psychoanalysis, nonverbal forms of communication seemed to hold much promise. Creative arts therapies were nurtured in a few long-term psychiatric hospitals such as St. Elizabeths in Washington, D.C., the Menninger Clinic in Topeka, Kansas, and Chestnut Lodge in Rockville, Maryland, and by psychiatrists such as Jacob Moreno, who had introduced action-oriented techniques into psychotherapy in the 1930s. In addition, creative arts therapies were utilized as forms of relaxation/activities therapy for returning World War II veterans.

These factors led to the development of the field of activities therapy in the 1950s. The music therapy association formed in 1950. During the 1960s, the general atmosphere of social consciousness, the Vietnam War, and the dearth of jobs in the artistic field brought a number of artists with clinical backgrounds into the health field. By the late 1960s, the field of creative arts therapies was developing rapidly and establishing university-based graduate programs. The dance therapy association was formed in 1966, the art therapy association in 1969, and the drama and poetry therapy associations in 1979. By this time, the creative arts therapies had diversified their interests well beyond psychoanalysis into behavior therapy, special education, and humanistic approaches. These associations are now members of the National Coalition of Arts Therapy Associations (NCATA).

CLINICAL CONDITIONS SUBJECT TO TREATMENT

1. *Type of trauma.* The creative arts therapies have been utilized with all types of trauma, though there are no data to indicate whether their efficacy varies according to type of traumatic event, single versus repeated traumati-

zation, or age of traumatization (Cohen & Cox, 1995; Dayton, 1997; Golub, 1985; Kluft, 1992; Spring, 1993; Winn, 1994).

2. *State of the disorder.* Clinical experience suggests that the creative arts therapies have been helpful for clients with acute trauma, particularly children, in accessing memories of their trauma or abuse (Cattanach, 1992; Kaufman & Wohl, 1992; Malchiodi, 1990). Artwork and anatomically correct puppets are most often used (DiLeo, 1986). The creative arts therapies have been used with clients with chronic posttraumatic stress disorder (PTSD) to address associated conditions of demoralization and hopelessness (Dintino & Johnson, 1996; Feldman, Johnson, & Ollayos, 1994). No empirical studies have been conducted in these areas.

3. *Associated (comorbid) disorders.* The creative arts therapies have been used to improve associated conditions of depression and substance abuse, though no empirical studies have been conducted.

4. *Personality traits and habits.* There are few reports regarding the creative arts therapies in the treatment of personality traits among PTSD clients.

5. *Psychosocial problems.* The creative arts therapies have been applied to problems of social withdrawal, marital relationships, work adjustment, and interpersonal communication skills, though no empirical studies have been conducted.

SPECIFIC TREATMENT GOALS

The creative arts therapies have been used both to target specific PTSD symptoms and to address other, associated conditions and functional problems. Exposure-based methods address reexperiencing and avoidance symptoms, and relaxation and distraction-based methods target hyperarousal symptoms. Group interaction methods aim to improve interpersonal relationships, communication skills, and agoraphobic conditions. Creativity/performance-based methods aim to increase self-esteem and reduce shame caused by victimization.

The multifaceted aspects of creative arts therapy treatment lend themselves to broadly defined treatment goals. For example, Cruz and Essen (1994) note that many adult survivors of childhood trauma can benefit from the inclusion of arts therapies into their overall psychotherapy treatment program. Goals that can be attained by the effective use of expressive therapies include improving communication skills, sublimating impulses, experiencing feelings as a highly valuable and powerful aspect of the self, and working through traumatic material.

A number of specific approaches to the creative arts therapies (e.g., Art Therapy [Cohen, Barnes, & Rankin, 1995]; Guided Imagery and Music [Blake & Bishop, 1994]; Developmental Transformations [Dintino & Johnson, 1996]; Journal Therapy [Adams, 1997]) have been applied to the treatment of PTSD, though all are treatments for psychological distress in general. Currently, no PTSD-specific treatment approach has been designed.

TREATMENT INTERVENTIONS

Conceptual Framework

The source of therapeutic effect of the creative arts therapies has not been established through empirical research. Practitioners in the field emphasize the special role of the nonverbal form of intervention, which specifically involves the invocation of kinesthetic cues to memories or images, as well as the benefits of creativity and spontaneity to ameliorate feelings of hopelessness or worthlessness (Levy, 1995). First, the symbolic media of the arts may provide more complete access to implicit (as opposed to explicit) memory systems, as well as visual–kinesthetic schemas usually processed by the nondominant hemisphere of the brain (Johnson, 1987). It seems possible that traumatic experience and associated distorted schemas may be stored in these nonlexical forms. By more completely accessing the traumatic schema, the creative arts therapies may increase the impact of therapeutic processes such as desensitization, cognitive reframing, and habituation.

Second, the utilization of creative and socially valued artistic methods may have therapeutic effects in the psychosocial domain. Thus, Bloom (1997) recognized the importance of creative arts therapies in recovery from PTSD, by providing a safe space within which to explore feelings and a normative avenue for maintaining human health and balance, and serving a vital role in intrapsychic and interpersonal change (p. 128). Creative arts therapies may improve PTSD clients' self-esteem, hope, and prosocial behavior, and reduce feelings of shame and guilt, through the association of traumatic material to adaptive and aesthetic modes of expression.

Though, presumably, these nonverbal and creative components serve as the unique elements in this form of treatment, the creative arts therapies clearly utilize more generic therapeutic processes that overlap with many more established trauma treatments. For example, relaxation is used in nearly all forms of creative arts therapies. Exposure to traumatic memories, imagery, and cues is very common, possibly resulting in progressive desensitization during the course of treatment. Cognitive interventions, including identification of distorted cognitions, cognitive reprocessing, and reframing, are also common in these therapies. The use of journaling, writing, and storytelling are common narrative techniques used in the creative arts therapies. Finally, distraction may be a significant factor in a number of approaches that use bodily exercise, action tasks, or symbolic activities.

Conversely, more established forms of trauma therapy have incorporated creative or nonverbal techniques such as journaling, role playing, guided imagery, or muscle relaxation.

Indications

The three populations often identified that may benefit uniquely from the creative arts therapies are (1) children, (2) traumatized clients that have difficulty expressing their feelings verbally, and (3) highly intellectualized clients whose use of language obstructs their processing of traumatic material in a complete way.

The basis of the claim that creative arts therapies may benefit children lies in longstanding clinical use of art, puppets, and play in the treatment and assessment of children, particularly in the play therapy literature. For children, who are often unable to focus or attend to an abstract verbal discussion regarding their personal experiences, engagement in play is often the only, or the best, way to access these experiences (Briggs & Lehman, 1989; Cattanach, 1992; Gerber, 1994; Hagood, 1994; Wohl & Kaufman, 1985).

The theoretical and clinical basis of the claim that creative arts therapies help traumatized, inexpressive persons lies in the concept of alexithymia, about which much has been written in the trauma field (Krystal, 1988). The inability to put feelings into words appears to be relatively common in patients with posttraumatic stress disorder (Krystal, Giller, & Cicchetti, 1986). Presumably, the use of nonverbal modes of expression may allow clients to access and then process their traumatic memories more fully (Kluft, 1992).

The basis of the third claim, that creative arts therapies help intellectualized persons, appears to be largely clinical, driven by clients' satisfaction with creative expressions such as poems, paintings, music, or role plays, which they feel allow them to access a fuller emotional expression of their trauma story. These higher functioning, highly verbal clients may have voiced their frustration with the limits of other, verbal therapies. It is assumed that for these clients, verbalization and/or intellectualization has served to maintain avoidance of the traumatic material.

Techniques

Given the numerous formats and models in the creative arts therapies, it is a difficult task to describe them adequately. Nevertheless, we can outline some general principles. Generally, a typical session, whether with an individual, family, or group, begins with discussion about how clients are doing and what problems or concerns they have been facing. Then, instead of exploring these issues in continued verbal discussion, the therapist guides the client(s) into the use of a particular art medium, such as painting, dancing, role playing, or listening to or creating poetry or music, as a means of working on the presenting problem. Often, the therapist leads the client in warm-up or relaxation exercises in order to help prepare for the work and/or focus on the issue. For example, in art therapy, the client may be asked to draw or scribble randomly on a sheet of paper; in dance/movement therapy, the client may be guided through slow breathing exercises, stretching, or even running around the room; in music therapy, a client listens to music, sings a familiar song, or makes random noises on an instrument; or in poetry therapy, the client might write spontaneously for 5 minutes or listen to a poem. These activities typically open up and relax the client, and indicate to the therapist the client's mood or level of anxiety regarding the presenting issue. In the art therapy session, for example, the therapist may then ask the client to look at one of his or her scribbles to see if it reminds him or her of anything, and then to develop a picture from it. The creative arts therapist attempts to understand the client's behavior in terms of the particular art medium: for example, the art therapist attends to the expressive qualities of different colors, lines, forms, patterns, and arrangements; the dance/movement therapist assesses the meaning of different movement patterns and qualities, rhythms, energy flow, articulation of body parts, and use of space; the poetry therapist attends to word choice, images, or metaphors selected; and the music therapist attends to the rhythm, harmony, pitch, timbre, and meter of the client's musical productions. Cultural and social contexts are always taken into account in these observations. Each discipline has developed assessment procedures that give the therapist information about different clients with different diagnoses.

The main part of the session is spent participating in the arts medium. Sometimes the therapist participates with the client or group; at other times, he or she acts as a facilitator of the client's expressive activity. In psychodrama, the director rarely participates. Sometimes the problem is worked on directly; for example, when a man is having trouble with memories of physical abuse by his father, the drama therapist takes on the role of his father, and they role-play the scene. At other times, the client merely draws, sings, or improvises, and issues linked to the trauma are addressed by the therapist as they emerge. For example, the art therapist may ask the client to draw a picture of her home before the abuse began, or a picture of her feelings of anger, or her perception of her own body. The music therapist may help the client to produce an improvised song concerning the impact of the rape on her life. The client in poetry therapy may write and then read a poem written as a letter to a buddy who died in Vietnam. In each of these activities, in addition to the client's conscious thoughts that arise about the subject, it is believed that the presence of the rhythms, melodies, colors, and actions of the arts media enhances the possibility that new aspects of the situation will emerge.

Often, the therapist will leave it up to the client to make observations about how he or she is feeling and what the artwork means. At other times, the therapist may facilitate the client's exploration and questions about the poem, artwork, or song. The concretization of the client's issues in the art form tends to serve as a distancing tool, allowing the client to reflect on his or her own behavior in real-life situations. In time, some therapists point out possible underlying meanings or clarify vague, undeveloped meanings or themes evident in the client's artwork. In doing so, these therapists are guided by their particular theoretical framework, be it psychoanalytic, cognitive-behavioral, or Gestalt. In institutions, the course of therapy is determined by the client's length of stay. In outpatient situations or in private practice, creative arts therapy may be brief, such as 6–8 weeks, when a particular problem can be focused on readily, or it can be a long-term commitment of 6 months to several years.

While many creative arts therapists are familiar with several arts media, each therapist generally specializes in one or two. In most cases, the selection of the particular medium is based on the client's preference. However, in institutions where creative arts therapists work in teams, more sophisticated assessments have been developed that help the team select the best modality for the client. For example, in working with people with PTSD, such as Vietnam veterans or sexually abused women, art is often used to help elicit the visual aspect of the repressed images. Drama and poetry are often used in the later stages of therapy, when the client has become aware of the traumas and wishes to rejoin the world by expressing to others what happened (Johnson, 1987).

Appropriate Outcome Measures

Evidence from clinical case studies indicates that improvement has most often been noted in (1) the primary symptoms of PTSD and (2) global clinical improvement. Noted less often are improvements in functional behaviors or clinical service utilization.

Empirical and Clinical Evidence

There is a dearth of experimental research on the creative arts therapies, largely due to the lack of training of its practitioners in research methodology and the relatively few available doctoral-level programs in the creative arts therapies. The mean effect size of dance/movement therapy for core psychiatric symptoms, based on meta-analyses, has been estimated as 0.37 (range = 0.15 to 0.54; Cruz & Sabers, 1998). However, no estimates are available with specifically PTSD populations, nor to our knowledge have any meta-analyses been completed on the other creative arts therapy modalities. Most empirical work has been done on assessment, particularly in the discipline of art therapy. In a review of the empirical literature on graphic indicators of sexual abuse, Trowbridge (1995) found 12 studies that met inclusion criteria. In summarizing the results of this meta-analysis, she wrote, "Presence of the following indicators in children's drawings warrants further investigation: genitalia, hands omitted, fingers omitted, and head only drawn" (p. 492).

We found few empirical studies of the creative arts therapies in the treatment of trauma. Morgan and Johnson (1995) used a single-case experimental (A-B-A) design that demonstrated significant reductions in PTSD symptoms and frequency of nightmares after an art therapy intervention with four Vietnam veterans. Johnson, Lubin, James, and Hale (1997) found that the creative arts therapies produced higher rates of short-term symptom reduction among Vietnam veterans in an inpatient PTSD program, though the program, as a whole, showed modest therapeutic effects. The art therapy group was found to be most beneficial for the more symptomatic veterans.

Most of the evidence of efficacy is derived from clinical reports and case studies. Significant reductions in PTSD symptoms and other functional measures are commonly reported. The creative arts therapies have been cited as helpful in the reduction of alexithymia (Duey, 1991; James & Johnson, 1996; Loveszy, 1991), increase in emotional control (Cohen, Barnes, & Rankin, 1995; Slotoroff, 1994), improvement in interpersonal relationships (Henderson, 1991; Stember, 1978), decrease in dissociation and anxiety (Austin, 1996; Duey, 1991; Greenberg & van der Kolk, 1989; Jacobson, 1994; Mayers, 1995; Riley, 1996), decrease in nightmares (Morgan & Johnson, 1995), improved body image (Simonds, 1992), and reduction of depression (Clendenon-Wallen, 1991; Goldstein, 1990; Lindberg, 1995). In the nomenclature used for this guideline, all of these reports would be coded as Level D or E in terms of support.

Feasibility

The creative arts therapies are conducted in individual and group therapy settings in institutions and private practices. They require a minimum of specialized equipment. The major limitation to feasibility is the unavailability of fully trained therapists, particularly in rural areas.

Combinations with Other Treatment Modalities

The creative arts therapies have often been used as adjuncts to other forms of psychotherapy. For example, the treatment guidelines of the International Society for the Study of Dissociation (1997) note the following:

> Like other victims of childhood trauma, DID [dissociative identity disorder] patients are often uniquely responsive to nonverbal approaches. Art therapy, occupational therapy, sand tray therapy, movement therapy, other play therapy derivatives, and recreational therapy are reported as helpful toward achieving treatment goals, including integration. Nonverbal therapies need to be conducted by appropriately trained persons and be well timed and well integrated into the overall treatment plan. Many psychotherapists find nonverbal techniques (such as patients' drawings and journals) useful as part of ongoing psychotherapy. (p. 6)

No empirical data are available regarding the advantages of combined over single-treatment formats.

Cost to Individuals and Societies

The costs of the creative arts therapies consist only of the hourly fees of its practitioners.

Professional Organization and Credentialing

There are approximately 15,000 trained creative arts therapists in the United States, and several thousand in other parts of the world. Creative arts therapists are trained in specialized university programs, usually a 2-year master's degree (music therapists may receive training at the bachelor's or master's degree level). Several PhD programs also exist. All therapists are required to have substantial training in the particular art form before beginning their training, either in university courses or through professional experience as an artist, dancer, actor, poet, or musician. They then study psychology, learning theory, psychotherapy, group dynamics, counseling, and are trained in the special techniques, methods, and theories that have been developed to integrate the art forms with the healing process.

Creative arts therapists work in many different settings, such as psychiatric hospitals or outpatient mental health clinics, where they serve as members of the treatment team. In some locations, their services may be part of the daily activities of the treatment; in others, they are specifically referred and the client is billed separately for their services. Creative arts therapists also work in special education settings for the emotionally disturbed and mentally retarded, where they may provide one of several adjunctive services offered to clients. Increasingly, creative arts therapists are being employed in physical rehabilitation settings, working with traumatically brain injured, physically handicapped, or substance-abusing clients. Many creative arts therapists also work in nursing homes and geriatric centers. Finally, increasingly, creative arts therapists are working independently in private practice where they offer their services for a fee and act as primary therapists. Creative arts therapists are credentialed by their national associations and independent boards, and are referred to as Registered or Certified. In a number of states, they are also licensed as professional counselors. Scholarship from the faculties of over 100 universities is regularly reported in the eight professional journals in the field.

Availability of Treatment Manuals or Training Options

Information about training opportunities is available from the respective national associations (see Addresses of Professional Organizations on page 314).

Acceptability to Clients: Ethical and Gender Considerations

Clinical experience has indicated good client acceptance. Ethical practices consistent with all other mental health disciplines are advocated. Gender sensitivity is an important factor in initial screening, and requires that clients be asked if they have a preference for a male or female therapist. During ongoing treatment, there should be periodic discussion of the impact of the therapist's gender.

Known Risks and Side Effects

There are no known risks or side effects specific to the creative arts therapies when used by appropriately educated and trained therapists. Occasionally, clients may become overwhelmed when accessing traumatic material too quickly or too intensively, though these reactions can often be prevented through specific structuring techniques within the session (Cohen, 1996).

CONCLUSIONS AND RECOMMENDATIONS

Despite relatively wide use and application, the efficacy of the creative arts therapies has not been established through empirical research. Creative arts therapy professionals claim that these treatment modalities may be useful as either primary or adjunctive interventions (Johnson, 1987).

There is clinical consensus that the use of the creative arts may be helpful as an adjunct to the treatment of PTSD under the following conditions: (1) The arts therapy is conducted by a practitioner educated and trained in that approach; (2) the therapy is conducted with the permission of the client; and (3) the therapy is conducted in conjunction with other ongoing treatments and therapists. The exact source of therapeutic benefits of the creative arts therapies in the treatment of PTSD has not been identified, and is likely to be a combination of generic psychological processes (such as exposure, relaxation, and cognitive processing) and specific nonverbal and creative elements.

There is currently insufficient evidence to differentiate the impact of the creative arts therapies on PTSD, comorbid disorders, or associated disruptive symptoms. Similarly, there is insufficient evidence to make statements regarding their cost-effectiveness.

Recommendations

1. The recognition, justification, and further development of the creative arts therapies in the treatment of psychological trauma will be most fully encouraged by more sophisticated empirical inquiries using control groups and randomized assignment.

2. Creative arts therapy treatments designed as specific treatments for PTSD would presumably have heightened therapeutic effects over nonspecific creative arts therapy approaches. The design of such treatments is recommended.
3. Greater attention to the possible contraindications (e.g., types of clients, types of symptoms, stages of treatment) is needed.

ACKNOWLEDGMENTS

I gratefully acknowledge the contributions of the members of the Creative Arts Subcommittee: Kay Adams, Leslie Armeniox, Barry Cohen, Tian Dayton, and Peter Jampel.

REFERENCES

Adams, K. (1997). *The way of the journal.* Denver, CO: Sidran Press.
Austin, D. (1996). The role of improvised music in adult psychodynamic music therapy. *Music Therapy, 14,* 35–41.
Blake, R., & Bishop, S. (1994). The Bonny Method of Guided Imagery and Music in the treatment of posttraumatic stress disorder with adults in the psychiatric setting. *Music Therapy Perspectives, 12,* 125–129.
Bloom, S. (1997). *Creating sanctuary.* New York: Routledge.
Briggs, F., & Lehmann, K. (1989). Significance of children's drawings in cases of sexual abuse. *Early Child Development and Care, 47,* 131–147.
Cattanach, A. (1992). *Play therapy with abused children.* London: Jessica Kingsley.
Clendenon-Wallen, J. (1991). The use of music therapy to influence the self-confidence of adolescents who are sexually abused. *Music Therapy Perspectives, 9,* 17–31.
Cohen, B. (1996). Art and the dissociative person. In L. K. Michelson & W. J. Ray (Eds.), *Handbook of dissociation: Theoretical, empirical, and clinical perspectives* (pp. 131–149). New York: Plenum Press.
Cohen, B., Barnes, M., & Rankin, A. (1995). *Managing traumatic stress through art.* Lutherville, MD: Sidran Press.
Cohen, B., & Cox, C. (1995). *Telling without talking: Art as a window into the world of multiple personality.* New York: Norton.
Cruz, F., & Essen, L. (1994). *Adult survivors of childhood emotional, physical, and sexual abuse.* Northvale, NJ: Jason Aronson.
Cruz, R., & Sabers, D. (1998). Dance/movement therapy is more effective than previously reported. *Arts in Psychotherapy, 25,* 101–104.
Dayton, T. (1997). *Heartwounds: The impact of unresolved trauma and grief on relationships.* Deerfield Beach, FL: Health Communication.
DiLeo, C. (1986). *Children's drawings as diagnostic aids.* New York: Norton.
Dintino, C., & Johnson, D. (1996). Playing with the perpetrator: Gender dynamics in developmental drama therapy. In S. Jennings (Ed.), *Drama therapy: Theory and practice* (Vol. 3, pp. 205–220). London: Routledge.

Duey, C. J. (1991). Group music therapy for women with multiple personalities. In K. E. Bruscia (Ed.), *Case studies in music therapy*. Phoenixville, PA: Barcelona.

Feldman, S., Johnson, D., & Ollayos, M. (1994). The use of writing in the treatment of PTSD. In J. Sommer & M. Williams (Eds.), *The handbook of post-traumatic therapy* (pp. 366–385). Westport, CT: Greenwood.

Gerber, J. (1994). The use of art therapy in juvenile sex offender-specific treatment. *Arts in Psychotherapy, 21,* 367–374.

Goldstein, S. L. (1990). A songwriting assessment for hopelessness in depressed adolescents: A review of the literature and a pilot study. *Arts in Psychotherapy, 17,* 117–124.

Golub, D. (1985). Symbolic expression in post-traumatic stress disorder: Vietnam combat veterans in art therapy. *Arts in Psychotherapy, 12,* 285–296.

Greenberg, M., & van der Kolk, B. (1989). Retrieval and integration with the "painting cure." In B. van der Kolk (Ed.), *Psychological trauma* (pp. 191–216). Washington, DC: American Psychiatric Press.

Hagood, M. (1994). Diagnosis or dilemma: Drawings of sexually abused children. *Art Therapy: Journal of the American Art Therapy Association, 11*(1), 37–42.

Henderson, H. (1991). Improvised song in the treatment of a 13-year-old sexually abused girl from the Xhosa tribe in South Africa. In K. Bruscia (Ed.), *Case studies in music therapy* (pp. 57–61). Phoenixville, PA: Barcelona.

International Society for the Study of Dissociation. (1997). *Treatment guidelines.* Washington, DC: ISSD Publications.

Jacobson, M. (1994). Abreacting and assimilating traumatic, dissociated memories of MPD patients through art therapy. *Art Therapy: Journal of the American Art Therapy Association, 11*(1), 4–52.

James, M., & Johnson, D. (1996). Drama therapy for the treatment of affective expression in post-traumatic stress disorder. In D. Nathanson (Ed.), *Knowing feeling: Affect, script, and psychotherapy* (pp. 303–326). New York: Norton.

Johnson, D. (1987). The role of the creative arts therapies in the diagnosis and treatment of psychological trauma. *Arts in Psychotherapy, 14,* 7–14.

Johnson, D., Lubin, H., Hale, K., & James, M. (1997). Single session effects of treatment components within a specialized inpatient posttraumatic stress disorder program. *Journal of Traumatic Stress, 10,* 377–390.

Kaufman, B., & Wohl, A. (1992). *Casualties of childhood: A developmental perspective on sexual abuse using projective drawings.* New York: Brunner/Mazel.

Kluft, E. (Ed.). (1992). *Expressive and functional therapies in the treatment of multiple personality disorder.* Springfield, IL: C. C. Thomas.

Krystal, H. (1988). *Integration and self-healing: Affect, trauma, alexithymia.* Hillsdale, NJ: Analytic Press.

Krystal, J., Giller, E., & Cicchetti, D. (1986). Assessment of alexithymia in post-traumatic stress disorder and somatic illness: Introduction of a reliable measure. *Psychosomatic Medicine, 48,* 84–94.

Levy, F. (Ed.). (with J. Fried & F. Leventhal). (1995). *Dance and other expressive art therapies: When words are not enough.* New York and London: Routledge.

Lindberg, K. A. (1995). Songs of healing: Songwriting with an abused adolescent. *Music Therapy, 13,* 93–108.

Loveszy, R. (1991). The use of Latin music, puppetry, and visualization in reducing the physical and emotional pain of a child with severe burns. In K. Bruscia (Ed.), *Case studies in music therapy* (pp. 88–102). Phoenixville, PA: Barcelona.

Malchiodi, C. (1990). *Breaking the silence: Art therapy with children from violent homes*. New York: Brunner/Mazel.

Mayers, K. S. (1995). Songwriting as a way to decrease anxiety and distress in traumatized children. *Arts in Psychotherapy, 22,* 495–498.

Morgan, C., & Johnson, D. (1995). Use of a drawing task in the treatment of nightmares in combat-related PTSD. *Art Therapy: Journal of the American Art Therapy Association, 12*(4), 244–247.

Riley, S. (1996). An art psychotherapy stress reduction group for therapists dealing with severely abused client population. *Arts in Psychotherapy, 23,* 407–416.

Simonds, S. (1992). Sexual abuse and body image: Approaches and implications for treatment. *Arts in Psychotherapy, 19,* 289–294.

Slotoroff, C. (1994). Drumming technique for assertiveness and anger management in the short term psychiatric setting for adult and adolescent survivors of trauma. *Music Therapy Perspectives, 12,* 111–116.

Spring, D. (1993). *Shattered images: Phenomenological language of sexual trauma*. Chicago: Magnolia Street.

Trowbridge, M. M. (1995). Graphic indicators of sexual abuse in children's drawings: A review of the literature. *Arts in Psychotherapy, 22,* 485–494.

ADDRESSES OF PROFESSIONAL ORGANIZATIONS

American Art Therapy Association
1202 Allanson Road
Mundelein, IL 60060

American Dance Therapy Association
2000 Century Plaza, Suite 108
10632 Little Patuxent Parkway
Columbia, MD 21044

American Music Therapy Association
8455 Colesville Road, Suite 1000
Silver Spring, MD 20910

American Society for Group Psychotherapy and Psychodrama
301 North Harrison Street, Suite 508
Princeton, NJ 08540

National Association for Drama Therapy
5505 Connecticut Avenue, NW, Suite 280
Washington, DC 20015

National Association for Poetry Therapy
PO Box 551
Port Washington, NY 11050

II

TREATMENT GUIDELINES

15

Psychological Debriefing

Jonathan I. Bisson, Alexander McFarlane, and Suzanna Rose

DESCRIPTION

Psychological debriefing (PD) has been widely advocated for routine use following major traumatic events. Several methods of PD have been described, although most researchers consider a PD to be a single-session semistructured crisis intervention designed to reduce and prevent unwanted psychological sequelae following traumatic events by promoting emotional processing through the ventilation and normalization of reactions and preparation for possible future experiences. PD was initially described as a group intervention, one part of a comprehensive, systematic, multicomponent approach to the management of traumatic stress, but it has also been used with individuals and as a stand-alone intervention. Its purpose is to review the impressions and reactions of clients shortly after a traumatic incident. The focus of a PD is on the present reactions of those involved. Psychiatric "labeling" is avoided, and emphasis is placed on normalization. Participants are assured that they are normal people who have experienced an abnormal event.

GENERAL STRENGTH OF THE EVIDENCE

Identified studies vary greatly in their quality, but, overall, the quality of the studies, including the randomized controlled trials, is poor. The studies provide little evidence that early PD prevents psychopathology following trauma but confirm that it is well received overall by participants. Some negative outcomes following individual PD were found, but, overall, the impact of early PD was neutral when all the identified studies were considered collectively. The only positive randomized, controlled trial involved a combination of group PD and education conducted 6 to 9 months after a hurricane.

COURSE OF TREATMENT

PD has generally been described as a group intervention lasting up to a few hours shortly after (often within a few days) a traumatic event, and as one component of a critical-incident stress management program. It has also been described as a one-time intervention for individuals and as one component of a treatment package for chronic PTSD.

RECOMMENDATIONS

Indications

Given the current state of knowledge neither one-time group or individual PD can be advocated as being able to prevent the subsequent development of PTSD following a traumatic event (AHCPR Level B). However, there may be benefits to aspects of PD, particularly when it is employed as part of a comprehensive management program (AHCPR Level C). There appears to be good evidence that it is a well-received intervention for most people (AHCPR Level A), and even though it may not prevent later psychological sequelae, it may still be useful for screening, education, and support. It may be that appeals for "flexibility" in the therapeutic approach to immediate trauma survivors, such as those published following the Kings Cross Fire (Turner, Thompson, & Rosser, 1989), are important. The possibility that group PD, in combination with an educational session several months after a traumatic event, may be effective has been raised by one positive study but clearly needs replicating.

Contraindications

Some studies of individual PD have raised the possibility that the intense reexposure involved in the PD can retraumatize some individuals without allowing adequate time for habituation, resulting in a negative outcome (individual; AHCPR Level B). Therefore, if PD or any similar intervention is to be employed, it is essential that it is provided by experienced, well-trained practitioners, that it not be mandatory, and that potential participants be properly clinically assessed. If employed, the intervention should be accompanied by clear and objective evaluation procedures to ensure that it is meeting set objectives.

SUMMARY

The absence of rigorous research in this area is disappointing. It is essential that efforts be made to determine what, if anything, should be offered to individuals following traumatic events. The results of randomized, controlled trials, and other trials, indicate that one-time PD for individuals following traumatic events does not prevent the development of later psychological sequelae, but it is a well-received intervention for most people. It would be premature to conclude that PD should be discontinued as a possible intervention following trauma, but there is an urgent need for randomized, controlled trials, especially with group PD as part of a comprehensive traumatic-stress management program, and with alternative early interventions. Given the current state of knowledge, it would seem most appropriate to focus on detecting individuals who develop PTSD (perhaps through detecting acute stress disorder) or other disorders following traumatic events and offering them treatments that have been shown to work. The role of education is unclear and needs further evaluation, but basic education about trauma psychology, potential symptoms, and how to seek help without considering the traumatic event in detail may represent an appropriate way of detecting individuals who require more complex intervention.

REFERENCE

Turner, S. W., Thompson, J. A., & Rosser, R. M. (1989). The King's Cross Fire: Planning a "phase two" psychosocial response. *Disaster Management, 2,* 31–37.

SUGGESTED READINGS

Mitchell, J. T. (1983). When disaster strikes . . . *Journal of Emergency Medical Services, 8,* 36–39.

Raphael, B., Meldrum, L., & McFarlane, A. C. (1995). Does debriefing after psychological trauma work? *British Medical Journal, 310,* 1479–1480.

Rose, S. (1997). Psychological debriefing: History and methods. *Counselling—The Journal of the British Association of Counselling, 8,* 148–151.

Wessely S., Rose S., & Bisson J. (1998). *A systematic review of brief psychological interventions ("debriefing") for the treatment of immediate trauma related symptoms and the prevention of posttraumatic stress disorder* [CD-ROM]. Oxford, UK: Update Software.

16

Cognitive-Behavioral Therapy

Barbara Olasov Rothbaum, Elizabeth A. Meadows,
Patricia Resick, and David W. Foy

DESCRIPTION

Chapter 4 focused on a review of the published literature on cognitive-behavioral treatments (CBT) for posttraumatic stress disorder (PTSD). Due to the strength of the literature base in this area, only empirical studies were included. Eight different cognitive-behavioral treatments for PTSD were reviewed, along with several additional studies of treatment programs that combined one or more of these eight treatments. These included exposure therapy (EX; flooding/imaginal/*in vivo*/prolonged/directed), systematic desensitization (SD), stress inoculation training (SIT), cognitive processing therapy (CPT), cognitive therapy (CT), assertiveness training (AT), biofeedback (BIO), relaxation training (Relax), combined SIT/EX, combined EX/Relax/CT, and combined CT/EX.

GENERAL STRENGTH OF THE EVIDENCE

Table 4.1 in Chapter 4 contains many of the important details to determine the methodological rigor and thus the strength of the conclusions to be drawn from each study, including the gold standards ratings and Agency for Health Care Policy and Research (AHCPR) ratings. The reader is referred to Foa and Meadows (1997) for a critical review of treatments of PTSD, evaluating studies in terms of the gold standards for clinical studies. These gold

320

standards include (1) clearly defined target symptoms; (2) reliable and valid measures; (3) blind evaluators; (4) assessor training; (5) manualized, replicable, specific treatment programs; (6) unbiased (random) assignment to treatment; and (7) treatment adherence. Many of these CBT studies fare particularly well on this classification according to methodological rigor. The studies are discussed here by treatment technique.

Exposure Therapy

EX has been tested in 12 studies reviewed in Table 4.1, all finding positive results for this treatment with PTSD. These are also generally methodologically controlled studies, eight of which received the AHCPR Level A rating, with several meeting many of the gold standards for clinical outcome studies (Foa & Meadows, 1997); thus, the strength of evidence for exposure is very conclusive.

Five of six studies of exposure with *Vietnam veterans* found positive effects for EX, and four of these were well-controlled. Two very well-controlled studies examined EX with female *sexual assault survivors*. Both of these received AHCPR Level A ratings and met all seven of the gold standards for clinical outcome studies; thus, firm conclusions can be drawn from the results that EX was efficacious with female sexual assault survivors. Four studies examined the efficacy of EX for a *mixed variety* of traumas. Two were very well controlled and two were moderately well-controlled; all found EX helpful for these trauma survivors.

In summary, the evidence is very compelling from many well-controlled trials with a mixed variety of trauma survivors that EX is effective. In fact, no other treatment modality has such strong evidence for its efficacy. Overall, EX receives an AHCPR Level A rating.

Systematic Desensitization

Six studies have examined SD for posttrauma reactions, although most of these studies suffer from methodological problems. The only well-controlled study of SD found no difference between SD and the other treatments. In this study, however, not all of the traumas would necessarily meet DSM criteria, as many were due to loss of a loved one. Four of the remaining five studies examined SD with Vietnam veterans, although none were well controlled, and several used a large number of sessions over a long period of time. The only study of SD with female assault survivors is confounded by the fact that many were recent survivors, so their symptoms would be expected to decrease naturally with time; no PTSD measures were used; and it is not clear that all subjects participated in the same study at the same site.

In summary, although several studies have found that SD was effective in reducing posttrauma symptoms, the studies are not well controlled, and in some cases, we have reasons to doubt the validity of the findings. Thus, SD has not received strong support from well-controlled studies and has been largely abandoned in favor of exposure without relaxation and receives a Level B– or Level C+ rating.

Stress Inoculation Training

Four studies found SIT effective, but only two were well-controlled, and all were with female sexual assault survivors, leaving open the question of SIT's efficacy with other trauma populations. The strength of the two controlled studies earns SIT a Level A rating with female sexual assault survivors.

Cognitive Processing Therapy

The only published study investigating CPT received a Level B rating. CPT was effective in reducing PTSD and related symptoms in 19 female sexual assault survivors as compared to a naturally occurring wait-list control group. CPT is designed specifically for female sexual assault survivors; thus, it would have to be modified if applied to other trauma populations.

Cognitive Therapy

CT has been effective in reducing posttrauma symptoms and receives support from two controlled studies, which were rated Level A .

Assertiveness Training

Only one less well-controlled study, rated a Level B, has tested AT for PTSD, finding that it was not significantly different from comparison treatments for female sexual assault survivors. Thus, AT has not received strong support in the treatment of PTSD.

Biofeedback and Relaxation Training

Only one study has examined BIO in a controlled design. BIO was not supported, as the comparison treatment was more effective. Relax is generally included as a control treatment and has been found less effective than comparison treatments in four studies. Thus, BIO and Relax have not received support as effective treatments for PTSD and are not rated.

Combination Approaches

Combination treatments have not resulted in significantly more improvements on PTSD and related symptoms when compared to the single treatments in two well-controlled studies. They have been shown to be effective in a well-controlled study compared to an assessment control for female sexual assault survivors soon after the assault, who did not yet meet PTSD criteria, and in another study when compared to Relax. In uncontrolled investigations, combination approaches were effective for sexually abused girls and for survivors of motor vehicle accidents. In summary, combination approaches have received support as effective treatments for PTSD in studies rated Level A, but do not appear to be more effective than their single components.

COURSE OF TREATMENT

CBT techniques are generally very short-term, averaging approximately 8–12 sessions, meeting once or twice weekly.

RECOMMENDATIONS

Comparing the numbers and types of studies supporting each type of treatment, EX has the most studies and the greatest number of well-controlled studies to support its use. EX has been tested in 12 studies reviewed in Table 4.1 in Chapter 4, all finding positive results for this treatment with PTSD. These are also generally methodologically controlled studies, eight of which received the AHCPR Level A rating, with many meeting many of the gold standards for clinical outcome studies (Foa & Meadows, 1997); thus, the strength of evidence for EX is very conclusive. In one study, EX was superior to SIT and SIT/PE. Additionally, EX has been tested in a wider range of trauma populations and more studies than any of the other treatments. Thus, we strongly recommend the use of some form of EX in the treatment of PTSD unless otherwise indicated. In conclusion, the evidence is very compelling from many well-controlled trials with a mixed variety of trauma survivors that EX is effective. In fact, no other treatment modality has such strong evidence for its efficacy.

Four studies have examined the efficacy of SIT. All four studies found SIT effective, but only two were well-controlled, and all were with female sexual assault survivors, leaving open the question of SIT's efficacy with other trauma populations. The use of SIT for non-assault-related PTSD has not yet been studied, although there is no reason it should not be effective with these populations as well. CPT was found effective in one published study, but due to its focus on rape-related issues, it would be inappropriate with other trauma-related populations unless modified for use with them. CT has been effective in reducing posttrauma symptoms and receives support from two controlled studies. AT has not received strong support in the treatment of PTSD. SD, which has generally been replaced by EX, would not be recommended. BIO and Relax may be useful as anxiety management components within a more comprehensive program but have not received support as effective treatments for PTSD and are therefore not recommended.

Each of the treatments reviewed has its limitations. These include the following:

1. *Exposure.* Some trauma survivors are reluctant to confront trauma reminders and to tolerate the high anxiety and temporarily increased symptoms that sometimes accompany exposure. Thus, not everyone may be a candidate for EX. There is some preliminary evidence that EX is not effective for patients who were perpetrators of harm, especially when guilt is the primary emotion. There is also evidence that individuals whose primary emotional response is anger may not profit as much from EX as individuals whose primary emotional response is anxiety. However, EX has received the strongest evidence for PTSD; thus, it should be considered the first line of treatment unless reasons exist for ruling it out.

2. *Systematic desensitization.* Due to findings that longer exposures tend to outperform shorter ones and that the use of relaxation during EX does not enhance treatment effectiveness, SD has largely fallen out of favor relative to EX.

3. *Stress inoculation training.* To date, SIT has only been examined in female assault survivors; thus, its efficacy with regard to PTSD caused by other traumas is not known. Some SIT elements may be inappropriate for some clients (i.e., relaxation training may lead to relaxation-induced anxiety in some). Also, with its many components, therapists require a great deal of training.

4. *Cognitive processing therapy.* CPT was specifically designed as a treatment for rape victims; thus, it may be inappropriate for other trauma victims.

5. *Cognitive therapy.* CT received support from two controlled studies. This initial evidence offers some support for the use of CT for treating PTSD. However, many PTSD clinicians and researchers feel strongly that an exposure component is recommended.

6. *Assertiveness training.* At most, AT should be considered a component of treatment rather than a comprehensive treatment for PTSD.

7. *Biofeedback.* BIO has not been demonstrated to be as effective as other treatments and is not recommended as a treatment for PTSD.

8. *Relaxation.* Relax may lead to relaxation-induced anxiety in some clients and has been found to be less effective than the other therapies. Relax is not recommended as a treatment for PTSD.

9. *Combined programs.* These generally have not been shown to be better or worse than the individual treatments comprising the combination program. This may be due to the decrease in time spent on each component, but this has yet to be tested. Combined programs also are generally more complicated to deliver.

SUMMARY

The evidence is very compelling from many well-controlled trials with a mixed variety of trauma survivors that EX is effective. In fact, no other treatment modality has such strong evidence for its efficacy. SIT, CPT, CT, and combination approaches have some evidence for their efficacy, but all have some drawbacks in study populations (all female assault survivors), methodological rigor, or efficacy relative to comparison treatments.

REFERENCE

Foa, E. B., & Meadows, E. A. (1997). Psychosocial treatments for post-traumatic stress disorder: A critical review. *Annual Review of Psychology, 48,* 449–480.

SUGGESTED READINGS

The reader is referred to the following sources of information on cognitive behavioral treatment for PTSD:

Foa, E. B., & Rothbaum, B. O. (1998). *Treating the trauma of rape: Cognitive-behavioral therapy for PTSD.* New York: Guilford Press.

Follette, V. M., Ruzek, J. I., & Abueg, F. R. (Eds.). (1998). *Cognitive-behavioral therapies for trauma.* New York: Guilford Press.

Foy, D. W. (Ed.). (1992). *Treating PTSD.* New York: Guilford Press.

Resick, P. A., & Schnicke, M. K. (1993). *Cognitive processing therapy for rape victims: A treatment manual.* Newbury Park, CA: Sage.

17

Pharmacotherapy

Matthew J. Friedman, Jonathan R. T. Davidson,
Thomas A. Mellman, and Steven M. Southwick

DESCRIPTION

There are many compelling findings to suggest that a number of key psy-chobiological systems are dysregulated in PTSD patients. The strongest evi-dence shows alteration of adrenergic and hypothalamic–pituitary–adreno-corticol (HPA) mechanisms, heightened physiological reactivity, and sleep disturbances. PTSD-related abnormalities have also been detected or in-ferred about the serotonin, opioid, dopamine, thyroid, corticotropin releasing factor (CRF) and glutamatergic systems. Finally, the very frequent comorbid-ity with pharmacologically responsive disorders (e.g., major depression, pan-ic) makes pharmacotherapy an important treatment option to be considered in most cases of PTSD.

Despite these scientific findings, pharmacotherapy for PTSD has pri-marily been guided by empirical evidence that a specific drug has efficacy against a specific symptom. Indeed, at present, very few data in all psychiatric disorders, including PTSD, link psychobiological abnormalities to specific drug effects. In research (and in clinical practice), almost every class of psy-chotropic agent has been prescribed for PTSD patients. Most studies involve antidepressants: selective serotonin reuptake inhibitors (SSRIs), monoamine oxidase inhibitors (MAOIs), tricyclic antidepressants (TCAs), and other sero-tonergic agents (trazodone and nefazodone). Antiadrenergic drugs tested in-clude alpha-2 receptor agonists (clonidine and guanfacine) and the beta-receptor antagonist (propranolol). Tests of mood-stabilizing anticonvulsants (carbamazepine and valproate) were initially based on a rationale related to their antikindling properties. Other drugs tested include benzodiazepine, anxiolytics, and antipsychotic agents.

GENERAL STRENGTH OF THE EVIDENCE

The strength of the evidence is best for the different classes of antidepressant agents that have been tested in most of the randomized clinical trials on pharmacotherapy. Clinical trials without randomization or controls have been carried out on antidepressants, antiadrenergic agents, anticonvulsants, and benzodiazepines. The only evidence for other drugs is based mostly on anecdotal observations and case reports.

COURSE OF TREATMENT

Earlier research findings suggest that controlled drug trials in PTSD should last at least 8–12 weeks, because shorter trials, generally, had been ineffective. More recent and much larger scale studies (with SSRIs) have raised questions about this belief, since clinically significant PTSD symptom reduction has been observed within 2–5 weeks. This clearly is a question requiring further research.

RECOMMENDATIONS

The strength of evidence for each recommendation is indicated in parentheses (i.e., AHCPR Levels A–F). The data on which these recommendations are based can be found in Tables 5.2–5.4 in Chapter 5.

1. *SSRIs (sertraline—Level A; fluoxetine—Level A/B; paroxetine, fluvoxamine— Level B)*. SSRIs can be recommended as a first-line treatment for PTSD in nonveterans. They not only reduce DSM-IV PTSD symptoms and produce global improvement but also are effective against comorbid disorders and associated symptoms. Evidence from large, positive, double-blind trials has led to recent FDA approval for sertraline as an indicated treatment for PTSD. Therefore, it is given a full AHCPR Level A rating. Since there has only been one small, randomized clinical trial with fluoxetine published in a peer-reviewed journal, the level of evidence for fluoxetine (in Table 5.4) can only be considered an AHCPR Level A/B at this time. SSRIs have fewer side effects and greater safety than other antidepressants but may produce insomnia, agitation, gastrointestinal symptoms, and sexual dysfunction. Results

with veterans are difficult to interpret because of the severity and chronicity of PTSD in the veteran cohorts that have been tested thus far.

2. *MAOIs (phenelzine—Level A/B; moclobemide—Level B).* MAOIs have been shown to be effective for B symptoms and global improvement, with some efficacy against C symptoms; however, they have not been tested extensively. They are also effective antidepressants and antipanic agents. Of the two published, randomized clinical trials with phenelzine, one has serious methodological flaws. Therefore, the level of evidence supporting efficacy of this drug can only be Level A/B (see Table 5.4) pending further studies. Compliance with dietary restrictions is an important limitation of MAOI treatment. Furthermore, they are contraindicated in patients likely to use alcohol, illicit drugs, or certain drugs prescribed for other clinical conditions. Cardiovascular, hepatotoxic, and other side effects also must be monitored with MAOIs. If the reversible MAO-A inhibitor moclobemide proves safe and efficacious in future trials, it certainly will advance the argument that MAOIs should be considered first-line drugs for PTSD in the future.

3. *TCAs (imipramine/amitriptyline/desipramine—Level A).* TCAs have a similar spectrum of action (e.g., reduction of B symptoms and global improvement) as MAOIs but are less effective. Although they have fewer serious side effects than MAOIs, they may produce hypotension, cardiac arrhythmias, anticholinergic side effects, sedation, and arousal.

4. *Antiadrenergic agents (clonidine/guanfacine/propranolol—Level C).* Antiadrenergic agents appear to reduce arousal, reexperiencing, and possibly dissociative symptoms but have not been tested adequately in clinical trials. They are generally safe, although blood pressure and pulse rate must be monitored routinely. Special caution must be observed when prescribing these agents for patients with low blood pressure or those who receive antihypertensive medications. A few case reports suggest that tolerance is less likely to occur with guanfacine than with clonidine. Propranolol may sometimes produce depressive symptoms or psychomotor slowing.

5. *Anticonvulsants (carbamazepine/valproate—Level B).* These drugs have shown efficacy in reducing D symptoms (both drugs), B symptoms (carbamazepine only) and C symptoms (valproate only). They have been tested in several open clinical trials but not in any randomized clinical trials. Both drugs have proven efficacy in bipolar affective disorders, and both may cause significant side effects, especially carbamazepine.

6. *Benzodiazepines (alprazolam—Level B; clonazepam—Level C).* These are both effective anxiolytics and antipanic agents. Among PTSD patients, they produce their typical antiarousal effects without reducing either B or C symptoms. Discretion and caution should be exercised when considering their use for patients with past or present alcohol/drug abuse/dependency. They also may produce psychomotor slowing and exacerbate depressive symptoms. They do not appear to have any advantage over other classes of drugs and, therefore, cannot be recommended for use as monotherapy in

PTSD at this time. They may be beneficial as adjunctive treatment in time-limited treatment of disrupted sleep or for quick relief of global anxiety.

7. *Other serotonergic agents (nefazodone—Level B; trazodone—Level C; cyproheptadine/buspirone—Level F).* Open label trials with nefazodone indicate that it may improve sleep and reduce anger. Trazodone appears useful as an adjunct to SSRI treatment because it reverses SSRI-induced insomnia through a pharmacological mechanism of action that is synergistic with that of SSRIs. Since reports on the beneficial effects of both cyproheptadine and buspirone are anecdotal, there is no basis for recommending either drug at this time.

8. *Antipsychotics (thioridazine/clozapine/risperidone—Level F).* These drugs cannot be recommended for routine use in PTSD because only a few clinical anecdotes indicating their effectiveness have been published. They may ultimately prove to have a unique role for patients who are refractory to first- and second-line drugs—especially when these patients exhibit extreme hypervigilance, paranoid symptoms, agitation, or psychosis. They have many side effects, some of which are serious.

SUMMARY

The best evidence supports the use of SSRIs as first-line drugs for PTSD. There is also good evidence suggesting that MAOIs are moderately, and TCAs mildly effective agents, although both may produce adverse side effects. Evidence supporting the use of antiadrenergic and anticonvulsants agents is weak, not because of negative findings, but because there have been no randomized trials with either class of drugs. There is evidence to suggest that benzodiazepines are not useful for treating PTSD B or C symptoms. Finally, antipsychotic agents cannot be recommended for routine use, because only a few case reports have appeared in the literature.

18

Treatment of Children and Adolescents

Judith A. Cohen, Lucy Berliner, and John S. March

DESCRIPTION

Both psychosocial and medication management have been recommended, alone and in combination, for children and adolescents suffering from post-traumatic stress disorder (PTSD). Empirical evidence favors cognitive-behavioral psychotherapy over other forms of psychotherapy; support for medication management is weak at best. All recommended treatment approaches incorporate psychoeducation, including parents, usually at the beginning of treatment. While empirical evidence does not support a preference for individual, family, or group therapy, in most cases, treatment likely will be administered as individual therapy. For abused children, interventions may initially be delivered as individual therapy and subsequently be reinforced by rehearsal and practice with parents. Group therapy in the school setting may be optimal for children who have experienced a trauma that is held in common, for example, a hurricane or school shooting.

GENERAL STRENGTH OF THE EVIDENCE

As of this writing, cognitive-behavioral treatment (CBT) approaches have the strongest empirical evidence for efficacy in resolving PTSD symptoms in children. CBT may, therefore, be considered the first-line approach, either alone or in combination with other forms of treatment. Most CBT interventions for children have included exposure, cognitive-restructuring, anxiety-management, and psychoeducational components, but it is unclear from the existing research which of these components are the "active ingredients." For example, it is not yet established how much and how explicit the exposure component needs to be or how many repetitions are necessary to obtain therapeutic effect, nor even if exposure per se is necessary for symptomatic improvement. Similarly, the relative importance of including cognitive-restructuring or anxiety-management components in CBT interventions has not been adequately empirically evaluated in children. Eye movement desensitization and reprocessing (EMDR) may or may not prove useful, depending on further comparisons, especially those with CBT. Other psychosocial treatments, such as psychodynamic psychotherapy, art therapy, or group psychotherapy, are supported by anecdotal evidence but cannot on this basis be recommended as first-line treatments for pediatric PTSD. Similarly, due to the lack of adequate empirical data, clinicians must rely on expert judgment to determine the appropriateness and type of psychopharmacological interventions.

COURSE OF TREATMENT

There currently is no empirical evidence regarding the optimal length of treatment with psychotherapy or medication. As with most cognitive-behavioral interventions for pediatric mental disorders, the majority of empirically evaluated interventions have been between 8 and 16 sessions. However, some children, especially those who have experienced prolonged victimization, poor premorbid adjustment, comorbid conditions, or exhibit chronic PTSD with predominantly dissociative features, may require much longer interventions. Given that PTSD may be a chronic waxing and waning condition in children, judgment based on clinical improvement of symptoms and success in achieving appropriate developmental expectations should determine treatment length.

RECOMMENDATIONS

Children and adolescents with PTSD would likely benefit from treatment focused on PTSD symptomatology. Of the available treatments, CBT has the most empirical support and is therefore the initial treatment of choice. The particular format of CBT should be dictated by the nature of the trauma, with specific protocols focused on either abuse or sudden trauma. Because of their favorable side-effect profile and evidence supporting effectiveness in treating both depressive and anxiety disorders, SSRIs often are the first psychotropic medication chosen for treating pediatric PTSD, especially when dictated by SSRI-responsive comorbidity. Clonidine may be helpful for some children and adolescents with prominent hyperarousal symptoms, especially elevated startle responses.

Recommendation ratings are as follows:

Psychotherapy

CBT	A
EMDR	B–C
Dynamic psychotherapy	D
Debriefing	E
Family psychotherapy	E
Group psychotherapy	E
Art therapy	E

Medication

Propranolol	B
Clonidine	C
SSRI	D
TCA	D
Buspirone	D
Atypical antidepressants	E

Contraindications are those common to each treatment class and/or unique to each treatment.

SUGGESTED READINGS

Cohen, J. A., & Mannarino, A. P. (1996). A treatment outcome study for sexually abused preschool children: Initial findings. *Journal of the American Academy of Child and Adolescent Psychiatry, 35*(1), 42–50.

Deblinger, E., & Heflin, A. H. (1996). *Cognitive behavioral interventions for treating sexually abused children.* Thousand Oaks, CA: Sage.

Donnelly, C. L., Amaya-Jackson, L., & March, J. S. (1999). Psychopharmacology of pediatric posttraumatic stress disorder. *Journal of Child Adolescent Psychopharmacology, 9*(3), 203–220.

March, J., Amaya-Jackson, L., Murry, M., & Schulte, A. (1998). Cognitive-behavioral psychotherapy for children and adolescents with post-traumatic stress disorder following a single incident stressor. *Journal of the American Academy of Child and Adolescent Psychiatry, 37*(6), 585–593.

March, J., Amaya-Jackson, J., & Pynoos, R. (1996). Pediatric post-traumatic stress disorder. In J. Weiner (Ed.), *Textbook of child and adolescent psychiatry* (2nd ed.). Washington, DC: American Psychiatric Press.

19

Eye Movement Desensitization and Reprocessing

Claude M. Chemtob, David F. Tolin, Bessel A. van der Kolk, and Roger K. Pitman

DESCRIPTION

Eye movement desensitization and reprocessing (EMDR) is an integrative treatment for posttraumatic stress disorder (PTSD) during which the patient is asked to hold in mind a disturbing image, an associated negative cognition, and bodily sensations associated with a traumatic memory, while tracking the clinician's moving finger in front of his or her visual field. Variations of the procedure are repeated until distressing aspects of the traumatic memory are reduced and more adaptive cognitions emerge regarding the trauma. Similar procedures are used to install alternate positive cognitions, coping strategies, and adaptive behaviors.

GENERAL STRENGTH OF THE EVIDENCE

EMDR was found to be an efficacious treatment for PTSD. It is assigned an AHCPR Level A/B rating. The "A" component of the rating means that based upon a review of seven published, randomized, controlled studies with overall large effect sizes, one of which included children, EMDR was found to be more efficacious for PTSD than wait-list, routine-care, and active-treatment controls. The "B" component means that additional studies that employ more extensive controls addressing the limitations of studies to date, and that compare EMDR to other focused PTSD treatments, are needed to establish the highest level of confidence in EMDR's efficacy. As might be expected for any treatment, the evidence is stronger for the beneficial effect of EMDR on persons with single-event civilian trauma than on multiply traumatized, treatment-refractory, chronically ill war veterans.

Support for EMDR's therapeutic efficacy does not necessarily imply support for the postulated role of eye movements. Randomized dismantling studies provide little support for the hypothesis that eye movements are critical to the effects of EMDR. However, methodological limitations of these studies preclude a final conclusion regarding this issue.

RECOMMENDATIONS

Clinical

It is important to distinguish the treatment of a single traumatic memory from the treatment of PTSD. In some early studies, this distinction was not preserved, leading to unrealistic expectations. Accordingly, the number of EMDR sessions administered should be consistent with the complexity of the trauma and the number of traumatic memories. Studies demonstrating EMDR's efficacy have generally followed the structured procedure articulated by Shapiro (1995). Clinical deviations from this procedure may not produce comparable results.

Because inadequate data are available to identify which patients will respond more or less favorably to EMDR compared to other treatments, choice of treatment modality needs to be based upon such considerations as the skills and training of the therapist, and the desires of the patient. Few data are available regarding any contraindications to EMDR. Patients with comorbid psychopathology (e.g., substance abuse) or acute problems (e.g., suicide potential) should undergo comprehensive clinical assessment and treatment planning, with careful consideration of all options. Skill in EMDR supplements but does not replace general skill in the treatment of psychopathology.

Research

Additional, properly designed dismantling studies need to be conducted in order to identify what components of EMDR are beneficial. Comparisons of EMDR with other PTSD treatments in larger samples are indicated. These should not be restricted to efficacy, but should also examine other important issues such as treatment efficiency, and patient tolerance and comfort, which may be advantages of this therapy. EMDR's apparent efficacy in the treatment of childhood PTSD needs to be further explored. EMDR has resulted in the training of an extraordinarily large number of practitioners in a highly standardized treatment modality. These therapists represent a potentially valuable resource for mounting large, field-based effectiveness trials of PTSD treatment.

REFERENCE

Shapiro, F. (1995). *Eye movement desensitization and reprocessing: Basic principles, protocols, and procedures.* New York: Guilford Press.

SUGGESTED READINGS

Feske, U. (1998). Eye movement desensitization and reprocessing treatment for posttraumatic stress disorder. *Clinical Psychology: Science and Practice, 5,* 171–181.
Lohr, J. M., Tolin, D. F., & Lilienfeld, S. O. (1998). Efficacy of eye movement desensitization and reprocessing: Implications for behavior therapy. *Behavior Therapy, 29,* 123–156.
Shapiro, F. (1999). Eye movement desensitization and reprocessing (EMDR) and the anxiety disorders: Clinical and research implications of an integrated psychotherapy treatment. *Journal of Anxiety Disorders, 13,* 35–67.
Spector, J., & Read, J. (1999). The current status of eye movement desensitization and reprocessing (EMDR). *Clinical Psychology and Psychotherapy, 6,* 165–174.

20

Group Therapy

David W. Foy, Shirley M. Glynn, Paula P. Schnurr,
Mary K. Jankowski, Melissa S. Wattenberg, Daniel S. Weiss,
Charles R. Marmar, and Fred D. Gusman

DESCRIPTION

Group therapy for posttraumatic stress disorder (PTSD) offers cohesion, encouragement, and support from other members in either "covering" or "uncovering" formats, referring to whether or not traumatic experiences are addressed directly. Representative of the "covering" strategy is *supportive group therapy*, designed to maintain interpersonal comfort and to provide a context that orients members toward current coping. There are two "uncovering" types. *Psychodynamic groups* aim to give each member new understanding about what it means to have been exposed to trauma and to have reacted the way he or she did, and about the continuing issues presented by the experience. *Cognitive-behavioral group therapy* emphasizes systematic, prolonged exposure and cognitive restructuring applied to members' traumatic experiences.

GENERAL STRENGTH OF THE EVIDENCE

Group treatment for PTSD is recommended as potentially effective based upon consistent positive evidence from 14 recent studies. The Levels of Evidence range from 2 studies using randomized control designs (AHCPR Level A), and 5 studies using nonrandomized control designs (AHCPR Level B), to

7 studies using single-group designs in which pre–post differences were examined (AHCPR Level C). Evidence does not presently favor one type over the others.

COURSE OF TREATMENT

"Uncovering" groups are more likely to be conducted as "closed" or cohort groups, while supportive groups are amenable to an "open" format in which members can be added after the group begins. Groups are typically planned for a duration of 10–52 weeks, are composed of six to eight members and two therapists, last 90 minutes per session, and meet on a weekly basis.

RECOMMENDATIONS

The Level of Evidence for the specific indications and contraindications that follow is anecdotal (Level D), taken from experienced clinicians' judgment and rationally derived criteria used in the 14 published studies on group therapy. Indications for group therapy include flexible personal schedule, in order to meet group at appointed times; ability to establish interpersonal trust with other group members and leaders; prior group experience, including 12-step groups; completion of a preparatory course of individual therapy; not actively suicidal or homicidal; shares similar traumatic experiences with other group members; compatible for gender, ethnicity, and sexual orientation with other members; willingness to abide by rules of group confidentiality; not severely paranoid or sociopathic; stable living arrangements.

Contraindications for group therapy include active psychosis; severe organicity or limited cognitive capacity; pending litigation or compensation-seeking.

For assignment to "uncovering" groups, the following indications apply: Individual can tolerate high anxiety arousal or other strong affects; no active suicidality or homicidality; substance abuse or other comorbidities are under control; individual accepts rationale for trauma uncovering work; willingness to self-disclose personal traumatic experiences; no current life crises.

SUMMARY

Since the inception of PTSD as a diagnostic entity almost 20 years ago, less than 20 published studies have evaluated group therapy techniques for treating the disorder. Despite methodological limitations of these studies, positive treatment outcomes were reported, lending general support for the use of group therapy with trauma survivors. While three distinct types of group therapy are represented in the literature, treatment outcome findings do not presently favor a particular type.

SUGGESTED READINGS

Alexander, P. C., Neimeyer, R. A., Follette, V. M., Moore, M. K., & Harter, S. (1989). A comparison of group treatments of women sexually abused as children. *Journal of Consulting and Clinical Psychology, 57,* 479–483.

Resick, P. A., & Schnicke, M. K. (1992). Cognitive processing therapy for sexual assault victims. *Journal of Consulting and Clinical Psychology, 60,* 748–756.

Tutty, L. M., Bidgood, B. A., & Rothery, M. A. (1993). Support groups for battered women: Research on their efficacy. *Journal of Family Violence, 8,* 325–343.

21

Psychodynamic Therapy

Harold S. Kudler, Arthur S. Blank Jr.,
and Janice L. Krupnick

DESCRIPTION

Psychodynamic treatment seeks to reengage normal mechanisms of adaptation by addressing what is unconscious and, in tolerable doses, making it conscious. This is accomplished by exploring the psychological meaning of a traumatic event. It may include sifting and sorting through wishes, fantasies, fears, and defenses stirred up by the event. Psychodynamic treatment requires insight and courage, and is best approached in the context of a therapeutic relationship that emphasizes safety and honesty. Transference and countertransference are universal phenomena that should be recognized by therapists but may or may not be explicitly addressed in the therapy depending on treatment modality and therapist judgment. The therapist–patient relationship, in itself, is a crucial factor in the patient's response.

GENERAL STRENGTH OF THE EVIDENCE

Only a few empirical investigations with randomized designs, controlled variables, and validated outcome measures have been reported. Case reports and tightly reasoned scholarly works comprise the bulk of the psychodynamic literature. These can neither provide ultimate tests for psychodynamic hypotheses nor can they define the limits of psychopathology, theory, or technique, yet they are an essential part of the scientific effort to understand the human impact of psychological trauma.

COURSE OF TREATMENT

Formal psychoanalysis involves four to five 45- to 50-minute sessions each week over the course of 2 to 7 (or more) years. Psychodynamic psychotherapy most commonly involves one to two meetings per week and can be relatively short-term (a few months) or open-ended (lasting years). Brief psychodynamic psychotherapy involves meetings once or twice a week for an average of 12 to 20 sessions. Supportive psychotherapy can be brief (12–20 sessions) and focal or long-term and open-ended. Supportive psychotherapy typically involves one session per week, but more- or less-frequent sessions may be necessary depending on the patient's needs and tolerance.

RECOMMENDATIONS

The decision to undertake psychodynamic psychotherapy, and the choice of modality, depends on the patient's attributes, the presence of maladaptive psychological defenses, the focalization of the problem, and the patient's goals for treatment. The indications for more expressive treatment include strong motivation, significant suffering, ability to regress in the service of the ego, tolerance for strong affect and frustration, psychological mindedness, intact reality testing, ability to form meaningful and enduring relationships, reasonably good impulse control, and ability to sustain a job (AHCPR Level C/D). Patients who are significantly lacking in one or more of these attributes are more likely to benefit from more supportive, less insight-oriented treatment (AHCPR Level D). All psychodynamic psychotherapies combine expressive and supportive elements. Formal psychoanalysis is primarily an expressive psychotherapy that aims at decreasing symptoms, increasing self-understanding, improving ego strength, and bringing about fundamental change in the patient's intrapsychic balance (by focusing on long-standing conflicts, relationship problems, and developmental issues in the context of analysis of the transference). Psychodynamic psychotherapy, primarily expressive technique, differs from formal psychoanalysis in that it does not aim at fundamental changes in intrapsychic structure and does not necessarily center upon interpretation of the transference. Brief psychodynamic psychotherapy (either expressive or supportive) may be indicated when the situation is relatively acute and the patient's issues are focal (AHCPR Level B/C). Contraindications to expressive therapies include long-standing ego weakness, acute life crisis, poor tolerance for anxiety and/or frustration, poor capacity for insight, poor reality testing, severely impaired object relations, limited impulse control, low intelligence or organic cognitive dysfunction, difficulty with self-observation, and tenuous ability to form a therapeutic alliance. These attributes do not preclude psychodynamic psychotherapy, but modifications of technique are indicated in order to help the patient take part in treatment (AHCPR Level D).

SUGGESTED READINGS

Briere, J. (1996). *Therapy for adults molested as children: Beyond survival* (2nd ed.). New York: Springer.

Gabbard, G. O. (1994). *Psychodynamic psychiatry in clinical practice: The DSM-IV edition*. Washington, DC: American Psychiatric Press.

Herman, J. (1992). *Trauma and recovery*. New York: Basic Books.

Krystal, H. (Ed.). (1968). *Massive psychic trauma*. New York: International Universities Press.

Lindy, J. (1988). *Vietnam: A casebook*. New York: Brunner/Mazel.

Shengold, L. (1989). *Soul murder: The effects of childhood abuse and deprivation*. New Haven, CT: Yale University Press.

van der Kolk, B. A., McFarlane, A. C., & Weisaeth, L. (Eds.). (1996). *Traumatic stress: The effects of overwhelming experience on mind, body, and society*. New York: Guilford Press.

22

Inpatient Treatment

Christine A. Courtois and Sandra L. Bloom

DESCRIPTION

Inpatient treatment for posttraumatic stress disorder (PTSD) is available on general psychiatric units and in specialty units and treatment tracks. Specialty programs are distinguished by a treatment philosophy that incorporates attention to the traumatization as it relates to the individual's symptoms and functioning, and by selective admissions criteria, an organized and sequenced course of treatment within a therapeutic community, and a staff with specialized training. To date, specialty programs have been organized for two primary populations: combat veterans and adult survivors of childhood trauma. These individuals are likely to have had multiple traumatic episodes and to suffer from prolonged chronic forms of PTSD, with associated psychiatric and medical conditions. Inpatient treatment for PTSD is multimodal in that it incorporates many different interventions; it can thus be considered a "metatherapy" rather than one specific treatment. It is generally reserved for the stabilization of severe crises involving imminent harm to self and others and/or decompensation and the inability to function (especially when of short-term duration—several days to a 2-week length of stay). Longer lengths of stay (2–12 weeks) often involve planned rather than crisis admissions for conditions involving severe symptomatology and/or serious destabilization. Inpatient treatment is one component in the continuum of care that is available on a short- or moderate-term basis and episodically, as needed.

342

GENERAL STRENGTH OF THE EVIDENCE

A limited amount of research (none of it randomized with control groups) has been conducted to assess the efficacy of specialized inpatient PTSD treatment. Most of the research has been conducted within the VA on the treatment of combat veterans; little is available on the treatment of adult abuse survivors. Research efforts are complicated by the fact that the treatment is a metatherapy with numerous therapeutic interventions and components to evaluate. Available research involves a pre–post design that assesses PTSD and other symptoms at admission and discharge and, in some studies, at various follow-up points postdischarge. To date, only three studies have utilized control or comparison groups.

Research evidence suggests that inpatient treatment is effective in reducing PTSD and other psychiatric symptoms for a period of time but that gains are not permanent in many cases. Yet treatment success should not be measured as symptom reduction only. Attention needs to be directed to improvements in the individual's overall quality of life and object relations. Treatment focus and length of stay have emerged as important variables. Treatment that is oriented to present-day functioning, with general attention to the impact of traumatization, is preferable to treatment that is exclusively trauma-focused. A moderate-term length of stay (in the range of 2 to 12 weeks) is preferable to an overly short stay or one that is extended and leads to regression. Additional research is needed. To quote Fontana and Rosenheck (1997, p. 763), "The chronicity of the disorders poses its own hindrances to successful treatment beyond those posed by the disorders themselves. An important ongoing task for clinicians and researchers is to continue to devise and test specific interventions and programs that will result in improvements that go beyond this chronic level." Additionally, assessment of the impact of the overall milieu and the treatment philosophy are as important as assessing specific techniques.

COURSE OF TREATMENT

A multidisciplinary assessment is conducted upon admission to determine reasons for hospitalization and treatment goals, and to review the patient's psychosocial history, including significant stressors, personal strengths and deficits, and pre- and posttrauma risk factors. Because inpatient treatment is often due to imminent danger to self or others and/or severe decompensation, treatment begins with attention to safety, stabilization, and ability to function. The patient is incorporated into the therapeutic milieu and actively engaged in the treatment process as soon as possible. A variety of treatment modalities (adjunctive assessments and consultations; individual and group treatment; education; cognitive-behavioral interventions, including skills building for self-management of emotions and symptoms; expressive therapy; couple and family education and therapy; psychopharmacology; collaboration and consultation with outpatient providers; active safety and discharge planning) are utilized and based upon a posttrauma philosophical orientation. Inpatient treatment follows the sequenced model of posttrauma treatment. The focus on safety, stabilization, symptom management, personal functioning, and reconnection to others is primary. Directed attention to the traumatic events or memories occurs only as needed and after the patient is sufficiently stabilized and has developed functional coping skills.

RECOMMENDATIONS

Recommendations are based on the limited research data on inpatient treatment and on the evolving consensus model of posttrauma treatment (primarily in outpatient settings but applicable to inpatient treatment as well).

A "second generation" posttrauma treatment approach of carefully sequenced multimodal milieu treatment of moderate length (2 to 12 weeks) in a context of personal and social safety, with a present and future orientation as well as a trauma-responsive approach, is recommended as the inpatient model of choice. Findings of available studies and authoritative writing on posttrauma treatment suggest the need for careful assessment and treatment planning, with differential goals and treatment strategies determined by the individual's object relations, ego strength and self-capacity, severity of symptoms, degree of social connection, and level of functioning and disability.

Indications

Inpatient treatment should be considered when the individual is in imminent danger of harming self or others, has destabilized or relapsed significantly in the ability to function, is in the throes of major psychosocial stressors, suffers from debilitating symptoms of PTSD and comorbid conditions, and/or is in need of specialized observation/evaluation in a secure environment (AHCPR Level C, D, E).

> Moderate-term length of stay (ranging from 2 to 12 weeks) (Level B, C, D, E)
> Present-day focus, but trauma responsive (Level B, C, D, E)
> Sequenced, with safety and stabilization as preliminary foci (Level C, D, E)
> Interventions individually tailored and not all aimed at symptom reduction (Level B, C, D, E)
> Multidisciplinary and multimodal (Level C, D, E)

Contraindications

Inpatient treatment on a specialty unit is contraindicated for individuals who are unwilling or unable to participate in milieu treatment based on a post-trauma treatment model, for those who are better off not focusing on the trauma, for those who are actively psychotic and/or characterologically impaired to such a degree that they are unable or unwilling to maintain safety within the therapeutic context, and for those who have conditions (e.g., substance abuse, eating disorders) that are life threatening and must be stabilized first (Level C, D, E).

SUMMARY

A short- or moderate-length model of inpatient PTSD treatment, with attention to personal and social safety, stabilization, life skills, and social connection, has several significant advantages. It assists in and complies with utilization review and cost-containment efforts, and makes efficient use of mental health resources. It empowers patients to be partners in treatment and encourages them to move to a less restrictive (and less regressive) level of care once their crises and symptoms are stabilized. It operates in collaboration with the patient's residential and outpatient provider(s), and functions as one component (albeit a very crucial one in times of destabilization) of the continuum of treatment options for chronic trauma survivors. It responds to the long-term treatment needs of patients with prolonged PTSD and associated psychiatric and medical conditions, and anticipates the need for episodic, intensive treatment in a secure environment. Within the environment, it provides a philosophy and treatment model, tailored to the traumatized patient, that is not usually available on more general units. This orientation ensures that the traumatic origin of the patient's difficulties and pathology is not ignored yet has a whole-person focus that extends beyond the traumatization. A focus on the past trauma is only in the interest of the future, to a life less encumbered by the trauma, or what Shalev (1997) labeled "healing forward."

REFERENCES

Fontana, A., & Rosenheck, R. (1997). Effectiveness and cost of the inpatient treatment of posttraumatic stress disorders: Comparison of three models of treatment. *American Journal of Psychiatry, 154*(6), 758–776.

Shalev, A. Y. (1997). Discussion: Treatment of war-related posttraumatic stress disorder: Learning from experience. *Journal of Traumatic Stress, 10,* 415–422.

SUGGESTED READINGS

Bloom, S. L. (1994). The sanctuary model: Developing generic inpatient programs for the treatment of psychological trauma. In M. B. Williams & J. F. Sommer (Eds.), *Handbook of post-traumatic therapy* (pp. 474–494). Westport, CT: Greenwood Press.

Bloom, S. L. (1997). *Creating sanctuary: Toward the evolution of sane societies*. New York: Routledge.

Herman, J. L. (1992). *Trauma and recovery: The aftermath of violence—from domestic to political terror*. New York: Basic Books.

23

Psychosocial Rehabilitation

Walter Penk and Raymond B. Flannery Jr.

DESCRIPTION

Psychosocial rehabilitation techniques are recommended for the treatment of posttraumatic stress disorder (PTSD) among traumatized adults. A class of seven such techniques is reviewed here: (1) health education and psychoeducational techniques, (2) self-care/independent-living skills training, (3) supported housing, (4) family skills training, (5) social skills training, (6) vocational rehabilitation, and (7) case management.

Currently, these psychosocial rehabilitation techniques are suggested only as an adjunct to accompany other forms of treating PTSD, since psychosocial rehabilitation traditionally is not trauma-focused. However, as noted in this review, manualized approaches are being developed in which such techniques are being adapted to address PTSD symptoms. If empirically validated, such rehabilitation may evolve from an adjunctive to an independent form of treatment for PTSD. Considering that the context of these techniques consists of the everyday environments of social interactions, psychosocial rehabilitation techniques contain considerable promise for generalizing skills learned in the clinic for coping with PTSD to the everyday world of adjusting in the home, at work, and in the community.

GENERAL STRENGTH OF THE EVIDENCE

Such techniques are effective; however, none of the seven classes of psychosocial rehabilitation techniques listed here have been tested at either of the higher Level A or B categories for Level of Evidence of the Agency for Health Care Policy and Research (AHCPR). No studies have been completed among persons with PTSD using randomized, controlled clinical trials or with placebo-like comparisons. However, all such techniques have been supported by surveys and studies meeting the Level C criteria; that is, naturalistic studies and clinical observations show that psychosocial rehabilitation techniques are beneficial in treating PTSD.

COURSE OF TREATMENT

Course of treatment varies and is operationally defined as no longer needed when problems addressed by a particular class of psychosocial rehabilitation have been fully resolved. For example, if the person with PTSD identifies homelessness as a problem and plans on eliminating homelessness as a personal goal, then supported housing techniques should continue until homelessness is resolved. A checklist is presented for occasions when clients have identified specific kinds of problems for which psychosocial rehabilitation techniques may be initiated, continued, discontinued, and resumed. When to initiate such techniques should be decided by the client and individually tailored to each person's stage in recovery, which may be constantly changing (see Wang, Wilson, & Mason, 1996, for a stage-by-stage analysis in recovery).

RECOMMENDATIONS

Psychosocial rehabilitation techniques are recommended when clients and clinicians identify the following kinds of problems associated with diagnosis of PTSD: persistent high-risk behaviors (e.g., substance abuse); lack of self-care and independent living skills; homelessness; interaction with a family that does not understand PTSD; socially inactive; unemployed; and encounters with barriers to various forms of treatment and rehabilitation services. Psychosocial rehabilitation techniques designed to resolve such problems should occur concurrently or shortly after a course of treatment for PTSD. Clients and clinicians should routinely determine whether such problems are associated with core symptoms of PTSD and, if so, then ensure that rehabilitation techniques are used as a contextual vehicle for alleviating PTSD symptoms. Generalizing skills for coping with PTSD from clinic to home is the fundamental goal of psychosocial rehabilitation techniques, provided that such interventions are client-centered and client-focused.

Much of the rehabilitation literature has focused on persons with serious mental disorders, such as schizophrenia. With regard to PTSD, our basic recommendation for deciding if psychosocial rehabilitation services are to be implemented is, first, to determine whether the client has identified that a particular problem exists, and, if so, then for client and clinician to adapt appropriate rehabilitation services for PTSD and for ever-evolving stages in recovery (Wang, Wilson, & Mason, 1996).

Psychosocial rehabilitation techniques are indicated when persons identify their problems, then set personal goals to address high-risk behaviors such as substance abuse; to improve self-care and independent living skills; to eliminate homelessness; to become employed; to improve social skills and relationships with family and friends; and to improve access to available, appropriate psychosocial rehabilitation services. Psychosocial rehabilitation techniques are contraindicated when client and clinician conclude that such problems are resolved.

SUMMARY

While psychosocial rehabilitation techniques hold considerable promise for improving treatment of PTSD, effectiveness needs to be empirically validated with and without trauma-specific adaptations. Clients and clinicians collaboratively should adapt proven psychosocial rehabilitation services to address consumer-identified problems and undertake systematic comparisons of their relative effectiveness for PTSD.

REFERENCE

Wang, S., Wilson, J. P., & Mason, J. W. (1996). Stages of decompensation in combat-related PTSD. *Integrative Physiolgical and Behavioral Science, 31,* 237–253.

SUGGESTED READINGS

Anthony, W. A., & Spaniol, L. (1994). *Readings in psychiatric rehabilitation.* Boston: Center for Psychiatric Rehabilitation.

Cook, J. A. (1998). *The Employment Intervention Demonstration Program (EIDP).* Chicago: EIDP Coordinating Center, University of Illinois at Chicago.

International Association of Psychosocial Rehabilitation Services. (1994). (Ed.). *An introduction to psychiatric rehabilitation.* Columbia, MD: Author.

Liberman, R. P., Wallace, C. J., Blackwell, G. A., Eckman, T. A., Vaccaro, T. V., & Kuehnel, T. G. (1993). Innovations in skills training: The UCLA social and independent living skills modules. *Innovations and Research, 2,* 43–59.

24

Hypnosis

Etzel Cardeña, Jose Maldonado,
Onno van der Hart, and David Spiegel

DESCRIPTION

Hypnosis is a procedure generally established by an induction, during which
suggestions for alterations in behavior and mental processes including sensations, perceptions, emotions, and thoughts are provided. An induction procedure typically entails instructions to disregard extraneous concerns and to focus on the experiences and behaviors that the therapist suggests or that may
arise spontaneously. Although many inductions use some type of relaxation
instructions, others instead emphasize mental alertness and physical activity.
Hypnosis can bring about a narrow focus of attention, enhanced suggestibility, and alterations in consciousness (e.g., in time perception, in body image).
Individuals differ in their level of responsiveness to hypnotic suggestions, and
it is generally believed that hypnotic techniques are especially useful for individuals with at least moderate levels of hypnotizability. Hypnosis is not a
therapy per se, but an adjunct to psychodynamic, cognitive-behavioral, or
other therapies, and has been shown to enhance significantly their efficacy
for a variety of clinical conditions (Kirsch, Capafons, Cardeña, & Amigó,
1998; Spiegel & Spiegel, 1987). The use of hypnosis in clinical practice requires appropriate professional training and credentialing. Healthcare professionals should only use its techniques within their own areas of professional
expertise.

GENERAL STRENGTH OF THE EVIDENCE

The literature contains only one randomized, controlled clinical trial of hypnosis with patients with various types of posttraumatic symptomatology (Brom, Kleber, & Defares, 1989). This study showed that hypnosis significantly decreased intrusion and avoidance symptoms. However, the considerable literature supporting the efficacy of hypnosis for posttraumatic conditions is mostly based on service and case studies, some going back to the 19th century (AHCPR Level C).

COURSE OF TREATMENT

Hypnotic techniques can be easily integrated with diverse approaches to the treatment of traumatic stress syndromes. In a three-stage model of treatment, hypnotic techniques can be used in the following ways:

1. In the initial stage, hypnosis can be used to stabilize the patient by providing techniques to enhance relaxation and establish cues to induce a calm state outside of the therapeutic context. Specific suggestions may also be used to enhance ego strength and a sense of safety, to contain traumatic memories, and to reduce, or at least better control symptoms such as anxiety and nightmares. Finally, hypnosis is widely believed to intensify the therapist–client relationship, which can then be used for therapeutic purposes.

2. In the second stage, working through and resolving traumatic memories, various hypnotic techniques can be used to help pace and control the investigation, integration, and resolution of traumatic memories. In this context, the patient may learn to modulate the emotional and cognitive distance from the traumatic material and better integrate traumatic memories. Projective and restructuring techniques such as an imaginary split-screen to represent different aspects of the traumatic experience may be especially advantageous in this stage.

3. Finally, the goals of the third stage include achieving a more adaptive integration of the traumatic experience into the patient's life, maintaining more adaptive coping responses, and furthering personal development. Hypnotic techniques can be helpful in providing strategies to focus intentionally and shift attention as necessary; they can also be helpful in self-integration through, for instance, rehearsals in fantasy of a more adaptive self-image, new activities, and so on.

Throughout these three basic stages, hypnosis can be used to facilitate eight important tasks for PTSD patients: (1) confronting the traumatic material; (2) confessing embarrassing emotions or deeds; (3) facilitating the conscious experience of aspects of the trauma that might have been dissociated; (4) confessing painful or embarrassing deeds or emotions; (5) providing appropriate consolation and sympathy for painful experiences; (6) condensing various aspects of trauma into representative and more manageable images; (7) enhancing concentration and mental control instead of falling prey to unbidden and distressing mental episodes; and (8) facilitating an adaptive congruence in various areas of the patient's personal and social life. In the case of clients without a history of chronic pathology, who have undergone a recent traumatic event, our observation has been that hypnotic techniques can facilitate recovery in a matter of a few sessions. Chronic and more complicated clinical pictures typically require lengthier treatment.

RECOMMENDATIONS

Indications

There are a number of indications for the use hypnosis in the treatment of PTSD:

1. Hypnotic techniques may be especially valuable for symptoms often associated with PTSD, such as dissociation and nightmares, for which they have been successfully used (AHCPR Level C).
2. PTSD patients who manifest at least moderate hypnotizability may benefit from the addition of hypnotic techniques to their treatment (AHCPR Level D).
3. Hypnotic techniques can be easily integrated into diverse approaches, including psychodynamic or cognitive-behavioral therapies and pharmacotherapy. Although clinical observations suggest the value of such integration for PTSD, we need data that directly evaluate whether its addition enhances the efficacy of those treatments.
4. Because confronting traumatic memories may be very difficult for some PTSD patients, hypnotic techniques may provide them with a means to modulate the emotional and cognitive distance from such memories as they are worked-through therapeutically (AHCPR Level D).
5. For PTSD patients who may have experienced dissociative phenomena at the time of a traumatic event, a similar state induced in hypnosis may potentially enhance a fuller recall of those events, especially if no strong cues to the event exist (AHCPR Level F).

Contraindications

1. In the rare cases of individuals who are refractory or minimally responsive to hypnotic suggestions, hypnotic techniques may not be beneficial. There is some evidence that hypnotizability is related to treatment outcome.
2. Some PTSD patients may resist the use of hypnosis because of mis-

taken preconceptions or other reasons. If this resistance is not overcome after dispelling mistaken assumptions about hypnosis, other suggestive techniques that do not involve the term "hypnosis" or an induction procedures, such as emotional self-regulation therapy (ESRT), may be employed (AHCPR Level F).

3. For patients with low blood pressure or proneness to fall asleep, a hypnotic procedure that emphasizes alertness rather than relaxation may be employed (AHCPR Level F).

Potential complications of using hypnosis for PTSD include exaggerated confidence in the veracity of memories produced during hypnosis and the possible creation of pseudomemories, or "false memories," especially among highly suggestible individuals given misleading information. A number of studies have shown that hypnosis facilitates improved recall of both true and confabulated material, with no change in overall accuracy. Providing accurate information about the nature of hypnosis and memory, and warning patients about the potentially unwarranted confidence in memories obtained through hypnosis or other techniques, may minimize this concern. Clinicians should be especially careful with patients who may want to use hypnotic techniques to access "unremembered" episodes of previous abuse.

There may also be legal ramifications in the use of hypnosis for accessing memories of traumatic events, for instance, in the case of witnesses to crime. The ability of victims to testify in court may be challenged if they have been hypnotized. In these situations, it is wise to discuss such issues in advance with the attorneys and police officials involved in the case, and to electronically record all contacts with the patient.

REFERENCES

Brom, D., Kleber, R. J., & Defares, P. B. (1989). Brief psychotherapy for post-traumatic stress disorder. *Journal of Consulting and Clinical Psychology, 57,* 607–612.

Kirsch, I., Capafons, A., Cardeña, E., & Amigó, S. (Eds.). (1998). *Clinical hypnosis and self-regulation therapy: A cognitive-behavioral perspective.* Washington, DC: American Psychological Association.

Spiegel, H., & Spiegel, D. (1987). *Trance and treatment: Clinical uses of hypnosis.* Washington, DC: American Psychiatric Press.

SUGGESTED READINGS

Brown, D. P., & Fromm, E. (1986). *Hypnotherapy and hypnoanalysis.* Hillsdale, NJ: Erlbaum.

Hammond, D. F., Garver, R. B., Crasilneck, H. B., Frischholz, E., Gravitz, M. A., Hibler, N. S., Olson, J., Scheflin, A., Spiegel, H., & Wester, W. (1995). *Clinical hypnosis and memory: Guidelines for clinicians and for forensic hypnosis.* Des Plaines, IL: American Society of Clinical Hypnosis.

25

Marital and Family Therapy

David S. Riggs

DESCRIPTION

Marital and family therapy has been recommended for the treatment of traumatized adults. Typically, these treatments are suggested as an adjunct to other forms of treatment that are designed to address the symptoms of posttraumatic stress disorder (PTSD) more directly. Marital and family treatments for trauma survivors fall into one of two general categories: systemic approaches designed to treat marital or family disruption, and supportive approaches designed to help family members offer support for an individual being treated for PTSD. Of the two approaches, the systemic treatments have received more attention in the literature, and the descriptions of these interventions are more detailed than are those of supportive approaches.

GENERAL STRENGTH OF THE EVIDENCE

Only a couple of empirical investigations of marital or family therapy were found in the literature (only one that included a randomized, controlled trial). In general, information regarding the efficacy of marital and family approaches for treating trauma survivors encompasses clinical descriptions based on the experience of a single clinician or clinic. Few of these descriptions include any systematic assessment of the efficacy of the approach (e.g., standardized measurement), and none have been replicated across clinics.

COURSE OF TREATMENT

Marital and family treatments of trauma survivors are typically seen as time-limited, problem-focused interventions. These specific courses of treatment vary depending on the format and philosophy of the treatment. The goals of these treatments are typically to foster communication and mutual support around posttrauma reactions and symptoms.

RECOMMENDATIONS

At the present time, then, it is recommended that marital and family therapy be used as adjuncts to treatments that are focused on the alleviation of PTSD symptoms and not be seen as treatments for PTSD themselves. However, as marital and family disruption is frequently a problem among trauma survivors, it is also recommended that clinicians evaluate the need for marital and family therapy when treating trauma survivors. When such a need is identified, it is recommended that marital and family therapy occur concurrently or following treatment of the survivor's PTSD symptoms. Finally, it is recommended that marital and family therapy focus on improving communication and reducing conflict among family members. This may entail communication about current problems or issues related to the trauma and its aftermath.

Indications	Strength of evidence
Marital or family distress	E
Intact system prior to trauma	E
Traumatized individual(s) also in treatment for individual symptoms	E
Traumatized client in agreement with intervention involving others	E
Marital/family treatment will help individual recovery	E

Contraindications	
Family violence	D
Lack of commitment to family/marriage	E

SUGGESTED READINGS

Figley, C. R. (1989). *Helping traumatized families.* San Francisco: Jossey-Bass.

Johnson, S. M., & Williams-Keeler, L. (1998). Creating healing relationships for couples dealing with trauma: The use of emotionally focused marital therapy. *Journal of Marital and Family Therapy, 24,* 25–40.

26

Creative Therapies

David Read Johnson

DESCRIPTION

The creative arts therapies are the intentional use by a trained therapist of art, music, dance/movement, drama, and poetry in psychotherapy, counseling, special education, or rehabilitation.

Practitioners in the field emphasize the special role of the nonverbal form of intervention, which specifically involves the invocation of kinesthetic cues to memories or images, as well as the benefits of creativity and spontaneity in ameliorating feelings of hopelessness or worthlessness. First, the symbolic media of the arts may provide more complete access to implicit (as opposed to explicit) memory systems, as well as visual–kinesthetic schemas that are usually processed by the nondominant hemisphere of the brain. It seems possible that traumatic experience and associated distorted schemas may be stored in these nonlexical forms. By more completely accessing the traumatic schema, the creative arts therapies may increase the impact of therapeutic processes such as desensitization, cognitive reframing, and habituation.

Second, the utilization of creative and socially valued artistic methods may have therapeutic effects in the psychosocial domain. Creative arts therapies may improve PTSD clients' self-esteem, hope, and prosocial behavior, and reduce feelings of shame and guilt, through the association of traumatic material to adaptive and aesthetic modes of expression.

Though, presumably, these nonverbal and creative components serve as the unique elements in this form of treatment, the creative arts therapies clearly utilize more generic therapeutic processes that overlap with many more established trauma treatments, such as relaxation, exposure, desensitization, cognitive interventions, narrative techniques, and distraction.

GENERAL STRENGTH OF THE EVIDENCE

Most empirical work has been done on assessment, particularly in the discipline of art therapy. Presence of the following indicators in children's drawings warrants further investigation: genitalia, hands omitted, fingers omitted, and head only.

We found few empirical studies of the creative arts therapies in the treatment of trauma. Most of the evidence of efficacy derives from clinical reports and case studies. Significant reductions in PTSD symptoms and other functional measures are commonly reported. The creative arts therapies have been cited as helpful in the reduction of alexithymia, increase in emotional control, improvement in interpersonal relationships, decrease in dissociation and anxiety, decreased nightmares, improved body image, and reduction of depression.

RECOMMENDATIONS

Three populations are often identified that may benefit uniquely from the creative arts therapies: (1) For children who are often unable to focus or attend to an abstract verbal discussion regarding their personal experiences, engagement in play often is the only or best way to access these experiences; (2) for traumatized clients who have difficulty expressing their feelings verbally, the use of nonverbal modes of expression may allow them to access and then process traumatic memories more fully; and (3) for highly intellectualized clients whose use of language obstructs their processing of traumatic material, the arts media may aid in circumventing their avoidant defenses. Despite relatively wide use and application, the efficacy of the creative arts therapies has not been established through empirical research. The creative arts therapies may be helpful as an adjunct to treatment under the following conditions: (1) The arts therapy is conducted by a practitioner trained in that approach; (2) the therapy is conducted with the permission of the client; and (3) the therapy is conducted in conjunction with other ongoing treatments and therapists. The exact source of therapeutic benefits of the creative arts therapies in the treatment of PTSD has not been identified and is likely to be a combination of generic psychological processes (such as exposure, relaxation, and cognitive processing) and specific nonverbal and creative elements.

There is currently insufficient evidence to differentiate the impact of the creative arts therapies on PTSD, comorbid disorders, or associated disruptive symptoms. Similarly, there is insufficient evidence to make statements regarding their cost-effectiveness.

1. The recognition, justification, and further development of the creative arts therapies in the treatment of psychological trauma will be most fully encouraged by more sophisticated empirical inquiries using control groups and randomized assignment.
2. Creative arts therapy treatments designed to be specific for PTSD would presumably have heightened therapeutic effects over nonspecific creative arts therapy approaches. The design of such treatments is recommended.
3. Greater attention to the possible contraindications (e.g., types of clients, types of symptoms, stages of treatment) is needed.

SUGGESTED READINGS

Cohen, B., & Cox, C. (1995). *Telling without talking: Art as a window into the world of multiple personality*. New York: Norton.

Dayton, T. (1997). *Heartwounds: The impact of unresolved trauma and grief on relationships*. Deerfield Beach, FL: Health Communication.

Feldman, S., Johnson, D., & Ollayos, M. (1994). The use of writing in the treatment of PTSD. In J. Sommer & M. Williams (Eds.), *The handbook of post-traumatic therapy* (pp. 366–385). Westport, CT: Greenwood Press.

Johnson, D. (1987). The role of the creative arts therapies in the diagnosis and treatment of psychological trauma. *Arts in Psychotherapy, 14*, 7–14.

Kaufman, B., & Wohl, A. (1992). *Casualties of childhood: A developmental perspective on sexual abuse using projective drawings*. New York: Brunner/Mazel.

Malchiodi, C. (1990). *Breaking the silence: Art therapy with children from violent homes*. New York: Brunner/Mazel.

27

Integration and Summary

Arieh Y. Shalev, Matthew J. Friedman,
Edna B. Foa, and Terence M. Keane

In this book, we have attempted to provide critical reviews of the various treatment approaches to posttraumatic stress disorder (PTSD). Each chapter is dedicated to a specific approach, leaving unaddressed the important clinical questions of how patients' needs dictate choices between treatment approaches or their integration. While the treatment guidelines for any given approach indicate the degree of empirical support available for that treatment, empirical data on combination treatments in PTSD are extremely rare and mostly descriptive. Similarly, there are only few systematic comparisons between treatment modalities (see, e.g., Brom, Kleber, & Defares, 1989; Foa, Rothbaum, Riggs., & Murdock, 1991).

Despite the scarce empirical studies, many PTSD patients do receive more than one form of therapy (e.g., pharmacotherapy and some form of psychotherapy). As no current intervention claims to have curative effect on PTSD (as would be true for other mental disorders), treatment combinations, hierarchy, and integration are important topics to be considered.

It can be argued that PTSD is a relatively "new" disorder; therefore, it is only a matter of time before knowledge on treatment combinations and integration will become available. While this may be true, studies of treatment combinations are few, even in more established disorders such as depression and obsessive–compulsive disorder (OCD), and panic disorder. This may be due not only to focused theoretical or commercial interests but also to the fact that well-controlled studies of combined therapies are complex, expensive, and require very large samples. Moreover, such studies have not always been conclusive. For example, the results of the National Institute of

Mental Health (NIMH) collaborative study of the treatment of depression (Imber et al., 1990), in which two forms of psychotherapy, cognitive therapy and interpersonal therapy, were compared with pharmacotherapy and with placebo-management condition, suggested that patient and disease characteristics contributed to the general outcome as much as factors related to treatment modality (Elkin et al., 1989). Moreover, there are many ways in which several treatment modalities can be combined, and therefore an almost endless number of combinations to study. For example, the failure to find that the combination of cognitive-behavioral therapy and pharmacotherapy were not more effective than cognitive-behavioral therapy alone in treating OCD may have been due to the fact that the treatments were introduced simultaneously rather than sequentially (Kozak, Leibowitz, & Foa, 2000). At present, therefore, the integration of treatment techniques remains the art of the clinician.

As many clinicians know, the exercise of such "art" has many constraints. Not all clinicians are skilled in providing different techniques: Psychologists customarily do not prescribe medication, and few psychiatrists are adequately trained in cognitive-behavioral therapy. Moreover, not all patients desire, or have the resources to engage in more than one form of therapy. Importantly, as with other mental disorders, the patients with PTSD that present to clinics pose unique and heterogeneous problems that require flexible solutions, including amendments to treatment protocols. Epitomizing these clinical dilemmas is the dictum: *Science is mainly generic, whereas Reality is always specific.* By analogy, when implementing the treatments discussed in the various chapters of this book in one's clinical practice, it is not a generic "PTSD" that one treats, but rather a particular PTSD patient, or group of patients, in a particular life situation and clinical setting.

QUESTIONS ADDRESSED IN THIS CHAPTER

- How should one choose among treatment modalities?
- What can one expect from treatment, and how does one define realistic goals?
- How can one combine various treatment techniques?
- How does one approach complex clinical pictures and comorbid conditions?
- How long should a treatment be followed? Booster sessions? Follow-up?
- Are there features of PTSD that require a special approach that cuts across treatment modalities?
- How does one make sense of clinical difficulties and assess failure?

In this concluding chapter, we provide an overview to assist the clinician in evaluating the information provided in each of the previous chapters. We also attempt to help the clinician know how to optimize the treatment of individual patients with PTSD. To this end, we address the above questions. We begin, however, by outlining what we have learned from each of the chapters and what questions are left open.

GENERAL ISSUES

One of the first general lessons learned from this book is that there is a need for more research. Most chapters conclude that the available empirical evidence does not permit strong conclusions about the efficacy of the treatment approach addressed. In many chapters, therefore, the ensuing recommendations are tentative and based on clinical impression and expert opinion. Lack of evidence, however, should not be confounded with negative evidence (i.e., evidence of lack of efficacy), and the reader should not conclude that only treatments that are heavily researched are likely to help his or her patients. Indeed, although lack of evidence limits the degree to which a particular treatment can be endorsed in these practice guidelines, it should not be interpreted to mean that a lightly researched treatment is ineffective.

A second general point is that most treatment approaches described earlier are not specific to PTSD, but rather are based on principles, theories, or basic experiments that apply for other mental disorders as well. By analogy, when clinicians are called to choose between treatment options, they must firstly use their general skills and knowledge as diagnostician and therapist. *The treatment of PTSD, therefore, is to be applied by skilled clinicians only.*

Finally, as noted in the Introduction, diagnosis and careful evaluation must precede treatment. In the case of PTSD these should include the following:

1. Formal diagnoses of PTSD and comorbid disorders.
2. Determination of the most disturbing problem, which may or may not be the PTSD symptoms themselves (e.g., marriage breaking up, violence, depression).
3. Evaluation of the patient's resources (e.g., stable family, work, housing) and his or her deficiencies (e.g., substance misuse, poverty, ongoing traumatization).
4. Evaluation of the patient's motivation and ability to commit to the prescribed course of the selected therapy and to its particular demands (e.g., complete homework assignments in cognitive-behavioral therapy, adhere to the medication regimen). *Indeed, engaging patients*

with PTSD in the therapeutic process (or in complying with prescribed medication) is the first and critical stage of the treatment.

OVERVIEW OF THE CHAPTERS

Acute Interventions and Debriefing

Various early interventions have been employed with individuals who have undergone recent traumatic experiences. The only treatment modality addressed in this chapter is psychological debriefing (PD). The available empirical data suggest that debriefing does not reduce the incidence of PTSD or the severity of PTSD symptoms, as recorded several months to 1 year following trauma. The reader should not, however, conclude that any early treatment of trauma survivors is of no help. Indeed, studies indicate efficacy of front-line treatment of soldiers with combat stress reactions (Solomon & Benbenishty, 1986), early cognitive treatment of road accident victims (Bryant, Harvey, Dang, Sackville, & Basten, 1998), and female assault survivors. Thus, while some early interventions may be useful, others are not.

It is important to note that PD is often employed with groups of trauma survivors who do not have formal diagnoses of PTSD, and sometimes with entire cohorts of survivors regardless of their levels of distress. Consequently, the question of whether preventive treatment should be provided to all trauma survivors or only to those with identifiable symptoms (or dysfunction) remains open. Other questions left unanswered include the following: (1) Is any single and short "immediate" intervention expected to have enough power to reverse the complex causation of PTSD? (2) What is the optimal time for introducing preventive interventions? and (3) Should such interventions be clinical in nature or should they address situational and social stressors that occur shortly after the trauma (e.g., relocation, uncertainty, pain, and rejecting attitudes of others)?

Given the paucity of controlled trials on PD and the many complex questions that have yet to be systematically addressed, in this regard, it is much too early to conclude that PD is an ineffective intervention for all acutely traumatized individuals. Even if subsequent studies confirm these early findings, however, and indicate that PD reduces neither the incidence nor severity of PTSD, we must be careful not to misinterpret the practical implications of such results. These same studies have also shown that the vast majority of people who receive PD report that this intervention facilitated their recovery from acute posttraumatic distress. Since most traumatized people do not develop PTSD, one possibility is that PD is very useful for many posttraumatic survivors but not for those at greatest risk for developing PTSD. In short, whether PD is effective, what clinical outcomes should be expected, when PD should be administered, who should receive it, and whether it can prevent the later development of PTSD are still open questions.

Cognitive-Behavioral Therapy

The various forms of behavioral, cognitive, and cognitive-behavioral techniques (CBT) are the most studied interventions for PTSD. Rothbaum and colleagues (Chapters 4 and 16) concluded that CBT techniques are clearly effective. However, not all patients who receive CBT benefit from treatment, and it is yet unclear what factors predict success. First, as with any other treatment, the therapists must be trained in the various interventions that come under the heading of CBT, and some interventions (e.g., cognitive therapy) require more training than others (e.g., relaxation). Second, the treatment is demanding for both the therapist and the patient, since it requires that the therapist be disciplined and focus on employing the particular intervention rather than attend to issues that are extraneous to the treatment goals. Third, the patient needs to be motivated and able to adhere to treatment requirements, including active engagement with the treatment demands both during the session and at home. Most of the studies have been conducted in specialty clinics, where therapists are highly trained and experienced in motivating their patients to comply with treatment demands. Foa and her colleagues are conducting a study to examine the transportability of exposure therapy and cognitive therapy to community clinics that serve female survivors of rape. Preliminary results are encouraging: After 2 weeks of intensive training, counselors in those clinics are achieving outcomes comparable to those of experts. It should be noted, however, that throughout the study, the community counselors have been supervised regularly by experts in CBT.

It is important to note that the administration of CBT, like the administration of any therapy for PTSD, needs to adhere to general, responsible clinical practices such as careful assessment of suicidality that may dictate preliminary therapy (e.g., the administration of medication or short-term hospitalization). Likewise, patients inundated with personal problems may require attention for those problems before attending to their PTSD symptoms. This means that whereas some patients are ready to participate in a straight CBT protocol, others require a global treatment plan in which CBT is only one of several therapeutic components.

While several CBT studies compare the efficacy of specific interventions (e.g., cognitive therapy, exposure) and their combinations, no studies have examined the combination of CBT with other treatment approaches (e.g., pharmacotherapy, marital therapy). Most studies have only monitored relatively short-term follow-up (up to 1 year); therefore, the long-term stability of CBT effects on PTSD have not yet been established. Thus, we do not know to what extent patients require "booster sessions" in order to maintain the treatment effects beyond 1 year. Also, because CBT programs routinely include several components, the relative contribution of each to the program success is as yet unknown. In this respect, we do not know to what extent it is crucial to focus the treatment on the recollections of the traumatic event (reliving or imaginal exposure) or on its current consequences (e.g., avoidance and negative self-perception). Finally, studies indicate that exposure therapy has modest effects on male Veterans with PTSD as compared to female assault victims. Is this differential efficacy due to gender differences, trauma differences (e.g., combat vs. sexual trauma), or does it suggest differences in PTSD severity or comorbidity? We do not have answers to these questions because information about factors that predict treatment response is scarce. Such information., however, is crucial for the clinical management of patients and decisions about treatment implementation.

It is important to note that CBT therapists routinely measure and monitor progress during therapy (e.g., by repeated evaluation of subjective distress during exposure, inspecting homework diaries during cognitive therapy). Our knowledge about all treatments would be greatly enhanced if this practice were adopted by therapists using other approaches.

Pharmacotherapy

Research has identified a number of pharmacological agents capable of significantly reducing PTSD symptoms, mainly among the antidepressants. Questions remain regarding other categories of drugs, including antiadrenergic agents, anticonvulsants, the new generation of antipsychotics, and drugs yet to be tested that normalize neuropeptide components of the human stress response. Importantly, the pharmacotherapy of PTSD, like that of most other anxiety disorders, seems capable of controlling symptoms yet does not have clear effect on the course of the disorder. In that sense, hopes for recovery, as opposed to remission, are not supported by current research. Pharmacotherapy, however, may open the way for psychological and social therapies through which the patient may gain further advantage (e.g., by challenging avoidance). It is also notable that the agents currently recommended as first-line treatment for PTSD—the selective serotonin reuptake inhibitors (SSRIs)—have other applications (such as major depression, obsessive–compulsive disorder, panic disorder, eating disorders, etc.). These, and other drugs, should therefore be considered neuromodulators rather than "antidepressants."

Among questions left open in drug therapy of PTSD is how to handle treatment resistance. Would augmentation techniques, such as the ones used in resistant depression, also work in PTSD? Another important question concerns the maintenance of treatment effects across time. As a clinician, one sees many PTSD patients who continue to take medication prescribed years earlier. This is particularly true for drugs that induce sleep and other tranquilizers. Research on relapse following discontinuation of pharmacotherapy has been very productive in other areas of psychiatry and should be conducted for PTSD as well. Another clinical observation is that patients with PTSD are often treated with several compounds. Unfortunately, there has been no research on pharmacotherapy with more than one drug, despite the fact that polypharmacy is a common clinical practice. Clearly, this is an important future area for research.

Unlike many other disorders, PTSD has an identifiable starting point; hence, it may be amenable to preventive pharmacotherapy. Preventive pharmacotherapy, however, has not been studied (yet one is often tempted to treat a recent trauma survivor with medication; e.g., in order to reduce insomnia or intense physiological arousal). New agents are being developed, including some that affect important psychobiological abnormalities not targeted by current drugs in use, such as modulators of the "stress" axes of the brain (e.g., corticotropin-releasing factor, hypothalamic–pituitary–adrenal and locus coeruleus norepinephrine systems). The clinician should remain attentive to innovations and news in this field.

Treatment of Children and Adolescents

Most treatment modalities for adults have been tried with children, with various degrees of success and lesser degrees of evidential certainty, due to fewer systematic studies. This chapter underscores several important issues related to childhood trauma and its treatment. First, the provision of treatment to a traumatized child requires the identification of a trauma-related disorder and a help-seeking behavior by a caring adult. Yet for many traumatized children, the traumas are inflicted by the caregivers themselves or occur in an environment that may misinterpret or overlook children's symptoms. Thus, many traumatized children do not have access to treatment. Second, many studies on childhood traumatization have focused on the reactions to one-time, salient events (e.g., hurricanes, bus kidnapping), which are much less frequent than ongoing, long-term trauma associated domestic violence, abuse, or neglect. Many children are exposed to extremely traumatic events that go unnoticed for years. Chapter 6 focuses on treatment of children whose traumatic experiences have ended before the start of treatment (because research with children has emphasized such traumas). We have very little data on the efficacy of interventions for the child who is exposed to ongoing traumas. Finally, developmental arrest, personality changes, and incubation of future vulnerabilities may be frequent consequences of childhood trauma that are as clinically significant as overt PTSD symptoms. Unfortunately, little is known about the incidence, prevalence, prevention, or treatment of such consequences.

Eye Movement Desensitization and Reprocessing

Research suggest that EMDR is more effective than wait-list controls and techniques such as applied muscle relaxation and standard clinical care at a health maintenance organization (HMO) clinic. However, as noted in Table 6.1 of Chapter 6, most of the existing studies suffer from methodological problems that limit the interpretation of their results. Of particular concern is the absence of a blind, independent assessor in all but one study, and the absence of PTSD diagnosis in many of the studies' patients. The efficacy of EMDR relative to CBT has been examined in only one study, indicating the superiority of the latter (see Chapter 4). Several studies comparing the efficacy of exposure therapy (the most investigated psychosocial treatment for PTSD) and EMDR are being conducted, and their results will certainly advance our knowledge in this area. Such studies are of particular theoretical and practical interest because EMDR, as well as most of the studied CBT programs, included a variant of exposure to the traumatic memory. It is of value to know to what extent such exposure is a necessary component of an effective treatment for PTSD and whether the length of exposure (prolonged vs. interrupted) influences therapeutic outcome.

It is important to note that several of the eight stages of EMDR include components that overlap with other therapies, such as obtaining a patient's history, treatment planning, establishing a therapeutic relationship, education about PTSD, assessment, identifying maladaptive and adaptive cognitions, and imaging the traumatic memory. At the same time, as noted in Chapter 7, the studies evaluating the role of the unique component of EMDR (i.e., the eye movements) failed to find this component an essential ingredient of the treatment. Future studies will further shed light on this issue.

In summary, research suggests that EMDR is an effective treatment for PTSD. Whether its efficacy stems from the fact that it is yet another variant of exposure therapy (with some ingredients of cognitive therapy) or that it is based on new principles is unclear.

Group Therapy

Interestingly, studies of the efficacy of group psychotherapy seem to indicate that interventions addressing the trauma directly produce similar effects to those of interventions that do not address the trauma, such as assertive training and supportive interventions: All active group interventions yielded significant improvement relative to no-treatment or wait-list controls. Moreover, similar effect size was evident across group therapies despite major differences in outcome measures. As noted by the authors of Chapter 8, "Group psychotherapy, regardless of the nature of the therapy, is associated with favorable outcomes in a range of symptom domains" (p. 168). If true, does group therapy act via nonspecific effects? Or is group therapy, of any sort, particularly useful in PTSD because it provides a unique format in which individuals can normalize their posttraumatic distress, receive social support through the group process, and acquire the empowerment needed to overcome the adverse consequences of their symptoms?

Aware of these issues, the authors of Chapter 8 suggest that future research should evaluate specific group processes in controlled studies with larger samples, in which patients are randomly assigned to different conditions. Such studies are likely to inform us about the extent to which generic aspects of group processes, such as verbalizing, sharing, providing and receiving support, and structuring communication, are responsible for the across-the-board positive outcome found in the various studies.

Psychodynamic Therapy

Chapter 9 provides a thoughtful review of theory and treatment techniques. In this way, it allows the reader to reflect on the role of basic interpersonal processes and interaction between therapist and patient in the treatment of PTSD. Indeed, one of the strengths of the psychodynamic approach is its focus on generic elements of therapeutic encounters, including therapy for PTSD. On the other hand, there is very little empirical research on the efficacy of psychodynamic treatment for PTSD. This is partly due to the fact that typical goals of psychodynamically oriented psychotherapy are to affect factors such as the capacity for human relatedness or one's incomplete view of one's past rather than reduction of symptoms of specific disorders such as PTSD (which is the aim of therapies such as CBT and medication), for which we do not have satisfactory assessment methodology. Given the current emphasis of the practice guidelines on PTSD, Chapter 9 does not focus on those patients for whom such therapies might provide the best approach: the repeatedly traumatized, deeply injured, and chronically impaired survivors of protracted interpersonal trauma, sometimes diagnosed with "complex PTSD." Such patients' most salient problems have less to do with DSM-IV PTSD symptoms and more to do with interpersonal and intrapsychic deficiencies, mistrust of others, self-devaluation, dissociation, somatization, impulsivity, self-destructive behavior, and poor affective modulation. It should be clearly stated, therefore, that the effectiveness of psychodynamic psychotherapies for "complex PTSD" and related problems is simply not addressed in this book. This is yet another, open question requiring further research.

Inpatient Treatment

Inpatient treatment, rather than being a form of treatment, is a setting and a milieu within which many forms of therapy can be provided to handle crisis situations. It is often, therefore, a "platform" used for the treatment of acute episodes or exacerbation related to the course of PTSD and comorbid disorders. Moreover, those who require inpatient admission are often the most severe cases of PTSD, whose conditions need to be stabilized before specific interventions can take place. As such, the expected outcome of inpatient admission is not limited to "treating PTSD" but often extends to comorbid conditions, adverse social behavior, homelessness, and social drift (Shalev, 1997). Indeed, inpatient interventions are not treatments unto themselves but serve a specific function in the longitudinal course of ongoing outpatient therapy. This function may be for crisis intervention, relapse prevention, diagnostic reassessment, or a specific set of intense procedures designed to inform or accelerate resumption of postdischarge treatment. At its best, inpatient treatment should be carefully coordinated with outpatient therapy, and discharge planning should be initiated as soon as possible after admission. Improvements on some PTSD outcome indices have been noted in some reports of inpatient admissions, yet, in general, such assessments have not been systematically carried out utilizing instruments with satisfactory psychometric properties.

Little is known about deliberate and planned inpatient admissions designed to intensely address PTSD symptoms, or to engage the patient in pharmaco- or psychotherapy in this setting. Nor do we know much about how to ensure continuity of care between inpatient and outpatient treatment, which may be important in securing the long-term success of inpatient treatment. These are all important questions that have had little systematic evaluation. It should be noted, however, that such interventions have recently been provided successfully to inpatient cohorts of Australian Vietnam veterans hospitalized at the Australian Department of Veterans Affairs Center for War-Related PTSD (Creamer, Morris, Biddle, & Elliott, 1999), with more positive results.

Psychosocial Rehabilitation

Psychosocial rehabilitation techniques have proved valuable with severe mentally ill (SMI) patients, especially with regard to work therapy and case management. Indeed, an emerging empirical literature demonstrates the efficacy of such approaches with schizophrenic and affectively disordered patients in a variety of public-sector programs. Since PTSD is often a comorbid disorder for such patients (Mueser et al., 1998), and since severe and chronic PTSD patients are often found among SMI cohorts and in homeless shelters (Friedman & Rosenheck, 1996), it makes sense to design and test psychosocial rehabilitation programs. Such treatments would have some distinctive therapeutic components given the unique social avoidance, hyperarousal, and other psychopathology of PTSD in comparison to other psychiatric disorders. Most importantly, patients referred for such treatment would be evaluated primarily in terms of self-care, independent living, family function, social skills, and maintenance of gainful employment, rather than in terms of reduced PTSD symptoms. We hope that these specific areas will be evaluated systematically and that rehabilitation techniques specific to PTSD-related impairments will be developed and studied.

Hypnosis

As noted in Chapter 12, hypnosis is one of the oldest psychotherapy techniques that have been applied to trauma-related disturbances. This rich history makes hypnosis a natural candidate when the therapist considers therapeutic options. Yet despite this fascinating history on which the authors rely in their clear description of how to integrate hypnosis into the general treatment of PTSD, we have very little empirical evidence for the efficacy of this technique. The authors recommend hypnosis as an adjunctive procedure rather than as a stand-alone treatment; this, too, awaits empirical support.

Marital and Family Therapy

Marital and family therapy for PTSD encompasses two approaches: supportive and active (or "systemic"). One problem with assessing family therapy for PTSD is that reduction in PTSD symptoms may not be the appropriate outcome measure for this therapy. While PTSD-related distress may be alleviated when family relationships improve, such an outcome is not specific to PTSD and can be seen in other disorders such as schizophrenia.

The impact of PTSD on families is extensive. Treating vicarious traumatization of family members, therefore, may be very important. On the other hand, family therapy that focuses primarily on the PTSD sufferer, without fortifying the family, may not address other family members' needs for support. It would seem that there is a critical role for marital and family therapy that attempts to achieve a clinically meaningful balance between addressing dysfunctional symptoms and behavior of the PTSD patient and the distress of family members whose needs also require attention. This is a very important area for future research.

Creative Therapies

As with hypnosis, rehabilitation, and marital and family therapies, creative arts therapies address important dimensions of PTSD and may often be effective during impasses that other treatment techniques fail to affect. The reader, therefore, is invited to consider the information provided about these techniques and their specific targets, as these may apply for his or her patients. Better efficacy on PTSD symptoms may be achieved once a breakthrough is attained via creative arts therapies. Interestingly, creative arts therapies do not escape from the typical problems of treating PTSD, that is, the balance between addressing current problems (e.g., alexithymia) or delving into past trauma, and between uncovering and reshaping traumatic material and finding new, "future-oriented" ways of expression. While the techniques described in Chapter 14 may capture the imagination of the therapist, it is important to keep in mind that, as with many other therapies discussed in this volume, empirical evidence for the efficacy of creative arts therapies with PTSD and other related symptoms is not available.

Now that we have briefly reviewed the chapters on each specific treatment emphasized the importance of defining relevant and achievable goals at the outset of treatment, and described dimensions of therapy that cut across specific treatment approaches, we are ready to tackle the key questions enunciated at the beginning of this chapter. Here, there are very few experimental data to guide our answers. But practicing clinicians cannot wait for slow-paced scientific research to come to the rescue. Patients suffering from PTSD demand treatment immediately. Decisions must be made about choice of treatment, treatment combinations, reasonable expectations from treatment, length of treatment and follow-up, PTSD-specific treatment issues that cut across treatment modalities, how to approach complex clinical pictures and comorbid conditions, how to make sense of clinical difficulties and, most importantly, how to assess failure.

CHOOSING A GOAL FOR TREATMENT

As noted earlier, the choice of treatment should be informed by the patient's needs, abilities, and preferences. The first step in making a decision about choice of treatment involves defining the treatment goals and considering whether or not they are obtainable. With most patients, PTSD symptoms will be among the main targets. But in some patients, comorbid symptoms and conduct may need to be addressed first. For many patients, symptom reduction is the major focus of treatment. For some, however, stabilization and prevention of relapse may take precedence. In some cases, the initial goal of treatment is to help patients realize that they need to address their PTSD problems by seeking psychological or medical treatment (e.g., instead of drinking or acting out). For others, stressful life events or adverse life conditions may have to be addressed first, in order to bring reactivation or deterioration of PTSD to a halt. Finally, while the patients themselves are the identified focus, treatment may need to involve other individuals, such as family members and others who are reciprocally involved in a significant relationship that has been adversely affected by the expression of PTSD symptoms.

  • *How should one choose among treatment modalities?* Currently, there are no clear guidelines for choosing among treatment modalities.

However, several criteria for making such choices can be recommended. Among those, expected efficacy should be the first one, since without such efficacy, the core concept of "treatment" is violated. That is why this practice guideline has placed such emphasis on efficacy throughout this volume. Following efficacy, one should evaluate the effectiveness of specific treatments on associated disorders and conditions. Potential difficulties, side effects, and negative effects of treatment must also be considered. Acceptability and consent should come next, followed by an evaluation of cost, length, and cultural appropriateness of the treatment. Finally, one should evaluate one's own resources and skills, as well as potential forensic implications of treatment. These general considerations have special implications for the treatment of traumatized survivors with PTSD.

Criteria for choosing treatment of PTSD

- Expected efficacy against PTSD
- Associated disorders and conditions
- Difficulties, side effects, negative effects
- Acceptability and consent
- Cultural appropriateness
- Length, cost, and availability of resources
- Legal, administrative, and forensic implications

Efficacy, as used here, relates specifically to prevention, amelioration, or eradication of PTSD symptoms. All things being equal, the treatment selected should be one that has proven successful in empirical trials.

Associated disorders and conditions relate to all or some dimensions and associated features of PTSD, such as depression, suicidality, violent behavior, or drinking habits. In some cases, treatment may have to stabilize an unstable condition (or patient) to prevent adverse events (loss of job) or conduct (drinking) before addressing PTSD per se. For example, suicidal behavior may require hospitalization; alcohol dependence, detoxification; depression, antidepressant medication; and marital disruption, couple therapy. Whenever possible, it is desirable to select a treatment that might be expected to ameliorate the urgent problem and the PTSD simultaneously. For example, an SSRI would be a good choice for both depression and PTSD. Systemic marital therapy might address the marital crisis and PTSD simultaneously. Hospitalization would be indicated for suicidal symptoms but might also provide an opportunity to initiate PTSD treatment. And combined alcoholism/PTSD group treatment might be the best choice when drinking behavior is the most urgent problem.

Side effects include those effects pertinent to each treatment technique (e.g., loss of appetite with some drugs) as well as those pertinent to PTSD (e.g., reactivation of symptoms during explorative therapy). Difficulties, side

effects, and negative effects may also result from interactions between therapists and traumatized patients. One should remember that PTSD is associated with increased physiological and psychological reactivity, which can be
specific (e.g., related to one's traumatic experiences) or nonspecific (e.g., generated by environmental demands).

Contrasting with prevalent views, *acceptability* and *consent* are neither cat-
egorical (yes or no) nor a priori statements given by the patient at the outset
of therapy. Acceptability and consent, particularly in PTSD, are dynamic
processes that are often fragile and brittle. Trust may have to be renewed, or
regained, explicitly or implicitly, at each treatment encounter, particularly in
survivors of dehumanizing, man-made traumata. Furthermore, patient preference must be weighed carefully in the choice of treatment. For example.,
some patients may be strongly opposed to any type of trauma focus (e.g., exposure) treatment that will necessitate intense work on traumatic memories.
Others may refuse to take medications. In both cases, therapists' beliefs about
what treatments are best must be subordinated to the likelihood that a patient
will accept and comply with the treatment that has been prescribed. Acceptability across *cultural boundaries* is particularly relevant in the case of refugees,
who may or may not be prepared to accept the way in which their suffering is
appraised and treated in another culture (e.g., as a mental disorder). Cross-
gender problems may be seen in survivors of gender-related traumata. Indeed, many trauma survivors may wonder how much their therapist can
"truly understand" and genuinely relate to their traumatic experiences,
which they often perceive as ineffable.

Conceptually, issues of *cost* and *availability of resources* are extremely important in many societies, especially in poorer nations and in inner-city ghet-
tos within wealthier nations. The cost of some SSRIs may be prohibitive in
Third-World countries and poor provinces. The likelihood of finding a skilled
psychologist or psychiatrist is very low in disaster areas in Africa or in Central
and South America. Child psychiatrists are rare across the world. Indeed, in
any mass disaster, the number of victims is likely to overwhelm the best efforts
to provide skilled professional help. While such shortages may exist in other
conditions as well (e.g., AIDS), there are currently no simplified treatment protocols for PTSD, such as, for example, those emerging for the prevention of
AIDS in poorer countries. The development of low-cost treatment for traumatized survivors with PTSD is a major task for the future of our field.

Finally, for many traumatized individuals, *legal, administrative,* or *forensic*
elements are likely to be (or to become) associated with the treatment. Prevalent examples are litigation, financial coverage for the treatment, recognition
of disability and entitlement for pension, reparations, and/or compensation.
There are many ways in which such elements can be linked with, or affect,
the conduct of treatment and its expected outcome. Therapists should
identify such issues and make their implications for therapy explicit in each
individual case.

• *What to expect from treatment and how to define realistic goals?* Given the variety of expected outcomes, it is important to clearly define specific goals for the treatment of PTSD and share these goals with the patient. Treatment goals should, first of all, be *realistic* (i.e., both desirable and obtainable). In most cases, a reduction of PTSD symptoms will be among the central targets, but clinicians should be aware of the effect size of each therapy as a boundary to expectations. In other cases, comorbid symptoms and behaviors may take precedence. In some instances, stabilization and prevention of relapse is paramount. Sometimes, a preliminary goal should be set, such as getting the patient to choose psychological or medical treatment instead of, for example, isolation, drinking, or acting out. Other times, current stressors and life events may have to be addressed first (e.g., in order to bring a reactivation to an end). Finally, significant others whose distress, conduct, or attitudes are associated with the patient's condition may join the treatment. In general, one may recommend to see the therapy of PTSD as *oriented toward changing behavior, rather than symptoms.*

In all instances, treatment goals should be *predefined, adhered to,* and *evaluated,* such that if one treatment modality fails, this can be acknowledged, the causes sought out, and alternatives offered. The need to tie treatment techniques to desired goals is of paramount importance, as presented in the various chapters within this practice guideline. When empirical evidence is missing, it becomes a matter of clinical wisdom to choose the right tool. Such choices should be *explicit,* based on information contained in each of the book chapters, *patient-oriented,* and *flexible.* Given PTSD's chronic course, attention should be given to long-term goals, for which continuity of care and the right sequencing of interventions is mandatory.

• *How can one combine various treatment techniques?* Combined treatments are the rule rather than exception for PTSD, despite the fact that there is very few empirical data support this practice. Indeed, in one of the few studies pertinent to this question, Foa and associates (1991) found that both psychological exposure and stress inoculation therapy (SIT) had better outcomes than a combined approach in which rape survivors received both prolonged exposure and SIT concurrently. Although this provocative result raises as many questions as it answers (e.g., would the prolonged exposure and SIT combination have proven superior had treatment been extended beyond the brief, 9-week experimental protocol?), it clearly shows that combined treatments demand systematic evaluation in rigorous clinical trials. In practice, most CBT approaches combine several different modalities, as do most pharmacotherapeutic approaches in which PTSD patients frequently receive two or more different types of drugs. Another common clinical occurrence is that many PTSD patients who receive some sort of individual psychotherapy also receive at least one medication. Such patients may receive group, marital, or family therapy, in addition to individual psychotherapy and drug treatment. Although there are generally good clinical indications for prescribing combined treatments, we must recognize that such clinical practices must eventually be tested in rigorous experimental protocols.

An etiological treatment approach postulates that given the complex psychological, biological, and social abnormalities associated with this disorder, it is not unreasonable to consider different therapeutic approaches to target different symptoms. Such an approach sees each (e.g., individual, drug, group, etc.) treatment as complementary and of equal value. On the other hand, a pragmatic rationale for combining treatments might consider individual psychotherapy the major vehicle for improvement, with other treatments playing an adjunctive role (e.g., pharmacotherapy reducing intrusion or arousal symptoms so that individual psychotherapy can progress; or couple therapy keeping social support intact so that psychotherapy will not be disrupted by a marital crisis).

The lack of empirical evidence supporting combined approaches should not be interpreted as evidence against the efficacy of such treatments. Given the importance of this issue and the widespread prevalence of combined PTSD treatment in current clinical practice, we strongly recommend that treatments be introduced one at a time. After the therapist has chosen (and the patient has accepted) a specific initial treatment, there must be an adequate clinical trial of this approach to determine its effectiveness. If clinical goals are achieved, there is no need for additional treatments. If treatment is ineffective, or if it produces intolerable side effects, it must be discontinued and a different approach initiated. In the usual clinical scenario, however, patients achieve enough improvement to suggest that the initial treatment was effective but insufficient improvement to be satisfied with the results. This is the time to introduce a second treatment, while maintaining the first treatment as initially prescribed. Again, treatment success (or failure) will be determined if predefined goals have been achieved. If so, efforts should be made to reduce or terminate the first treatment, since it may have been superceded by the more potent, second treatment.

A common problem is that once started, a treatment may be maintained indefinitely even though its usefulness is questionable. We believe that combined treatments probably have a very important place in PTSD treatment and must be clarified by future research. We also believe that any treatment, combined or not, should be evaluated periodically to ensure that it is still needed to maintain desirable clinical outcomes.

• *How to approach complex clinical pictures and comorbid conditions?* We have already discussed complex clinical conditions in which psychiatric crises must be addressed before initiating treatment for PTSD. These include suicidal behavior, alcohol dependence, incapacitating depression, and marital disruption (see the section on choosing treatment for PTSD). We have also discussed combined treatments in which two or more clinical approaches have been prescribed for PTSD. These two issues must be reconsidered when PTSD is associated with at least one comorbid psychiatric disorder. This is a very common challenge in the diagnosis and treatment of PTSD, since 80% of all PTSD patients will have had at least one other DSM-IV Axis I psychiatric disorder in the course of their lives (Kessler, Sonnega, Bromet, Hughes, & Nelson, 1995). Most commonly, PTSD is associated with comorbid affective (e.g., depression, dysthymia) or anxiety (panic, social phobia, obsessive–compulsive) disorders or alcohol/drug abuse/dependency. In addition, the high prevalence of PTSD among severely mentally ill patients with schizophrenia and chronic affective illness is beginning to be recognized (Mueser et al., 1998). Finally, comorbid personality, and dissociative and somatoform disorders (often associated with prolonged childhood trauma) are another treatment challenge frequently seen in clinical practice.

As with so many important clinical questions under discussion, there are no empirical data to guide recommendations for treating PTSD associated with comorbid conditions. On the other hand, there is a rich empirical literature on treatment of many of these comorbid conditions themselves (e.g., depression, panic disorder, OCD, etc.). Therefore, we draw on such clinical findings in order to make a few suggestions.

The efficacy of pharmacotherapy for affective disorders, panic, social phobia, OCD, and schizophrenia is well-established. Cognitive-behavioral treatment is also very effective in depression and the aforementioned anxiety disorders. Finally, detoxification and a variety of alcohol/drug rehabilitation protocols are widely available. In short, empirical support for the efficacy of treatments for the DSM-IV Axis I disorders most frequently comorbid with PTSD is generally stronger than support for treatment of PTSD itself. This is at least partly due to the fact that clinical trials in PTSD have only been carried out during the past 10–15 years, whereas treatment research for these comorbid disorders has extended over a much longer time frame.

There are several ways to design a treatment plan when PTSD is associated with a comorbid disorder. Given the dictum "less is more," pharmacotherapists and CBT practitioners should start with a single treatment that might be expected to normalize both disorders simultaneously. For example, an SSRI would appear to be a logical first choice when PTSD is comorbid with depression, panic disorder, or OCD. Similarly, a CBT protocol for PTSD could incorporate specific modules that address panic, social phobia, and OCD. CBT can also incorporate relapse prevention components (Foy, Ruzek, Glynn, Riney, & Gusman, 1997) to address alcohol/drug abuse/dependency. Finally, we recommend simultaneous treatment of PTSD and comorbid chemical abuse/dependency (Kofoed, Friedman, & Peck, 1993) rather than the conventional approach, in which they are treated sequentially, usually starting with detoxification and alcohol/drug rehabilitation before progressing to PTSD treatment (except in extreme cases when the severity of addiction or chemical dependency makes PTSD treatment impossible).

These guidelines do not apply when the therapist's choice of PTSD treatment is without proven efficacy with the comorbid disorder. Indeed, if the preferred approach is EMDR, psychodynamic, group, or marital therapy, a separate treatment must be prescribed for the comorbid disorder. If the co-morbid disorder is the first order of business because of urgency or severity, it must be addressed before PTSI) treatment can begin. For example, if PTSD is comorbid with severe depression, antidepressant medication might be the best initial step. PTSD treatment should be delayed until depressive symp-toms are under control. At that point, EMDR, psychodynamic, group, or marital therapy can be initiated. As detailed previously (see the section on combined treatments), we recommend that all treatments (whether for the comorbid disorder or for PTSD) be introduced one at a time and be given an adequate clinical trial before adding or discontinuing other treatments. We also reiterate our recommendation that all treatments (for PTSD as well as for comorbid disorders) be evaluated periodically to ensure that they are still needed to maintain desirable clinical outcomes.

   • *How long should a treatment be followed?* We know very little about long-term maintenance of favorable treatment outcomes for two ma-jor reasons: because we lack the relevant scientific data, and because of the nature of PTSD itself. First, with few exceptions, most posttreatment out-come studies rarely monitor clinical status beyond 6 months. Clearly, long-term research is needed to help us develop reasonable expectations for longi-tudinal maintenance of therapeutic gains. With regard to pharmacotherapy, the classic research design is a discontinuation study in which successfully medicated patients are randomized to a placebo or continuation drug condi-tion to determine relapse rates with and without treatment over a long follow-up period. With regard to CBT, EMDR, and other time-limited psychotherapies, the operative questions are (1) how long can the beneficial outcomes from treatment be sustained; and (2) can treatment benefits be for-tified by periodic booster sessions, and, if so, how often and for how tong should such booster sessions be scheduled?

   Second, people who have recovered from an episode of PTSD are at greater risk for subsequent episodes if exposed to traumatic or trauma-related stimuli in the future. It is our hope that the coping skills acquired from psychotherapy will make individuals less vulnerable to future relapse than people with PTSD who have not received such treatment. An important fo-cus for the future, therefore, must be to design interventions that will foster resilience and prevent relapse. In the long run, such treatments will be much more valuable than approaches limited to amelioration of current sympto-matology.

   • *Are there features of PTSD that require special attention beyond the active ingredient of treatment?* No matter what treatment or combination of treatments seem best, there are several unique features of PTSD that diagnosticians and therapists must keep in mind. The initial assessment must be approached cautiously, since patients are asked to retrieve and relate traumatic memories against which they have developed a wide variety of cognitive, emotional, and behavioral defenses. Clinicians must respect such defenses, establish an atmosphere of trust and security, and show patience as reluctant patients' traumatic narratives unfold. The understandable ambivalence exhibited by PTSD patients between their desire for symptom relief and their fear that therapy, itself, will be toxic, by reexposing them to into intolerable thoughts, memories, and feelings, is the usual context in which the therapeutic contract must be negotiated. Realistic treatment goals must be carefully discussed. The staging and pace of treatment must be carefully considered. For severe and chronic PTSD, especially when associated with protracted trauma (as in childhood sexual abuse), it is often necessary to evaluate issues of safety and security in the home environment as well as in the therapist's office. For example, trauma-focused psychotherapy is not advisable for patients who continue to be traumatized (e.g., because of ongoing domestic violence or physical/sexual abuse). In such cases, the initial phase of treatment is the establishment of safety and security. It is only after this has been achieved that exposure or some other trauma-focused treatment can be initiated. It is important to remember in this regard that, for reasons addressed previously, trauma-focused treatment is not necessarily the treatment of choice for everyone.

Trust is an important concern for all PTSD patients, so therapists must demonstrate trustworthiness as well as professional competence. Negotiating a therapeutic contract that clearly specifies the process, time frame, and goals of treatment is one way to accomplish this. Another way is to avoid making promises that may be difficult to keep. For example, one should never promise a full recovery, since it is unlikely to occur and the risk of relapse is an ever-present possibility, even following complete remission of symptoms. This is another way to build trust, establish credibility, and generate appropriate expectations.

Attention to these matters is a prerequisite for any effective therapeutic alliance with PTSD patients.

• *How to understand treatment resistance and failure?* As with many mental disorders, PTSD, particularly in its chronic phase, is often resistant to treatment. Despite repeated descriptions of difficulties and poor treatment outcomes in PTSD, *treatment resistance* is poorly defined for this disorder. Specifically, the following questions have not received convincing answers: Which treatments are being "resisted," which symptoms are particularly tenacious, when is it clear that a treatment is ineffective, and what should by done in such case (e.g., add more treatment, change dose, or start a new therapeutic approach)? These questions are especially difficult to answer because of the heterogeneity of treatment approaches to PTSD and traumatized populations (e.g., survivors of prolonged atrocities, along with survivors of short incidents).

It is not surprising, therefore, in more recent studies (e.g., Davidson et al., 1998) to find not only larger effect size of treatment but also an unexpected placebo response. At the same time, CBT has proven effective with a variety of PTSD patients, including those with prolonged PTSD. With the advent of specific treatment protocols, better quantification of outcome, and delivery of treatment to larger numbers of individuals, treatment resistance might be better described.

For the time being, the known reasons for treatment resistance in PTSD include those seen in other disorders (e.g., chronicity, comorbidity, poor compliance, adverse life circumstances), along with more specific, yet poorly explored reasons (e.g., extreme or repeated traumatization, traumatization during critical developmental stages, etc.). No clear guidelines can be given to clinicians who encounter treatment resistance in their patients except to use their clinical wisdom to probe and eventually improve their approach to the patient, to find out what could have gone wrong (too fast or too slow an exploration, incomplete mapping of current life stressors, lack of home practice, over- or underdosage of medication), and to use the variety of options offered in this book to refine and enrich their versatility as therapists.

CONCLUSION

These practice guidelines are a work in progress. Although there has been considerably more research on CBT, pharmacotherapy, and EMDR than other treatments, on balance, we know relatively little about PTSD monotherapy and next to nothing about combined treatment approaches. The good news is the rapid growth of rigorous clinical research in recent years. Indeed, we fully expect that many questions posed throughout this book will have solid empirical answers within the foreseeable future. Until that time, we hope that the analyses of treatment research and recommendations by experts within this practice guideline will assist clinicians in the trenches and promote more effective treatment of PTSD.

REFERENCES

Bryant, R. A., Harvey, A. G., Dang, S. T., Sackville, T., & Basten, C. (1998). Treatment of acute stress disorder: A comparison of cognitive-behavioral therapy and supportive counselling. *Journal of Consulting and Clinical Psychology, 66*(5), 862–866.

Brom, D., Kleber, R. J., & Defares, P. B. (1989). Brief psychotherapy for posttraumatic stress disorders. *Journal of Consulting and Clinical Psychology, 57*(5), 607–612.

Creamer, M., Morris, P., Biddle, D., & Elliott, P. (1999). Treatment outcome in Australian veterans with combat-related posttraumatic stress disorder: A cause for cautious optimism? *Journal of Traumatic Stress, 12*(4), 545–558.

Davidson, J., Landburg, P. D., Pearlstein, T., Weisler, R., Sikes, K., & Farfel, G. (1997). Double-blind comparison of sertraline and placebo in patients with posttraumatic stress disorder (PTSD). *American College of Neuropsychopharmaology Abstracts.*

Elkin, I., Shea, M. T., Watkins, J. T., Imber, S. D., Sotsky, S. M., Collins, J. F., Glass, D. R., Pilkonis, P. A., Leber, W. R., & Docherty, J. P. (1989). National Institute of Mental Health Treatment of Depression Collaborative Research Program: General effectiveness of treatments. *Archives of General Psychiatry, 46*(11), 971–982.

Foa, E. B., Hearst-Ikeda, D., & Perry, K. J. (1995). Evaluation of a brief cognitive-behavioral program for the prevention of chronic PTSD in recent assault victims. *Journal of Consulting and Clinical Psychology, 63*, 948–955.

Foa, E. B., Rothbaum, B. O., Riggs, D. S., & Murdock, T. B. (1991). Treatment of posttraumatic stress disorder in rape victims: a comparison between cognitive-behavioral, procedures and counseling. *Journal of Consulting and Clinical Psychology, 59*, 715–723.

Foy, D. W., Ruzek, J. I., Glynn, S. M., Riney, S. A., & Gusman, F. D. (1997). Trauma focus group therapy for combat-related PTSD. *In Session: Psychotherapy in Practice, 3*, 59–73.

Friedman, M. J., & Rosenheck, R. A. (1996). PTSD as a persistent mental illness. In S. Soreff (Ed.), *The seriously and persistently mentally ill: The state-of-the-art treatment handbook* (pp. 369-389). Seattle, WA: Hogrefe & Huber.

Imber, S. D., Pilkonis, P. A., Sotsky, S. M., Elkin, I., Watkins, J. T., Collins, J. F., Shea, M. T., Leber, W. R., & Glass, D. R. (1990). Mode-specific effects among three treatments for depression. *Journal of Consulting and Clinical Psychology, 58*(3), 352–359.

Kessler, R. C., Sonnega, A., Bromet, E., Hughes, M., & Nelson, C. B. (1995). Posttraumatic stress disorder in the National Comorbidity Survey. *Archives of General Psychiatry, 52*, 1048–1060.

Kofoed, L., Friedman, M. J., & Peck, R. (1993). Alcoholism and drug abuse in patients with PTSD. *Psychiatric Quarterly, 64*, 151–171.

Kozak, M. J., Liebowitz, M. R., & Foa, E. B. (2000). Cognitive behavior therapy and pharmacotherapy for OCD: The NIIMH-sponsored collaborative study. In W. K. Goodman, M. V. Rudorfer, &. J. D. Maser (Eds.), *Obsessive–compulsive disorder: Contemporary issues in treatment.* Mahwah, NJ: Erlbaum.

Mueser, K. T., Goodman, L. B., Trumbette, S. L., Osher, F. C., Vidaver, R., Auciello, P., & Foy, D. W. (1998). Trauma and posttraumatic stress disorder in severe mental illness. *Journal of Consulting and Clinical Psychology, 66*, 493–499.

Shalev, A. Y. (1997). Discussion: Treatment of prolonged posttraumatic stress disorder—learning from experience [Comment]. *Journal of Traumatic Stress, 10*, 415–423.

Solomon, Z., & Benbenishty, R. (1986). The role of proximity, immediacy, and expectancy in frontline treatment of combat stress reaction among Israelis in the Lebanon War. *American Journal of Psychiatry, 143*, 613–617.

Index

Abreaction, 176, 254–255, 265
    fractionated, 256
Accelerated information processing model,
    140
Acute stress disorder (ASD)
    diagnosis, 109
    predictive utility, 54
ADIS-R. *See* Assessment methods
Adrenergic hyperreactivity and PTSD,
    85–86
    effectiveness of antiadrenergic agents in
        open trials and case reports, 93–94,
        98, 100
    evidence strength, 328
Alexithymia, 180
    and creative arts therapies, 309
Anticonvulsants and PTSD
    effectiveness in open trials and case
        reports, 96, 98, 101, 102
    evidence strength, 328
Antipsychotics and PTSD, 96, 101
    evidence strength, 329
Anxiety
    and exposure therapy, 79
    hierarchy, 64, 65
    management and SIT, 65
Arousal symptoms of PTSD, 19
Assaultive violence, and PTSD, 21
Assertiveness training (AT), 320
    and fear inhibition, 66
    studies, 76–77
        evidence strength, 322
    treatment limitations, 79, 324
Assessment methods for PTSD, 31–32
    dichotomous vs. continuous measures, 25
    psychometric theory and principles, 22–23
    psychophysiological measures, 29–30
    self-report questionnaires, 26
        Impact of Event Scale—Revised (IES-
            R), 26–27

Keane PTSD Scale of the MMPI-2, 27
Los Angeles Symptom Checklist
    (LASC), 29
Mississippi Scale for Combat-Related
    PTSD, 27
Penn Inventory for Posttraumatic Stress,
    27–28
Posttraumatic Diagnostic Scale (PTDS),
    28
PTSD Checklist (PCL), 28
standardization, 30–31
structured diagnostic interviews, 23
    Anxiety Disorders Interviews
        Schedule—Revised (ADIS-R), 24
    Clinician-Administered PTSD Scale
        (CAPS), 25–26, 239
    limitations, 24
    PTSD Interview, 24
    PTSD Symptom Scale Interview (PSS-
        I), 26
    Structured Clinical Interview for DSM
        (SCID), 23–24, 239
    Structured Interview for PTSD (SI-
        PTSD), 25
Assimilation/accommodation vs.
    overaccommodation, 62–63
Attention-deficit/hyperactivity disorder
    (ADHD) and PTSD, 110, 117
Avoidance symptoms of PTSD, 19

Behavioral theory/therapy. *See also* Learning
    theory
    contingency management for avoidance
        and other behavioral problems, 61
    exposure as treatment for reexperiencing,
        61
Benzodiazepines (BZD) and PTSD, 89, 101
    effectiveness in open trials and case
        reports, 95–96, 102
    evidence strength, 328–329

380

risks with comorbid alcohol/drug abuse dependence, 95
Biofeedback therapy for PTSD (BIO), 60, 66, 320
study, 77
evidence strength, 322
treatment limitations, 79, 324
Borderline personality disorder (BPD) and PTSD, 110

Case management and PTSD, 5
indications, 237–238
Children/adolescents and PTSD, 330, 332, 365
and ADHD, 110
assessment, 127
and borderline personality disorder, 110
clinical issues, 6
cognitive-behavioral techniques
cognitive therapy, 113
controlled exposure, 112
stress management, 112–113
comorbidity, 109–110, 117
developmental level importance, 6, 107–108, 126
factors predicting symptom levels, 107
moderator and mediator variables, 107
indications/contraindications for interventions, 129–130
lack of prevalence data, 20
literature summary
clinical evidence, 116–117
empirical evidence, 117–126
strength of evidence, 330–331
"omen formation," 108, 113
and physiological abnormalities, 117
prevention–intervention model, 116
and revictimization, 192
theoretical position, 106–107
treatment guidelines, 126–130
treatment length, 115, 331
treatment setting, 128
treatment techniques, 126
cognitive-behavioral, 112–113, 128–129, 331
combined approaches, 125–126
cost-effectiveness, 131
EMDR, 113, 152
inclusion of parents, 114, 124, 127
integrated, 114–115
pharmacotherapy, 113–114, 331–332
psychoanalytic/psychodynamic approaches, 111–112
psychoeducation, 111, 128
psychological debriefing, 111, 116
trauma-focused ("play therapy"), 110–111, 116–117, 124
CISD. See Psychological debriefing

Clinical research issues
ages/developmental stages focus, 130–131
clinical wisdom vs. scientific knowledge, 17, 173, 360
limitations of research in psychosocial rehabilitation techniques, 238–239
coding system for evaluating treatment approaches, 13–14, 17
competing treatments comparison issues, 150
features of well-controlled studies, 67, 320–321
assessor training, 10–11
blind evaluators, 10
defined target symptoms, 10
manualized/specific treatment programs, 11
reliable/valid measures, 10
treatment adherence, 11
unbiased assignment to treatment, 11
lack of evidence vs. lack of efficacy, 361
limitations
ease of study of some treatment approaches, 11
inclusion and exclusion criteria, 4, 10, 11
methodological in assessing effectiveness of group therapy, 168–170, 172–173
methodological shortcomings in psychological debriefing studies, 53
milieu therapy study challenges, 210
psychodynamic research and conventional research paradigms, 194
PTSD and pharmacotherapy issues, 96–97
validation techniques for self-help books, 231
Cognitive processing therapy (CPT)
cognitive therapy component, 65, 320
exposure therapy component, 65
study, 76
evidence strength, 322
treatment limitations, 79, 324
Cognitive therapy (CT), 320
and assertiveness training, 66
and automatic (dysfunctional) thoughts, 66
and children, 113
as component of cognitive processing therapy, 65
studies, 76
evidence strength, 322
treatment limitations, 79, 324
Cognitive-behavioral group therapy
techniques, 156
literature, 167–168
and principles of habituation and extinction, 160
and trauma processing, 159

Cognitive-behavioral group therapy
    techniques *(continued)*
    vs. psychodynamic approaches, 159–160
Cognitive-behavioral therapy (CBT) for
    PTSD
    combination approaches in studies, 77,
        320, 322–323, 363–364
    limitations, 79–80, 324
    and comorbidity, 80
    contributions to debriefing, 42
    efficacy, 13
    and hypnosis, 252–253
    literature, treatment outcome studies, 67,
        68–73, 320–321
    and pharmacotherapy for disruptive
        symptoms, 102
    as preventative measure, 54
    treatment goals, symptom reduction, 7
    treatments, 63
        for children, 112–113, 128–129
        limitations, 78–80
        vs. EMDR, 77
        vs. psychodynamic psychotherapy, 183
Combat veterans and PTSD
    combat fatigue concept, 180
    communalization of experiences
        importance, 193
    and marital therapy, 290–291
    General S. L. Marshall's debriefing
        method, 40
    Mississippi Scale for Combat-Related
        PTSD assessment method, 27
    narcotherapy, 266–267
    outcome research source, 217–218
    PIE model, 40
    and randomized clinical trials (RCTs), 4
    shell shock and hypnosis, 265
    and SSRI treatment, 98
    trauma-based inpatient approach, 200
    and treatment resistance, 15–16
    veterans' "rap groups," 156
    Vietnam War, 20
    war neuroses concept, 266
        and hypnosis, 267
Comorbidity with PTSD, 2,7
    importance in assessment, 31
    and treatment setting, 14
"Concreting" memories/pseudomemories
    retrieved through hypnosis, 262–263
Corticotropin-releasing factor (CRF) levels
    (elevated), 86, 97
Countertransference
    countertransference vicarious
        traumatization cycle, 193
    importance in treating trauma survivors,
        178–179
Creative therapies and PTSD, 302, 356–357,
    369–340

clinical conditions subject to treatment
    comorbid disorders, 304
    personality traits/habits, 304
    psychosocial problems, 304
    state of the disorder, 304
    type of trauma, 303–304
conceptual framework, nonverbal
    intervention, 305
definition, 303
empirical and clinical evidence, 308–309
    strength of, 357
gender considerations, 311
history, 303
indications, 306, 311, 357–358
outcome measures, 308
overlap with other treatments, 305,
    309–310
professional organization/credentialing,
    310
role of therapist, 307–308
techniques, 306–308
treatment goals, 304–305
Critical incident stress debriefing (CISD),
    39
Critical interaction therapy
    goals, 288
    sequence of interventions, 289

Depressive disorder (MDD) and PTSD, 109
Diagnostic utility determination
    "gold standard," 22
    test sensitivity/specificity, 22–23
Disasters, and PTSD risk, 20
Disorders of extreme stress not otherwise
    specified (DESNOS), and
    trauma/trauma histories, 1–2
Dissociation, 250
    at time of trauma as predictor of PTSD,
        251
    chronic and repeated trauma, 251
    levels, 251
    and use of hypnosis, 265
Dual representation theory, 60
    elements of emotional processing, 63

Effect size, 12
Eight-process model to treat PTSD, 259
    concentration, 260–261
    condensation, 260
    confession, 260
    confrontation, 259–260
    congruence, 261
    conscious experience, 260
    consolation, 260
    control, 261
Emotional numbing symptoms of PTSD, 19
Emotional processing theory and PTSD
    fear structures, 61

mechanisms in improvement changes
  corrections of erroneous probability
    estimates, 62
  imaginal reliving, 62, 64
  variants, 64
Emotionally focused couple therapy (EFT),
    289
  nine steps, 290
Event interpretation theory, 66
Exposure therapy (EX), 64, 320
  for children, 112, 128
  and combined treatments, 64
  as component of cognitive processing
    therapy, 65
  effectiveness, 75
  evidence strength, 321
  and hypnosis, 255
  imaginal vs. *in vivo*, 74–75
  studies, 67, 74–75, 78
  treatment limitations, 78–79, 324
  vs. psychosocial rehabilitation, 226
Eye movement desensitization and
    reprocessing (EMDR) for PTSD
  and children, 113, 152, 333, 366
  history/development, 139–140
  literature summary
    additional study details, 144–146
    criteria for inclusion, 143
    dismantling studies, 149–151
    evidence strength, 333–334
    limitations, 147
    studies using control treatments or
      newly initiated standard care,
      148–149
    studies using wait-list or continuing
      standard care control, 147–148
  procedural alternatives, 140, 142
  recommendations
    clinical, 334
    research, 334–335
  study vs. biofeedback, 77
  subjective level (units) of disturbance
    (SUD) scale, 141
  theory, 140
  trauma memories as "targets," 141
  treatment efficacy for PTSD, 13
  treatment fidelity and efficacy, 151
  treatment goals, symptom reduction, 7
  treatment stages
    assessment, 141
    body scan, 142
    closure, 142
    desensitization/reprocessing, 142
    patient history/treatment planning,
      141
    positive cognition installation, 142
    preparation, 141
    reevaluation, 142

validity of positive cognition (VoC) scale,
    141
  vs. cognitive-behavioral therapy, 77

Fear structures, and fear activation during
    treatment for PTSD, 61
Flooding technique, 64, 320
  imaginal flooding (IMF), 73
  in vivo flooding (IVF), 73

Gender
  considerations and creative therapies, 311
  and development of interpersonal
    psychotherapy, 184
  differences in development of PTSD,
    20–21
  and PTSD treatment response, 5
Glutamatergic dysregulation and PTSD, 86
"Gold standard." *See* Clinical research
    issues/features of well controlled
    studies; Diagnostic utility determination
Group therapy and PTSD, 336, 366
  "covering" vs. "uncovering" methods, 156
  cross-types comparisons, 165–166, 168
  group types
    cognitive-behavioral, 156
    psychodynamic, 156, 158–159
    supportive, 156, 157–158
  indications/contraindications for group
    therapy, 171
  literature summary, 160, 161–164
    cognitive-behavioral model, 167–168
    evidence strength, 336–337
    methodological limitations, 168–170
    psychodynamic group model, 167
    recommendations, 337
    supportive group model, 160, 167
  principles of group process, 156
  research areas, 172–174
  "survivor helping survivor" model, 155
  "trauma focus" groups, 157
  trauma-survivor–group assignment, 171
  trauma focus vs. supportive, 172
Guidelines development process, 3–4
  rating system, 3

Hypnosis, 247, 350, 369
  clinical use, 248–249, 270, 352
    contraindications, 271, 352–353
    for "re-education," 265–266
    synergistic effect, 252
    as a tool to remove traumatic memories,
      176, 185, 252–253
  "ego therapy" approach, 267
Hypnosis–dissociation–trauma triad,
    250–251
Hypnotic Induction Profile (HIP), 248
Hypnotic inductions, 248

Hypnotic phenomena, 249
Hypnotic-like phenomena, 249
Hypnotizability/hypnotic
    susceptibility/responsiveness, 249
    and life cycle, 249–250
    and PTSD individuals, 251,252
    and PTSD literature summary, 264–
        265
        as an "empirically supported
            treatment," 270
        evidence strength, 351
        history, 265–268
        recent studies, 268–270
    techniques for PTSD treatment
        eight-process model, 259–261
        phase-oriented model, 253–259
        and transference issues, 255, 261–262
    treatment efficacy for PTSD, 13, 265
        rationale, 252–253
        and unrealistic confidence in reported
            memory, 253, 262–264
        pseudomemory creation, 262
        and "war neuroses," 267
Hypothalamic–pituitary–adrenocortical
    (HPA) enhanced negative feedback and
    PTSD, 86

Information processing theory, 62, 63. See
    also Dual representation theory
    accelerated information-processing model,
        140
    impact of "overwhelming events," 180
    influence on EMDR, 140
Inpatient treatment of PTSD, 342, 345,
    367–368
    admission criteria, 206, 219, 344
    central paradigms
        life-span development model, 201
        social learning theory, 201
        therapeutic community/milieu
            psychiatry, 201, 205–206, 210
    contraindications, 203, 345
    and cost containment, 201, 202, 218
    course of treatment, 343–344
    goals, 202, 218–219
    literature summary, 211–214
        challenges of studying milieu therapy,
            210
        clinical studies, 217
        empirical studies, 210, 215–217
        evidence strength, 343
    as "metatherapy," 218
    partial hospitalization, 203
    programs and techniques, 204–208
    "second generation" model, 201, 216, 344
    trauma-based approach, 200, 204, 207
        comprehensive treatment orientation
            reasons, 200–201

"healing forward," 219
"social healing for social wounds," 205
transtheoretical and multimodal, 207
vs. general psychiatric units, 209
Interpersonal psychotherapy (IPT),
    184–185

Jargon vs. behaviorally anchored
    terminology, 31, 43, 317

Koach program (Israel), 292

Lamotrigene, clinical antikindling
    significance, 86
LASC. See Assessment methods
Learning theory
    and development/maintenance of PTSD
        symptoms, 60–61
    reexperiencing as conditioned emotional
        response, 61
Level of evidence. See Clinical research
    issues/coding

Marital and family therapy and PTSD, 354,
    369
    course of treatment, 355
    indications/contraindications, 294–295,
        355
        family violence, 295–296, 297
        other considerations, 296–297
    limitation of studies, 280, 293–294, 297
        evidence strength, 354
        and original source data, 283–284
    shared characteristics
        multiple participants, 280
        systemic focus, 280
    supportive treatment approaches, 281,
        282, 293–293
        rationale, 283
    and symptom chronicity, 298
        rationale, 282–283
    systemic treatment approaches,
        281–282
        family interventions, 284–288
        marital interventions, 288–292
Massage therapy and PTSD, for children,
    123
Monoamine oxidase inhibitors (MAOI) and
    PTSD, 88, 89, 90, 100
    effectiveness in open trials and case
        reports, 94–95
    evidence strength, 328
Multiple Stressors Debriefing Model, 46

Object relations
    as predictor of treatment outcomes, 215
    theory, 181
Opioid dysregulation and PTSD, 85

Pharmacotherapy for PTSD, 98, 326–327,
    329, 364–365
  and children, 113–114, 129
    clinical trials, 122
  and comorbid disorders, 102
  efficacy of drugs in treatment, 99–101
  ethnophamacological concerns, 97
  literature summary, 88–90
    open trials and case reports, 90, 91–92
  psychotherapeutical approaches, vs.
      cognitive-behavioral therapy, 80
  research issues, 96–97
  state of current knowledge, 13, 85
  synergy with psychodynamic treatments,
      194
  techniques, 87–88
  treatment goals, symptom reduction, 7
Phase model of trauma treatment with
    hypnosis, 351–352
  personality reintegration/rehabilitation
      phase, 259
    spiritual dimension, 259
  stabilization and symptom reduction
      phase, 254
  treatment of traumatic memories phase,
      254–256
    affect bridge, 258
    age regression, 257–258
    imaginal memory containment,
        258–259
    projective techniques, 256–257
    relaxation, 256
    restructuring, 257
Posttraumatic stress disorder (PTSD), 1
  acute vs. chronic, 18
  animal model
    limitations, 84
    and sensitization/kindling, 86
  assessment. See also Assessment methods
    purposes, 21
    special considerations, 376–377
  comorbidity, 2, 7, 80, 87, 200, 206
    in children, 109–110, 117
  complex PTSD, 192, 374–376
  core features, 109
  corticotropin-releasing factor importance,
      86
  delayed onset, 18
  diagnostic criteria, 18–19, 236, 361–362
    arousal symptoms, 19
    avoidance/emotional numbing
        symptoms, 19
    reexperiencing symptoms, 19
    symptoms, 1, 85
  disruptive symptoms, 79, 85, 87, 102, 205
  dissociation at time of trauma as predictor,
      251
  engaging the patient, 361–362

  high-risk populations, 20
  "learned helplessness" symptoms, 232
  pathways to homelessness, 232
  prevalence, 19–21
  psychobiological aspects, 5, 84
  and psychophysiological functions, 29–30,
      43
    in children, 117
  subtypes, 97, 108–109
  susceptibility factors, 6
  symptom relapses, 6, 208, 376
Posttraumatic stress disorder treatment, 7
  in children
    nature of the stressor, 107
    pulsed intervention, 115
  clinical considerations, 17
    chemical abuse/dependency, 8
    comorbidity, 7, 102, 374–376
    concurrent medical conditions, 8
    disability/functional impairment, 8–9
    inpatient indications, 9, 14
    suicidality, 8, 14, 218
  clinical issues
    age, 6
    children, 6
    elder adults, 6
    gender, 5
    PTSD chronicity, 5, 298
    single vs. multiple traumas, 4–5
    trauma type, 4
  coding system, 13–14, 17
  combined treatment, 373–374
    in inpatient trauma-focused therapy,
        207
    studies, 13, 359–360
  considerations
    choices among treatment modalities,
        370–372
    costs, 87, 131, 201, 218
    readiness, 16
    resistance, 15–16, 377–378
    treatment management, 15
    treatment settings, 14
  effective plan, 170
  efficacy studies, 9–10, 13, 371
  follow-up, 376
  "magic bullet," 97
  managed care impact, 199, 202, 207, 235,
      270
  in nonindustrial countries, 2
  "one-stop shopping" model, 236–237,
      241
  optimization, 361
  practitioner training, 14, 199–200, 361
  therapeutic goals, 370, 373
    assessment/therapeutic process
        enrichment, 7
    functional improvements, 7, 9

Posttraumatic stress disorder treatment
(continued)
   intrapsychic change in psychodynamic
      psychotherapy, 187
   symptom reduction, 7
   trauma-focused, 110–111, 116–117, 200
PSS-I. *See* Assessment methods
Psychoanalysis, 182
   indications/factors, 192–193
Psychoanalytic/psychodynamic
      psychotherapy, 339, 367
   abreaction, 176, 180, 185
   and biological psychiatry, 181–182
   and catharsis, 42, 177
   contraindications, 340–341
   and death instinct, 180
   free association, 177
   fundamental rule, 182
   goals, 187
   and group therapies, 185
   and hypnosis, 252–253
   indications, 177, 190–191, 340
   observing ego, 191
   literature summary
      clinical studies, 187–190
      empirical studies, 186–187
      evidence strength, 339–340
   psychic balance concept, 177
   repetition compulsion and posttraumatic
      dreams, 180
   stimulus barrier
      as "holding environment," 181
      and trauma, 179–180
   symptom definition, 177
   synergy with pharmacological treatments,
      194
   theory statement, 176–182
   transference concept, 177–178, 190
   treatment efficacy for PTSD, 13
      in children, 111–112, 128
   treatment techniques, 182–185
Psychobiological abnormalities in PTSD,
      84–85
Psychodynamic group therapy, 156
   and appropriate affective involvement,
      158
   literature, 167
   restructuring self–other representations,
      160
   techniques, 158–159
   vs. cognitive-behavioral group therapy,
      159–160
Psychodynamic psychotherapy techniques,
      182–183
   brief psychodynamic therapy, 183–184
   and core conflictual relationship theme,
      191–192
   as expressive therapy, 183

and trauma survivors, vs. cognitive-
      behavioral therapies, 183
Psychoeducation
   and children, 111
   and parents, 114
   and debriefing, 42
   and exposure therapy, 64
   and family support, 233–234
Psychological debriefing (PD), 317, 362–363
   acute preventive interventions as social
      movement interventions, 40
   as acute psychological first aid, 55, 111,
      116
   catharsis, 42
   and children, 111
   cognitive behavioral therapies
      cognitive schemas and traumatic
         memories, 42
      desensitization concept, 42
   crisis intervention, 41
   critical incident stress debriefing (CISD),
      39, 43
      seven-phase technique, 44
   eclectic model, 42
   evidence strength, 317–318
   grief counseling, 41–42
   group psychotherapy, 41
   immediate vs. long-term protective value,
      50
   indications/contraindications, 318
   individual, 46
      and retraumatization, 55
   literature summary
      methodological shortcomings, 53, 56,
         319
      open trials and case reports, 49–50
      randomized controlled clinical trials,
         47–48
      studies without control or comparison
         groups, 50–51
   manualized, 42
   General S. L. Marshall's debriefing
      method, 40
   Multiple Stressors Debriefing Model, 46
   and other interventions, 46–47
      common features of one-time
         interventions, 51–53
   Proximity, Immediacy, and Expectancy
      (PIE) model, 40
   psychoeducation, 42
   recommendations, 54–55
   screening function, 111, 116, 128
   stages
      disengagement, 45–46
      emotional reactions, 45
      expectations and facts, 44–45
      future planning/coping, 45
      introduction, 44

normalization, 45
thoughts and impressions, 45
Psychosocial rehabilitation for PTSD, 347,
   368–369
  advocacy, 242
  checklist, 228, 348
  client self-direction importance, 225, 228,
    238, 241
  clinical trials for children, 118, 122,
    123–125
  clinical wisdom vs. scientific knowledge,
    limitation of research
    approaches, 238–239
  and creative therapies, 304
  literature summary, 230, 238
    case management, 237–238
    evidence strength, 347–348
    family support techniques, 233–234
    physical health and education services,
      230–231
    self-care/independent living skills
      techniques, 231–232
    social skills training, 234–235
    supported housing techniques, 232–233
    vocational rehabilitation techniques,
      235–237, 239
  practice importance, 229
  as problem-focused approach, 224
  recommendations, 348–349
  services, 224, 225
  techniques, and other mental disorders,
    224, 227, 230
  Telehealth/Telemedicine applications, 235
  theoretical rationales
    social connections reestablishment,
      226–227
    stage theories of treatment, 225–226,
      229
  trauma-focused techniques, 239–240
  treatment goals, functional improvement,
    7
  vs. reexperiencing trauma, 226, 230
  wide-scale "needs assessment," 240–241
  PTDS. *See* Assessment methods

Race, and differences in development of
    PTSD, 21
Rape victims, and risk for PTSD, 20,21
Reexperiencing symptoms of PTSD, 19
Relaxation training for PTSD, 60, 66, 320
  combined with exposure therapy, 64
  and hypnosis, 256
  studies, 77
    evidence strength, 322
    treatment limitations, 79, 324

Sanctuary® model program, 216
SCID. *See* Assessment methods

Self psychology theory, and psychological
    trauma, 180–181
Sensitization/kindling and PTSD, 86
Seratonin reuptake inhibitors (SSRI) and
    PTSD, 88, 89, 90, 99
  and children, 129, 331
  current treatment knowledge, 13, 98
  effectiveness in open trials and case
    reports, 90, 93, 98
  evidence strength, 327–328
  and other serotonergic agents, 93, 99
    evidence strength, 329
Serotonergic dysregulation and PTSD, 86
SI-PTSD. *See* Assessment methods
Social psychiatry movement, and disaster
    research, 42–43
Social-cognitive theories
  affective expression and trauma memory
    processing, 63. *See also* Dual
    representation theory
  and information processing concerns,
    62
State-dependent memory theory, 253
Stress inoculation training (SIT), 65, 320
  compared to exposure therapy, 74
  studies, 75–76
    evidence strength, 322
    limitations of, 78
    treatment limitations, 79, 324
Suicidality, as an associated feature of PTSD,
    8, 218
Supportive group therapy, 156
  current coping context, 157
  functions in different treatment settings,
    158
  literature, 160, 167
  techniques, 157–158
Supportive psychotherapy, 184
Systematic desensitization therapy (SD), 60,
    64–65, 320
  and imaginal exposure, 64
    vs. *in vivo* exposure, 65
  and principle of reciprocal inhibition,
    64
  studies, 75
    evidence strength, 321–322
    vs. hypnosis and psychodynamic
      psychotherapy, 268
    treatment limitations, 79, 324

Therapist considerations
  legal ramifications of trauma work,
    263–264
  role in creative therapies, 307–308
  therapeutic relationship, 15, 179
  training, 14, 199–200, 361
Thyroid activity (increased) and PTSD,
    86–87

Transference concept, 178–179, 190
  issues, 255, 261–262
  "traumatic transference," 262
Trauma, as process of objectification, 251
Traumatic experiences
  and disorders, 1
  imaginal reliving, 62
  and initial levels of distress as predictors of
      PTSD, 54
  and medical illness, 8
  memories, validity of, 16
  "omen formation" in children, 108, 113
  as a pathogen, 176
  prevalence, 19
  prevention/minimization of posttraumatic
      reactions, 39

and PTSD, 49
  as public health delivery system
      challenge, 20
  and recovery, 18–19
  single vs. multiple, 4–5, 107, 151, 251
  survivor's guilt, 113
Tricyclic antidepressants (TCA) and PTSD,
    101
  effectiveness in open trials and case
      reports, 95
  evidence strength, 328
Two-factor theory of conditioned fear and
    operant avoidance, 60

Veterans. See Combat veterans